The Complete Atlas of Britain

Published by The Automobile Association

1st Edition   Apr 1979
2nd Edition   Jan 1980
3rd Edition   Jan 1981
4th Edition   Oct 1981
5th Edition   Jan 1983
6th Edition   Mar 1984
7th Edition   Oct 1984
Reprinted   May 1985
8th Edition ©The Automobile Association Oct 1985

Produced by the Cartographic Department, Publications Division of the
Automobile Association.

Based on the Ordnance Survey maps, with the permission of the Controller of
Her Majesty's Stationery Office, Crown Copyright Reserved.

Printed and bound in Spain by Artes Graficas Toledo, S.A.-Toledo.
D. L. TO: 1304 -1985

The contents of this book are believed correct at the time of printing.
Nevertheless, the publisher can accept no responsibility for errors or omissions,
or for changes in the details given.

Published by the Automobile Association, Fanum House, Basing View,
Basingstoke, Hampshire RG21 2EA.

ISBN 0 86145 302 6

Contents

Journey Planning

The Motoring Atlas of Great Britain combines superb maps with accurate and practical routefinding aids. These aids are designed to help the motorist complete a journey as quickly and with as little stress as possible.

ALERTNESS

Whether a journey is undertaken for business or pleasure, it is essential that the driver should set out feeling alert and confident, and that he should remain so until his destination is reached. A tired, frustrated driver is a potential danger to himself, to his passengers, and to other road users. The driver will feel more confident, and will certainly have a less troublesome journey, if he has planned his journey in advance.

MILEAGE

One of the fundamental considerations to be taken into account when planning a journey of any sort is that of the mileage involved. The mileage chart on page x which gives the distances between a selection of towns in Great Britain, can be used to make a rough calculation of the total journey length. From this an indication of the journey time may be gained.

ROUTE PLANNING

Once an indication of the journey length and time has been ascertained it is necessary to decide on a general route, and for this the route planning maps on pages II–VII are an invaluable guide. They depict principal routes throughout the country, and pinpoint the larger conurbations on those routes. Detailed routes can be worked out from the maps in the main atlas section of this book. The driver may find it useful to make a note of road numbers and route directions before setting out, as this can reduce his need to stop and consult the atlas.

MOTORAIL

If the journey involved is very long, the motorist may find it both more convenient and less exhausting to take advantage of the British Rail Motorail service. The cost of transporting a car and a family of four by rail is between 10% and 20% higher than travelling by road, but there may be considerable gains in travelling time, and saving in vehicle wear and tear. Details of the Motorail Service can be obtained from British Rail stations.

RADIO

Frequent radio bulletins are issued by the BBC and Independent Local Radio stations on road conditions, possible hold-ups, etc. and these can be of great assistance to the driver. By tuning to the local stations of areas being passed through it may be possible to avoid delays, and be prepared to make running changes to the route. The maps and accompanying text on pages viii–ix give details of the wavelengths and reception areas of all local radio stations in Great Britain.

ROAD SIGNS

Considerable help in negotiating the nation's highways can be obtained by understanding the various types of road direction signs. They are illustrated, and their functions described, on page xii. The principal benefit of the system is that primary route signs indicate the most straightforward route between one major town and another. It should be remembered that the shortest route is not necessarily the quickest. The driver is advised, where possible, to avoid driving through towns and built-up-areas, even if such routes appear to be more direct from the map. Delays caused by traffic lights, one-way systems, pedestrians, etc, will almost certainly be encountered in such areas.

THE NATIONAL GRID

The National Grid system, which is explained on page xiii, enables the driver to pinpoint any town or village in the atlas after having first found the reference number of that place by consulting the index. There is a separate index for London. A series of plans of principal towns and cities in Great Britain will be found between pages 153 and 206.

MOTORWAYS

When planning routes, many drivers will consider using motorways. They have several advantages over other types of road; not only are they faster, but they are also very easy to follow and allow a more consistent speed to be maintained. Drivers should, however, be fully conversant with the special rules for motorway driving, which are contained in the Highway Code. Perhaps the most ignored of these is that the outside lanes of a motorway should be used for overtaking only; there is no such thing as a 'fast lane'. Beginning on page 114 is a series of maps of the principal motorways in Great Britain.

Route Planning Maps

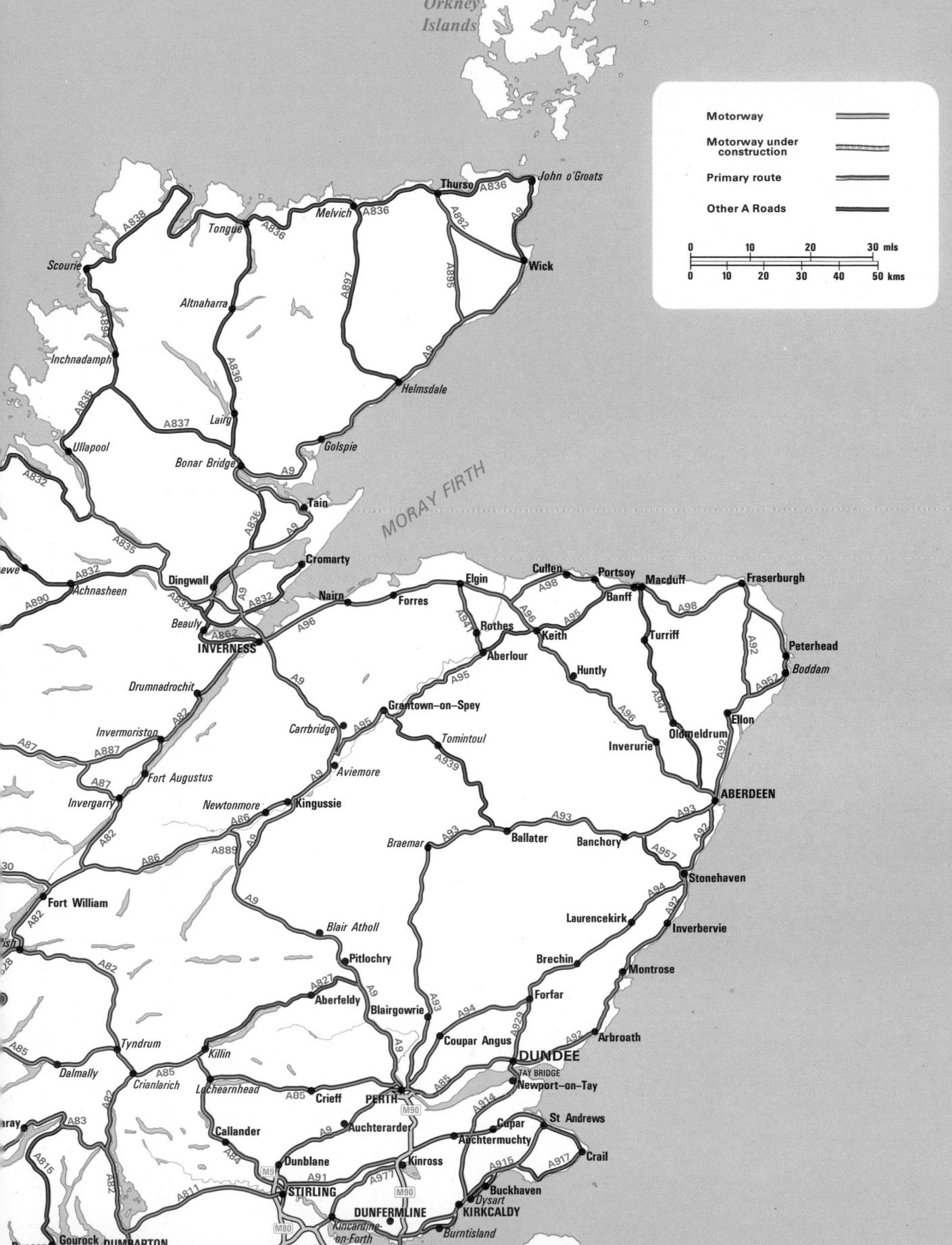

Orkney Islands

Motorway	
Motorway under construction	
Primary route	
Other A Roads	

0   10   20   30 mls
0   10   20   30   40   50 kms

John o'Groats
Thurso   A836
Melvich   A836   A9
Tongue   A836   A882   Wick
Scourie   A897   A895
Altnaharra
A838
A894
Inchnadamph   A836
A835   Helmsdale
Lairg   A9
Ullapool   A837
Bonar Bridge   Golspie
A832   A9
ewe   A832   Tain
A890   Cromarty
Achnasheen   Nairn   Forres   Elgin   Cullen   Portsoy   Macduff   Fraserburgh
A832   A832   A98   Banff
Dingwall   A96   A941   Rothes   A98
Beauly   A862   A96   Keith   Turriff   A92
INVERNESS   A941   Peterhead
Aberlour   Huntly   A952   Boddam
Drumnadrochit   A9   A95
A82   Grantown-on-Spey   A96   A947   Ellon
Invermoriston   Carrbridge   A95   Oldmeldrum   A92
A87   A887   Inverurie
A87   Fort Augustus   Aviemore   A939   Tomintoul   ABERDEEN
Invergarry   Newtonmore   Kingussie   A93   A957
A82   A86   A889   A9   A93   Ballater   Banchory   Stonehaven
30   A86   Braemar   A94   A92
Fort William   A9   Laurencekirk   Inverbervie
A82   Blair Atholl   Brechin   Montrose
sh   A82   Pitlochry   A94   A92   Arbroath
A827   Aberfeldy   A929   Forfar
Tyndrum   A9   Blairgowrie   A93   Coupar Angus   A92
Killin   A85   A9   DUNDEE
Dalmally   A85   Lochearnhead   Crieff   TAY BRIDGE
Crianlarich   A85   PERTH   Newport-on-Tay   St Andrews
ray   A82   Callander   A9   Auchterarder   M90   Cupar   Crail
A83   A84   A914   Auchtermuchty   A917
A815   Dunblane   Kinross   A915
A811   M9   A91   A977   M90   Buckhaven
Dunoon   Gourock   DUMBARTON   STIRLING   Dysart
GREENOCK   A82   ERSKINE   M80   Kincardine-   KIRKCALDY
BRIDGE   on-Forth   Burntisland
FALKIRK   M9   FORTH BRIDGE
Linlithgow   EDINBURGH   Dunbar

III

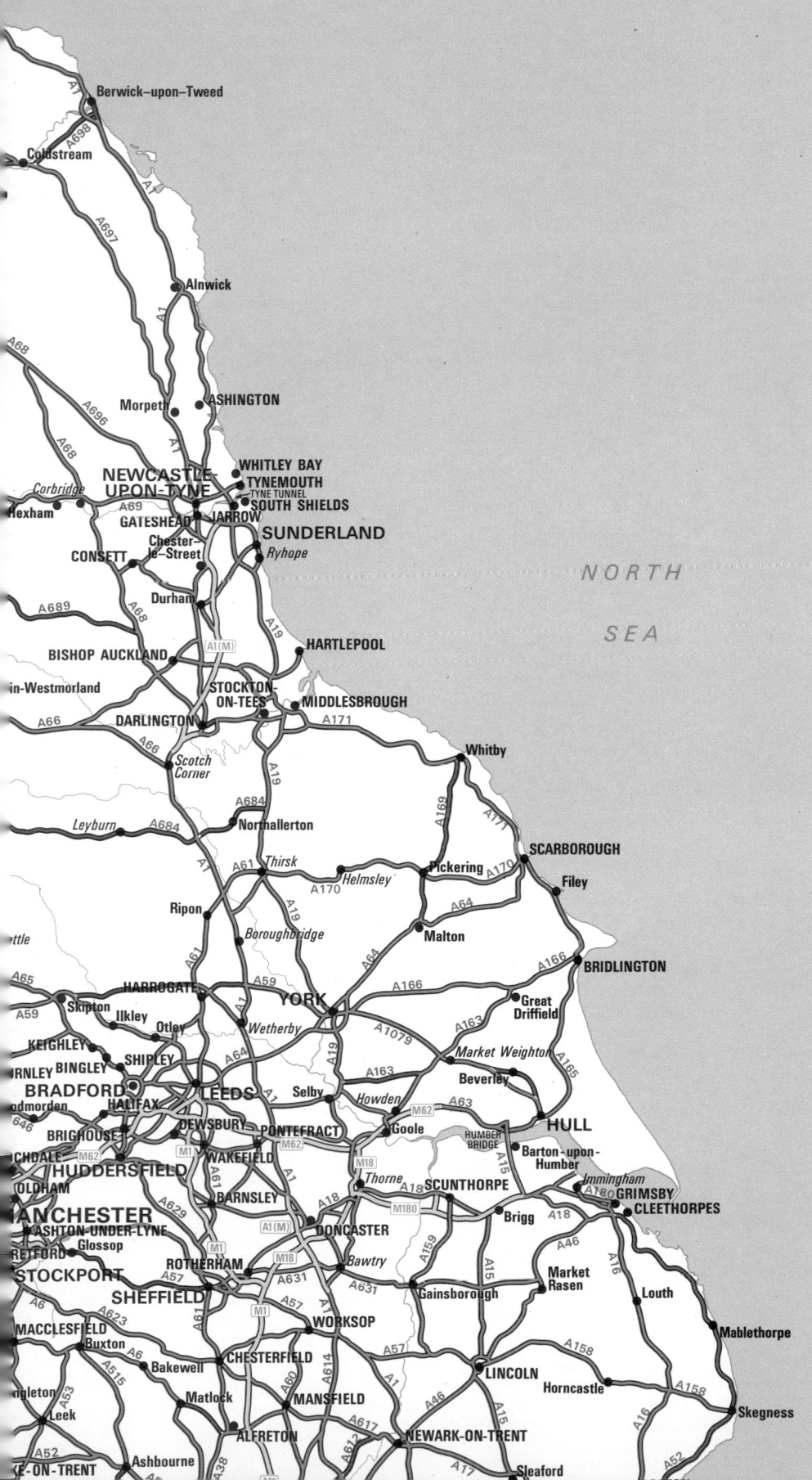

Berwick-upon-Tweed

Coldstream

Alnwick

Morpeth   ASHINGTON

Corbridge   WHITLEY BAY
NEWCASTLE   TYNEMOUTH
UPON-TYNE   TYNE TUNNEL
Hexham   SOUTH SHIELDS
GATESHEAD JARROW
        SUNDERLAND
CONSETT   Chester-   Ryhope
          le-Street
          Durham

BISHOP AUCKLAND
in-Westmorland   STOCKTON-   HARTLEPOOL
          ON-TEES   MIDDLESBROUGH
DARLINGTON

Scotch   Whitby
Corner

Leyburn   Northallerton

Thirsk   Pickering   SCARBOROUGH
Helmsley   Filey
Ripon

Boroughbridge   Malton
        BRIDLINGTON
HARROGATE
Skipton   YORK   Great
Ilkley Otley Wetherby   Driffield
KEIGHLEY
SHIPLEY   Market Weighton
BINGLEY   Beverley
BRADFORD LEEDS Selby Howden
HALIFAX   HULL
DEWSBURY PONTEFRACT Goole HUMBER
BRIGHOUSE   BRIDGE Barton-upon-
        Humber
HUDDERSFIELD WAKEFIELD   Thorne Immingham GRIMSBY
OLDHAM   BARNSLEY   SCUNTHORPE CLEETHORPES
ANCHESTER
ASHTON-UNDER-LYNE DONCASTER Brigg
Glossop
RETFORD
STOCKPORT ROTHERHAM Bawtry   Market
        Rasen Louth
SHEFFIELD   Gainsborough
MACCLESFIELD   Mablethorpe
Buxton WORKSOP
CHESTERFIELD   LINCOLN Horncastle
Bakewell   Skegness
Matlock MANSFIELD
Leek   NEWARK-ON-TRENT
E-ON-TRENT Ashbourne   ALFRETON   Sleaford

NORTH

SEA

NORTH SEA

V

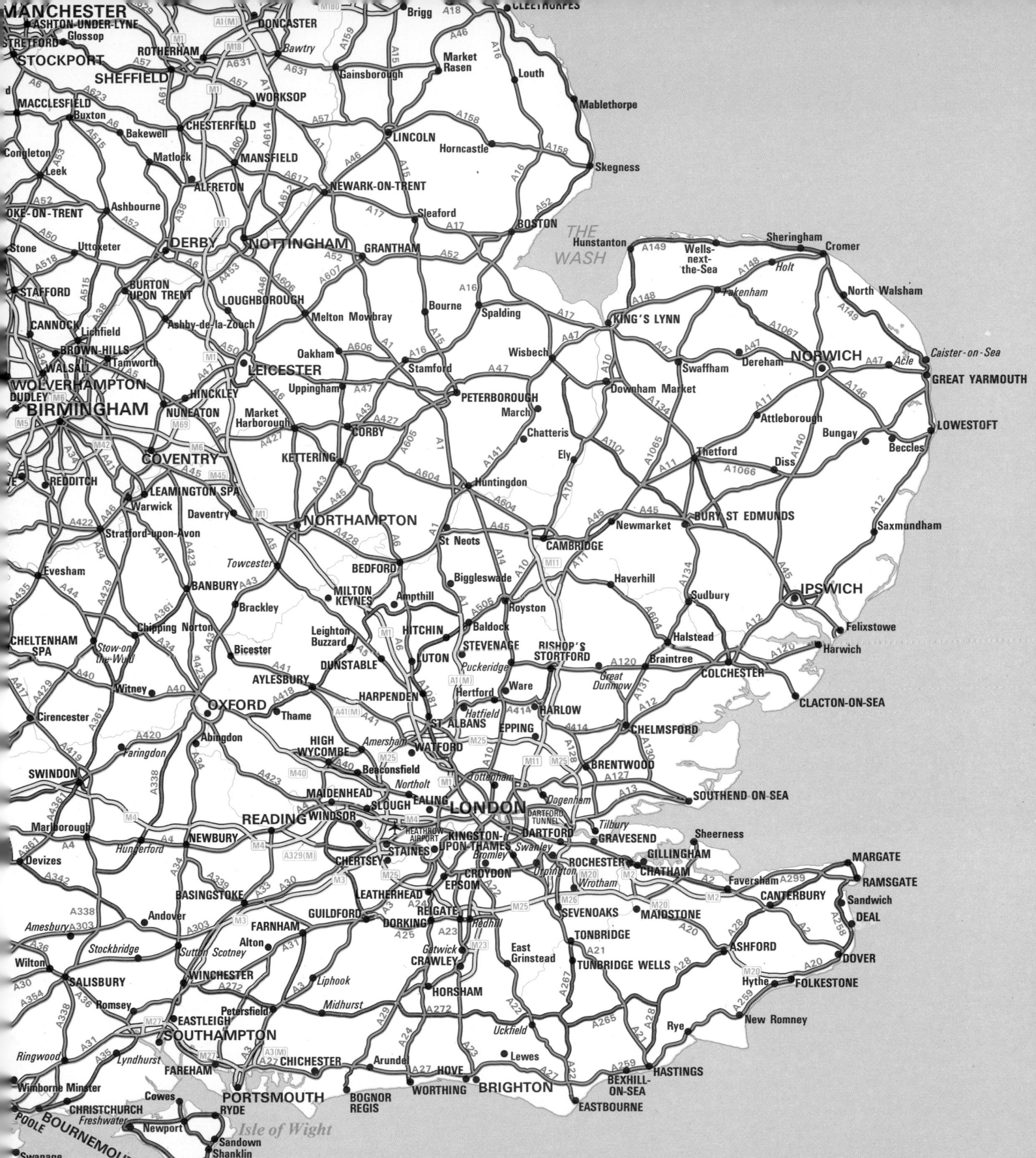

BBC Local Radio

Motoring information by radio

Most radio stations, including three of the national networks, give motoring information. Many of them include such details as part of their scheduled programmes, but information is also frequently given as it comes in. Both the BBC and ILR (Independent Local Radio) include in their programmes information on road and weather conditions.

Under normal circumstances any car radio should be able to receive local radio broadcasts within the reception areas shown on these maps. In some regions, particularly fringe areas, either the VHF, or the Medium Wave signal, may prove to be stronger.

It should be noted that in some parts of the country reception areas overlap; this applies particularly in the North Midlands and Northern England. The VHF/FM signal can sometimes vary over a very small area depending on local topography, and MW reception coverage is considerably reduced at night.

Regional Networks

Wales
Radio Wales 340 ● 882 ● —
Radio Cymru (Welsh Language Service) — ● ●
92.5-94.5
(S. Wales area 96.8)
(Occasional local programmes are broadcast on R. Clwyd (457 ● 657 MW) & R. Gwent (95.1 & 103.0 VHF/FM))

Scotland
Radio Scotland 370 ● 810 ●
92.5-94.6 (N.W. Scotland 97.7-99.3)
(Occasional local programmes are broadcast on 92.5-94.6 VHF/FM by R. Aberdeen (also on 303 ● 990 MW), R. Highland, (with R. nan Eilean), R. Orkney, R. Shetland, R. Solway (also on 513 ● 585 MW) and R. Tweed)

National Networks

R1 275/285 ● 1089/1053 ●
88.1-90.1 (at certain times)
R2 330/433 ● 909/693 ●
88.1-90.1 (carries R1 at certain times)
R4 1500 ● 200 (92.5-94.7 – England)

Local MW frequencies

R1	Bournemouth	202 ●	1485
	Merseyside	271 ●	1107
R2	Cardigan Bay	303 ●	990
R4	Aberdeen	207 ●	1449
	Carlisle	202 ●	1485
	London	417 ●	720
	Newcastle-upon-Tyne and area	498 ●	603
	Plymouth	388 ●	774
	Redruth	397 ●	756

BBC Local Radio

1 Bedfordshire
Radio Bedfordshire
Bedford area 258 ● 1161 ● 103.1
Luton area 476 ● 630 ● 103.1

2 Bristol
Radio Bristol 194 ● 1548 ● 95.5
Bristol area 194 ● 1548 ● 104.4
Taunton area 227 ● 1323 ● 95.5

3 Cambridgeshire
Radio Cambridgeshire 292 ● 1026 ● 96.0
Peterborough and N. Cambridgeshire area 207 ● 1449 ● 103.9

4 Cleveland
Radio Cleveland 194 ● 1548 ● 96.6
Whitby area 194 ● 1548 ● 95.8

5 Cornwall
Radio Cornwall
East Cornwall 457 ● 657 ● 95.2
West Cornwall 476 ● 630 ● 96.4
Isles of Scilly area 476 ● 630 ● 97.3

6 Cumbria
Radio Cumbria 397 ● 756 ● 95.6
Whitehaven area 206 ● 1458 ● 95.6

7 Derby
Radio Derby 269 ● 1116 ● 96.5
Derby only 269 ● 1116 ● 94.2

8 Devon
Radio Devon
Exeter area 303 ● 990 ● 97.0
Torbay area 206 ● 1458 ● 97.5
Plymouth area 351 ● 855 ● 97.5
Barnstaple & N. Devon area 375 ● 801 ● 103.9
Okehampton area — ● — ● 96.2

9 Furness
Radio Furness 358 ● 837 ● 96.1

10 Humberside
Radio Humberside 202 ● 1485 ● 96.9

11 Kent
Radio Kent 290 ● 1035 ● 96.7
Tunbridge Wells 187 ● 1602 ● 96.7
East Kent 388 ● 774 ● 102.8

12 Lancashire
Radio Lancashire 351 ● 855 ● 96.4
Lancaster area 193 ● 1557 ● 103.3

13 Leeds
Radio Leeds 388 ● 774 ● 92.4
Wharfedale area 388 ● 774 ● 95.3

14 Leicester
Radio Leicester 358 ● 837 ● 95.1

15 Lincolnshire
Radio Lincolnshire 219 ● 1368 ● 94.9

16 London
Radio London 206 ● 1458 ● 94.9

17 Manchester
Radio Manchester 206 ● 1458 ● 95.1

18 Merseyside
Radio Merseyside 202 ● 1485 ● 95.8

19 Newcastle
Radio Newcastle 206 ● 1458 ● 95.4
NE Northumberland 206 ● 1458 ● 96.3

20 Norfolk
Radio Norfolk 351 ● 855 ● 95.1
King's Lynn area 344 ● 873 ● 96.7

21 Northampton
Radio Northampton 271 ● 1107 ● 96.6
Corby area 271 ● 1107 ● 103.3

22 Nottingham
Radio Nottingham 197 ● 1521 ● 95.4
Central Nottinghamshire area 189 ● 1584 ●

23 Oxford
Radio Oxford 202 ● 1485 ● 95.2

24 Sheffield
Radio Sheffield 290 ● 1035 ● 97.4
Sheffield city 290 ● 1035 ● 88.6

25 Shropshire
Radio Shropshire 397 ● 756 ● 96.0
Ludlow area — ● — ● 95.0

26 Solent
Radio Solent 300 ● 999 ● 96.1
Bournemouth area 221 ● 1359 ● 96.1

27 Stoke-on-Trent
Radio Stoke-on-Trent 200 ● 1503 ● 94.6

28 Sussex
Radio Sussex
Brighton area 202 ● 1485 ● 95.3
East Sussex area 258 ● 1161 ● 103.1
Reigate/Crawley area 219 ● 1368 ● 102.7

29 West Midlands
Radio WM 206 ● 1458 ● 95.6
Wolverhampton area 362 ● 828 ● 95.6

30 York
Radio York 450 ● 666 ● 90.2
Scarborough area 238 ● 1260 ● 97.2

Channel Islands
Radio Guernsey 269 ● 1116 ● —
Radio Jersey 292 ● 1026 ● 88.8

IBA Local Radio

Independent Local Radio

1 Aberdeen
North Sound 290 ● 1035 ● 96.9

2 Ayr
West Sound 290 ● 1035 ● 96.2
Girvan area 290 ● 1035 ● 97.1

3 Birmingham
BRMB Radio 261 ● 1152 ● 94.8

4 Bournemouth
2CR 362 ● 828 ● 97.2

5 Bradford/Halifax/ Huddersfield
Pennine Radio
Bradford area 235 ● 1278 ● 96.0
Halifax/Huddersfield area 196
● 1530 ● 103.4

6 Brighton
Southern Sound 227 ● 1323 ●
103.4

7 Bristol
Radio West 238 ● 1260 ● 96.3

8 Bury St Edmunds
Saxon Radio 240 ● 1251 ● 96.3

9 Cardiff
CBC 221 ● 1359 ● 96.0

10 Coventry
Mercia Sound 220 ● 1359 ● 95.9

11 Dundee/Perth
Radio Tay
Dundee area 258 ● 1161 ● 95.8
Perth area 189 ● 1584 ● 96.4

12 Edinburgh
Radio Forth 194 ● 1548 ● 96.8

13 Exeter/Torbay
Devon Air Radio
Exeter area 450 ● 666 ● 95.8
Torbay area 314 ● 954 ● 95.1

14 Glasgow
Radio Clyde 261 ● 1152 ● 95.1

15 Gloucester & Cheltenham
Severn Sound 388 ● 774 ● 95.0

16 Great Yarmouth & Norwich
Radio Broadland 261 ● 1152 ●
97.6

17 Guildford
County Sound 203 ● 1476 ● 96.6

18 Hereford/Worcester
Radio Wyvern
Hereford area 314 ● 954 ● 95.8
Worcester area 196 ● 1530 ●
96.2

19 Humberside
Viking Radio 258 ● 1161 ●
102.7

20 Inverness
Moray Firth Radio 271 ● 1107 ●
95.9

21 Ipswich
Radio Orwell 257 ● 1170 ● 97.1

22 East Kent
Invicta Sound 497 ● 603 ● 95.1
Thanet area 497 ● 603 ● 95.9
Dover/Folkestone 497 ● 603 ●
97.0
Ashford area 497 ● 603 ● 96.3

23 Leeds
Radio Aire 362 ● 828 ● 94.6

24 Leicester
Leicester Sound 238 ● 1260 ●
97.1

25 Liverpool
Radio City 194 ● 1548 ● 96.7

26 London
Capital Radio (General) 194 ●
1548 ● 95.8
LBC (News & Information) 261
● 1152 ● 97.3

27 Luton/Bedford
Chiltern Radio
Luton area 362 ● 828 ● 97.6
Bedford area 379 ● 792 ● 95.5

28 Maidstone & Medway
Invicta Sound 241 ● 1242 ●
103.8

29 Manchester
Piccadilly Radio 261 ● 1152 ●
97.0

31 Nottingham
Radio Trent 301 ● 999 ● 96.2

32 Peterborough/ Northampton
Hereward Radio
Peterborough area 225 ● 1332
● 95.7
Northampton area 193 ● 1557 ●
102.8

33 Plymouth
Plymouth Sound 261 ● 1152 ●
96.0

34 Portsmouth
Radio Victory 257 ● 1170 ● 95.0

35 Preston & Blackpool
Red Rose Radio 300 ● 999 ●
97.3

36 Reading
Radio 210 210 ● 1431 ● 97.0

37 Reigate & Crawley
Radio Mercury 197 ● 1521 ●
103.6

38 Sheffield/Rotherham/ Barnsley
Radio Hallam
Sheffield area 194 ● 1548 ● 95.2
Rotherham area 194 ● 1548 ●
95.9
Barnsley area 230 ● 1305 ● 95.6

39 Southend/Chelmsford
Essex Radio
Southend area 210 ● 1431 ●
95.3
Chelmsford area 220 ● 1359 ●
96.4

40 Stoke-on-Trent
Signal Radio 257 ● 1170 ● 104.3

41 Swansea
Swansea Sound 257 ● 1170 ●
95.1

42 Swindon/West Wiltshire
Wiltshire Radio
Swindon area 258 ● 1161 ● 96.4
West Wiltshire 320 ● 936 ● 97.4

43 Teesside
Radio Tees 257 ● 1170 ● 95.0

44 Tyne & Wear
Metro Radio 261 ● 1152 ● 97.0

45 Wolverhampton & Black Country
Beacon Radio 303 ● 990 ● 97.2

46 Wrexham & Deeside
Marcher Sound/
Sain-Y-Gororau 238 ● 1260 ●
95.4

Isle of Man
Manx Radio (Not run by IBA)
219 ● 1368 ● 96.9/89.0

Inverness ● ▲ 20
Aberdeen
1
11 ▲
Perth ● ▲
Edinburgh
Glasgow ▲ 14 12
2
Carlisle ●
Newcastle Upon Tyne
44 ▲
Middlesbrough
43 ▲
19
35 ▲
5 ▲ 23 Leeds ● Hull
Manchester
25 ● 29 ▲ 38 ▲
Liverpool ● Sheffield
Lincoln
Nottingham ●
31 ▲
Norwich
16 ▲
Telford ● 40 ▲
45 ▲ Leicester ●
Birmingham ● 3 ▲ 24 ▲ 32 ▲
10 Cambridge ●
8 ▲
18 ▲ 27 ▲ 21 ▲
15 ▲
Swansea ● 41 ▲ Oxford ●
9 ▲ 39 ▲
Cardiff ● 26 ▲
Bristol ● 42 ▲ 28 ▲
7 ▲ 36 ▲ 17 ▲ LONDON 22 ▲
Southampton ●
34 ▲ 6 ▲
Exeter ●
33 ▲ 13 ▲
Plymouth ●

IX

Mileage Chart

The distances between towns on the mileage chart are given to the nearest mile, and are measured along the normal AA recommended routes. It should be noted that AA recommended routes do not necessarily follow the shortest distances between places but are based on the quickest travelling time, making maximum use of motorways or dual-carriageway roads.   © The Automobile Association 1980

Aberdeen
470 | Aberystwyth
605 222 | Barnstaple
430 119 179 | Birmingham
610 271 205 184 | Brighton
511 129 101 85 151 | Bristol
468 218 256 101 132 156 | Cambridge
532 110 141 107 186 45 191 | Cardiff
234 233 368 197 372 275 252 295 | Carlisle
520 48 203 133 247 106 235 67 282 | Carmarthen
525 265 292 146 123 193 49 228 309 289 | Colchester
588 207 93 160 118 61 181 123 352 185 204 | Dorchester
591 320 277 202 78 198 121 234 393 298 111 203 | Dover
130 333 468 293 474 373 337 395 98 382 390 451 457 | Edinburgh
584 200 41 157 174 81 233 119 346 181 270 53 249 446 | Exeter
176 445 578 402 582 484 462 505 209 493 518 561 599 135 556 | Fort William
149 327 466 291 471 372 349 393 97 376 404 447 490 45 444 103 | Glasgow
477 110 130 51 145 35 121 61 245 112 173 111 194 341 108 449 337 | Gloucester
572 227 177 146 44 107 96 143 337 203 117 99 100 436 148 541 431 101 | Guildford
465 79 148 55 177 53 144 58 230 85 204 130 227 328 128 440 324 31 132 | Hereford
457 106 327 151 330 232 246 209 221 155 305 309 347 325 305 431 319 199 289 155 | Holyhead
361 224 319 136 281 227 157 246 155 273 211 290 278 229 297 362 245 194 240 197 215 | Hull
105 496 632 453 636 537 501 558 260 544 551 613 623 158 610 66 175 505 594 490 486 393 | Inverness
285 187 328 151 327 229 217 251 49 238 264 307 347 148 301 258 144 199 290 185 178 134 309 | Kendal
336 174 310 115 260 216 143 236 122 220 198 291 265 205 288 331 215 181 221 168 163 59 367 72 | Leeds
396 196 261 96 212 166 93 205 180 229 147 228 212 263 239 389 275 132 175 155 200 48 427 144 71 | Lincoln
361 110 272 98 274 178 195 200 125 158 238 256 295 222 250 332 220 146 236 116 104 126 385 78 72 128 | Liverpool
555 277 234 167 50 158 85 194 357 255 76 160 43 422 206 565 454 151 57 184 312 243 589 311 230 179 259 | Maidstone
354 129 261 88 265 167 153 188 118 178 205 243 283 218 239 325 214 133 224 121 123 97 379 72 43 88 34 251 | Manchester
277 242 355 170 317 263 195 283 93 291 249 332 316 145 333 302 186 236 281 238 234 87 308 80 63 121 141 286 113 | Middlesbrough
239 271 383 198 347 291 224 311 58 320 279 356 348 107 361 243 150 262 306 265 260 121 268 96 91 155 170 315 141 37 | Newcastle
480 171 206 54 132 114 50 137 243 177 96 143 149 344 184 453 341 77 94 91 200 151 503 199 131 88 147 114 135 192 216 | Northampton
501 281 317 161 179 217 62 252 284 297 60 240 167 365 295 492 379 183 155 206 309 153 528 247 173 106 232 135 183 224 258 112 | Norwich
402 161 244 59 194 151 82 170 187 193 139 206 202 268 222 397 281 118 157 121 174 92 432 163 73 36 107 177 71 132 156 66 123 | Nottingham
497 156 174 63 108 74 82 109 260 173 124 102 148 361 152 470 354 49 70 80 218 188 523 217 171 126 164 105 153 230 253 41 144 104 | Oxford
696 313 110 272 288 195 346 232 462 294 383 166 362 561 112 669 559 221 262 239 419 411 723 414 401 352 366 319 355 449 477 295 407 336 265 | Penzance
83 379 516 339 521 420 385 443 144 427 434 497 507 43 494 105 60 424 478 373 370 277 115 194 251 310 269 474 263 192 153 388 413 316 407 607 | Perth
624 241 66 199 218 125 275 164 391 222 311 94 290 488 45 597 486 149 191 167 347 341 651 342 328 280 294 247 281 378 410 224 336 265 193 78 535 | Plymouth
324 145 282 109 284 188 197 209 88 195 253 266 305 187 260 295 182 156 245 140 136 121 347 42 69 123 29 268 32 105 124 157 229 123 175 373 231 301 | Preston
547 182 119 112 86 52 141 99 313 160 164 40 163 412 91 520 412 74 63 105 268 250 574 266 232 189 217 120 203 292 316 103 200 166 62 204 459 132 226 | Salisbury
376 164 271 87 229 179 119 202 161 226 175 245 240 250 249 371 255 146 193 148 158 68 407 121 34 46 76 205 36 106 136 102 150 45 143 364 291 293 80 205 | Sheffield
412 76 223 48 224 128 142 110 178 126 193 204 243 276 201 387 272 95 185 53 104 164 438 132 116 121 64 207 69 189 216 96 205 85 113 315 321 242 88 165 114 | Shrewsbury
571 205 142 128 63 75 133 123 339 181 156 54 155 437 114 547 436 99 50 130 296 253 599 293 235 193 241 112 227 319 108 192 171 67 227 483 155 251 23 205 190 | Southampton
387 110 221 44 222 125 139 149 156 160 192 205 242 252 191 360 248 94 184 86 122 118 413 107 90 89 55 205 44 164 191 93 176 51 111 313 297 243 64 166 52 34 191 | Stoke
241 344 479 307 483 386 361 406 109 393 420 464 503 130 457 192 88 353 443 338 332 259 269 161 232 292 234 426 229 164 355 295 371 572 152 502 198 423 269 287 447 261 | Stranraer
552 168 49 126 152 48 203 87 318 149 239 41 224 415 32 524 412 76 124 94 274 269 578 269 256 207 221 181 208 306 335 152 264 193 121 145 461 73 228 67 221 169 89 170 429 | Taunton
325 200 313 128 275 221 153 241 117 249 208 287 274 191 291 325 208 190 237 193 190 38 354 93 24 72 100 243 71 49 83 144 86 185 406 238 340 83 247 60 144 252 119 228 263 | York
543 240 220 118 53 119 60 155 307 216 63 127 77 405 170 513 402 104 30 135 263 215 569 259 196 161 201 37 199 252 280 67 115 128 56 283 453 215 218 85 167 162 76 156 419 167 209 | LONDON

Index to Motorways

Index to Town Plans

Road Signs

Considerable help in negotiating the nation's highways can be obtained by understanding the various types of road direction signs illustrated on this page. The principal benefit of the sign system is that the primary route signs (green) indicate the most straightforward route between one town and another. These signs do not necessarily indicate the most direct route, but it should be remembered that direct routes may not be the quickest, or the easiest to follow.

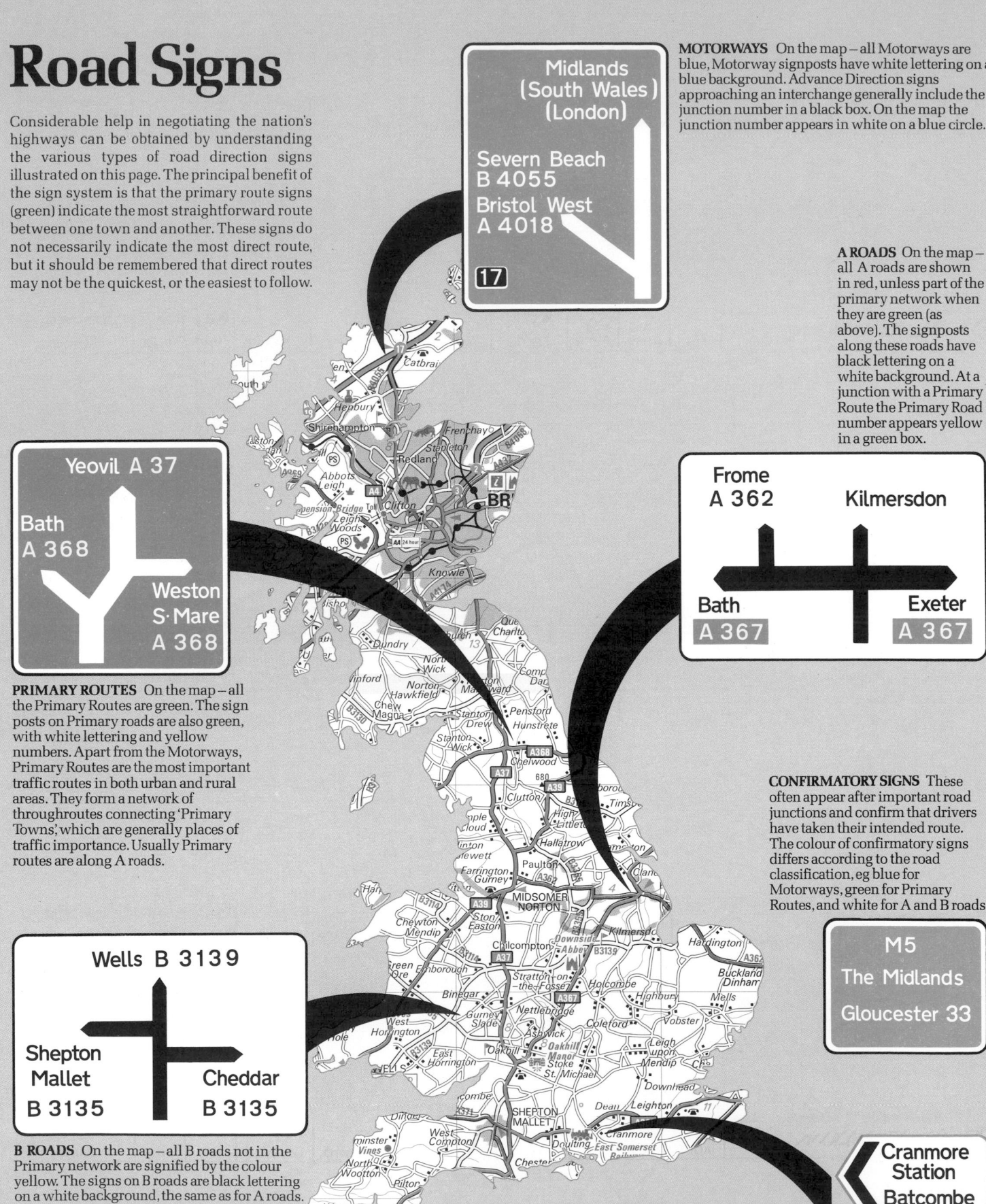

MOTORWAYS On the map—all Motorways are blue. Motorway signposts have white lettering on a blue background. Advance Direction signs approaching an interchange generally include the junction number in a black box. On the map the junction number appears in white on a blue circle.

A ROADS On the map—all A roads are shown in red, unless part of the primary network when they are green (as above). The signposts along these roads have black lettering on a white background. At a junction with a Primary Route the Primary Road number appears yellow in a green box.

PRIMARY ROUTES On the map—all the Primary Routes are green. The sign posts on Primary roads are also green, with white lettering and yellow numbers. Apart from the Motorways, Primary Routes are the most important traffic routes in both urban and rural areas. They form a network of throughroutes connecting 'Primary Towns', which are generally places of traffic importance. Usually Primary routes are along A roads.

CONFIRMATORY SIGNS These often appear after important road junctions and confirm that drivers have taken their intended route. The colour of confirmatory signs differs according to the road classification, eg blue for Motorways, green for Primary Routes, and white for A and B roads.

B ROADS On the map—all B roads not in the Primary network are signified by the colour yellow. The signs on B roads are black lettering on a white background, the same as for A and B roads.

UNCLASSIFIED ROADS On the map—all unclassified roads are white. New signposts along unclassified roads are usually of the Local Direction type. These have black lettering on a white background with a blue border. Local Direction signs may also appear in addition to Primary and non-Primary signs and indicate the route to local districts and amenities.

The National Grid

To locate a place in this atlas, first look up the name of the town or village required in the index, which starts on page 227. Each entry is followed by the page number on which the place can be found, and its National Grid reference.

Eg:	Hyssington	*40*	SO 3194
	Hythe (Hants.)	*11*	SU 4207
	Hythe (Kent)	*15*	TR 1635

Hythe is on page 15 with National Grid reference TR 1635.

When the required place name and its reference have been found in the index:

a) turn to the page number indicated,
b) find the location using the last four numbers,

Taking Hythe (Kent) as our example:

Take the first figure of the reference 1, this refers to the numbered grid line running along the bottom of the page. Having found this line, the second figure 6, tells you the distance to move in tenths to the right of this line. A vertical line through this point is the first half of the reference.

The third figure 3, refers to the numbered grid lines on the left hand side of the page, finally the fourth figure 5, indicates the distance to move in tenths above this line. A horizontal line drawn through this point to intersect with the first line gives the precise location of the place in question. See example below.

NATIONAL GRID EXPLANATION

The National Grid provides a system of reference common to maps of all scales. The grid covers Britain with an imaginary network of 100 kilometre squares. Each square is identified by two letters eg. TR. Every 100 kilometre square is then sub-divided into 10 kilometre squares which appear as a network of blue lines on the map pages. These blue lines are numbered left to right 0-9 and bottom to top 0-9. These 10 kilometre squares can be further divided into tenths to give a place reference to the nearest kilometre.

Legend

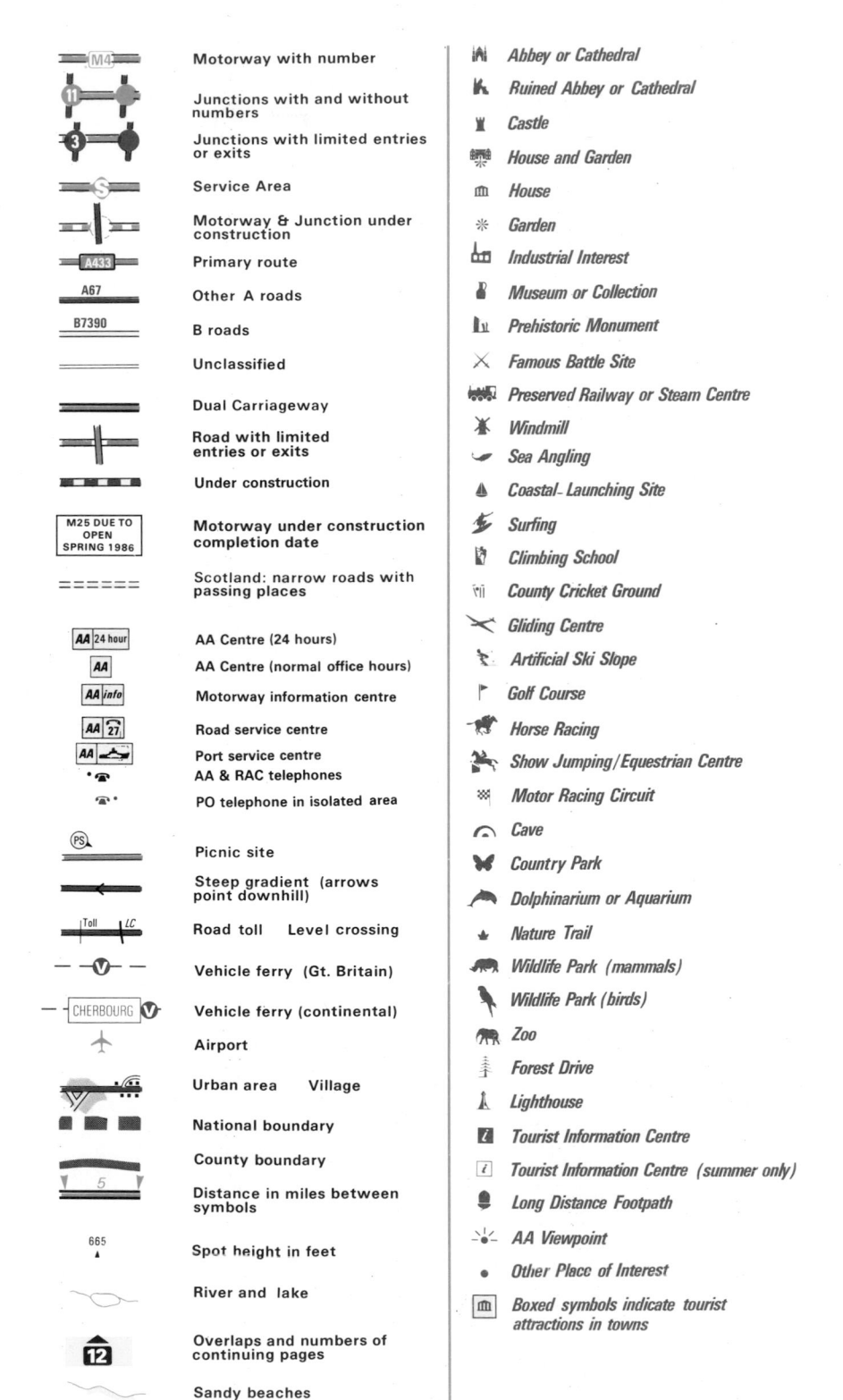

Motorway with number	
Junctions with and without numbers	
Junctions with limited entries or exits	
Service Area	
Motorway & Junction under construction	
Primary route	
Other A roads	
B roads	
Unclassified	
Dual Carriageway	
Road with limited entries or exits	
Under construction	
Motorway under construction completion date	
Scotland: narrow roads with passing places	
AA Centre (24 hours)	
AA Centre (normal office hours)	
Motorway information centre	
Road service centre	
Port service centre	
AA & RAC telephones	
PO telephone in isolated area	
Picnic site	
Steep gradient (arrows point downhill)	
Road toll Level crossing	
Vehicle ferry (Gt. Britain)	
Vehicle ferry (continental)	
Airport	
Urban area Village	
National boundary	
County boundary	
Distance in miles between symbols	
Spot height in feet	
River and lake	
Overlaps and numbers of continuing pages	
Sandy beaches	

Abbey or Cathedral

Ruined Abbey or Cathedral

Castle

House and Garden

House

Garden

Industrial Interest

Museum or Collection

Prehistoric Monument

Famous Battle Site

Preserved Railway or Steam Centre

Windmill

Sea Angling

Coastal Launching Site

Surfing

Climbing School

County Cricket Ground

Gliding Centre

Artificial Ski Slope

Golf Course

Horse Racing

Show Jumping/Equestrian Centre

Motor Racing Circuit

Cave

Country Park

Dolphinarium or Aquarium

Nature Trail

Wildlife Park (mammals)

Wildlife Park (birds)

Zoo

Forest Drive

Lighthouse

Tourist Information Centre

Tourist Information Centre (summer only)

Long Distance Footpath

AA Viewpoint

Other Place of Interest

Boxed symbols indicate tourist attractions in towns

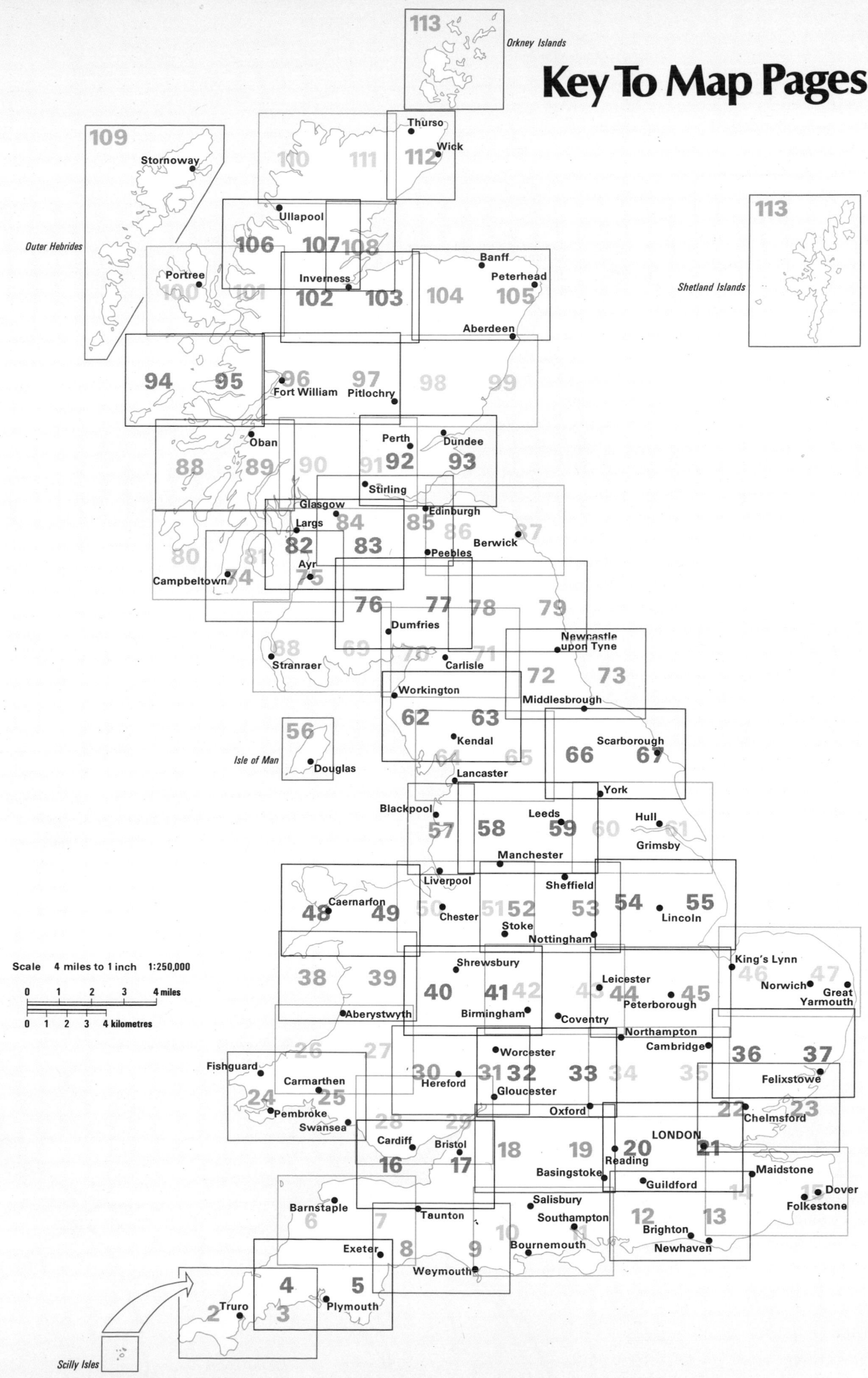

Key To Map Pages

113 Orkney Islands

113 Shetland Islands

109 Stornoway
Outer Hebrides

110 **111** **112** Thurso Wick

Ullapool

106 **107** **108** Banff Peterhead
Portree Inverness

100 **101** **102** **103** **104** **105** Aberdeen

94 **95** **96** **97** **98** **99**
Fort William Pitlochry

88 **89** **90** **91** **92** **93** Oban Perth Dundee

Stirling

Glasgow Edinburgh
Largs **84** **85** **86** **87**
82 **83** Berwick
80 **81** Ayr Peebles
Campbeltown **74** **75**

76 **77** **78** **79**
Dumfries

68 **69** **70** **71** Newcastle upon Tyne
Stranraer Carlisle **72** **73**
Workington Middlesbrough

62 **63**
Kendal Scarborough
56 **64** **65** **66** **67**
Isle of Man Lancaster
Douglas York
Blackpool Leeds Hull
57 **58** **59** **60** **61**
Manchester Grimsby
Liverpool Sheffield
Caernarfon **51** **52** **53** **54** **55**
48 **49** **50** Chester Stoke Lincoln
Nottingham

Shrewsbury King's Lynn
38 **39** Leicester **46** **47**
40 **41** **42** **43** **44** **45** Norwich Great Yarmouth
Aberystwyth Birmingham Peterborough
Coventry Northampton
Worcester Cambridge **36** **37**
Fishguard **26** **27** **30** **31** **32** **33** **34** **35** Felixstowe
Carmarthen Hereford
24 **25** Gloucester **22** **23**
Pembroke Oxford Chelmsford
Swansea **28** **29** LONDON
Cardiff Bristol **21**
16 **17** **18** **19** **20** Maidstone
Basingstoke Reading **14** **15** Dover
Guildford Folkestone
Barnstaple Salisbury
6 **7** Taunton Southampton **12** **13** Brighton
Exeter **8** **9** **10** **11** Bournemouth Newhaven
Weymouth

2 **4** **5**
3 Truro Plymouth

Scilly Isles

Scale   4 miles to 1 inch   1:250,000

0   1   2   3   4 miles

0   1   2   3   4 kilometres

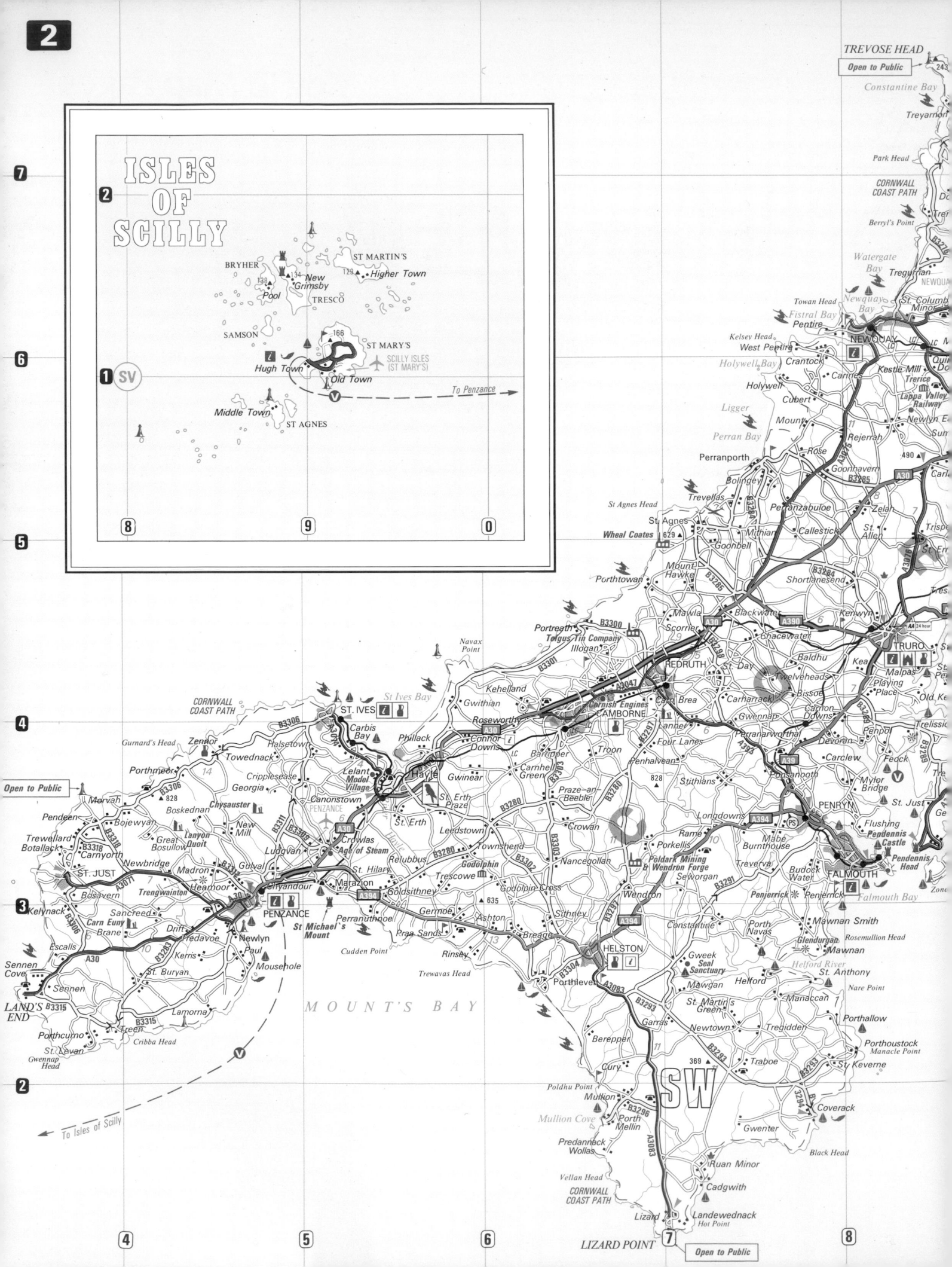

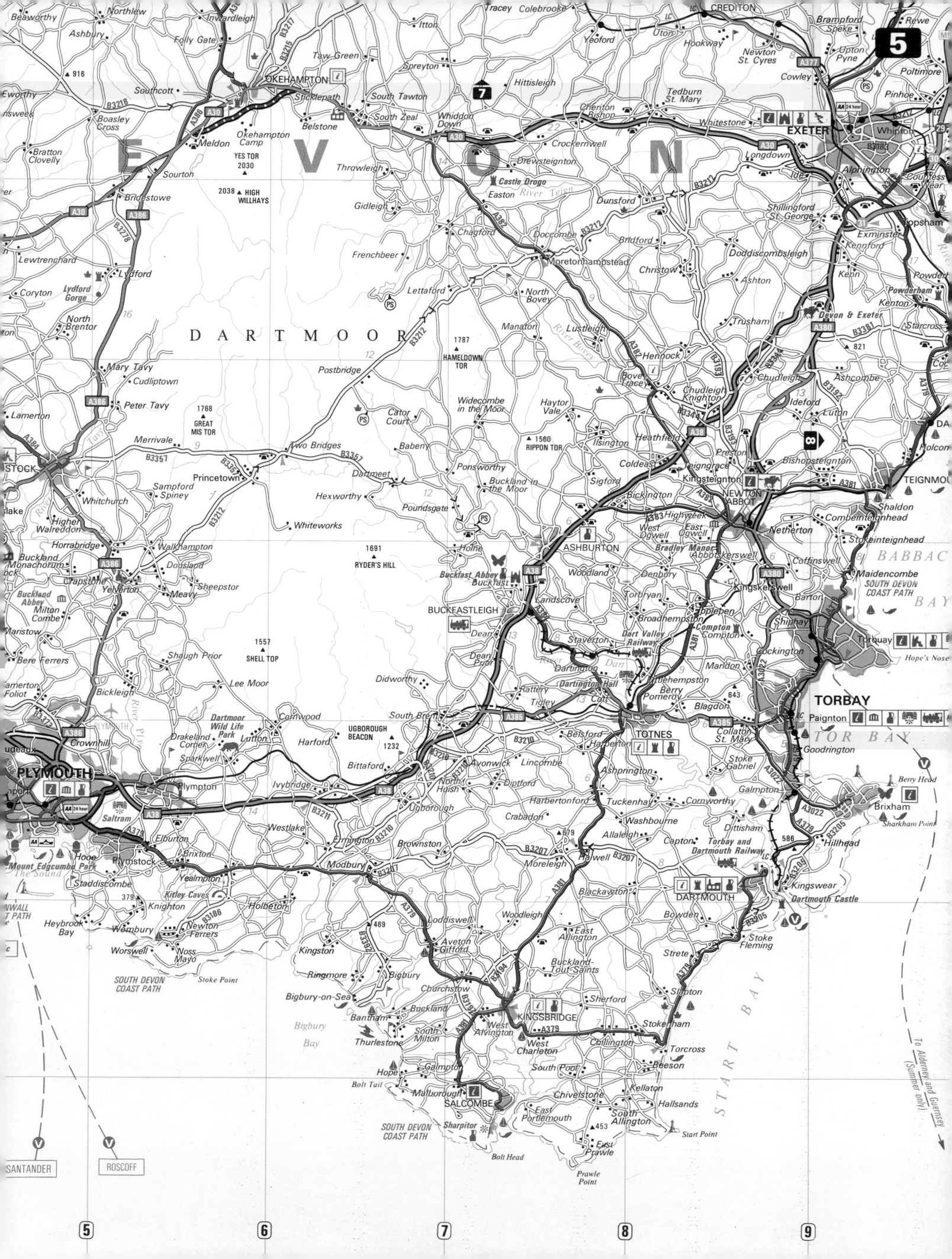

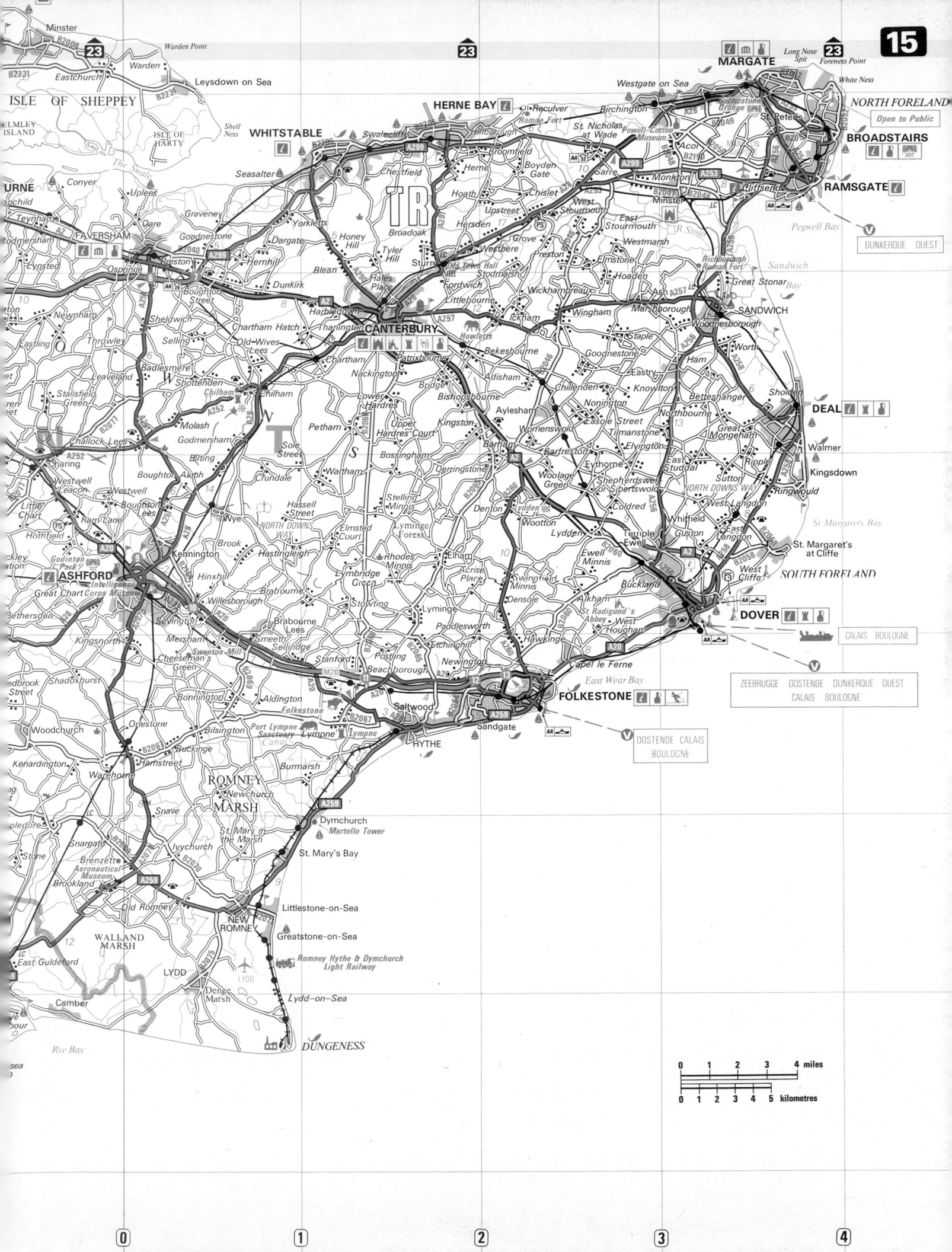

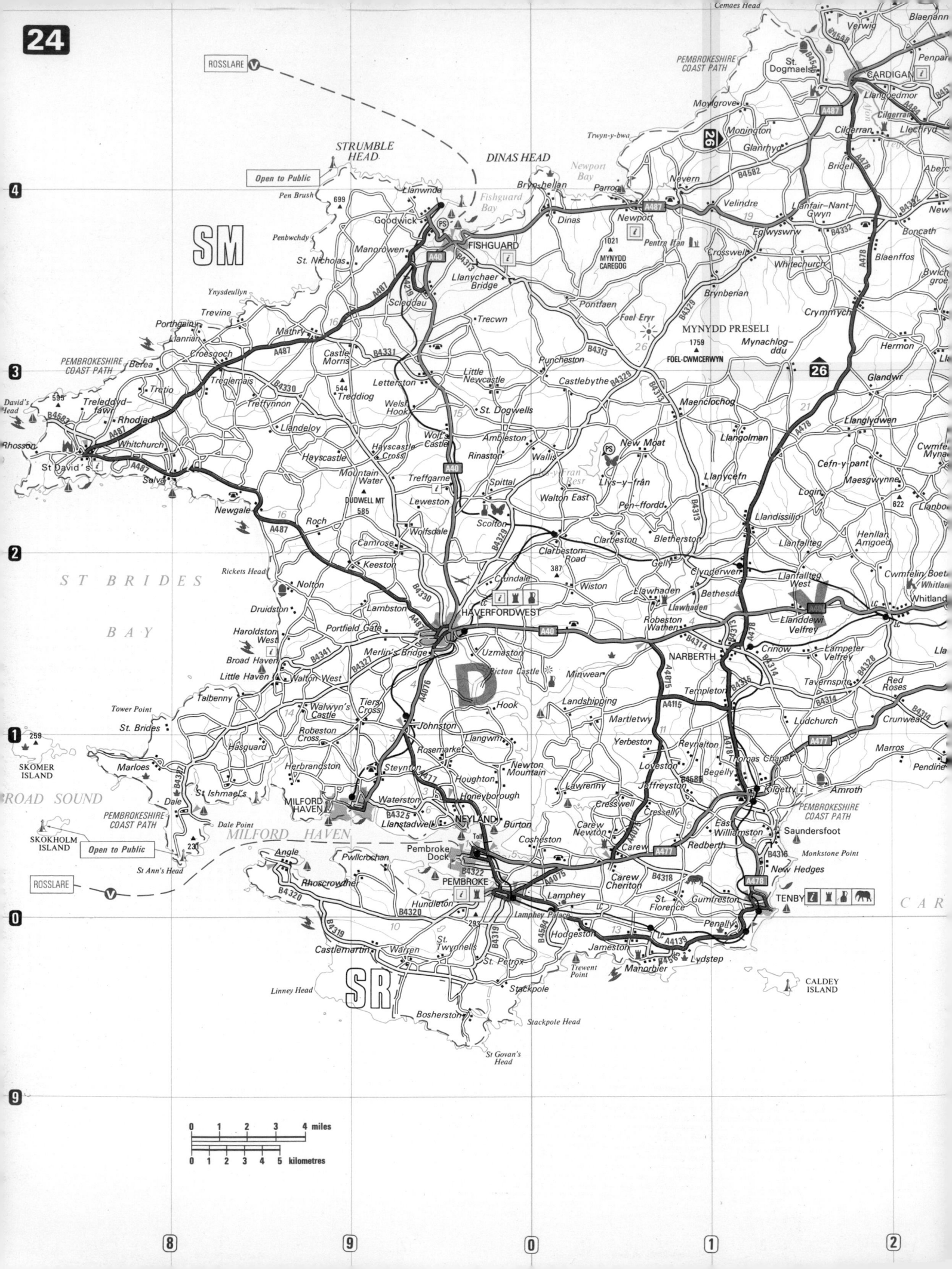

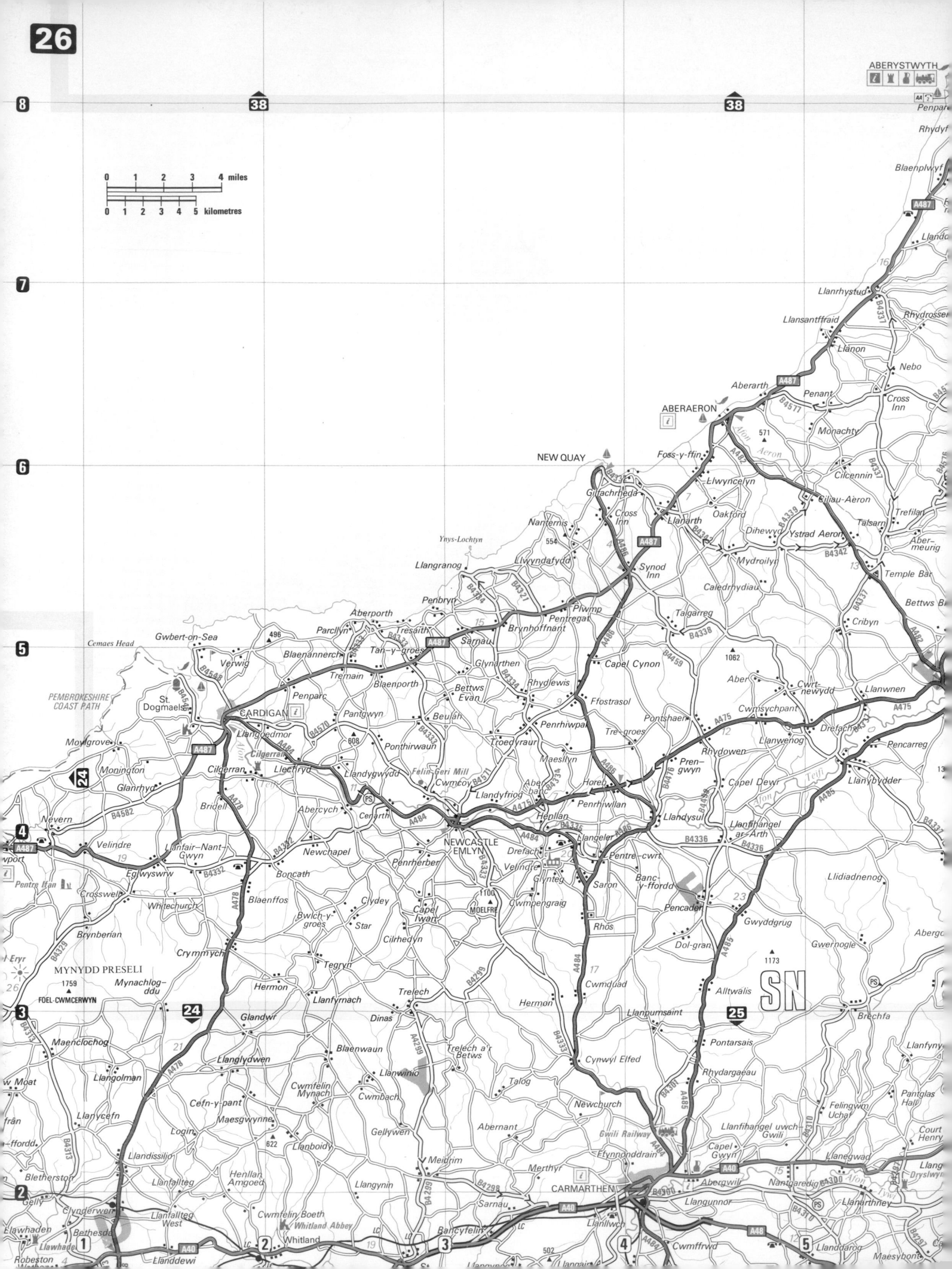

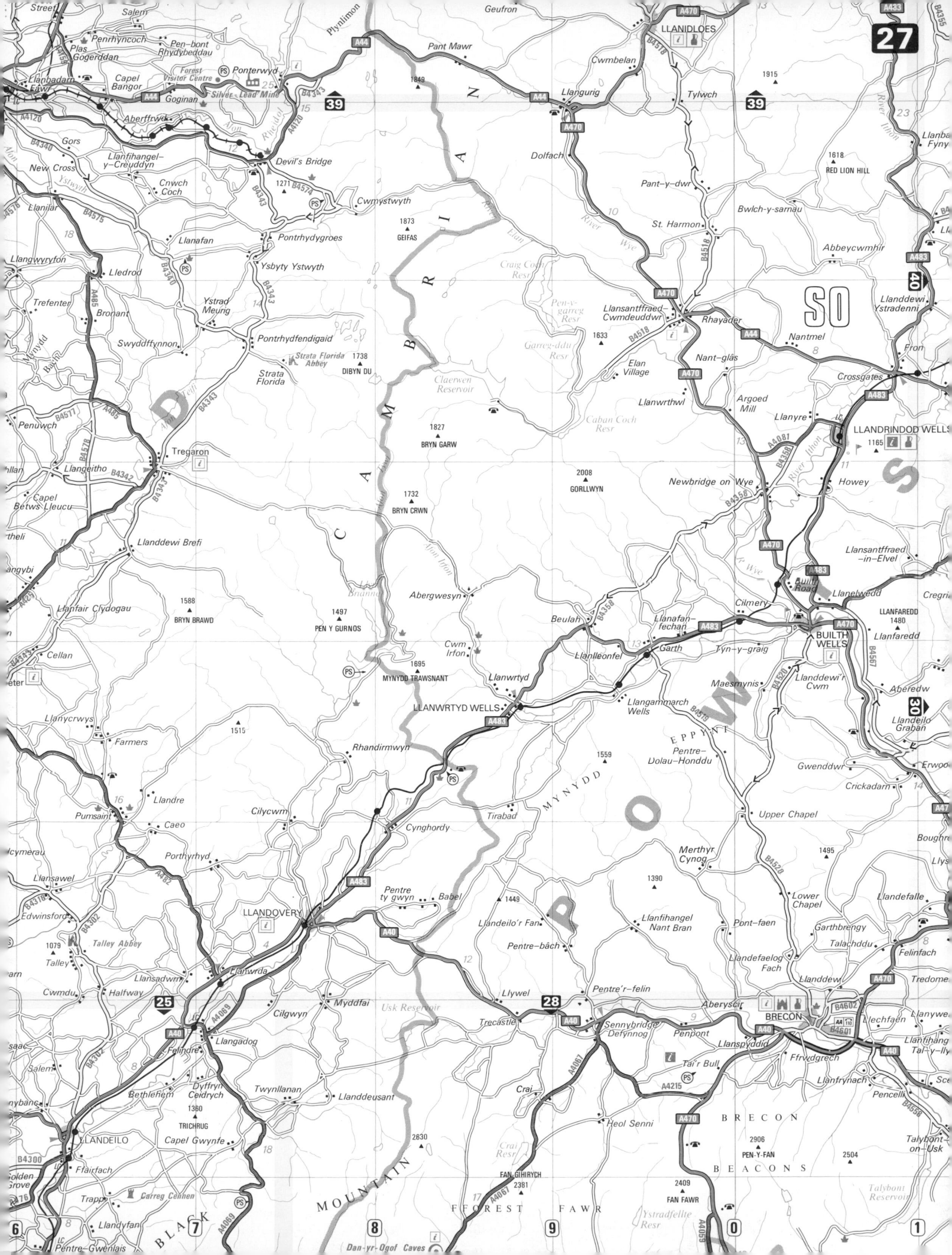

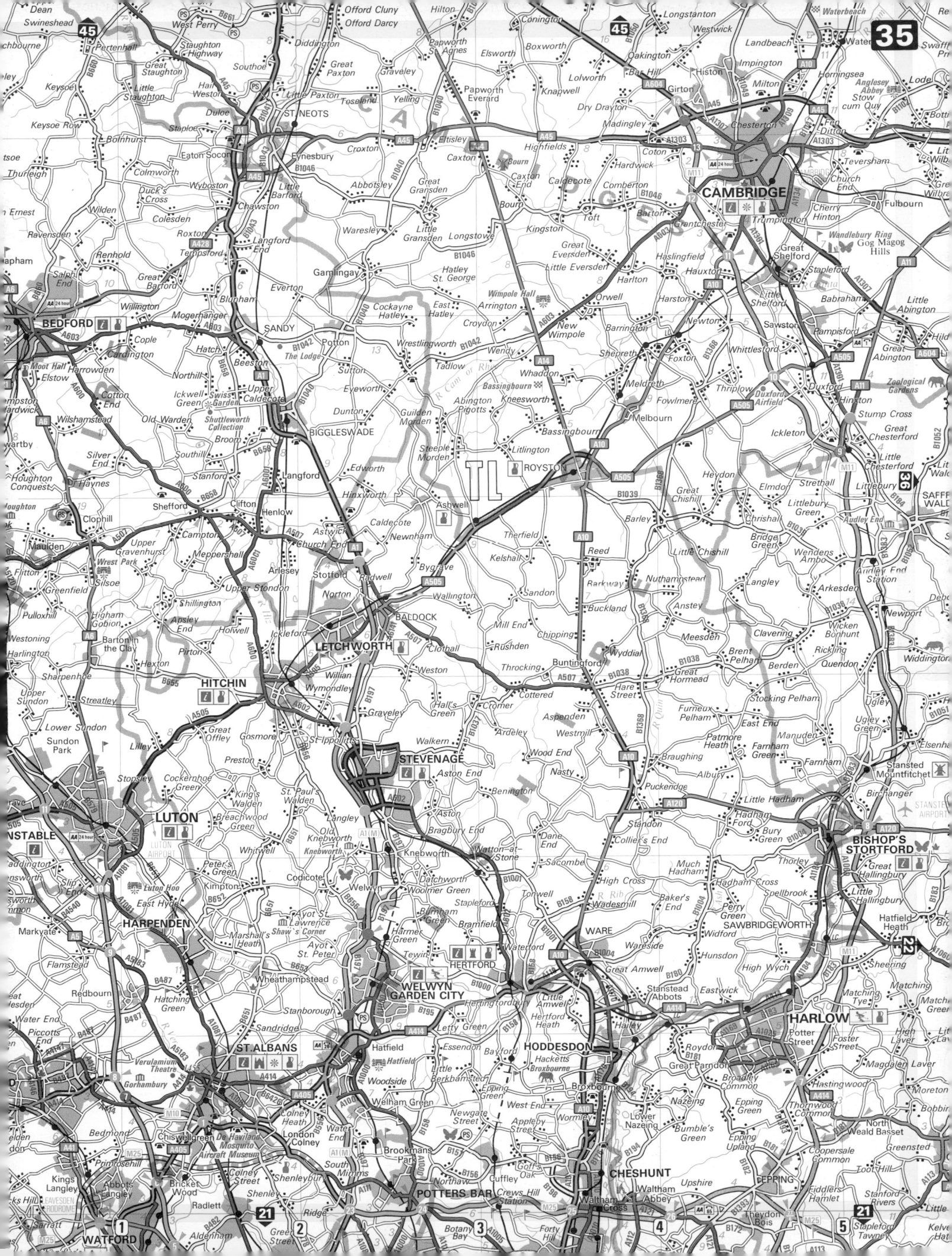

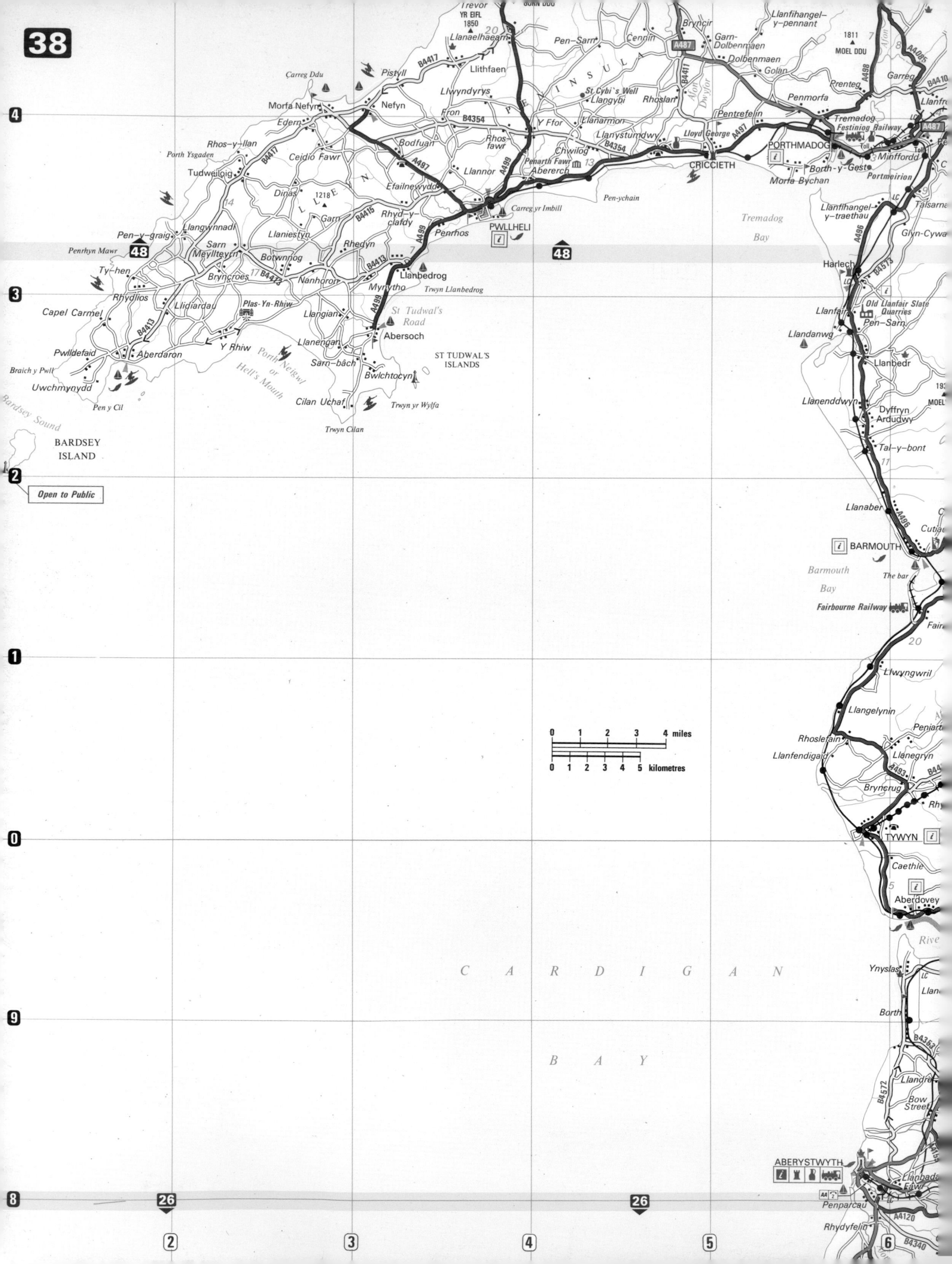

4

3

2

1

0

9

8

Trevor
YR EIFL
1850
Llanaelhaearn
Pistyll
Carreg Ddu
Morfa Nefyn
Nefyn
Edern
Rhos-y-llan
Porth Ysgaden
Tudweiliog
Dinas
1218
Garn
Llangwnnadl
Sarn
Meyllteyrn
Bryncroes
Ty-hen
Rhydlios
Llidiardau
Capel Carmel
B4413
Pwlldefaid
Aberdaron
Braich y Pwll
Uwchmynydd
Pen y Cil

Bardsey Sound

BARDSEY
ISLAND

Open to Public

Llithfaen
Llwyndyrys
Fron
B4354
Y Ffor
Bodfuan
Rhos-fawr
Ceidio Fawr
A487
Efailnewydd
Rhyd-y-clafdy
B4415
Botwnnog
Rhedyn
Nanhoron
B4413
Mynytho
Llanbedrog
Trwyn Llanbedrog
Llangian
Llanengan
Abersoch
Sarn-bach
Bwlchtocyn
Cilan Uchaf
Trwyn yr Wylfa
Trwyn Cilan

St Tudwal's
Road

ST TUDWAL'S
ISLANDS

Porth Neigwl
or
Hell's Mouth

LLEYN

PENINSULA

Pen-Sarn
Cennin
Llangybi
St Cybi's Well
Llanarmon
Llanystumdwy
Chwilog
Penarth Fawr
Abererch
Llannor
Penrhos
PWLLHELI
Carreg yr Imbill

Pen-ychain

48

Bryncir
Garn-Dolbenmaen
Dolbenmaen
Golan
Penmorfa
Lloyd George
CRICCIETH
Morfa Bychan
Borth-y-Gest

MOEL DDU
1811

Prenteg
Tremadog
Festiniog Railway
PORTHMADOG
Minffordd
Portmeirion
Talsarnau
Glyn-Cywa

Garreg
B4410

A487

A4085

A4411

A487

A496

Llanfihangel-y-pennant

Llanfihangel-y-traethau

Tremadog
Bay

Harlech
Old Llanfair Slate
Quarries
Llanfair
Pen-Sarn
Llandanwg
Llanbedr
Llanenddwyn
Dyffryn Ardudwy
Tal-y-bont
Llanaber
Cutiau
BARMOUTH
Barmouth
Bay
The bar
Fairbourne Railway
Fair

Llwyngwril
Llangelynin
Peniart
Rhoslefain
Llanegryn
Llanfendigaid
Bryncrug
Rhy
TYWYN
Caethle
Aberdovey
Ynyslas
Borth
Llandre
Bow Street

ABERYSTWYTH
Penparcau
Rhydyfelin

C A R D I G A N

B A Y

0 1 2 3 4 miles
0 1 2 3 4 5 kilometres

2 **3** **4** **5** **6**

TG

TM

Scale:
0 1 2 3 4 miles
0 1 2 3 4 5 kilometres

NORWICH

GREAT YARMOUTH

CROMER

SHERINGHAM

LOWESTOFT

WYMONDHAM

BECCLES

BUNGAY

DISS

Cley next the Sea, Salthouse, Weybourne, West Runton, East Runton, Overstrand, Sidestrand, Newgate, Kelling, Kelling Park, Bodham Street, Upper Sheringham, Beeston Regis, Felbrigg, Felbrigg Hall, Trimingham, Holt, West Beckham, East Beckham, Gresham, Aylmerton, Crossdale Street, Northrepps, Gimingham, Mundesley, Hempstead, Baconsthorpe, Bessingham, Sustead, Thorpe Market, Southrepps, Paston, Stow Mill, Thornage, Hunworth, Edgefield, Matlaske, Hanworth, Thurgarton, Roughton, Bradfield, Trunch, Knapton, Bacton, Keswick, Walcott, Stody, Edgefield Street, Plumstead, Aldborough, Alby Hill, Erpingham, Suffield, Antingham, Swafield, Edingthorpe, Ridlington, Happisburgh, Briston, Little Barningham, Wickmere, Calthorpe, Colby, Witton, Crostwight, Happisburgh Common, Whimpwell Green, Cornusty, Saxthorpe, Itteringham, Ingworth, Felmingham, North Walsham, Spa Common, Lessingham, Sea Palling, Blickling, Blickling Hall, Aylsham, Banningham, Tuttington, Westwick, Worstead, Honing, Briggate, East Ruston, Stalham, Ingham, Waxham, Heydon, Oulton, Oulton Street, Burgh next Aylsham, Skeyton, Brampton, Swanton Abbot, Sloley, Dilham, Smallburgh, Low Street, Stalham Green, Hickling, Horsey, Guestwick, Wood Dalling, Southgate, Marsham, Scottow, Lamas, Little Hautbois, Fairstead, Sutton, Hickling Green, Hickling Heath, Themelthorpe, Reepham, Cawston, Eastgate, Buxton Heath, Buxton, Funstead, Barton Turf, Catfield, Somerton, Sall, Brandiston, Hevingham, Stratton Strawless, Sco Ruston, Beeston Hall, Neatishead, Irstead, Potter Heigham, Bawdeswell, Sparham, Norfolk Wildlife Park Alderford, Swannington, Waterloo, Horstead, Coltishall, Hoveton, Ludham, Martham, Hemsby, Lyng, Lenwade, Felthorpe, St. Helena, Belaugh, Horning, Bastwick, Repps, Rollesby, Ormesby St. Margaret, Scratby, Morton, Attlebridge, Horsford, Newton St. Faith, Frettenham, Crostwick, Wroxham, Woodbastwick, Upper Street, Thurne, Clippesby, Burgh St. Margaret, Filby, Ormesby St. Michael, California, Primrose Green, Ringland, Drayton, Horsham St. Faith, Spixworth, Rackheath, Salhouse, Ranworth, Thrigby, Mautby, Caister, Roman Town, Caister-on-Sea, Hockering, Honingham, Taverham, Costessey, Hellesdon, New Rackheath, New Costessey, Catton, Sprowston, Little Plumstead, Panxworth, South Walsham, Fairhaven, Billockby, Stokesby, West End, West Caister, Easton, Bawburgh, Colney, Bowthorpe, Thorpe End Garden Village, Great Plumstead, North Burlingham, Upton, Acle, Runham, Great Yarmouth, East Tuddenham, Colton, Marlingford, Little Melton, Eaton, Thorpe St. Andrew, Brundall, Postwick, Blofield, South Burlingham, Beighton, Damgate, Tunstall, Stracey Arms Wind Pump, Halvergate, Brandon Parva, Barford, Cringleford, Lakenham, Arminghall, Surlingham, Bramerton, Rockland St. Mary, Cantley, Freethorpe, Freethorpe Common, Limpenhoe, Berney Arms, Berney Arms Station, Burgh Castle, Gorleston on Sea, Wramplingham, High Green, Hethersett, Keswick, Caistor St. Edmund, Framingham Pigot, Framingham Earl, Kirby Bedon, Hellington, Yelverton, Claxton, Ashby St. Mary, Langley Street, Hardley Street, Pettitts Rural Industries, Reedham, Berney Arms, Burgh Bradwell, Belton, Kimberley, Crownthorpe, Ketteringham, Swardeston, East Carleton, Dunston, Stoke Holy Cross, Bergh Apton, Chedgrave, Thurton, Norton Subcourse, Lower Thurlton, St Olaves Priory, Fritton, Hobland Hall, Hopton on Sea, Wicklewood, Hackford, Morley St. Botolph, Suton, Ashwellthorpe, Mulbarton, Swainsthorpe, Howe, Bracon Ash, East Poringland, Shotesham, Brooke, Mundham, Loddon, Hales, Thurlton, Thorpe, Herringfleet, Somerleyton, Somerleyton Hall, Blundeston, Corton, Besthorpe, Spooner Row, Toprow, Flordon, Hapton, Rainthorpe Hall, Tasburgh, Saxlingham Nethergate, Kirstead Green, Seething, Woodton, Hedenham, Raveningham, Hales Hall, Thwaite St. Mary, Maypole Green, Haddiscoe, Somerleyton, Lowestoft End, Tacolneston, Forncett St. Mary, Tharston, Upper Tasburgh, Hempnall, Stockton, Toft Monks, Oulton Broad, Kirby Cane, Wheatacre, Barnby, Carlton Colville, Bunwell, Forncett End, Forncett St. Peter, Hempnall Green, Stratton St. Michael, Fritton, Topcroft, Ditchingham, Broome, Geldeston, Aldeby, Burgh St. Peter, Kirkley, Pakefield, Carleton Rode, Aslacton, Great Moulton, Shelton, Shelton Green, Topcroft Street, Great Green, Bungay, Mettingham, Barsham, Ringsfield, Worlingham, Beccles, North Cove, Transport Museum, Gisleham, Old Buckenham, Tibenham, Long Stratton, Wacton, Morningthorpe, Woodton, Denton, Alburgh, Earsham, Ringsfield Corner, Mutford, Ellough, Rushmere, New Buckenham, Banham, Tivetshall St. Margaret, North Green, Hardwick, Bush Green, Ditchingham, Homersfield, Ilketshall St. Margaret, Ilketshall St. Andrew, Hulver Street, Kessingland, International Motor Museum, Kenninghall, Winfarthing, Gissing, Tivetshall St. Mary, Pulham Market, Wortwell, Redenhall, Flixton, St. Margaret South Elmham, St. Michael South Elmham, Redisham, Shadingfield, Sotterley, Henstead, Suffolk Wildlife Park, Benacre, Shelfanger, Ferstield, Burston, Rushall, Harleston, Needham, Pulham St. Mary, Starston, St. Cross South Elmham, All Saints, Cox Common, Brampton Station, Stoven, Clay Common, Wrentham, Redgrave, Wortham, Roydon, Palgrave, Diss, Scole, Billingford, Dickleburgh, Thorpe Abbotts, Brockdish, Needham, Weybread, Withersdale Street, Mendham, St. James South Elmham, Rumburgh, Spexhall, Shadingfield, South Cove, Covehithe, Bressingham, Live Steam Museum, Oakley, Hoxne, Billingford Mill, Fressingfield, Metfield, Wissett, Holton, Uggeshall, Wangford, Mount Pleasant, Reydon, Blyford, Chediston, South Lopham, Stuston, Wingfield, Westhall, Cheston

Roads: A149, A148, A140, A1151, A1062, A1064, A47, A11, A146, A143, A144, A1066, A12, A145, A1065, B1145, B1149, B1354, B1155, B1156, B1159, B1160, B1140, B1135, B1332, B1134, B1077, B1108, B1113, B1127, B1062, B1123, B1124, B1152, B1158, B1074

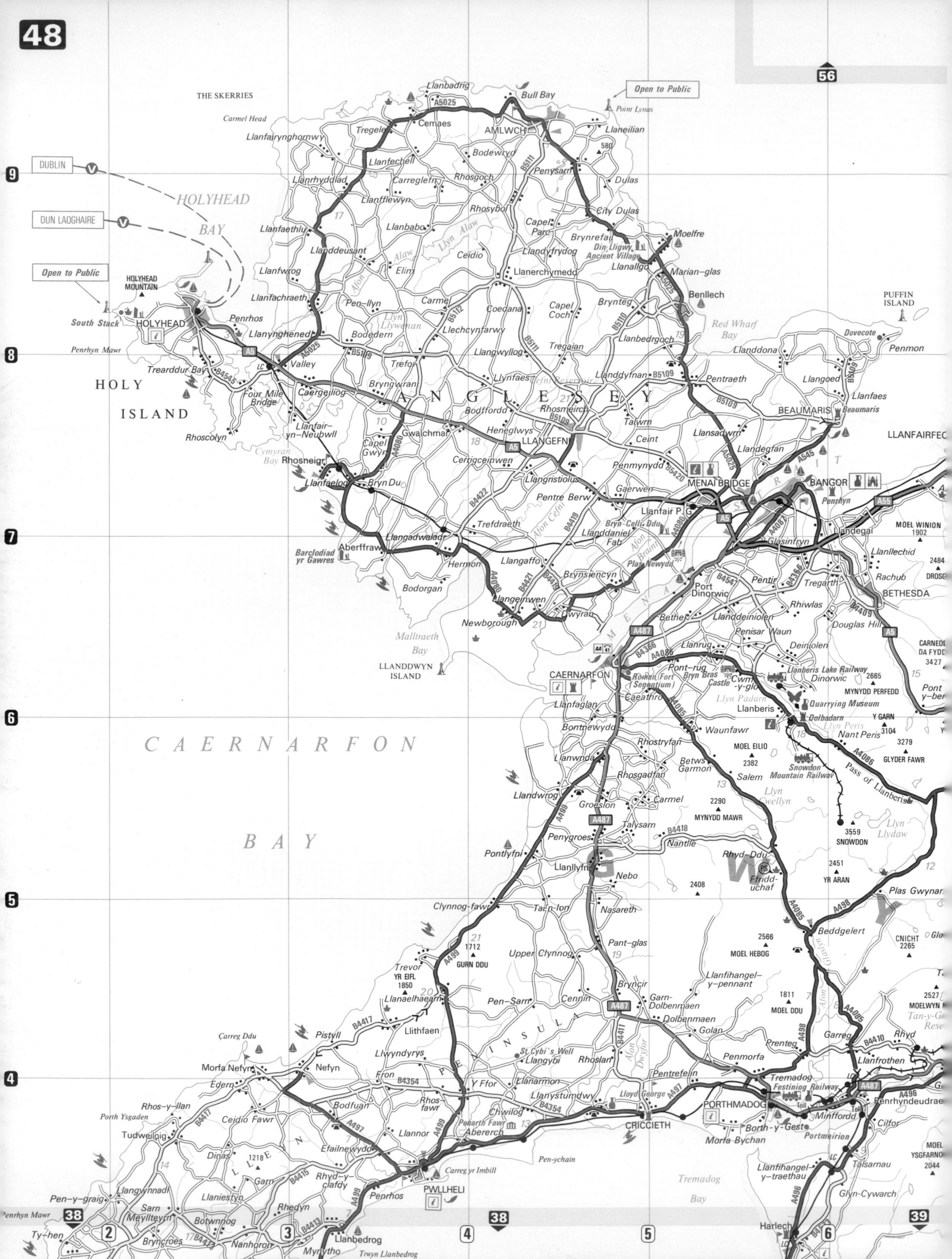

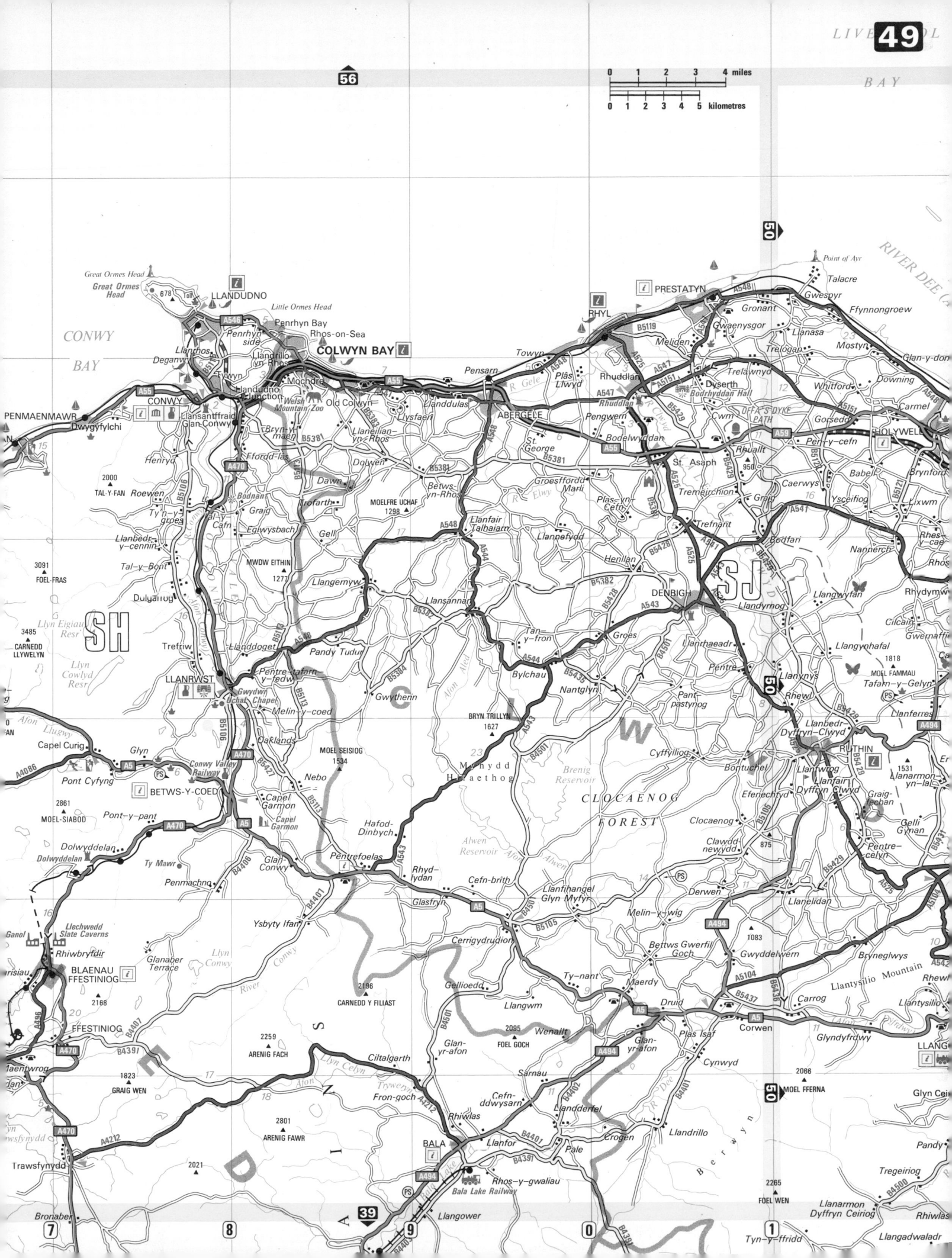

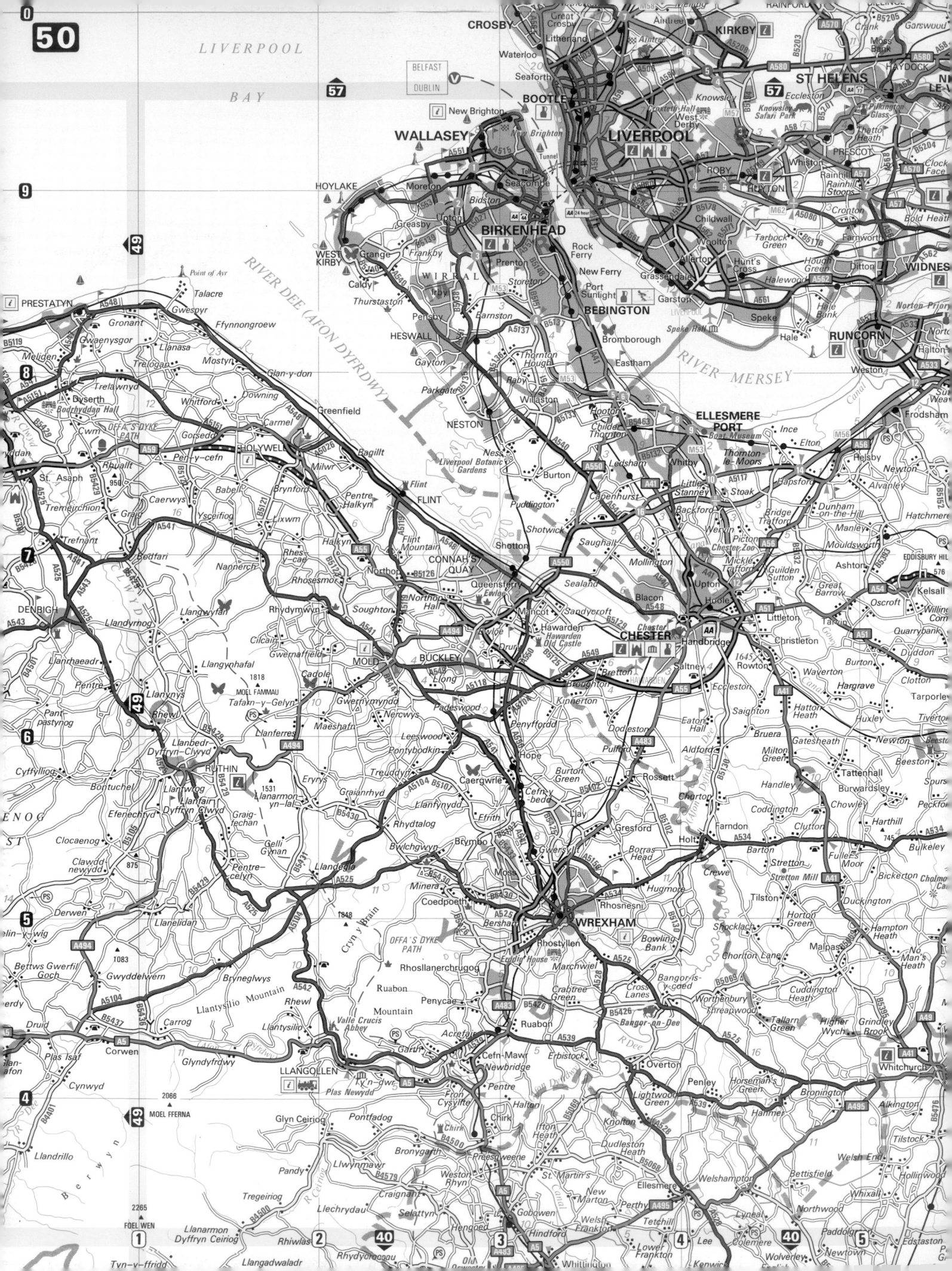

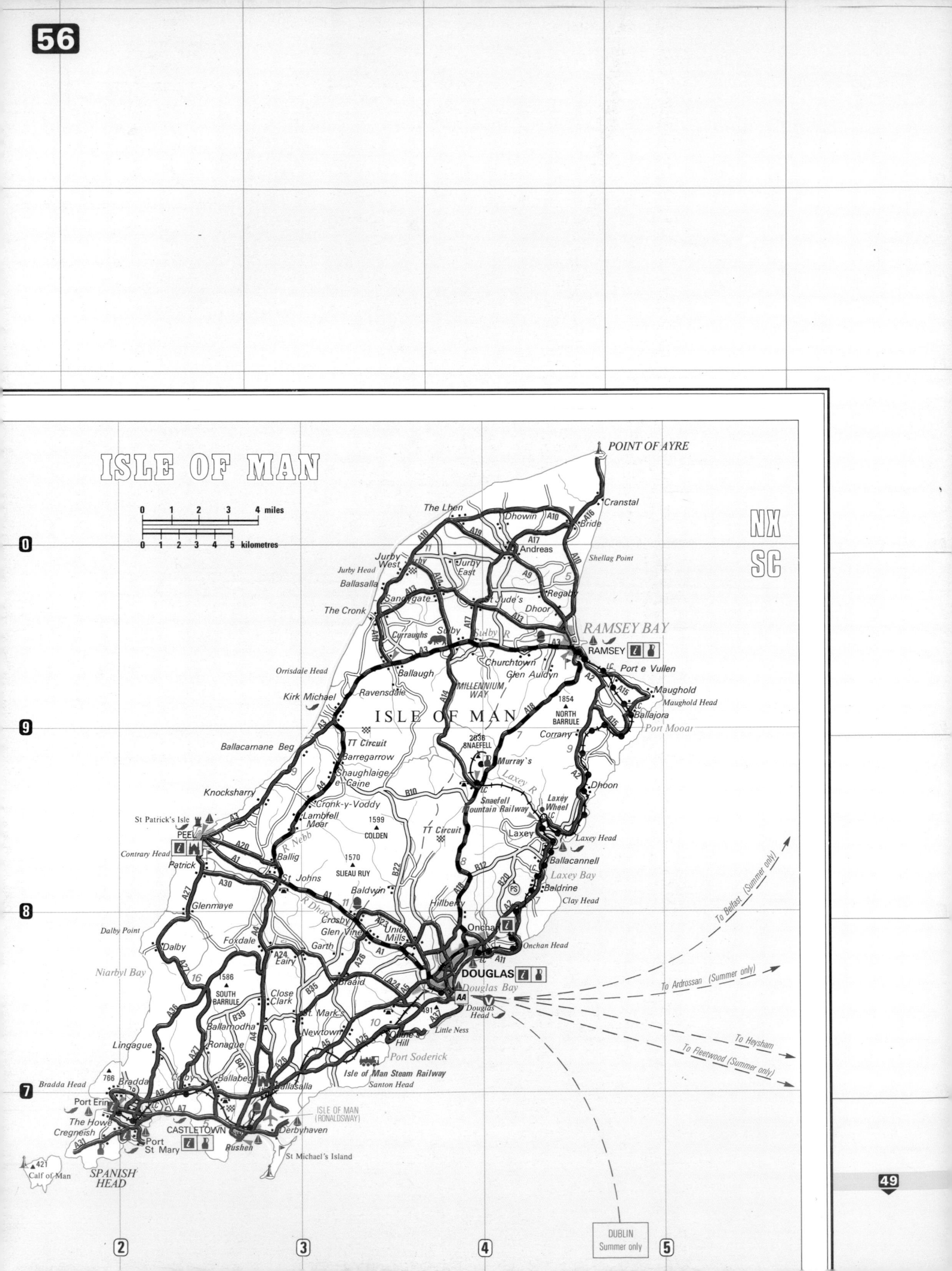

ISLE OF MAN

POINT OF AYRE

NX
SC

The Lhen
Dhowin   A10
Cranstal
A16
Bride
A19
A17
A10   Andreas
Jurby   Jurby
West   A9   Shellag Point
Jurby Head   Jurby   Jurby
East
Ballasalla
A13   A9   Regaby
Sandygate   St Jude's
The Cronk   A17   Dhoor
Curraughs   Sulby   Sulby R   RAMSEY BAY
A3
Orrisdale Head   Ballaugh   Churchtown   RAMSEY
Glen Auldyn   Port e Vullen
Kirk Michael   Ravensdale   A2
MILLENNIUM   Maughold
WAY   A18   Maughold Head
1854   A5   Ballajora
NORTH
BARRULE   Port Mooar
ISLE OF MAN
Ballacarnane Beg   Corrany
TT Circuit   2836   A18   9
Barregarrow   SNAEFELL
Shaughlaige-   Murray's   A2   Dhoon
e-Caine   Laxey R
Knocksharry   B10   Snaefell   Laxey
Mountain Railway   Wheel
Cronk-y-Voddy
St Patrick's Isle   Lambfell   1599   TT Circuit   Laxey
Mear   COLDEN   Laxey Head
PEEL   A7   Ballacannell
Contrary Head   A20   Ballig   1570   8   Baldrine
Patrick   A1   SLIEAU RUY   B12   B20
St Johns   Baldwin   Laxey Bay
A30   11   PS   Clay Head
Glenmaye   Crosby   Hillberry   Baldrine
Dalby Point   Foxdale   Glen Vine   Union   Onchan
Mills   Onchan Head
Dalby   A24   Eairy   A26   A1
1586   Garth   A5
16   SOUTH   Braaid   DOUGLAS
BARRULE   Close   A24   Douglas Bay
Clark   St Mark's   A1   AA   Douglas Head
Ballamodha   Newtown   A26   10   Little Ness
Lingague   Ronague   Glline   To Belfast (Summer only)
Hill
Port Soderick
Ballabeg   Isle of Man Steam Railway   To Ardrossan (Summer only)
766   Bradda   Colby   Ballasalla   Santon Head
Bradda Head   A5   To Heysham
Port Erin   A7   ISLE OF MAN
The Howe   (RONALDSWAY)   To Fleetwood (Summer only)
Cregneish   CASTLETOWN   Derbyhaven
Port   Rushen
421   St Mary   St Michael's Island
Calf of Man
SPANISH
HEAD

DUBLIN
Summer only

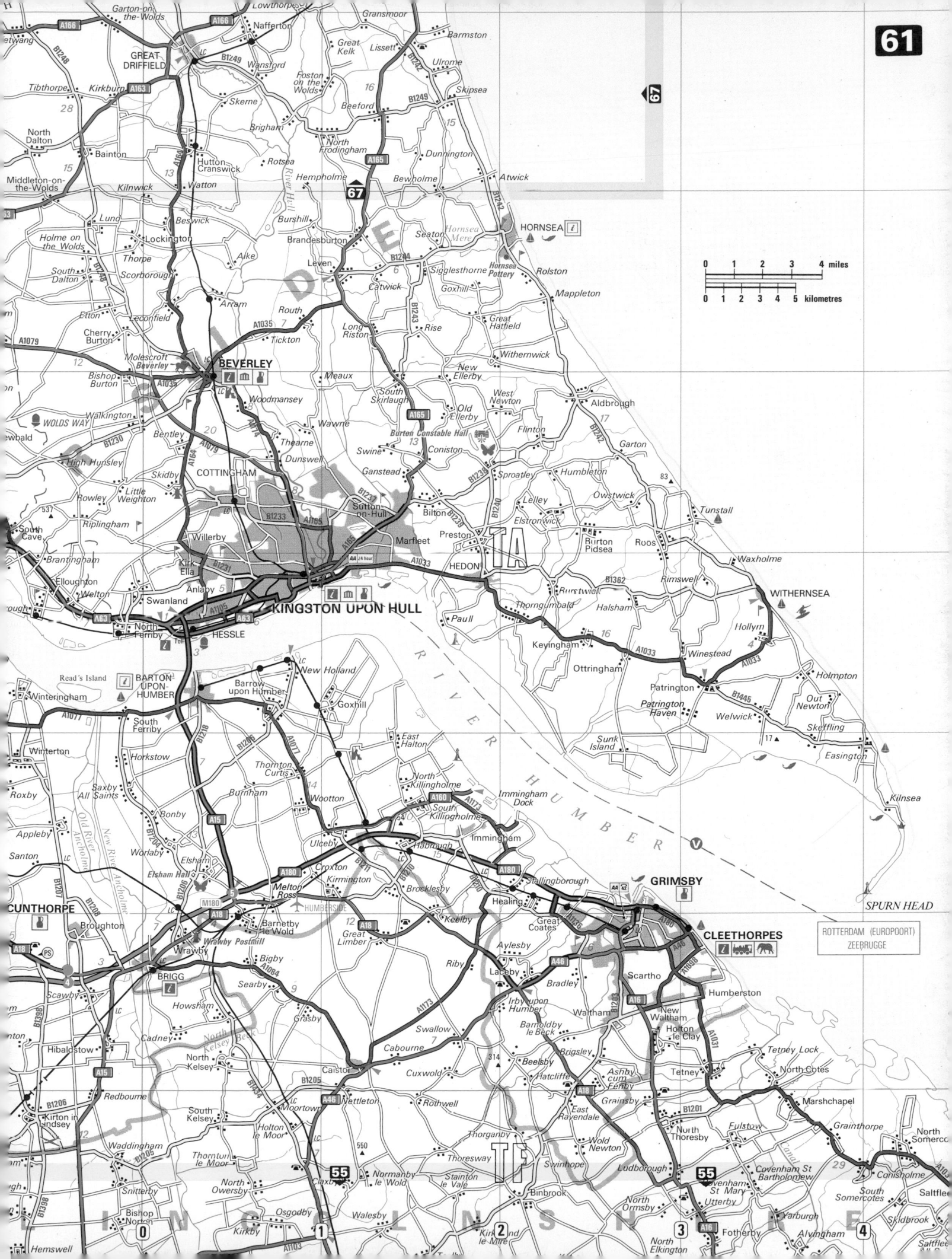

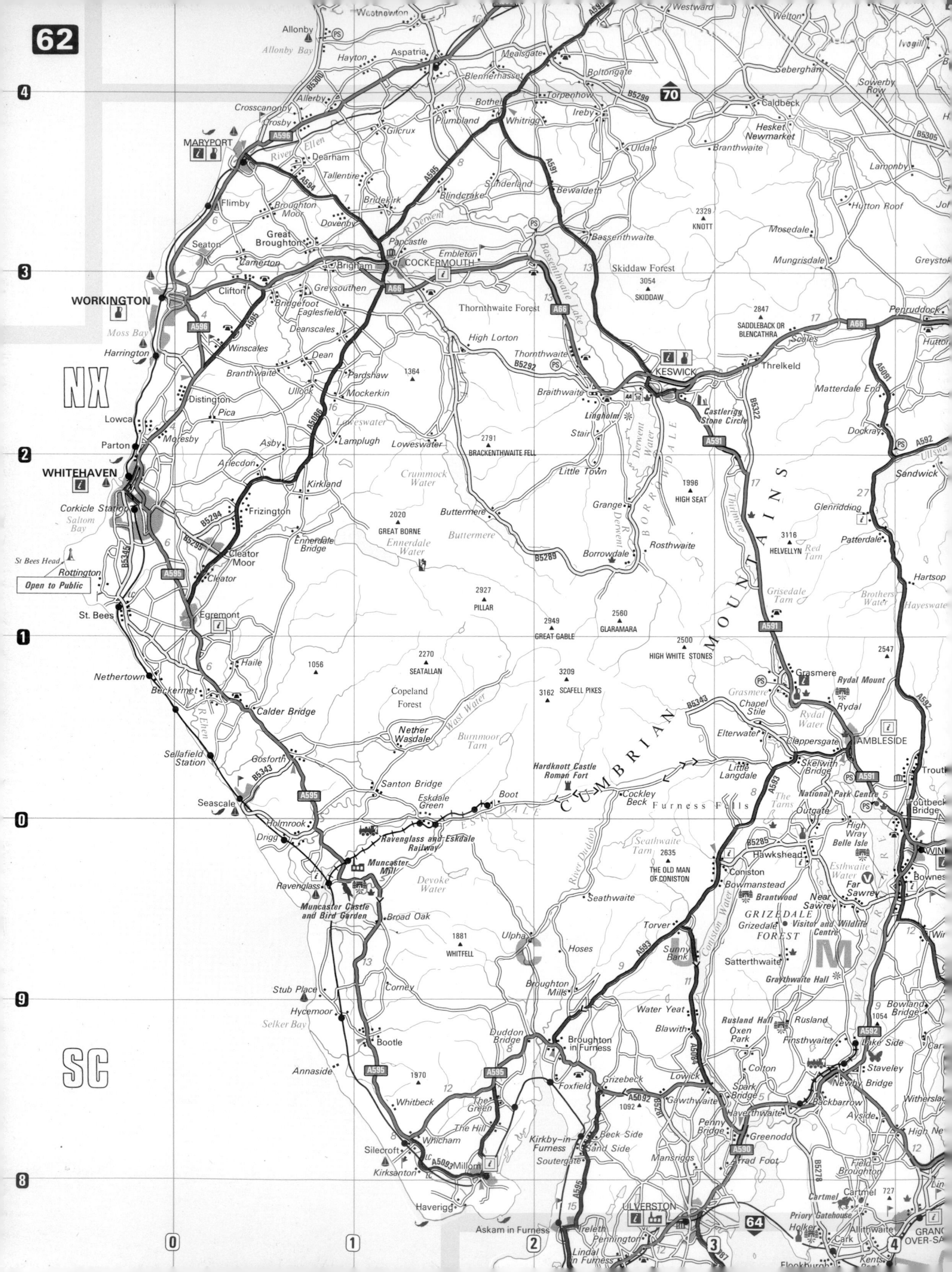

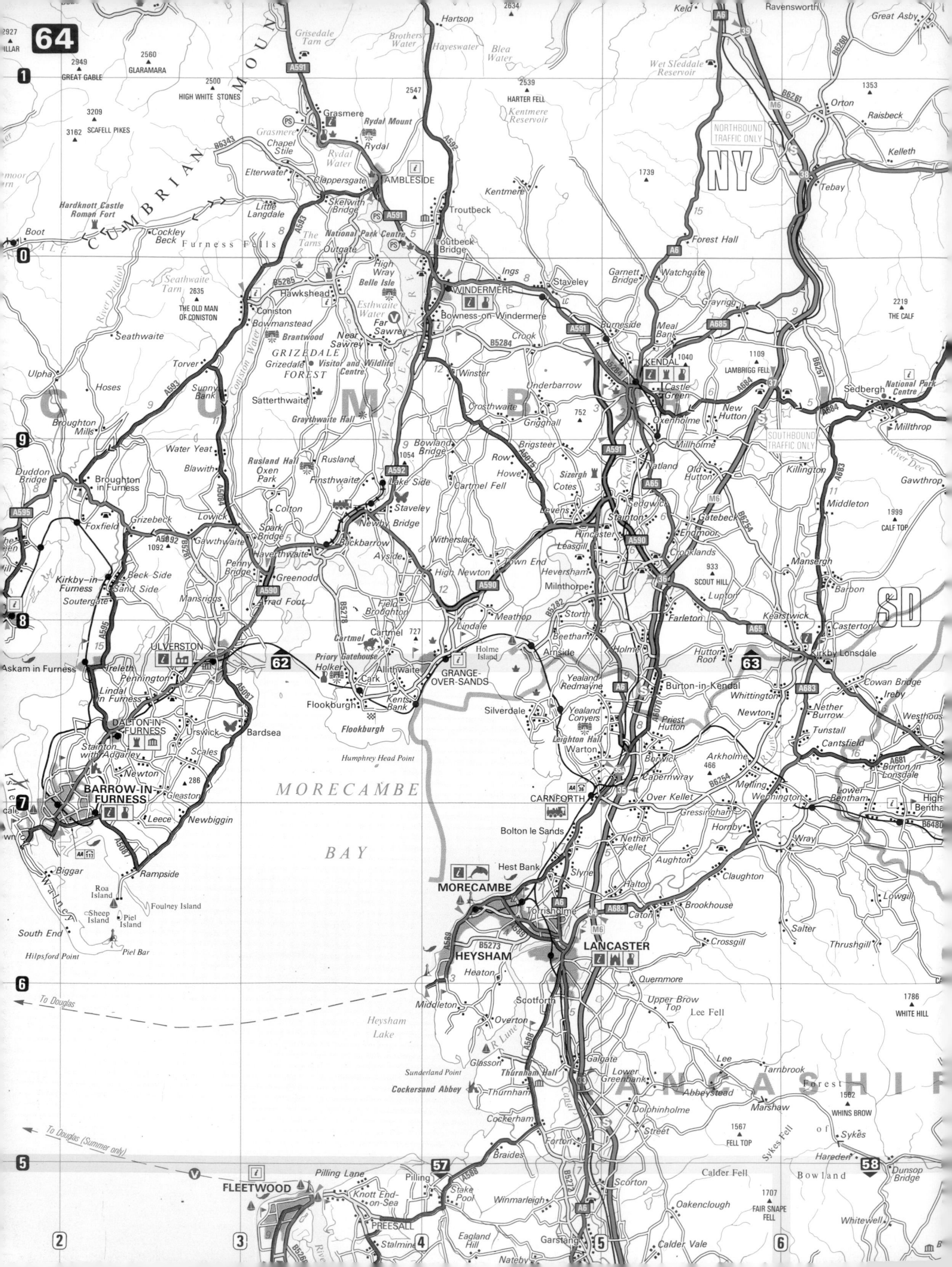

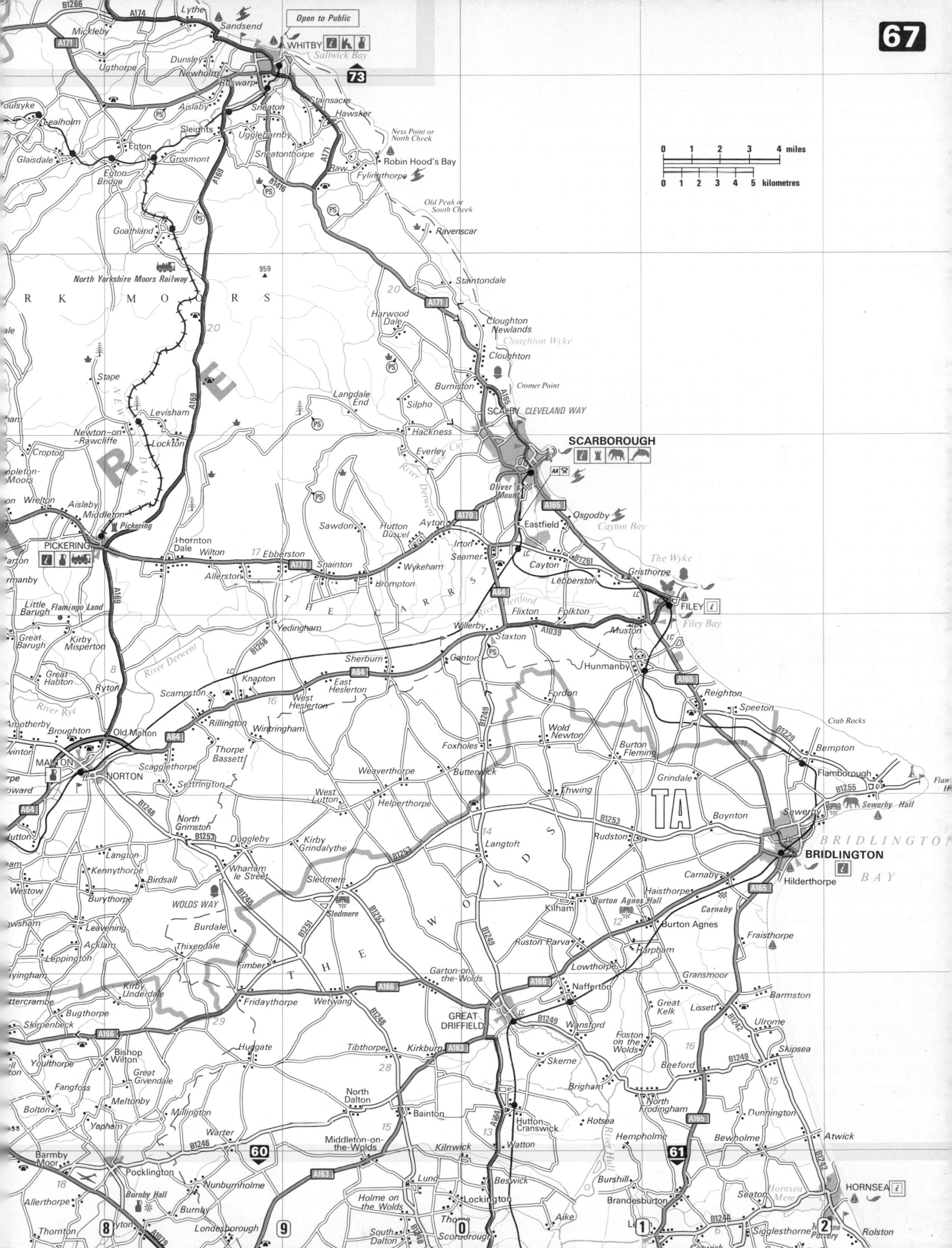

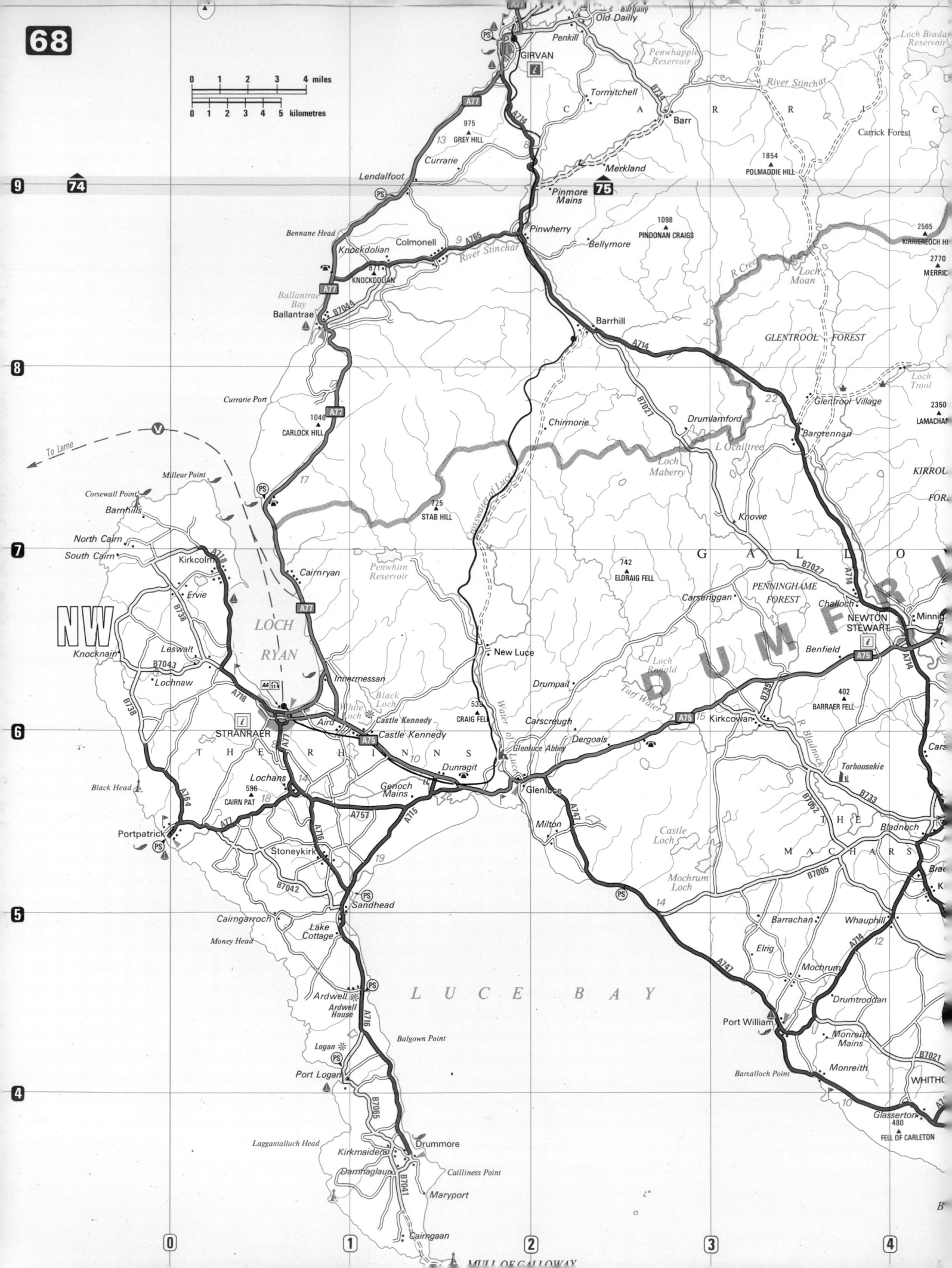

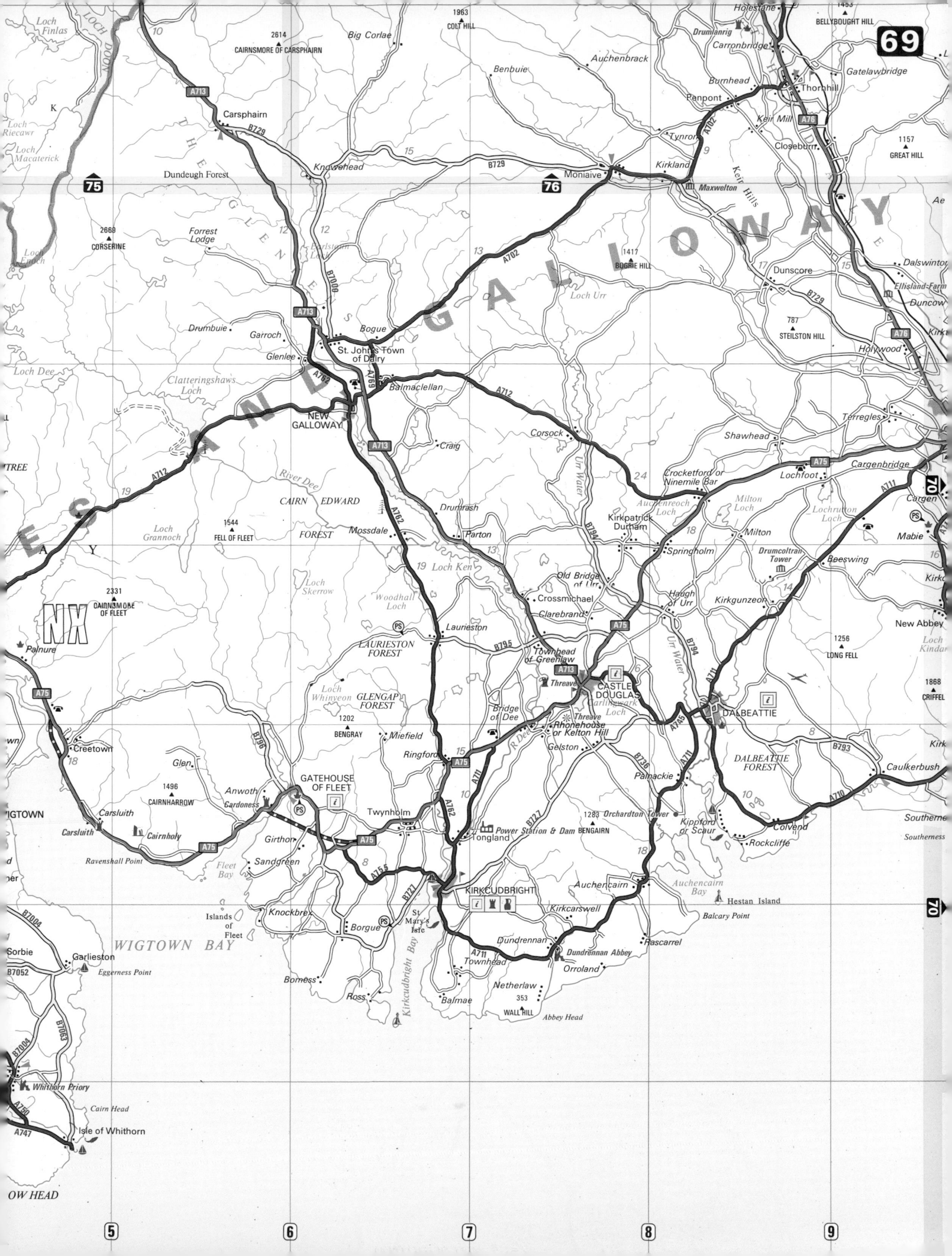

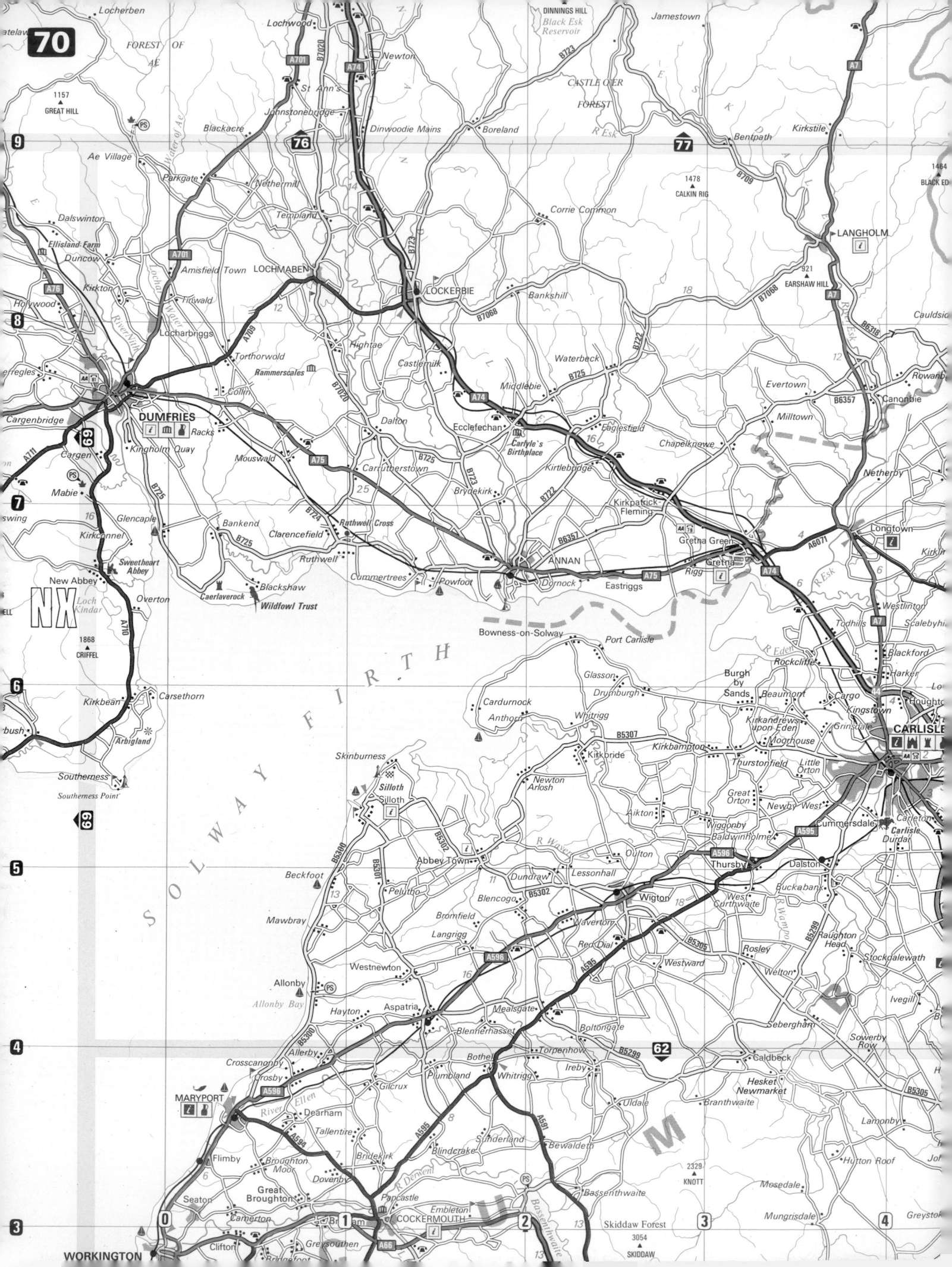

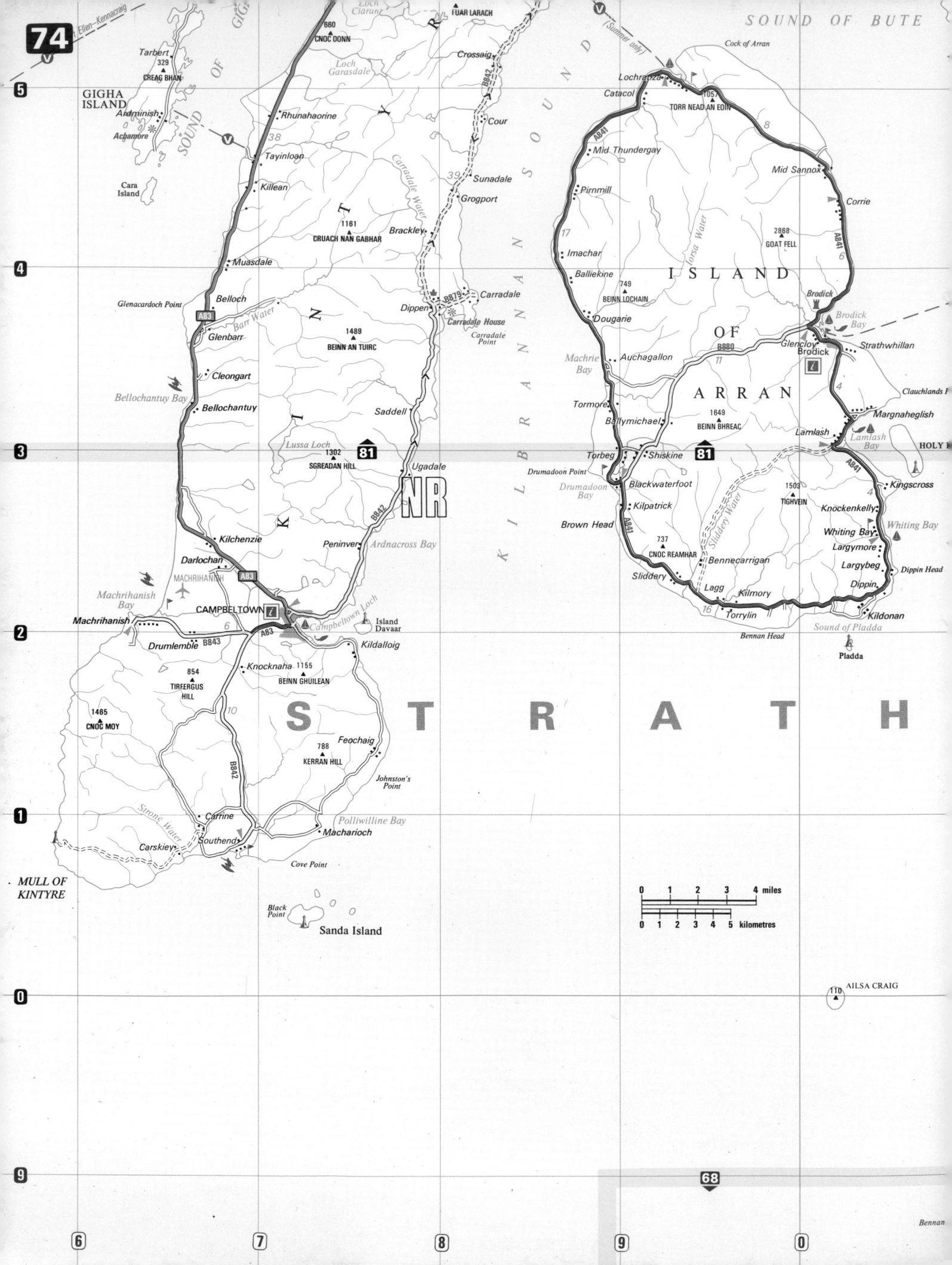

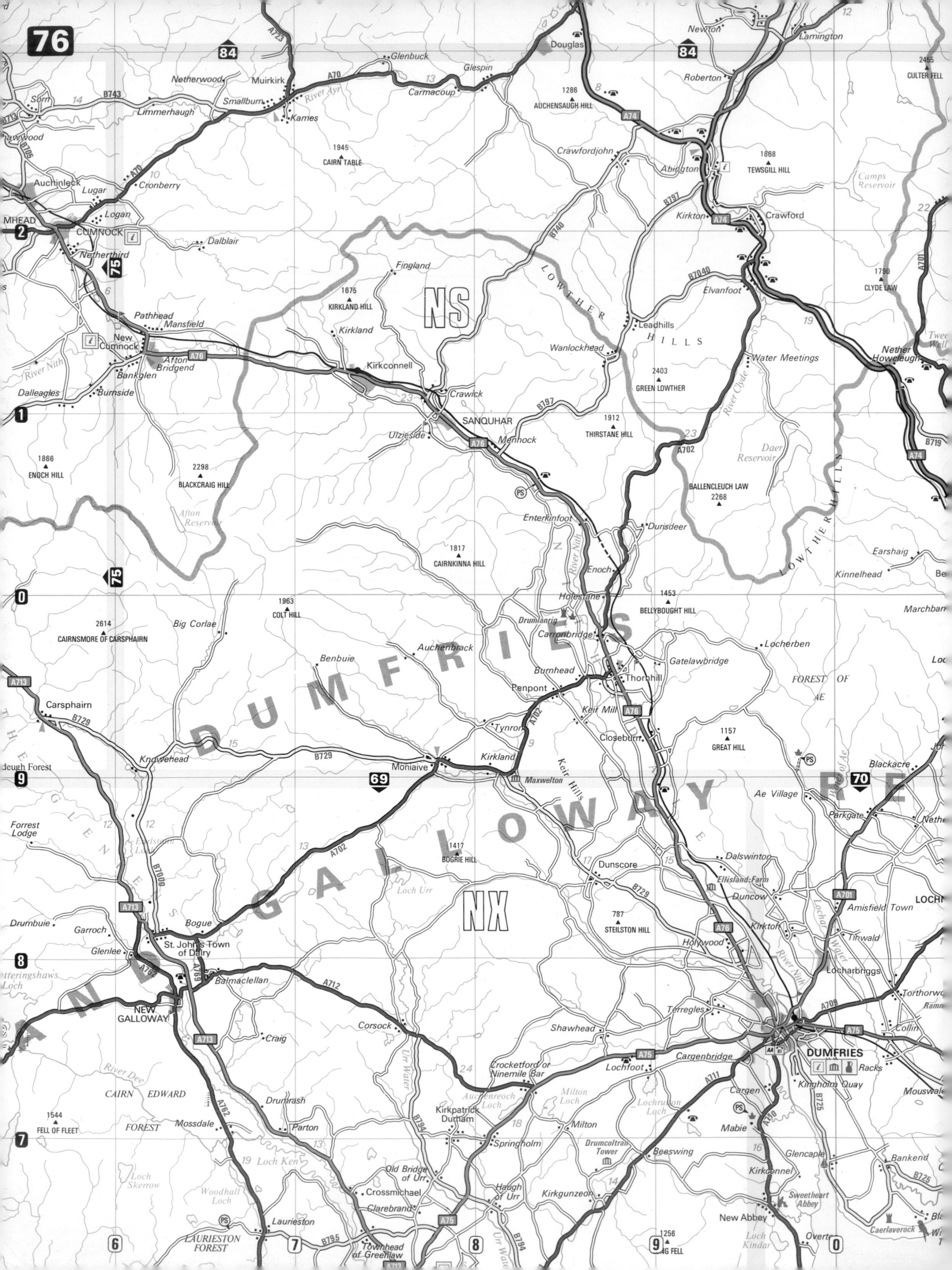

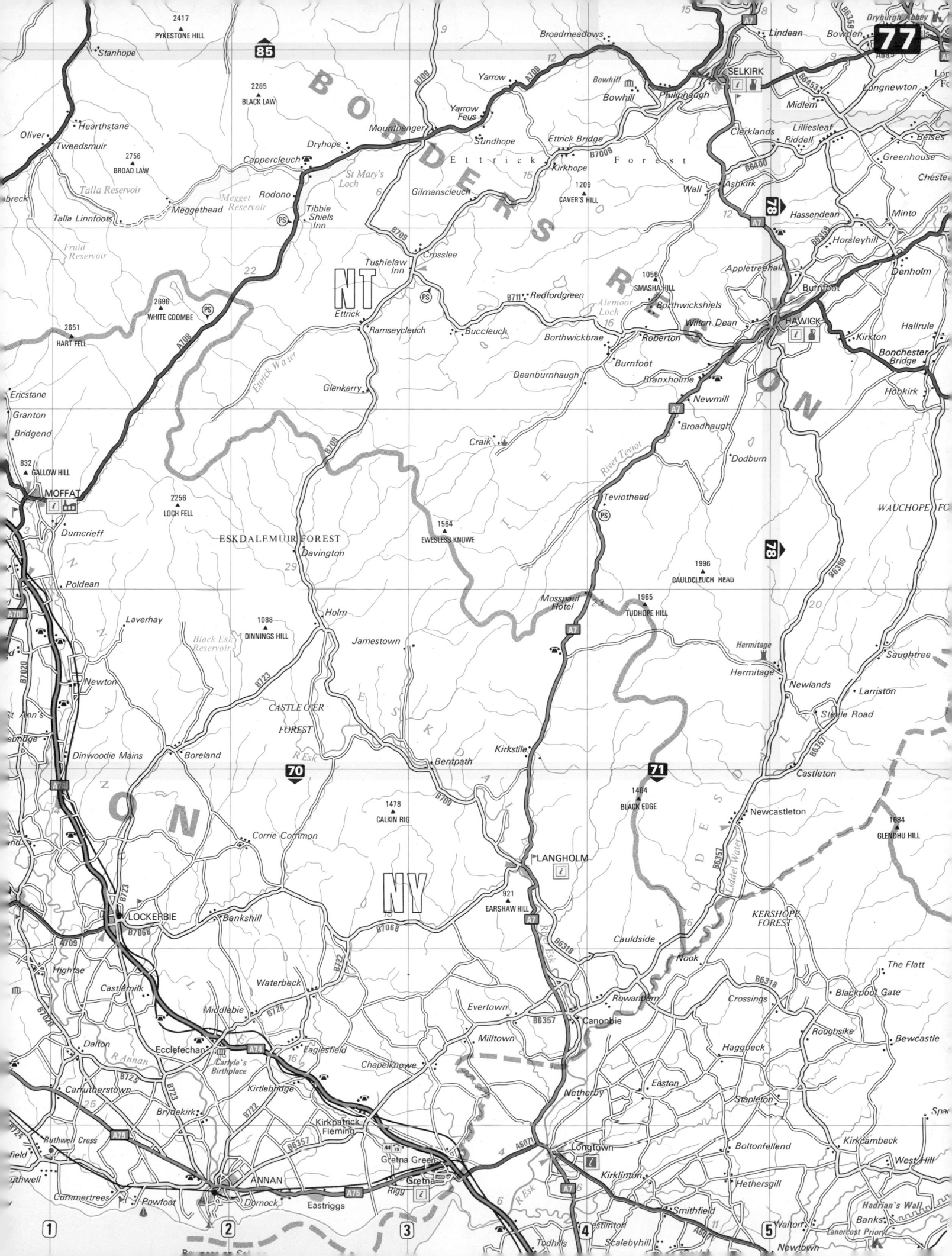

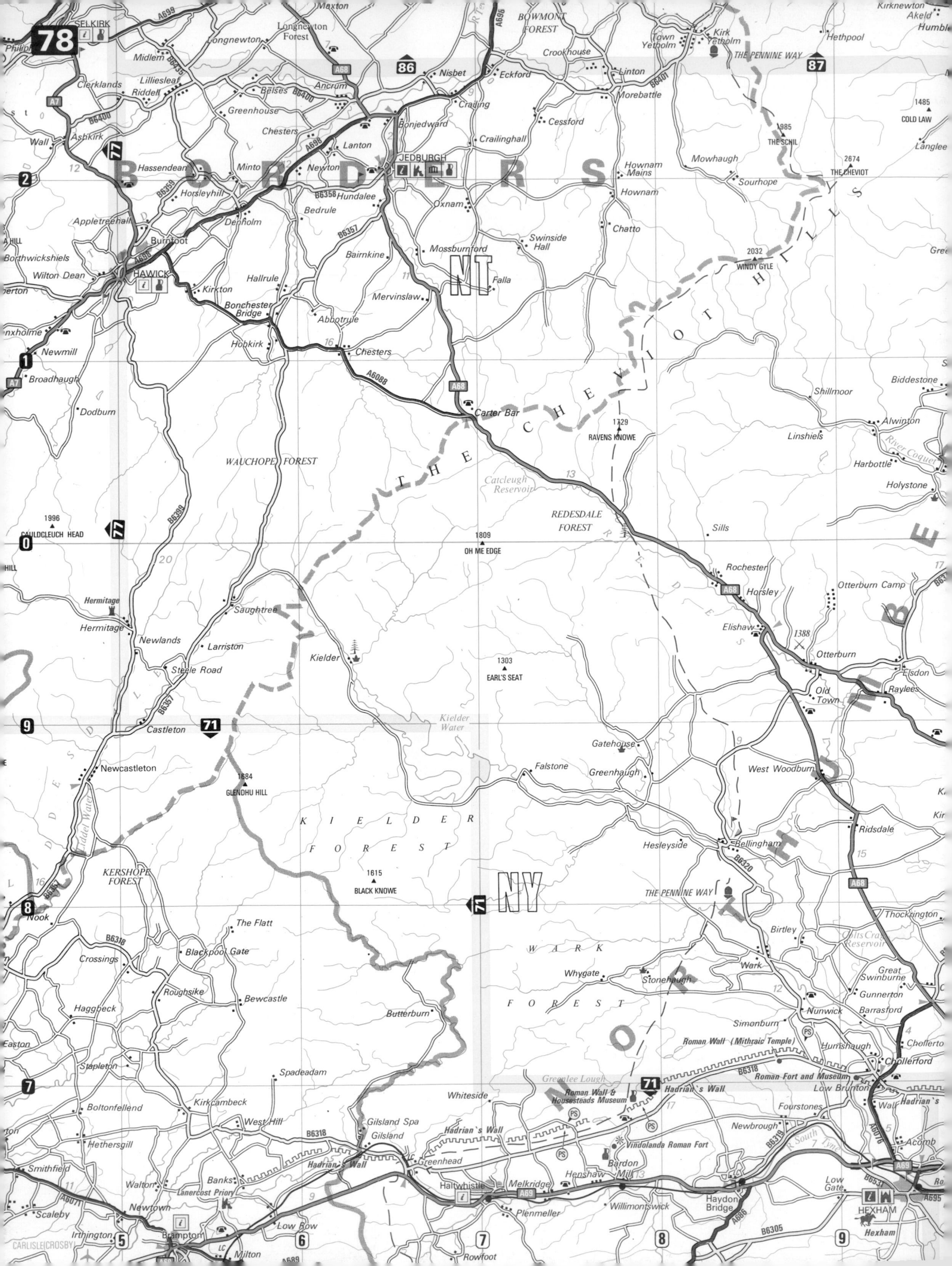

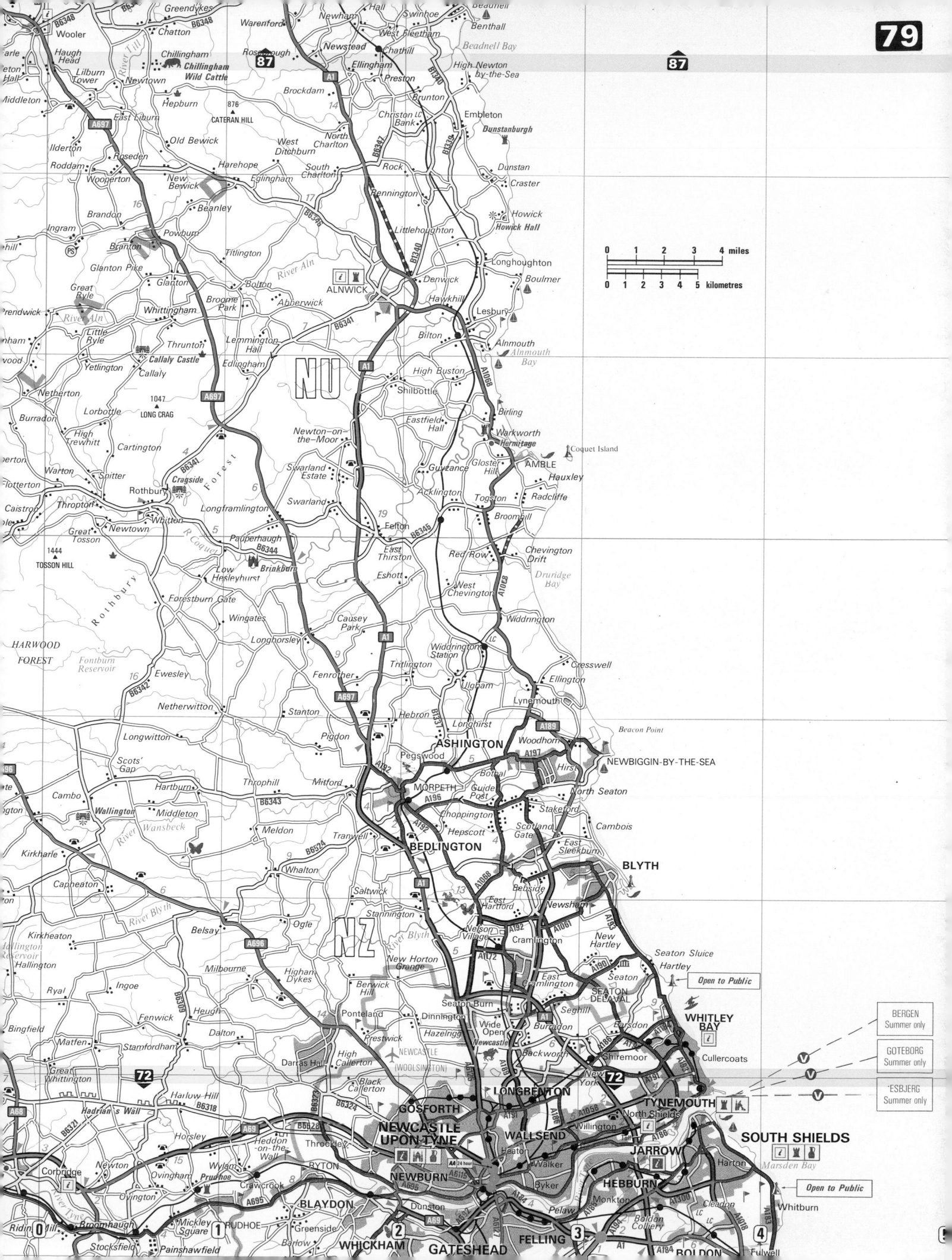

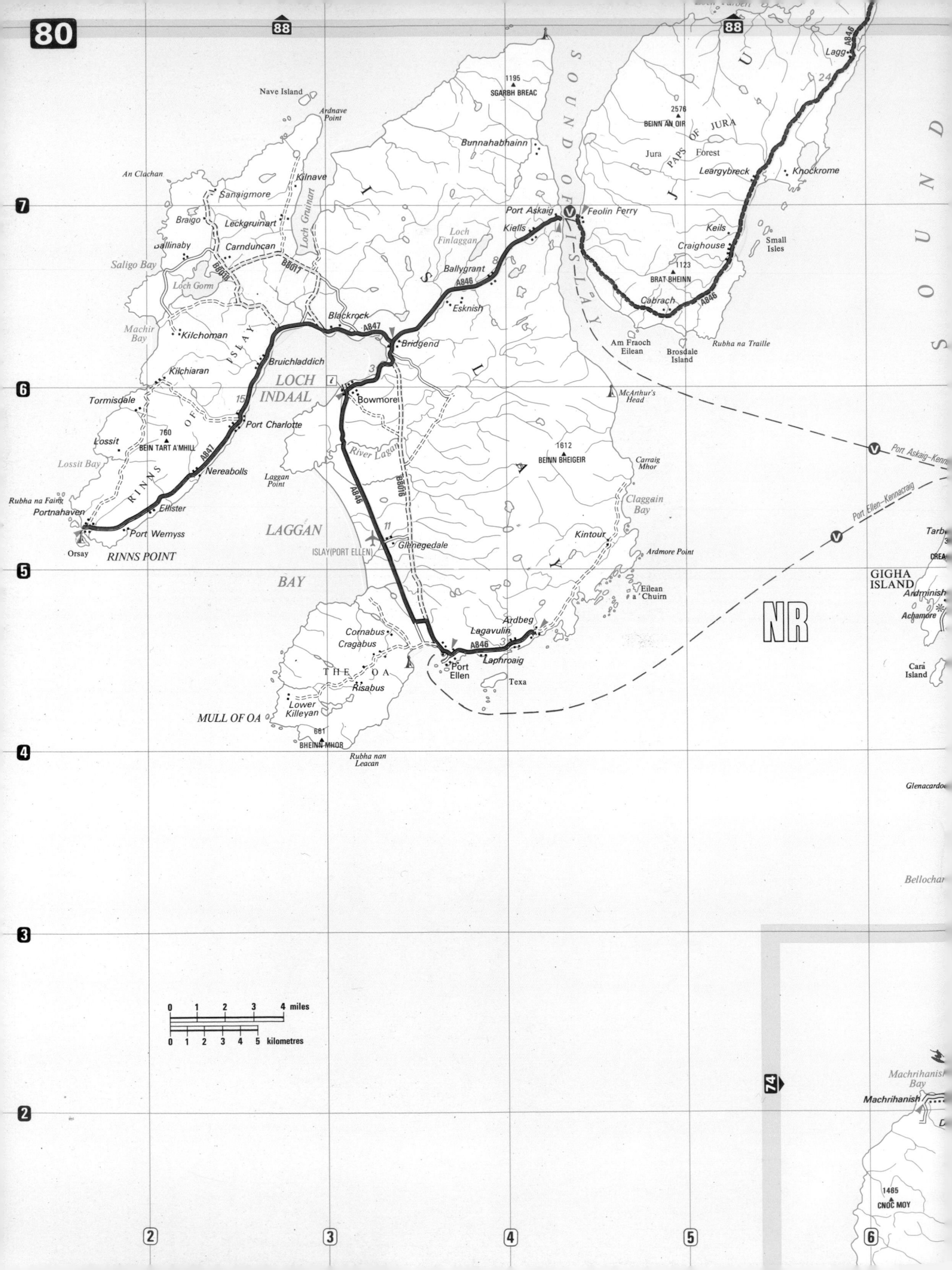

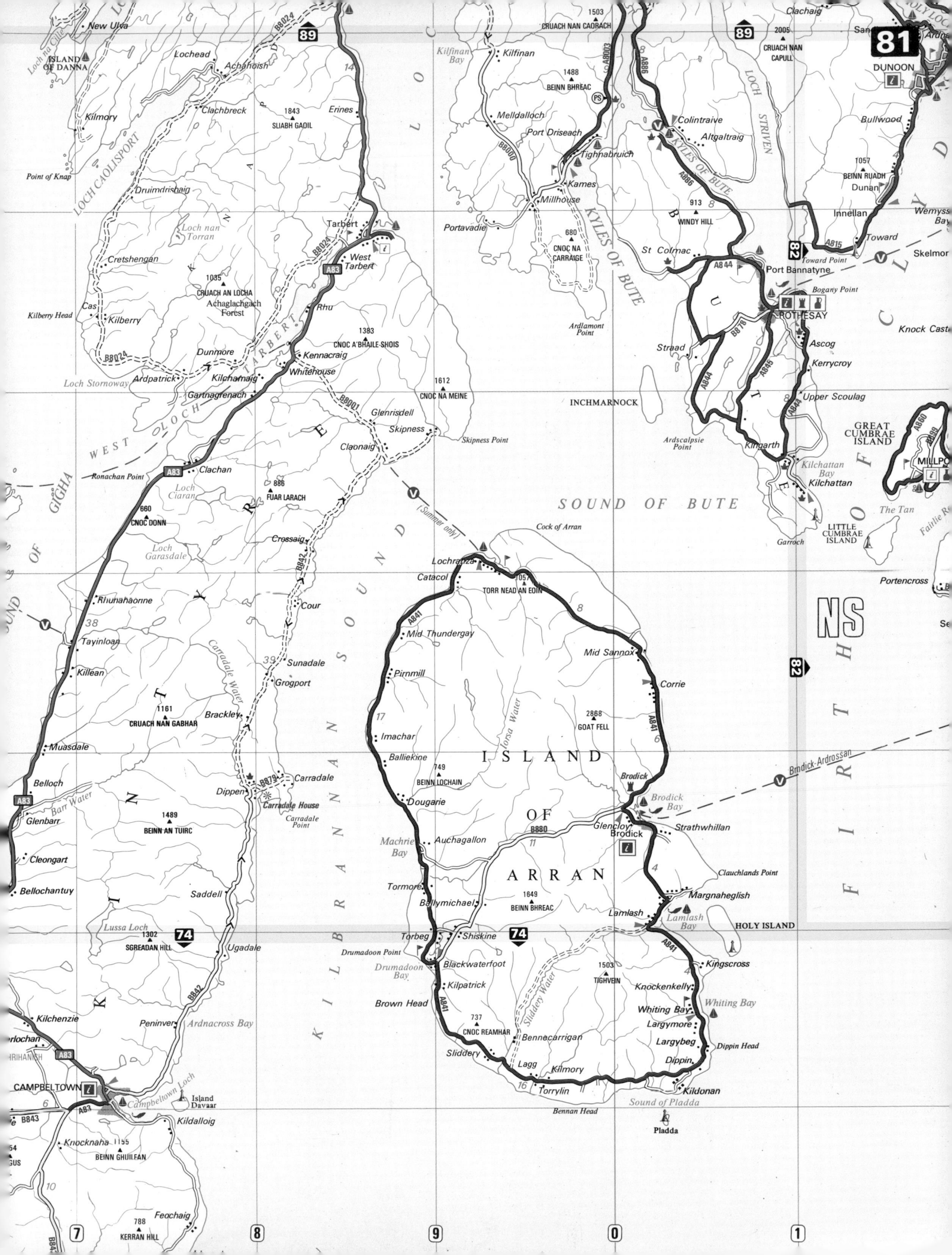

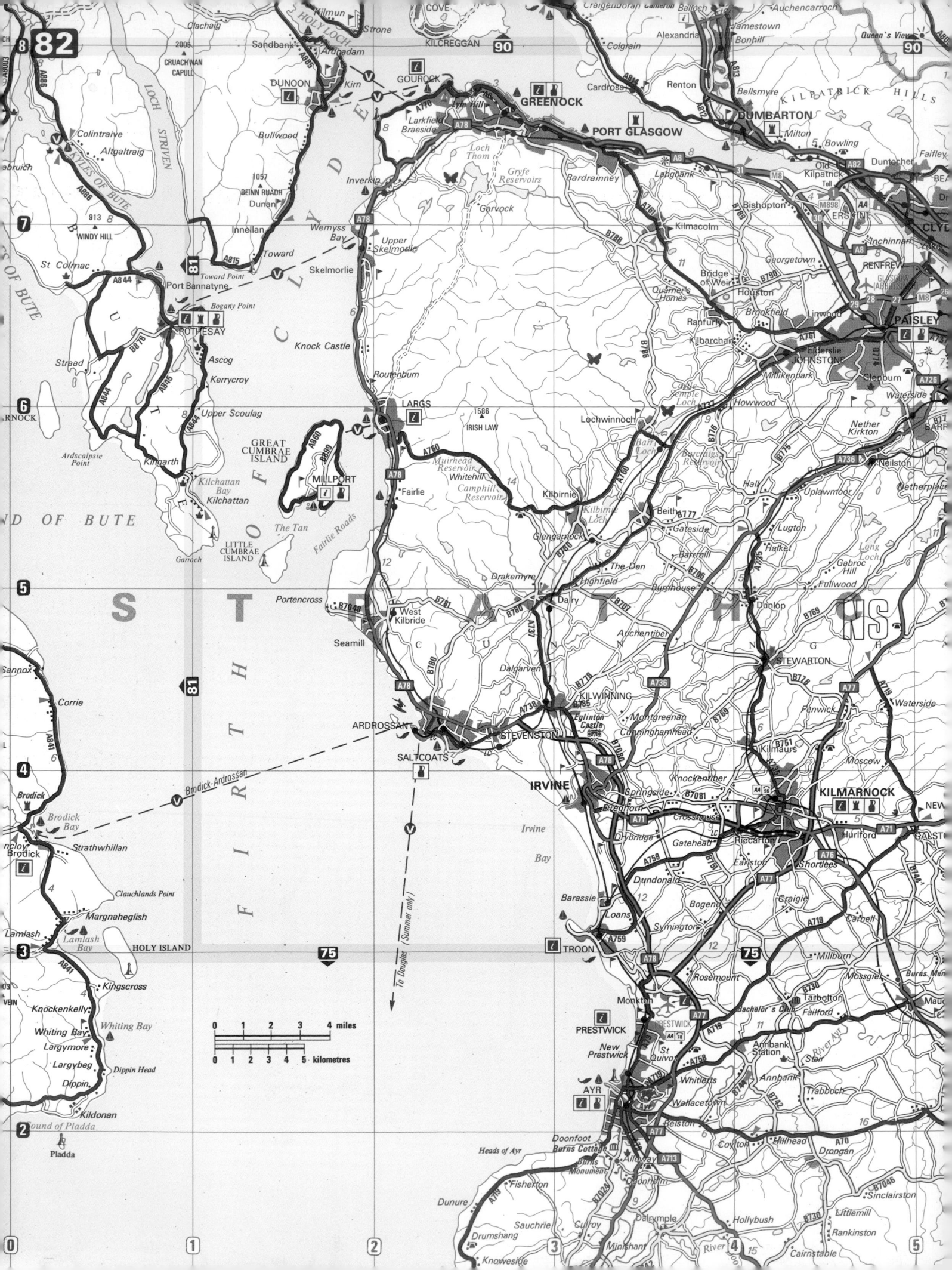

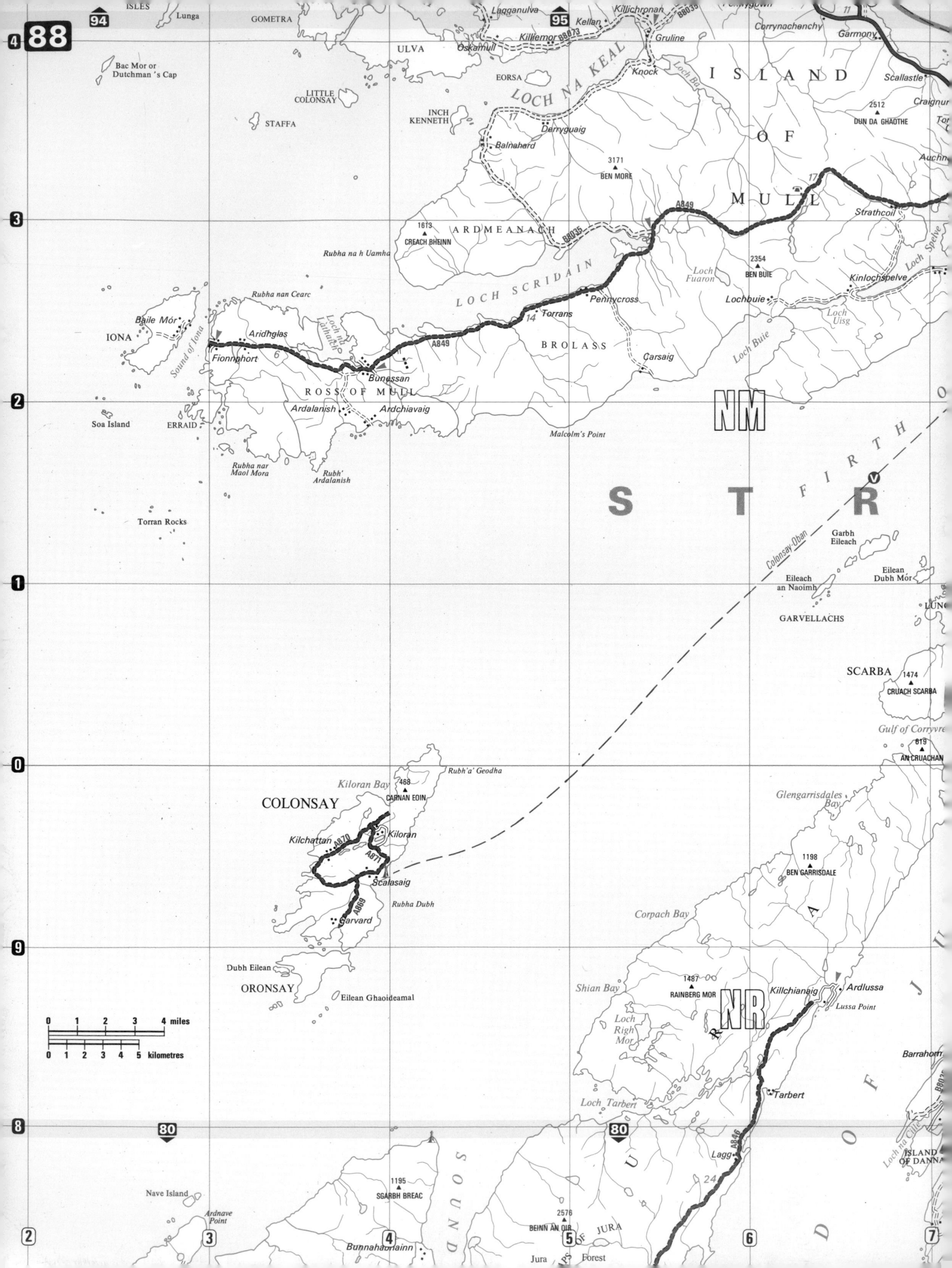

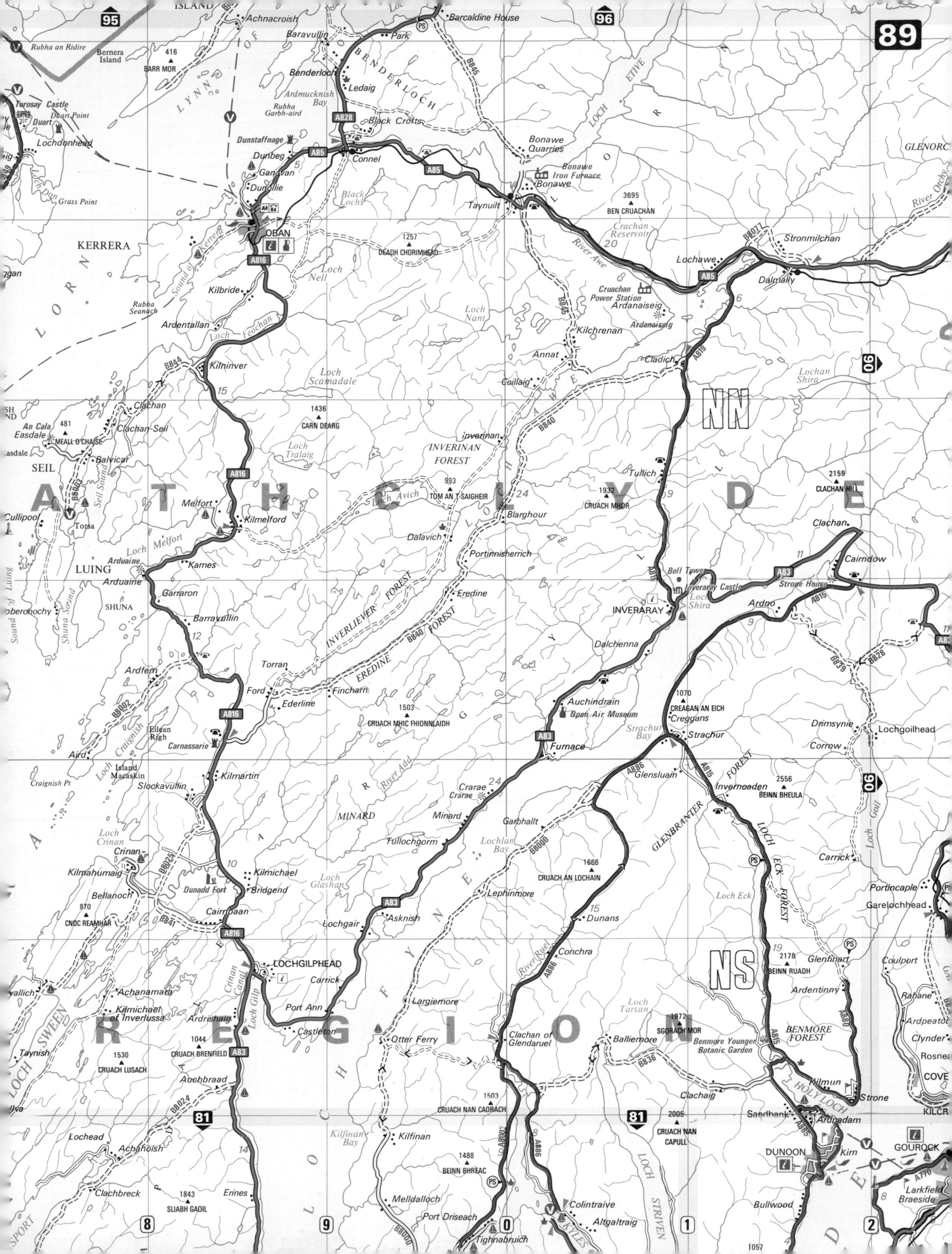

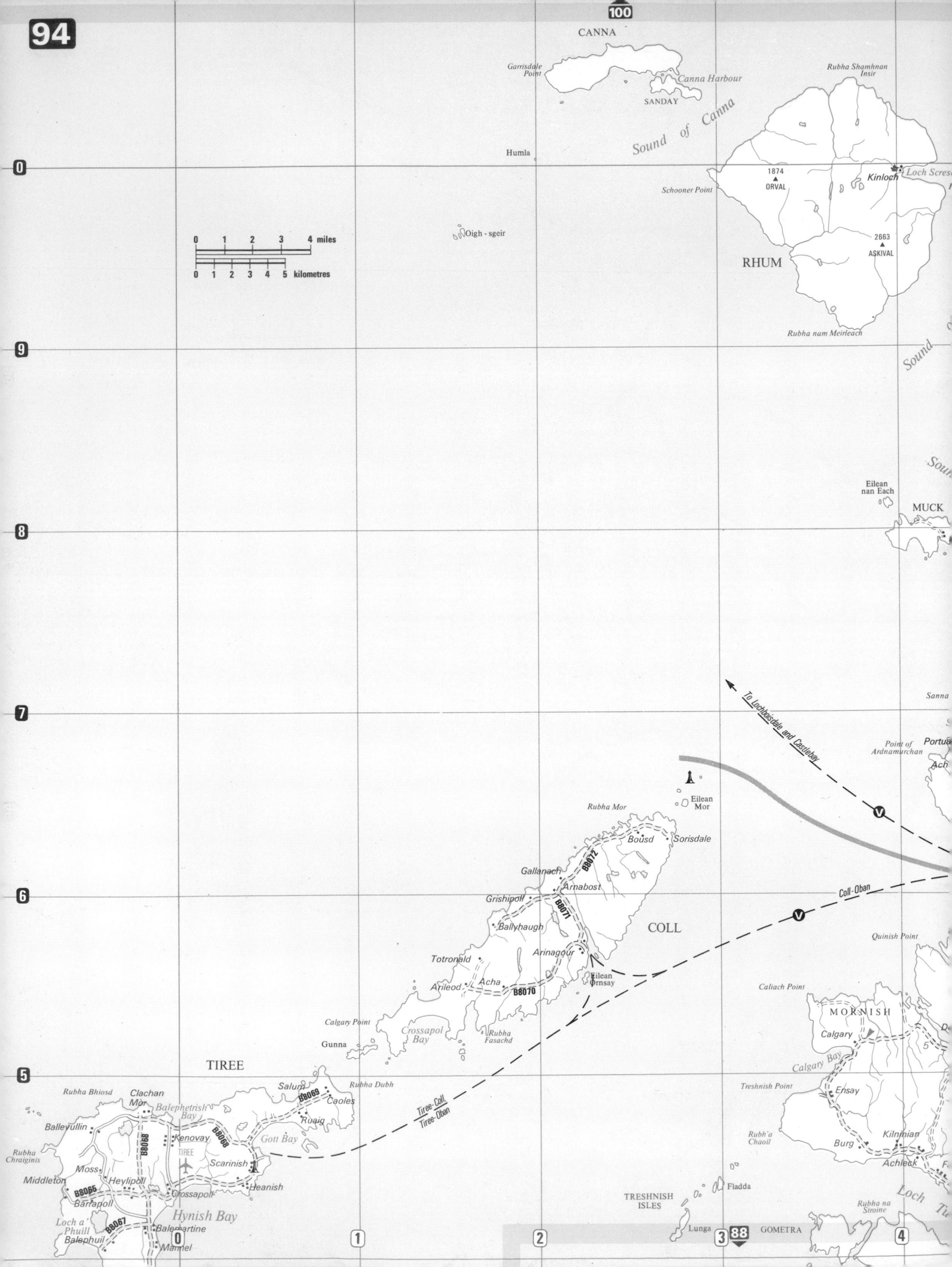

100

CANNA

Garrisdale
Point

Canna Harbour

SANDAY

Sound of Canna

Rubha Shamhnan
Insir

Humla

Schooner Point

1874
▲
ORVAL

Kinloch Loch Screse

Oigh - sgeir

2663
▲
ASKIVAL

RHUM

Rubha nam Meirleach

0

0   1   2   3   4 miles

0 1 2 3 4 5   kilometres

9

Eilean
nan Each

MUCK

8

Sanna

7

To Lochboisdale and Castlebay

Point of
Ardnamurchan Ach

Portua

Rubha Mor

Eilean
Mor

Bousd Sorisdale

Gallanach

B8072

Arnabost

Coll-Oban

Grishipoll

B8071

Ballyhaugh

COLL

Quinish Point

Totronald

Arinagour

Calgary Point

Arileod Acha

Eilean
Ornsay

B8070

Caliach Point

MORNISH

Calgary

Crossapol
Bay

Rubha
Fasachd

Calgary Bay

Gunna

Treshnish Point

Ensay

5

Rubha Bhiosd Clachan
Mor

Salum

B8069

Rubha Dubh

TIREE

Balleyullin

*Balephetrish
Bay*

Caoles

Ruaig

Rubh'a
Chaoil

Burg

Kilninian

Kenovay

B8068

Gott Bay

Tiree-Coll
Tiree-Oban

Achleck

Rubha
Chraiginis

Moss

TIREE

B8068

Scarinish

Middleton

Heylipoll

Fladda

B8065

Crossapoll

Heanish

TRESHNISH
ISLES

Rubha na
Stroine

Balfapoll

Loch a'
Phuill

B8067

Balemartine

Hynish Bay

Balephuil

Mannel

1   **2**   **3** **88** GOMETRA   **4**

Lunga

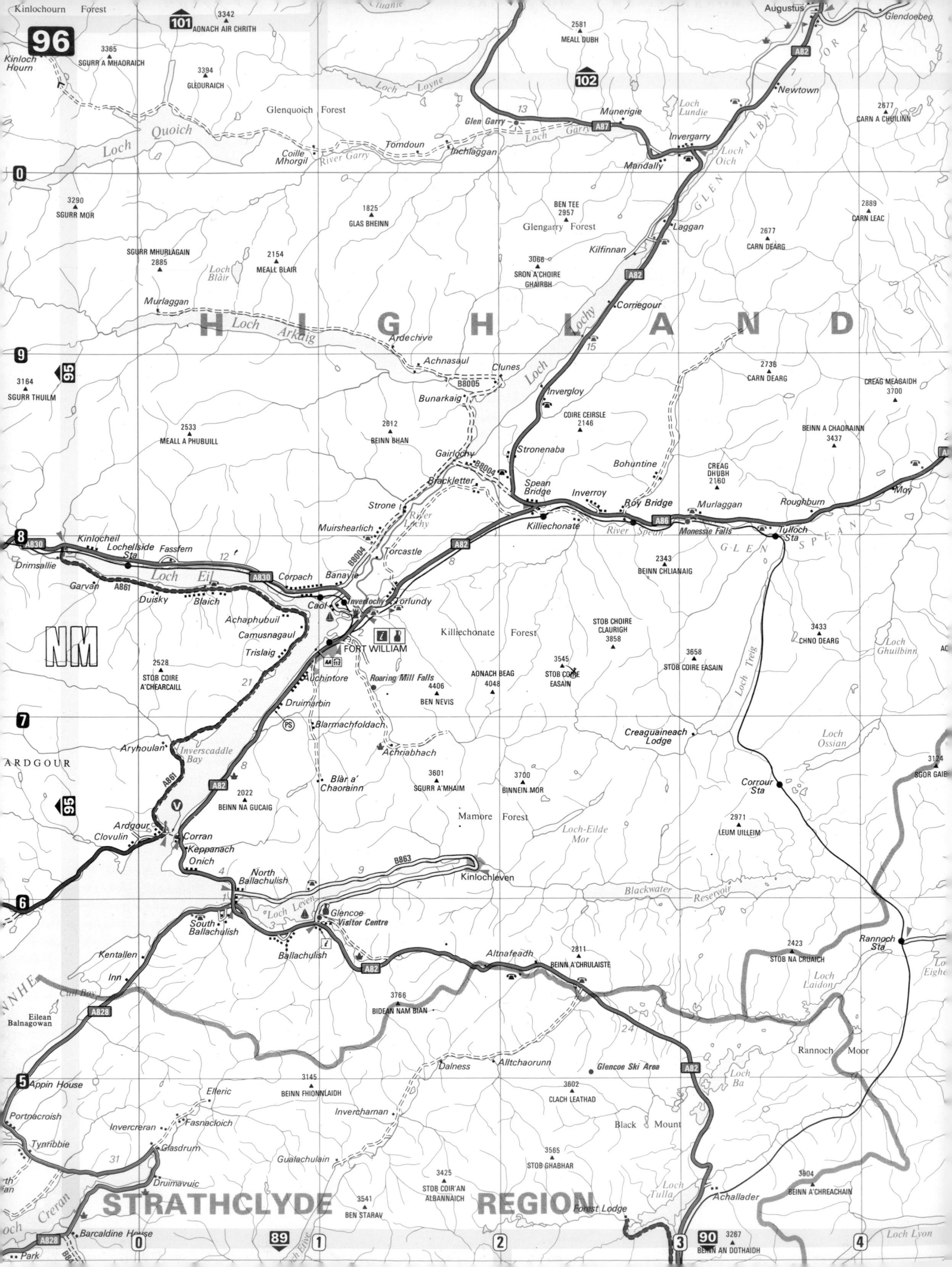

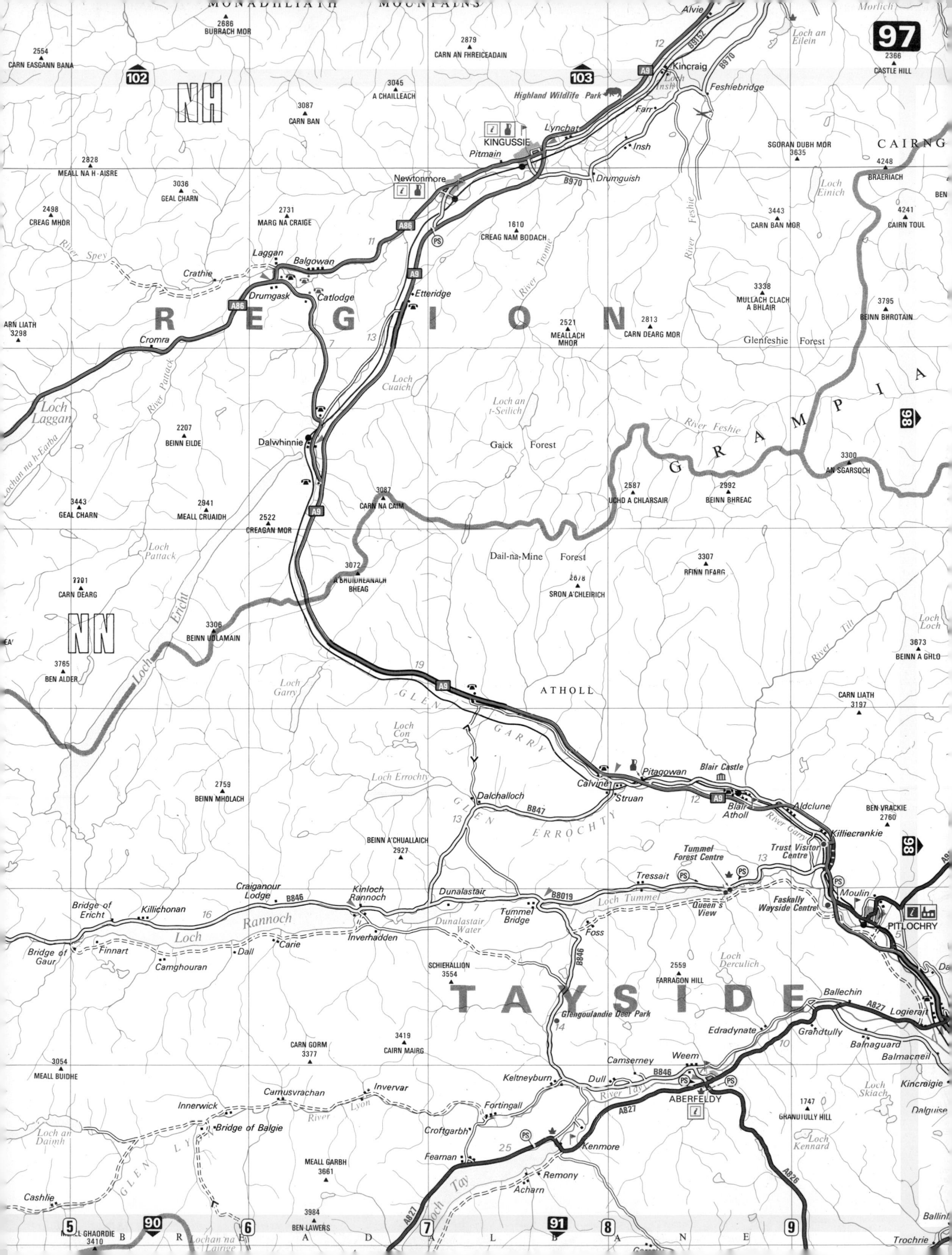

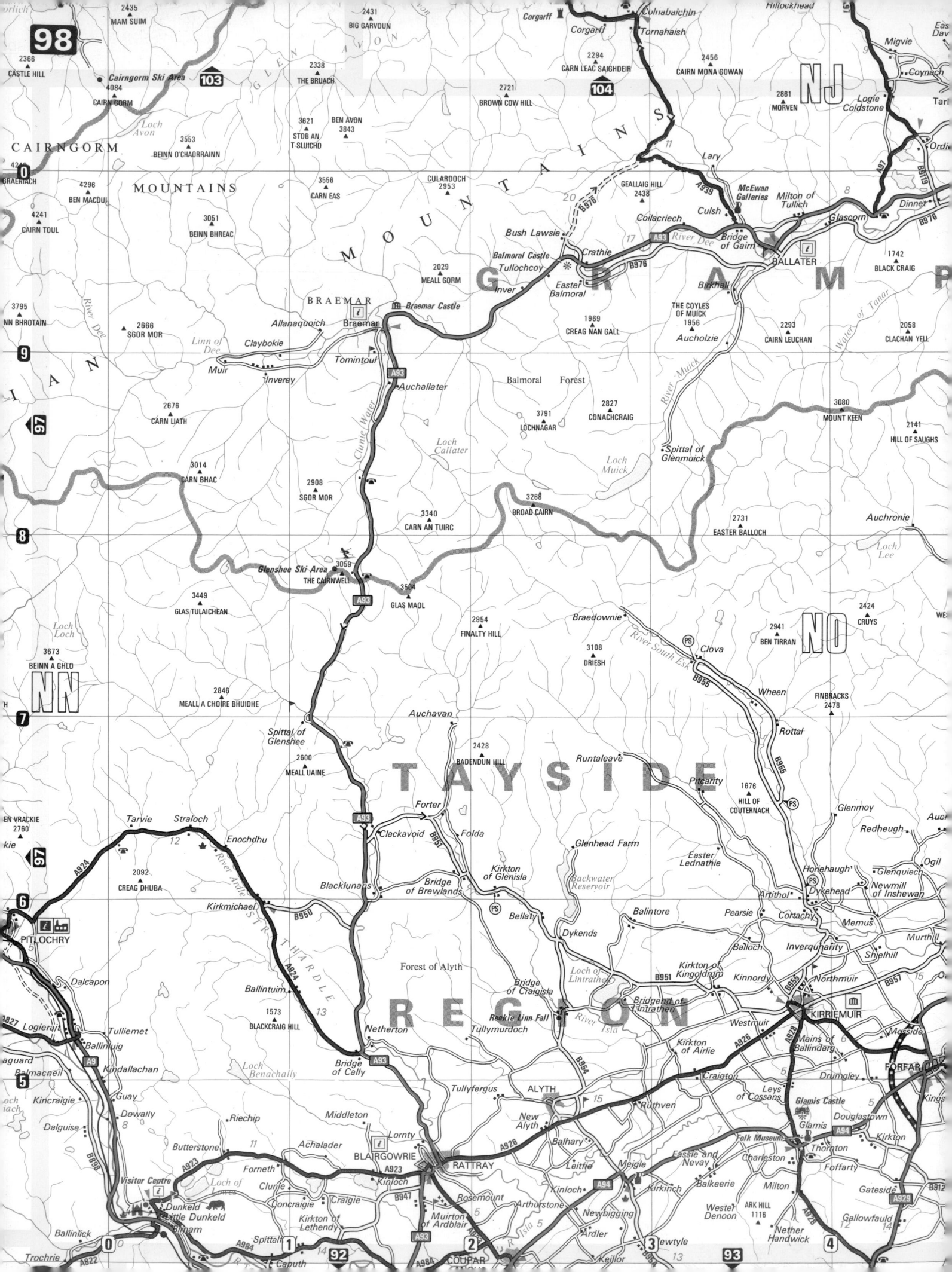

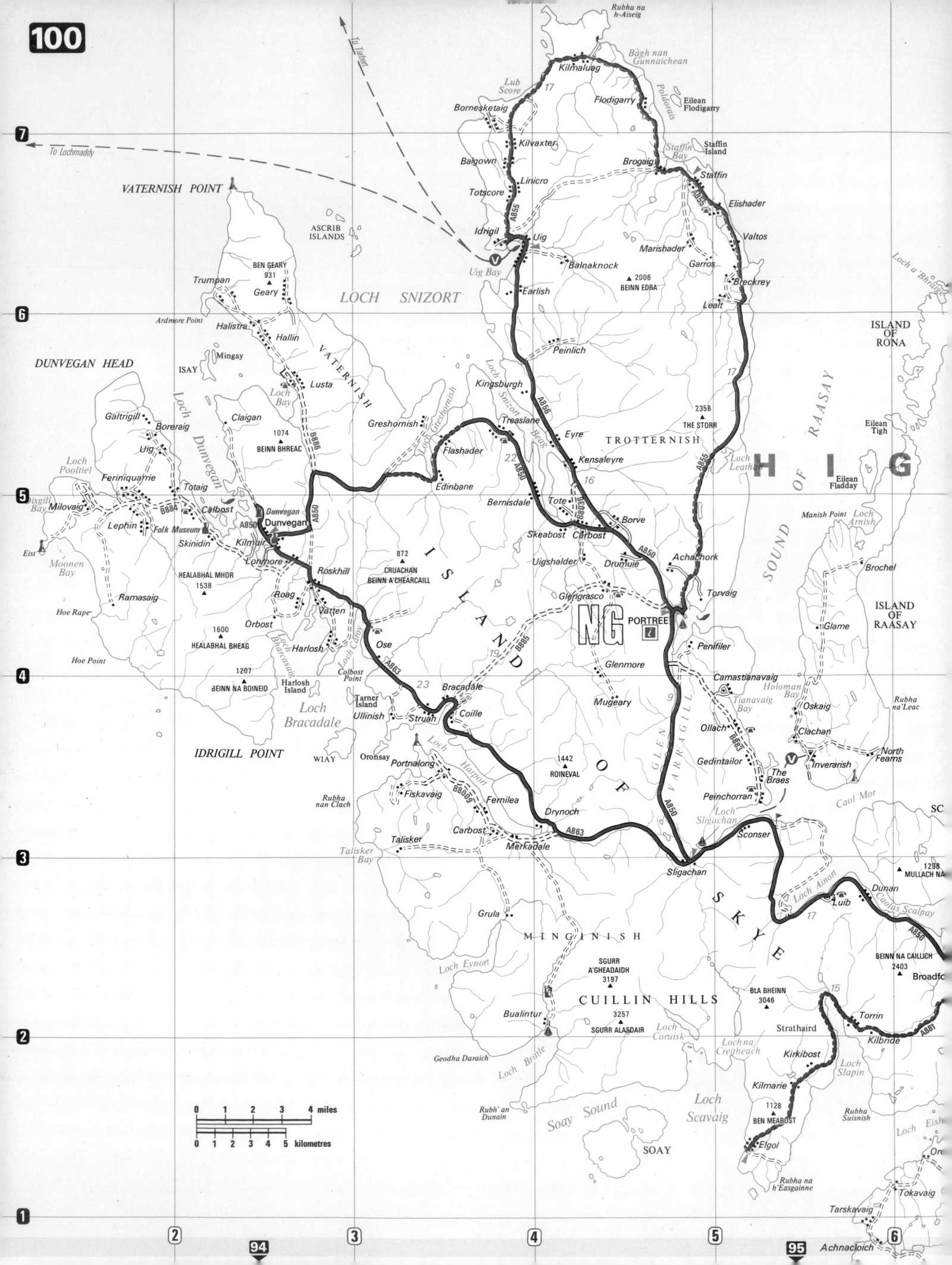

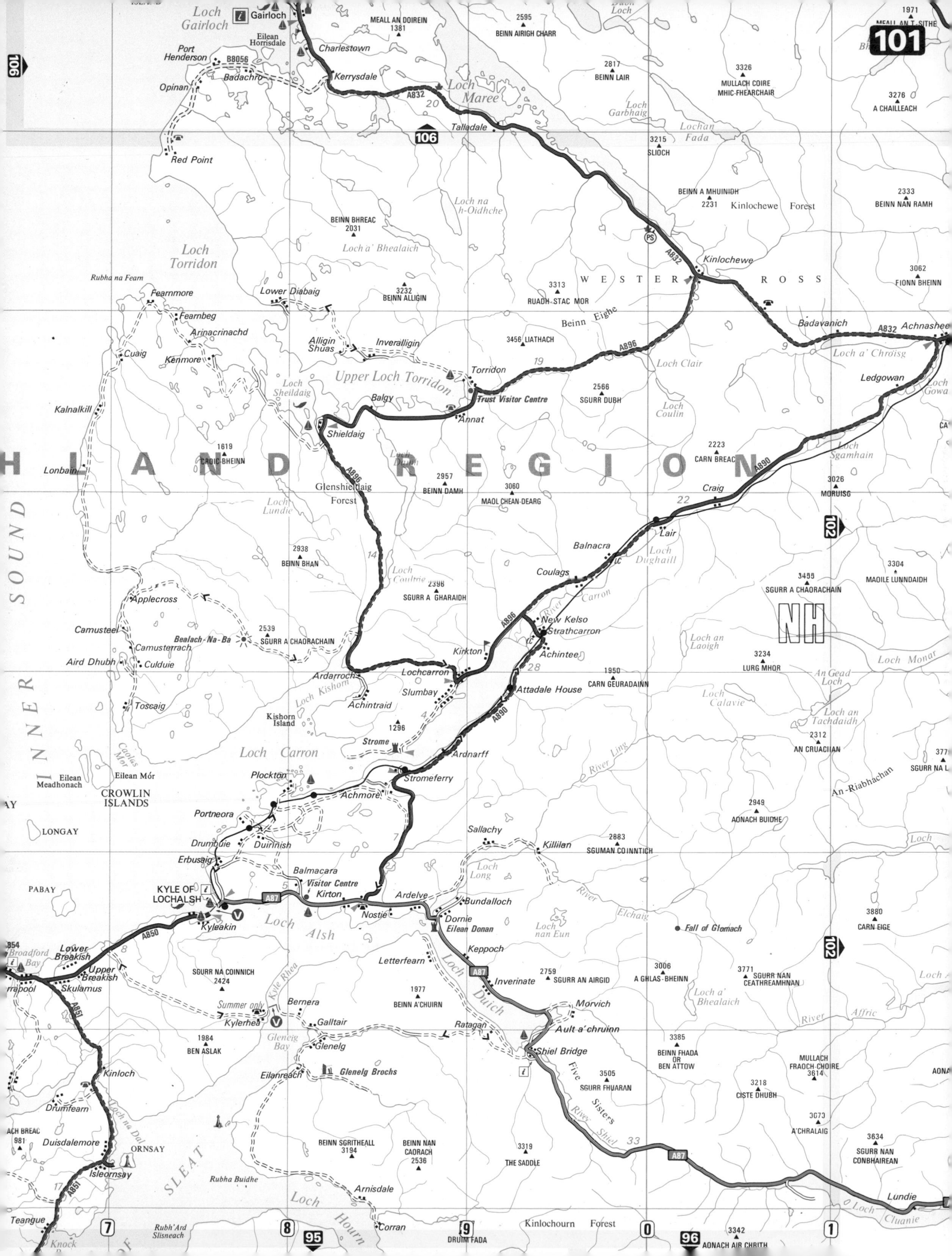

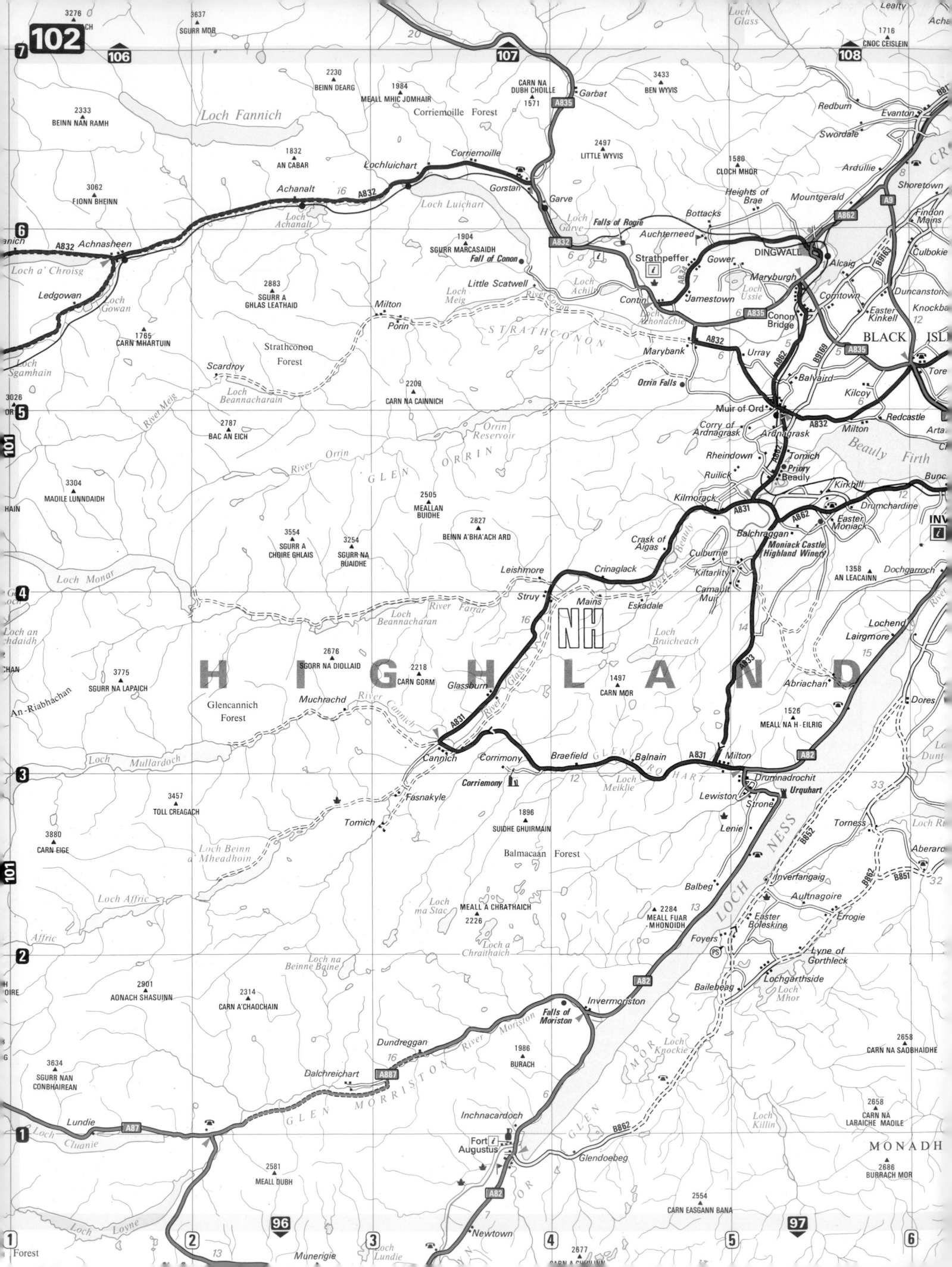

ROSEHEARTY • Sandhaven • Kinnaird Head • FRASERBURGH
Troup Head • Gamrie Bay • Crovie • Pennan • Quarry Head • Peathill • Percyhorner • Pitblae • Fraserburgh Bay • Cairnbulg Point
Boyndie Bay • Head of Garness • MACDUFF • Silverford • Gardenstown • New Aberdour • Egypt • Mid Ardlaw • Inverallochy
BANFF • Duff • Greenskairs • Longmanhill • Gamrie • Dubford • Boyndie • Gowanhill • St. Combs • Inzie Head
Keilhill • Minnonie • Cushnie • Netherbrae • Glasslaw • Ladysford • Memsie • Rathen • Crofts of Savoch • Loch of Strathbeg
Gorrachie • Milltown of Craigston • Craigmaud • Hillhead of Auchentumb • Strichen • New Leeds • Crimond • Rattray Head • Blackhill
Muirden • New Byth • Bonnykelly • Denhead • Leys • Backfolds • Kirktown • St Fergus
Fintry • Garmond • Ironside • Fetterangus • Rora • Scotstown Head
Kirkton • TURRIFF • Cuminestown • Howe of Teuchar • Balthangie • Fedderate • Toux • Dunshillock • Mintlaw • Inverugie • Kirkton
Colp • Darra • Culsh • Maud • Deer Abbey • Old Deer • Longside • Flushing • Torterston • PETERHEAD
Birkenhills • Crofts of Inverthernie • Muirtack • Maryhill • New Deer • Drum • Backhill of Clackriach • Bulwark • Stuartfield • Inverquhomery • Millbreck • Nether Kinmundy • Little Dens • Hillhead of Cocklaw • Burnhaven
Steinmanhill • Gourdas • Lethenty • Kirkton • Crofts of Meikle Ardo • Barrack • Knaven • Nethermuir • Crichie • Kinnadie • Clola • Blackhill • Sandford Bay
Kirktown of Auchterless • Monkshill • Brownhill • Cairnorrie • Auchnagatt • Fortree • Skelmuir • Kinharrachie • Smallburn • NK • Sandfordhill • Boddam • Buchan Ness
Titty • Backhill • Cottown • Ardo • Skelmonae • Inkhorn • Milton Coldwells • Blackhill • Stonegate Crofts • Teuchan • Coldwells
Badenscoth • Gordonstown • Fyvie • Woodhead • Crofts of Haddo • Quilquox • Drumwhindle • Arthrath • Auchleuchries • Muirtack • Hatton
Redhill • Rothiebrisbane • Collynie • Methlick • Haddo • R Ythan • Drumwhindle • Toll of Birness • Cruden Bay
Rothienorman • Petty • Cromblet • Barthol Chapel • Earlsford • Ythanbank • Hilton • Birness • Bogbrae • Chapel Hill • Bay of Cruden
Rothmaise • Newseat • St Katherines • Folla Rule • Wedderlairs • Inverebrie • Bromfield • Leask • Whinnyfold
Tocher • Cross of Jackston • Balgove • Tarves • Kinharrachie • ELLON • Artrochie • Auchmacoy
Kirkton of Rayne • Meikle Wartle • Jackstown • Craigdam • FORMARTINE • Ythsie • Kirkton of Logie Buchan • Collieston
Old Rayne • Durno • Daviot • OLDMELDRUM • Fingask • Auquhorthies • Tolquhon Castle • Esslemont • Meikle Tarty
Whiteford • Cairnbrogie • Pitmeddan • Pitmedden • Tipperty • Newburgh
Pittodrie • Pitcaple • Balhalgardy • Kirktown of Bourtie • Mill of Kingoodie • Udny Green • Cultercullen • Foveran
Inveramsay • Hillbrae • Hattoncrook • Affleck • Pettymuk • Minnes • Tillycorthie • Drums
Burgh Muir • INVERURIE • Whiterashes • Nether Crimond • Tillygreig • Craigie • Delfrigs
Bograxie • Port Elphinstone • Straloch • Causeyend • Balmedie
Burnhervie • Kinmuck • Newmachar • Whitecairns • Belhelvie
Grantlodge • Balbithan • Kippundy • Cothall • Milton of Potterton • Blackdog
Monymusk • Clovenstone • KINTORE • Wester Fintray • Hatton of Fintray • Mundurno
Kemnay • Cottown • Balbithan • Whitecairns
Craigearn • Lauchintilly • Leylodge • Overton • Blackburn • Dyce • Bridge of Don
Castle Fraser • Lyne of Skene • Clinterty • Stoneywood • ABERDEEN • To Lerwick
Sauchen • Achath • East Auchronie • Craibstone • Bankhead • Denmore
Dunecht • Kirkton of Skene • Buckburn • Old Aberdeen
Corsindae • Loch of Skene • Northfield • Mastrick • Kittybrewster • ABERDEEN
Echt • Westhill • Garlogie
South Kirkton • Elrick • Kingswells • Mannofield • Torry • Nigg
Landerberry • Redhill • Easter Ord • Blacktop • Nether Anguston

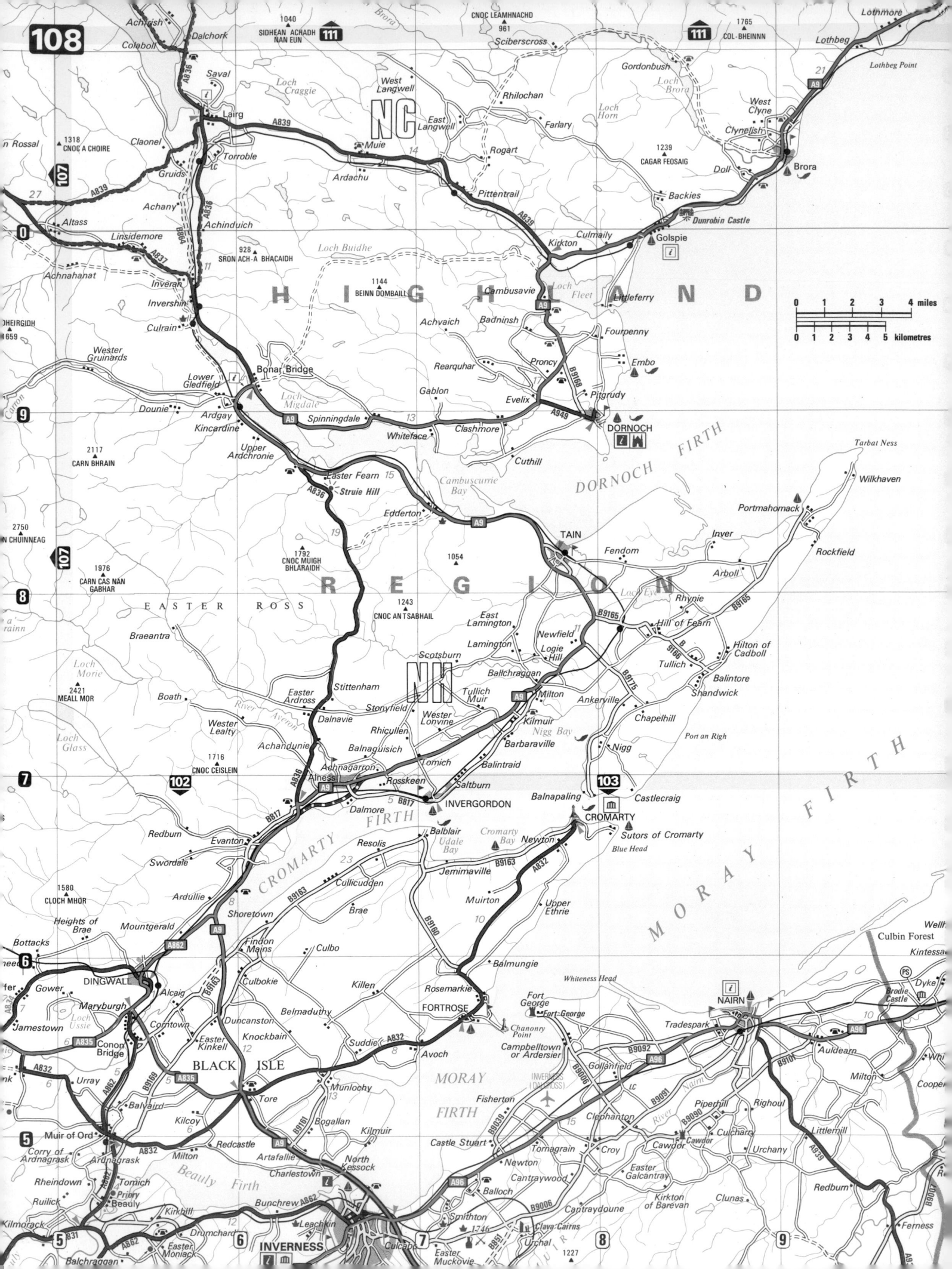

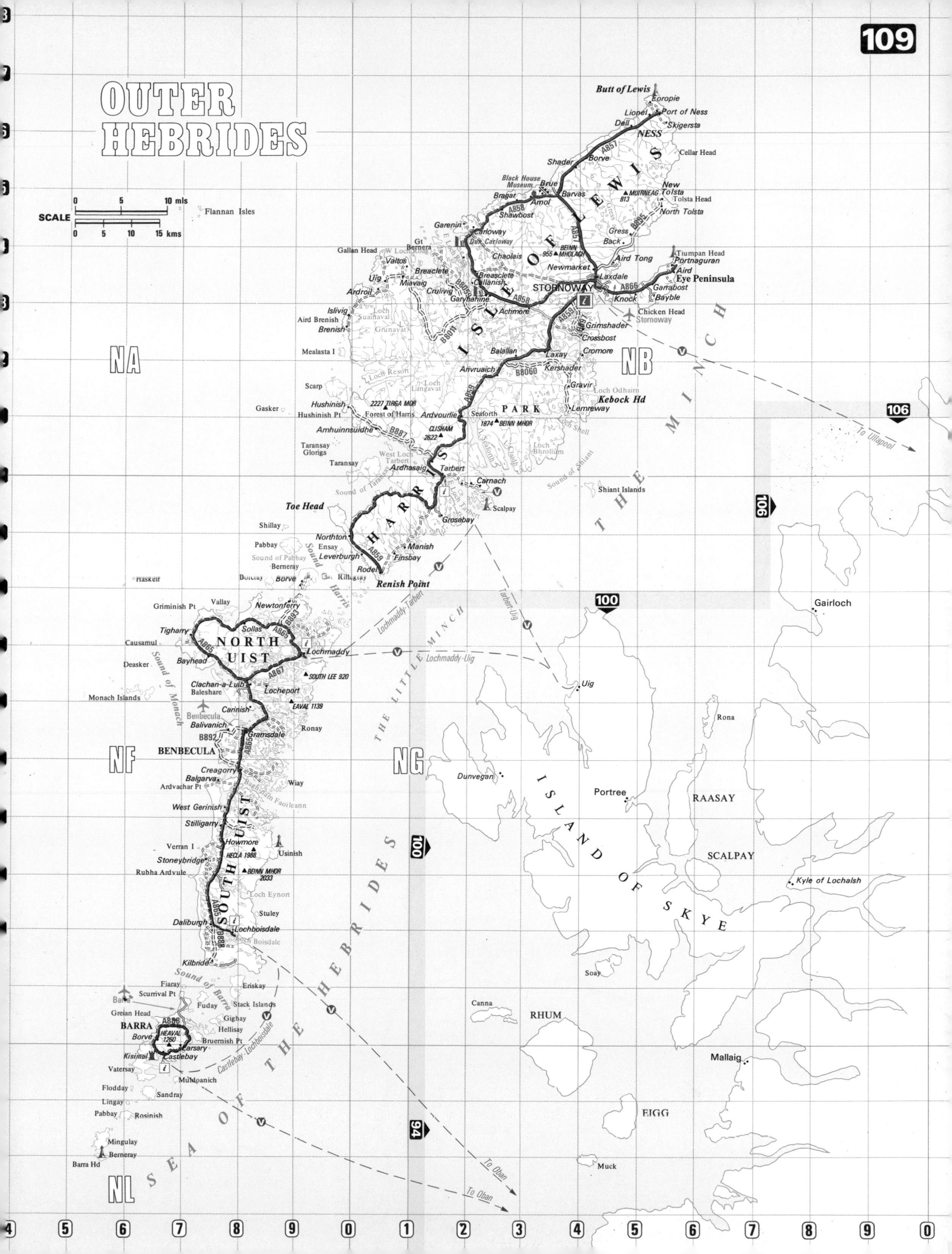

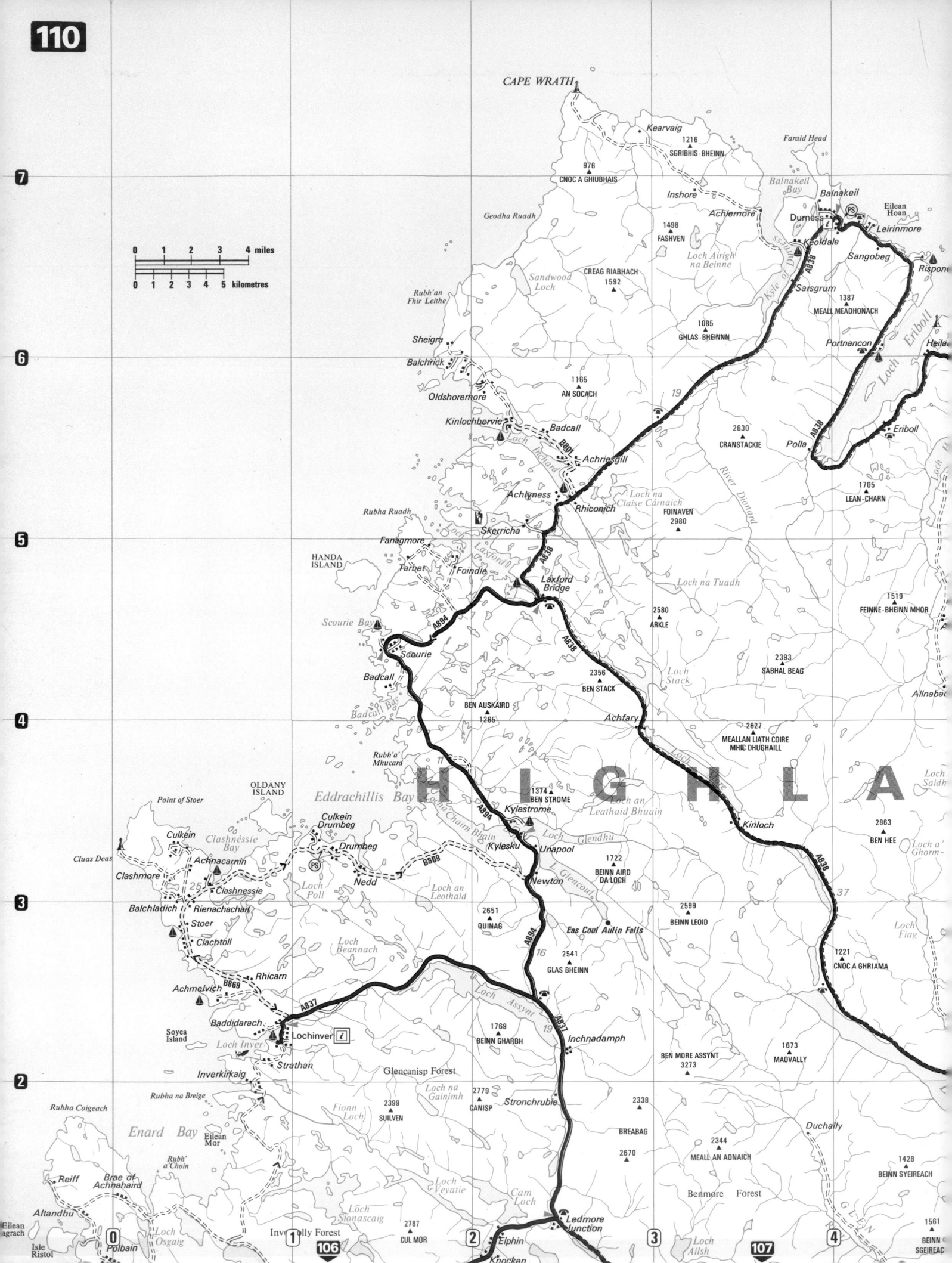

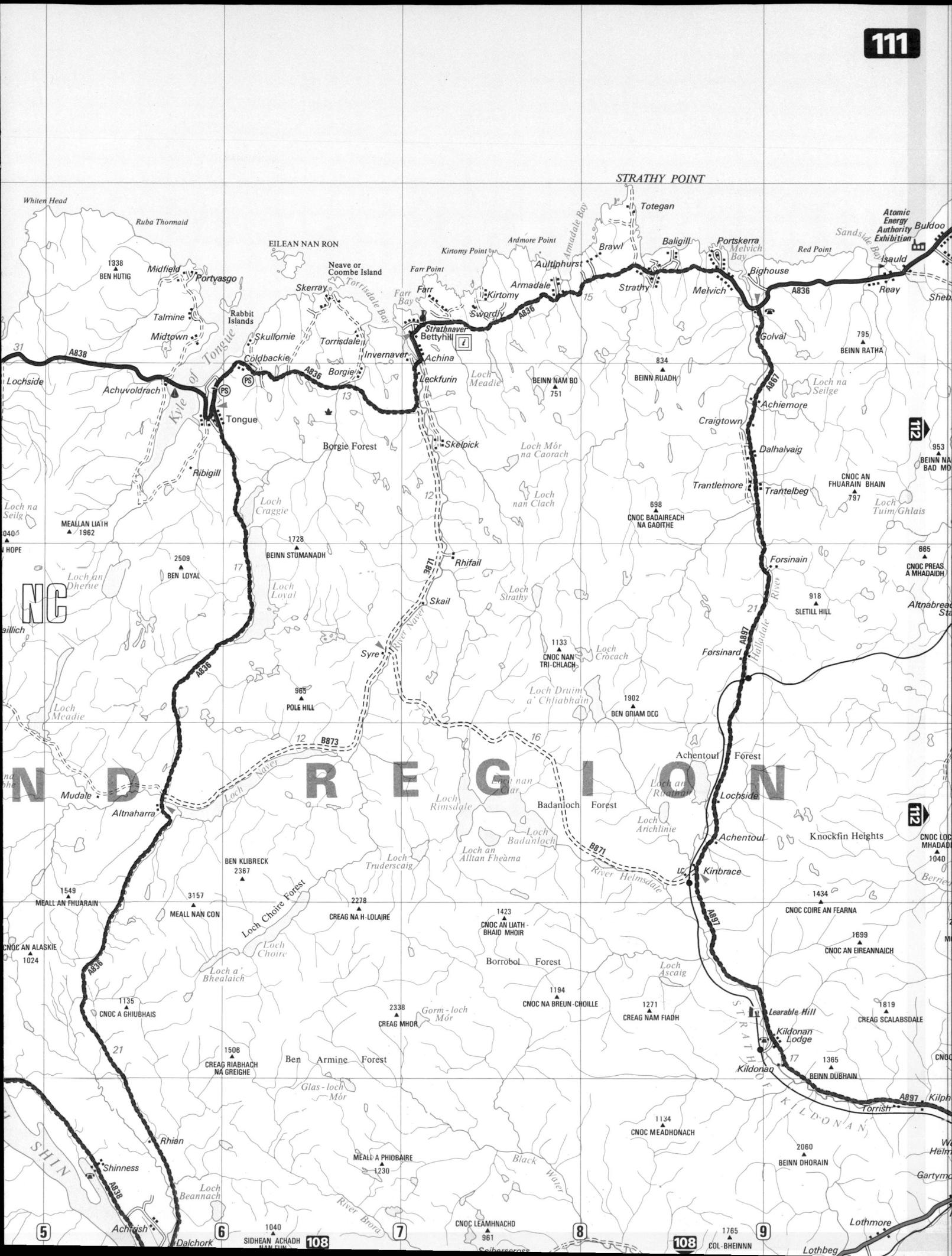

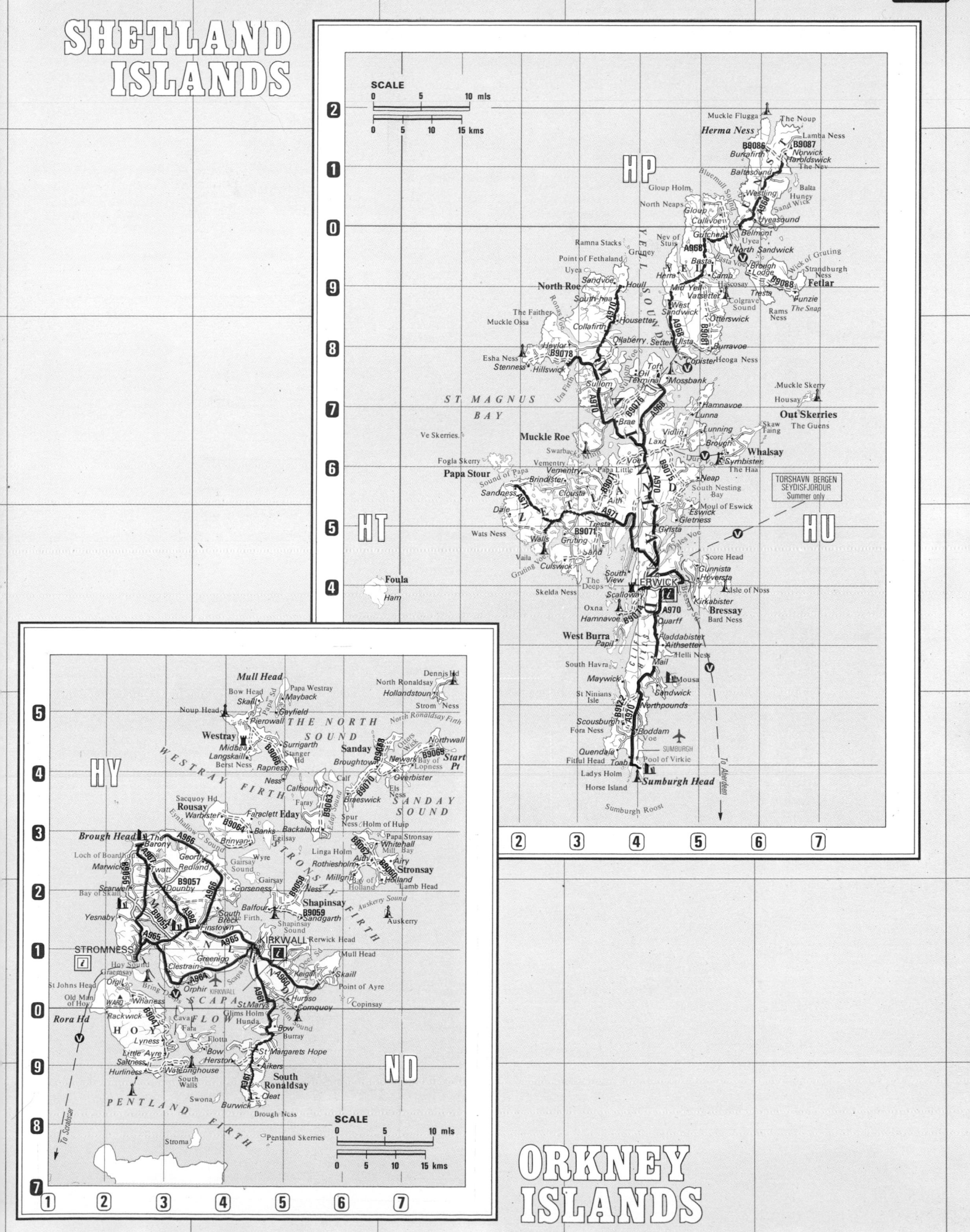

SHETLAND ISLANDS

ORKNEY ISLANDS

SCALE
0 5 10 mls
0 5 10 15 kms

HP

HT

HU

Shetland Islands labels (main map):

Muckle Flugga, The Noup, *Herma Ness*, Lamba Ness, B9086, B9087, Burrafirth, Norwick, Haroldswick, The Nev, Baltasound, UNST, Gloup Holm, Westing, Balta, Hungy, Sand Wick, Uyeasound, North Neaps, Gloup, Cullivoe, Nev of Stuis, Gutcher, Belmont, Uyea, A968, Ramna Stacks, Gruney, North Sandwick, Brough Lodge, Strandburgh Ness, Point of Fethaland, Uyea, Basta, V, Brough, Wick of Gruting, **North Roe**, Sandvoe, Houll, Herra, Basta Voe, Camb, B9068, **Fetlar**, South-hea, YELL, Mid Yell, Hascosay, Tresta, Funzie, The Faither, The Snap, Muckle Ossa, Collafirth, Olaberry, Housetter, Setter, Ulsta, West Sandwick, Vatsetter, Colgrave Sound, Rams Ness, Esha Ness, Heylor, B9078, Setter, Burravoe, Heoga Ness, Stenness, Hillswick, Olaberry, Toft, Copister, Muckle Skerry, *ST MAGNUS BAY*, Sullom, Oil Terminal, Mossbank, Housay, Ve Skerries, Brae, Vidlin, Hamnavoe, Out Skerries, Fogla Skerry, Swarback's Mint, Laxo, Lunna, Lunning, Skaw Taing, The Guens, Muckle Roe, Vementry, Voe, Neap, Brough, Whalsay, Papa Stour, Papa Little, South Nesting Bay, V, Symbister, The Haa, **Papa Stour**, Brindister, Clousta, Aith, MAINLAND, Moul of Eswick, TORSHAVN BERGEN SEYDISFJORDUR Summer only, Sandness, Dale, Tresta, Eswick, Gletness, Walls, B9071, Sand, Girlsta, Score Head, Gunnista, Hoversta, Wats Ness, Gruting, Vaila, Culswick, The Deeps, South View, LERWICK, Isle of Noss, V, Foula, Ham, Skelda Ness, Scalloway, Kirkabister, Bressay, Oxna, Hamnavoe, Quarff, Bard Ness, West Burra, Papil, Fladdabister, Aithsetter, Helli Ness, South Havra, Mail, Mousa, St Ninians Isle, Maywick, V, Sandwick, Northpounds, Scousburgh, Fora Ness, Boddam, SUMBURGH, Quendale, Pool of Virkie, Fitful Head, Toab, To Aberdeen, Ladys Holm, Sumburgh Head, Horse Island, Sumburgh Roost

Road numbers: A970, A968, B9076, B9075, A971

ORKNEY ISLANDS

HY

ND

Orkney Islands labels (inset map):

Mull Head, Papa Westray, North Ronaldsay, Dennis Hd, Bow Head, Skaill, Mayback, Hollandstoun, Noup Head, Geyfield, Pierowall, *THE NORTH SOUND*, Strom Ness, Northwall, **Westray**, Surrigarth, Stanger, **Sanday**, Otters Wick, Midbea, Langskaill, Rapness, Ness, Broughton, Newark, Bay of Lopness, Start Pt, Berst Ness, Calf, Overbister, Sacquoy Hd, Calfsound, Faray, Els Ness, *SANDAY SOUND*, **Rousay**, Warbister, Faraclett Eday, Backaland, *WESTRAY FIRTH*, Egilsay, Spur Ness, Holm of Huip, Brough Head, The Barony, Georth, Redland, Twatt, Wyre, Banks, Brinyan, Linga Holm, Papa Stronsay, Whitehall, Loch of Boardho, A966, *EYNHALLOW SOUND*, Gairsay Sound, Rothiesholm, Airy, **Stronsay**, Marwick, Scarwell, B9057, Dounby, Gairsay, Corseness, Auth, Bay of Holland, Holland, Bay of Skaill, Yesnaby, A986, *STRONSAY FIRTH*, Millgren, Lamb Head, A965, Finstown, South Breck, Balfour, Shapinsay Sound, Sandgarth, Auskerry, **Shapinsay**, STROMNESS, Greenigo, B9059, Mull Head, Clestrain, KIRKWALL, Kaigan, Skaill, Berwick Head, Hoy Sound, A964, Orphir, Deer Sound, Point of Ayre, Graemsay, Bring Deeps, KIRKWALL, *SCAPA FLOW*, St Marys, Glims Holm, Hurliso, Copinsay, St Johns Head, Cava, Fara, St Marys, Cornquoy, Old Man of Hoy, WARD, Whaness, Flotta, Bow, Burray, Rora Hd, HOY, Lyness, Bow, Herston, V, Rackwick, Little Ayre, Saltness, Waulkhouse, Aikers, South Ronaldsay, Cleat, Hurliness, South Walls, Swona, Burwick, Brough Ness, To Scrabster, *PENTLAND FIRTH*, Stroma, Pentland Skerries

Road numbers: A966, B9056, B9057, A986, A965, A964, B9059

SCALE
0 5 10 mls
0 5 10 15 kms

Motorway Maps

The maps on the following pages depict the principal motorways in Great Britain and are arranged in easy-to-follow strips. Enlarged details of many motorway junctions have been included to help the driver approach these without hesitation. The motorway guide opposite gives an overall picture of the system and enables the driver to plan extended use of motorways.

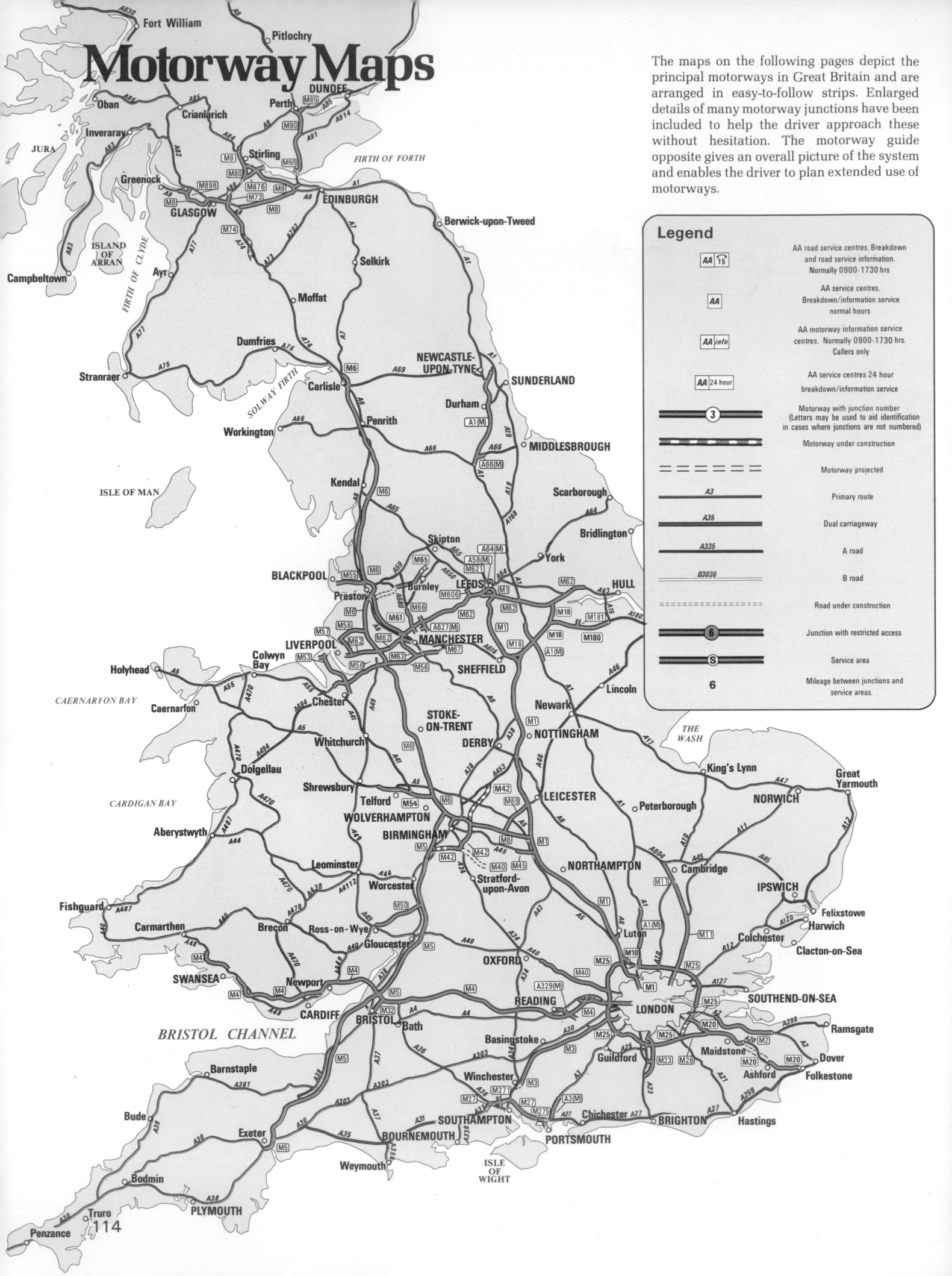

Legend

AA 15	AA road service centres. Breakdown and road service information. Normally 0900-1730 hrs
AA	AA service centres. Breakdown/information service normal hours
AA info	AA motorway information service centres. Normally 0900-1730 hrs. Callers only
AA 24 hour	AA service centres 24 hour breakdown/information service
——3——	Motorway with junction number (Letters may be used to aid identification in cases where junctions are not numbered)
— — —	Motorway under construction
– – –	Motorway projected
A3	Primary route
A35	Dual carriageway
A335	A road
B3036	B road
= = =	Road under construction
——6——	Junction with restricted access
——S——	Service area
6	Mileage between junctions and service areas.

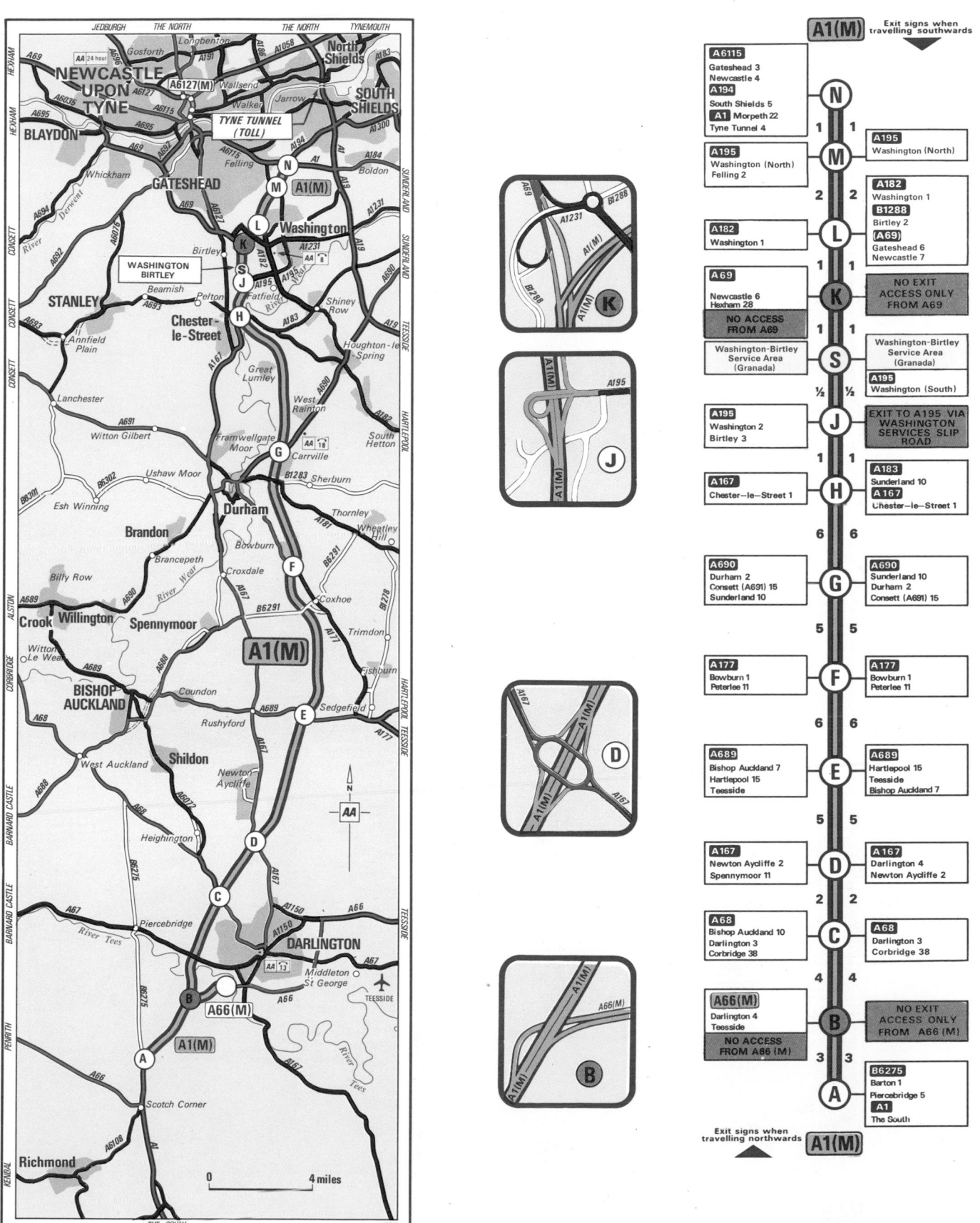

SOUTH MIMMS–HATFIELD–BALDOCK A1(M)

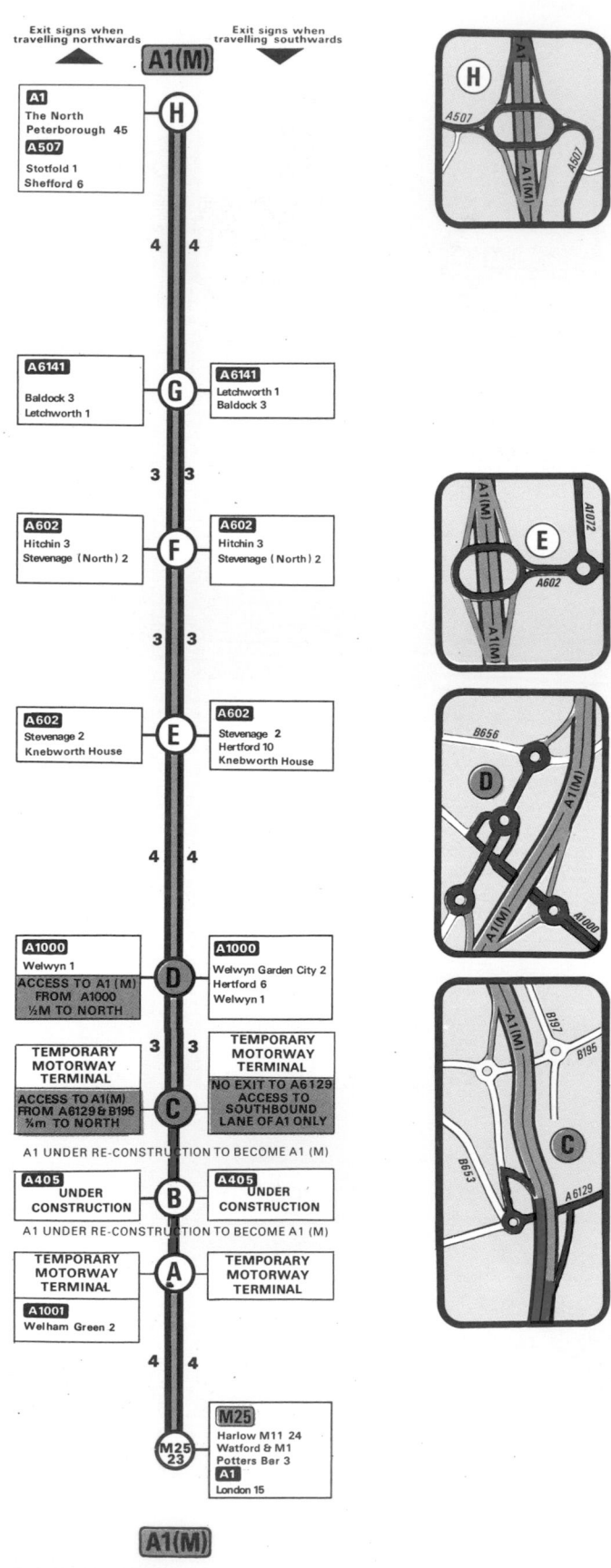

A1(M)

A1
The North
Peterborough 45
A507
Stotfold 1
Shefford 6

H

4 4

A6141
Baldock 3
Letchworth 1

G

A6141
Letchworth 1
Baldock 3

3 3

A602
Hitchin 3
Stevenage (North) 2

F

A602
Hitchin 3
Stevenage (North) 2

3 3

A602
Stevenage 2
Knebworth House

E

A602
Stevenage 2
Hertford 10
Knebworth House

4 4

A1000
Welwyn 1
**ACCESS TO A1(M)
FROM A1000
½M TO NORTH**

D

A1000
Welwyn Garden City 2
Welwyn 1

**TEMPORARY
MOTORWAY
TERMINAL**
**ACCESS TO A1(M)
FROM A6129 & B195
¾m TO NORTH**

3 3

C

**TEMPORARY
MOTORWAY
TERMINAL**
**NO EXIT TO A6129
ACCESS TO
SOUTHBOUND
LANE OF A1 ONLY**

A1 UNDER RE-CONSTRUCTION TO BECOME A1 (M)

A405
**UNDER
CONSTRUCTION**

B

A405
**UNDER
CONSTRUCTION**

A1 UNDER RE-CONSTRUCTION TO BECOME A1 (M)

**TEMPORARY
MOTORWAY
TERMINAL**

A

**TEMPORARY
MOTORWAY
TERMINAL**

A1001
Welham Green 2

4 4

M25
23

M25
Harlow M11 24
Watford & M1
Potters Bar 3
A1
London 15

A1(M)

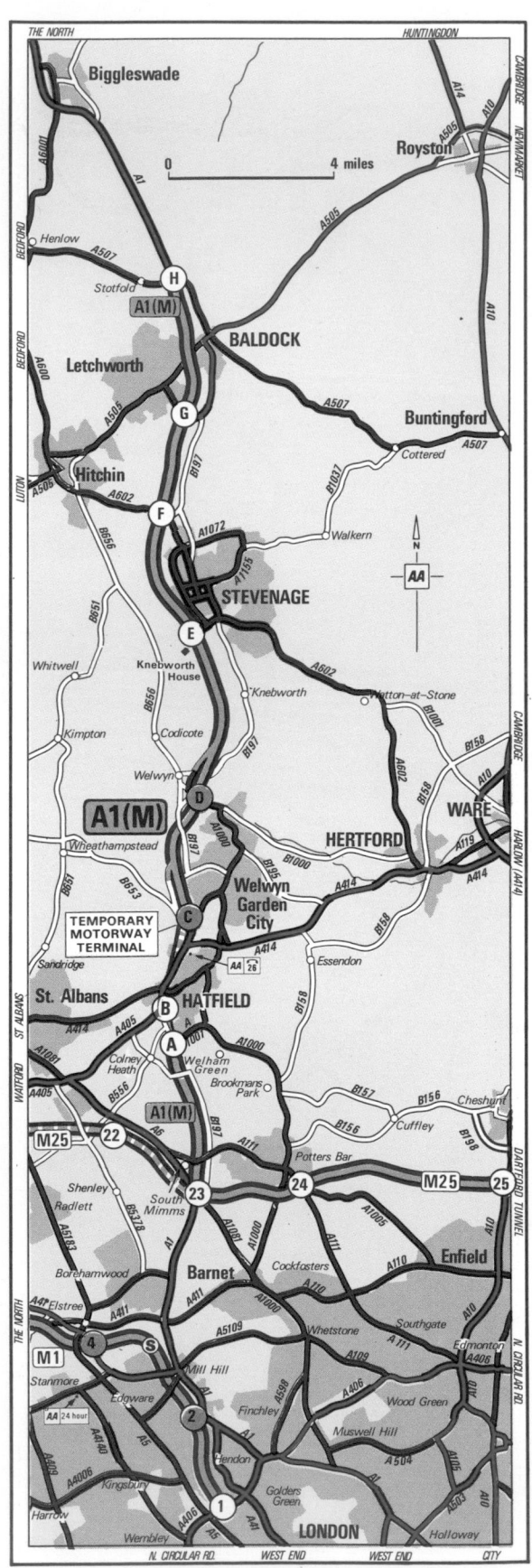

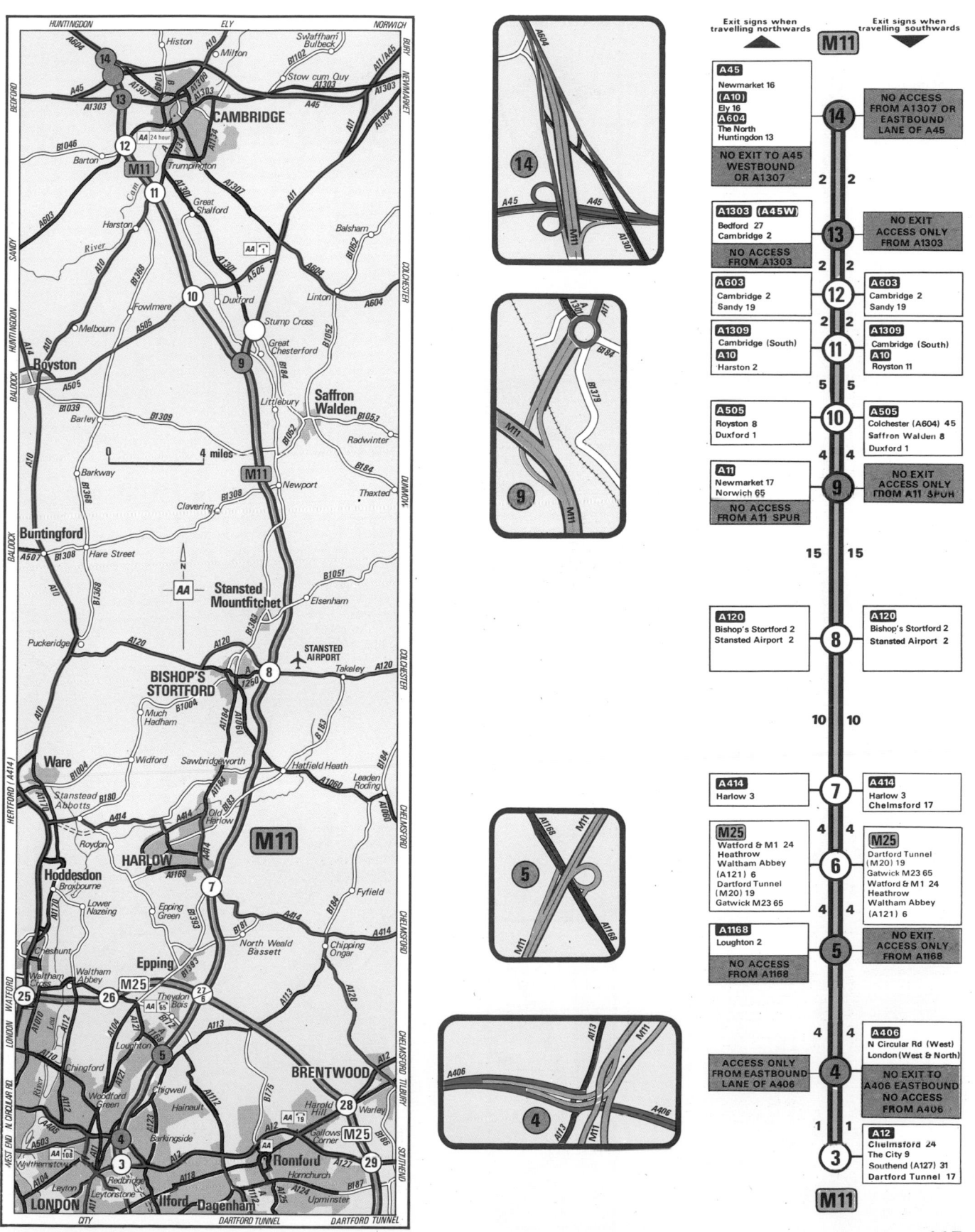

Exit signs when travelling northwards ▲ | M11 | Exit signs when travelling southwards ▼

A45
Newmarket 16
(A10)
Ely 16
A604
The North
Huntingdon 13

NO EXIT TO A45
WESTBOUND
OR A1307

(14)

NO ACCESS
FROM A1307 OR
EASTBOUND
LANE OF A45

2   2

A1303 (A45W)
Bedford 27
Cambridge 2

NO ACCESS
FROM A1303

(13)

NO EXIT
ACCESS ONLY
FROM A1303

2   2

A603
Cambridge 2
Sandy 19

(12)

A603
Cambridge 2
Sandy 19

2   2

A1309
Cambridge (South)
A10
Harston 2

(11)

A1309
Cambridge (South)
A10
Royston 11

5   5

A505
Royston 8
Duxford 1

(10)

A505
Colchester (A604) 45
Saffron Walden 8
Duxford 1

4   4

A11
Newmarket 17
Norwich 65

NO ACCESS
FROM A11 SPUR

(9)

NO EXIT
ACCESS ONLY
FROM A11 SPUR

15   15

A120
Bishop's Stortford 2
Stansted Airport 2

(8)

A120
Bishop's Stortford 2
Stansted Airport 2

10   10

A414
Harlow 3

(7)

A414
Harlow 3
Chelmsford 17

4   4

M25
Watford & M1 24
Heathrow
Waltham Abbey
(A121) 6
Dartford Tunnel
(M20) 19
Gatwick M23 65

(6)

M25
Dartford Tunnel
(M20) 19
Gatwick M23 65
Watford & M1 24
Heathrow
Waltham Abbey
(A121) 6

4   4

A1168
Loughton 2

NO ACCESS
FROM A1168

(5)

NO EXIT.
ACCESS ONLY
FROM A1168

4   4

ACCESS ONLY
FROM EASTBOUND
LANE OF A406

(4)

A406
N Circular Rd (West)
London (West & North)

NO EXIT TO
A406 EASTBOUND
NO ACCESS
FROM A406

1   1

(3)

A12
Chelmsford 24
The City 9
Southend (A127) 31
Dartford Tunnel 17

M11

117

LONDON–MILTON KEYNES M1

Exit signs when travelling northwards ▲

Exit signs when travelling southwards ▼

M1

Northbound	Exit	Southbound
A509 Newport Pagnell 3 Milton Keynes 4 Woburn Sands 4	(14)	**A509** Newport Pagnell 3 Milton Keynes 4
5		5
A421 Bedford 10 Milton Keynes (South)	(13)	**A421** Bedford 10 Woburn 3
7		7
A5120 Woburn 6	(12)	**A5120** Toddington 1
1		1
Toddington Service Area (Granada)	(S)	Toddington Service Area (Granada)
4		4
A505 Dunstable 2 Luton 3	(11)	**A505** Dunstable 2 Luton 3
3		3
A6 Harpenden 4 Luton & Airport 2	(10)	**A6** Harpenden 4 Luton & Airport
2		2
A5 Harpenden 4 Whipsnade 7	(9)	**A5** Whipsnade 7
5		5
A4147 Hemel Hempstead 3	(8)	**A4147** Hemel Hempstead 3
1		1
NO EXIT ACCESS ONLY FROM M10	(7)	**M10** Hatfield 10 St Albans 4 — NO ACCESS
2		2
ACCESS FROM M25 UNDER CONSTRUCTION	(6A)	**M25** UNDER CONSTRUCTION
1		1
A405 Hatfield 8 St Albans 4	(6)	**A405** Watford 5
3		2
A41 Watford 3 Aylesbury 24	(5)	**A41** Harrow 7
4		4
NO EXIT. ACCESS ONLY FROM A41	(4)	**A41** Edgware 2 — NO ACCESS
2		2
Scratchwood Service Area (Trusthouse Forte)	(S)	Scratchwood Service Area (Trusthouse Forte)
2		2
NO EXIT ACCESS ONLY FROM A1	(2)	**A1** N Circular Rd East City 12 Dartford Tunnel 32 — NO EXIT TO A41 NO ACCESS TO M1
2		2
	(1)	**A406** (East) N Circular Road E West End (A41) **A406** (West) N Circular Road W Heathrow 17

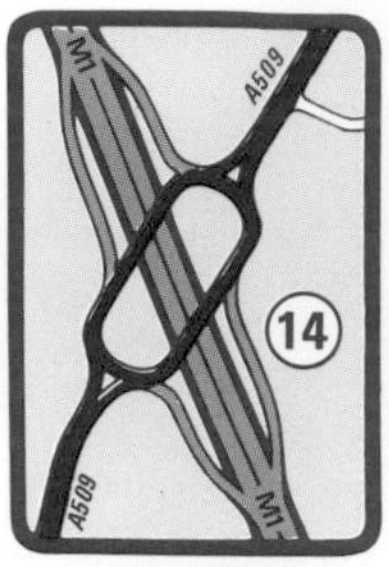

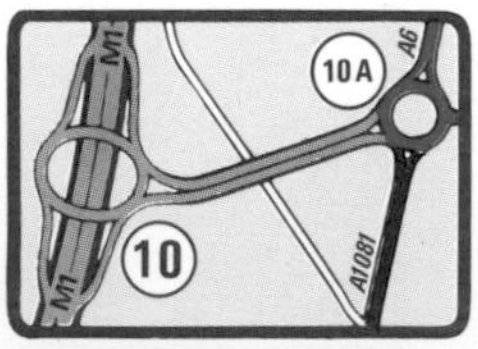

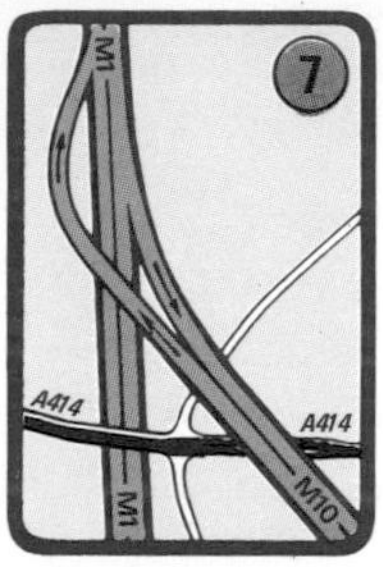

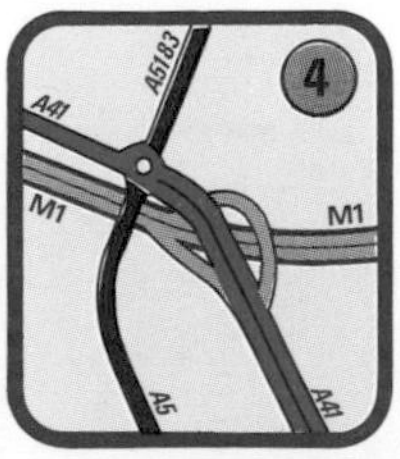

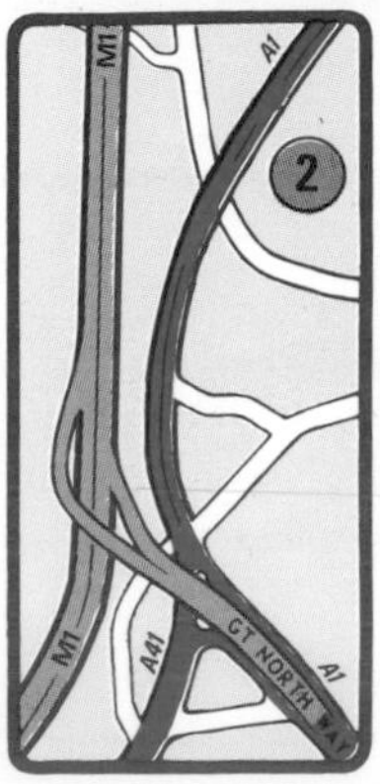

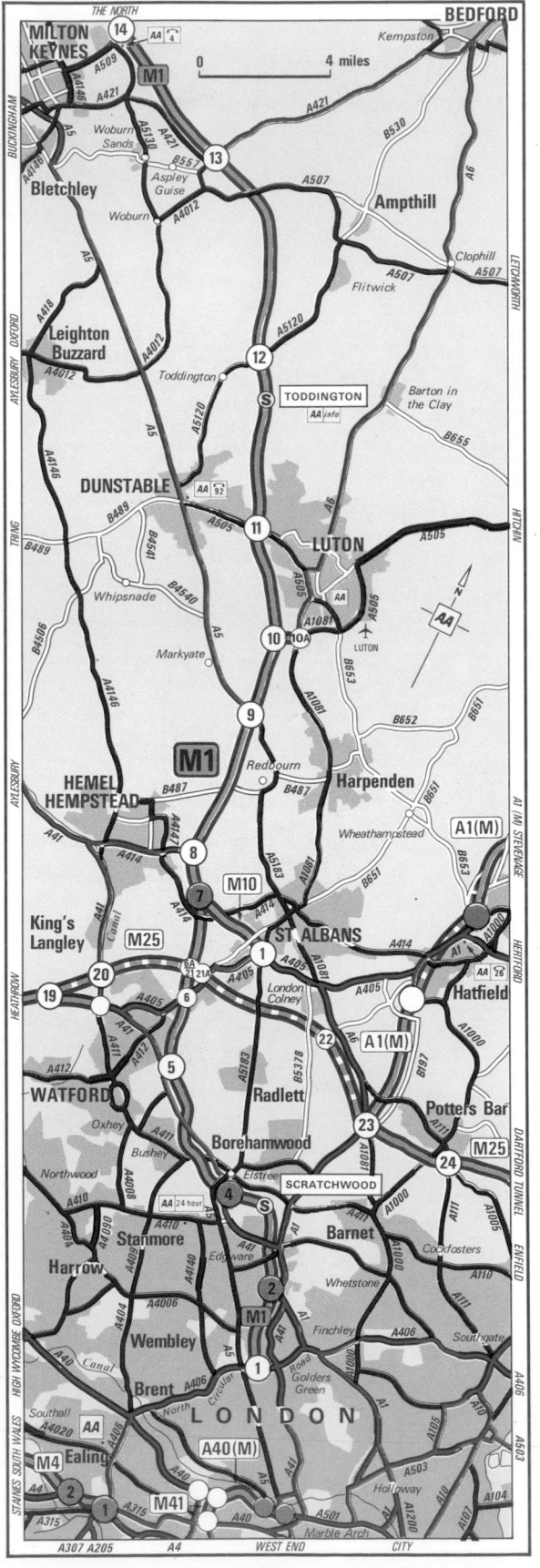

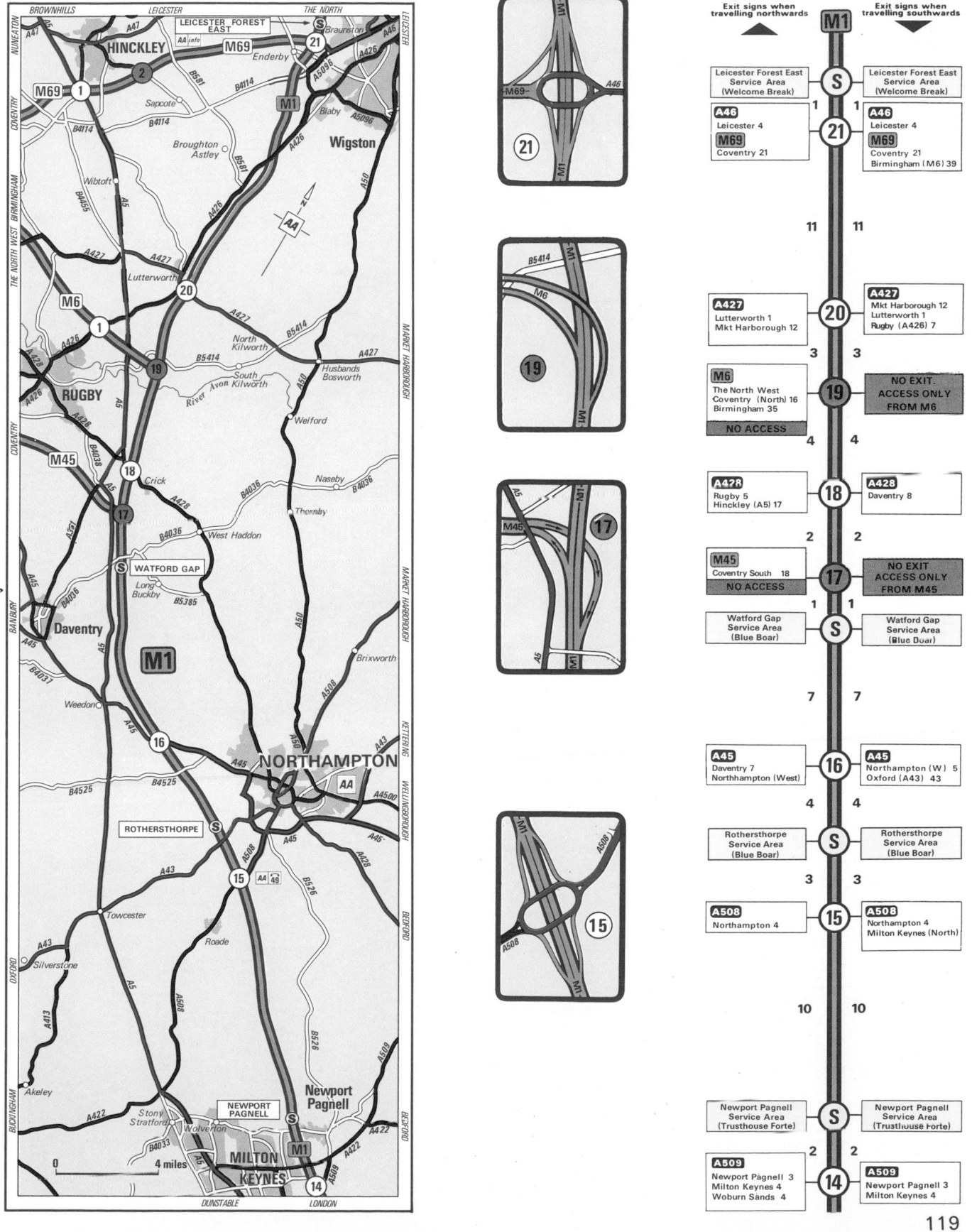

Exit signs when travelling northwards ▲   **M1**   Exit signs when travelling southwards ▼

Northwards		Southwards
Leicester Forest East Service Area (Welcome Break)	**S**	Leicester Forest East Service Area (Welcome Break)
	1	1
A46 Leicester 4 **M69** Coventry 21	**21**	**A46** Leicester 4 **M69** Coventry 21 Birmingham (M6) 39
	11	11
A427 Lutterworth 1 Mkt Harborough 12	**20**	**A427** Mkt Harborough 12 Lutterworth 1 Rugby (A426) 7
	3	3
M6 The North West Coventry (North) 16 Birmingham 35 NO ACCESS	**19**	NO EXIT. ACCESS ONLY FROM M6
	4	4
A428 Rugby 5 Hinckley (A5) 17	**18**	**A428** Daventry 8
	2	2
M45 Coventry South 18 NO ACCESS	**17**	NO EXIT ACCESS ONLY FROM M45
	1	1
Watford Gap Service Area (Blue Boar)	**S**	Watford Gap Service Area (Blue Boar)
	7	7
A45 Daventry 7 Northhampton (West)	**16**	**A45** Northampton (W) 5 Oxford (A43) 43
	4	4
Rothersthorpe Service Area (Blue Boar)	**S**	Rothersthorpe Service Area (Blue Boar)
	3	3
A508 Northampton 4	**15**	**A508** Northampton 4 Milton Keynes (North)
	10	10
Newport Pagnell Service Area (Trusthouse Forte)	**S**	Newport Pagnell Service Area (Trusthouse Forte)
	2	2
A509 Newport Pagnell 3 Milton Keynes 4 Woburn Sands 4	**14**	**A509** Newport Pagnell 3 Milton Keynes 4

LEICESTER–BOLSOVER M1

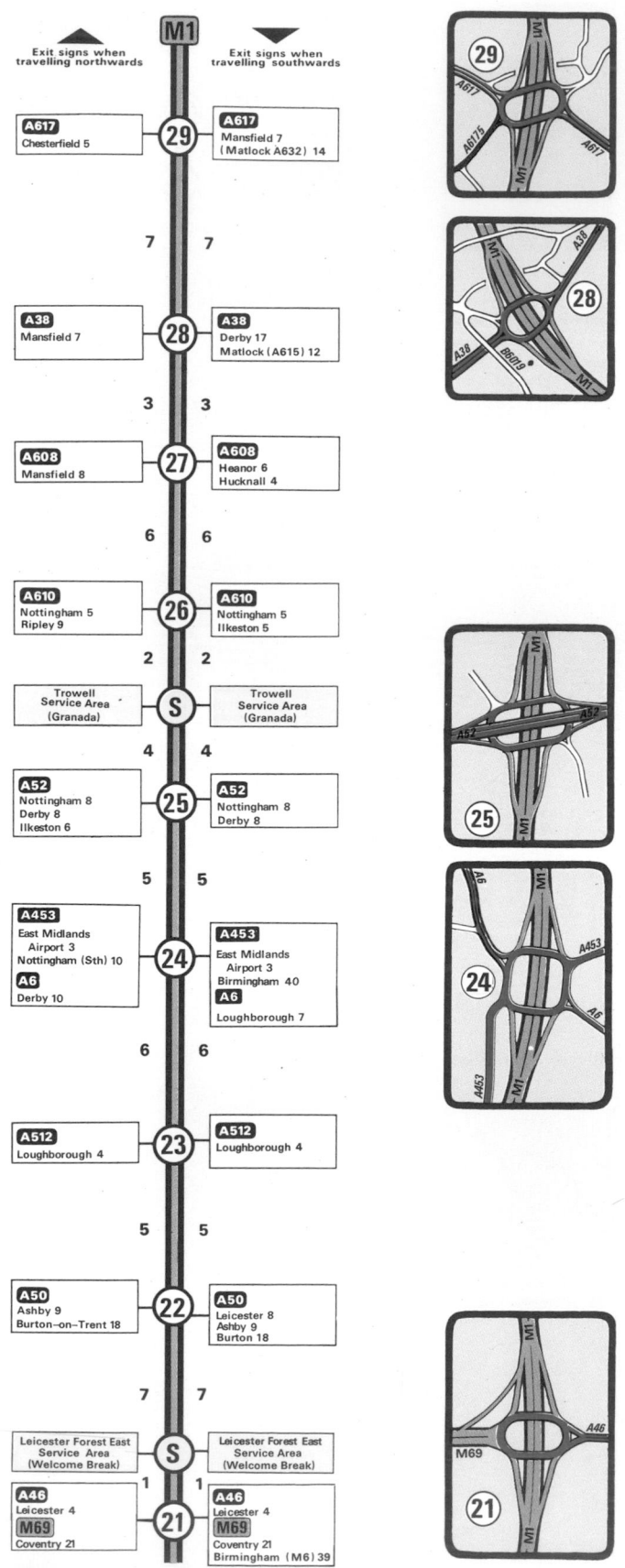

M1

▲ Exit signs when travelling northwards   ▼ Exit signs when travelling southwards

Northbound	Jct	Southbound
A617 Chesterfield 5	29	**A617** Mansfield 7 (Matlock A632) 14
	7 7	
A38 Mansfield 7	28	**A38** Derby 17 Matlock (A615) 12
	3 3	
A608 Mansfield 8	27	**A608** Heanor 6 Hucknall 4
	6 6	
A610 Nottingham 5 Ripley 9	26	**A610** Nottingham 5 Ilkeston 5
	2 2	
Trowell Service Area (Granada)	S	Trowell Service Area (Granada)
	4 4	
A52 Nottingham 8 Derby 8 Ilkeston 6	25	**A52** Nottingham 8 Derby 8
	5 5	
A453 East Midlands Airport 3 Nottingham (Sth) 10 **A6** Derby 10	24	**A453** East Midlands Airport 3 Birmingham 40 **A6** Loughborough 7
	6 6	
A512 Loughborough 4	23	**A512** Loughborough 4
	5 5	
A50 Ashby 9 Burton-on-Trent 18	22	**A50** Leicester 8 Ashby 9 Burton 18
	7 7	
Leicester Forest East Service Area (Welcome Break)	S	Leicester Forest East Service Area (Welcome Break)
	1 1	
A46 Leicester 4 **M69** Coventry 21	21	**A46** Leicester 4 **M69** Coventry 21 Birmingham (M6) 39

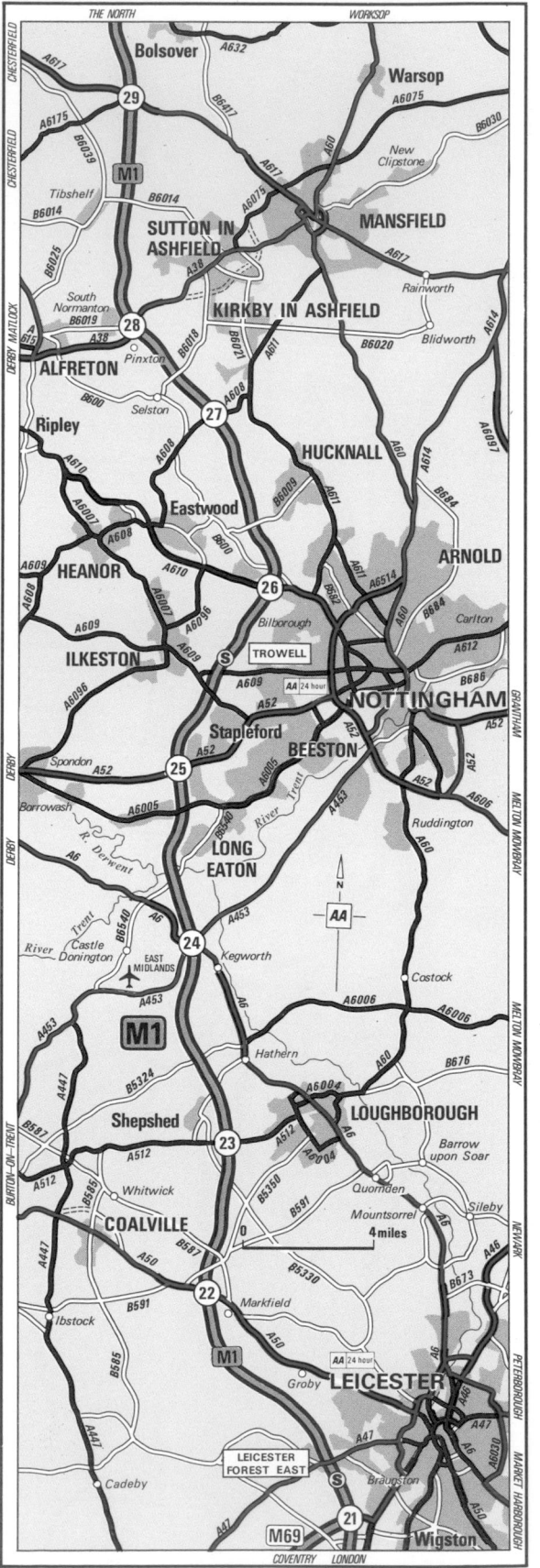

120

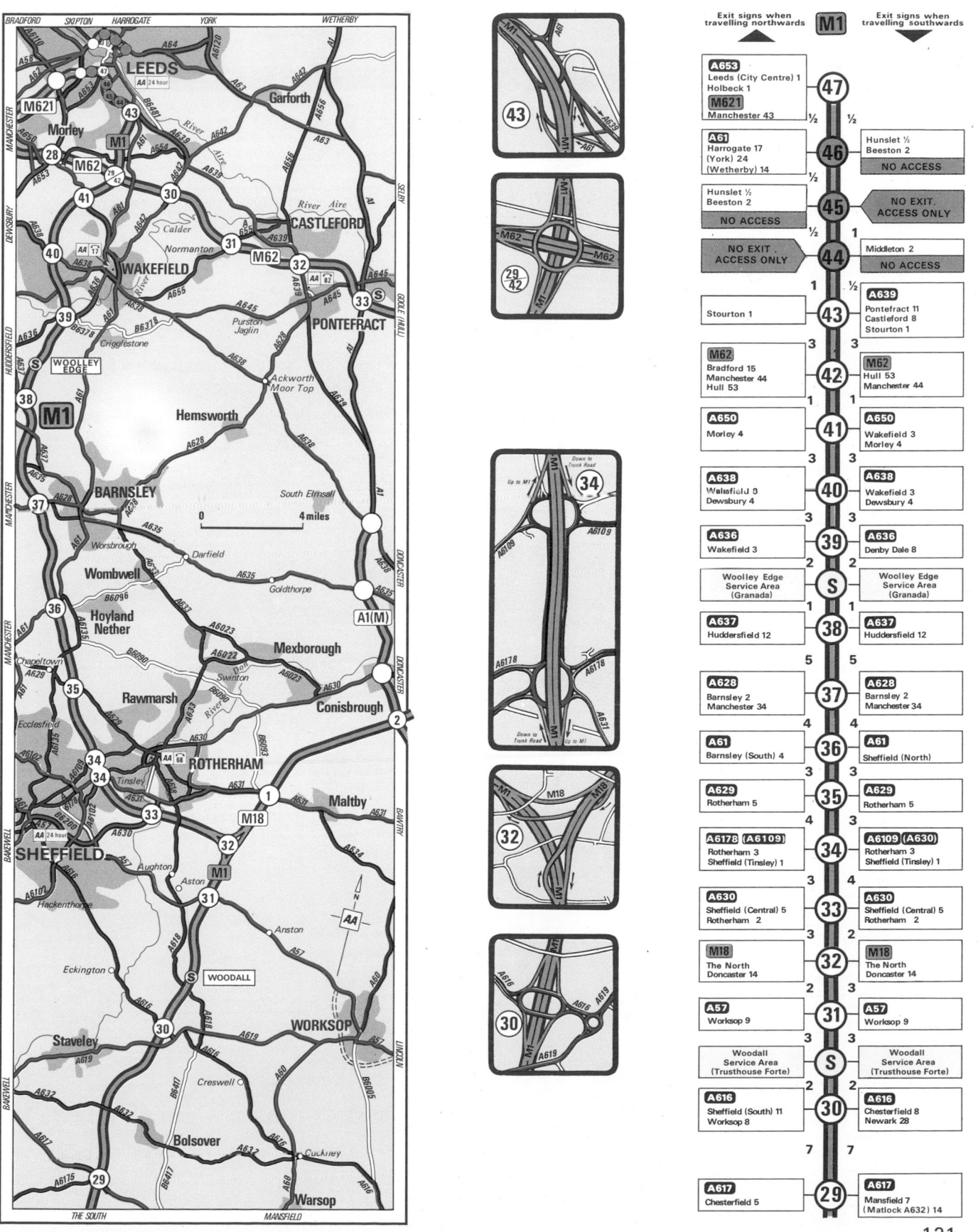

Exit signs when travelling northwards ▲

Exit signs when travelling southwards ▼

M1

47
½ ½

A653
Leeds (City Centre) 1
Holbeck 1
M621
Manchester 43

46
½ ½

A61
Harrogate 17
(York) 24
(Wetherby) 14

Hunslet ½
Beeston 2
NO ACCESS

45
½

Hunslet ½
Beeston 2
NO ACCESS

NO EXIT.
ACCESS ONLY

44
1

NO EXIT.
ACCESS ONLY

Middleton 2
NO ACCESS

43
1 ½

Stourton 1

A639
Pontefract 11
Castleford 8
Stourton 1

42
3 3

M62
Bradford 15
Manchester 44
Hull 53

M62
Hull 53
Manchester 44

41
1 1

A650
Morley 4

A650
Wakefield 3
Morley 4

40
3 3

A638
Wakefield 3
Dewsbury 4

A638
Wakefield 3
Dewsbury 4

39
3 3

A636
Wakefield 3

A636
Denby Dale 8

S
2 2

Woolley Edge
Service Area
(Granada)

Woolley Edge
Service Area
(Granada)

38
1 1

A637
Huddersfield 12

A637
Huddersfield 12

37
5 5

A628
Barnsley 2
Manchester 34

A628
Barnsley 2
Manchester 34

36
4 4

A61
Barnsley (South) 4

A61
Sheffield (North)

35

A629
Rotherham 5

A629
Rotherham 5

34
4 3

A6178 (A6109)
Rotherham 3
Sheffield (Tinsley) 1

A6109 (A630)
Rotherham 3
Sheffield (Tinsley) 1

33
3 4

A630
Sheffield (Central) 5
Rotherham 2

A630
Sheffield (Central) 5
Rotherham 2

32
3 3

M18
The North
Doncaster 14

M18
The North
Doncaster 14

31
2 2

A57
Worksop 9

A57
Worksop 9

S
3 3

Woodall
Service Area
(Trusthouse Forte)

Woodall
Service Area
(Trusthouse Forte)

30
2 2

A616
Sheffield (South) 11
Worksop 8

A616
Chesterfield 8
Newark 28

29
7 7

A617
Chesterfield 5

A617
Mansfield 7
(Matlock A632) 14

121

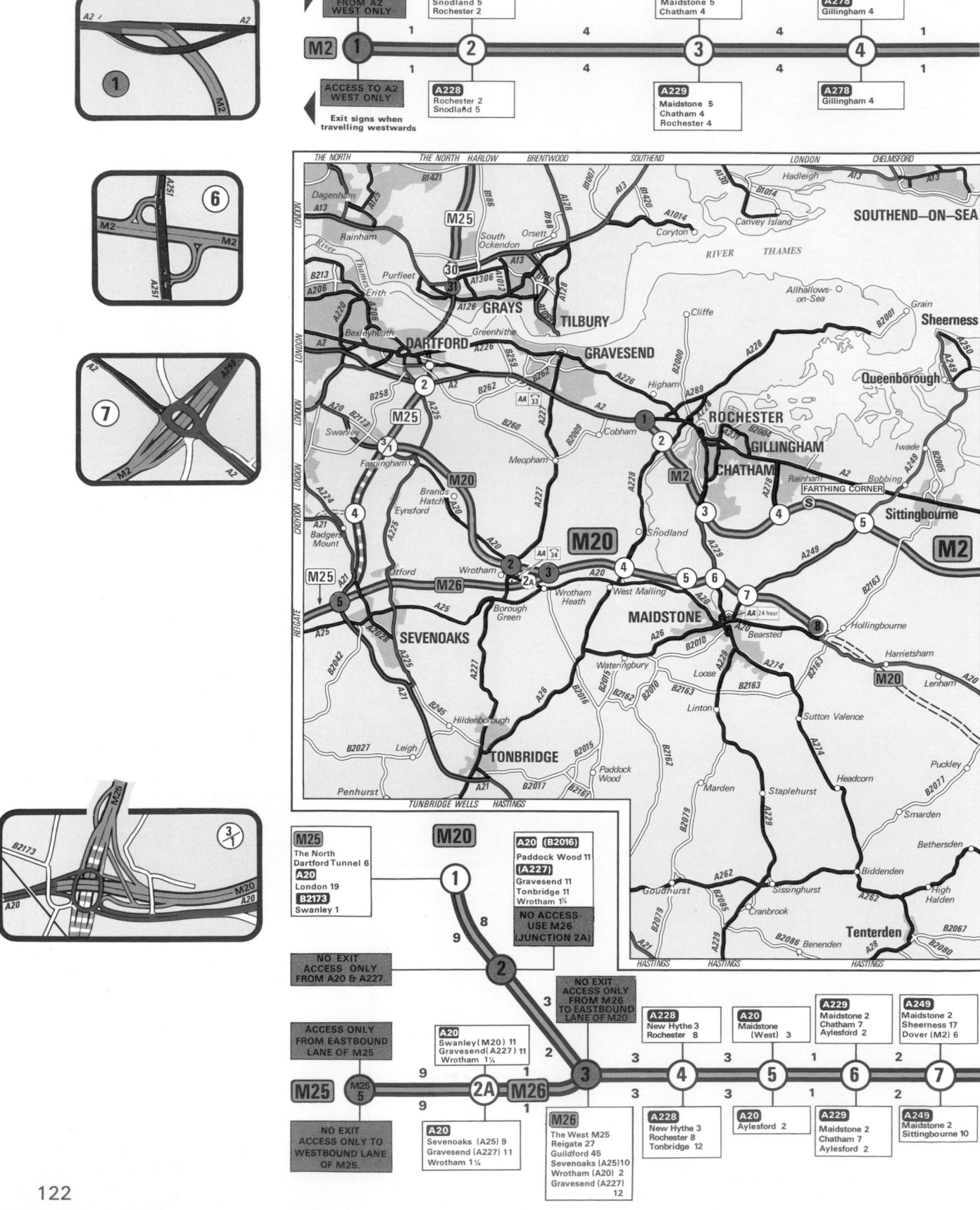

Exit signs when travelling eastwards

ACCESS TO M2 FROM A2 WEST ONLY	A228 Snodland 5 Rochester 2	A229 Maidstone 5 Chatham 4	A278 Gillingham 4

M2 ——(1)—— 1 ——(2)—— 4 ——(3)—— 4 ——(4)—— 1

ACCESS TO A2 WEST ONLY	A228 Rochester 2 Snodland 5	A229 Maidstone 5 Chatham 4 Rochester 4	A278 Gillingham 4

Exit signs when travelling westwards

Inset maps (left column): 1, 6, 7, 3/1

Map labels

THE NORTH · THE NORTH · HARLOW · BRENTWOOD · SOUTHEND · LONDON · CHELMSFORD

SOUTHEND-ON-SEA

Dagenham · Rainham · Purfleet · Erith · Bexleyheath · DARTFORD · Greenhithe · Swanley · Farningham · Brands Hatch · Eynsford · Badgers Mount · Otford · SEVENOAKS · Borough Green · Wrotham · Wrotham Heath · West Malling · Snodland · MAIDSTONE · Bearsted · Hollingbourne · Harrietsham · Lenham

GRAYS · TILBURY · GRAVESEND · Cliffe · Allhallows-on-Sea · Grain · Sheerness · Queenborough · Iwade · ROCHESTER · GILLINGHAM · CHATHAM · Rainham · Bobbing · Sittingbourne · FARTHING CORNER

RIVER THAMES

Cobham · Meopham · Wateringbury · Loose · Linton · Sutton Valence · Headcorn · Marden · Staplehurst · Puckley · Smarden · Bethersden

Hildenborough · Leigh · Penhurst · TONBRIDGE · Paddock Wood · Goudhurst · Cranbrook · Benenden · Sissinghurst · Biddenden · High Halden · Tenterden

TUNBRIDGE WELLS · HASTINGS · HASTINGS · HASTINGS · HASTINGS

M20 / M26 diagram

M25 The North Dartford Tunnel 6 · A20 London 19 · B2173 Swanley 1	M20	A20 (B2016) Paddock Wood 11 (A227) Gravesend 11 Tonbridge 11 Wrotham 1¼ · NO ACCESS USE M26 (JUNCTION 2A)

(1) 8 / 9

NO EXIT ACCESS ONLY FROM A20 & A227.

(2)

3 / 2

A20 Swanley (M20) 11 Gravesend (A227) 11 Wrotham 1¼	NO EXIT ACCESS ONLY FROM M26 TO EASTBOUND LANE OF M20	A228 New Hythe 3 Rochester 8	A20 Maidstone (West) 3	A229 Maidstone 2 Chatham 7 Aylesford 2	A249 Maidstone 2 Sheerness 17 Dover (M2) 6

ACCESS ONLY FROM EASTBOUND LANE OF M25

M25 ——(M25 5)—— 9 / 9 ——(2A) M26—— 9 / 9 ——(3)—— 3/3 ——(4)—— 3/3 ——(5)—— 1/1 ——(6)—— 2/2 ——(7)

NO EXIT ACCESS ONLY TO WESTBOUND LANE OF M25.

A20 Sevenoaks (A25) 9 Gravesend (A227) 11 Wrotham 1¼	M26 The West M25 Reigate 27 Guildford 45 Sevenoaks (A25)10 Wrotham (A20) 2 Gravesend (A227) 12	A228 New Hythe 3 Rochester 8 Tonbridge 12	A20 Aylesford 2	A229 Maidstone 2 Chatham 7 Aylesford 2	A249 Maidstone 2 Sittingbourne 10

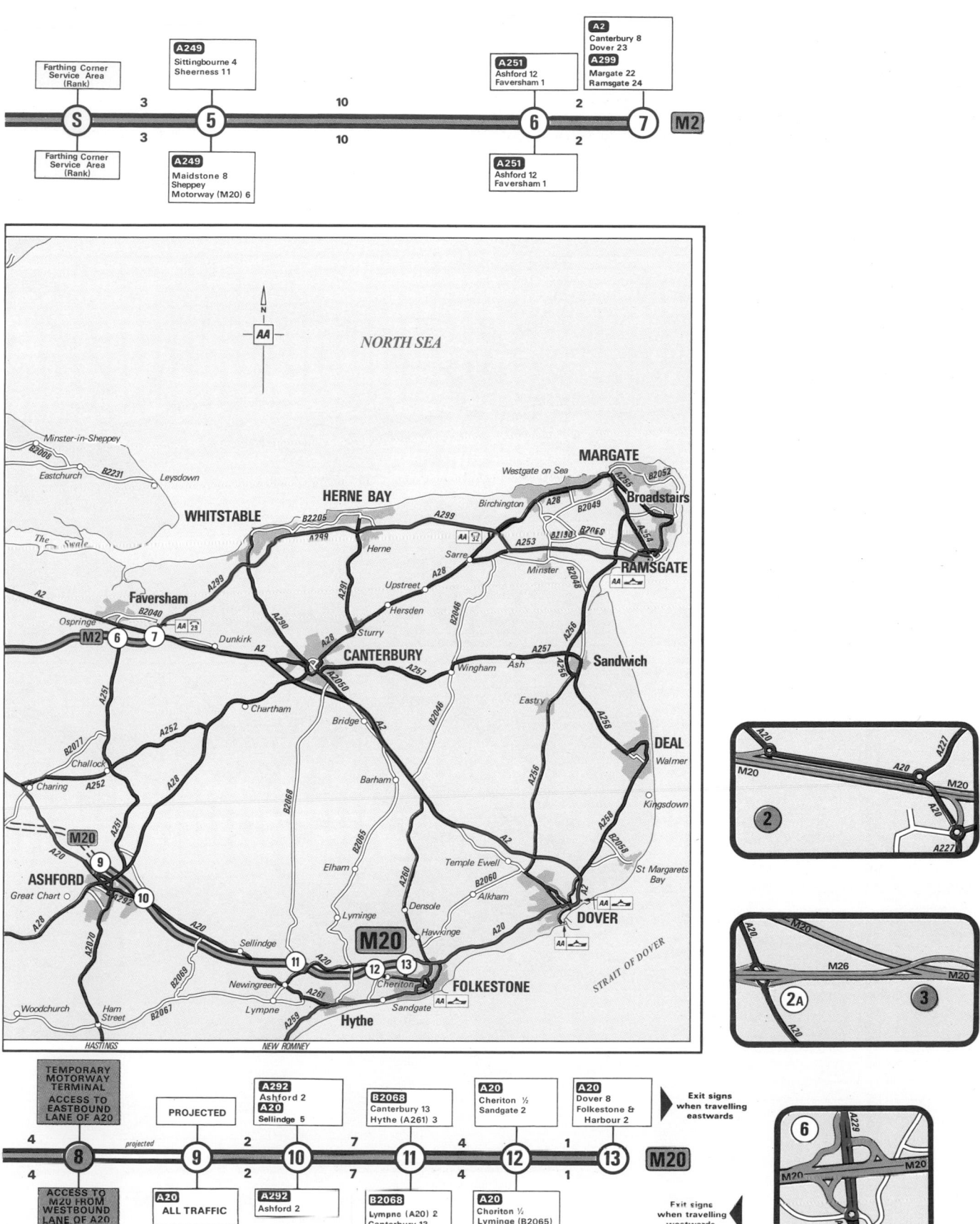

A249
Sittingbourne 4
Sheerness 11

A249
Maidstone 8
Sheppey
Motorway (M20) 6

Farthing Corner
Service Area
(Rank)

Farthing Corner
Service Area
(Rank)

A251
Ashford 12
Faversham 1

A251
Ashford 12
Faversham 1

A2
Canterbury 8
Dover 23

A299
Margate 22
Ramsgate 24

S   3   5   10   6   2   7   M2
3   10   2

NORTH SEA

Minster-in-Sheppey

Eastchurch   *Leysdown*

WHITSTABLE   **HERNE BAY**   *Westgate on Sea*   **MARGATE**   *Broadstairs*

Birchington

Herne   *Sarre*   **RAMSGATE**

Upstreet   *Minster*

Faversham   *Hersden*

Osprey   *Dunkirk*   *Sturry*   *Wingham*   *Ash*   **Sandwich**

M2   6   7   **CANTERBURY**

Chartham   *Eastry*   **DEAL**

Bridge   *Walmer*

Challock   *Barham*   *Kingsdown*

Charing   *Temple Ewell*   *St Margarets Bay*

M20   *Elham*   *Densole*   *Alkham*

9   *Lymnge*   *Hawkinge*   **DOVER**

ASHFORD   M20

Great Chart   10   *Sellindge*   *STRAIT OF DOVER*

11   12   13   *Cheriton*   **FOLKESTONE**

Newingreen   *Sandgate*

Woodchurch   *Ham Street*   *Lympne*   **Hythe**

HASTINGS   *NEW ROMNEY*

**TEMPORARY
MOTORWAY
TERMINAL**
ACCESS TO
EASTBOUND
LANE OF A20

ACCESS TO
M20 FROM
WESTBOUND
LANE OF A20

PROJECTED

ALL TRAFFIC

A292
Ashford 2
A20
Sellindge 5

A20
Ashford 2

B2068
Canterbury 13
Hythe (A261) 3

B2068
Lympne (A20) 2
Canterbury 13

A20
Cheriton ½
Sandgate 2

A20
Choriton ½
Lyminge (B2065)
4

A20
Dover 8
Folkestone &
Harbour 2

*Exit signs
when travelling
eastwards*

*Exit signs
when travelling
westwards*

4   8   *projected*   9   2   10   7   11   4   12   1   13   M20
4   2   4   1

2

2A   M26   3

6

123

LONDON-BASINGSTOKE-SOUTHAMPTON M3

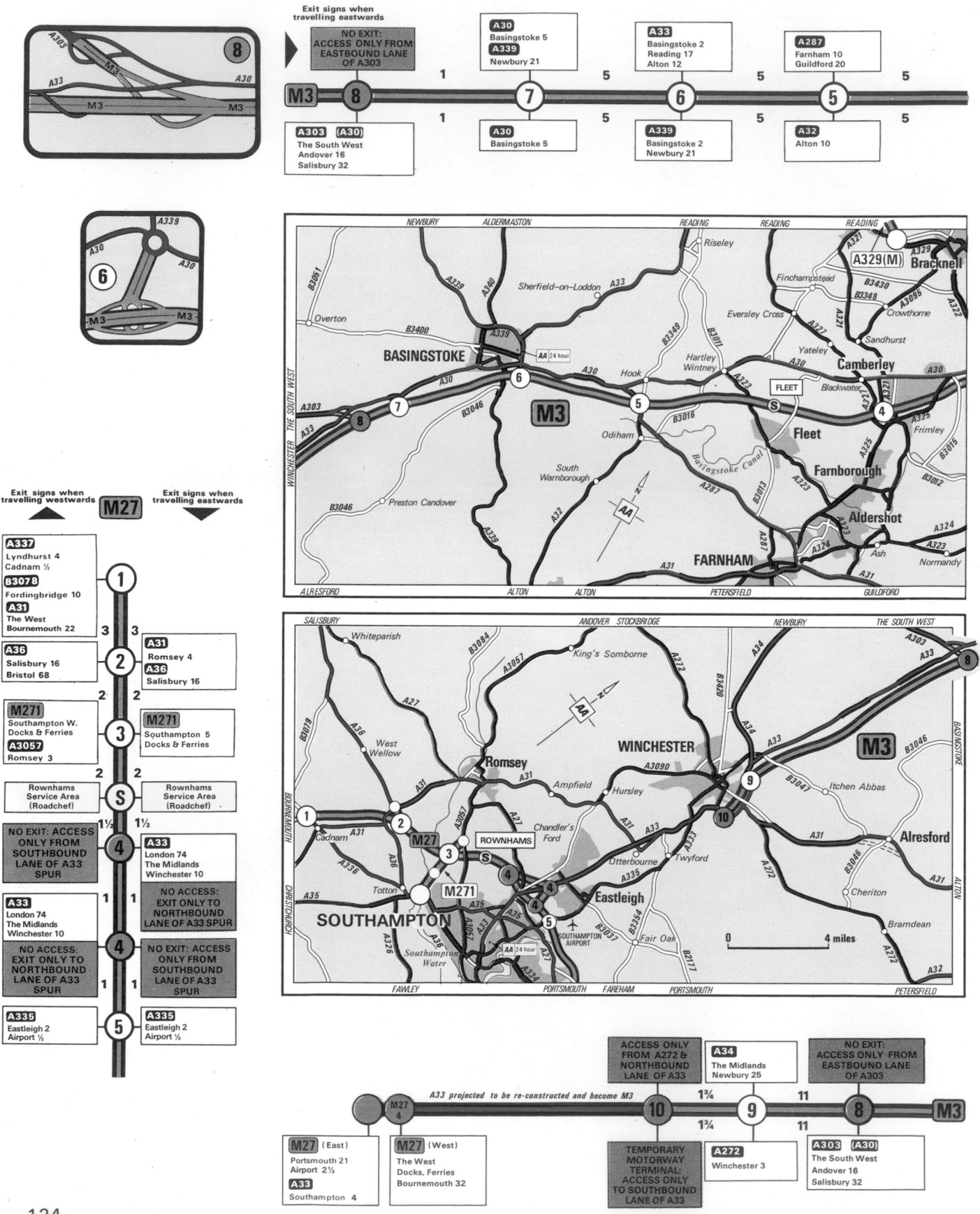

Exit signs when travelling eastwards

NO EXIT: ACCESS ONLY FROM EASTBOUND LANE OF A303

A30 Basingstoke 5 / A339 Newbury 21

A33 Basingstoke 2 / Reading 17 / Alton 12

A287 Farnham 10 / Guildford 20

M3 8   1   7   5   6   5   5   5

A303 (A30) The South West / Andover 16 / Salisbury 32

A30 Basingstoke 5

A339 Basingstoke 2 / Newbury 21

A32 Alton 10

Exit signs when travelling westwards   M27   Exit signs when travelling eastwards

A337 Lyndhurst 4 / Cadnam ½ — B3078 Fordingbridge 10 — A31 The West / Bournemouth 22

1

A36 Salisbury 16 / Bristol 68

2

A31 Romsey 4 — A36 Salisbury 16

M271 Southampton W. Docks & Ferries — A3057 Romsey 3

3

M271 Southampton 5 Docks & Ferries

Rownhams Service Area (Roadchef)   S   Rownhams Service Area (Roadchef)

NO EXIT: ACCESS ONLY FROM SOUTHBOUND LANE OF A33 SPUR

4

A33 London 74 / The Midlands / Winchester 10

A33 London 74 / The Midlands / Winchester 10

NO ACCESS: EXIT ONLY TO NORTHBOUND LANE OF A33 SPUR

NO ACCESS: EXIT ONLY TO NORTHBOUND LANE OF A33 SPUR

4

NO EXIT: ACCESS ONLY FROM SOUTHBOUND LANE OF A33 SPUR

A335 Eastleigh 2 / Airport ½

5

A335 Eastleigh 2 / Airport ½

A33 projected to be re-constructed and become M3

M27 4   10   1¾   9   11   8   M3
              1¾   11

ACCESS ONLY FROM A272 & NORTHBOUND LANE OF A33

A34 The Midlands / Newbury 25

NO EXIT: ACCESS ONLY FROM EASTBOUND LANE OF A303

M27 (East) Portsmouth 21 / Airport 2½ — A33 Southampton 4

M27 (West) The West / Docks, Ferries / Bournemouth 32

TEMPORARY MOTORWAY TERMINAL: ACCESS ONLY TO SOUTHBOUND LANE OF A33

A272 Winchester 3

A303 (A30) The South West / Andover 16 / Salisbury 32

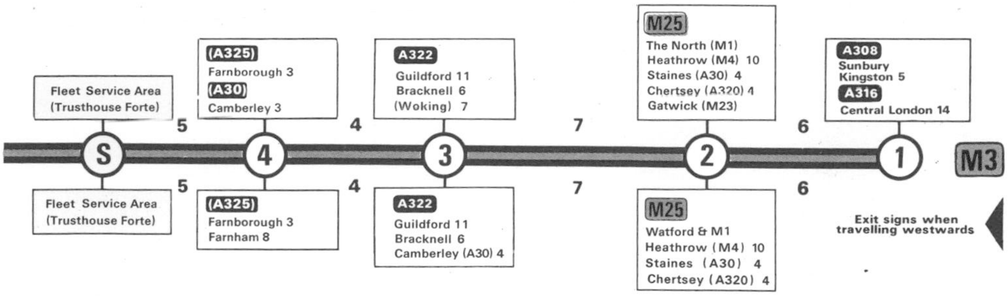

M3

Top junction strip (M3, westward direction — top row signs):

Junction	Sign details
S	Fleet Service Area (Trusthouse Forte)
5	
4	(A325) Farnborough 3, (A30) Camberley 3
4	
3	A322 Guildford 11, Bracknell 6, (Woking) 7
7	
2	M25 The North (M1), Heathrow (M4) 10, Staines (A30) 4, Chertsey (A320) 4, Gatwick (M23)
6	
1	A308 Sunbury, Kingston 5; A316 Central London 14

Bottom junction strip (eastward direction — lower row signs):

Junction	Sign details
S	Fleet Service Area (Trusthouse Forte)
5	
4	(A325) Farnborough 3, Farnham 8
4	
3	A322 Guildford 11, Bracknell 6, Camberley (A30) 4
7	
2	M25 Watford & M1, Heathrow (M4) 10, Staines (A30) 4, Chertsey (A320) 4
6	
1	

M3

Exit signs when travelling westwards ◀

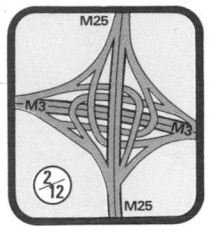

Selected Junctions on M23

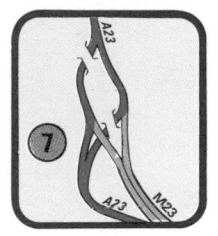

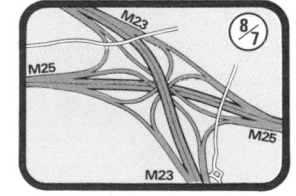

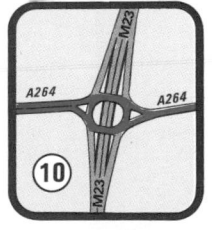

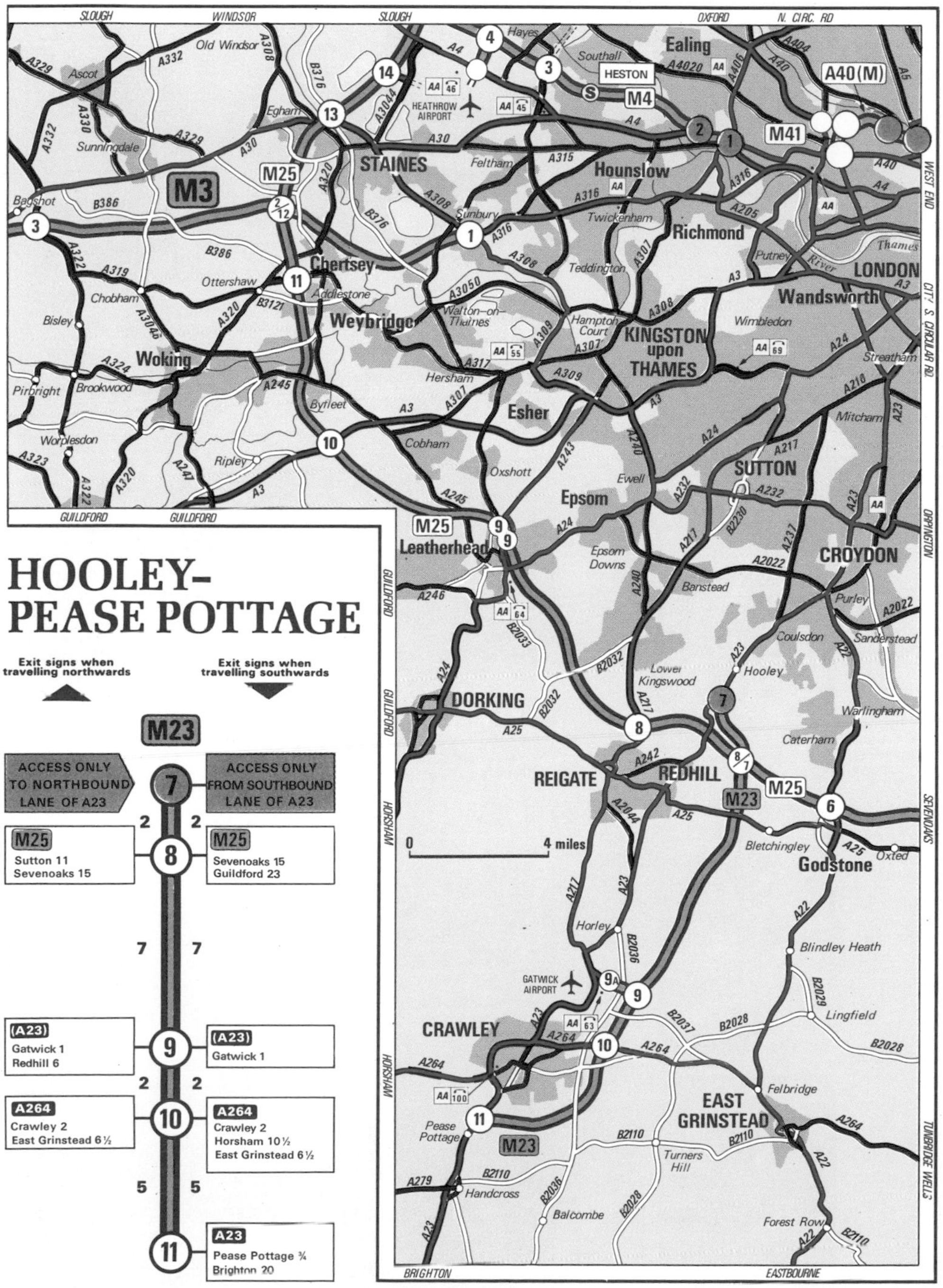

HOOLEY–
PEASE POTTAGE

Exit signs when travelling northwards ▲   Exit signs when travelling southwards ▼

M23

Junction	Northbound signs		Southbound signs
7	ACCESS ONLY TO NORTHBOUND LANE OF A23		ACCESS ONLY FROM SOUTHBOUND LANE OF A23
	2		2
8	M25 Sutton 11, Sevenoaks 15		M25 Sevenoaks 15, Guildford 23
	7		7
9	(A23) Gatwick 1, Redhill 6		(A23) Gatwick 1
	2		2
10	A264 Crawley 2, East Grinstead 6½		A264 Crawley 2, Horsham 10½, East Grinstead 6½
	5		5
11			A23 Pease Pottage ¾, Brighton 20

0 ___ 4 miles

LONDON–THEALE (M4) BRACKNELL–READING (A329(M))

Exit signs when travelling westwards
M4
Exit signs when travelling eastwards
A4 Theale 2
12
A4 Reading 5
5 5
A33 Reading 4 Basingstoke 14
11
A33 Reading 4 Basingstoke 14
6 6
A329(M) Reading 7 Wokingham 3 Bracknell 7
10
A329(M) Reading 7 Wokingham 3 Bracknell 7
7 7
A423(M) Oxford 33 Henley 10 A308(M) Maidenhead 2
8/9
A423(M) A308(M) Maidenhead 2
3 3
A4 Slough (West)
7
A4 Slough (West)
2 2
A355 Slough (Central) 2 Windsor (A332) 3
6
A355 Slough (Central) 2 Windsor (A332) 3 Eton 3
4 4
A4 Langley 1 The South West (M3) B470 Eton 5
5
A4 B470 Langley 1 Staines (A3044) 6
2 2
M25 Gatwick M23 40 Heathrow Terminal 4 & Cargo 5 Watford & M1 20 Oxford M40 43
4B
M25 Watford & M1 20 Oxford M40 43 Heathrow Terminal 4 & Cargo 5 Gatwick M23 40
2 2
(A408) Heathrow 2 Uxbridge 5
4
(A408) Heathrow Uxbridge 5 Hayes 2
2 2
A312 Feltham 4 Hayes 2
3
A312 Feltham 4 Hounslow (A3006) 3
1 1
Heston Service Area (Granada)
S
Heston Service Area (Granada)
4 4
A4 A4 & local traffic
A205 South Circular Road A406 North Circular Road (M1) The North
M4 EXIT /ACCESS IS TO OR FROM WESTBOUND LANE OF A4 ONLY
2
M4 EXIT /ACCESS IS TO OR FROM EASTBOUND LANE OF A4 ONLY
½ ½
ACCESS ONLY FROM WESTBOUND LANE OF A4
1
ACCESS ONLY TO EASTBOUND LANE OF A4

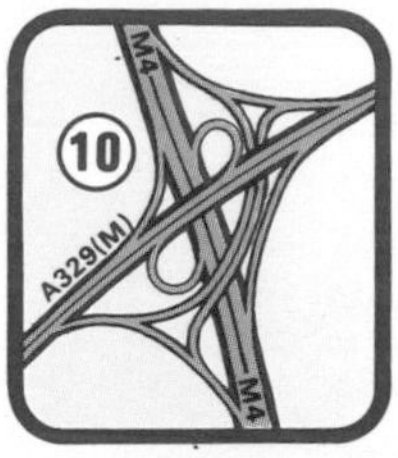

10
M4
A329(M)

M4
A423(M)
A308(M)
8/9

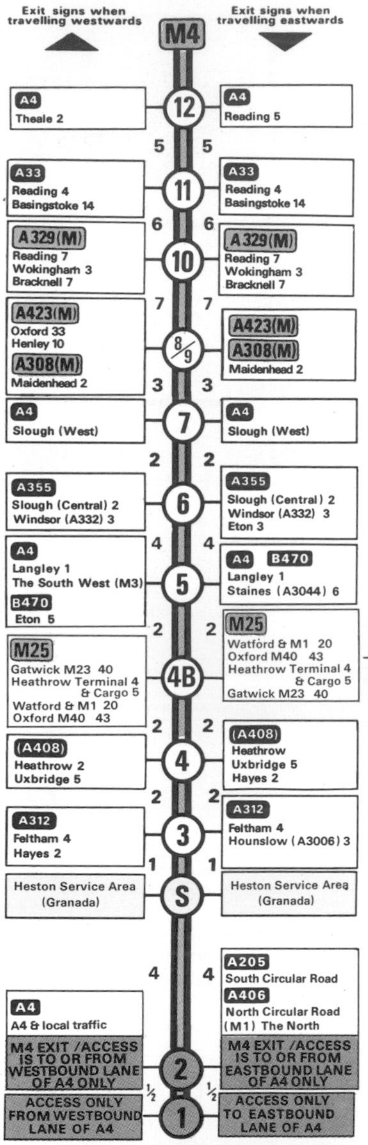

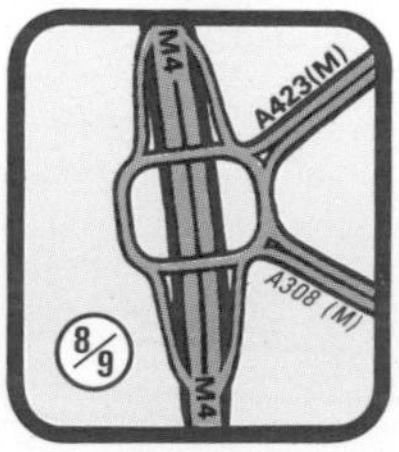

Note: Full turning manoeuvres between M25 and M4 may not be available until late 1985 or early 1986

A3044
M4
A408
4
To London Airport

A4
Up to M4
Up to M4
Down to A4
Down to A4
M4
2

GREAT WEST ROAD
A205 South Circular
North Circular
A406
M4
A315
A3000
1

Exit signs when travelling westwards
A329(M)
Exit signs when travelling eastwards
A4 Reading 1½
C
2 2
A329 Winnersh 1¼ Woodley 1½ Earley 1¼
B
Winnersh 1¼ Woodley 1½
2 2
M4 South Wales Newbury 25 London 34 Slough 14
M4 10
M4 London 34 South Wales
3 3
A
A329 Bracknell 2½ Wokingham 1½

NEWBURY
OXFORD
Theale
Pangbourne
Purley
0 4 miles
READING
Sonning Common
Riseley
Arborfield
Henley-on-Thames
Wokingham
Twyford
Mill End
Crowthorne
Binfield
Bracknell
Marlow
MAIDENHEAD
Ascot
Winkfield
Bourne End
Burnham
WINDSOR
Eton
SLOUGH
Datchet
Langley
Iver Heath
Gerrards Cross
STAINES
HEATHROW AIRPORT LONDON
Uxbridge
SUNBURY
Hayes
Hillingdon
Feltham
HESTON
Northwood
Hounslow
EALING
KINGSTON upon THAMES
Richmond
Wembley
Putney
Wimbledon
Fulham
Hampstead
Hendon
Finchley
Clapham
Streatham
LONDON
CITY
CHELMSFORD
BASINGSTOKE
THE SOUTH WEST
CHERTSEY
ESHER
GUILDFORD
DORKING REIGATE
REDHILL
HIGH WYCOMBE
BEACONSFIELD
AMERSHAM WATFORD
RICKMANSWORTH
THE NORTH

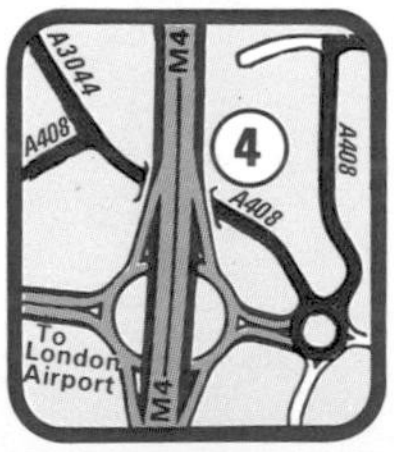

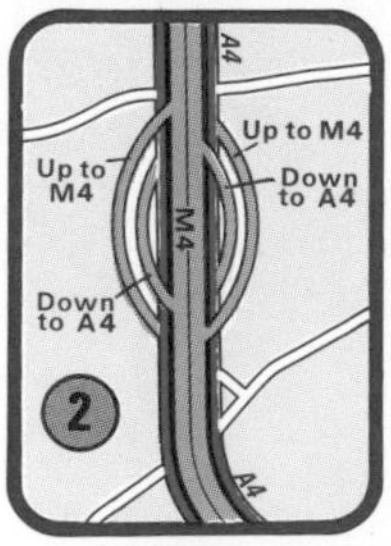

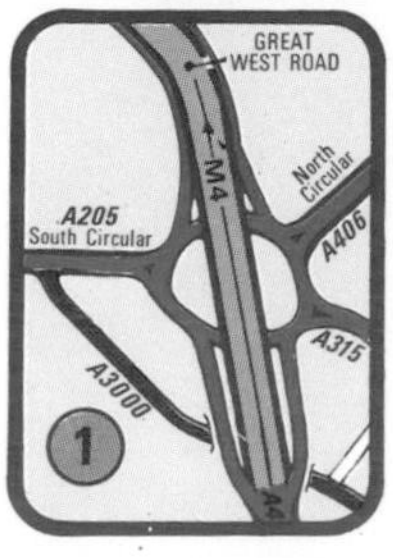

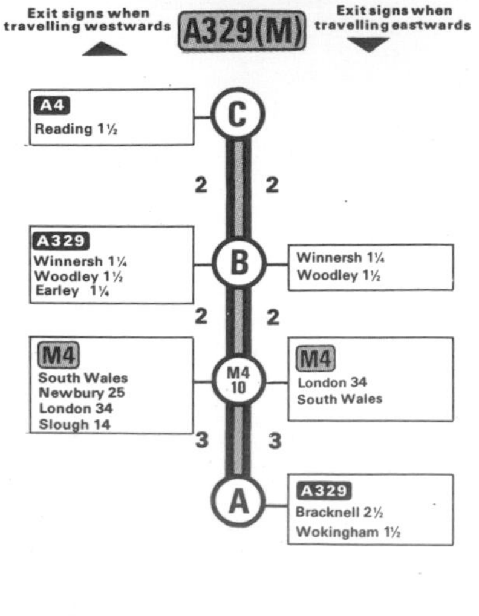

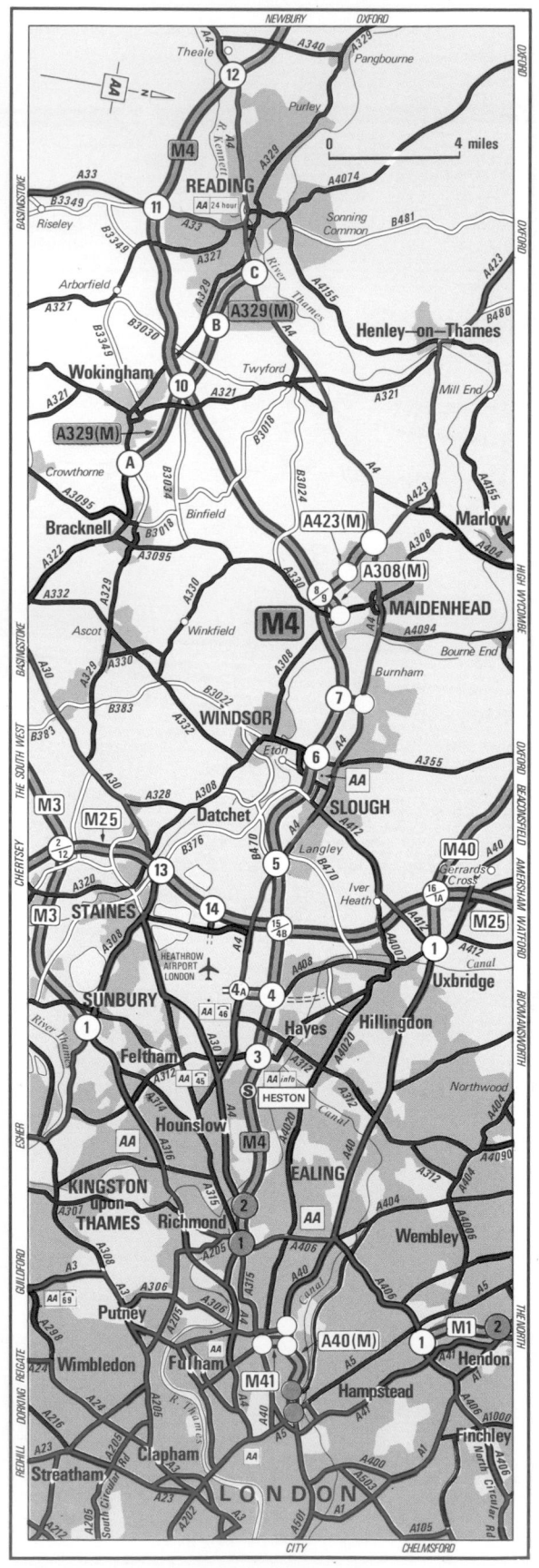

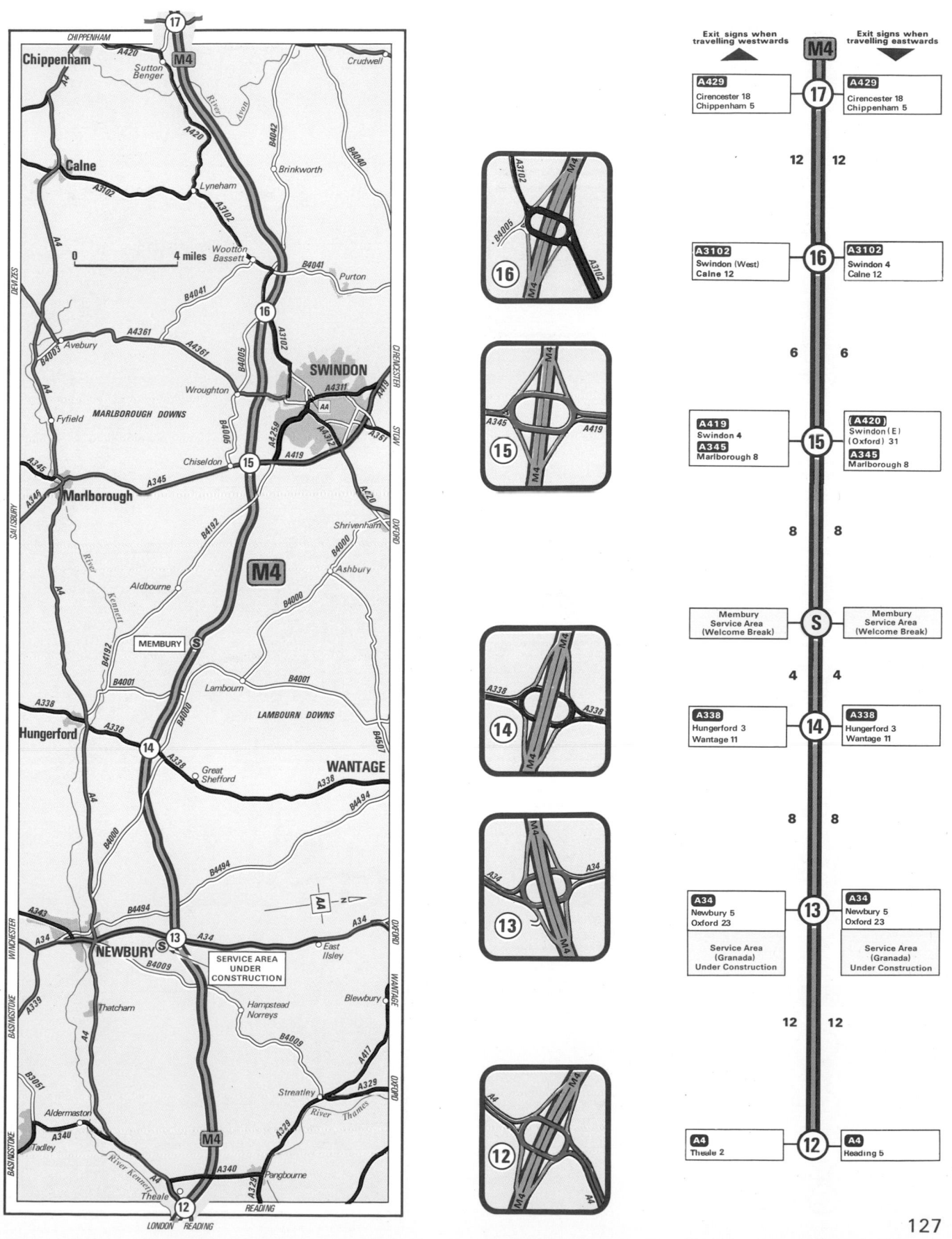

CHIPPENHAM–CARDIFF M4 BRISTOL PARKWAY M32

▲ Exit signs when travelling westwards M4 Exit signs when travelling eastwards ▲

Westward	Jct	Eastward
A48(M) Cardiff 9 — NO ACCESS FROM A48 (M)	29	NO EXIT. ACCESS ONLY FROM A48 (M)
2		
A48 Newport 2 / A467 Risca 5 Brynmawr 20	28	A48 Newport 2 / A467 Risca 5 Brynmawr 20
1		1
B4591 High Cross ½	27	B4591 High Cross ½
2		2
A4042 Cwmbran 4 Newport (Centre) 1	26	A4042 Cwmbran 4 Newport (Centre) 1
1		1
B4596 Caerleon 2	25	B4596 Caerleon 2
3		3
A455 A48 Newport (East) / A449 Monmouth 20	24	A449 Midlands (M50) Monmouth 20 / A48 Newport 4
4		4
B4245 Magor 1	23	B4245 Magor 1
8		8
A466 (A48) Chepstow 2	22	A466 Chepstow 2 Gloucester (A48) 30
SEVERN BRIDGE TOLLBOOTHS		SEVERN BRIDGE TOLLBOOTHS
3		3
Aust Service Area (Rank)		Aust Service Area (Rank)
A403 Avonmouth 9	21	A403 Avonmouth 9
5		5
M5 The South West The Midlands Bristol (West)	20	M5 The Midlands The South West Bristol (West) & Airport
3		3
M32 Bristol 6	19	M32 Bristol 6
7		7
A46 Bath 11 Stroud 20	18	A46 Bath 11 Stroud 20
9		9
Leigh Delamere Service Area (Granada)	S	Leigh Delamere Service Area (Granada)
2		2
A429 Cirencester 18 Chippenham 5	17	A429 Cirencester 18 Chippenham 5

▲ Exit signs when travelling northwards M32 Exit signs when travelling southwards ▼

Northward	Jct	Southward
M4 South Wales Midlands (M5) London 114 Swindon 35	M4 19	
¾		¾
A4174 Bristol East Filton 2	1	A4174 Bristol East Filton 2
2¾		2¾
Stapleton ½ Frenchay 2¼ Horfield 1½ Fishponds 1½	2	B4469 Fishponds 1½ Horfield 1½
1		1
	3	City Centre 1¼ Other Routes

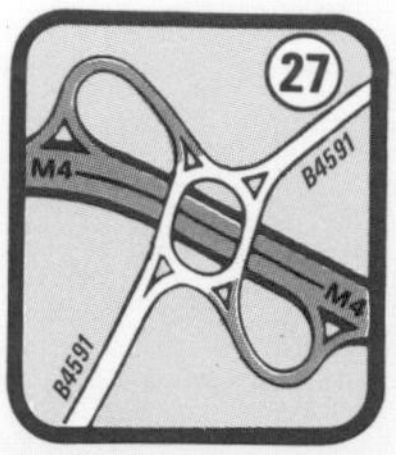

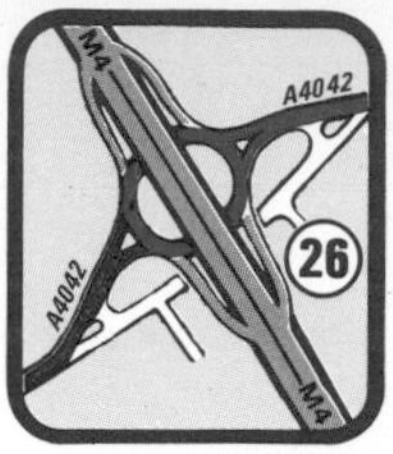

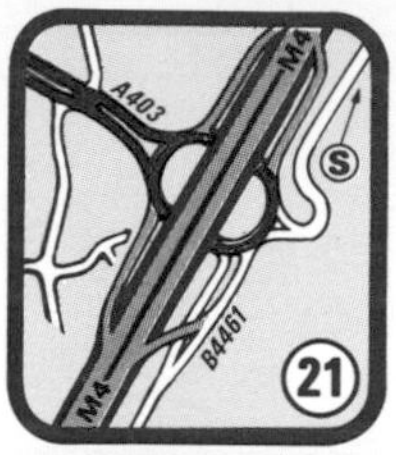

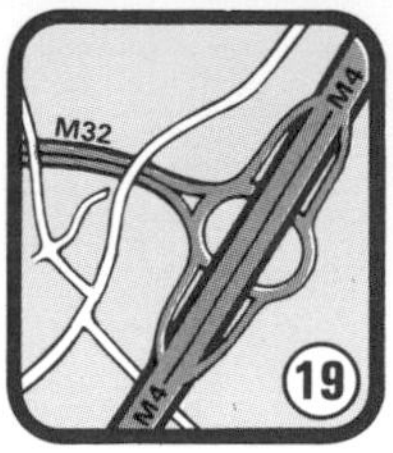

27

26

21

15/20

19

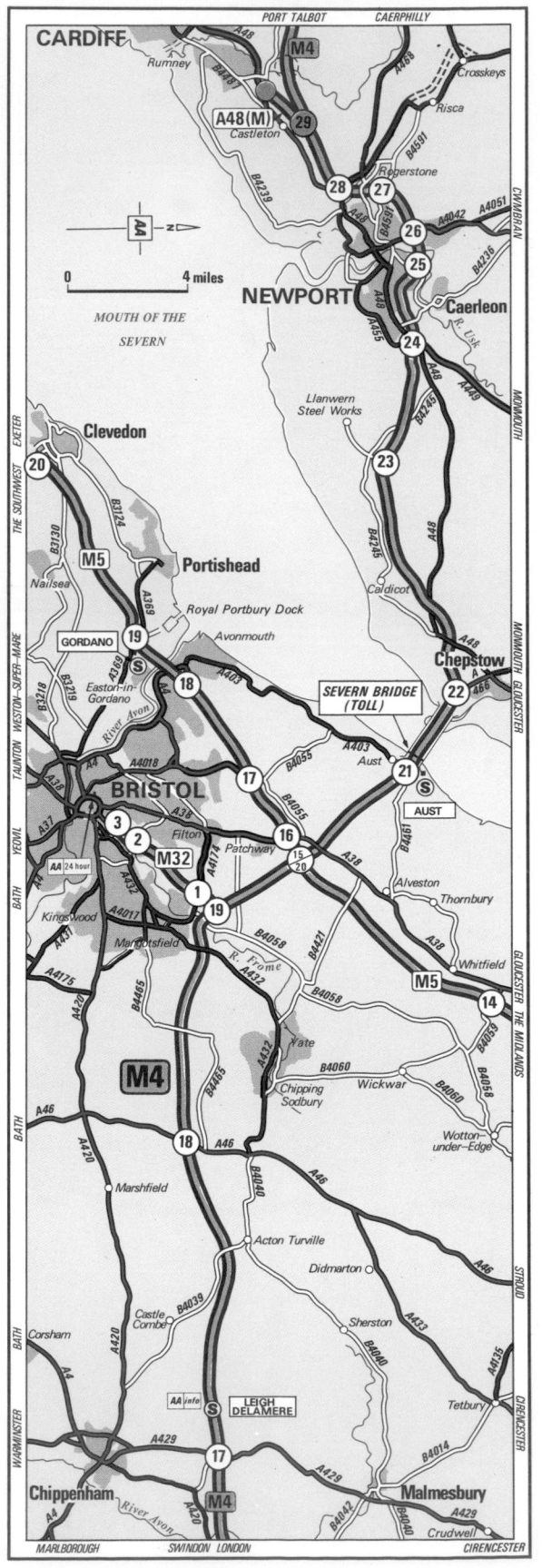

128

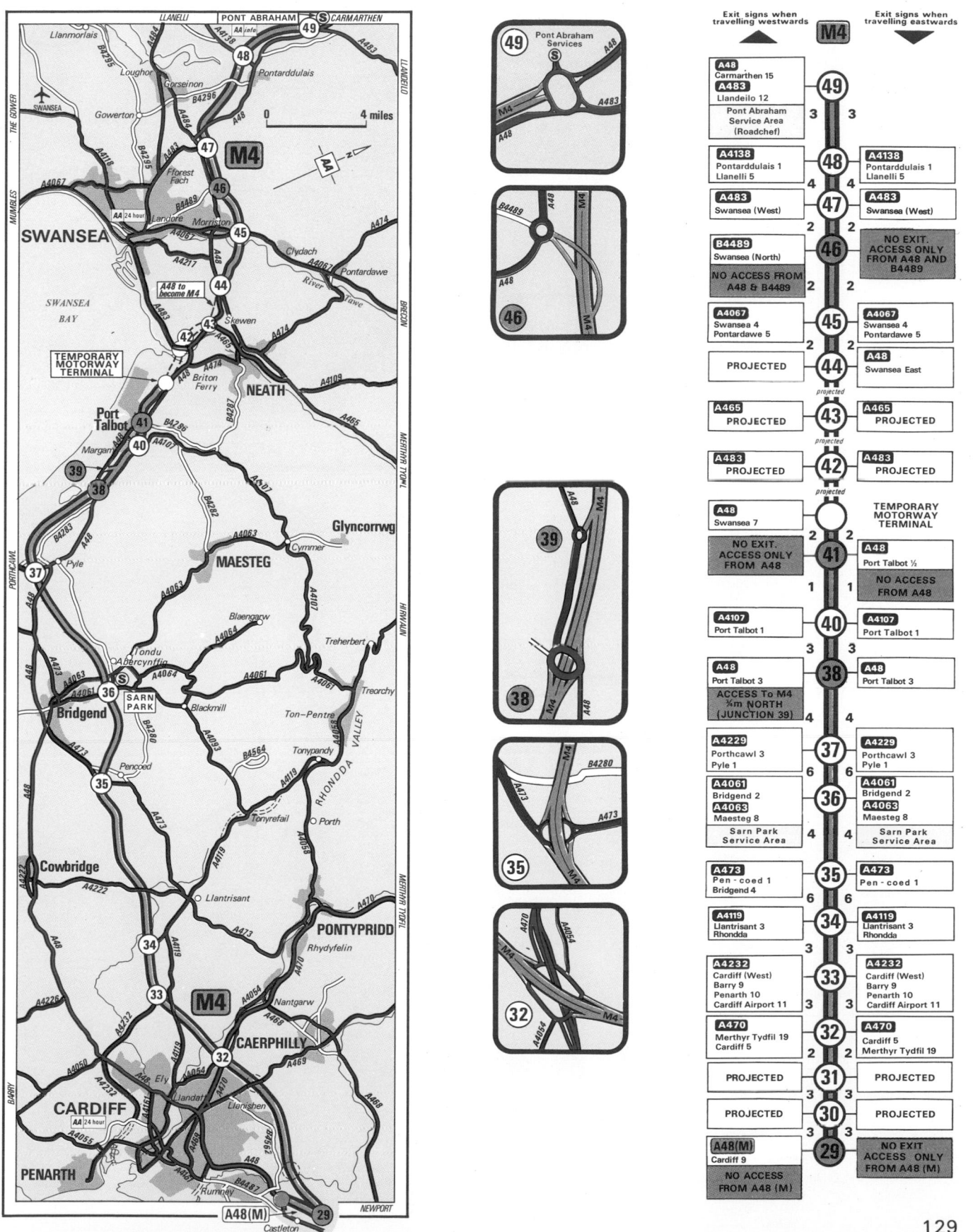

Exit signs when travelling westwards | M4 | Exit signs when travelling eastwards

Westward signs	Jct	Eastward signs
A48 Carmarthen 15 **A483** Llandeilo 12 Pont Abraham Service Area (Roadchef)	49	
A4138 Pontarddulais 1 Llanelli 5	48	**A4138** Pontarddulais 1 Llanelli 5
A483 Swansea (West)	47	**A483** Swansea (West)
B4489 Swansea (North) NO ACCESS FROM A48 & B4489	46	NO EXIT. ACCESS ONLY FROM A48 AND B4489
A4067 Swansea 4 Pontardawe 5	45	**A4067** Swansea 4 Pontardawe 5
PROJECTED	44	**A48** Swansea East
A465 PROJECTED	43	**A465** PROJECTED
A483 PROJECTED	42	**A483** PROJECTED
A48 Swansea 7 NO EXIT. ACCESS ONLY FROM A48	TEMPORARY MOTORWAY TERMINAL / 41	**A48** Port Talbot ½ NO ACCESS FROM A48
A4107 Port Talbot 1	40	**A4107** Port Talbot 1
A48 Port Talbot 3 ACCESS To M4 ¾m NORTH (JUNCTION 39)	38	**A48** Port Talbot 3
A4229 Porthcawl 3 Pyle 1	37	**A4229** Porthcawl 3 Pyle 1
A4061 Bridgend 2 **A4063** Maesteg 8 Sarn Park Service Area	36	**A4061** Bridgend 2 **A4063** Maesteg 8 Sarn Park Service Area
A473 Pen-coed 1 Bridgend 4	35	**A473** Pen-coed 1
A4119 Llantrisant 3 Rhondda	34	**A4119** Llantrisant 3 Rhondda
A4232 Cardiff (West) Barry 9 Penarth 10 Cardiff Airport 11	33	**A4232** Cardiff (West) Barry 9 Penarth 10 Cardiff Airport 11
A470 Merthyr Tydfil 19 Cardiff 5	32	**A470** Cardiff 5 Merthyr Tydfil 19
PROJECTED	31	PROJECTED
PROJECTED	30	PROJECTED
A48(M) Cardiff 9 NO ACCESS FROM A48 (M)	29	NO EXIT ACCESS ONLY FROM A48 (M)

BIRMINGHAM-CHELTENHAM M5 ROSS SPUR M50

Exit signs when travelling northwards ▲	M5	Exit signs when travelling southwards ▼
M6 London (M1) 120 Birmingham (NE,N) The North West Wolverhampton 10 Walsall 5	8	
2		3
A41 Birmingham (NW) West Bromwich 1	1	A41 Birmingham (NW) West Bromwich 1
3		3
A4123 Dudley 3 Wolverhampton 6	2	A4123 Birmingham (West) Dudley 3
3		3
A456 Birmingham (West & Central)	3	A456 Kidderminster 11
1		1
Frankley Service Area (Granada)	S	Frankley Service Area (Granada)
4		4
A38 Birmingham (SW) 10 A491 Stourbridge 9	4	A38 Birmingham (SW) 10 Bromsgrove 3
2½		2½
M42 UNDER CONSTRUCTION		ACCESS FROM M42 UNDER CONSTRUCTION
5		5
A38 Bromsgrove 5 Droitwich 2	5	A38 Droitwich 2
6		6
A449 Kidderminster 15 Worcester (North) 4	6	A4538 Evesham 14 A449 Worcester (North) 4
3		3
A44 Worcester (South) 3 Evesham 13	7	A44 Evesham 13 Worcester (South) 3
8		8
Strensham Service Area (Kennings)	S	Strensham Service Area (Kennings)
1		1
M50 South Wales Ross 23	8	M50 South Wales Ross 23
4		4
A438 Evesham 11 Tewkesbury 2	9	A438 Evesham 11 Tewkesbury 2
5		5
NO EXIT: ACCESS ONLY FROM A4019	10	A4019 Cheltenham 4 NO ACCESS FROM A4019

Exit signs when travelling northeastwards ▲	M50	Exit signs when travelling southwestwards ▼
M5 Midlands Worcester 12 Bristol 51	M5 8	
1½		1½
A38 Tewkesbury 3	1	A38 Malvern 11
9		9
A417 Gloucester 12	2	A417 Ledbury 5 Hereford (A438) 20
7½		7½
B4221 Newent 3½	3	B4221 Newent 3½
3½		3½
	4	A449 South Wales Ross 1½ Monmouth 11½

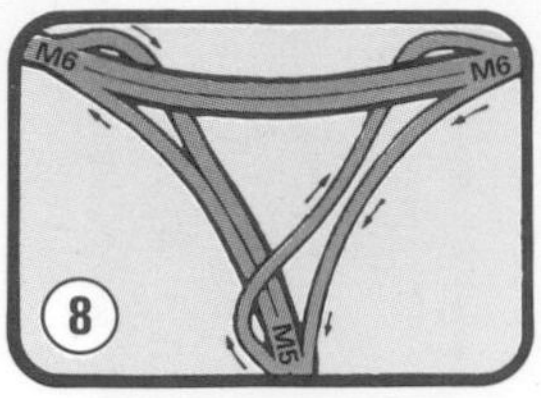

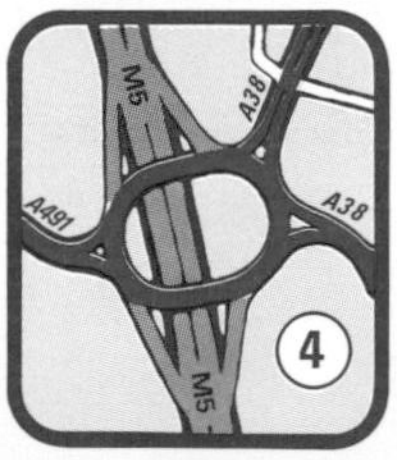

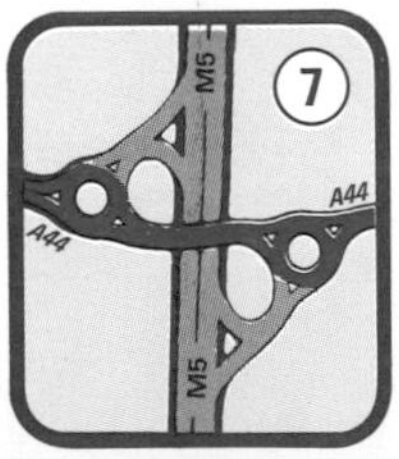

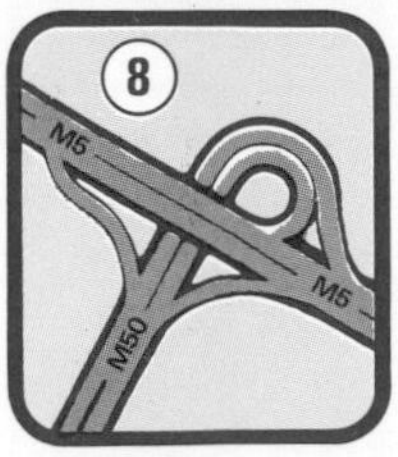

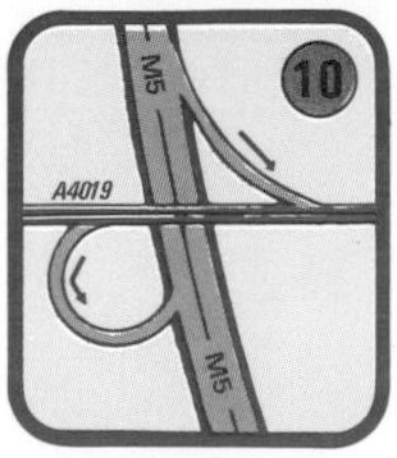

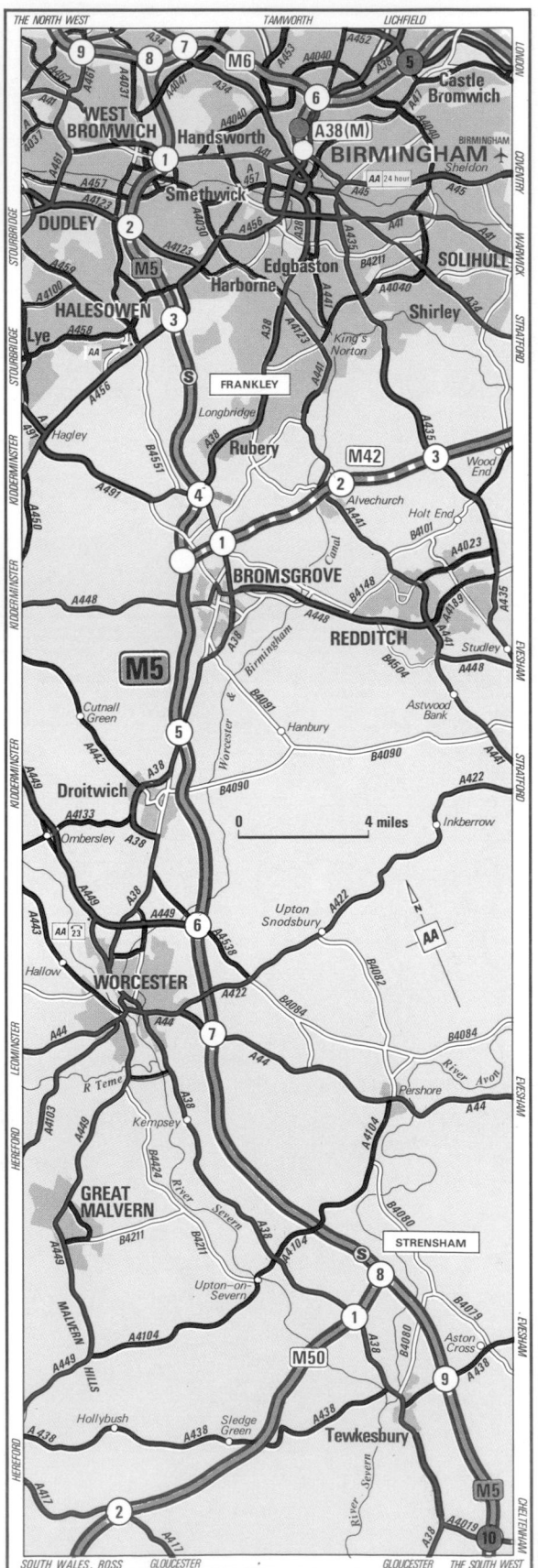

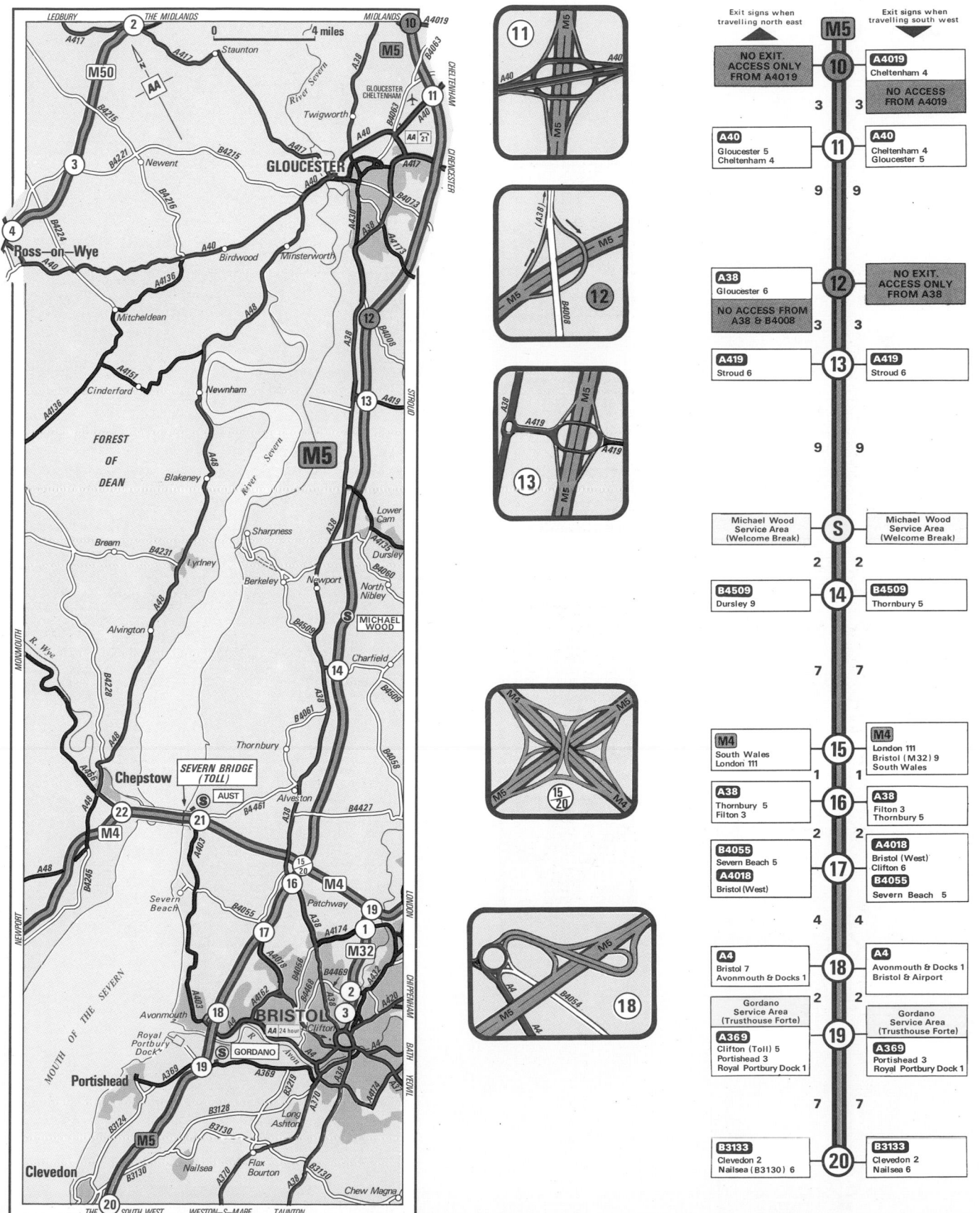

Exit signs when travelling north east | Exit signs when travelling south west

M5

⑩
NO EXIT. ACCESS ONLY FROM A4019 | **A4019** Cheltenham 4
NO ACCESS FROM A4019

3 | 3

⑪
A40 Gloucester 5 Cheltenham 4 | **A40** Cheltenham 4 Gloucester 5

9 | 9

⑫
A38 Gloucester 6 NO ACCESS FROM A38 & B4008 | NO EXIT. ACCESS ONLY FROM A38

3 | 3

⑬
A419 Stroud 6 | **A419** Stroud 6

9 | 9

Ⓢ
Michael Wood Service Area (Welcome Break) | Michael Wood Service Area (Welcome Break)

2 | 2

⑭
B4509 Dursley 9 | **B4509** Thornbury 5

7 | 7

⑮
M4 South Wales London 111 | **M4** London 111 Bristol (M32) 9 South Wales

1 | 1

⑯
A38 Thornbury 5 Filton 3 | **A38** Filton 3 Thornbury 5

2 | 2

⑰
B4055 Severn Beach 5 **A4018** Bristol (West) | **A4018** Bristol (West) Clifton 6 **B4055** Severn Beach 5

4 | 4

⑱
A4 Bristol 7 Avonmouth & Docks 1 | **A4** Avonmouth & Docks 1 Bristol & Airport

2 | 2

⑲
Gordano Service Area (Trusthouse Forte) **A369** Clifton (Toll) 5 Portishead 3 Royal Portbury Dock 1 | Gordano Service Area (Trusthouse Forte) **A369** Portishead 3 Royal Portbury Dock 1

7 | 7

⑳
B3133 Clevedon 2 Nailsea (B3130) 6 | **B3133** Clevedon 2 Nailsea 6

CLEVEDON–WATERLOO CROSS M5

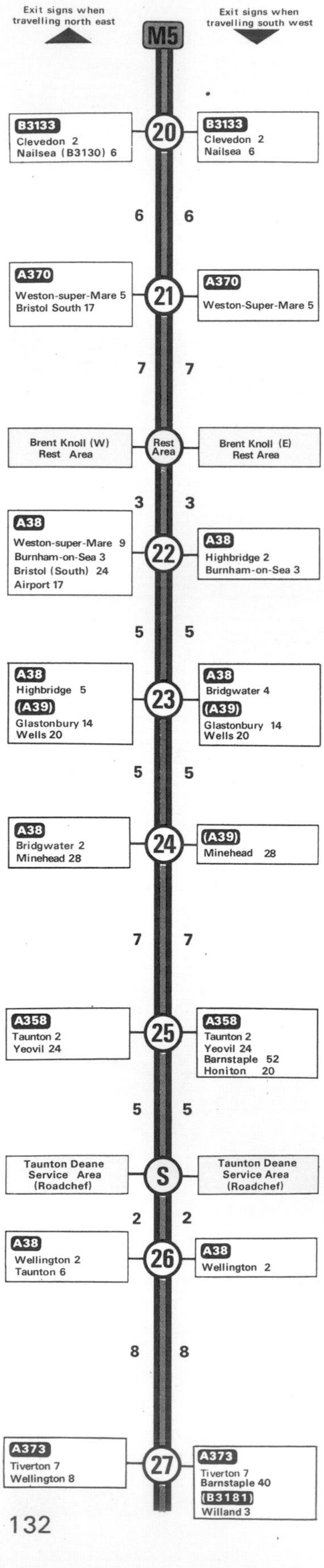

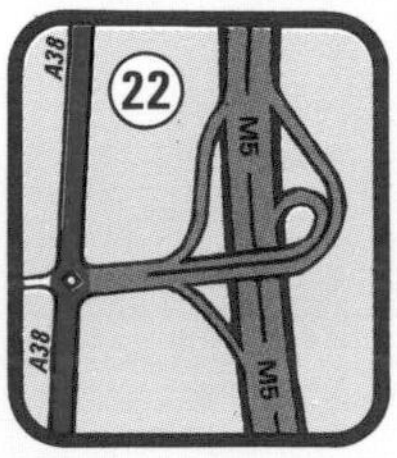

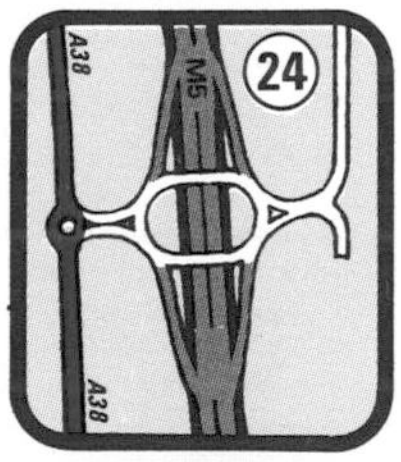

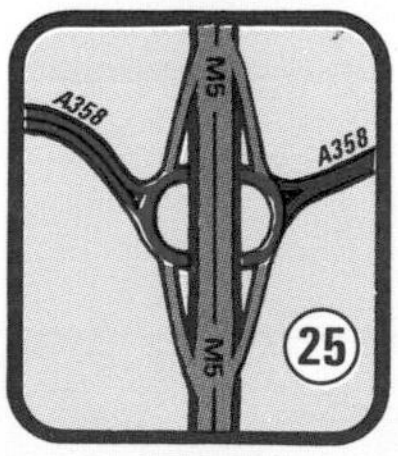

Exit signs when travelling north east
Exit signs when travelling south west
M5
B3133 Clevedon 2 Nailsea (B3130) 6
20
B3133 Clevedon 2 Nailsea 6
6 6
A370 Weston-super-Mare 5 Bristol South 17
21
A370 Weston-Super-Mare 5
7 7
Brent Knoll (W) Rest Area
Rest Area
Brent Knoll (E) Rest Area
3 3
A38 Weston-super-Mare 9 Burnham-on-Sea 3 Bristol (South) 24 Airport 17
22
A38 Highbridge 2 Burnham-on-Sea 3
5 5
A38 Highbridge 5 (A39) Glastonbury 14 Wells 20
23
A38 Bridgwater 4 (A39) Glastonbury 14 Wells 20
5 5
A38 Bridgwater 2 Minehead 28
24
(A39) Minehead 28
7 7
A358 Taunton 2 Yeovil 24
25
A358 Taunton 2 Yeovil 24 Barnstaple 52 Honiton 20
5 5
Taunton Deane Service Area (Roadchef)
S
Taunton Deane Service Area (Roadchef)
2 2
A38 Wellington 2 Taunton 6
26
A38 Wellington 2
8 8
A373 Tiverton 7 Wellington 8
27
A373 Tiverton 7 Barnstaple 40 (B3181) Willand 3

21
M5
A370
A370
M5

22
A38
M5
A38
M5

24
A38
M5
A38

A358
M5
A358
M5
25

BRISTOL
BRISTOL
BRISTOL
Chew Magna
Chew Valley Lake
BATH
Clevedon
Redhill
Blagdon Lake
Congresbury
Compton Martin
Churchill
MENDIP HILLS
Winscombe
WESTON–SUPER–MARE
Axbridge
Cheddar
Cheddar Reservoir
Draycott
WELLS
BRENT KNOLL Rest Area
Wedmore
East Brent
Mark
Burnham–on–Sea
BRIDGWATER BAY
Highbridge
Westhay
Ashcott
GLASTONBURY
Pawlett
Knowle
M5
BRIDGWATER
Cannington
Westonzoyland
Othery
LANGPORT
North Petherton
Lyng
MINEHEAD
QUANTOCK HILLS
West Monkton
TAUNTON
Wrantage
Hatch Beauchamp
Norton Fitzwarren
YEOVIL
BARNSTAPLE
Milverton
TAUNTON DEANE
Buckland St Mary
ANDOVER
Wellington
BLACK DOWN HILLS
Yarcombe
Waterloo Cross
Uffculme
0 4 miles
Monkton
TIVERTON
EXETER
HONITON

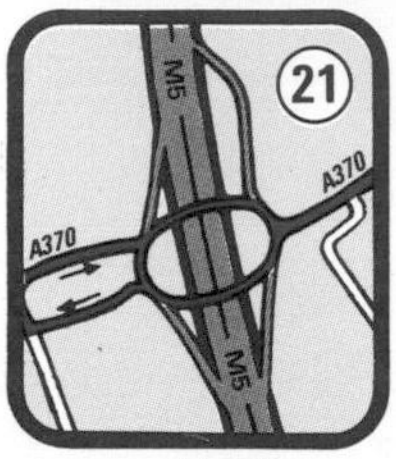

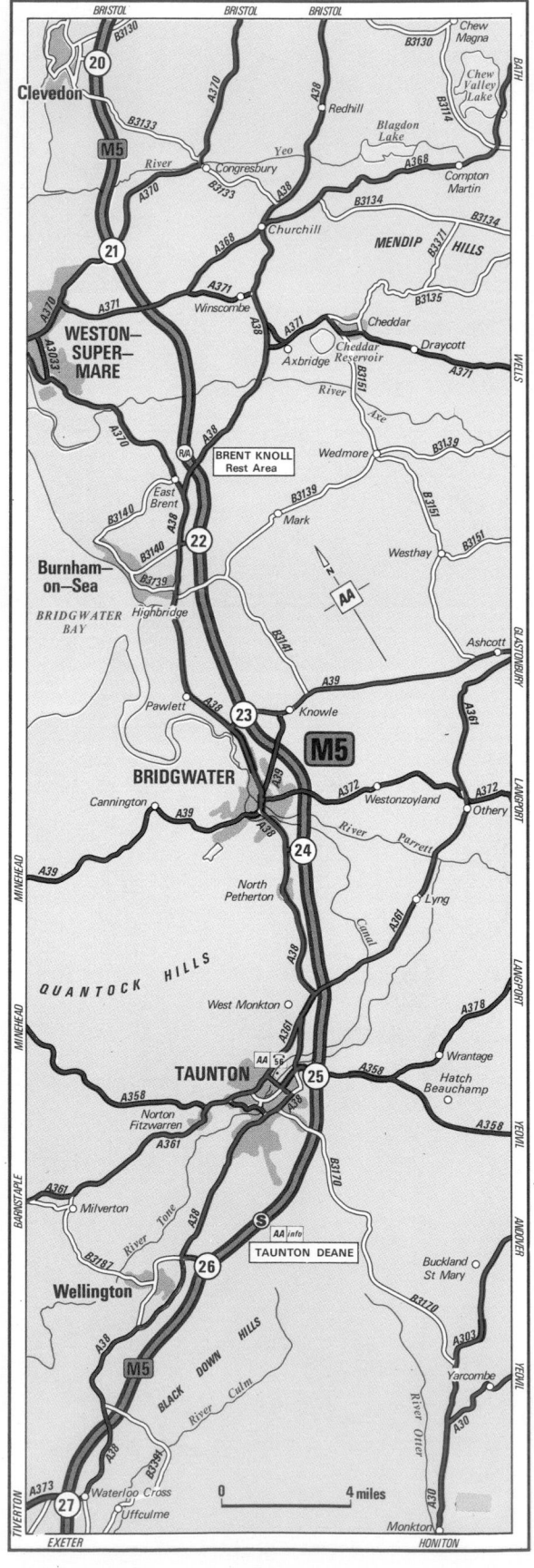

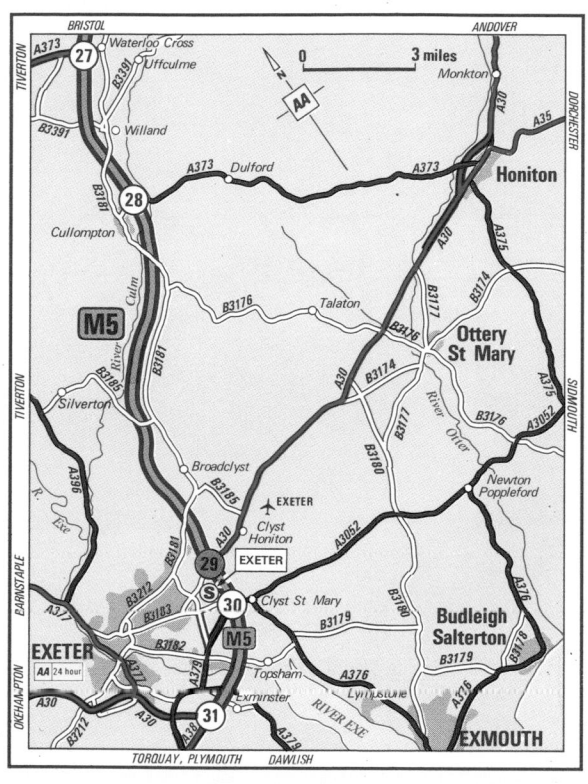

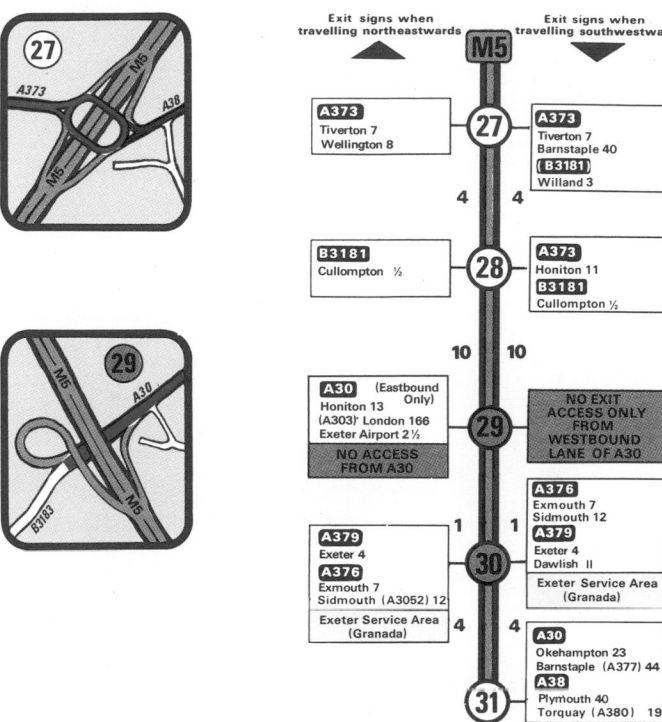

	Exit signs when travelling northeastwards		Exit signs when travelling southwestwards

M5

Northeastwards	Junction	Southwestwards
A373 Tiverton 7 Wellington 8	27	**A373** Tiverton 7 Barnstaple 40 **B3181** Willand 3
4		4
B3181 Cullompton ½	28	**A373** Honiton 11 **B3181** Cullompton ½
10		10
A30 (Eastbound Only) Honiton 13 (A303) London 166 Exeter Airport 2½ — NO ACCESS FROM A30	29	NO EXIT ACCESS ONLY FROM WESTBOUND LANE OF A30
		A376 Exmouth 7 Sidmouth 12 **A379** Exeter 4 Dawlish 11
1		1
A379 Exeter 4 **A376** Exmouth 7 Sidmouth (A3052) 12 Exeter Service Area (Granada)	30	Exeter Service Area (Granada)
4		4
	31	**A30** Okehampton 23 Barnstaple (A377) 44 **A38** Plymouth 40 Torquay (A380) 19

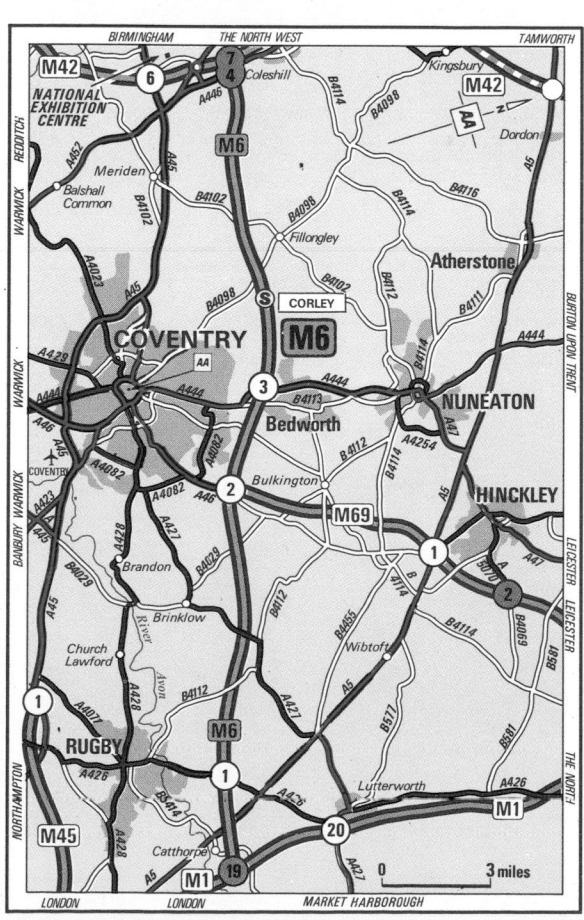

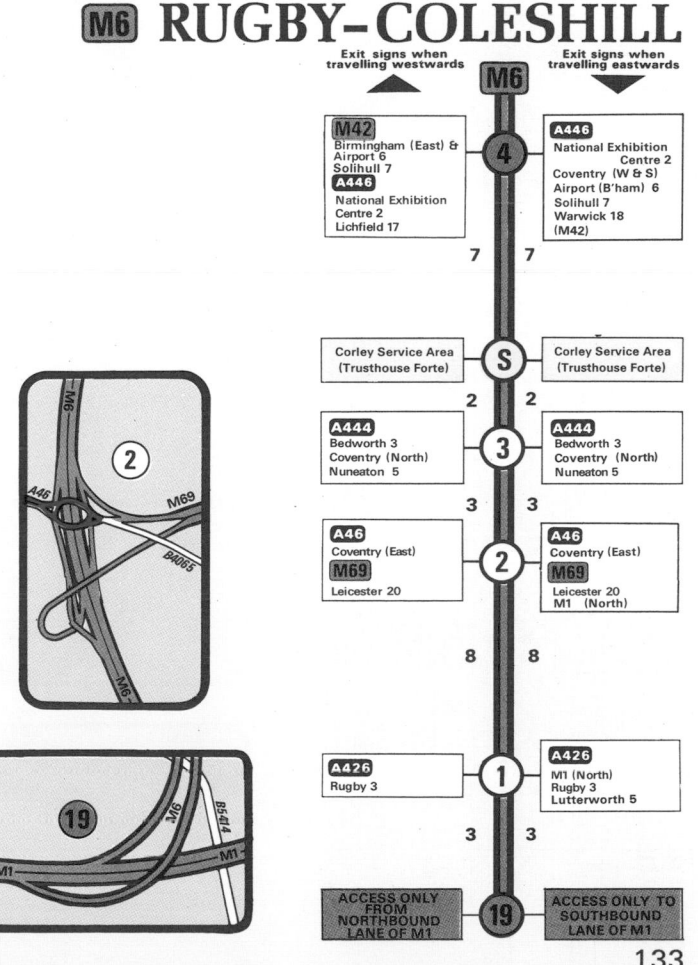

	Exit signs when travelling westwards		Exit signs when travelling eastwards

M6

Westwards	Junction	Eastwards
M42 Birmingham (East) & Airport 6 Solihull 7 **A446** National Exhibition Centre 2 Lichfield 17	4	**A446** National Exhibition Centre 2 Coventry (W & S) Airport (B'ham) 6 Solihull 7 Warwick 18 (M42)
7		7
Corley Service Area (Trusthouse Forte)	S	Corley Service Area (Trusthouse Forte)
2		2
A444 Bedworth 3 Coventry (North) Nuneaton 5	3	**A444** Bedworth 3 Coventry (North) Nuneaton 5
3		3
A46 Coventry (East) **M69** Leicester 20	2	**A46** Coventry (East) **M69** Leicester 20 M1 (North)
8		8
A426 Rugby 3	1	**A426** M1 (North) Rugby 3 Lutterworth 5
3		3
ACCESS ONLY FROM NORTHBOUND LANE OF M1	19	ACCESS ONLY TO SOUTHBOUND LANE OF M1

133

M6

Keele Service Area (Trusthouse Forte) — **S** — Keele Service Area (Trusthouse Forte)

3 — 3

A500
Stoke-on-Trent 5
Newcastle 2¾
— **15** —
A500
Stoke (South) 5
Stone 8
Eccleshall 10

11 — 11

A34
Eccleshall 6
Stone 6
Stafford ((North) 3
— **14** —
A34
Stafford (North) 3

5 — 5

A449
Stafford 3
— **13** —
A449
Stafford (South) 3

6 — 6

A5
Telford 16
— **12** —
A5
Telford 16
Cannock 4
Wolverhampton 9

3 — 3

A460
Cannock 3
— **11** —
A460
Wolverhampton 7

Hilton Park Service Area (Rank) — **S** — Hilton Park Service Area (Rank)

1 — 1

M54
North Wales
Wolverhampton 6
Telford 18
NO ACCESS FROM M54
— **10A** —
NO EXIT. ACCESS ONLY FROM M54

4 — 4

A454
Walsall 2
Wolverhampton 5
— **10** —
A454
Walsall 2

2 — 2

A461
Wednesbury 2
— **9** —
A461
Wednesbury 2

3 — 2

M5
The South West
Birmingham
(NW. W & SW)
West Bromwich 4
— **8** —
M5
The South West
Birmingham
(NW. W&SW)
West Bromwich 4

1 — 2

A34
Birmingham (North)
Walsall 4
— **7** —
A34
Birmingham
(North & NE)

4 — 4

A38(M)
Birmingham (Central) 3
A38
Birmingham (NE)
— **6** —
A38(M)
Birmingham (Central) 4
A38
Birmingham (NE)
Lichfield 14

3 — 3

A452
Birmingham (NE)
Sutton Coldfield 5
NO ACCESS FROM A452
— **5** —
NO EXIT. ACCESS ONLY FROM A452

2 — 2

ACCESS FROM M42 UNDER CONSTRUCTION
— **4A** —
M42
UNDER CONSTRUCTION

3 — 3

M42
Birmingham (East)
& Airport 6
Solihull 7
A446
National Exhibition
Centre 2
Lichfield 17
— **4** —
A446
National Exhibition
Centre 2
Coventry (W & S) 6
Airport (B'ham) 6
Solihull 7
Warwick 18
(M42)

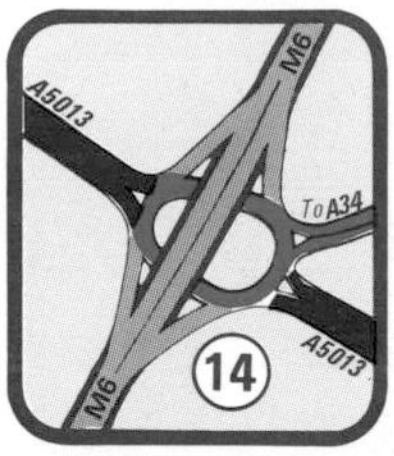

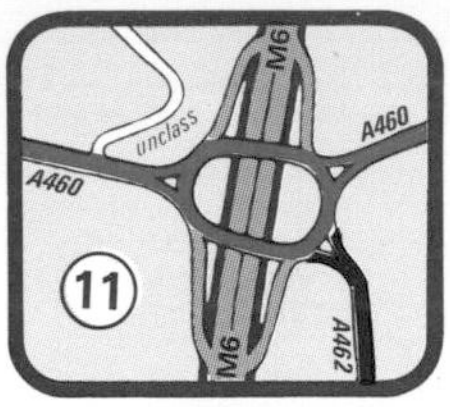

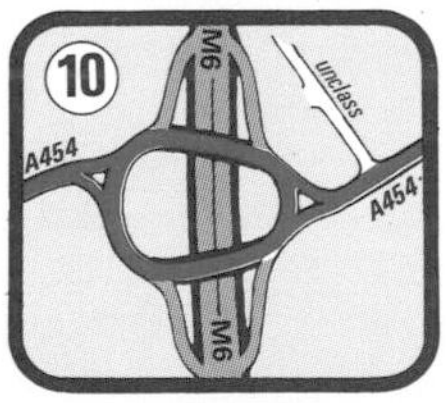

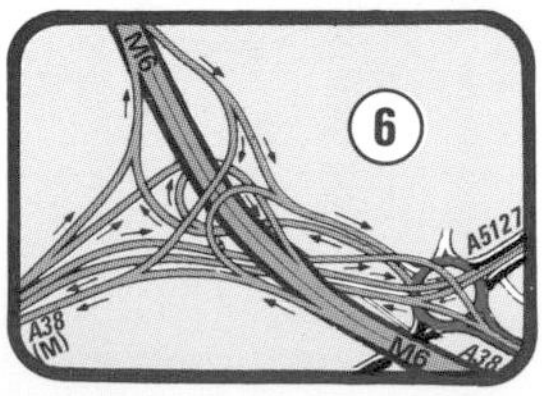

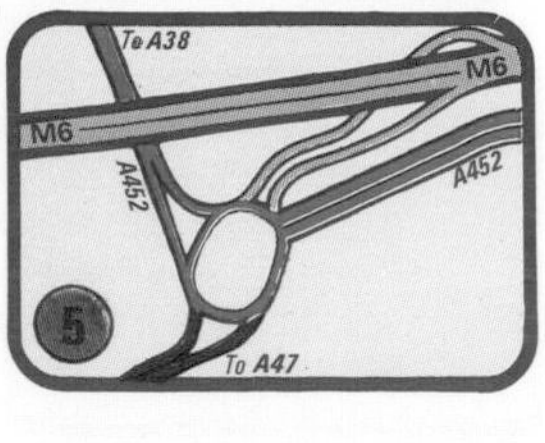

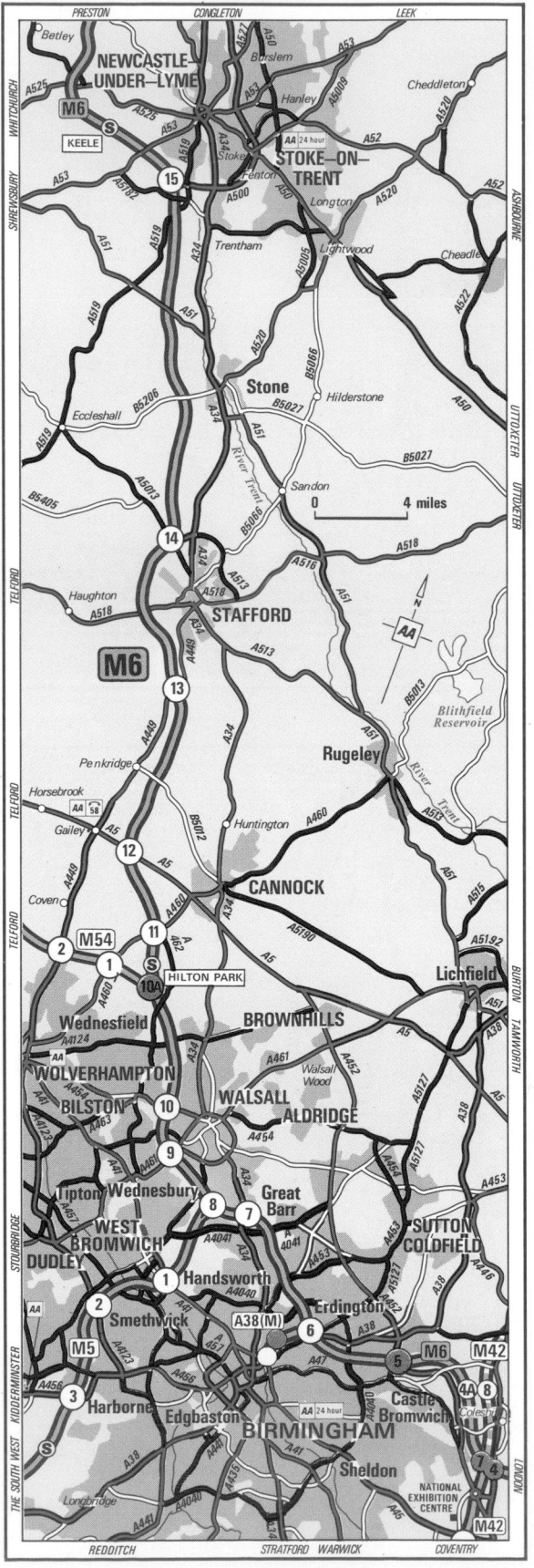

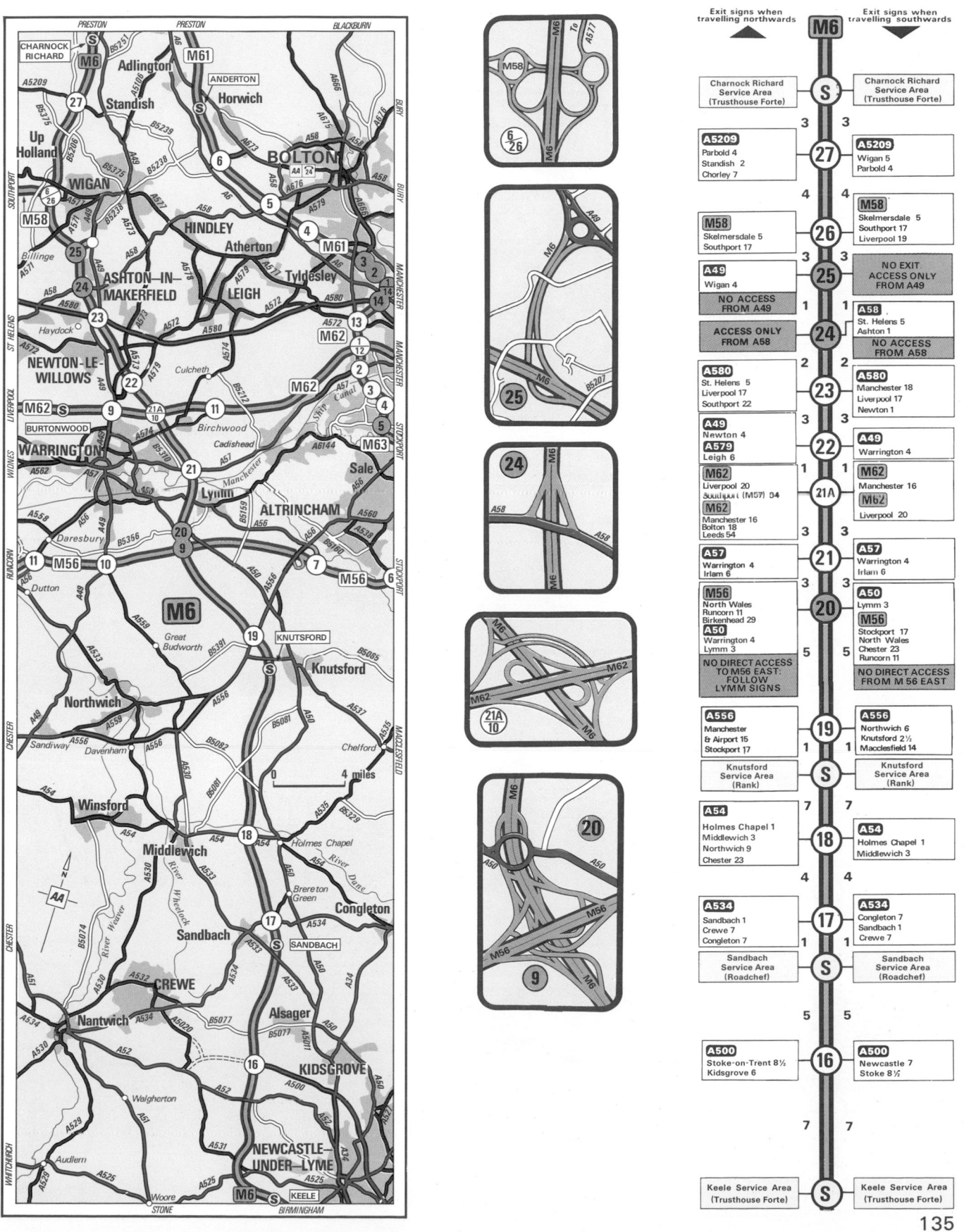

CHARNOCK RICHARD - KILLINGTON LAKE M6

PRESTON - BLACKPOOL M55

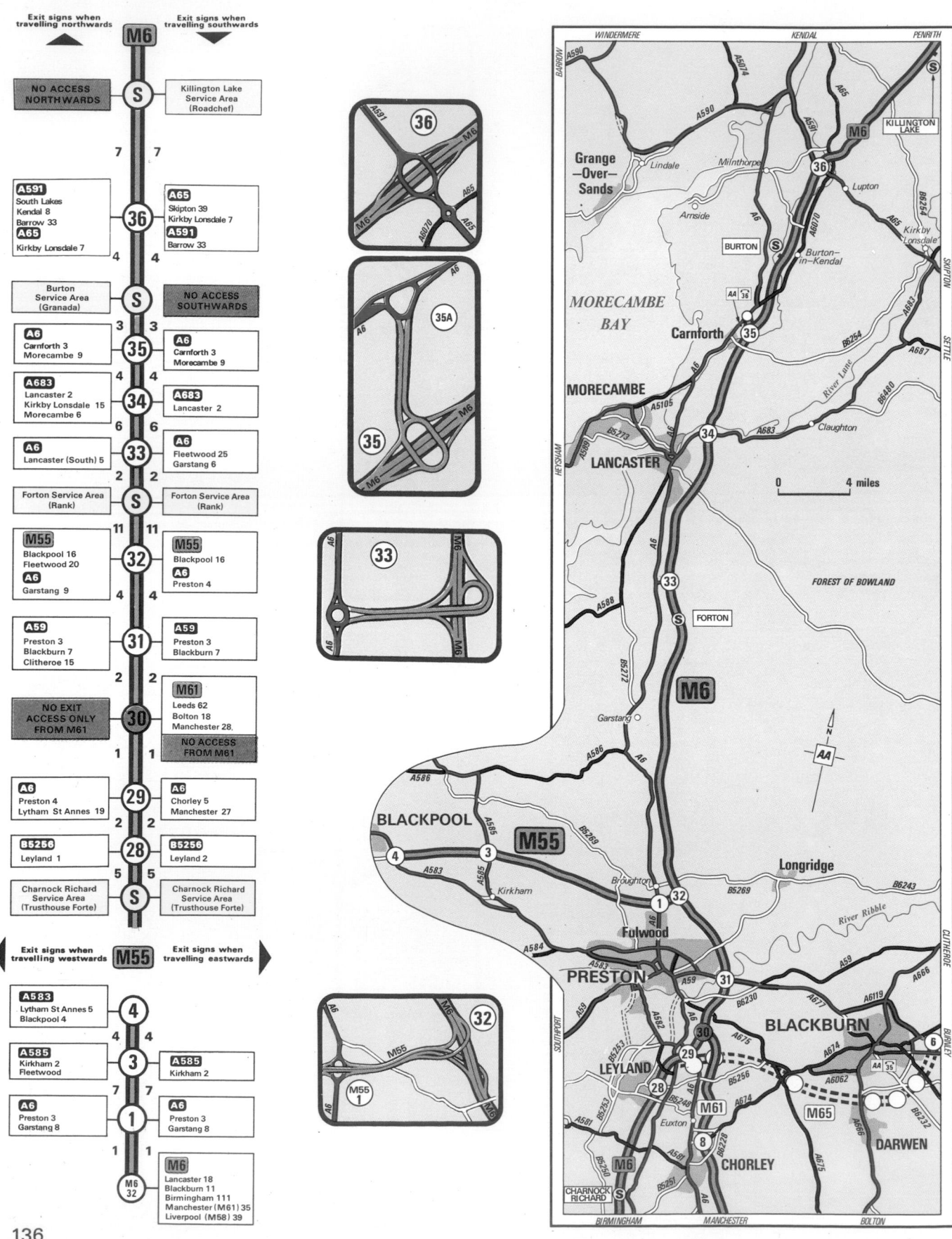

Exit signs when travelling northwards ▲
Exit signs when travelling southwards ▼

M6

Northwards	Jct	Southwards
NO ACCESS NORTHWARDS	(S)	Killington Lake Service Area (Roadchef)
7		7
A591 South Lakes Kendal 8 Barrow 33 / **A65** Kirkby Lonsdale 7	(36)	**A65** Skipton 39 Kirkby Lonsdale 7 / **A591** Barrow 33
4		4
Burton Service Area (Granada)	(S)	**NO ACCESS SOUTHWARDS**
3		3
A6 Carnforth 3 Morecambe 9	(35)	**A6** Carnforth 3 Morecambe 9
4		4
A683 Lancaster 2 Kirkby Lonsdale 15 Morecambe 6	(34)	**A683** Lancaster 2
6		6
A6 Lancaster (South) 5	(33)	**A6** Fleetwood 25 Garstang 6
2		2
Forton Service Area (Rank)	(S)	Forton Service Area (Rank)
11		11
M55 Blackpool 16 Fleetwood 20 / **A6** Garstang 9	(32)	**M55** Blackpool 16 / **A6** Preston 4
4		4
A59 Preston 3 Blackburn 7 Clitheroe 15	(31)	**A59** Preston 3 Blackburn 7
2		2
NO EXIT ACCESS ONLY FROM M61	(30)	**M61** Leeds 62 Bolton 18 Manchester 28 / **NO ACCESS FROM M61**
1		1
A6 Preston 4 Lytham St Annes 19	(29)	**A6** Chorley 5 Manchester 27
2		2
B5256 Leyland 1	(28)	**B5256** Leyland 2
5		5
Charnock Richard Service Area (Trusthouse Forte)	(S)	Charnock Richard Service Area (Trusthouse Forte)

◀ **Exit signs when travelling westwards** **M55** **Exit signs when travelling eastwards** ▶

Westwards	Jct	Eastwards
A583 Lytham St Annes 5 Blackpool 4	(4)	
4		4
A585 Kirkham 2 Fleetwood	(3)	**A585** Kirkham 2
7		7
A6 Preston 3 Garstang 8	(1)	**A6** Preston 3 Garstang 8
1		1
M6 32		**M6** Lancaster 18 Blackburn 11 Birmingham 111 Manchester (M61) 35 Liverpool (M58) 39

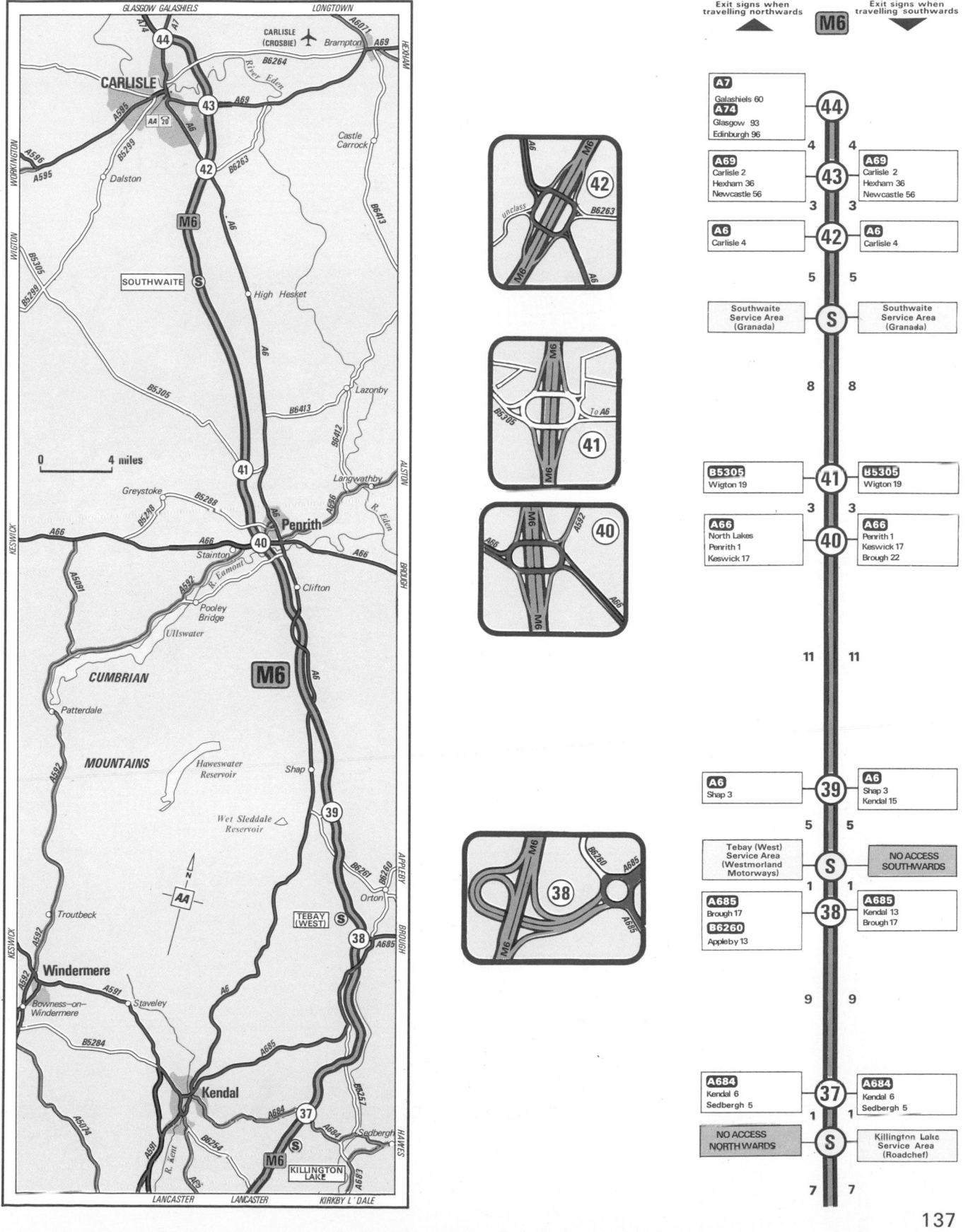

LONDON ORBITAL MOTORWAY M25

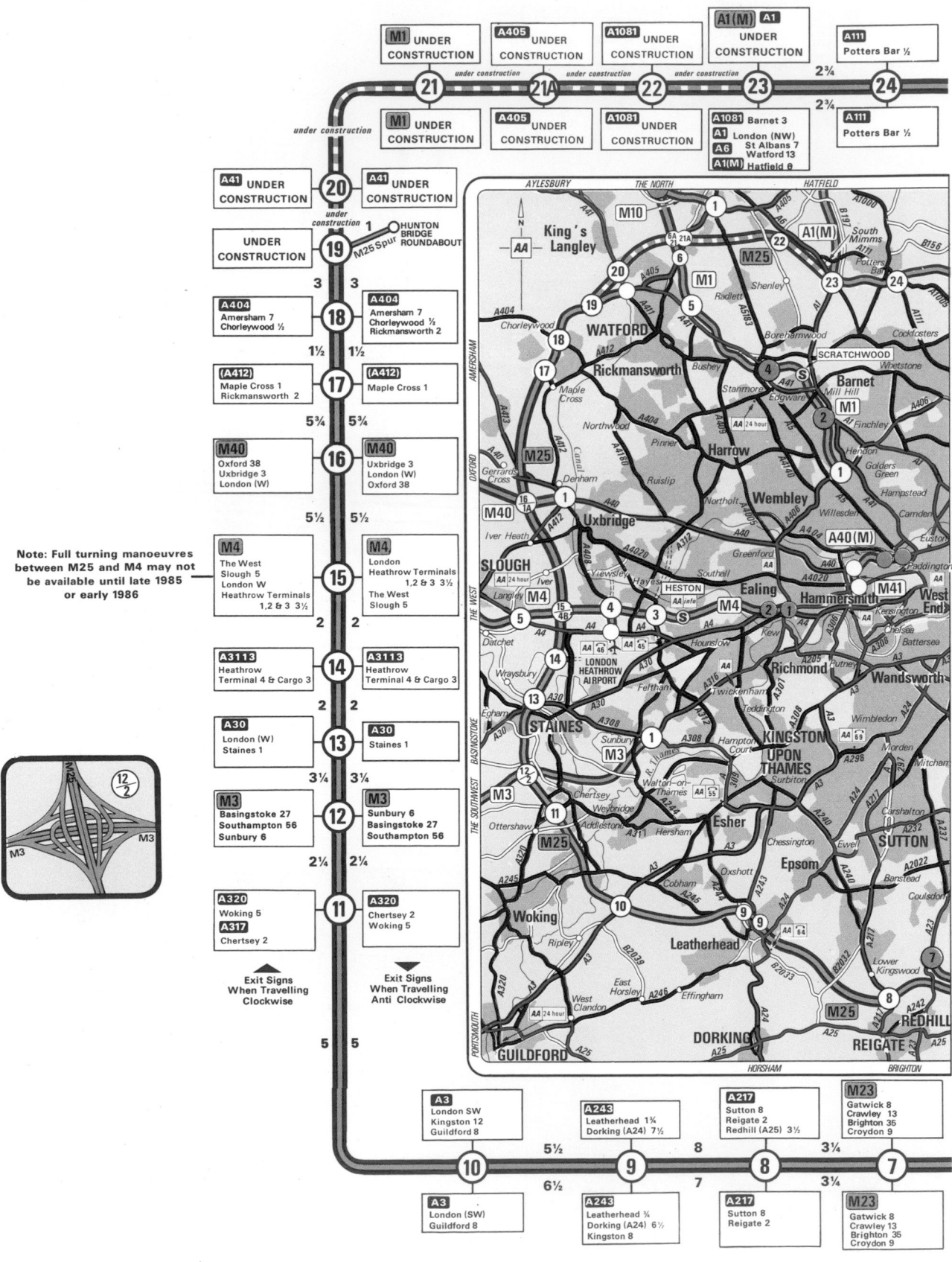

M1 UNDER CONSTRUCTION
A405 UNDER CONSTRUCTION
A1081 UNDER CONSTRUCTION
A1(M) A1 UNDER CONSTRUCTION
A111 Potters Bar ½

(21) (21A) (22) (23) 2¾ (24)

under construction   under construction   under construction   2¾

M1 UNDER CONSTRUCTION
A405 UNDER CONSTRUCTION
A1081 UNDER CONSTRUCTION
A1081 Barnet 3 / **A1** London (NW) / **A6** St Albans 7 / Watford 13 / **A1(M)** Hatfield 8
A111 Potters Bar ½

A41 UNDER CONSTRUCTION
(20)
A41 UNDER CONSTRUCTION

under construction

UNDER CONSTRUCTION
(19) 1 HUNTON BRIDGE ROUNDABOUT
M25 Spur

3   3

A404 Amersham 7 / Chorleywood ½
(18)
A404 Amersham 7 / Chorleywood ½ / Rickmansworth 2

1½   1½

(A412) Maple Cross 1 / Rickmansworth 2
(17)
(A412) Maple Cross 1

5¾   5¾

M40 Oxford 38 / Uxbridge 3 / London (W)
(16)
M40 Uxbridge 3 / London (W) / Oxford 38

5½   5½

Note: Full turning manoeuvres between M25 and M4 may not be available until late 1985 or early 1986

M4 The West / Slough 5 / London W / Heathrow Terminals 1,2 & 3 3½
(15)
M4 London / Heathrow Terminals 1,2 & 3 3½ / The West / Slough 5

2   2

A3113 Heathrow Terminal 4 & Cargo 3
(14)
A3113 Heathrow Terminal 4 & Cargo 3

2   2

A30 London (W) / Staines 1
(13)
A30 Staines 1

3¼   3¼

M3 Basingstoke 27 / Southampton 56 / Sunbury 6
(12)
M3 Sunbury 6 / Basingstoke 27 / Southampton 56

2¼   2¼

A320 Woking 5 / **A317** Chertsey 2
(11)
A320 Chertsey 2 / Woking 5

Exit Signs When Travelling Clockwise

Exit Signs When Travelling Anti Clockwise

5   5

(12/2)
M3 interchange diagram

A3 London SW / Kingston 12 / Guildford 8
A243 Leatherhead 1¾ / Dorking (A24) 7½
A217 Sutton 8 / Reigate 2 / Redhill (A25) 3½
M23 Gatwick 8 / Crawley 13 / Brighton 35 / Croydon 9

(10) 5½ (9) 8 (8) 3¼ (7)

6½   7   3¼

A3 London (SW) / Guildford 8
A243 Leatherhead ¾ / Dorking (A24) 6½ / Kingston 8
A217 Sutton 8 / Reigate 2
M23 Gatwick 8 / Crawley 13 / Brighton 35 / Croydon 9

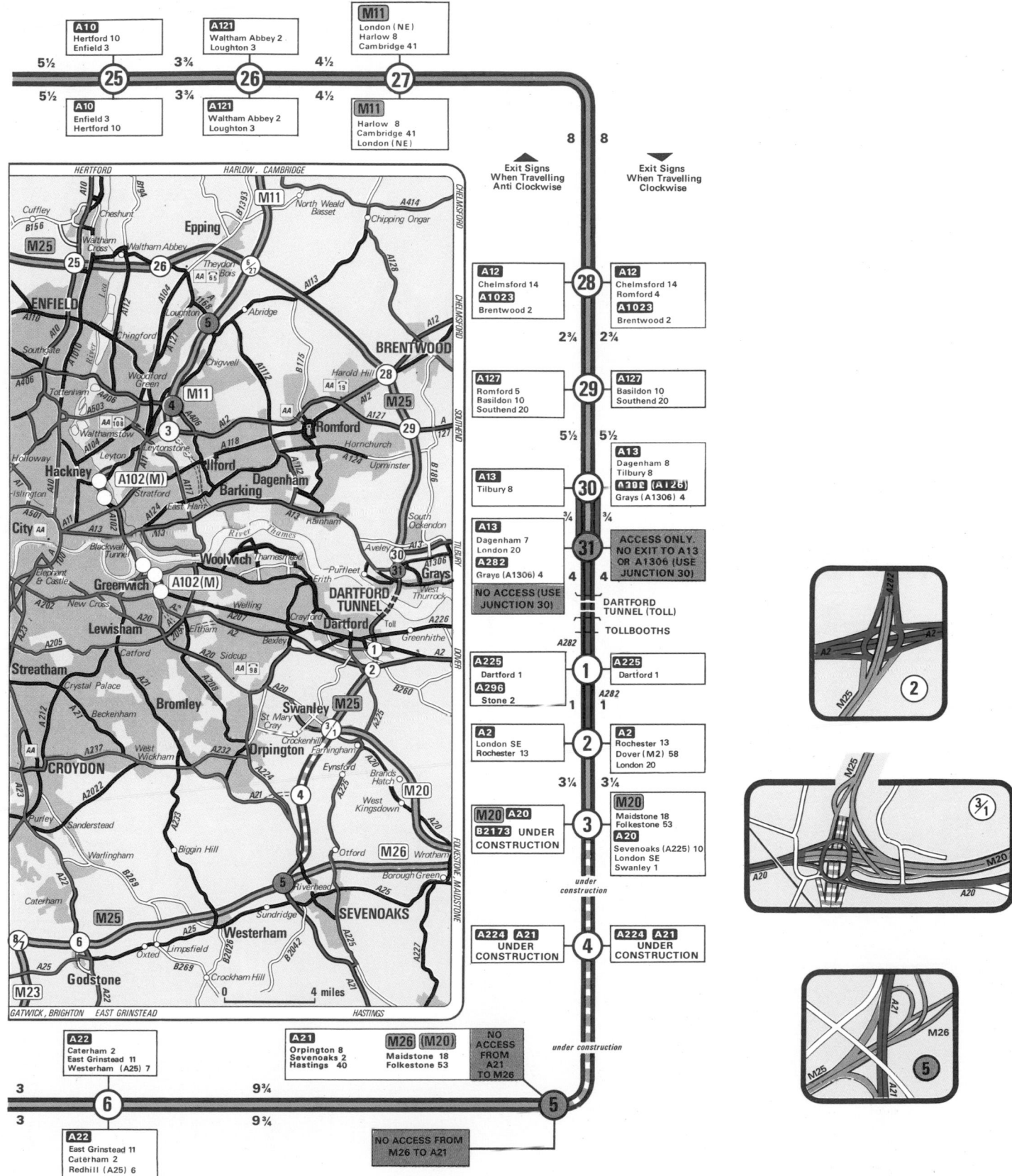

A10 | Hertford 10 | Enfield 3 — **25** — 5½
A121 | Waltham Abbey 2 | Loughton 3 — **26** — 3¾
M11 | London (NE) | Harlow 8 | Cambridge 41 — **27** — 4½

A10 | Enfield 3 | Hertford 10 — 5½
A121 | Waltham Abbey 2 | Loughton 3 — 3¾
M11 | Harlow 8 | Cambridge 41 | London (NE) — 4½

8   8

▲ Exit Signs
When Travelling
Anti Clockwise

▼ Exit Signs
When Travelling
Clockwise

28
A12 | Chelmsford 14 | A1023 | Brentwood 2
A12 | Chelmsford 14 | Romford 4 | A1023 | Brentwood 2
2¾   2¾

29
A127 | Romford 5 | Basildon 10 | Southend 20
A127 | Basildon 10 | Southend 20
5½   5½

30
A13 | Tilbury 8
A13 | Dagenham 8 | Tilbury 8 | A13 A126 | Grays (A1306) 4
¾   ¾

31
A13 | Dagenham 7 | London 20 | A282 | Grays (A1306) 4 | NO ACCESS (USE JUNCTION 30)
ACCESS ONLY. NO EXIT TO A13 OR A1306 (USE JUNCTION 30)
4   4

DARTFORD TUNNEL (TOLL)
TOLLBOOTHS
A282

1
A225 | Dartford 1 | A296 | Stone 2
A225 | Dartford 1
1   1
A282

2
A2 | London SE | Rochester 13
A2 | Rochester 13 | Dover (M2) 58 | London 20
3¼   3¼

3
M20 A20 | B2173 UNDER CONSTRUCTION
M20 | Maidstone 18 | Folkestone 53 | A20 | Sevenoaks (A225) 10 | London SE | Swanley 1

under construction

4
A224 A21 | UNDER CONSTRUCTION
A224 A21 | UNDER CONSTRUCTION

under construction

A22 | Caterham 2 | East Grinstead 11 | Westerham (A25) 7
A21 | Orpington 8 | Sevenoaks 2 | Hastings 40
M26 (M20) | Maidstone 18 | Folkestone 53
NO ACCESS FROM A21 TO M26

3   **6**   9¾
5

3   9¾

A22 | East Grinstead 11 | Caterham 2 | Redhill (A25) 6

NO ACCESS FROM M26 TO A21

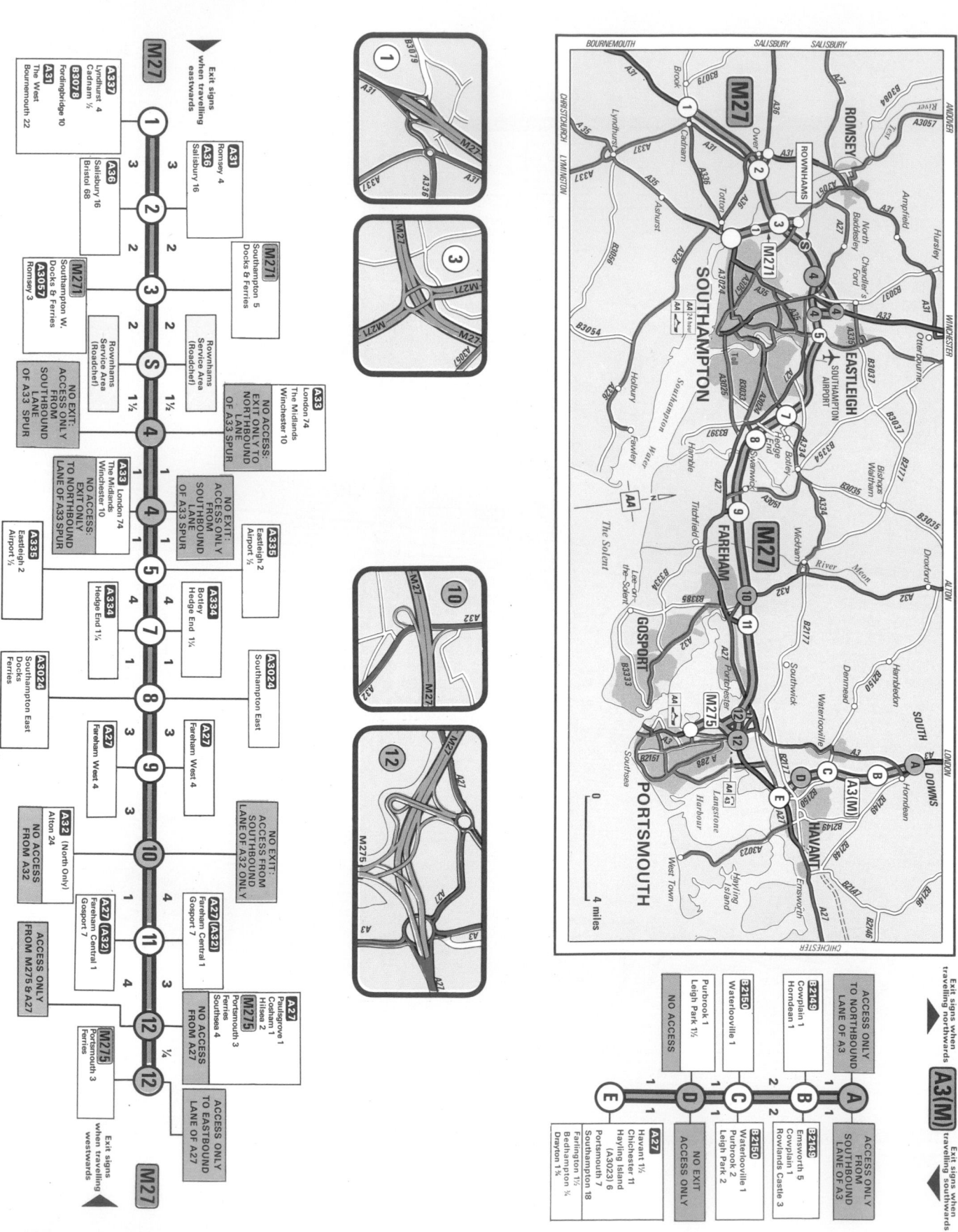

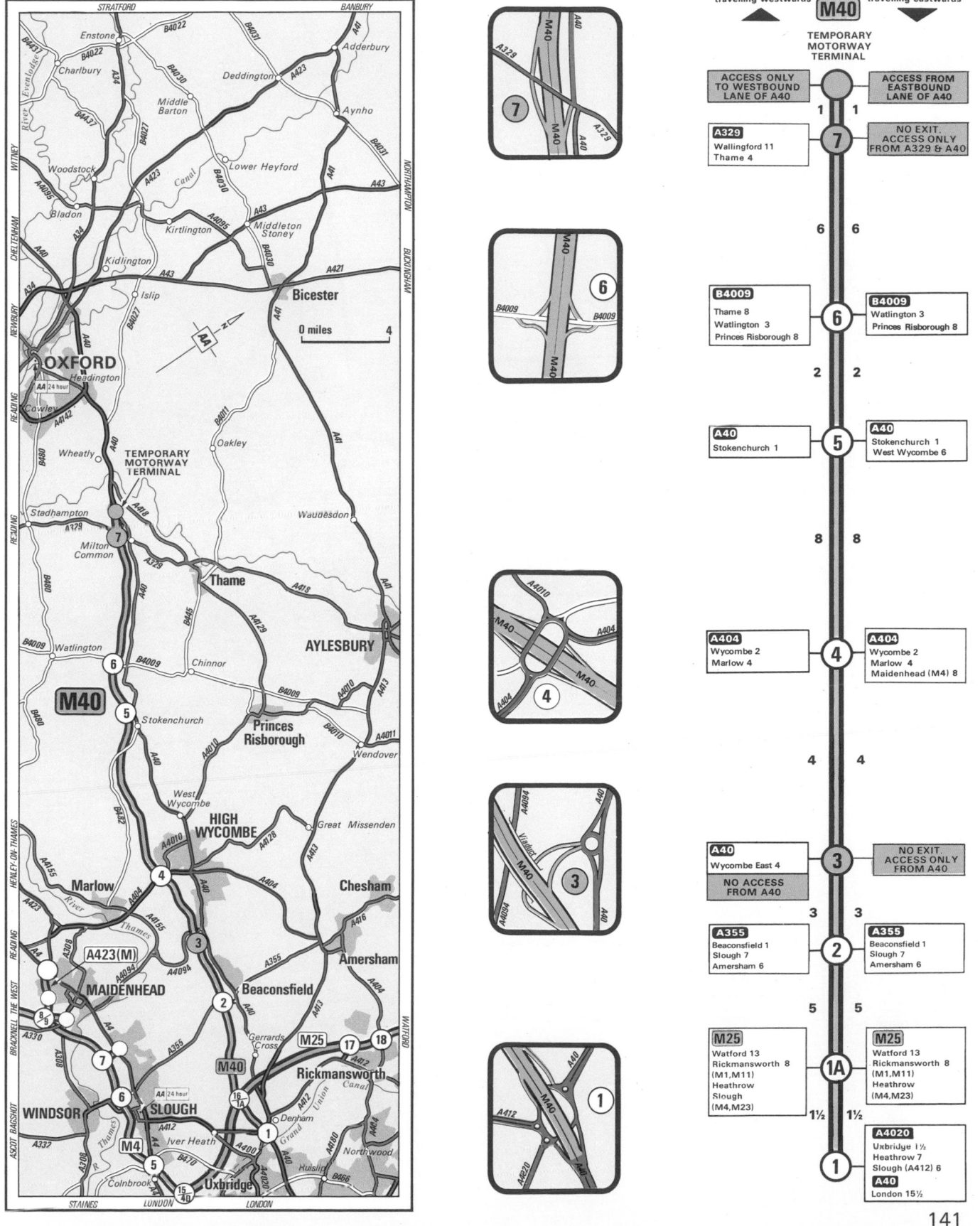

TEMPORARY
MOTORWAY
TERMINAL

| ACCESS ONLY TO WESTBOUND LANE OF A40 | 1 | 1 | ACCESS FROM EASTBOUND LANE OF A40 |

A329
Wallingford 11
Thame 4

⑦ NO EXIT.
ACCESS ONLY FROM A329 & A40

6   6

B4009
Thame 8
Watlington 3
Princes Risborough 8

⑥

B4009
Watlington 3
Princes Risborough 8

2   2

A40
Stokenchurch 1

⑤

A40
Stokenchurch 1
West Wycombe 6

8   8

A404
Wycombe 2
Marlow 4

④

A404
Wycombe 2
Marlow 4
Maidenhead (M4) 8

4   4

A40
Wycombe East 4

NO ACCESS FROM A40

③ NO EXIT.
ACCESS ONLY FROM A40

3   3

A355
Beaconsfield 1
Slough 7
Amersham 6

②

A355
Beaconsfield 1
Slough 7
Amersham 6

5   5

M25
Watford 13
Rickmansworth 8
(M1,M11)
Heathrow
Slough
(M4,M23)

1A

M25
Watford 13
Rickmansworth 8
(M1,M11)
Heathrow
(M4,M23)

1½   1½

①

A4020
Uxbridge 1½
Heathrow 7
Slough (A412) 6
A40
London 15½

BROMSGROVE–APPLEBY MAGNA M42

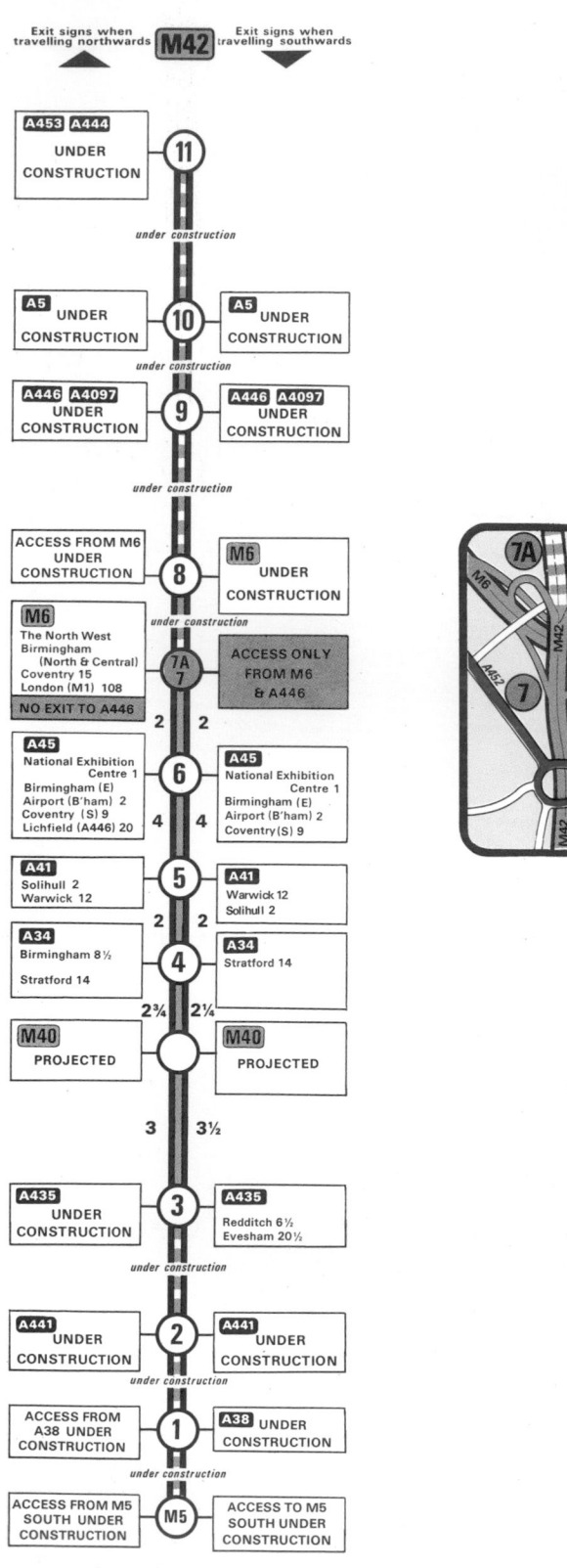

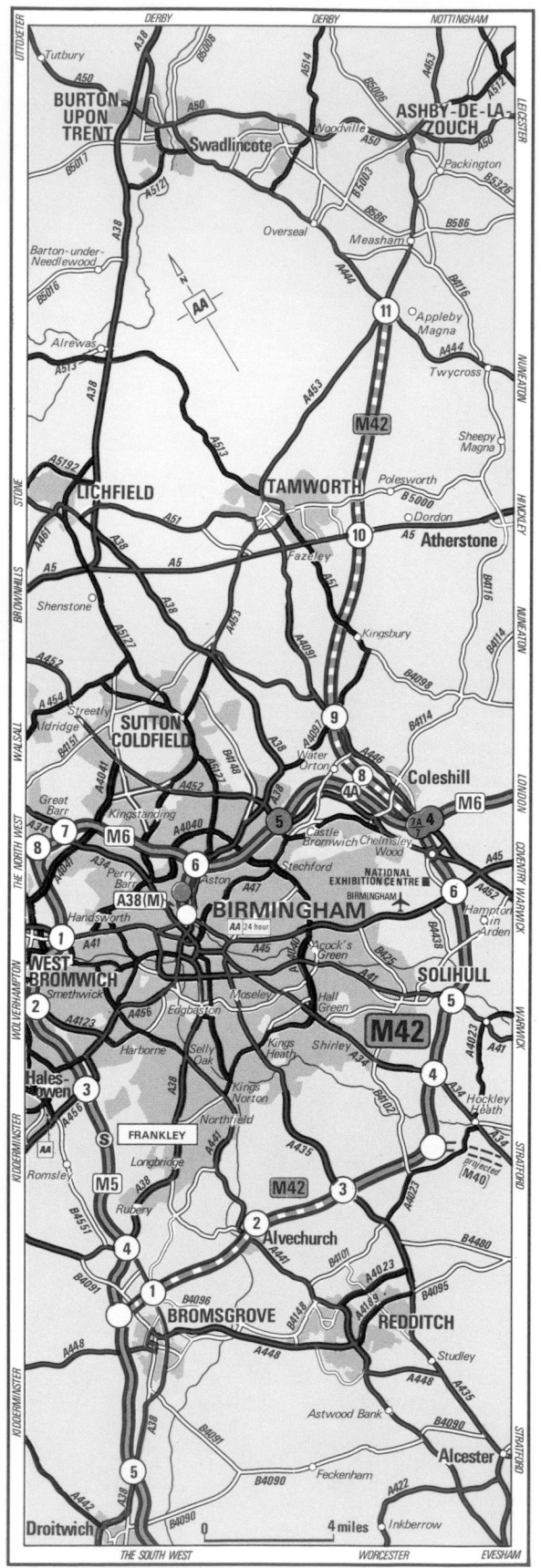

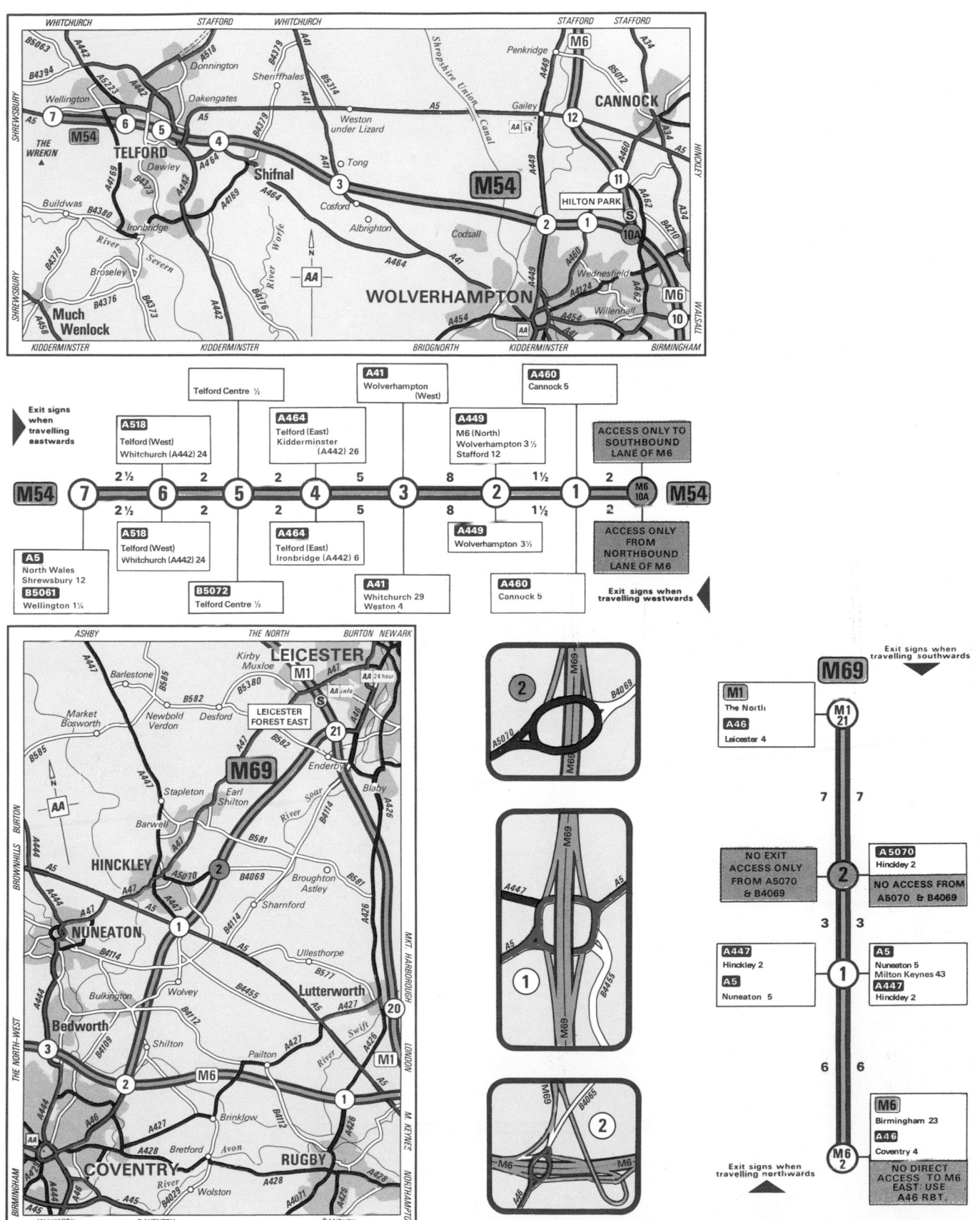

Exit signs when travelling eastwards

A518 Telford (West) Whitchurch (A442) 24

Telford Centre ½

A464 Telford (East) Kidderminster (A442) 26

A41 Wolverhampton (West)

A449 M6 (North) Wolverhampton 3½ Stafford 12

A460 Cannock 5

ACCESS ONLY TO SOUTHBOUND LANE OF M6

M54 — 7 — 2½ — 6 — 2 — 5 — 2 — 4 — 5 — 3 — 8 — 2 — 1½ — 1 — 2 — M6 10A — M54

A5 North Wales Shrewsbury 12
B5061 Wellington 1¼

A518 Telford (West) Whitchurch (A442) 24

B5072 Telford Centre ½

A464 Telford (East) Ironbridge (A442) 6

A41 Whitchurch 29 Weston 4

A449 Wolverhampton 3½

A460 Cannock 5

ACCESS ONLY FROM NORTHBOUND LANE OF M6

Exit signs when travelling westwards

Exit signs when travelling southwards

M69

M1 The North **A46** Leicester 4 — M1 21

7 — 7

NO EXIT ACCESS ONLY FROM A5070 & B4069 — 2 — **A5070** Hinckley 2 **NO ACCESS FROM A5070 & B4069**

3 — 3

A447 Hinckley 2 **A5** Nuneaton 5 — 1 — **A5** Nuneaton 5 Milton Keynes 43 **A447** Hinckley 2

6 — 6

M6 Birmingham 23 **A46** Coventry 4 — M6 2

Exit signs when travelling northwards

NO DIRECT ACCESS TO M6 EAST: USE A46 RBT.

143

LIVERPOOL–HUDDERSFIELD M62

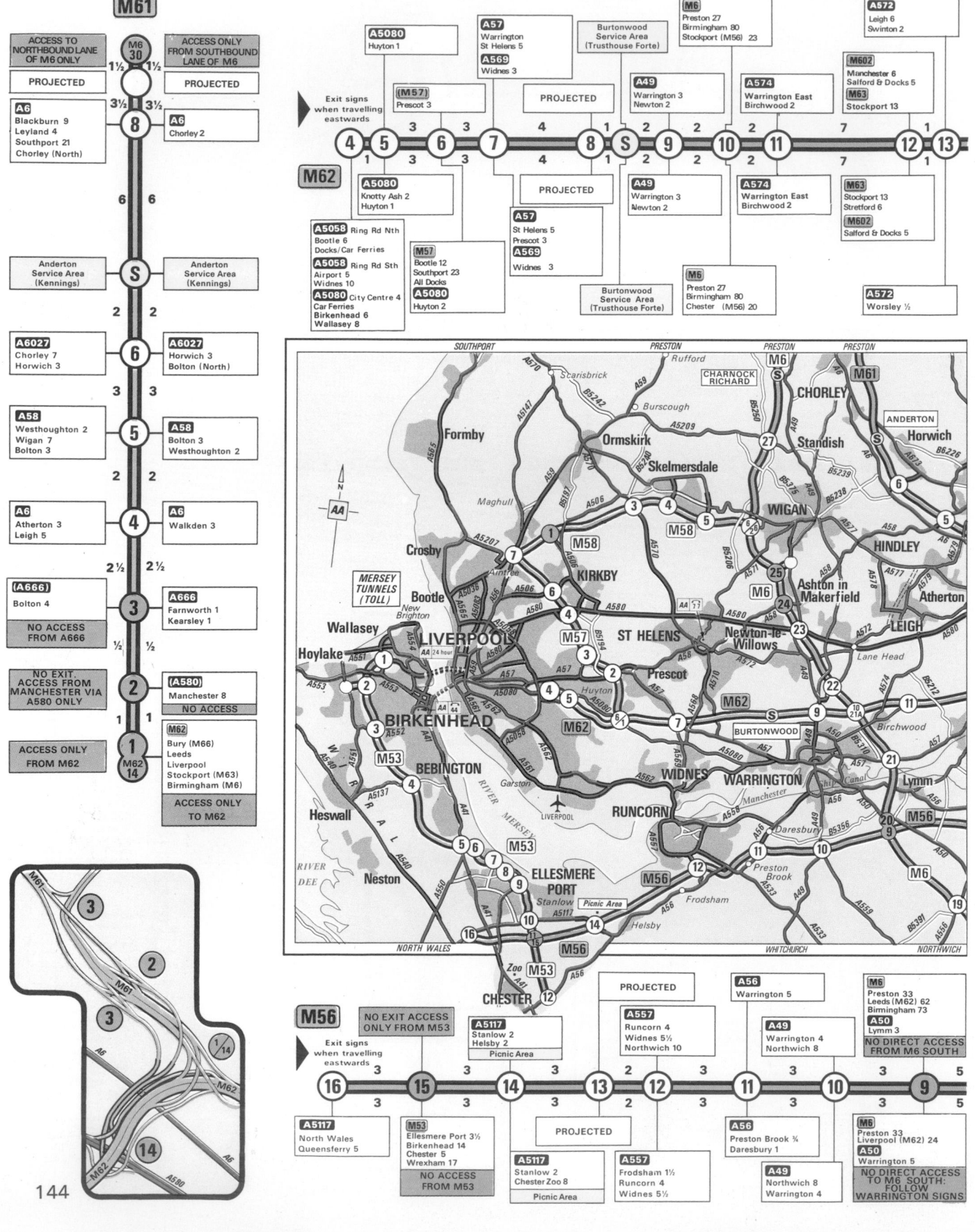

144

M56 NORTH CHESHIRE MOTORWAY

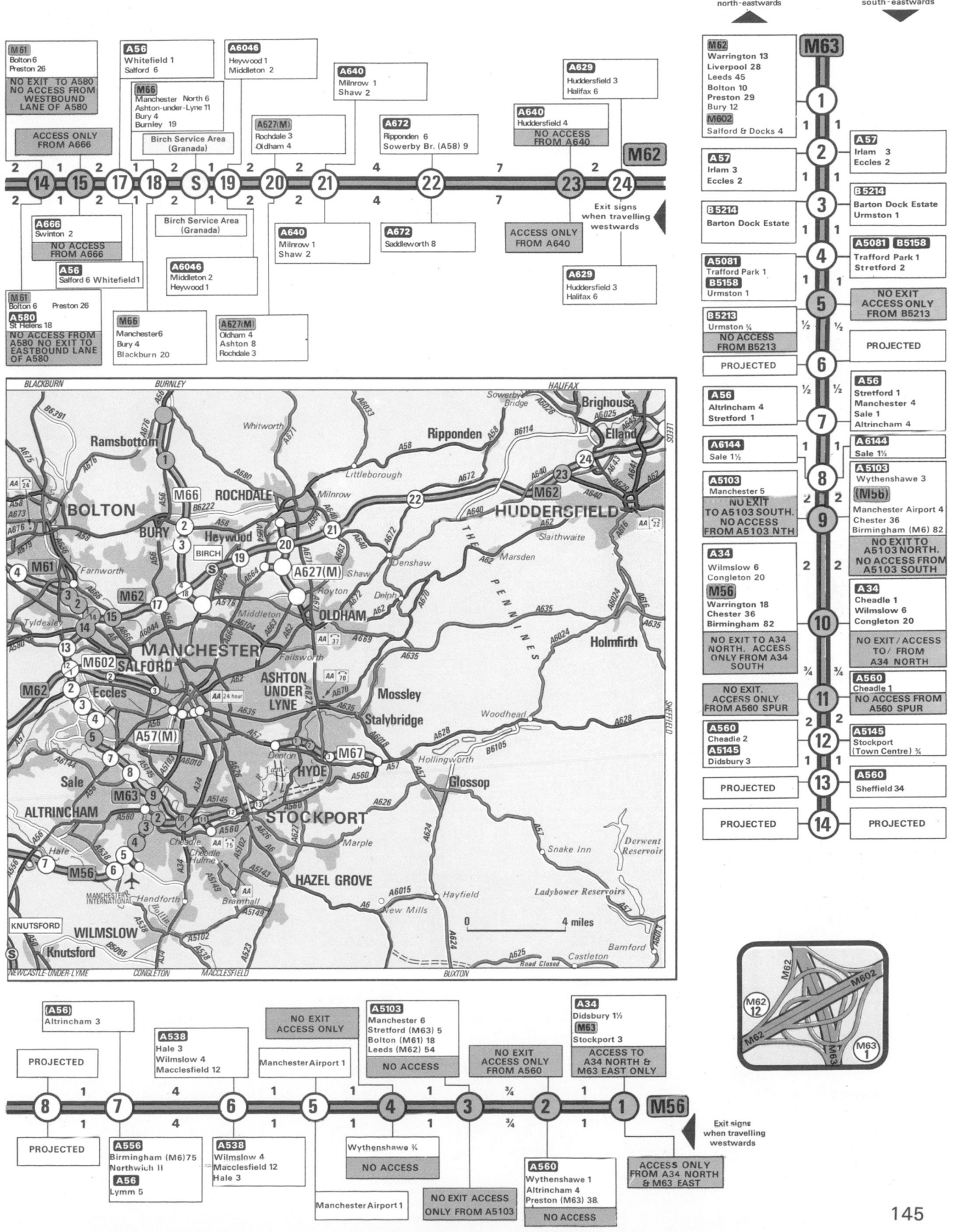

Exit signs when travelling north-eastwards

Exit signs when travelling south-eastwards

M63

M62
Warrington 13
Liverpool 28
Leeds 45
Bolton 10
Preston 29
Bury 12
M602
Salford & Docks 4

A57
Irlam 3
Eccles 2

B5214
Barton Dock Estate

A5081
Trafford Park 1
B5158
Urmston 1

B5213
Urmston ¾
NO ACCESS FROM B5213

PROJECTED

A56
Altrincham 4
Stretford 1

A6144
Sale 1½

A5103
Manchester 5
NO EXIT TO A5103 SOUTH. NO ACCESS FROM A5103 NTH

A34
Wilmslow 6
Congleton 20
M56
Warrington 18
Chester 36
Birmingham 82
NO EXIT TO A34 NORTH. ACCESS ONLY FROM A34 SOUTH

NO EXIT. ACCESS ONLY FROM A560 SPUR

A560
Cheadle 2
A5145
Didsbury 3

PROJECTED

PROJECTED

— right side —

A57
Irlam 3
Eccles 2

B5214
Barton Dock Estate
Urmston 1

A5081 **B5158**
Trafford Park 1
Stretford 2

NO EXIT ACCESS ONLY FROM B5213

PROJECTED

A56
Stretford 1
Manchester 4
Sale 1
Altrincham 4

A6144
Sale 1½

A5103
Wythenshawe 3
(M56)
Manchester Airport 4
Chester 36
Birmingham (M6) 82
NO EXIT TO A5103 NORTH. NO ACCESS FROM A5103 SOUTH

A34
Cheadle 1
Wilmslow 6
Congleton 20
NO EXIT/ACCESS TO/FROM A34 NORTH

A560
Cheadle 1
NO ACCESS FROM A560 SPUR

A5145
Stockport (Town Centre) ¾

A560
Sheffield 34

PROJECTED

Exit numbers (top, M63): 1, 2, 3, 4, 5, 6, 7, 8, 9, 10, 11, 12, 13, 14

Distances between (left of M63): 1, 1, 1, 1, ½, ½, ½, 1, 2, ¾
Distances between (right of M63): 1, 1, 1, 1, ½, ½, 2, 2, ¾, 2

M62 12 / M62 / M62 / M63 / M63 1 / M602

M61
Bolton 6
Preston 26
NO EXIT TO A580 NO ACCESS FROM WESTBOUND LANE OF A580

ACCESS ONLY FROM A666

A56
Whitefield 1
Salford 6

M66
Manchester North 6
Ashton-under-Lyne 11
Bury 4
Burnley 19

Birch Service Area (Granada)

A6046
Heywood 1
Middleton 2

A627(M)
Rochdale 3
Oldham 4

A640
Milnrow 1
Shaw 2

A672
Ripponden 6
Sowerby Br. (A58) 9

A629
Huddersfield 3
Halifax 6

A640
Huddersfield 4
NO ACCESS FROM A640

M62

Exit numbers (top): 2 1 2 1 2 1 1 1 4 7 2
(14) (15) (17) (18) (S) (19) (20) (21) (22) (23) (24)
Exit numbers (bottom): 2 1 2 1 2 1 2 1 7 7 2

Exit signs when travelling westwards

A666
Swinton 2
NO ACCESS FROM A666

A56
Salford 6 Whitefield 1

M61
Bolton 6 Preston 26
A580
St Helens 18
NO ACCESS FROM A580 NO EXIT TO EASTBOUND LANE OF A580

Birch Service Area (Granada)

A640
Milnrow 1
Shaw 2

A6046
Middleton 2
Heywood 1

M66
Manchester 6
Bury 4
Blackburn 20

A627(M)
Oldham 4
Ashton 8
Rochdale 3

A672
Saddleworth 8

ACCESS ONLY FROM A640

A629
Huddersfield 3
Halifax 6

(A56)
Altrincham 3

PROJECTED

A538
Hale 3
Wilmslow 4
Macclesfield 12

NO EXIT ACCESS ONLY

Manchester Airport 1

A5103
Manchester 6
Stretford (M63) 5
Bolton (M61) 18
Leeds (M62) 54
NO ACCESS

NO EXIT ACCESS ONLY FROM A560

A34
Didsbury 1½
M63
Stockport 3
ACCESS TO A34 NORTH & M63 EAST ONLY

Exit numbers (M56): 8, 7, 6, 5, 4, 3, 2, 1
Distances top: 1, 4, 1, 1, 1, ¾, 1
Distances bottom: 1, 4, 1, 1, 1, ¾, 1

M56

Exit signs when travelling westwards

PROJECTED

A556
Birmingham (M6) 75
Northwich 11
A56
Lymm 5

A538
Wilmslow 4
Macclesfield 12
Hale 3

Wythenshawe ¾
NO ACCESS

Manchester Airport 1

NO EXIT ACCESS ONLY FROM A5103

A560
Wythenshawe 1
Altrincham 4
Preston (M63) 38
NO ACCESS

ACCESS ONLY FROM A34 NORTH & M63 EAST

145

HUDDERSFIELD-HULL M62

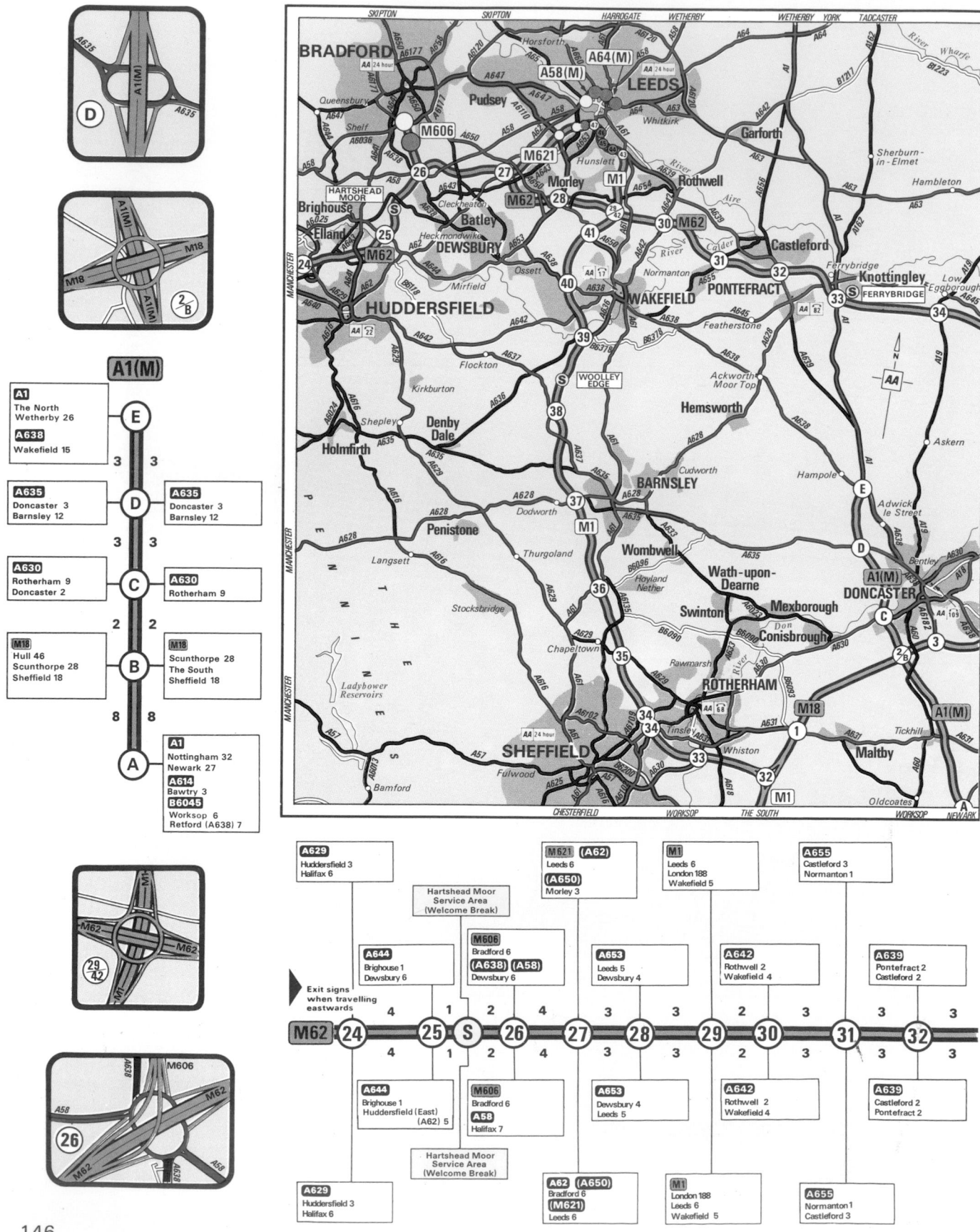

A1(M)

A1
The North
Wetherby 26
A638
Wakefield 15

E

3   3

A635
Doncaster 3
Barnsley 12

D

A635
Doncaster 3
Barnsley 12

3   3

A630
Rotherham 9
Doncaster 2

C

A630
Rotherham 9

3   3

M18
Hull 46
Scunthorpe 28
Sheffield 18

B

M18
Scunthorpe 28
The South
Sheffield 18

2   2

8   8

A

A1
Nottingham 32
Newark 27
A614
Bawtry 3
B6045
Worksop 6
Retford (A638) 7

Exit signs when travelling eastwards

A629 Huddersfield 3 Halifax 6		A644 Brighouse 1 Dewsbury 6		Hartshead Moor Service Area (Welcome Break)	M606 Bradford 6 (A638) (A58) Dewsbury 6	M621 (A62) Leeds 6 (A650) Morley 3		A653 Leeds 5 Dewsbury 4	M1 Leeds 6 London 188 Wakefield 5		A642 Rothwell 2 Wakefield 4		A655 Castleford 3 Normanton 1		A639 Pontefract 2 Castleford 2	
M62	**24**	4	**25**	1	**S**	2	**26**	4	**27**	3	**28**	3	**29**	3	**30**	3	**31**	3	**32**	3
		4		1		2		4		3		3		2		3		3		3
A629 Huddersfield 3 Halifax 6		A644 Brighouse 1 Huddersfield (East) (A62) 5		Hartshead Moor Service Area (Welcome Break)	M606 Bradford 6 A58 Halifax 7	A62 (A650) Bradford 6 (M621) Leeds 6		A653 Dewsbury 4 Leeds 5	M1 London 188 Leeds 6 Wakefield 5		A642 Rothwell 2 Wakefield 4		A655 Normanton 1 Castleford 3		A639 Castleford 2 Pontefract 2	

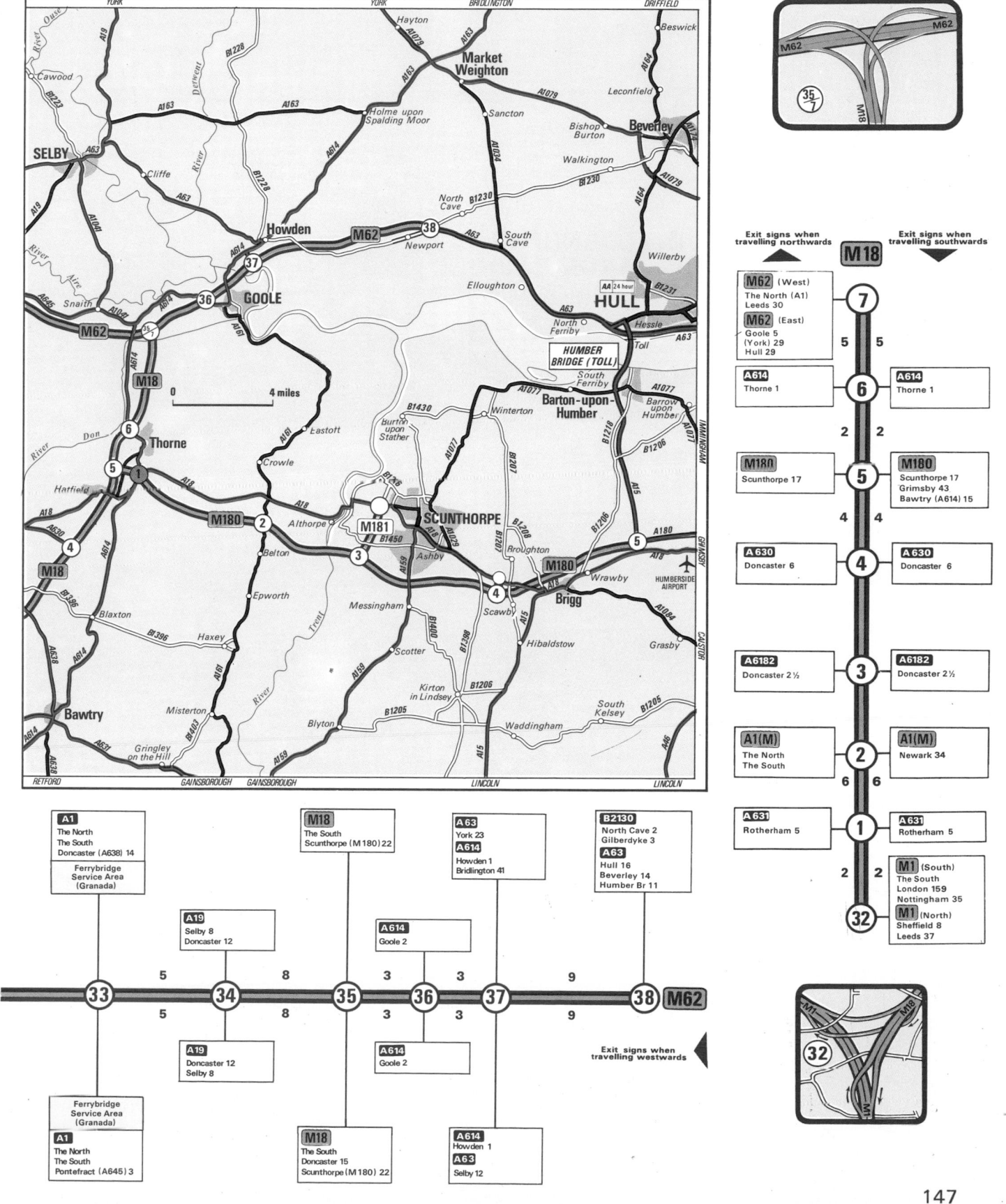

EDINBURGH–DUNBLANE [M9]

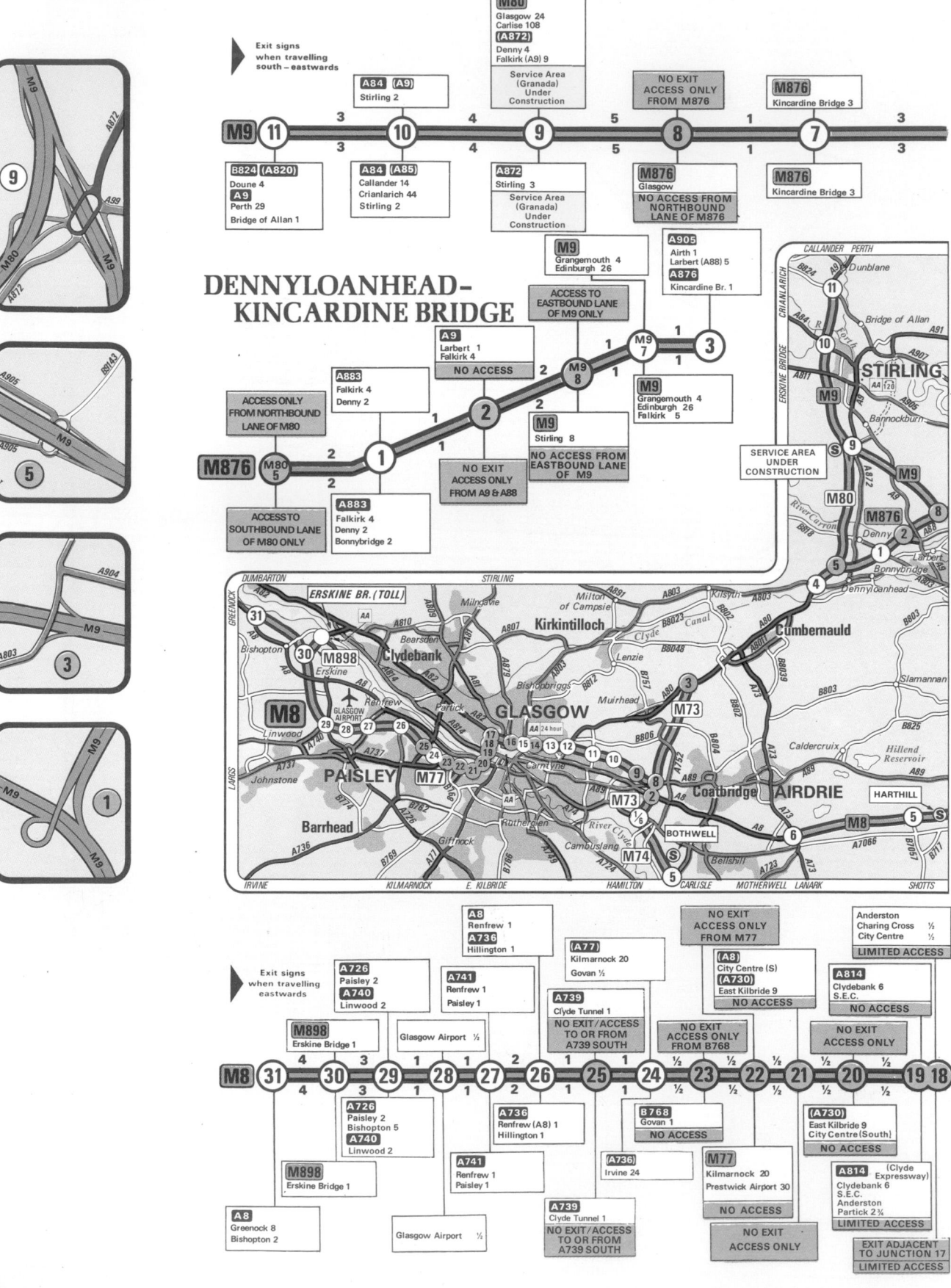

Exit signs when travelling south – eastwards

M80
Glasgow 24
Carlise 108
(A872)
Denny 4
Falkirk (A9) 9
Service Area (Granada) Under Construction

(A84) (A9)
Stirling 2

NO EXIT ACCESS ONLY FROM M876

M876
Kincardine Bridge 3

M9 ⑪ 3 ⑩ 4 ⑨ 5 ⑧ 1 ⑦ 3
3   4   5   1   3

B824 (A820)
Doune 4
A9
Perth 29
Bridge of Allan 1

A84 (A85)
Callander 14
Crianlarich 44
Stirling 2

A872
Stirling 3
Service Area (Granada) Under Construction

M876
Glasgow
NO ACCESS FROM NORTHBOUND LANE OF M876

M876
Kincardine Bridge 3

DENNYLOANHEAD– KINCARDINE BRIDGE

M9
Grangemouth 4
Edinburgh 26

A905
Airth 1
Larbert (A88) 5
A876
Kincardine Br. 1

ACCESS TO EASTBOUND LANE OF M9 ONLY

A9
Larbert 1
Falkirk 4
NO ACCESS

ACCESS ONLY FROM NORTHBOUND LANE OF M80

A883
Falkirk 4
Denny 2

M9 ⑦ 1 ③
M9 ⑧ 1
2   1
M876 M80⑤ 2 ① 1 ② 2
2   1   2

NO EXIT ACCESS ONLY FROM A9 & A88

M9
Stirling 8
NO ACCESS FROM EASTBOUND LANE OF M9

M9
Grangemouth 4
Edinburgh 26
Falkirk 5

ACCESS TO SOUTHBOUND LANE OF M80 ONLY

A883
Falkirk 4
Denny 2
Bonnybridge 2

SERVICE AREA UNDER CONSTRUCTION

Exit signs when travelling eastwards

A8
Renfrew 1
A736
Hillington 1

(A77)
Kilmarnock 20
Govan ½

NO EXIT ACCESS ONLY FROM M77

Anderston ½
Charing Cross
City Centre ½
LIMITED ACCESS

A726
Paisley 2
A740
Linwood 2

A741
Renfrew 1
Paisley 1

A739
Clyde Tunnel 1
NO EXIT/ACCESS TO OR FROM A739 SOUTH

(A8)
City Centre (S)
(A730)
East Kilbride 9
NO ACCESS

A814
Clydebank 6
S.E.C.
NO ACCESS

M898
Erskine Bridge 1

Glasgow Airport ½

NO EXIT ACCESS ONLY

M8 31 4 30 3 29 2 28 27 26 2 25 24 1 23 ½ 22 ½ 21 ½ 20 ½ 19 18
4   3   2   2   1   ½   ½   ½   ½

A726
Paisley 2
Bishopton 5
A740
Linwood 2

A736
Renfrew (A8) 1
Hillington 1

B768
Govan 1
NO ACCESS

(A730)
East Kilbride 9
City Centre (South)
NO ACCESS

M898
Erskine Bridge 1

A741
Renfrew 1
Paisley 1

(A736)
Irvine 24

M77
Kilmarnock 20
Prestwick Airport 30
NO ACCESS

A814
(Clyde Expressway)
Clydebank 6
S.E.C.
Anderston
Partick 2¾
LIMITED ACCESS

A8
Greenock 8
Bishopton 2

Glasgow Airport ½

A739
Clyde Tunnel 1
NO EXIT/ACCESS TO OR FROM A739 SOUTH

NO EXIT ACCESS ONLY

EXIT ADJACENT TO JUNCTION 17
LIMITED ACCESS

148

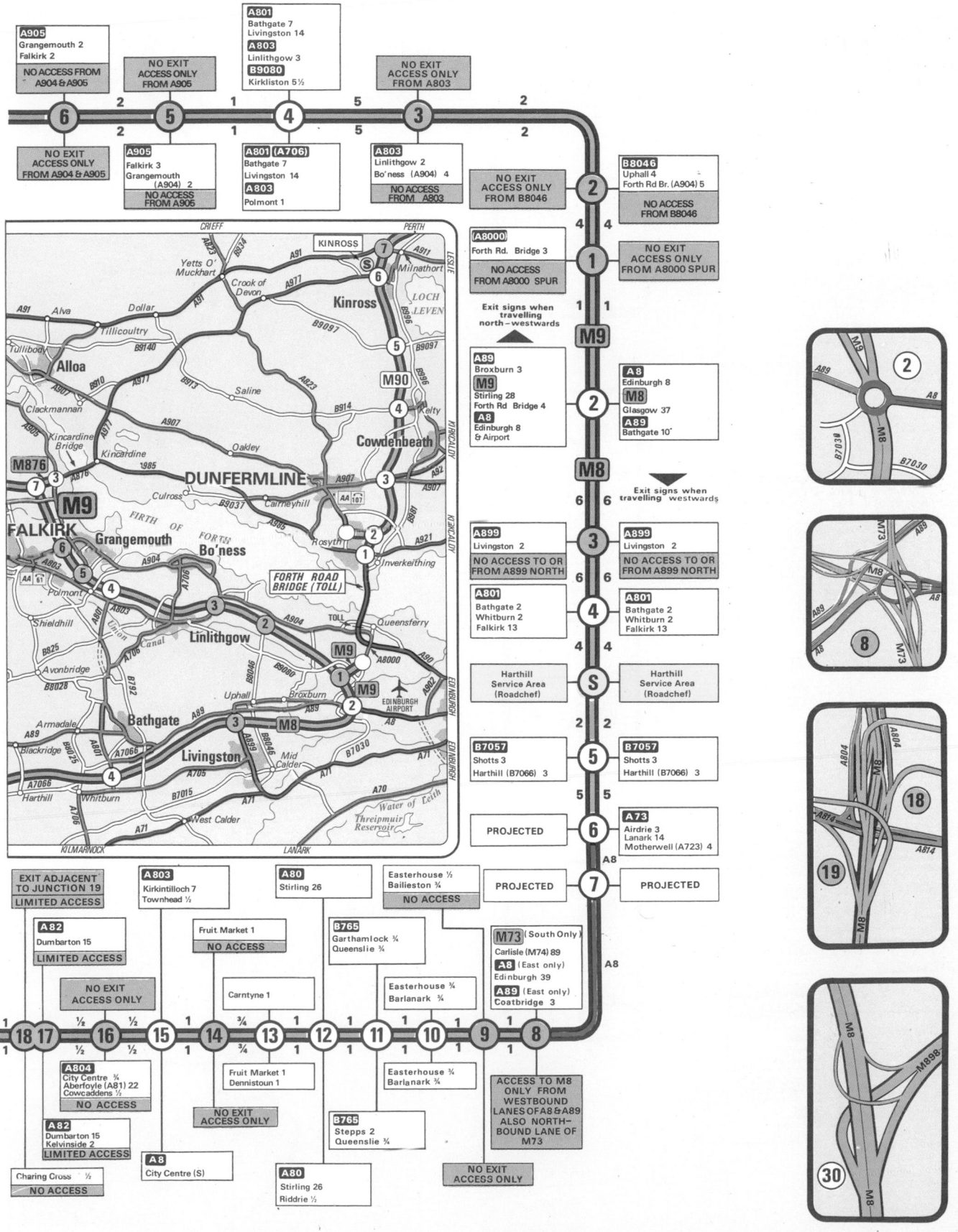

A905
Grangemouth 2
Falkirk 2
NO ACCESS FROM A904 & A905

A801
Bathgate 7
Livingston 14
A803
Linlithgow 3
B9080
Kirkliston 5½

NO EXIT
ACCESS ONLY
FROM A905

NO EXIT
ACCESS ONLY
FROM A803

6 2 **5** 1 **4** 5 **3** 2

2 2 1 5 2

NO EXIT
ACCESS ONLY
FROM A904 & A905

A905
Falkirk 3
Grangemouth
(A904) 2
NO ACCESS
FROM A905

A801 (A706)
Bathgate 7
Livingston 14
A803
Polmont 1

A803
Linlithgow 2
Bo'ness (A904) 4
NO ACCESS
FROM A803

NO EXIT
ACCESS ONLY
FROM B8046

B8046
Uphall 4
Forth Rd Br. (A904) 5
NO ACCESS
FROM B8046

2 2

4 4

(A8000)
Forth Rd. Bridge 3
NO ACCESS
FROM A8000 SPUR

NO EXIT
ACCESS ONLY
FROM A8000 SPUR

1

2

Exit signs when
travelling
north–westwards ▲

M9

1 1

A89
Broxburn 3
M9
Stirling 28
Forth Rd Bridge 4
A8
Edinburgh 8
& Airport

A8
Edinburgh 8
M8
Glasgow 37
A89
Bathgate 10

2

M8

Exit signs when
travelling westwards ▼

6 6

A899
Livingston 2
NO ACCESS TO OR
FROM A899 NORTH

A899
Livingston 2
NO ACCESS TO OR
FROM A899 NORTH

3

6 6

A801
Bathgate 2
Whitburn 2
Falkirk 13

A801
Bathgate 2
Whitburn 2
Falkirk 13

4

4 4

Harthill
Service Area
(Roadchef)

Harthill
Service Area
(Roadchef)

S

2 2

B7057
Shotts 3
Harthill (B7066) 3

B7057
Shotts 3
Harthill (B7066) 3

5

5 5

PROJECTED

A73
Airdrie 3
Lanark 14
Motherwell (A723) 4

6

PROJECTED

7

PROJECTED

A8

M73 (South Only)
Carlisle (M74) 89
A8 (East only)
Edinburgh 39
A89 (East only)
Coatbridge 3

A8

EXIT ADJACENT
TO JUNCTION 19
LIMITED ACCESS

A803
Kirkintilloch 7
Townhead ½
NO ACCESS

A80
Stirling 26

Easterhouse ½
Baillieston ¾
NO ACCESS

A82
Dumbarton 15
LIMITED ACCESS

Fruit Market 1
NO ACCESS

B765
Garthamlock ¾
Queenslie ¾

NO EXIT
ACCESS ONLY

Carntyne 1

Easterhouse ¾
Barlanark ¾

18 ½ **17** ½ **16** 1 **15** ¾ **14** 1 **13** 1 **12** 1 **11** 1 **10** 1 **9** 1 **8**

1 ½ ½ 1 ¾ 1 1 1 1

A804
City Centre ¾
Aberfoyle (A81) 22
Cowcaddens ½
NO ACCESS

Fruit Market 1
Denniston 1

Easterhouse ¾
Barlanark ¾

ACCESS TO M8
ONLY FROM
WESTBOUND
LANES OF A8 & A89
ALSO NORTH-
BOUND LANE OF
M73

A82
Dumbarton 15
Kelvinside 2
LIMITED ACCESS

A8
City Centre (S)

B765
Stepps 2
Queenslie ¾

Charing Cross ½
NO ACCESS

A80
Stirling 26
Riddrie ½

NO EXIT
ACCESS ONLY

2

8

18

19

30

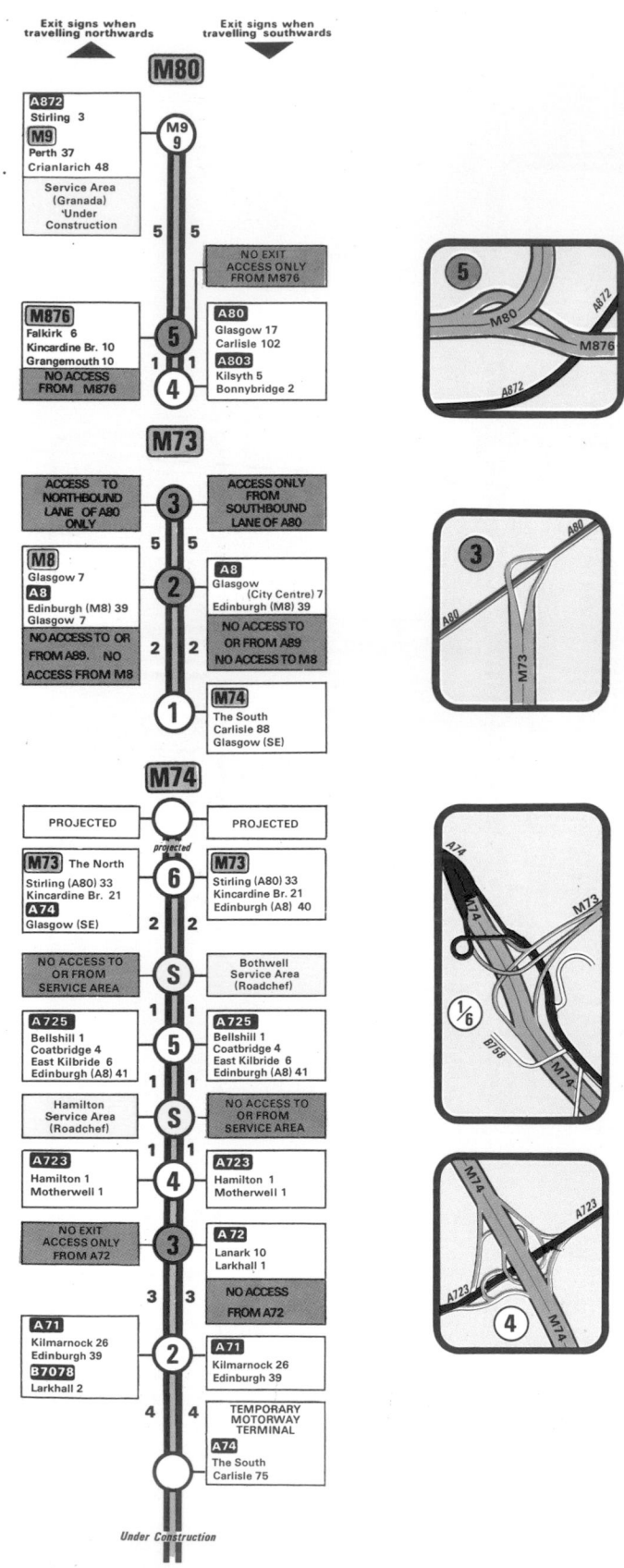

Exit signs when travelling northwards / **Exit signs when travelling southwards**

M80

Northbound		Southbound
A872 Stirling 3 **M9** Perth 37 Crianlarich 48 Service Area (Granada) Under Construction	M9 9	
	5 5	
		NO EXIT ACCESS ONLY FROM M876
M876 Falkirk 6 Kincardine Br. 10 Grangemouth 10 NO ACCESS FROM M876	5 / 1 1 / 4	**A80** Glasgow 17 Carlisle 102 **A803** Kilsyth 5 Bonnybridge 2

M73

Northbound		Southbound
ACCESS TO NORTHBOUND LANE OF A80 ONLY	3	ACCESS ONLY FROM SOUTHBOUND LANE OF A80
	5 5	
M8 Glasgow 7 **A8** Edinburgh (M8) 39 Glasgow 7 NO ACCESS TO OR FROM A89. NO ACCESS FROM M8	2 / 2 2	**A8** Glasgow (City Centre) 7 Edinburgh (M8) 39 NO ACCESS TO OR FROM A89 NO ACCESS TO M8
	1	**M74** The South Carlisle 88 Glasgow (SE)

M74

Northbound		Southbound
PROJECTED	○ projected	PROJECTED
M73 The North Stirling (A80) 33 Kincardine Br. 21 **A74** Glasgow (SE)	6 / 2 2	**M73** Stirling (A80) 33 Kincardine Br. 21 Edinburgh (A8) 40
NO ACCESS TO OR FROM SERVICE AREA	S	Bothwell Service Area (Roadchef)
A725 Bellshill 1 Coatbridge 4 East Kilbride 6 Edinburgh (A8) 41	1 / 5 / 1	**A725** Bellshill 1 Coatbridge 4 East Kilbride 6 Edinburgh (A8) 41
Hamilton Service Area (Roadchef)	S	NO ACCESS TO OR FROM SERVICE AREA
A723 Hamilton 1 Motherwell 1	4	**A723** Hamilton 1 Motherwell 1
NO EXIT ACCESS ONLY FROM A72	3	**A72** Lanark 10 Larkhall 1
	3 3	NO ACCESS FROM A72
A71 Kilmarnock 26 Edinburgh 39 **B7078** Larkhall 2	2 / 4 4	**A71** Kilmarnock 26 Edinburgh 39
		TEMPORARY MOTORWAY TERMINAL **A74** The South Carlisle 75

Under Construction

Inset diagrams: 5, 3, 1/6, 4

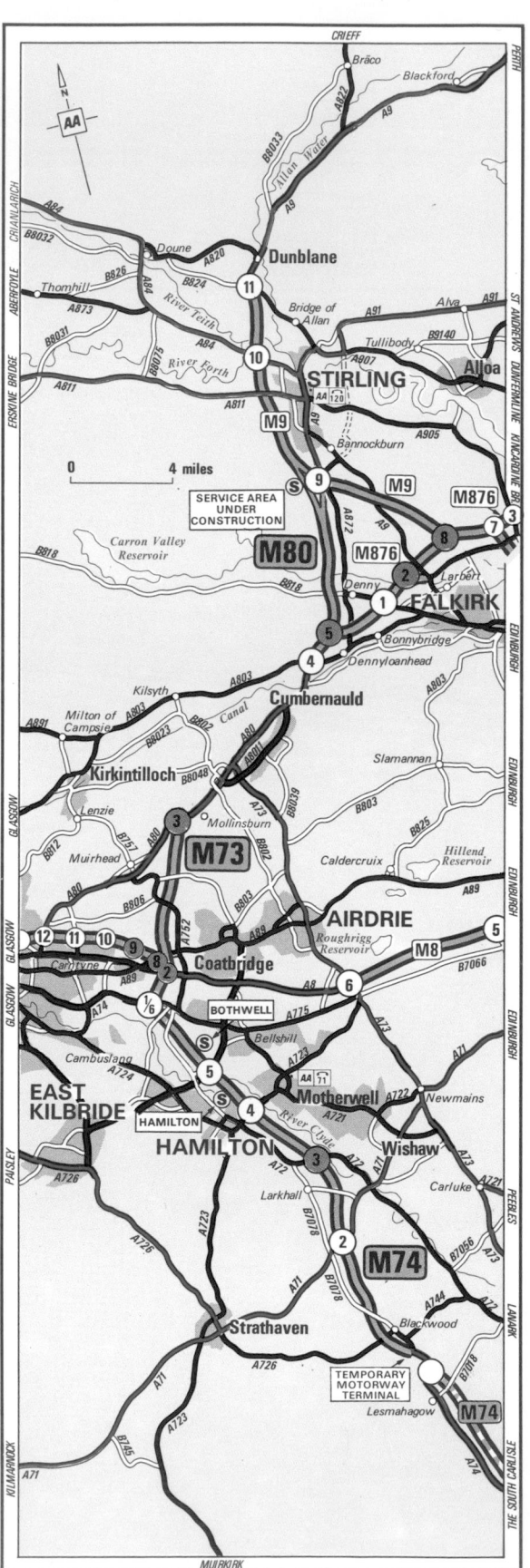

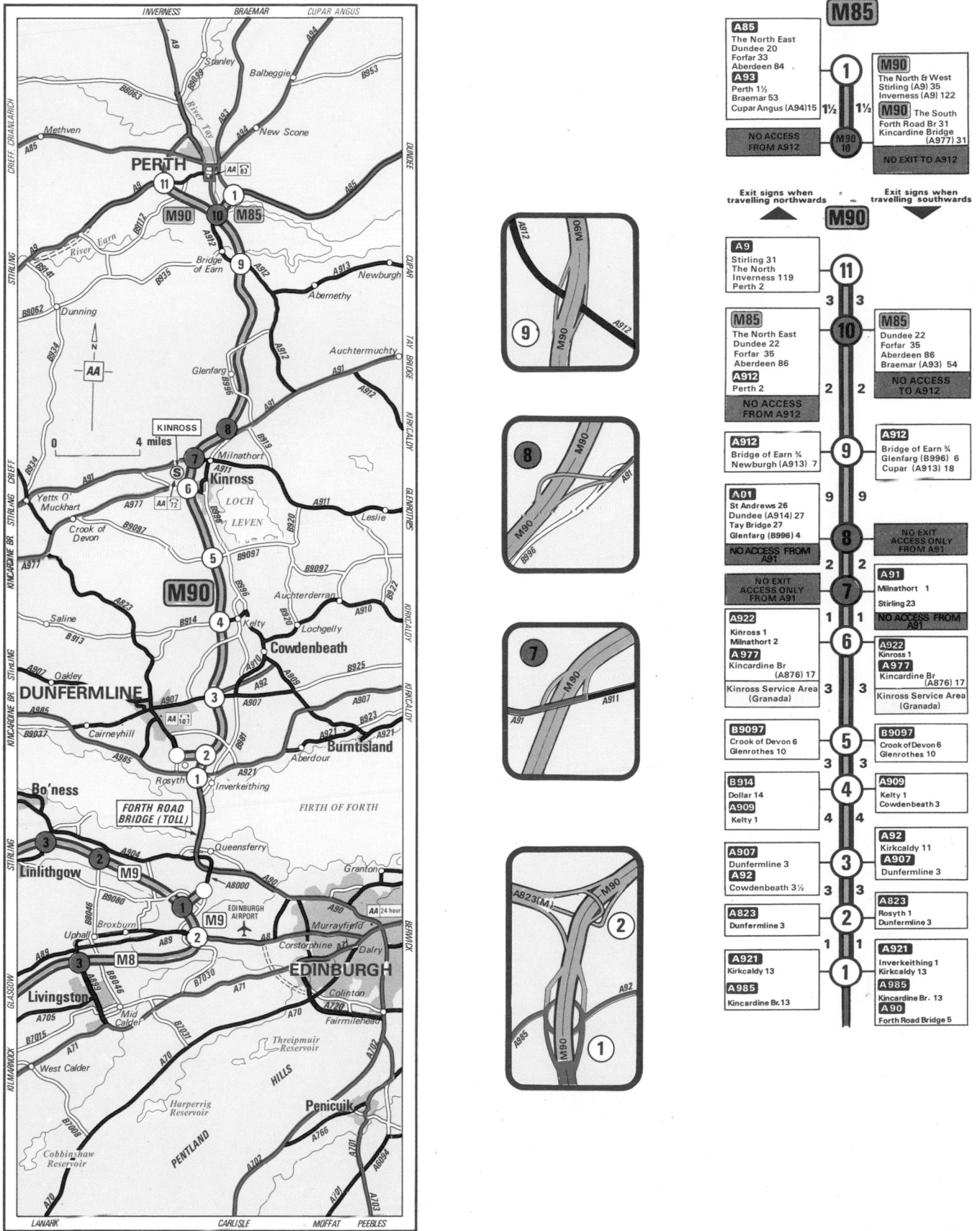

LEYLAND-COLNE M65

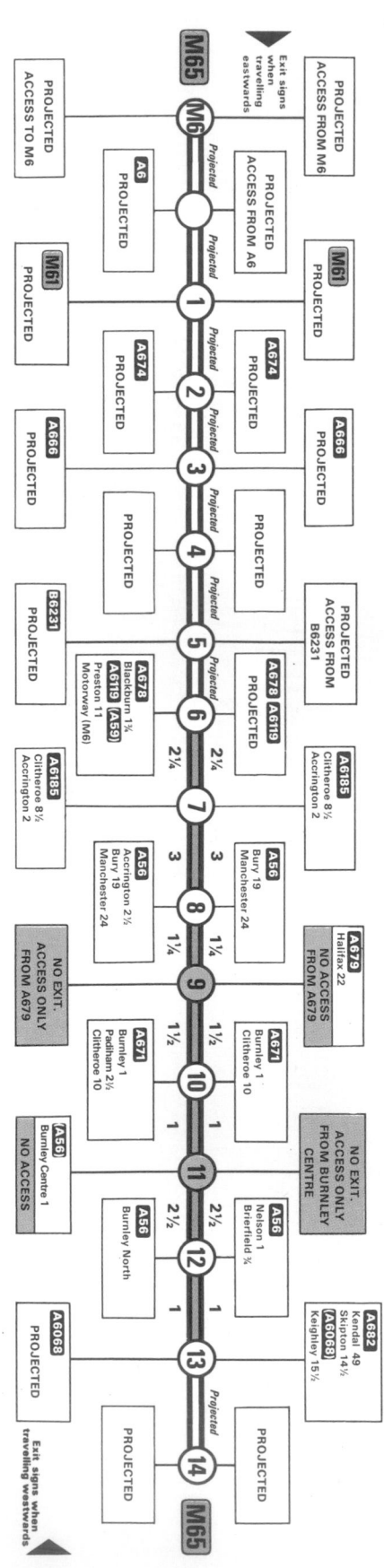

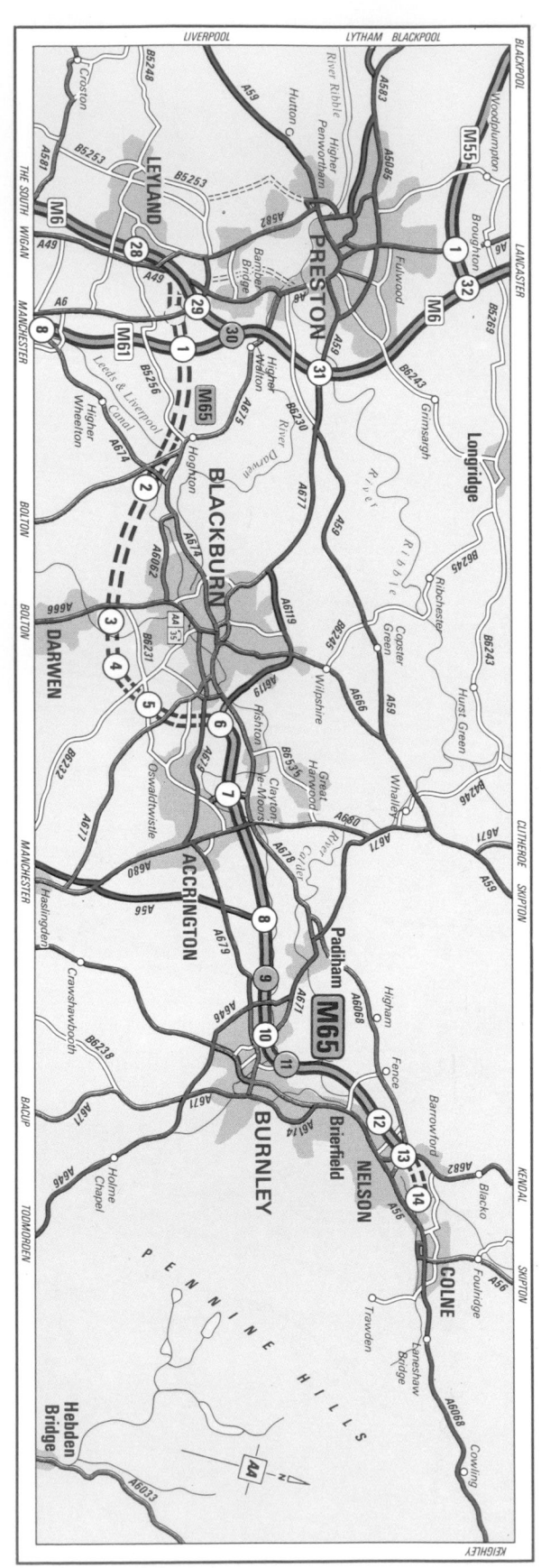

Aberdeen

Stirling

Greenock Glasgow Edinburgh
Paisley

Whitley Bay
Newcastle North Shields
Durham

York Beverley
Blackpool Leeds Hull

Liverpool Manchester
Sheffield
Chester Lincoln
Nottingham

Leicester
Nuneaton Hinckley Norwich
Ludlow Birmingham Coventry
Rugby Huntingdon
Ely
Stratford Cambridge

Witney Oxford
Swansea Neath Abingdon
Port Caerphilly
Talbot Cardiff Windsor Margate
Barry Bristol Ramsgate
Bath Canterbury

Salisbury Winchester Dover
Southampton Eastleigh Lewes
Poole Christchurch Hove Brighton
Bournemouth Chichester

Plymouth

Aberdeen

Granite gives Aberdeen its especial character; but this is not to say that the city is a grim or a grey place, the granites used are of many hues – white, blue, pink and grey. Although the most imposing buildings date from the 19th century, granite has been used to dramatic effect since at least as early as the 15th century. From that time dates St Machar's Cathedral, originally founded in AD580,

but rebuilt several times, especially after a devasting fire started on the orders of Edward III of England in 1336. St Machar's is in Old Aberdeen, traditionally the ecclesiastical and educational hub of the city, while 'New' Aberdeen (actually no newer) has always been the commercial centre. Even that definition is deceptive, for although Old Aberdeen has King's College, founded in 1494, New Aberdeen has Marischal College, founded almost exactly a century later (but rebuilt in 1844)

and every bit as distinguished as a seat of learning. Both establishments functioned as independent universities until they were merged in 1860 to form Aberdeen University. The North Sea oil boom has brought many changes to the city, some of which threatened its character. But even though high-rise buildings are now common, the stately façades, towers and pillars of granite still reign supreme and Union Street remains one of the best thoroughfares in Britain.

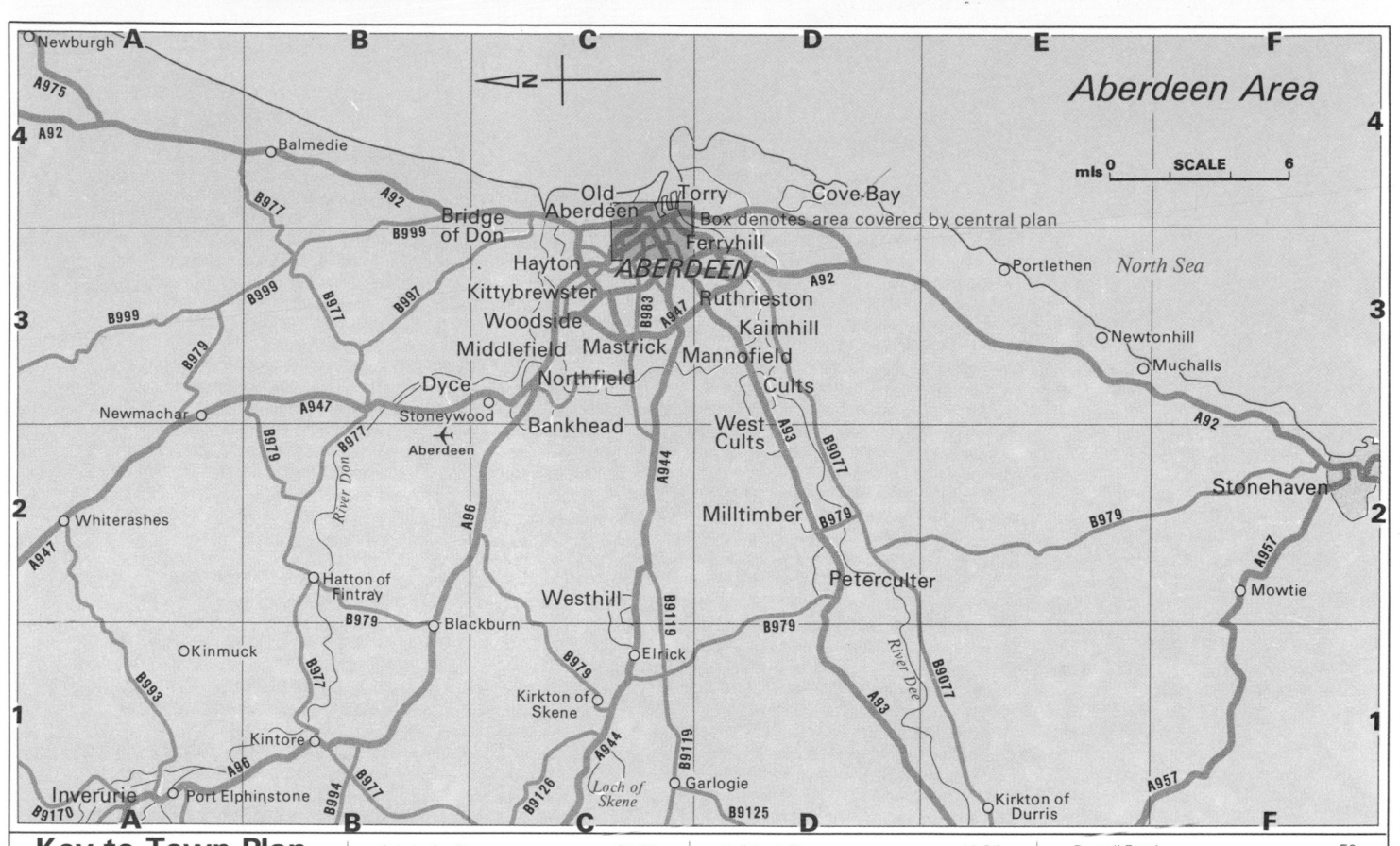

Aberdeen Area

Newburgh · Balmedie · Bridge of Don · Old Aberdeen · Torry · Cove Bay · Ferryhill · Portlethen · North Sea · Hayton · ABERDEEN · Kittybrewster · Ruthrieston · Woodside · Kaimhill · Middlefield · Mastrick · Mannofield · Newtonhill · Muchalls · Dyce · Northfield · Cults · Stoneywood · Bankhead · West Cults · Aberdeen · Milltimber · Stonehaven · Whiterashes · Peterculter · Mowtie · Hatton of Fintray · Westhill · Newmachar · Blackburn · Elrick · Kinmuck · Kirkton of Skene · Garlogie · Kintore · Loch of Skene · Kirkton of Durris · Inverurie · Port Elphinstone

mls 0 SCALE 6

Box denotes area covered by central plan

Roads: A975, A92, B977, B999, B997, A947, A96, B979, A944, B9119, B9126, B9125, B993, B9170, B994, B977, A957, B9077, A93, River Don, River Dee, A983, B983

Key to Town Plan and Area Plan

Town Plan
A A Recommended roads
Other roads
Restricted roads
Buildings of interest   Cinema
Car Parks   P
Parks and open spaces
A A Centre   AA
One Way Streets

Area Plan
A roads
B roads
Locations   Hattoncrook ○
Urban area

Street Index with Grid Reference

Aberdeen

Street	Grid
Abbotsford Lane	C2-D2
Academy Street	C4-D4
Advocates Road	E8
Affleck Street	D3
Albert Quay	F3
Albert Place	A5-A6
Albert Street	A4-A5
Albert Terrace	A4-A5
Albury Place	B2-C2
Albury Road	B2-C2-C3
Albyn Grove	A4
Albyn Lane	A3-A4-B4
Albyn Place	A4-B4
Alford Place	B4
Allan Street	A1-A2
Ann Street	C7-C8
Ashvale Place	A3-B3
Back Wyndd	D5
Baker Street	B6-C6
Balmoral Place	A1
Balmoral Road	A1-B1
Bank Street	D2
Beach Boulavard	F6
Belgrave Terrace	A6
Belmont Street	D5
Berryden Road	B8-C8
Bethany Gardens	B2
Blackfriars Street	D6
Bloomfield Place	A2-A1-B1
Bloomfield Road	A1-B1
Bon-Accord Crescent	C3-C4
Bon-Accord Crescent Lane	C3-C4
Bon-Accord Square	C4
Bon-Accord Street	C2-C3-C4
Bridge Place	D4
Broad Street	E5-E6
Broomhill Road	A1-A2
Caledonian Lane	C2

Street	Grid
Caledonian Place	C2-C3
Canal Road	D8
Canal Street	D8-E8
Carden Place	A5
Carmelite Street	D4
Caroline Place	B8-C8-C7
Castle Street	E5-F5
Castle Terrace	F5
Causeway End	D8
Chapel Street	B4-B5
Charles Street	C8-D8
Charlotte Street	C7-D7-D6
Claremont Street	A3
Clyde Street	F2-F3
College Street	D3-D4
Commerce Street	F4-F5
Commercial Quay	E3-F3
Constitution Street	F6
Cornhill Road	A8
Craibstone Lane	C3-C4
Craigie Loanings	A5-A6
Craigie Street	D7
Crimon Street	C5
Crombie Place	F1-F2
Crombie Road	F2
Crown Street	D2-D3-D4-C4
Crown Terrace	D3-D4
Cuparstone Row	A3-B3
Dee Place	C3-D3
Dee Street	C3-C4
Deemont road	C1-D1
Denburn Road	D5
Denburn Viaduct	C5-D5
Devanha Gardens	C1
Devanha Terrace	D1-D2
Diamond Street	C5-D5
Duff Street	F6-F7
East North Street	E6-F6
Errol Street	F8
Esslemont Avenue	A6-B6-B5
Exchange Street	E4-E5
Farmers Hill	C6-C7
Ferryhill Place	C2
Ferryhill Road	C2-D2
Ferryhill Terrace	C2-D2
Fonthill Road	A2-B2-C2
Fonthill Terrace	B1-B2
Forbes Street	B7-C7
Fraser Place	C8-D8
Fraser Road	C8
Fraser Street	C8
Frederick Street	E6-F6
Gallowgate	D7-E7-E6
George Street	C8-D8-D7-D6-D5
Gerrard Street	D7
Gilcomston Park	F1
Glenbervie Road	F1
Golden Square	C5
Gordon Street	C3-C4
Grampian Road	E1-F1
Great Southern Road	A1-B2-B1
Great Western Place	A3
Great Western Road	A2-A3
Grosvenor Place	A6
Guild Street	D4-E4
Hadden Street	E5
Hanover Street	F5-F6
Hardgate	A1-A2-B2-B3-B4
Hill Street	C7
Holburn Road	A2
Holburn Street	A1-A2-A3-B3-B4
Holland Street	C8

Street	Grid
Hollybank Place	A3-B3
Howburn Place	A3-B3-B2
Huntley Street	B5-C5-C4
Hutcheon Street	B8-C8-D8
Innes Street	D7-E7
Irvine Place	A2
James Street	F4-F5
Jasmine Place	F7
Jasmine Terrace	E7-F7
John Street	C6-D6-D7
Jopp's Lane	D6-D7
Justice Street	E5-F5-F6
Justice Mill Lane	B4
Jute Street	D8-E8
Kidd Street	B5-C5
King Street	E5-E6-E7-E8-F8
Kintore Place	B6-B7-C7
Langstone Place	C4
Leaside Road	B6
Lemon Street	F6
Little John Street	E6
Loanhead Terrace	A7
Loch Street	D6-D7
Maberley Street	C7-D7
Margaret Street	B5
Marischal Street	E5-F5-F4
Market Street	E3-E4-E5
Marywell Street	D3
Meal Market Street	E6
Mearns Street	F4-F5
Menzies Road	E1-E2-F2
Millburn Street	D2
Minster Lane	B5-C5
Mountholly	E7-E8
Mount Street	B7-B8
Nellfield Place	A2
Nelson Street	E7-E8
North Esplanade East	E3-F3
North Esplanade West	D1-D2-E2-E3
North Silver Street	C5
Northfield Place	B6
Old Ford Road	D2
Osborne Place	A5
Oscar Road	F1
Palmerston Place	D2
Palmerston Road	D2-D3-E3
Park Place	F6
Park Road	F7
Park Street	F6-F7
Polmuir Road	C1-C2
Portland Street	D2-D3
Poynernook Road	D2-E2-E3
Princes Street	E6-F6
Prospect Terrace	D1-D2
Queen Street	E5-E6
Raeburn Place	C6
Raik Road	E2-E3
Regent Road	F3-F4
Regent Quay	E5-F5
Rennies Wyndd	D4
Richmond Street	B6-B7
Richmond Terrace	B7
Riverside Drive	D1
Rose Street	B4-B5
Rosebank Place	B3
Rosebank Terrace	C3-D3
Rosemount Place	A7-A6-B6-B7 C7
Rosemount Terrace	B7-B8
Rosemount Viaduct	B6-C6-C5
Roslin Street	F7-F8
Roslin Terrace	E7-F7
Rubislaw Terrace	A4

Street	Grid
Russell Road	E2
St Andrew Street	C6-D6
St Clair Street	E7
St John's Place	D4
St Mary's Place	F2
St Nicholas Street	D5-E6
St Paul Street	D6-E6
School Hill	D5
Seaforth Road	F8
Ship Row	E4-E5
Short Loanings	B6
Sinclair Road	F2
Skene Square	C6-C7
Skene Street	A5-B5-C5
Skene Terrace	C5
South College Street	D1-D2-D3
South Crown Street	C1-D1-D2
South Esplanade East	F2
South Esplanade West	E1-E2
South Mount Street	B6-B7
Spa Street	C6
Spital Kings Crescent	E8
Spring Garden	D7
Spring Bank Street	C3-D3
Spring Bank Terrace	C3-D3
Stell Road	E3
Stirling Street	D4-E4
Summer Street	B4-B5-C5
Summerfield Terrace	E6-F6
Sycamore Place	B1-C1
The Green	D4-D5
Thistle Lane	B4-B5
Thistle Street	B4
Thomson Street	A7
Trinity Quay	E4
Upper Denburn	B6-C6
Upper Kirkgate	D5-D6-E6
Urquhart Lane	F7-F8
Urquhart Place	F7
Urquhart Road	F7
Urquhart Street	F7-F8
Union Bridge	D4-D5
Union Glen	B3
Union Grove	A3-B3
Union Row	B4-C4
Union Street	B4-C4-D4-D5
Union Terrace	C5-D5
Victoria Bridge	E3-E2-F2
Victoria Road	F1-F2
Victoria Street	A5-B4-B5
Virginia Street	E5-F5
Wales Street	F6
Walker Road	E1-F1
Wallfield Place	A6-A7
Watson Street	A7-A8
Waverley Lane	A4-A5
Waverley Place	A4-B4
Wellington Road	D3
West Mount Street	B7
West North Street	E6-E7-E8
Westburn Road	A8-B8
Whinhill Road	B1-C1-C2
Whitehall Place	A5-A6-B6
Willow Bank Road	B3-C3
Willowdale Place	E7
Windmill Brae	C4-D4
Woolmanhill	C6-D6

155

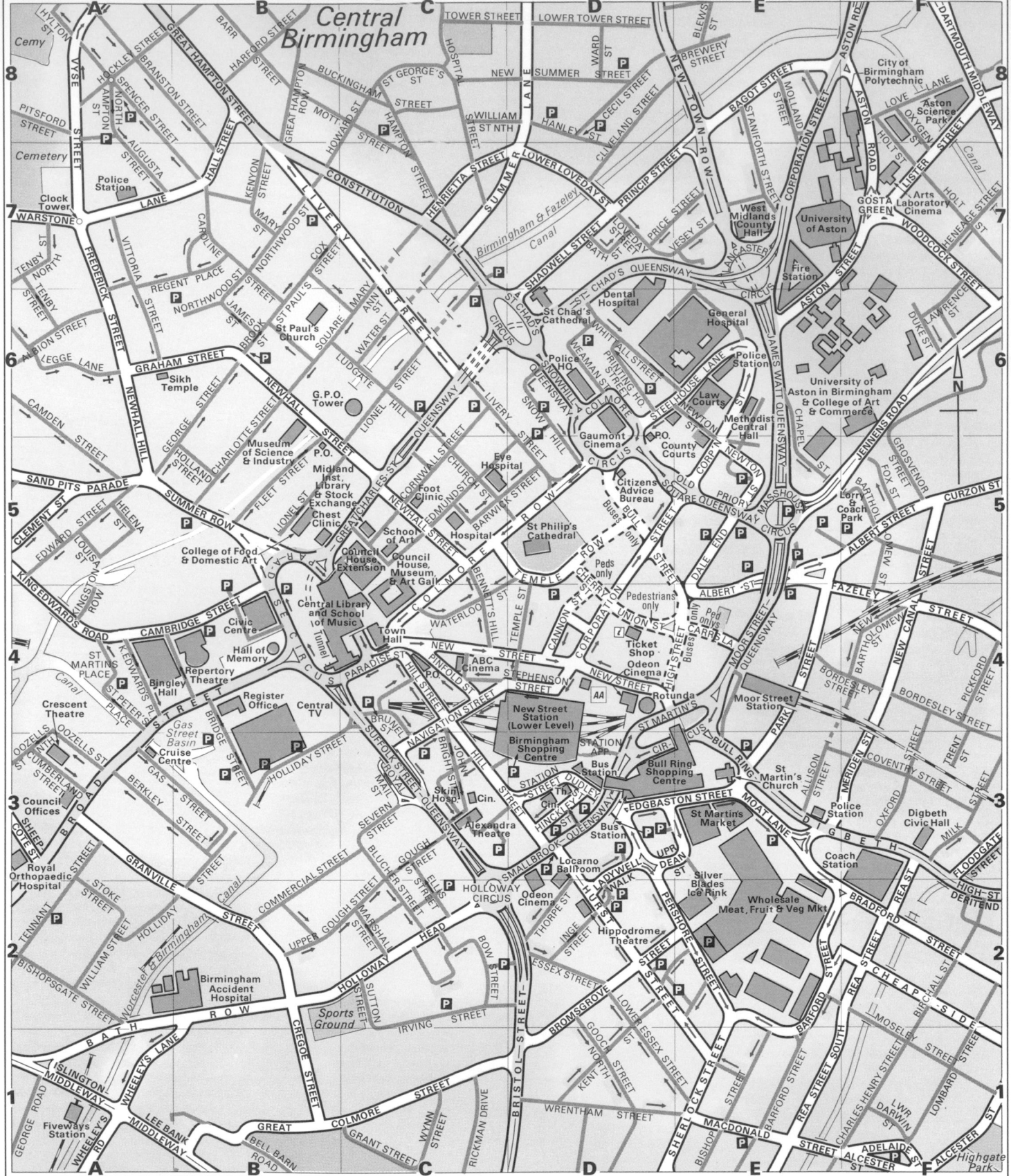

Birmingham

It is very difficult to visualise Birmingham as it was before it began the growth which eventually made it the second-largest city in England. When the Romans were in Britain it was little more than a staging post on Icknield Street. Throughout medieval times it was a sleepy agricultural centre in the middle of a heavily-forested region. Timbered houses clustered together round a green that was

eventually to be called the Bull Ring. But by the 16th century, although still a tiny and unimportant village by today's standards, it had begun to gain a reputation as a manufacturing centre. Tens of thousands of sword blades were made here during the Civil War. Throughout the 18th century more and more land was built on. In 1770 the Birmingham Canal was completed, making trade very much easier and increasing the town's development dramatically. All of that pales into near

insignificance compared with what happened in the 19th century. Birmingham was not represented in Parliament until 1832 and had no town council until 1838. Yet by 1889 it had already been made a city, and after only another 20 years it had become the second largest city in England. Many of Birmingham's most imposing public buildings date from the 19th century, when the city was growing so rapidly. Surprisingly, the city has more miles of waterway than Venice.

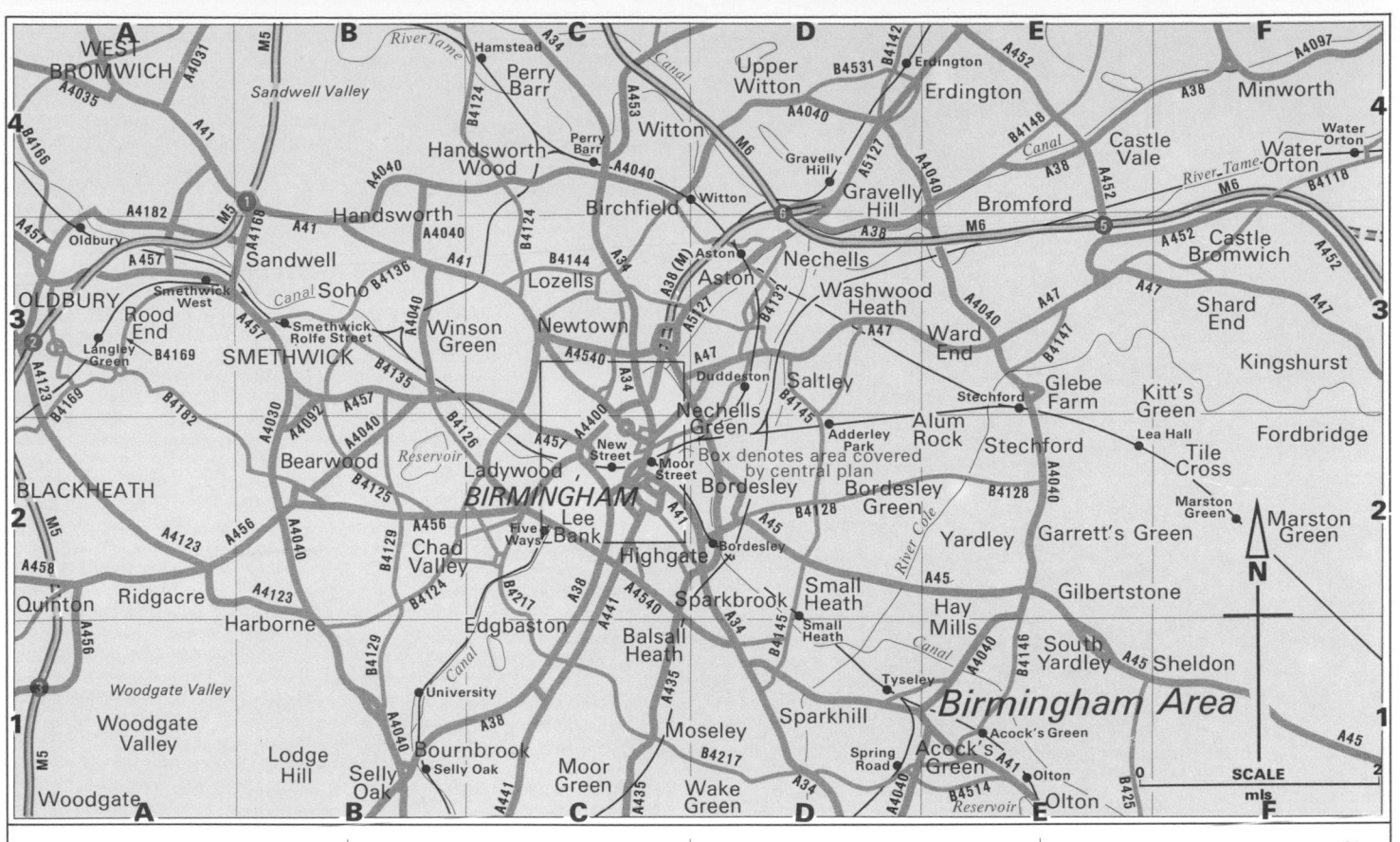

Key to Town Plan and Area Plan

Town Plan

AA Recommended roads	≡
Restricted roads	≡
Other roads	≡
Buildings of interest	Station ▢
AA Service Centre	AA
Car Parks	P
Parks and open spaces	▢
One Way Streets	→

Area Plan

A roads	—
B roads	—
Locations	Meer End○

Street Index with Grid Reference

Birmingham

Adelaide Street	F1
Albert Street	E4-E5-F5
Albion Street	A6
Alcester Street	F1
Allison Street	E3
Aston Road	E8-F8-F7
Aston Street	E6-E7-F7
Augusta Street	A7-A8
Bagot Street	E8
Barford Street	E1-E2-F2
Barr Street	B8
Bartholomew Street	F4-F5
Barwick Street	C5-D5
Bath Row	A1-A2-B2
Bath Street	D7
Bell Barn Road	B1
Bennett's Hill	C4-C5
Berkley Street	A3-B3
Birchall Street	F1-F2
Bishop Street	E1
Bishopsgate Street	A2
Blews Street	E8
Blucher Street	C2-C3
Bordesley Street	E4-F4-F3
Bow Street	C2
Bradford Street	E3-E2-F2
Branston Street	A8-B8-B7
Brewery Street	E8
Bridge Street	B3-B4
Bristol Street	C1-D1-D2-C2
Broad Street	A2-A3-A4-B4
Bromsgrove Street	D1-D2-E2
Brook Street	B6
Brunel Street	C3-C4
Buckingham Street	B8-C7-C8
Bull Ring	E3
Bull Street	D5-E5 E4
Cambridge Street	A4-B4-B5
Camden Street	A5-A6
Cannon Street	D4
Caroline Street	B6-B7
Carrs Street	E4
Cecil Street	D8
Chapel Street	E5-E6
Charles Henry Street	F1
Charlotte Street	B5-B6
Cheapside	F1-F2
Cherry Street	D4-D5
Church Street	C6-C5-D5
Clement Street	A5
Cliveland Street	D7-D8-E8
Colmore Circus	D5-D6
Colmore Row	C4-C5-D5
Commercial Street	B2-B3-C3
Constitution Hill	B7-C7
Cornwall Street	C5-C6
Corporation Street	D4-D5-E5-E6-E7-E8
Coventry Street	E3-F3
Cox Street	B7
Cregoe Street	B1-B2
Cumberland Street	A3
Curzon Street	F5
Dale End	E4-E5
Dartmouth Middleway	F7-F8
Digbeth	E3-F3
Dudley Street	D3
Duke Street	F6
Edgbaston Street	D3-E3
Edmund Street	C5-D5
Edward Street	A5
Ellis Street	C2-C3
Essex Street	D2
Fazeley Street	E5-E4-F4
Fleet Street	B5
Floodgate Street	F3
Fox Street	F5
Frederick Street	A6-A7
Gas Street	A3-B3
George Road	A1
George Street	A5-B5-B6
Gooch Street North	D1-D2
Gosta Green	F7
Gough Street	C3
Graham Street	A6-B6
Grant Street	C1
Granville Street	A3-A2-B2
Great Charles St Queensway	B5-C5-C6
Great Colmore Street	B1-C1-D1
Great Hampton Row	B8
Great Hampton Street	A8-B8
Grosvenor Street	F5-F6
Hall Street	B7-B8
Hampton Street	C7-C8
Hanley Street	D7-D8
Helena Street	A5
Heneage Street	F7
Henrietta Street	C7-D7
High Street	D4-E4
High Street Deritend	F2-F3
Hill Street	C4-C3-D3
Hinckley Street	D3
Hockley Street	A8-B8
Holland Street	B5
Holliday Street	A2-B2-B3-C3-C4
Holloway Circus	C2-C3-D3-D2
Holloway Head	B2-C2
Hult Street	F7-F8
Hospital Street	C7-C8
Howard Street	B7-C7-C8
Hurst Street	D3-D2-E2-E1
Hylton Street	A8
Inge Street	D2
Irving Street	C2-D2
Islington Middleway	A1
James Street	B6
James Watt Queensway	E5-E6
Jennens Road	E5-F5-F6
John Bright Street	C3-C4
Kent Street	D1-D2
Kenyon Street	B7
King Edward's Place	A4
King Edward's Road	A4-A5
Kingston Row	A4
Ladywell Walk	D2-D3
Lancaster Circus	E6-E7
Lawrence Street	F6-F7
Lee Bank Middleway	A1-B1
Legge Lane	A6
Lionel Street	B5-C5-C6
Lister Street	F7-F8
Livery Street	B7-C7-C6-D6-D5
Lombard Street	F1-F2
Louisa Street	A5
Love Lane	F8
Loveday Street	D7
Lower Darwin Street	F1
Lower Essex Street	D2-D1-E1
Lower Loveday Street	D7
Lower Tower Street	D8
Ludgate Hill	B6-C6
Macdonald Street	E1-F1
Marshall Street	C2
Mary Street	B7
Mary Ann Street	C6-C7
Masshouse Circus	E5
Meriden Street	E3-F3
Milk Street	F3
Moat Lane	E3
Molland Street	E8
Moor Street Queensway	E4-E5
Moseley Street	E2-F2-F1
Mott Street	B8-C8-C7
Navigation Street	C3-C4
New Street	C4-D4
New Bartholomew Street	F4
New Canal Street	F4-F5
Newhall Hill	A5-A6
Newhall Street	B6-B5-C5
New Summer Street	C8-D8
Newton Street	E5
New Town Row	D8-E8-E7
Northampton Street	A8
Northwood Street	B6-B7
Old Square	D5-E5
Oozells Street	A3-A4
Oozells Street North	A3-A4
Oxford Street	F3-F4
Oxygen Street	F7-F8
Paradise Circus	B4-B5
Paradise Street	B4-C4
Park Street	E3-E4
Pershore Street	D3-D2-E2
Pickford Street	F4
Pinfold Street	C4
Pitsford Street	A8
Price Street	D7-F7
Princip Street	D7-E7-E8
Printing House Street	D6
Priory Queensway	E5
Rea Street	E2-F2-F3
Rea Street South	E1-F1-F2
Regent Place	A7-B7
Rickman Drive	C1
Royal Mail Street	C3
St Chad's Circus	C7-C6-D6
St Chad's Queensway	D6-D7-F7
St George's Street	C8
St Martin's Circus	D3-D4-E4-E3
St Martin's Place	A4
St Paul's Square	B7-B6-C6
St Peter's Place	A4
Sand Pits Parade	A5
Severn Street	C3
Shadwell Street	D6-D7
Sheepcote Street	A3
Sherlock Street	D1-E1-E2
Smallbrook Queensway	C3-D3
Snow Hill	D5-D6
Snow Hill Queensway	D6
Spencer Street	A8-A7-B7
Staniforth Street	E7-E8
Station Approach	D3
Station Street	D3
Steelhouse Lane	D6-E6
Stephenson Street	C4-D4
Stoke Street	A2-A3
Suffolk Street Queensway	B4-C4-C3
Summer Row	A5-B5
Summer Lane	C7-D7-D8
Sutton Street	C2
Temple Row	C5-D5
Temple Street	D4-D5-D5
Tenby Street	A6-A7
Tenby Street North	A7
Tennant Street	A2-A3
Thorpe Street	D2-D3
Tower Street	C8-D8
Trent Street	F3-F4
Union Street	D4
Upper Dean Street	D3-E3
Upper Gough Street	B2-C2-C3
Vesey Street	D7-E7
Vittoria Street	A6-A7
Vyse Street	A7-A8
Ward Street	D8
Warford Street	B8
Warstone Lane	A7-B7
Water Street	C6
Waterloo Street	C4-C5-D5
Weaman Street	D6
Wheeley's Lane	A1-B1-B2
Wheeley's Road	A1
Whittall Street	D6-E6
William Street	A2
William Street North	C8-D8
Woodcock Street	F6-F7
Wrentham Street	D1-E1
Wynn Street	C1

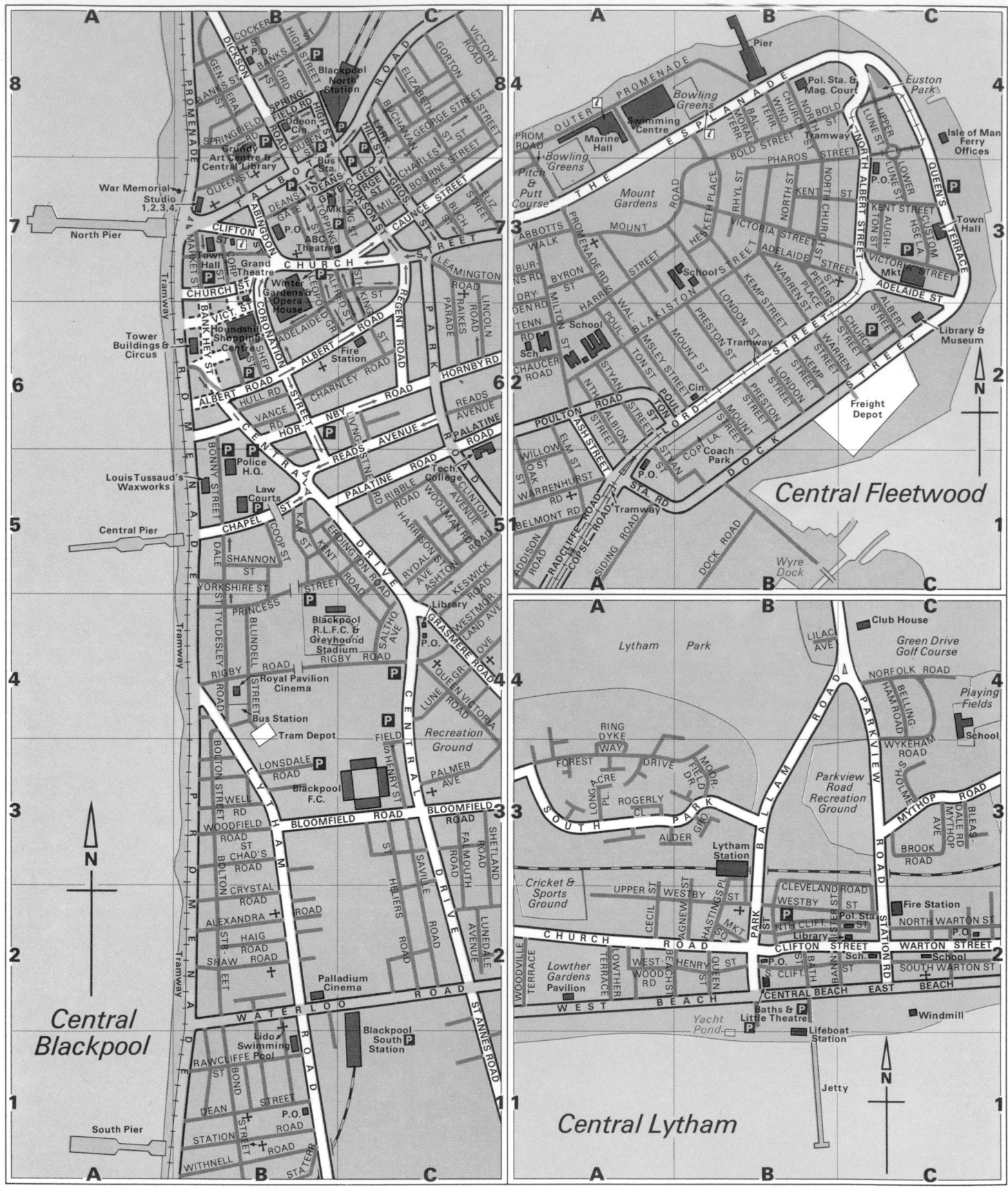

Blackpool

No seaside resort is regarded with greater affection than Blackpool. It is still the place where millions of North Country folk spend their holidays; its famous illuminations draw visitors from all over the world. It provides every conceivable kind of traditional holiday entertainment, and in greater abundance than any other seaside resort in Britain. The famous tower – built in the 1890s as a replica of the Eiffel Tower – the three piers, seven miles of promenade, five miles of illuminations, countless guesthouses, huge numbers of pubs, shops, restaurants and cafes play host to eight million visitors a year.

At the base of the tower is a huge entertainment complex that includes a ballroom, a circus and an aquarium. Other 19th-century landmarks are North Pier and Central Pier, the great Winter Gardens and Opera House and the famous trams that still run along the promenade – the only electric trams still operating in Britain. The most glittering part of modern Blackpool is the famous Golden Mile, packed with amusements, novelty shops and snack stalls. Every autumn it becomes part of the country's most extravagant light show – the illuminations – when the promenade is ablaze with neon representations of anything and everything from moon rockets to the Muppets. Autumn is also the time when Blackpool is a traditional venue for political party conferences.

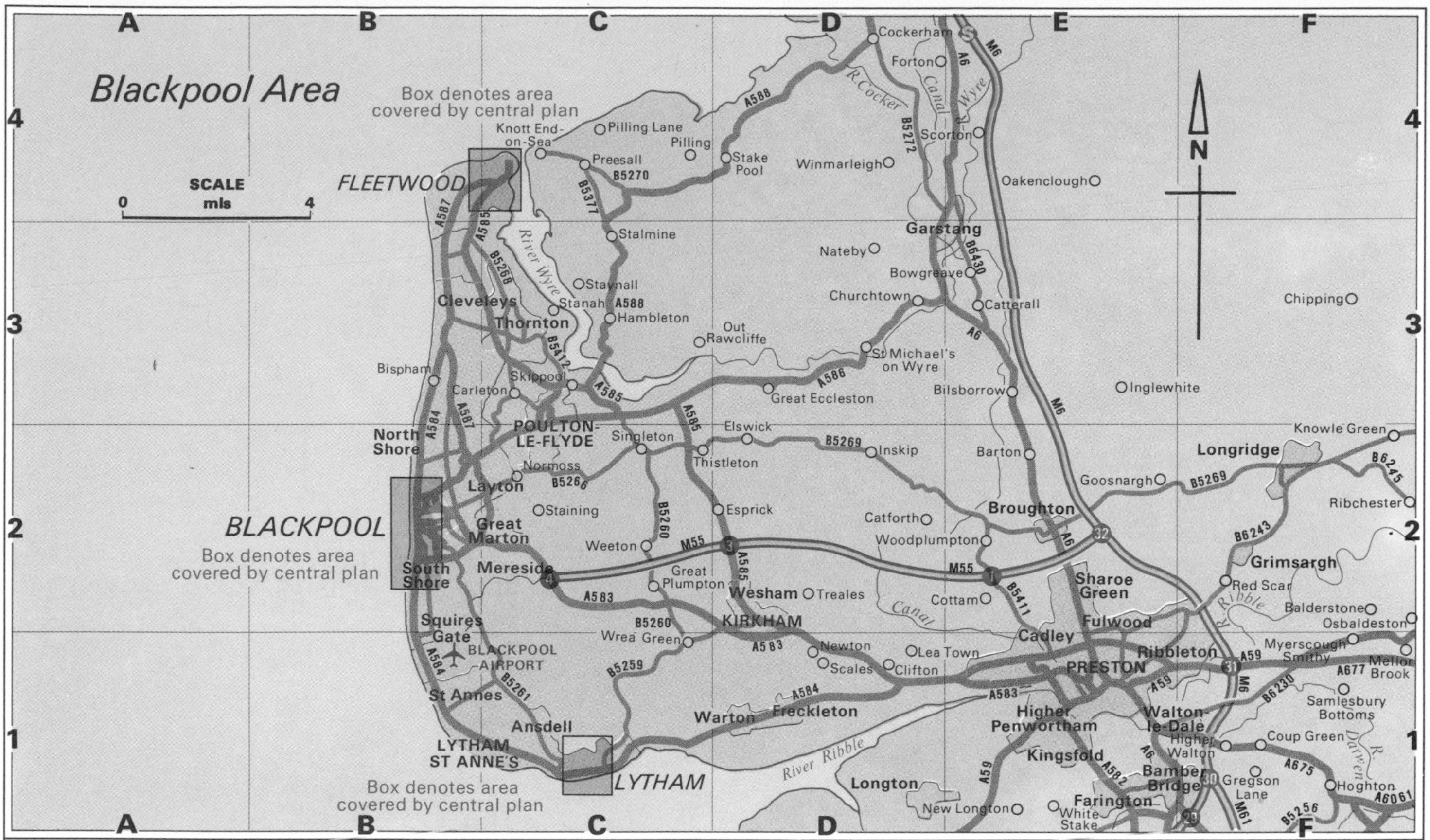

Blackpool Area

Box denotes area covered by central plan

FLEETWOOD

SCALE
mls
0 — 4

BLACKPOOL
Box denotes area covered by central plan

Box denotes area covered by central plan
LYTHAM

N

(Map labels include:) Cockerham, Forton, Pilling Lane, Pilling, Preesall, Knott End-on-Sea, Stake Pool, Winmarleigh, Oakenclough, Scorton, Garstang, Chipping, Stalmine, Nateby, Bowgreave, Staynall, Churchtown, Catterall, Stanah, Cleveleys, Thornton, Hambleton, Out Rawcliffe, St Michael's on Wyre, Bilsborrow, Inglewhite, Bispham, Carleton, Skippool, Great Eccleston, Knowle Green, North Shore, POULTON-LE-FLYDE, Singleton, Elswick, Inskip, Barton, Goosnargh, Longridge, Ribchester, Normoss, Thistleton, Grimsargh, Layton, Staining, Esprick, Catforth, Broughton, Red Scar, Balderstone, Osbaldeston, BLACKPOOL, Great Marton, Weeton, Great Plumpton, Woodplumpton, Mereside, Wesham, Treales, Cottam, Sharoe Green, Myerscough Smithy, Mellor Brook, South Shore, Squires Gate, KIRKHAM, Wrea Green, Newton, Lea Town, Cadley, Fulwood, Ribbleton, PRESTON, Scales, Clifton, BLACKPOOL AIRPORT, St Annes, Warton, Freckleton, Higher Penwortham, Walton-le-Dale, Higher Walton, Coup Green, Hoghton, Ansdell, LYTHAM ST ANNE'S, LYTHAM, River Ribble, Longton, Kingsfold, Bamber Bridge, Gregson Lane, Farington, New Longton, White Stake, River Wyre, River Cocker, Canal, Ribble, Darwen

---

LEGEND

Town Plan

AA recommended route	
Restricted roads	
Other roads	
Buildings of interest	School
Car parks	P
Parks and open spaces	
One way streets	

Area Plan

A roads	
B roads	
Locations	Wrea Green O
Urban area	

Street Index with Grid Reference

Blackpool

Abingdon Street	B7
Adelaide Street	B6-B7-C7
Albert Road	B6-C6
Alexandra Road	B2
Alfred Street	B7-C7-C6
Ashton Road	C4-C5
Bank Hey Street	B6-B7
Banks Street	B8
Bloomfield Road	B3-C3
Blundell Street	B4
Bolton Street	B2-B3-B4
Bond Street	B1-B2
Bonny Street	B5-B6
Buchanan Street	C7-C8
Caunce Street	C7-C8
Central Drive	B6-B5-C5-C4-C3-C2
Chapel Street	B5
Charles Street	C7-C8
Charnley Road	B6-C6
Church Street	B7-C7
Clifton Street	B7
Clinton Avenue	C5
Cocker Street	B8
Cookson Street	B8-B7-C7
Coop Street	B5
Coronation Street	B5-B6-B7
Corporation Street	B7
Crystal Road	B2
Dale Street	B4-B5
Deansgate	B7-C7
Dean Street	B1
Dickson Road	B7-B8
Erdington Road	B5-C5-C4
Elizabeth Street	C7-C8
Falmouth Road	C2-C3
Field Street	C3
General Street	B8
George Street	C7-C8
Gorton Street	C8
Grasmere Road	C4
Grosvenor Street	C7
Haig Road	B2
Harrison Street	C5
Henry Street	C3
High Street	B8
Hornby Road	B6-C6
Hull Road	B6
Kay Street	B5
Kent Road	B5-C5-C4
Keswick Road	C4-C5
King Street	C7
Larkhill Street	C8
Leamington Road	C7
Leopold Grove	B7-B6-C6
Lincoln Road	C6-C7
Livingstone Road	C5-C6
Lonsdale Road	B3
Lord Street	B8
Lunedale Avenue	C2
Lune Grove	C4
Lytham Road	B1-B2-B3-B4
Market Street	B7
Milbourne Street	C7-C8
Osbourne Road	B1
Palatine Road	B5-C5-C6
Palmer Avenue	C3
Park Road	C5-C6-C7
Princess Parade	A7-A8-B8-B7
Princess Street	B4-B5-C5
Promenade	B1-B2-B3-B4-B5-B6-A6-A7-B7-B8
Queen Street	B7-B8
Queen Victoria Road	C3-C4
Raikes Parade	C6-C7
Rawcliffe Street	B1
Reads Avenue	B5-C5-C6
Regent Road	C6-C7
Ribble Road	C5
Rigby Road	B4-C4
Rydal Avenue	C5
St Annes Road	C1-C2
St Chad's Road	B3
St Heliers Road	C2-C3
Salthouse Avenue	C4
Saville Road	C2-C3
Shannon Street	B5
Shaw Road	B2
Sheppard Street	B6
Shetland Road	C2-C3
South King Street	C6-C7
Springfield Road	B8
Station Road	B1
Station Terrace	B1
Talbot Road	B7-B8-C8
Topping Street	B7
Tyldesley Road	B4
Vance Road	B6
Victoria Street	B6
Victory Road	C8
Waterloo Road	B2-C2
Wellington Road	B3
Westmorland Avenue	C4
Woodfield Road	B3
Woolman Road	C5
Yorkshire Street	B5

Fleetwood

Abbotts Walk	A3
Adelaide Street	B3-C3-C2
Addison Road	A1
Albert Street	C2-C3
Ash Street	A1-A2
Aughton Street	C3
Balmoral Terrace	B4
Belmont Street	B4
Blakiston Street	A2-B2-B3
Bold Street	B4-C4
Burns Road	A3
Byron Street	A3
Chaucer Road	A2
Church Street	C2
Cop Lane	A1-B1-B2
Copse Road	A1
Custom House Lane	C3
Dock Road	B1
Dock Street	B1-B2-C2
Dryden Road	A2-A3
Elm Street	A1-A2
Harris Street	A2-A3-B3
Hesketh Place	B3
Kemp Street	B2-B3
Kent Street	B3-C3
London Street	B2-B3
Lord Street	A1-A2-B2-C2-C3
Lower Lune Street	C3
Milton Street	A2-A3
Mount Road	A3-B3
Mount Street	A2-B2
North Albert Street	C3-C4
North Albion Street	A1-A2
North Church Street	B3-B4
North Street	B3
Oak Street	A1-A2
Outer Promenade	A4-B4
Pharos Street	B3-C3-C4
Poulton Road	A2
Poulton Street	A2
Preston Street	B2
Promenade Road	A3-A4
Queen's Terrace	C3-C4
Radcliffe Road	A1
Rhyl Street	B3
St Peters Place	B2-B3
Siding Road	A1
Station Road	A1
Styan Street	A2-A1-B1
Tennyson Road	A2
The Esplanade	A3-A4-B4
Upper Lune Street	C4
Victoria Street	B3-C3
Walmsley Street	A3-A2-B2
Warrenhurst Road	A1
Warren Street	B3-B2-C2
Willow Road	A1
Windsor Terrace	B4

Lytham

Agnew Street	B2-B3
Alder Grove	A3-B3
Ballam Road	B2-B3-B4-C4
Bannister Street	C2
Bath Street	D2
Beach Street	B2
Bellingham Road	C4
Bleasdale Road	C3
Brook Road	B2
Cecil Street	C3
Central Beach	B2-C2
Church Road	A2-B2
Cleveland Road	B3-C3
Clifton Street	B2-C2
East Beach	C2
Forest Drive	A3-B3
Hastings Place	B2-B3
Henry Street	B2
Lilac Avenue	B4
Longacre Place	A3
Lowther Terrace	A2
Market Square	B2
Moorfield Drive	B3
Mythop Avenue	C3
Mythop Road	C3
Norfolk Road	C4
North Clifton Street	B2-C2
North Warton Street	C2
Park Street	C2
Parkview Road	C2-C3-C4
Queen Street	B2
Ring Dyke Way	A3
Rogerly Close	A3
South Clifton Street	B2-C2
Southolme	C3
South Park	A3-B3
South Warton Street	C2
Station Road	C2
Upper Westby Street	A2-B2
Warton Street	C2
West Beach	A2-B2
Westby Street	B2-C2
Westwood Road	A2
Woodville Terrace	A2
Wykeham Road	C3-C4

BLACKPOOL
Three piers, seven miles of promenade packed with entertainments galore and seemingly endless sandy beaches spread out beneath Blackpool's unmistakable tower which stands 518ft high in Britain's busiest and biggest holiday resort.

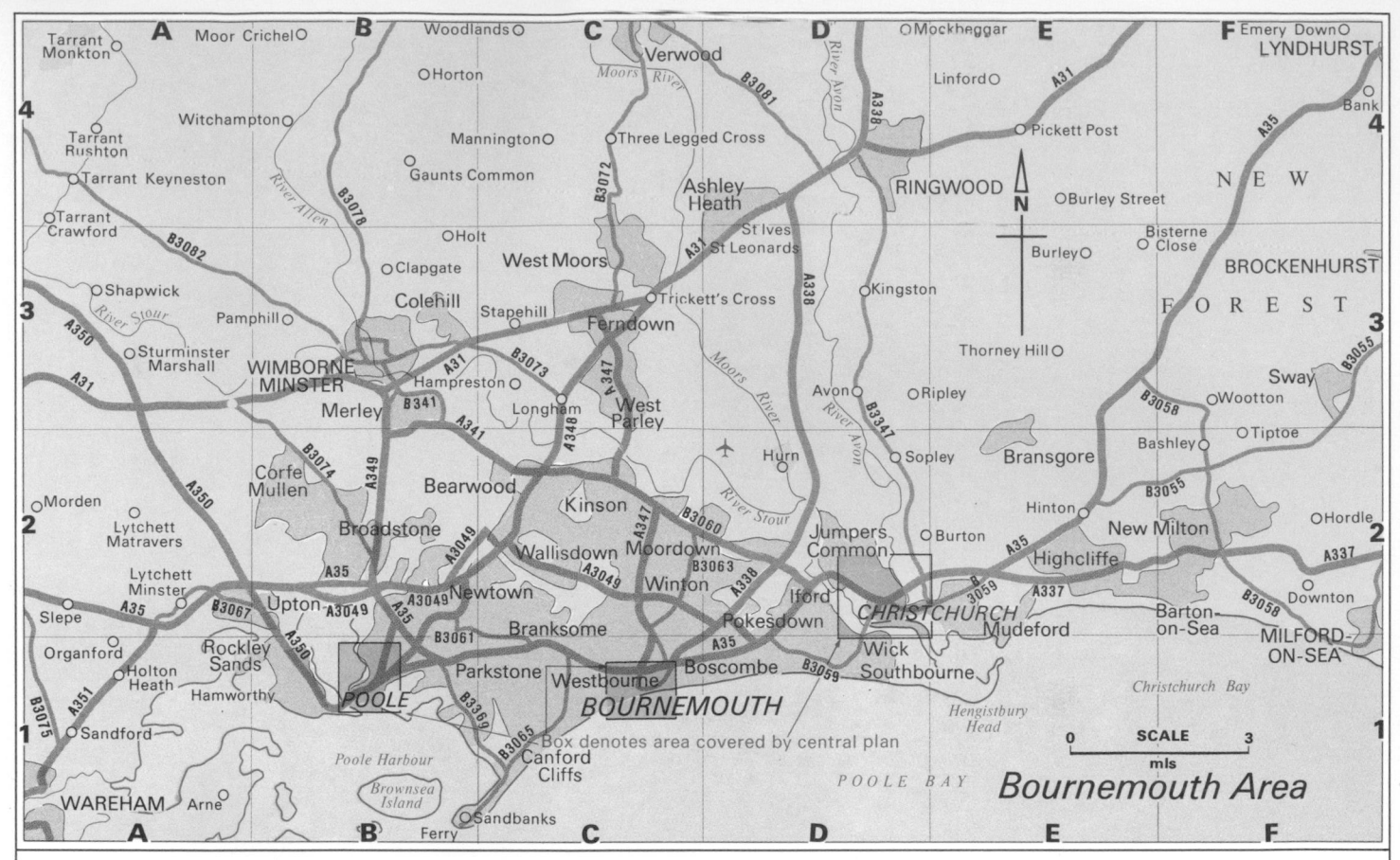

Bournemouth Area

Box denotes area covered by central plan

SCALE 0 ——— 3 mls

Street Index with Grid Reference

Bournemouth

Albert Road	C3-D3
Avenue Road	B3-C3
Bath Road	D2-E2-E3-E4-F4
Beacon Road	C1
Bodorgan Road	C4
Bourne Avenue	B3-C3
Bradley Road	B3-B4
Branksome Wood Road	A4
Cambridge Road	A2-A3
Central Drive	B4
Chine Crescent	A1-A2
Chine Crescent Road	A1-A2
Christchurch Road	F4
Cotlands Road	F4
Cranbourne Road	B2-C2
Crescent Road	A3-B3
Dean Park Crescent	C4-D4
Dean Park Road	C4
Durley Chine Road	A1-A2
Durley Gardens	A1-A2
Durley Road	A1-A2-B1
East Overcliff Drive	E2-F2-F3
Exeter Crescent	C2
Exeter Lane	C2-D2
Exeter Park Road	C2-D2
Exeter Road	C2-D2
Fir Vale Road	D3-D4
Gervis Place	C3-D3
Gervis Road	E3-F3
Glenfern Road	D3-E3-E4
Grove Road	E3-F3
Hahnemann Road	A1-B1-B2
Hinton Road	D2-D3-E2
Holdenhurst Road	F4
Lansdowne Road	E4-F4
Lorne Park Road	E4
Madeira Road	D4-E4
Marlborough Road	A2
Meyrick Road	F3-F4
Norwich Avenue	A2-A3-B3
Norwich Avenue West	A3
Old Christchurch Road	D3-D4-E4-F4
Parsonage Road	D3-E3
Poole Hill	A2-B2
Poole Road	A2
Priory Road	C1-C2

Richmond Hill	C3-C4
Russell Cotes Road	E2
St Michael's Road	B2-B1-C1
St Peter's Road	D3-E3
St Stephen's Road	B3-B4-C4-C3
Stafford Road	E4
Suffolk Road	A3-B3
Surrey Road	A3
Terrace Road	B2-C2
The Triangle	B2-B3
Tregonwell Road	B2-C2-C1
Undercliffe Drive	D1-D2-E1-E2-F2
Upper Hinton Road	D2-D3-E2
Upper Norwich Road	A2-B2
Upper Terrace Road	B2-C2
Wessex Way	A3-A4-B4-C4-D4-E4
West Cliff Gardens	B1
West Cliff Promenade	B1-C1-D1-C1
West Cliff Road	A1-B1
Westhill Road	A2-B2-B1-C1
Westover Road	D2-D3
West Promenade	C1-D1
Wimborne Road	C4
Wootton Gardens	E3-E4
Yelverton Road	C3-D3

Christchurch

Albion Road	A4
Arcadia Road	A4
Arthur Road	B3
Avenue Road	A3-B3-B4
Avon Road West	A3-A4-B4
Bargates	B2-B3
Barrack Road	A4-A3-B2-B3
Beaconsfield Road	B2-C3
Bridge Street	C2
Bronte Avenue	B4
Canberra Road	A4
Castle Street	B2-C2
Christchurch By-Pass	B2-C2-C3
Clarendon Road	A3-B3
Douglas Avenue	A2-B2
Endfield Road	A4
Fairfield	B3
Fairmile Road	A4-B4-B3
Flambard Avenue	A3-A4
Gardner Road	A3-B3
Gleadowe Avenue	A2-B2
Grove Road East	A3-B3

Grove Road West	A3
High Street	B2
Iford Lane	A1
Jumpers Avenue	A4
Jumpers Road	A3-A4-B4
Kings Avenue	A2-B2
Manor Road	B2
Millhams Street	B2-C2
Mill Road	B3-B4
Portfield Road	A3-B3
Queens Avenue	B1
Quay Road	B1
St John's Road	A2
St Margarets Avenue	B1
Sopers Lane	B1-B2
South View Road	B1
Stony Lane	C4-C3-C2
Stour Road	B3-B2-A1-A2
The Grove	A4
Tuckton Road	A1
Twynham Avenue	B2-B3
Walcott Avenue	A4-B4
Waterloo Place	C2
Wickfield Avenue	B1-B2
Wick Lane	A1-B1-B2
Willow Drive	A1-B1
Willow Way	A1-B1
Windsor Road	A3

Poole

Ballard Road	B1-C1
Church Street	A1
Dear Hay Lane	A2-B2
Denmark Road	C3
East Quay Road	B1
East Street	B1
Elizabeth Road	C3
Emerson Road	B1-B2
Esplanade	B3
Garland Road	C4
Green Road	B2-B1-C1
Heckford Road	C3-C4
High Street	A1-B1-B2
Hill Street	B2
Johns Road	C3-C4
Jolliffe Road	C4
Kingland Road	B2-C2
Kingston Road	C3-C4
Lagland Street	B1-B2

Longfleet Road	C3
Maple Road	C3-C4
Mount Pleasant Road	C2-C3
Newfoundland Drive	C1
New Orchard	A1-A2
North Street	B2
Old Orchard	B1
Parkstone Road	C3-C2
Perry Gardens	B1
Poole Bridge	A1
St Mary's Road	C3
Seldown Lane	C2-C3
Shaftesbury Road	C3
Skinner Street	B1
South Road	B2
Stanley Road	B1
Sterte Avenue	A4-B4
Sterte Road	B2-B3-B4
Stokes Avenue	B4-C4
Strand Street	A1-B1
Tatnam Road	B4-C4
The Quay	A1-B1
Towngate Bridge	B2-B3
West Quay Road	A1-A2-B2
West Street	A1-A2-B2
Wimborne Road	B3-C3-C4

LEGEND

Town Plan
AA Recommended route
Other roads
Restricted roads
Buildings of interest — Town Hall
AA Centre — AA
Car Parks — P
Parks and open spaces
One way streets — ←

Area Plan
A roads
B roads
Locations — Mudeford O
Urban area

Bournemouth

Until the beginning of the 19th century the landscape on which Bournemouth stands was open heath. Its rise began when a scattering of holiday villas were built by innovative trend-setters at a time when the idea of seaside holidays was very new. Soon a complete village had taken shape. In the next 50 years Bournemouth had become a major resort and its population catapulted to nearly 59,000.

Today's holidaymakers can enjoy Bournemouth's natural advantages – miles of sandy beaches, a mild climate and beautiful setting, along with a tremendous variety of amenities. These include some of the best shopping in the south – with shops ranging from huge departmental stores to tiny specialist places. Entertainments range from variety shows and feature films to opera, and the music of the world-famous Bournemouth Symphony Orchestra.

Poole has virtually been engulfed by the suburbs of Bournemouth, but its enormous natural harbour is still an attraction in its own right. At Poole Quay, some 15th-century cellars have been converted into a Maritime Museum, where the town's association with the sea from prehistoric times until the early 20th century is illustrated, and the famous Poole Pottery nearby offers guided tours of its workshops.

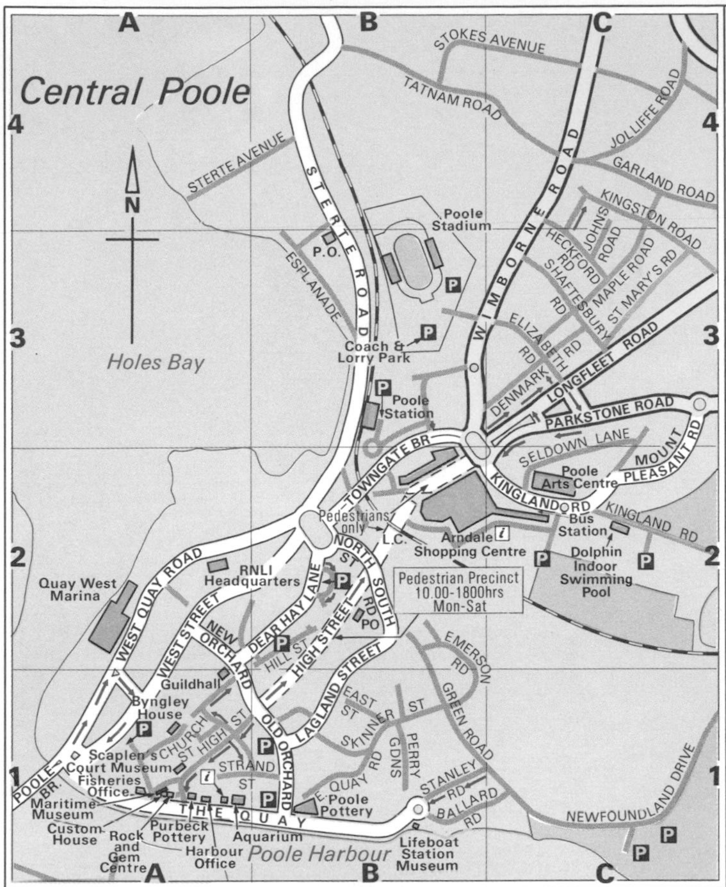

Central Poole
Holes Bay
Poole Harbour
Stokes Avenue
Tatnam Road
Sterte Avenue
Sterte Road
Esplanade
Poole Stadium
P.O.
Coach & Lorry Park
Poole Station
Wimborne Road
Jolliffe Road
Garland Road
Kingston Road
Heckford Rd
Johns Road
Shaftesbury Rd
Maple Road
St Mary's Rd
Elizabeth Rd
Longfleet Road
Denmark Rd
Parkstone Road
Towngate Br
Seldown Lane
Mount Pleasant Rd
Poole Arts Centre
Kingland Rd
Kingland Road
Bus Station
Pedestrians only
L.C.
Arndale Shopping Centre
Dolphin Indoor Swimming Pool
Pedestrian Precinct 10.00-1800hrs Mon-Sat
Quay West Marina
West Quay Road
RNLI Headquarters
North St
South Rd
West Street
Dear Hay Lane
New Orchard
High Street
Hill St
PO
Lagland Street
Emerson Rd
Green Road
Guildhall
Byngley House
Church St
High St
East St
Skinner St
Perry Gdns
Old Orchard
Strand St
Scaplen's Court Museum
Fisheries Office
Maritime Museum
Custom House
Rock and Gem Centre
Purbeck Pottery
Aquarium
Harbour Office
Poole Pottery
Quay Rd
Stanley Rd
Ballard Rd
The Quay
Lifeboat Station Museum
Newfoundland Drive
Poole Br.

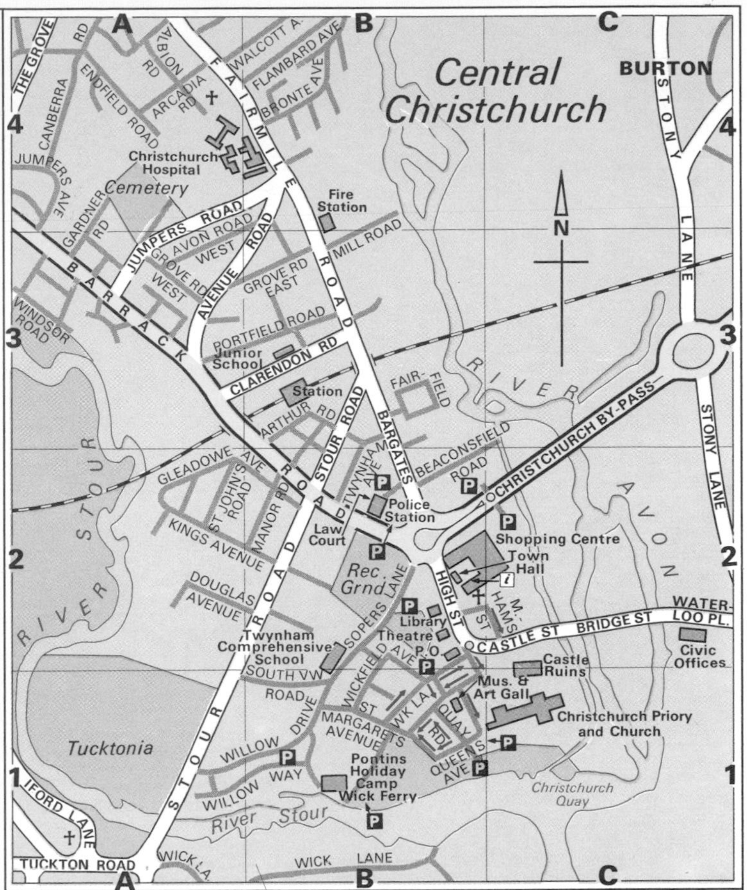

Central Christchurch
Burton
The Grove
Canberra Rd
Albion Rd
Arcadia Rd
Walcott A.
Flambard Ave
Bronte Ave
Endfield Road
Christchurch Hospital
Cemetery
Jumpers Ave
Gardner Rd
Fairmile Road
Fire Station
Jumpers Road
Avon Road West
Avenue Road
Mill Road
Grove Rd West
Grove Rd East
Barrack Road
Windsor Road
Portfield Road
Junior School
Clarendon Rd
Station
Arthur Rd
Stour Road
Bargates
Fairfield
Beaconsfield Road
Christchurch By-Pass
River Avon
Police Station
Law Court
Gleadowe Ave
St Johns Road
Manor Rd
Kings Avenue
Douglas Avenue
Rec. Grnd
Sopers Lane
Shopping Centre
Town Hall
High St
Library
Theatre
P.O.
Castle St
Bridge St
Waterloo Pl.
Castle Ruins
Civic Offices
Twynham Comprehensive School
South VW Road
Wickfield Ave
Margarets Avenue
Mus. & Art Gall.
Christchurch Priory and Church
Quay Rd
Queens Ave
River Stour
Tucktonia
Willow Drive
Willow Way
Pontins Holiday Camp
Wick Ferry
Christchurch Quay
Iford Lane
Tuckton Road
Wick La
Wick Lane
Stony Lane

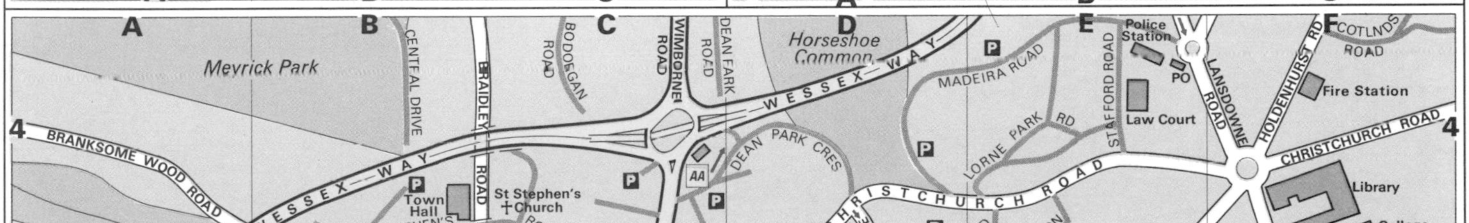

Central Bournemouth
Meyrick Park
Horseshoe Common
Central Drive
Braidley Road
Bodorgan Road
Wimborne Road
Dean Park Road
Wessex Way
Madeira Road
Stafford Road
Police Station
PO
Lansdowne Road
Holdenhurst Road
Cotlands Road
Fire Station
Law Court
Branksome Wood Road
Lorne Park Rd
Christchurch Road
Dean Park Cres
Library
College
Town Hall
St Stephen's Church
St Stephen's Road
Old Christchurch Road
Glenfern Road
Wootton Gardens
Surrey Road
Hospital
Town Hall
Railway Museum
Fir Vale Rd
Synagogue
Bath Road
Meyrick Road
Richmond Hill
Yelverton Road
St Peter's Rd
St Peter's Road
Gervis Road
Grove Road
Bourne Avenue
Crescent Rd
Upper Gardens
The Bourne
Albert Rd
PO
Parsonage Road
Wessex Way
Suffolk Road
Avenue Road
Pedestrians & Buses only
St Peter's Church
Norwich Ave West
Cambridge Rd
Norwich Ave
The Triangle
Gervis Place
Cinema
Hinton Road
Upper Hinton Rd
East Overcliff Drive
Upper Norwich Road
Terrace Rd
Upp Terrace Road
Exeter Road
Lower Gardens
Ice Rink
Westover Road
Cinemas
Russell Cotes Rd
Russell-Cotes Art Gallery and Museum
East Cliff
Poole Rd
Poole Hill
Tregonwell Road
Exeter Lane
Exeter Cres
Playhouse Theatre
Royal Bath Hotel
Pavilion
Undercliff Drive
Cranborne Rd
Exeter Park Rd
Marlborough Road
Durley Chine Road
Durley Road
Westhill
Winter Gardens
Royal Exeter Hotel
Rothesay Mus.
St Michael's Road
Chine Crescent Road
Chine Crescent
Hahnemann Road
Priory Road
Conference Centre
Pier Leisure Centre
Beacon Road
Westhill Road
West Cliff Road
Durley Gardens
West Cliff Gardens
West Cliff Promenade
West Promenade
Pier Theatre
Bournemouth Pier
Pedestrians only

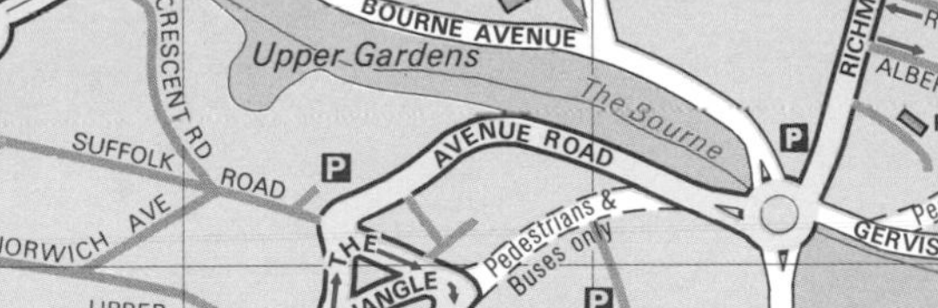

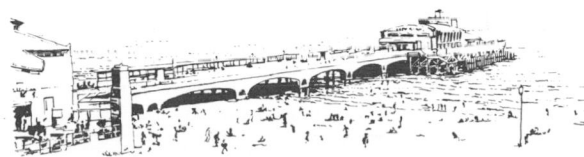

BOURNEMOUTH
The pier, safe sea-bathing, golden sands facing south and sheltered by steep cliffs, and plenty of amenities for the holiday maker make Bournemouth one of the most popular resorts on the south coast of England.

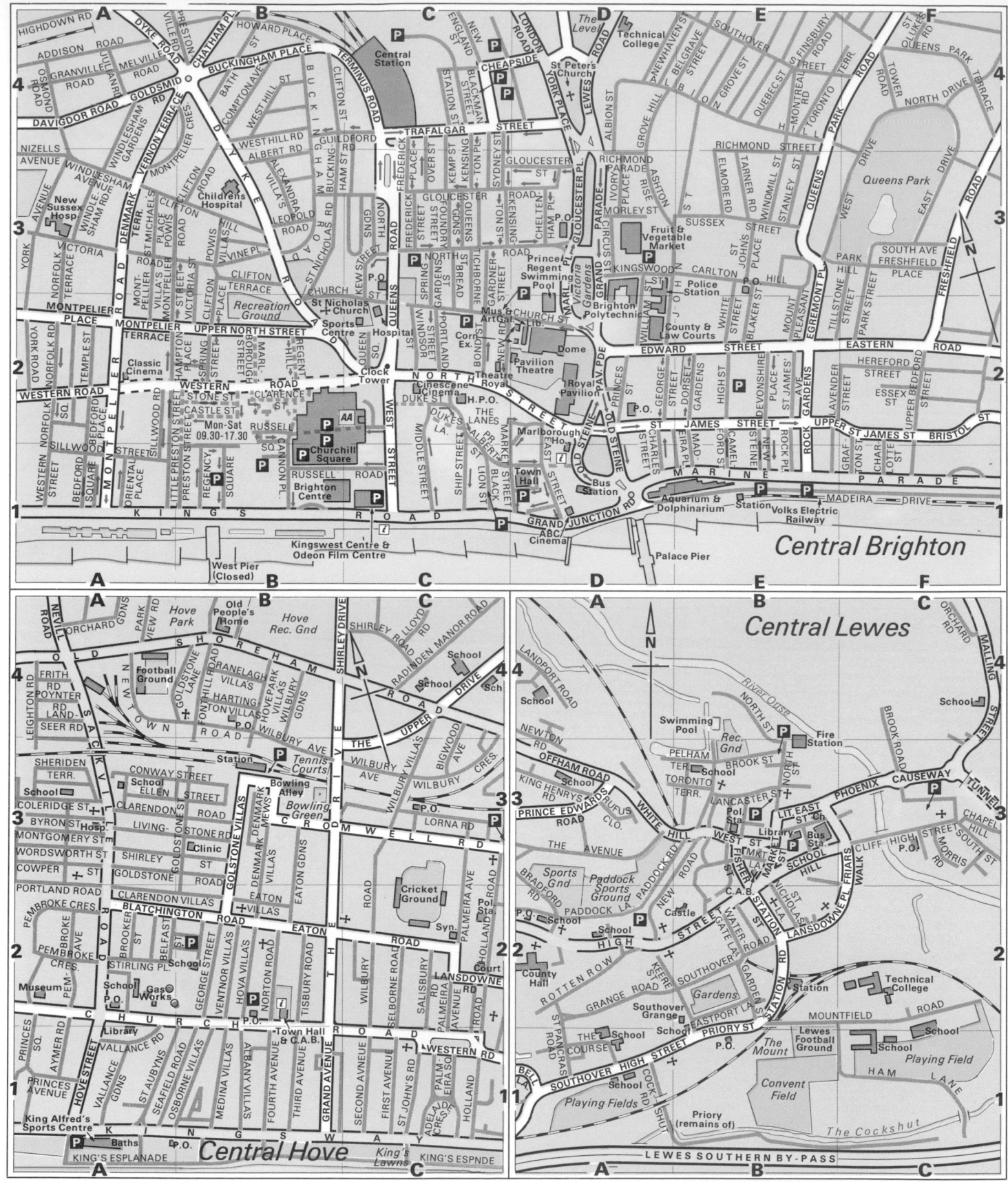

Brighton

Dr Richard Russell, from nearby Lewes, created the resort of Brighton almost singlehandedly. And he did it not by building houses or hotels, but by writing a book. His book, which praised the health-giving properties of sea-bathing and sea air, soon came to the attention of George, then Prince Regent and one day to become King George IV. He stayed at Brighthelmstone – as it was then known –

in 1783 and again in 1784. In 1786 the Prince rented a villa on the Steine – a modest house that was eventually transformed into the astonishing Pavilion. By 1800 – its popularity assured by royal patronage – the resort was described in a contemporary directory as 'the most frequented and without exception one of the most fashionable towns in the kingdom'.

Perhaps the description does not quite fit today, but Brighton is a perennially popular seaside

resort, as well as a shopping centre, university town and cultural venue. The Pavilion still draws most crowds, of course. Its beginnings as a villa are entirely hidden in a riot of Near Eastern architectural motifs, largely the creation of John Nash. Brighton's great days as a Regency resort *par excellence* are preserved in the sweeping crescents and elegant terraces, buildings which help to make it one of the finest townscapes in the whole of Europe.

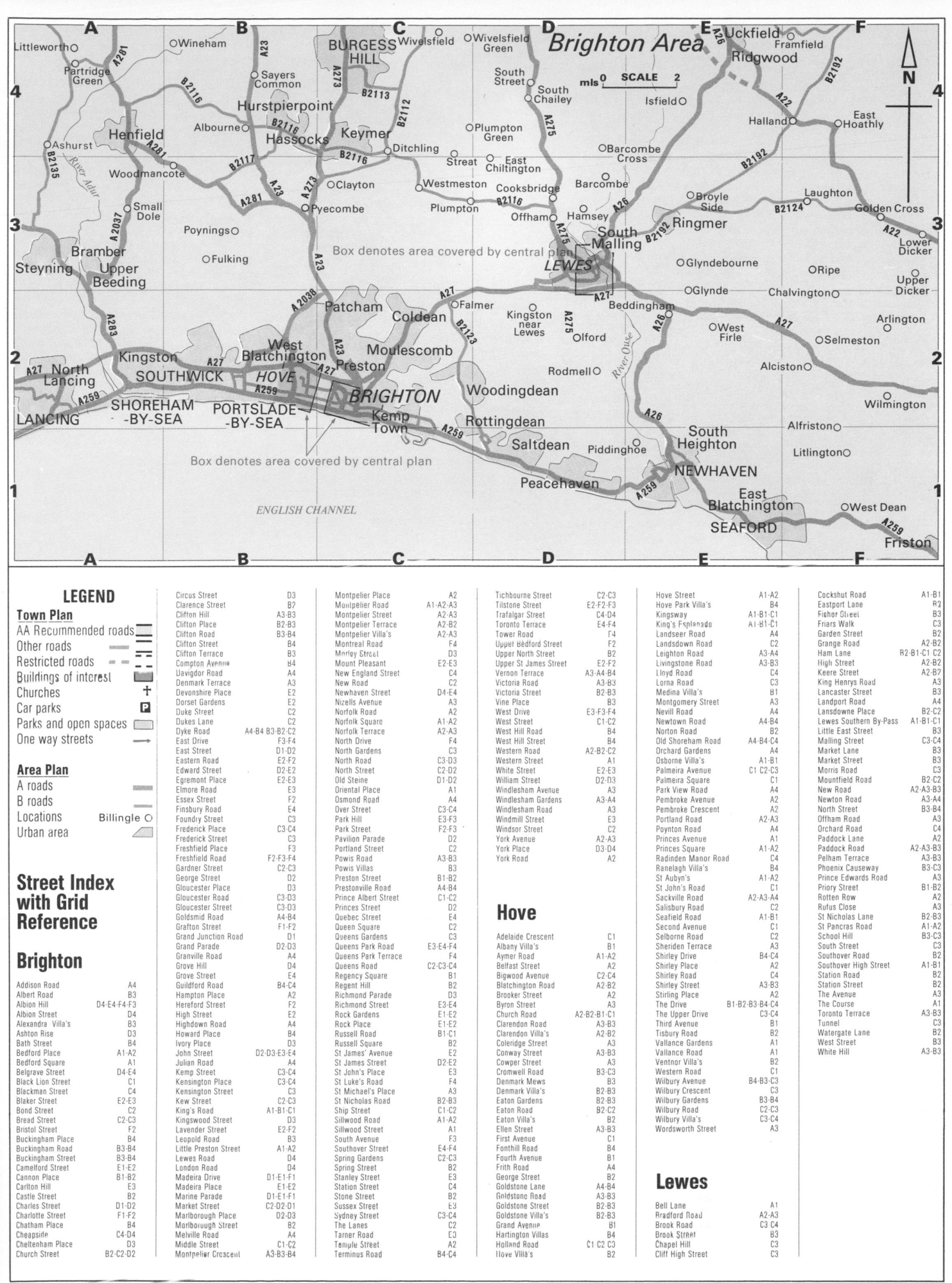

LEGEND

Town Plan
AA Recommended roads
Other roads
Restricted roads
Buildings of interest
Churches ✝
Car parks Ⓟ
Parks and open spaces
One way streets →

Area Plan
A roads
B roads
Locations Billingle ○
Urban area

Street Index with Grid Reference

Brighton

Addison Road	A4
Albert Road	B3
Albion Hill	D4-E4-F4-F3
Albion Street	D4
Alexandra Villa's	B3
Ashton Rise	D3
Bath Street	B4
Bedford Place	A1-A2
Bedford Square	A1
Belgrave Street	D4-E4
Black Lion Street	C1
Blackman Street	C4
Blaker Street	E2-E3
Bond Street	C2
Bread Street	C2-C3
Bristol Road	F2
Buckingham Place	B4
Buckingham Road	B3-B4
Buckingham Street	B3-B4
Camelford Street	E1-E2
Cannon Place	B1-B2
Carlton Hill	E3
Castle Street	B2
Charles Street	D1-D2
Charlotte Street	F1-F2
Chatham Place	B4
Cheapside	C4-D4
Cheltenham Place	D3
Church Street	B2-C2-D2
Circus Street	D3
Clarence Street	B7
Clifton Hill	A3-B3
Clifton Place	B2-B3
Clifton Road	B3-B4
Clifton Street	B4
Clifton Terrace	B3
Compton Avenue	B4
Davigdor Road	A4
Denmark Terrace	A3
Devonshire Place	E2
Dorset Gardens	E2
Duke Street	C2
Dukes Lane	C2
Dyke Road	A4-B4 B3-B2-C2
East Drive	F3-F4
East Street	D1-D2
Eastern Road	E2-F2
Edward Street	D2-E2
Egremont Place	E2-E3
Elmore Road	E3
Essex Street	F2
Finsbury Road	E4
Foundry Street	C3
Frederick Place	C3-C4
Frederick Street	C3
Freshfield Place	F3
Freshfield Road	F2-F3-F4
Gardner Street	C2-C3
George Street	D2
Gloucester Place	D3
Gloucester Road	C3-D3
Gloucester Street	C3-D3
Goldsmid Road	A4-B4
Grafton Street	F1-F2
Grand Junction Road	D1
Grand Parade	D2-D3
Granville Road	A4
Grove Hill	D4
Grove Street	E4
Guildford Road	B4-C4
Hampton Place	A2
Hereford Street	F2
High Street	E2
Highdown Road	A4
Howard Place	B4
Ivory Place	D3
John Street	D2-D3-E3-E4
Julian Road	A4
Kemp Street	C3-C4
Kensington Place	C3-C4
Kensington Street	C3
Kew Street	C2-C3
King's Road	A1-B1-C1
Kingswood Street	D3
Lavender Street	E2-F2
Leopold Road	B3
Little Preston Street	A1-A2
Lewes Road	D4
London Road	D4
Madeira Drive	D1-E1-F1
Madeira Place	E1-E2
Marine Parade	D1-E1-F1
Market Street	C2-D2-D1
Marlborough Place	D2-D3
Marlborough Street	B2
Melville Road	A4
Middle Street	C1-C2
Montpelier Crescent	A3-B3-B4
Montpelier Place	A2
Montpelier Road	A1-A2-A3
Montpelier Street	A2-A3
Montpelier Terrace	A2-B2
Montpelier Villa's	A2-A3
Montreal Road	F4
Morley Street	D3
Mount Pleasant	E2-E3
New England Street	C4
New Road	C2
Newhaven Street	D4-E4
Nizells Avenue	A3
Norfolk Road	A2
Norfolk Square	A1-A2
Norfolk Terrace	A2-A3
North Drive	F4
North Gardens	C3
North Road	C3-D3
North Street	C2-D2
Old Steine	D1-D2
Oriental Place	A1
Osmond Road	A4
Over Street	C3-C4
Park Hill	E3-F3
Park Street	F2-F3
Pavilion Parade	D2
Portland Street	C2
Powis Road	A3-B3
Powis Villas	B3
Preston Street	B1-B2
Prestonville Road	A4-B4
Prince Albert Street	C1-C2
Princes Street	D2
Quebec Street	E4
Queen Square	C2
Queens Gardens	C3
Queens Park Road	E3-E4-E2
Queens Park Terrace	F4
Queens Road	C2-C3-C4
Regency Square	B1
Regent Hill	B2
Richmond Parade	D3
Richmond Street	E3-E4
Rock Gardens	E1-E2
Rock Place	E1-E2
Russell Road	B1-C1
Russell Square	B2
St James' Avenue	E2
St James Street	D2-E2
St John's Place	E3
St Luke's Road	F4
St Michael's Place	A3
St Nicholas Road	B2-B3
Ship Street	C1-C2
Sillwood Road	A1-A2
Sillwood Street	A1
South Avenue	F3
Southover Street	E4-F4
Spring Gardens	C2-C3
Spring Street	B2
Stanley Street	E3
Station Street	C4
Stone Street	B2
Sussex Street	E3
Sydney Street	C3-C4
The Lanes	C2
Tarner Road	E3
Temple Street	A2
Terminus Road	B4-C4
Tichbourne Street	C2-C3
Tilstone Street	E2-F2-F3
Trafalgar Street	C4-D4
Toronto Terrace	E4-F4
Tower Road	F4
Upper Bedford Street	F2
Upper North Street	B2
Upper St James Street	E2-F2
Vernon Terrace	A3-A4-B4
Victoria Road	A3-B3
Victoria Road	B2-B3
Vine Place	B3
West Drive	E3-F3-F4
West Street	C1-C2
West Hill Road	B4
West Hill Street	B4
Western Road	A2-B2-C2
Western Street	A1
White Street	E2-E3
William Street	D2-D3
Windlesham Avenue	A3
Windlesham Gardens	A3-A4
Windlesham Road	A3
Windmill Street	E3
Windsor Street	C2
York Avenue	A2-A3
York Place	D3-D4
York Road	A2

Hove

Adelaide Crescent	C1
Albany Villa's	B1
Aymer Road	A1-A2
Belfast Street	A2
Bigwood Avenue	C2-C4
Blatchington Road	A2-B2
Brooker Street	A2
Byron Street	A2
Church Road	A2-B2-B1-C1
Clarendon Road	A3-B3
Clarendon Villa's	A2-B2
Coleridge Street	A3
Conway Street	A3-B3
Cowper Street	A3
Cromwell Road	B3-C3
Denmark Mews	B3
Denmark Villa's	B2-B3
Eaton Gardens	B2-B3
Eaton Road	B2-C2
Eaton Villa's	B2
Ellen Street	A3-B3
First Avenue	C1
Fonthill Road	B1
Fourth Avenue	B1
Frith Road	A4
George Street	B2
Goldstone Lane	A4-B4
Goldstone Road	A3
Goldstone Street	B2-B3
Goldstone Villa's	B2-B3
Grand Avenue	B1
Hartington Villas	A3
Holland Road	C1-C2-C3
Hove Villa's	B2
Hove Street	A1-A2
Hove Park Villa's	B4
Kingsway	A1-B1-C1
King's Esplanade	A1-B1-C1
Landseer Road	A4
Landsdown Road	C2
Leighton Road	A3-A4
Livingstone Road	A3-B3
Lloyd Road	C4
Lorna Road	C3
Medina Villa's	B1
Montgomery Street	A3
Nevill Road	A4
Newtown Road	A4-B4
Norton Road	B2
Old Shoreham Road	A4-B4-C4
Orchard Gardens	A4
Osborne Villa's	A1-B1
Palmeira Avenue	C1-C2-C3
Palmeira Square	C1
Park View Road	A4
Pembroke Avenue	A2
Pembroke Crescent	A2
Portland Road	A2-A3
Poynton Road	A4
Princes Avenue	A1
Princes Square	A1-A2
Radinden Manor Road	C4
Ranelagh Villa's	B4
St Aubyn's	A1-A2
St John's Road	C1
Sackville Road	A2-A3-A4
Salisbury Road	C2
Seafield Road	A1-B1
Second Avenue	C1
Selborne Road	C2
Sheriden Terrace	A3
Shirley Drive	B4-C4
Shirley Place	A2
Shirley Road	C4
Shirley Street	A3-B3
Stirling Place	A2
The Drive	B1-B2-B3-B4-C4
The Upper Drive	C3-C4
Third Avenue	B1
Tisbury Road	B2
Vallance Gardens	A1
Vallance Road	A1
Ventnor Villa's	B2
Western Road	C1
Wilbury Avenue	B4-B3-C3
Wilbury Crescent	C3
Wilbury Gardens	B3-B4
Wilbury Road	C2-C3
Wilbury Villa's	C3-C4
Wordsworth Street	A3

Lewes

Bell Lane	A1
Bradford Road	A2-A3
Brook Road	C3-C4
Brook Street	B3
Chapel Hill	C3
Cliff High Street	C3
Cockshut Road	A1-B1
Eastport Lane	B2
Fisher Street	B3
Friars Walk	C3
Garden Street	B2
Grange Road	A2-B2
Ham Lane	B2-B1-C1-C2
High Street	A2-B2
Keere Street	A2-B2
King Henrys Road	A3
Lancaster Street	B3
Landport Road	A4
Lansdowne Place	B2-C2
Lewes Southern By-Pass	A1-B1-C1
Little East Street	B3
Malling Street	C3-C4
Market Lane	B3
Market Street	B3
Morris Road	C3
Mountfield Road	B2-C2
New Road	A2-A3-B3
Newton Road	A2-B2
North Street	B3-B4
Offham Road	A3
Orchard Road	C4
Paddock Lane	A2
Paddock Road	A2-A3-B3
Pelham Terrace	A3-B3
Phoenix Causeway	B3-C3
Prince Edwards Road	A3
Priory Street	B1-B2
Rotten Row	A2
Rufus Close	A3
St Nicholas Lane	B2-B3
St Pancras Road	B3
School Hill	B3-C3
South Street	C3
Southover Road	B2
Southover High Street	A1-B1
Station Road	B2
Station Street	B2
The Avenue	A3
The Course	A1
Toronto Terrace	A3-B3
Tunnel	C3
Watergate Lane	B2
West Street	B3
White Hill	A3-B3

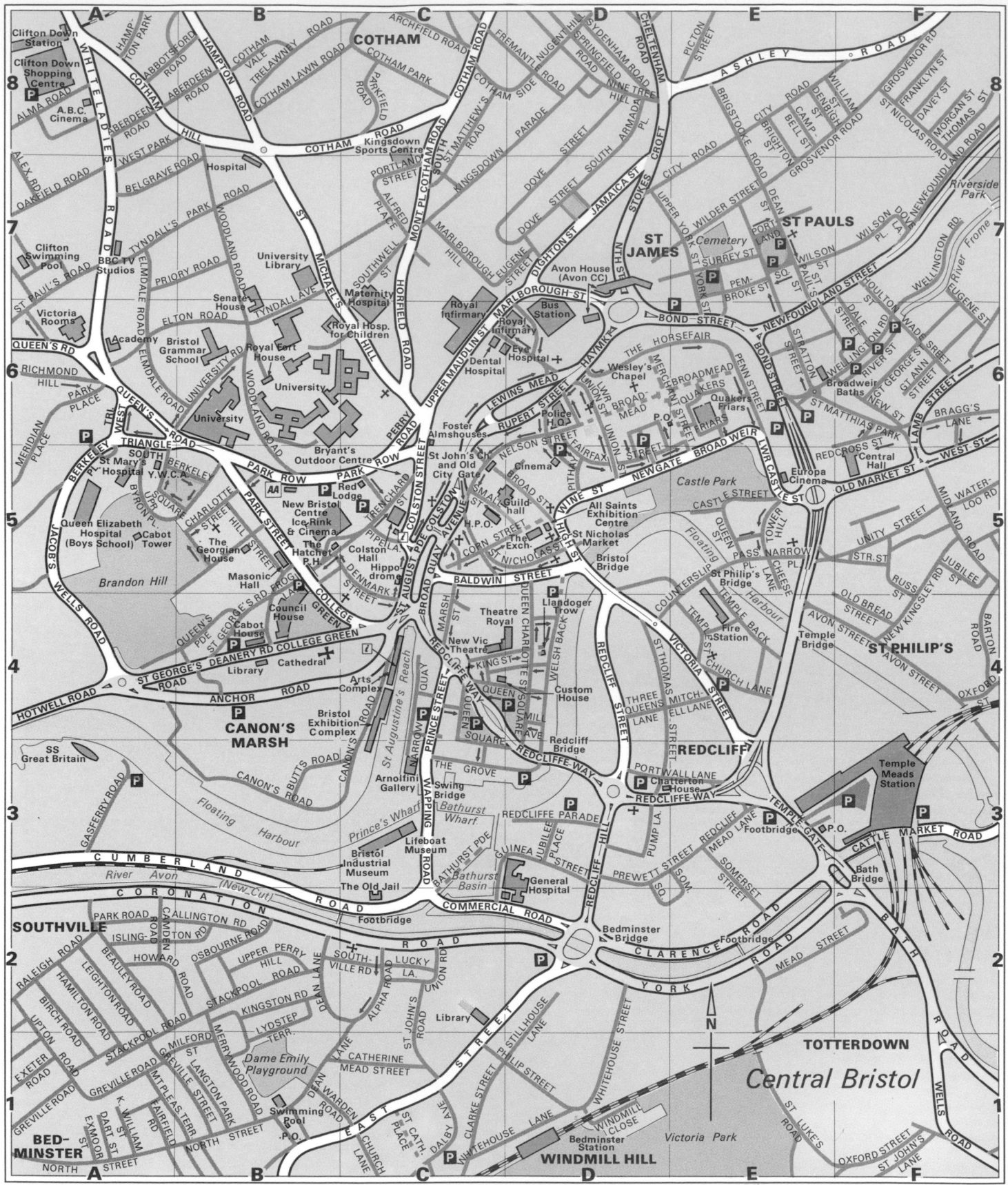

Bristol

One of Britain's most historic seaports, Bristol retains many of its visible links with the past, despite terrible damage inflicted during bombing raids in World War II. Most imposing is the cathedral, founded as an abbey church in 1140. Perhaps even more famous than the cathedral is the Church of St Mary Redcliffe. Ranking among the finest churches in the country, it owes much of

its splendour to 14th- and 15th-century merchants who bestowed huge sums of money on it.

The merchant families brought wealth to the whole of Bristol, and their trading links with the world are continued in today's modern aerospace and technological industries. Much of the best of Bristol can be seen in the area of the Floating Harbour – an arm of the Avon. Several of the old warehouses have been converted into museums, galleries and exhibition centres. Among them are

genuinely picturesque old pubs, the best-known of which is the Llandoger Trow. It is a timbered 17th-century house, the finest of its kind in Bristol. Further up the same street – King Street – is the Theatre Royal, built in 1766 and the oldest theatre in the country. In Corn Street, the heart of the business area, is a magnificent 18th-century corn exchange. In front of it are the four pillars known as the 'nails', on which merchants used to make cash transactions, hence 'to pay on the nail'.

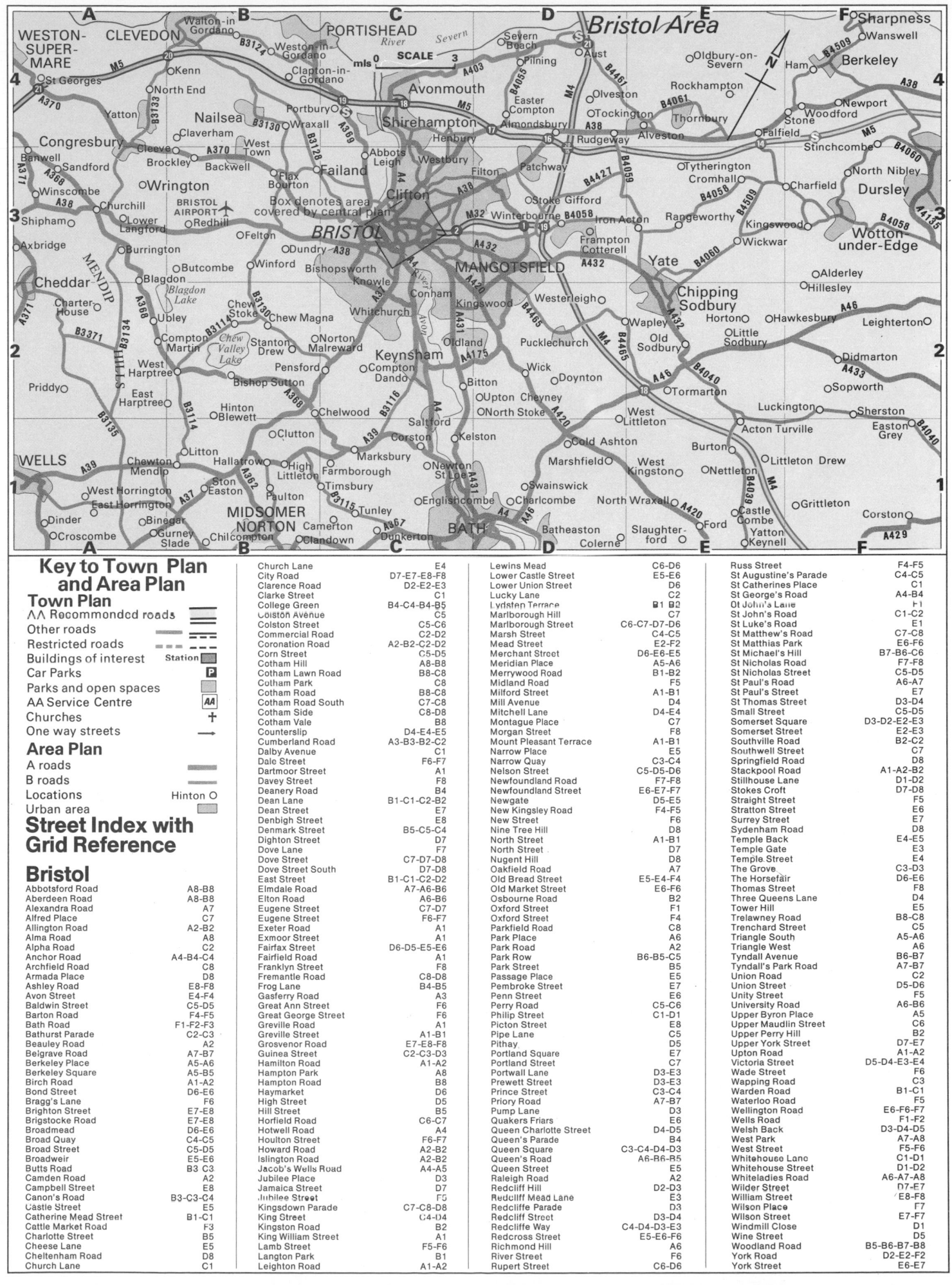

Key to Town Plan and Area Plan

Town Plan
- ∧∧ Recommended roads
- Other roads
- Restricted roads
- Buildings of interest — Station
- Car Parks — P
- Parks and open spaces
- AA Service Centre — AA
- Churches — †
- One way streets — →

Area Plan
- A roads
- B roads
- Locations — Hinton O
- Urban area

Street Index with Grid Reference

Bristol

Street	Grid Ref
Abbotsford Road	A8-B8
Aberdeen Road	A8-B8
Alexandra Road	A7
Alfred Place	C7
Allington Road	A2-B2
Alma Road	A8
Alpha Road	C2
Anchor Road	A4-B4-C4
Archfield Road	C8
Armada Place	D8
Ashley Road	E8-F8
Avon Street	E4-F4
Baldwin Street	C5-D5
Barton Road	F4-F5
Bath Road	F1-F2-F3
Bathurst Parade	C2-C3
Beauley Road	A2
Belgrave Road	A7-B7
Berkeley Place	A5-A6
Berkeley Square	A5-B5
Birch Road	A1-A2
Bond Street	D6-E6
Bragg's Lane	F6
Brighton Street	E7-E8
Brigstocke Road	E7-E8
Broadmead	D6-E6
Broad Quay	C4-C5
Broad Street	C5-D5
Broadweir	E5-E6
Butts Road	B3 C3
Camden Road	A2
Campbell Street	E8
Canon's Road	B3-C3-C4
Castle Street	E5
Catherine Mead Street	B1-C1
Cattle Market Road	F3
Charlotte Street	B5
Cheese Lane	E5
Cheltenham Road	D8
Church Lane	C1
Church Lane	E4
City Road	D7-E7-E8-F8
Clarence Road	D2-E2-E3
Clarke Street	C1
College Green	B4-C4-B4-B5
Colston Avenue	C5
Colston Street	C5-C6
Commercial Road	C2-D2
Coronation Road	A2-B2-C2-D2
Corn Street	C5-D5
Cotham Hill	A8-B8
Cotham Lawn Road	B8-C8
Cotham Park	C8
Cotham Road	B8-C8
Cotham Road South	C7-C8
Cotham Side	C8-D8
Cotham Vale	B8
Counterslip	D4-E4-E5
Cumberland Road	A3-B3-B2-C2
Dalby Avenue	C1
Dale Street	F6-F7
Dartmoor Street	A1
Davey Street	F8
Deanery Road	B4
Dean Lane	B1-C1-C2-B2
Dean Street	E7
Denbigh Street	E8
Denmark Street	B5-C5-C4
Dighton Street	D7
Dove Lane	F7
Dove Street	C7-D7-D8
Dove Street South	D7-D8
East Street	B1-C1-C2-D2
Elmdale Road	A7-A6-B6
Elton Road	A6-B6
Eugene Street	C7-D7
Eugene Street	F6-F7
Exeter Road	A1
Exmoor Street	A1
Fairfax Street	D6-D5-E5-E6
Fairfield Road	A1
Franklyn Street	F8
Fremantle Road	C8-D8
Frog Lane	B4-B5
Gasferry Road	A3
Great Ann Street	F6
Great George Street	F6
Greville Road	A1
Greville Street	A1-B1
Grosvenor Road	E7-E8-F8
Guinea Street	C2-C3-D3
Hamilton Road	A1-A2
Hampton Park	A8
Hampton Road	B8
Haymarket	D6
High Street	D5
Hill Street	B5
Horfield Road	C6-C7
Hotwell Road	A4
Houlton Street	F6-F7
Howard Road	A2-B2
Islington Road	A2-B2
Jacob's Wells Road	A4-A5
Jubilee Place	D3
Jamaica Street	D7
Jubilee Street	F5
Kingsdown Parade	C7-C8-D8
King Street	C4-D4
Kingston Road	B2
King William Street	A1
Lamb Street	F5-F6
Langton Park	B1
Leighton Road	A1-A2
Lewins Mead	C6-D6
Lower Castle Street	E5-E6
Lower Union Street	D6
Lucky Lane	C2
Lydston Terrace	B1 B2
Marlborough Hill	C7
Marlborough Street	C6-C7-D7-D6
Marsh Street	C4-C5
Mead Street	E2-F2
Merchant Street	D6-E6-E5
Meridian Place	A5-A6
Merrywood Road	B1-B2
Midland Road	F5
Milford Street	A1-B1
Mill Avenue	D4
Mitchell Lane	D4-E4
Montague Place	C7
Morgan Street	F8
Mount Pleasant Terrace	A1-B1
Narrow Place	E5
Narrow Way	C3-C4
Nelson Street	C5-D5-D6
Newfoundland Road	F7-F8
Newfoundland Street	E6-E7-F7
Newgate	D5-E5
New Kingsley Road	F4-F5
New Street	F6
Nine Tree Hill	D8
North Street	A1-B1
North Street	D7
Nugent Hill	D8
Oakfield Road	A7
Old Bread Street	E5-E4-F4
Old Market Street	E6-F6
Osbourne Road	B2
Oxford Street	F1
Oxford Street	F4
Parkfield Road	C8
Park Place	A6
Park Road	A2
Park Row	B6-B5-C5
Park Street	B5
Passage Street	E5
Pembroke Street	E7
Penn Street	E6
Perry Road	C5-C6
Philip Street	C1-D1
Picton Street	E8
Pipe Lane	C5
Pithay	D5
Portland Square	E7
Portland Street	C7
Portwall Lane	D3-E3
Prewett Street	D3-E3
Prince Street	C3-C4
Priory Road	A7-B7
Pump Lane	D3
Quakers Friars	E6
Queen Charlotte Street	D4-D5
Queen's Parade	B4
Queen Square	C3-C4-D4-D3
Queen's Road	A6-B6-B5
Queen Street	E5
Raleigh Road	A2
Redcliff Hill	D2-D3
Redcliff Mead Lane	E3
Redcliff Parade	D3
Redcliff Street	D3-D4
Redcliffe Way	C4-D4-D3-E3-E3
Redcross Street	E5-E6-F6
Richmond Hill	A6
River Street	F6
Rupert Street	C6-D6
Russ Street	F4-F5
St Augustine's Parade	C4-C5
St Catherines Place	C1
St George's Road	A4-B4
St John's Lane	F1
St John's Road	C1-C2
St Luke's Road	E1
St Matthew's Road	C7-C8
St Matthias Park	E6-F6
St Michael's Hill	B7-B6-C6
St Nicholas Road	F7-F8
St Nicholas Street	C5-D5
St Paul's Road	A6-A7
St Paul's Street	E7
St Thomas Street	D3-D4
Small Street	C5-D5
Somerset Square	D3-D2-E2-E3
Somerset Street	E2-E3
Southville Road	B2-C2
Southwell Street	C7
Springfield Road	D8
Stackpool Road	A1-A2-B2
Stillhouse Lane	D1-D2
Stokes Croft	D7-D8
Straight Street	F5
Stratton Street	E6
Surrey Street	E7
Sydenham Road	D8
Temple Back	E4-E5
Temple Gate	E3
Temple Street	E4
The Grove	C3-D3
The Horsefair	D6-E6
Thomas Street	F8
Three Queens Lane	D4
Tower Hill	E5
Trelawney Road	B8-C8
Trenchard Street	C5
Triangle South	A5-A6
Triangle West	A6
Tyndall Avenue	B6-B7
Tyndall's Park Road	A7-B7
Union Road	C2
Union Street	D5-D6
Unity Street	F5
University Road	A6-B6
Upper Byron Place	A5
Upper Maudlin Street	C6
Upper Perry Hill	B2
Upper York Street	D7-E7
Upton Road	A1-A2
Victoria Street	D5-D4-E3-E4
Wade Street	F6
Wapping Road	C3
Warden Road	B1-C1
Waterloo Road	F5
Wellington Road	E6-F6-F7
Wells Road	F1-F2
Welsh Back	D3-D4-D5
West Park	A7-A8
West Street	F5-F6
Whitehouse Lane	C1-D1
Whitehouse Street	D1-D2
Whiteladies Road	A6-A7-A8
Wilder Street	D7-E7
William Street	E8-F8
Wilson Place	F7
Wilson Street	E7-F7
Windmill Close	D1
Wine Street	D5
Woodland Road	B5-B6-B7-B8
York Road	D2-E2-F2
York Street	E6-E7

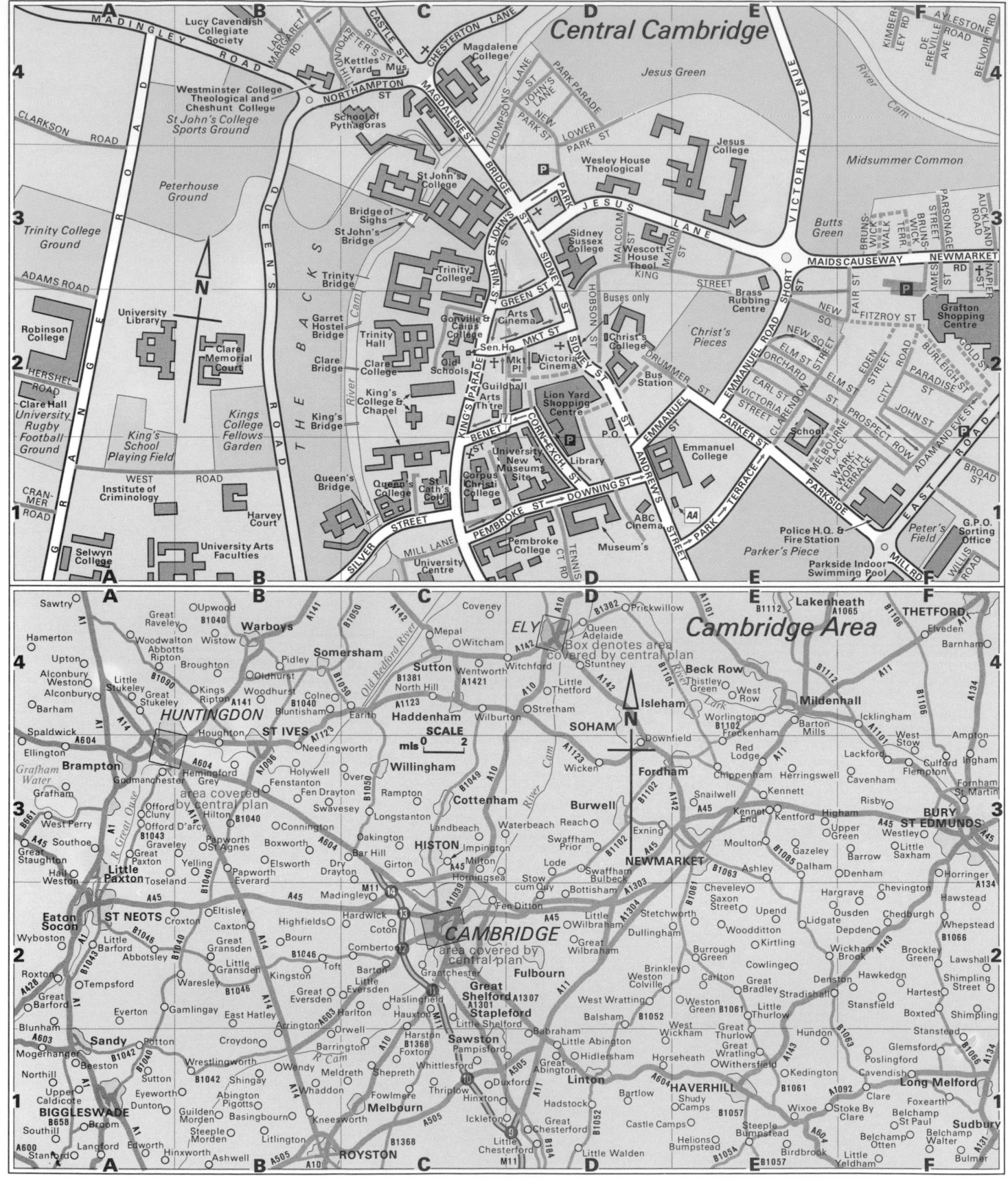

Cambridge

Few views in England, perhaps even in Europe, are as memorable as that from Cambridge's Backs towards the colleges. Dominating the scene, in every sense, is King's College Chapel. One of the finest Gothic buildings anywhere, it was built in three stages from 1446 to 1515.

No one would dispute that the chapel is Cambridge's masterpiece, but there are dozens of buildings here that would be the finest in any other town or city. Most are colleges, or are attached to colleges, and it is the university which permeates every aspect of Cambridge's landscape and life. In all there are 33 university colleges in the city, and nearly all have buildings and features of great interest. Cambridge's oldest church is St Bene't's, with a Saxon tower; its most famous is the Church of the Holy Sepulchre, one of only four round churches of its kind.

Huntingdon and **Ely** are both within easy driving distance of Cambridge. Oliver Cromwell and Samuel Pepys were pupils at Huntingdon Grammar School. The building is now a Cromwell museum. Ely also has strong Cromwellian connections – he and his family lived here for ten years. Ely's outstanding feature is the cathedral, a Norman foundation crowned by a stately octagonal lantern tower which contains the Stained Glass Museum.

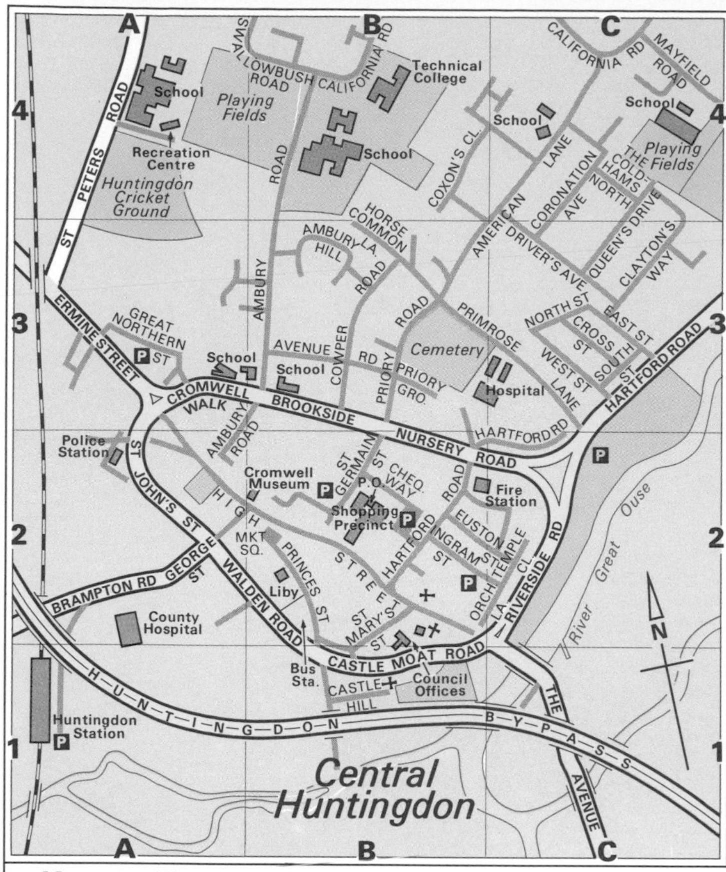

Central Huntingdon

(map — Central Huntingdon)

Labels visible: Swallowbush Road, California Road, Mayfield Road, Technical College, School, Playing Fields, Recreation Centre, Huntingdon Cricket Ground, St Peters Road, Ambury La., Horse Common, American Lane, Coronation Ave, North St, East St, Queen's Drive, Clayton's Way, Playing Fields, Coxon's Cl., Ambury Hill, Cowper Rd, Primrose Lane, Avenue Road, Cemetery, West St, South St, Cross St, Hartford Road, Great Northern St, School, Priory Gro., Priory, Hospital, Cromwell Walk, Brookside, Nursery Road, Hartford Rd, Police Station, St John's St, Ambury Road, Cromwell Museum, St Germain St, P.O. Way, Euston St, Ingram St, Fire Station, Shopping Precinct, Hartford Rd, Orch. Temple La., Riverside Rd, River Great Ouse, Brampton Rd, George St, Walden Road, High St, Princes St, Liby., MKT SQ., County Hospital, Castle Moat Road, Bus Sta., Castle Hill, Council Offices, St Mary's St, Huntingdon Station, Huntingdon By-Pass, The Avenue

Central Ely

(map — Central Ely)

Labels visible: Swimming Pool, Police Station, New Barn Rd, Prickwillow Road, Fire Station, Egremont Street, Nutholt Street, Newnham St, Lane, Archery Cres., Needham Crescent, Old Gaol, Cattle Mkt, Brays, Downham Road, Chapel, Health Centre, Council Offices, Street, Market Street, Butchers Row, P.O., The Vineyards, West Fen Rd, Library, Mkt Pl., High Street, Museum, Fore Hill, Palace Green, Cathedral, Bishop's Palace (School), Chapel, The King's School, Silver Street, Church Lane, The Range, Parade Lane, The Gallery, Barton Sq., The Park, Barton Road, Playing Fields, The King's School, Back Hill, Broad Street, Jubilee Terrace, Victoria St, Station Rd, Annesdale

---

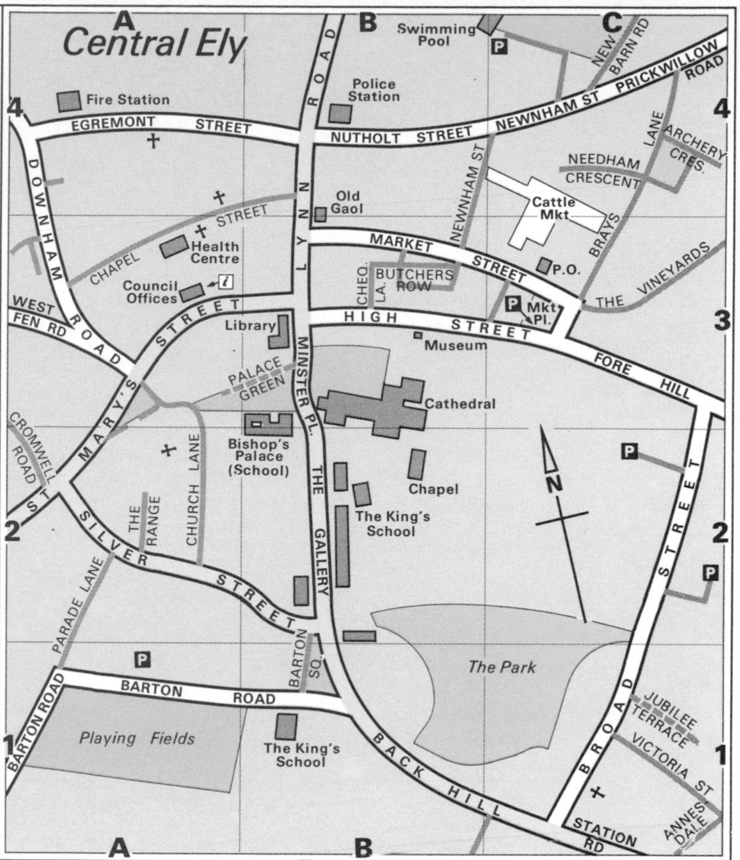

Key to Town Plan and Area Plan

Town Plan
- AA Recommended roads
- Restricted roads
- Other roads
- Buildings of interest — College
- Car Parks — P
- Parks and open spaces
- One Way Streets →

Area Plan
- A roads
- B roads
- Locations — Haslingfield ○
- Urban area

Street Index with Grid Reference

Cambridge

Adam and Eve Street	F1-F2
Adams Road	A2-A3
Auckland Road	F3
Aylestone Road	F4
Belvoir Road	F4
Benet Street	C1-C2-D2
Bridge Street	C3-D3
Broad Street	F1
Brunswick Terrace	F3
Brunswick Walk	F3
Burleigh Street	F2
Castle Street	C4
Chesterton Lane	C4-D4
City Road	F2
Clarendon Street	E1-E2-F2
Clarkson Road	A3-A4
Corn Exchange Street	D1-D2
Cranmer Road	A1
De Freville Avenue	F4
Downing Street	D1
Drummer Street	D2-E2
Earl Street	E2
East Road	F1-F2
Eden Street	F2
Elm Street	E2-F2
Emmanuel Road	E2
Emmanuel Street	D1-D2-E2
Fair Street	F2-F3
Fitzroy Street	F2
Gold Street	F2
Grange Road	A1-A2-A3-A4
Green Street	C2-D2-D3
Hershel Road	A2
Hobson Street	D2-D3
James Street	F3
Jesus Lane	D3-E3
John Street	F2
Kimberley Road	F4
King's Parade	C1-C2
King Street	D2-D3-E3
Lady Margaret Road	B4
Lower Park Street	D3-D4
Madingley Road	A4-B4
Magdalene Street	C4
Maids Causeway	E3-F3
Malcolm Street	D3
Manor Street	D3-E3
Market Street	D2
Melbourne Place	E1-E2-F2
Mill Lane	C1
Mill Road	F1
Napier Street	F3
Newmarket Road	F3
New Park Street	D4
New Square	E2-F2
Northampton Street	B4-C4
Orchard Street	E2-F2
Paradise Street	F2
Parker Street	E1-E2
Park Parade	D4
Parkside	E1-F1
Park Street	D3
Park Terrace	E1
Parsonage Street	F3
Pembroke Street	C1-D1
Pound Hill	B4-C4
Prospect Row	F1-F2
Queens Road	B1-B2-B3-B4
St Andrew's Street	D2-D1-E1
St John's Street	C3-D3
St Peter's Street	B4-C4
Short Street	E2-E3
Sidney Street	D2-D3
Silver Street	B1-C1
Tennis Court Road	D1
Thompson's Lane	C3-C4-D4
Trinity Street	C2-C3
Victoria Avenue	E3-E4
Victoria Street	E2
Warkworth Terrace	F1
West Road	A1-B1
Willis Road	F1

Huntingdon

Ambury Hill	B3
Ambury Road	A2-A3-B3-B4
American Lane	B3-B4-C4
Avenue Road	B3
Brampton Road	A2
Brookside	B2-B3
California Road	B4-C4
Castle Hill	B1
Castle Moat Road	B1-B2
Chequers Way	B2
Clayton's Way	C3-C4
Coronation Avenue	C3-C4
Cowper Road	B3
Coxon's Close	B4
Cromwell Walk	A3-B3
Cross Street	C3
Driver's Avenue	C3-C4
East Street	C3
Ermine Street	A3
Euston Street	B2-C2
George Street	A2
Great Northern Street	A3
Hartford Road	B2-C2-C3
High Street	A2-B2
Horse Common Lane	B3
Huntingdon Bypass	A2-A1-B1-C1
Ingram Street	B2-C2
Market Square	B2
Mayfield Road	C4
North Street	C3
Nursery Road	B3-B2-C2
Orchard Lane	B2-C2
Primrose Lane	B3-C3
Princes Street	B2
Priory Grove	B3
Priory Road	B3
Queens Drive	C3-C4
Riverside Road	C2
St Germain Street	B2
St John's Street	A2-A3
St Mary's Street	B1-B2

Ely

St Peters Road	A3-A4
South Street	C3
Swallowbush Road	A4-B4
The Avenue	C1
The Coldhams North	C4
Temple Close	C2
Walden Road	A2-B2-B1
West Street	C3

Annesdale	C1
Archery Crescent	C4
Back Hill	B1-C1
Barton Road	A1-B1
Barton Square	B1-B2
Brays Lane	C3-C4
Broad Street	C1-C2-C3
Butchers Row	B3
Chapel Street	A3-A4-B4
Chequers Lane	B3
Church Lane	A2-A3
Cromwell Road	A2-A3
Downham Road	A3-A4
Egremont Street	A4-B4
Fore Hill	C3
High Street	B3-C3
Jubilee Terrace	C1
Lynn Road	B3-B4
Market Street	B3-C3
Minster Place	B2-B3
Needham Crescent	C4
New Barn Road	C4
Newnham Street	B3-B4-C4
Nutholt Street	B4
Palace Green	A3-B3
Parade Lane	A1-A2
Prickwillow Road	C4
St Mary's Street	A2-A3-B3
Silver Street	A2-B2
Station Road	C1
The Gallery	B2
The Range	A2
The Vineyards	C3
Victoria Street	C1
West Fen Road	A3

CAMBRIDGE
Behind the gracious university college buildings beautiful lawns and gardens known as the Backs sweep down to the River Cam which, spanned by little bridges and shaded by willows, provides an idyllic setting for punting.

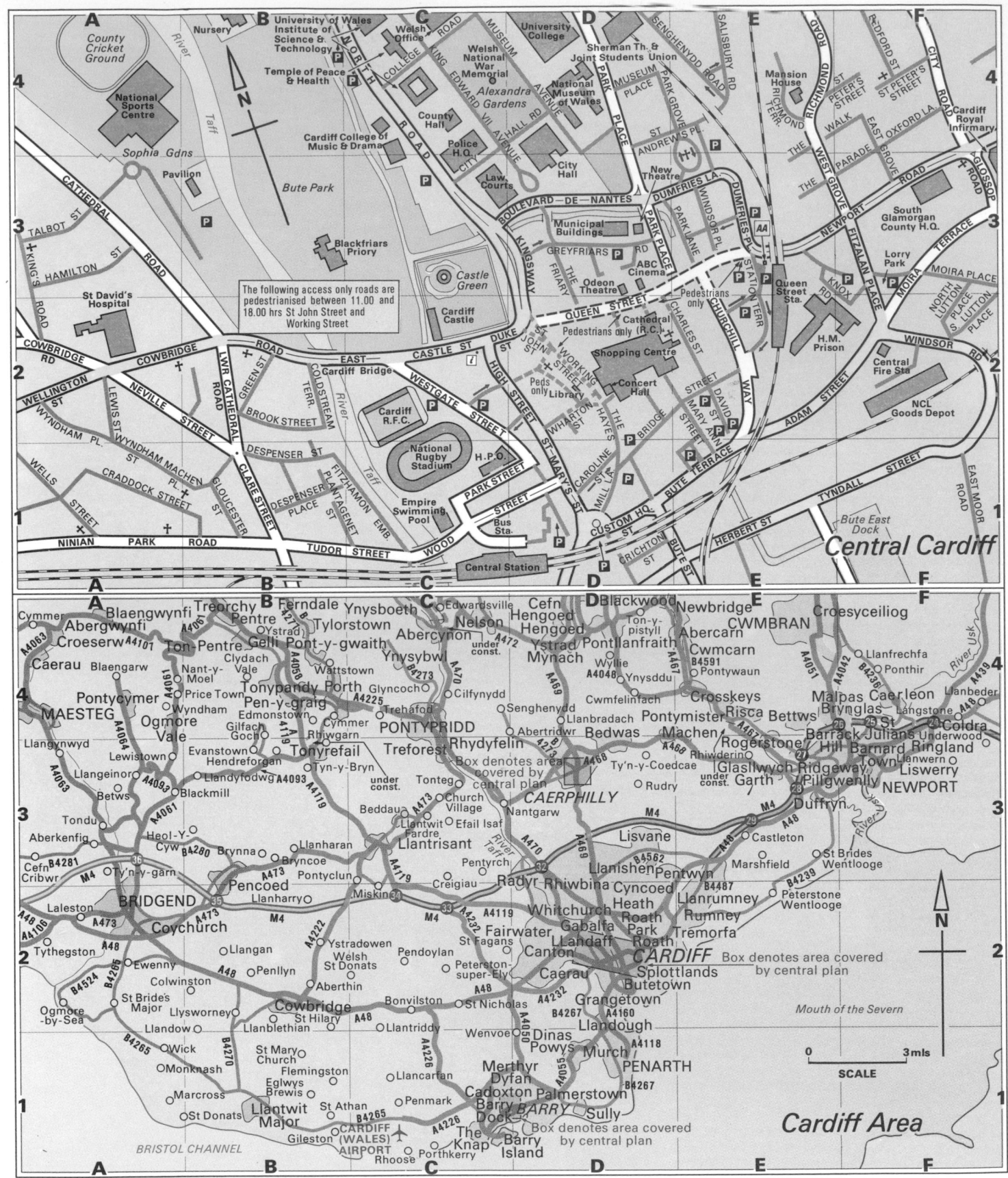

Central Cardiff

Cardiff Area

Cardiff

Strategically important to both the Romans and the Normans, Cardiff slipped from prominence in medieval times and remained a quiet market town in a remote area until it was transformed – almost overnight – by the effects of the Industrial Revolution. The valleys of South Wales were a principal source of iron and coal – raw materials which helped to change the shape and course of

the 19th-century world. Cardiff became a teeming export centre; by the end of the 19th century it was the largest coal-exporting city in the world.

Close to the castle – an exciting place with features from Roman times to the 19th century – is the city's civic centre – a fine concourse of buildings dating largely from the early part of the 20th century. Among them is the National Museum of Wales – a superb collection of art and antiquities from Wales and around the world.

Barry has sandy beaches, landscaped gardens and parks, entertainment arcades and funfairs. Like Cardiff it grew as a result of the demand for coal and steel, but now its dock complex is involved in the petrochemical and oil industries.

Caerphilly is famous for two things – a castle and cheese. The cheese is no longer made here, but the 13th-century castle, slighted by Cromwell, still looms above its moat. No castle in Britain – except Windsor – is larger.

168

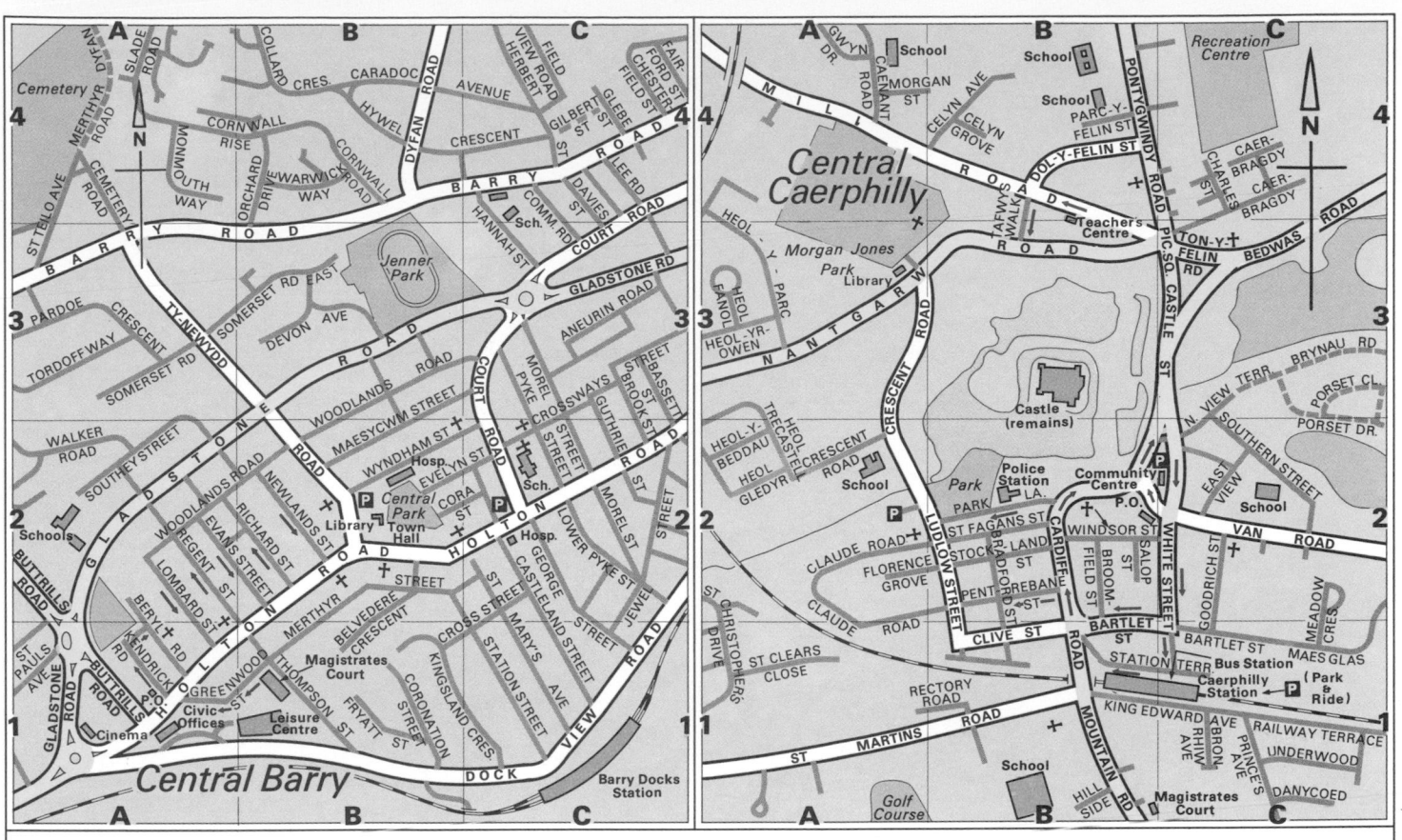

LEGEND

Town Plan

- AA recommended route
- Restricted roads
- Other roads
- Buildings of interest — Cinema ▪
- Car parks — P
- Parks and open spaces — ▲
- One way streets — ↳

Area Plan

- A roads
- B roads
- Locations — Glyncoch ○
- Urban area

Street Index with Grid Reference

Cardiff

Adam Street	E1-E2-F2
Bedford Street	F4
Boulevard de Nantes	C3-D3
Bridge Street	D1-D2-E2
Brook Street	B2
Bute Street	D1-E1
Bute Terrace	D1-E1
Caroline Street	D1
Castle Street	C2
Cathedral Street	A4-A3-B3-B2-A2
Charles Street	D2-E2
Churchill Way	E2-E3
City Hall Road	C3-C4-D4
City Road	F4
Clare Street	B1
Coldstream Terrace	B2
College Road	C4
Cowbridge Road	A2
Cowbridge Road East	A2-B2-C2
Craddock Street	A1-B1
Crichton Street	D1
Custom House Street	D1
David Street	E2
Despenser Place	B1
Despenser Street	B1
Duke Street	C2-D2
Dumfries Lane	D3-E3
Dumfries Place	E3
East Grove	F4-F3
East Moor Road	F1
Fitzalan Place	F3-F2
Fitzhamon Embankment	B1-C1
Glossop Road	F3
Gloucester Street	B1

Green Street	B2
Greyfriars Road	D3
Hamilton Street	A3
Herbert Street	E1
High Street	C2-D2
King Edward VII Avenue	C4-D4-D3-C3
King's Road	A2-A3
Kingsway	C3-D3-D2
Knox Road	E3-F3-F2
Lewis Street	A2
Lower Cathedral Road	B1-B2
Machen Place	A1-B1
Mary Ann Street	E1-E2
Mill Lane	D1
Moira Place	F3
Moira Terrace	F2-F3
Museum Avenue	C4-D4
Museum Place	D4
Neville Street	A2-B2-B1
Newport Road	E3-F3-F4
Ninian Park Road	A1-B1
North Lutton Place	F2-F3
North Road	B4-C4-C3
Oxford Lane	F4
Park Grove	D4-E4
Park Lane	D3-E3
Park Place	D4-D3-E3
Park Street	C1-D1
Plantagenet Street	B1-C1
Queen Street	D2-D3
Richmond Road	E4
Richmond Terrace	E4
St Andrew's Place	D4-E4
St John Street	D2
St Mary's Street	D1-D2
St Peter's Street	E4-F4
Salisbury Road	E4
Senghenydd Road	D4-E4
South Lutton Place	F2-F3
Station Terrace	E2-E3
The Friary	D2-D3
The Hayes	D1-D2
The Parade	E3-F3-F4
The Walk	E3-E4-F4
Talbot Street	A3
Tudor Street	B1-C1
Tyndall Street	E1-F1
Wellington Street	A2
Wells Street	A1
Westgate Street	C2-D2-D1
West Grove	E4-E3-F3
Wharton Street	D2
Windsor Place	E3
Windsor Road	F2
Wood Street	C1-D1
Working Street	D2
Wyndham Place	A2
Wyndham Street	A1-A2

Barry

Aneurin Road	C3
Barry Road	A3-A4-B3-B4-C4
Bassett Street	C2-C3
Belvedere Crescent	B1-B2
Beryl Road	A1-A2
Brook Street	C2-C3
Buttrills Road	A1-A2
Caradoc Avenue	B4-C4

Castleland Street	C1-C2
Cemetery Road	A3-A4
Chesterfield Street	C4
Collard Crescent	B4
Commercial Road	C3-C4
Cora Street	B2-C2
Cornwall Rise	A3-A4
Cornwall Road	B4
Coronation Street	B1
Court Road	C2-C3-C4
Crossways Street	C2-C3
Cross Street	B1-C1-C2
Davies Street	C3-C4
Devon Avenue	B3
Dock View Road	B1-C1-C2
Dyfan Road	B4
Evans Street	A2-B2
Evelyn Street	B2-C2
Fairford Street	C4
Field View Road	C4
Fryatt Street	B1
George Street	C1-C2
Gilbert Street	C4
Gladstone Road	A1-A2-B2-B3-C3
Glebe Street	C4
Greenwood Street	A1-B1
Guthrie Street	C3-C2
Hannah Street	C4-C3
Herbert Street	C4
Holton Road	A1-B1-B2-C2
Hywel Crescent	B4-C4
Jewel Street	C1-C2
Kendrick Road	A1
Kingsland Crescent	B1-C1
Lee Road	C4
Lombard Street	A1-A2
Lower Pyke Street	C2
Maesycwm Street	B2-B3-C3
Merthyr Dyfan Road	A4
Merthyr Street	B1-B2-C2
Monmouth Way	A4
Morel Street	C2-C3
Newlands Street	B2
Orchard Drive	B3-B4
Pardoe Crescent	A3
Pyke Street	C3-C2
Regent Street	A2-B2
Richard Street	A2-B2
St Mary's Avenue	C1-C2
St Pauls Avenue	A1
St Teilo Avenue	A3-A4
Slade Road	A4
Somerset Road	A3
Somerset Road East	A3-B3
Southey Street	A2-A3
Station Street	C1
Thomson Street	B1
Tordoff Way	A3
Ty-Newydd Road	A3-B3-B2
Walker Road	A2
Warwick Way	B4
Woodlands Road	A2-B2-B3-C3
Wyndham Street	B2-C2

Caerphilly

Bartlet Street	B2-B1-C1
Bedwas Road	C3-C4
Bradford Street	B1-B2

Broomfield Street	B2
Bronrhiw Avenue	C1
Brynau Road	D3
Caenant Road	A4
Caer Bragdy	C4
Cardiff Road	B1-B2
Castle Street	C3
Celyn Avenue	B4
Celyn Grove	B4
Charles Street	C4
Claude Road	A1-A2-B2
Clive Street	B1-B2
Crescent Rod	A2-A3-B3
Danycoed	C1
Dol-y-Felen Street	B4
East View	C2
Florence Grove	A2-B2
Goodrich Street	C1-C2
Gwyn Drive	A4
Heol Fanal	A3
Heol Gledyr	A2
Heol Trecastell	A2-A3
Hillside	B1
Heol-y-Beddau	A2
Heol-yr-Owen	A3
King Edward Avenue	B1-C1
Ludlow Street	A2-B2-B1
Maes Glas	C1
Meadow Crescent	C1-C2
Mill Road	A4-B4-B3
Morgan Street	A4-B4
Mountain Road	B1
Nantgarw Road	A3-B3
North View Terrace	C2-C3
Parc-y-Felin Street	B4
Park Lane	B2
Pentrebone Street	B2
Piccadilly Square	B2
Pontygwindy Road	B4-C4
Porset Close	C3
Porset Drive	C2-C3
Prince's Avenue	C1
Railway Terrace	C1
Rectory Road	A1-B1
St Christopher's Drive	A1-A2
St Clears Close	A1
St Fagans Street	B2
St Martins Road	A1-B1
Salop Street	B2
Southern Street	C2-C3
Station Terrace	B1-C1
Stockland Street	B2
Tafwy Walk	B3-B4
Ton-y-Felin Road	C3
Underwood	C1
Van Road	C2
White Street	C2
Windsor Street	B2

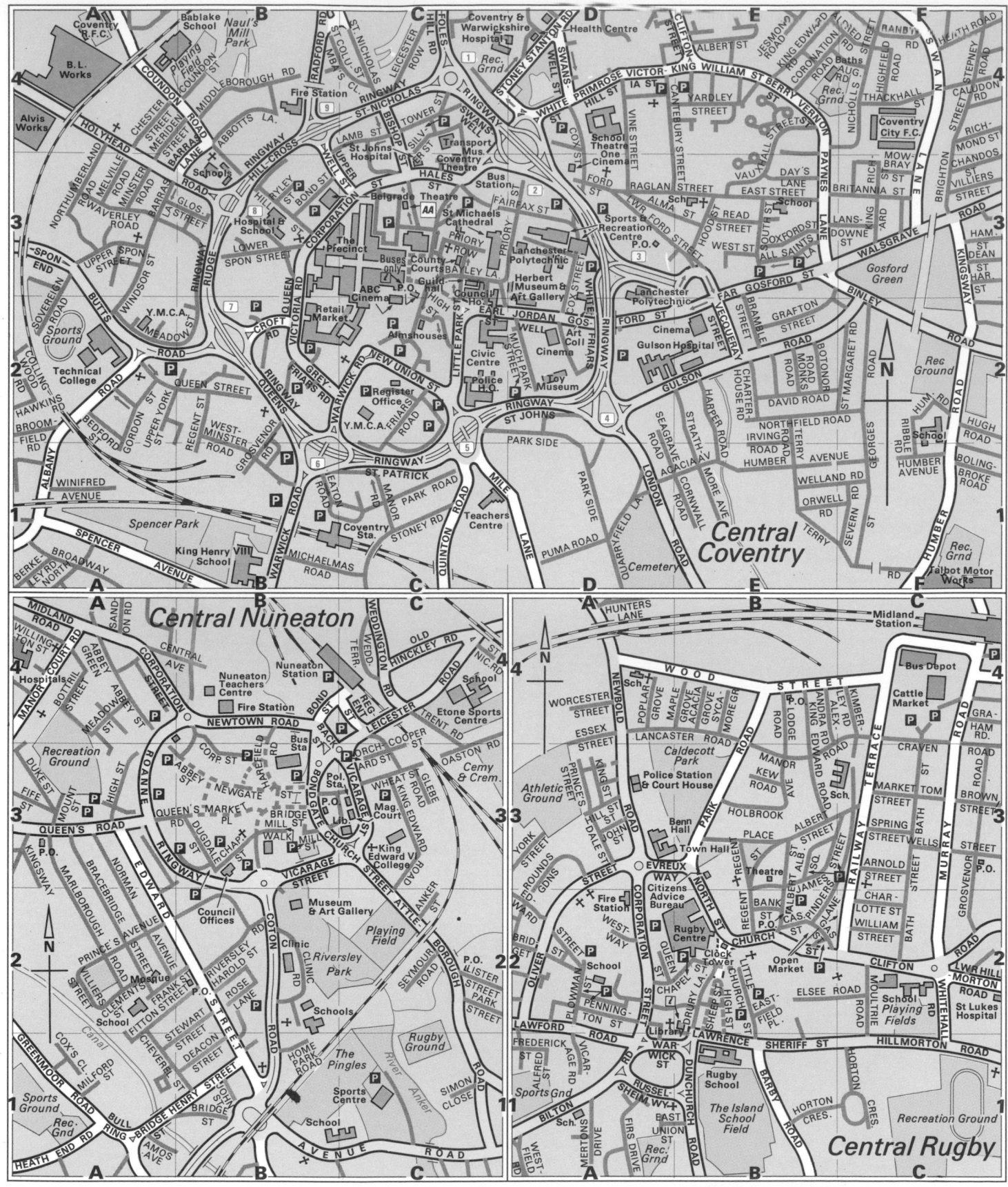

Coventry

Few British towns were as battered by the Blitz as Coventry. A raid in November 1940 flattened most of the city and left the lovely cathedral church a gaunt shell with only the tower and spire still standing. Rebuilding started almost immediately. Symbolising the creation of the new from the ashes of the old is Sir Basil Spence's cathedral, completed in 1962 beside the bombed ruins.

A few medieval buildings have survived intact in the city. St Mary's Guildhall is a finely restored 14th-century building with an attractive minstrels' gallery. Whitefriars Monastery now serves as a local museum. The Herbert Art Gallery and Museum has several collections. Coventry is an important manufacturing centre – most notably for cars – and it is also a university city with the fine campus of the University of Warwick some four miles from the centre.

Nuneaton is an industrial town to the north of Coventry with two distinguished old churches – St Nicholas' and St Mary's. Like Coventry it was badly damaged in the war and its centre has been rebuilt.

Rugby was no more than a sleepy market town until the arrival of the railway. Of course it did have the famous Rugby School, founded in 1567 and one of the country's foremost educational establishments. The railway brought industry – still the town's mainstay.

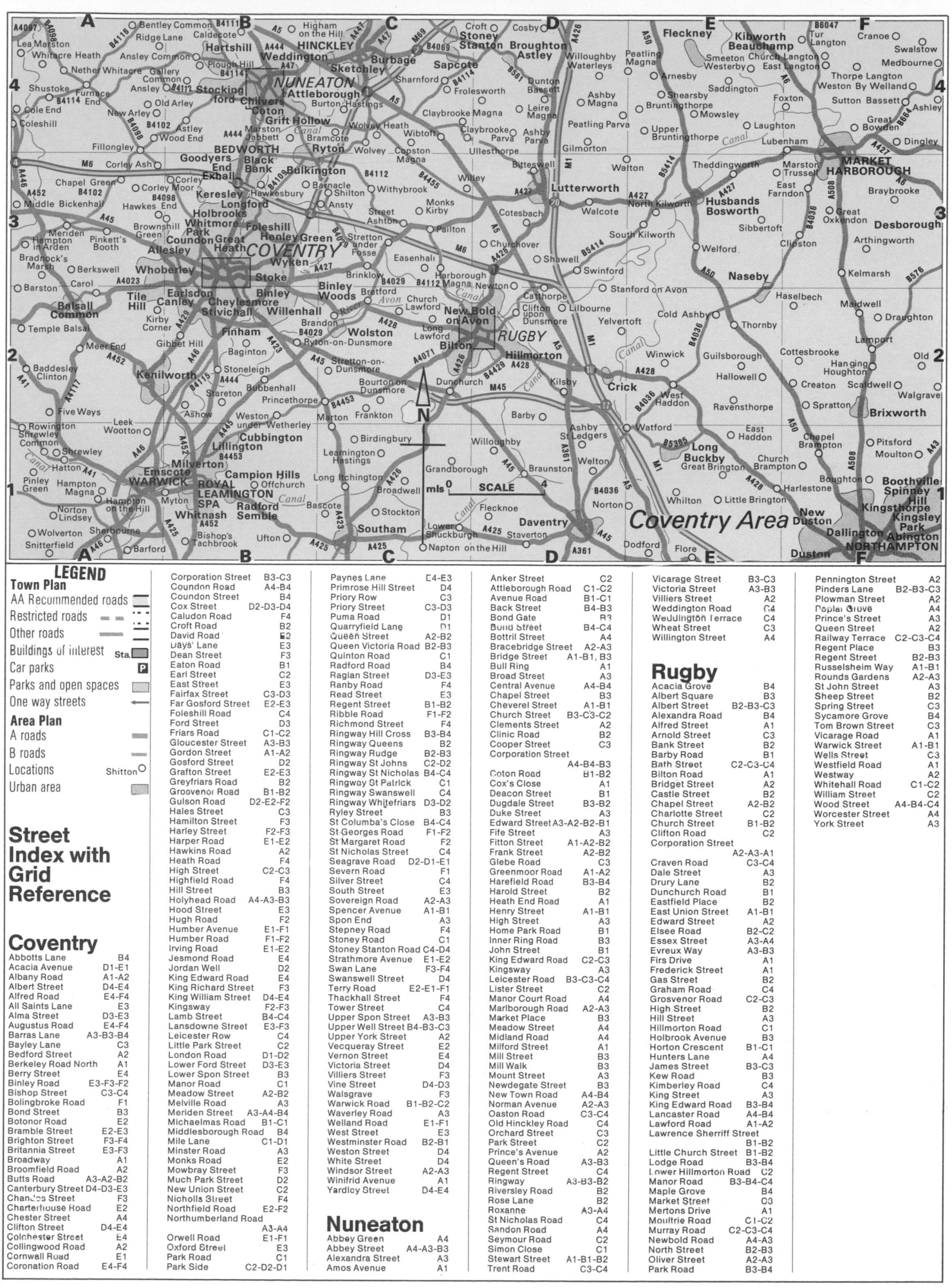

Coventry Area

SCALE
mls 0 _____ 4

N

LEGEND

Town Plan
AA Recommended roads
Restricted roads
Other roads
Buildings of interest   Sta.
Car parks   P
Parks and open spaces
One way streets

Area Plan
A roads
B roads
Locations   Shitton
Urban area

Street Index with Grid Reference

Coventry

Abbotts Lane	B4
Acacia Avenue	D1-E1
Albany Road	A1-A2
Albert Street	D4-E4
Alfred Road	E4-F4
All Saints Lane	E3
Alma Street	D3-E3
Augustus Road	E4-F4
Barras Lane	A3-B3-B4
Bayley Lane	C3
Bedford Street	A2
Berkeley Road North	A1
Berry Street	E4
Binley Road	E3-F3-F2
Bishop Street	C3-C4
Bolingbroke Road	F1
Bond Street	B3
Botonor Road	E2
Bramble Street	E2-E3
Brighton Street	F3-F4
Britannia Street	E3-F3
Broadway	A2
Broomfield Road	A2
Butts Road	A3-A2-B2
Canterbury Street	D4-D3-E3
Chandos Street	F3
Charterhouse Road	E2
Chester Street	A4
Clifton Street	D4-E4
Colchester Street	E4
Collingwood Road	A2
Cornwall Road	E1
Coronation Road	E4-F4
Corporation Street	B3-C3
Coundon Road	A4-B4
Coundon Street	B4
Cox Street	D2-D3-D4
Caludon Road	F4
Croft Road	B2
David Road	E2
Days' Lane	E3
Dean Street	F3
Eaton Road	B1
Earl Street	C2
East Street	E3
Fairfax Street	C3-D3
Far Gosford Street	E2-E3
Foleshill Road	C4
Ford Street	D3
Friars Road	C1-C2
Gloucester Street	B2
Gordon Street	A1-A2
Gosford Street	D2
Grafton Street	E2-E3
Greyfriars Road	B3
Grosvenor Road	B1-B2
Gulson Road	D2-E2-F2
Hales Street	C3
Hamilton Road	F3
Harley Street	F2-F3
Harper Road	E1-E2
Hawkins Road	A2
Heath Road	F4
High Street	C2-C3
Highfield Road	F4
Hill Street	B3
Holyhead Road	A4-A3-B3
Hood Street	E3
Hugh Road	F2
Humber Avenue	E1-F1
Humber Road	F1-F2
Irving Road	E1-E2
Jesmond Road	E4
Jordan Well	D2
King Edward Road	E4
King Richard Street	F3
King William Street	D4-E4
Kingsway	F2-F3
Lamb Street	B3-C4
Lansdowne Street	E3-F3
Leicester Row	C4
Little Park Street	C2
London Road	D1-D2
Lower Ford Street	D3-D4
Lower Spon Street	B3
Manor Road	C1
Meadow Street	A2-B2
Melville Road	A2
Meriden Street	A3-A4-B4
Michaelmas Road	B1-C1
Middlesborough Road	A4
Mile Lane	C1-D1
Minster Road	A4
Monks Road	E2
Mowbray Street	F3
Much Park Street	D2
New Union Street	C2
Nicholls Street	D4
Northfield Road	E2-F2
Northumberland Road	A3-A4
Orwell Road	E1-F1
Oxford Street	E3
Park Road	C1
Park Side	C2-D2-D1
Paynes Lane	E4-E3
Primrose Hill Street	D4
Priory Row	C3
Priory Street	C3-D3
Puma Road	D1
Quarryfield Lane	D1
Queen Street	A2-B2
Queen Victoria Road	B2-B3
Quinton Road	C1
Radford Road	B4
Raglan Street	D3-E3
Ranby Road	F4
Read Street	E4
Regent Street	B1-B2
Ribble Road	F1-F2
Richmond Street	F4
Ringway Hill Cross	B3-B4
Ringway Queens	B2
Ringway Rudge	B2-B3
Ringway St Johns	C2-D2
Ringway St Nicholas	B4-C4
Ringway St Patrick	C1
Ringway Swanswell	C4
Ringway Whitefriars	D3-D2
Ryley Street	D2
St Columba's Close	B4-C4
St Georges Road	F1-F2
St Margaret Road	F2
St Nicholas Street	C4
Seagrave Road	D2-D1-E1
Severn Road	F1
Silver Street	C4
South Street	E3
Sovereign Road	A2-A3
Spencer Avenue	A1-B1
Spon End	A3
Stepney Road	F4
Stoney Road	C1
Stoney Stanton Road	C4-D4
Strathmore Avenue	E1-E2
Swan Lane	F3-F4
Swanswell Street	D4
Terry Road	E2-E1-F1
Thackhall Street	F4
Tower Street	C4
Upper Spon Street	A3-B3
Upper Well Street	B4-B3-C3
Upper York Street	B2
Vecqueray Street	E2
Vernon Street	E4
Victoria Street	D4
Villiers Street	F3
Vine Street	D4-D3
Walsgrave	F3
Warwick Road	B1-B2-C2
Waverley Road	A3
Welland Road	E1-F1
West Street	E3
Westminster Road	B2-B1
Weston Street	D4
White Street	D4
Windsor Street	A2-A3
Winifrid Avenue	A1
Yardley Street	D4-E4

Nuneaton

Abbey Green	A4
Abbey Road	A4-A3-B3
Alexandra Street	A3
Amos Avenue	A1
Anker Street	C2
Attleborough Road	C1-C2
Avenue Road	B1-C1
Back Street	B4-B3
Bond Gate	B3
Bond Street	B4-C4
Bottril Road	B4
Bracebridge Street	A2-A3
Bridge Street	A1-B1, B3
Bull Ring	A1
Broad Street	A3
Central Avenue	A4-B4-B3
Chapel Street	B3
Cheverel Street	A1-B1
Church Street	B3-C3-C2
Clements Street	A2
Clinic Road	B2
Cooper Street	B2
Corporation Street	A4-B4-B3
Coton Road	B1-B2
Cox's Close	B1
Deacon Street	B1
Dugdale Street	B3-B2
Duke Street	A3
Edward Street	A3-A2-B2-B1
Fife Street	A3
Fitton Street	A1-A2-B2
Frank Street	A2-B2
Glebe Road	C3
Greenmoor Road	A1-A2
Harefield Road	B3-B4
Harold Street	B2
Heath End Road	A1
Henry Street	A1-B1
High Street	A3
Home Park Road	B1
Inner Ring Road	B3
John Street	B1
King Edward Road	C2-C3
Kingsway	A3
Leicester Road	B3-C3-C4
Lister Street	C2
Manor Court Road	A4
Marlborough Road	A2-A3
Market Place	B3
Meadow Street	A4
Midland Road	A4
Milford Street	A1
Mill Street	B3
Mill Walk	B3
Mount Street	A3
Newdegate Street	B3
New Town Road	A4-B4
Norman Avenue	A2-A3
Oaston Road	C3-C4
Old Hinckley Road	C4
Orchard Street	C3
Park Street	C2
Prince's Avenue	A2
Queen's Road	A3-B3
Regent Street	C4
Ringway	A3-B3-B2
Riversley Road	B2
Rose Lane	B2
Roxanne	A3-A4
St Nicholas Road	C4
Sandon Road	A4
Seymour Road	C2
Simon Close	A3
Stewart Street	A1-B1-B2
Trent Road	C3-C4
Vicarage Street	B3-C3
Victoria Street	A3-B3
Villiers Street	A2
Weddington Road	C4
Weddington Terrace	C4
Wheat Street	C3
Willington Street	A4

Rugby

Acacia Grove	B4
Albert Square	B3
Albert Street	B2-B3-C3
Alexandra Road	B4
Alfred Street	A1
Arnold Street	C3
Bank Street	B2
Barby Road	B1
Bath Street	C2-C3-C4
Bilton Road	A1
Bridget Street	A2
Castle Street	B2
Chapel Street	A2-B2
Charlotte Street	C2
Church Street	B1-B2
Clifton Road	C3
Corporation Street	A2-A3-A1
Craven Road	C3-C4
Dale Street	A3
Drury Lane	B2
Dunchurch Road	B1
Eastfield Place	B2
East Union Street	A1-B1
Edward Street	A2
Elsee Road	B2-C2
Essex Street	A3-A4
Evreux Way	A3-B3
Firs Drive	A1
Frederick Street	A1
Gas Street	B2
Graham Road	C4
Grosvenor Road	C2-C3
High Street	B2
Hill Street	A3
Hillmorton Road	C1
Holbrook Avenue	B3
Horton Crescent	B1-C1
Hunters Lane	A4
James Street	B3-C3
Kew Road	B3
Kimberley Road	C4
King Street	A3
King Edward Road	B3-B4
Lancaster Road	A4-B4
Lawford Road	A1-A2
Lawrence Sherriff Street	
Little Church Street	B1-B2
Lodge Road	B2
Lower Hillmorton Road	C2
Manor Road	B3-B4-C4
Maple Grove	B4
Market Street	C3
Mertons Drive	A1
Moultrie Road	C1-C2
Murray Road	C2-C3-C4
Newbold Road	A4-A3
North Street	B2-B3
Oliver Street	A2-A3
Park Road	B3-B4
Pennington Street	A2
Pinders Lane	B2-B3-C3
Plowman Street	A2
Poplar Grove	A4
Prince's Street	A3
Queen Street	A2
Railway Terrace	C2-C3-C4
Regent Place	B3
Regent Street	B2-B3
Russelsheim Way	A1-B1
Rounds Gardens	A2-A3
St John Street	A3
Sheep Street	B2
Spring Street	C3
Sycamore Grove	B4
Tom Brown Street	C3
Vicarage Road	A1
Warwick Street	A1-B1
Wells Street	C3
Westfield Road	A1
Westway	A2
Whitehall Road	C1-C2
William Street	C2
Wood Street	A4-B4-C4
Worcester Street	A4
York Street	A3

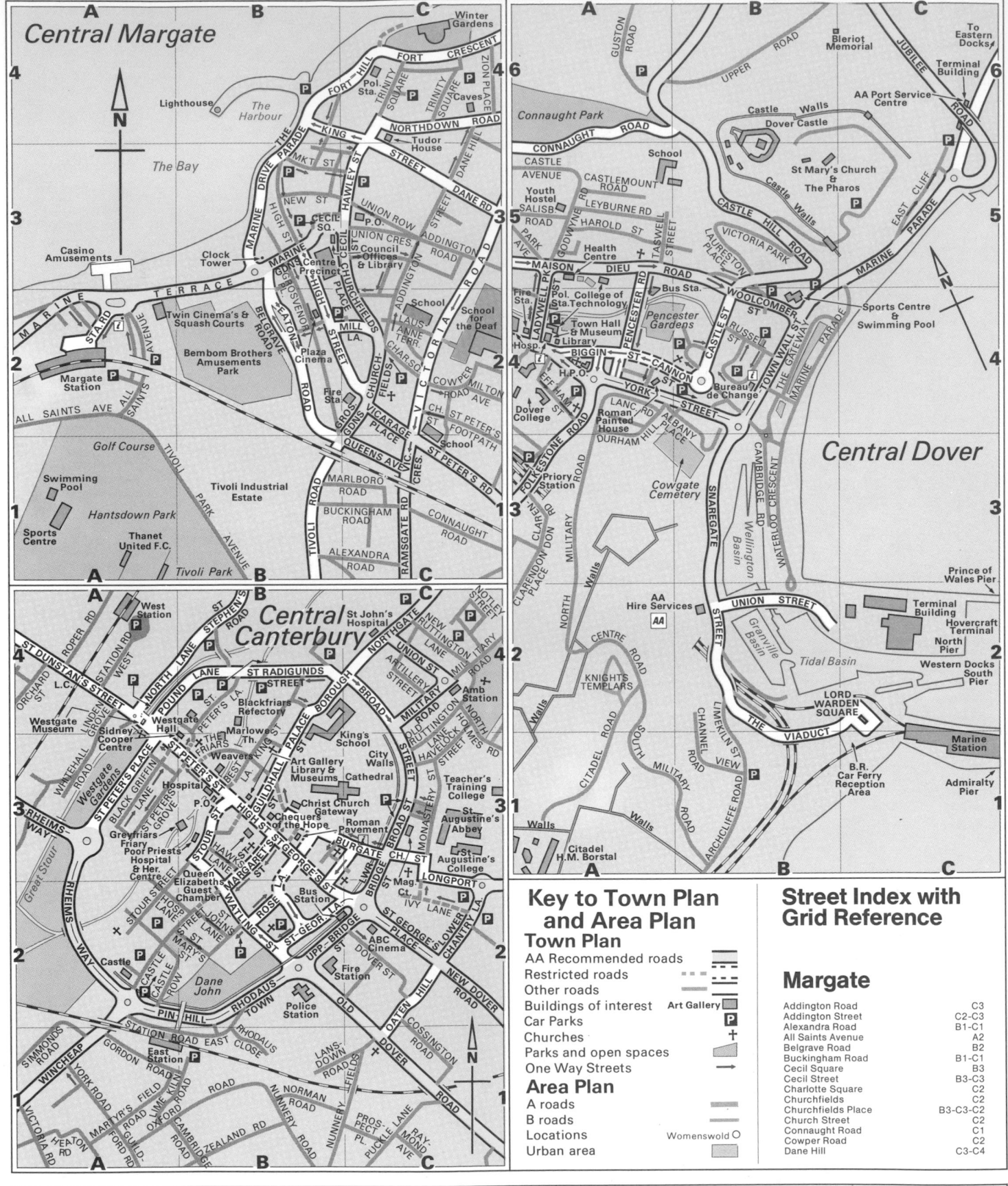

Key to Town Plan and Area Plan

Town Plan

AA Recommended roads	
Restricted roads	
Other roads	
Buildings of interest	Art Gallery
Car Parks	P
Churches	†
Parks and open spaces	
One Way Streets	→

Area Plan

A roads	
B roads	
Locations	Womenswold ○
Urban area	

Street Index with Grid Reference

Margate

Dover

Travellers tend to rush through Dover – it is one of the busiest passenger ports in England – and by so doing miss an exciting town with much of interest. Outstanding is the castle. Its huge fortifications have guarded the town since the 12th century, but within its walls are even older structures – a Saxon church and a Roman lighthouse called the Pharos. In the town itself, the town hall is housed within the walls of a 13th-century guest house called the Maison Dieu. The Roman Painted House in New Street consists of substantial remains of a Roman town house and include the best-preserved Roman wall paintings north of the Alps.

Canterbury is one of Britain's most historic towns. It is the seat of the Church in England, and has been so since St Augustine began his mission here in the 6th century. The cathedral is a priceless work of art containing many other works of art, including superb displays of medieval carving and stained glass. Ancient city walls – partly built on Roman foundations – still circle parts of the city, and a wealth of grand public buildings as well as charming private houses of many periods line the maze of lanes in the shadow of the cathedral.

Margate and *Ramsgate* both grew as commercial ports, but for many years they have specialised in catering for holidaymakers who like safe, sandy beaches and excellent facilities.

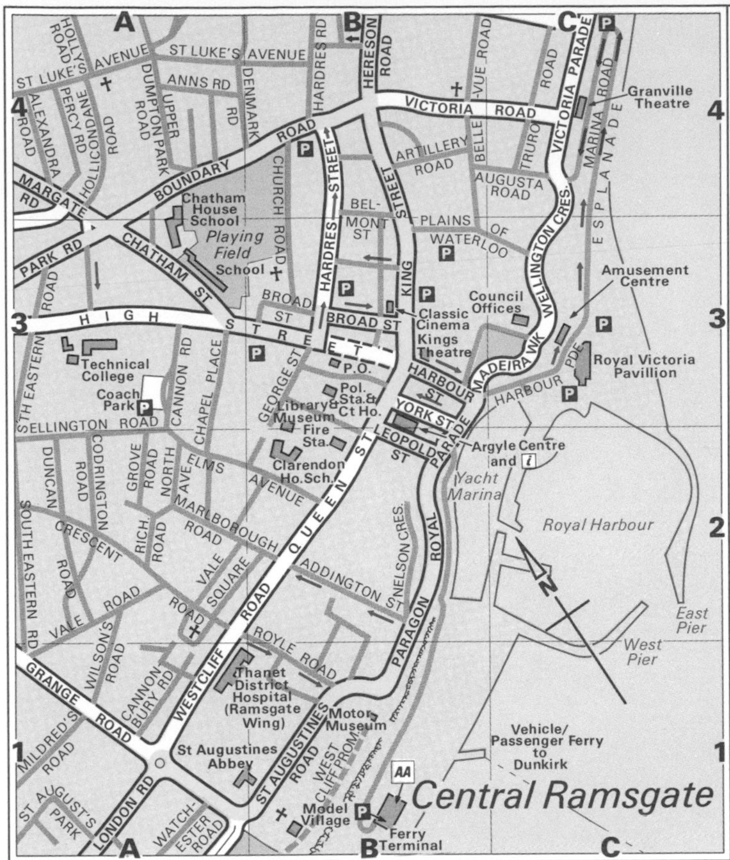

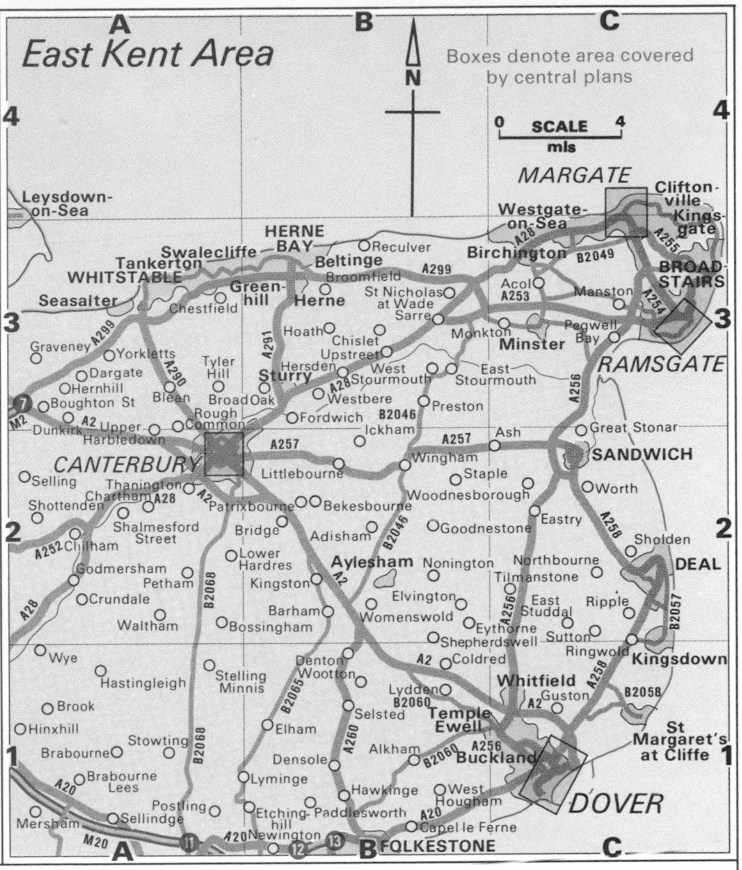

East Kent Area

Boxes denote area covered by central plans

SCALE 0 — 4 mls

Central Ramsgate

Dane Road	C3
Eaton Road	B1-B2-B3
Fort Crescent	C4
Fort Hill	B4-C4
Grosvenor Gardens	C1-C2
Grosvenor Place	B2-B3
Hawley Street	C2
High Street	B3-B2-C2
King Street	D4-C3
Lausanne Terrace	C2
Marine Drive	B3
Marine Gardens	B3
Marine Terrace	A2-A3-B3-B2
Market Street	B3-C3
Marlborough Road	B1-C1
Mill Lane	B2-C2
Milton Avenue	C2
New Street	B3
Northdown Road	C4
Queens Avenue	C1
Ramsgate Road	C1
St Peter's Footpath	C1-C2
St Peter's Road	C1
Station Road	A2
The Parade	B3-B4
Tivoli Park Avenue	A2-A1-B1
Tivoli Road	B1
Trinity Square	C4
Union Crescent	C3
Union Row	C3
Vicarage Crescent	C1
Vicarage Place	C1-C2
Victoria Road	C2-C3
Zion Place	C4

Canterbury

Artillery Street	C4
Best Lane	B3
Black Griffin Lane	A3
Borough	B4-C4
Broad Street	C4-C3
Burgate	B3-C3
Cambridge Road	A1-B1
Castle Row	A2-B2
Castle Street	A2-B2
Church Street	C3
Cossington Road	C2-C1
Dover Street	C2
Gordon Road	A1-B1
Guildford Road	A1
Guildhall Street	B3
Havelock Street	C3-C4
Hawks Lane	B3
Heaton Road	A1
High Street	B3
Hospital Lane	A2-B2
Ivy Lane	C2
King Street	B3-B4
Lansdown Road	B1-C1
Lime Kiln Road	A1-B1
Linden Grove	A3-A4
Longport	C2-C3
Lower Bridge Street	C2-C3
Lower Chantry Lane	C2
Martyr's Field Road	A1
Military Road	C4
Monastery Street	C3
New Dover Road	C2
New Ruttington Lane	C4
Norman Road	B1
Northgate	C4
North Holmes Road	C4-C3
North Lane	A4-B4
Notley Street	C4
Nunnery Fields	B1-C1
Nunnery Road	B1
Oaten Hill	C1-C2
Old Dover Road	B2-C2-C1
Old Ruttington Lane	C3-C4
Orchard Street	A4
Oxford Road	A1-B1
Palace Street	B3-B4
Pin Hill	A2-B2
Pound Lane	A4-B4
Prospect Place	C1
Puckle Lane	C1
Raymond Avenue	C1
Rheims Way	A2-A3
Rhodaus Town	B1
Roper Road	A4
Rose Lane	B2-B3
St Dunstan's Street	A4
St Georges Lane	A4
St George's Place	C2
St George's Street	B3-B2
St John's Lane	B2
St Margaret's Street	B2-B3
St Mary's Street	A2-B2
St Peters Grove	A3-B3
St Peter's Lane	B4
St Peter's Place	A3
St Peter's Street	A3-B3
St Stephen's Road	B4
St Rudlgunds Street	B4
Simmonds Road	A1-A2
Station Road East	A2-A1-B1
Station Road West	A4
Stour Street	A2-A3-B3
The Friars	B3
Union Street	C4
Upper Bridge Street	B2-C2
Victoria Road	A1
Watling Street	B2
Whitehall Road	A3
Wincheap	A1-A2
York Road	A1
Zealand Road	B1

Dover

Albany Place	A4-B4-B3
Archcliffe Road	B1
Biggin Street	A4
Cambridge Road	B3
Cannon Street	A4-B4
Castle Avenue	A5
Castle Hill Road	B5
Castlemount Road	A5
Castle Street	B4
Centre Road	A4
Channel View Road	B1-B2
Citadel Road	A1-A2
Clarendon Place	A2-A3
Clarendon Road	A3
Connaught Road	A5-A6
Durham Hill	A3-A4
East Cliff	C5
Effingham Street	A4
Folkestone Road	A3-A4
Godwyne Road	A5
Guston Road	A6
Harold Street	A5
Jubilee Road	C6
Knights Templars	A2
Ladywell Park Road	A4-A5
Lancaster Road	B5
Laureston Place	A5
Leyburne Road	A5
Limekiln Street	B1-B2
Lord Warden Square	C1-C2
Maison Dieu Road	A5-B5
Marine Parade	B4-C4-C5
North Military Road	A2-A3
Park Avenue	A5
Pencester Road	A4-A5
Russell Street	B4
Salisbury Road	A5
Snaregate Street	B2-B3
South Military Road	A2-A1-B1
The Gateway	B4
The Viaduct	B1-B2
Taswell Street	A5
Town Hall Street	B4
Union Street	B2
Upper Road	A6-B6
Victoria Park	B5
Woolcomber Street	B4
York Street	A4-B4

Ramsgate

Addington Street	B2
Alexandra Road	A4
Anns Road	A4
Artillery Road	B4
Augusta Road	B4-C4
Belle Vue Road	B4
Belmont Street	B4
Boundary Road	A3-A4-B4
Broad Street	B3
Cannonbury Road	A1
Canon Road	A3
Chapel Place	A2-A3
Chatham Street	A3
Church Road	B3-B4
Codrington Road	A2
Crescent Road	A2
Denmark Road	A4-B4
Duncan Road	A2
Ellington Road	A2-A3
Elms Avenue	A2-B2
Esplanade	C3-C4
George Street	B3
Grange Road	A1
Grove Road	A2
Harbour Parade	B3-C3
Harbour Street	B3
Hardres Street	B3-B4
Hereson Road	B4
High Street	A3-B3
Hollicondane Road	A4
Holly Road	A4
King Street	B3-B4
Leopold Street	B2 D0
London Road	A1
Madeira Walk	B3-C3
Margate Road	A3-A4
Marina Road	C4
Marlborough Road	A2-B2
Mildred's Road	A1
Nelson Crescent	B2
North Avenue	A2
Paragon Royal Parade	B1-B2-B3
Park Road	A3
Percy Road	A4
Plains of Waterloo	B3-C3
Queen Street	B2-B3
Richmond Road	A2
Royle Road	A2-B2-B1
St Augustines Road	A1-B1
St August's Park	A1
St Luke's Avenue	A4-B4
South Eastern Road	A1-A2-A3
Truro Road	C4
Upper Dumpton Park Road	A4
Vale Road	A1-A2
Vale Square	A2-B2
Victoria Parade	C4
Victoria Road	B4-C4
Watchester Road	A1
Wellington Crescent	C3-C4
West Cliff Promenade	B1
Westcliff Road	A1-A2-B2
Wilson's Road	A1-A2
York Street	B2-B3

DOVER
The famous White Cliffs of Dover provide exhilarating coastal walks with views out across the Channel. Paths to the north-east lead to Walmer and to the south-east, to Folkestone.

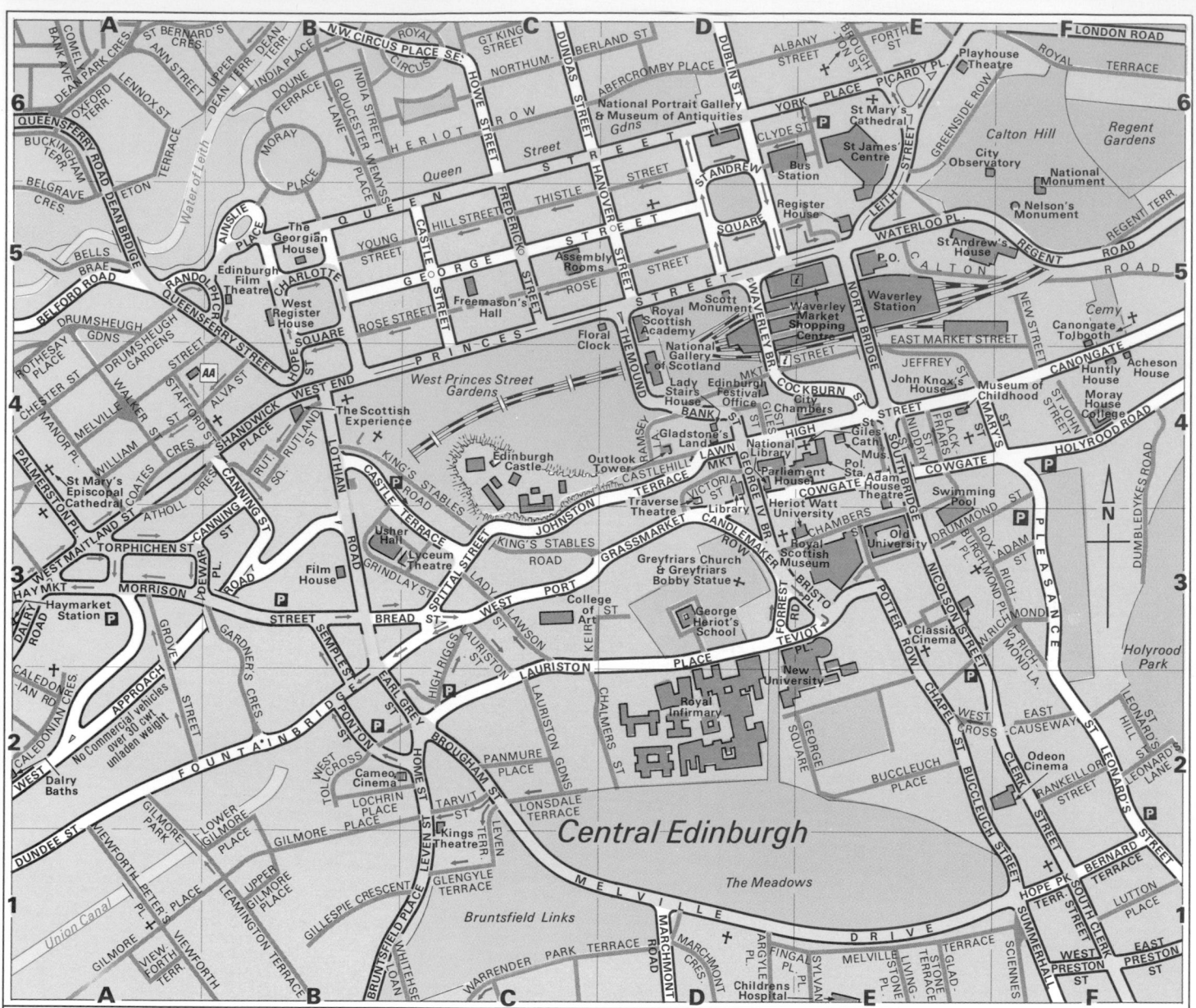

Key to Town Plan and Area Plan

Town Plan
A A Recommended roads	
Other roads	
Restricted roads	
Buildings of intrest	Gallery
Car Parks	P
Parks and open spaces	
One Way Streets	
Churches	+

Area Plan
A roads	
B roads	
Locations	Newcraighall O
Urban area	

Street Index with Grid Reference

Edinburgh

Abercromby Place	C6-D6
Adam Street	F3
Ainslie Place	B5
Albany Street	D6-E6
Alva Street	A4-B4
Ann Street	A6
Argyle Place	D1
Athol Crescent	A3-A4-B4
Bank Street	D4
Belford Road	A5
Belgrave Crescent	A5
Bells Brae	A5
Bernard Terrace	F1
Blackfriars Street	E4
Bread Street	B3-C3
Bristo Place	D3-E3
Brougham Street	C2
Broughton Street	E6
Bruntsfield Place	B1-C1
Buccleuch Place	E2
Buccleauch Street	E2-F2-F1
Buckingham Terrace	A5-A6
Caledonian Crescent	A2
Caledonian Road	A2
Calton Road	E5-F5
Candlemaker Row	D3
Canning Street	A3-B3-B4
Canongate	E4-F4-F5
Castle Hill	D4
Castle Street	C5
Castle Terrace	B4-B3-C3
Chalmers Street	C2-D2
Chambers Street	D3-E3
Charlotte Square	B4-B5
Chapel Street	E2
Chester Street	A4
Clerk Street	F1-F2
Clyde Street	D6-E6
Coates Crescent	A4-B4
Cockburn Street	D4-E4
Comely Bank Avenue	A6
Cowgate	D4-E4-F4
Dalry Road	A3
Dean Bridge	A5
Dean Park Crescent	A6
Dean Terrace	B6
Dewar Place	A3-B3
Doune Terrace	B6
Drummond Street	E3-F3-F4
Drumsheugh Gardens	A4-A5
Dublin Street	D6
Dumbiedykes Road	F3-F4
Dundas Street	C6
Dundee Street	A1-A2

Edinburgh

Scotland's ancient capital, dubbed the "Athens of the North", is one of the most splendid cities in the whole of Europe. Its buildings, its history and its cultural life give it an international importance which is celebrated every year in its world-famous festival. The whole city is overshadowed by the craggy castle which seems to grow out of the rock itself. There has been a fortress here since the 7th century and most of the great figures of Scottish history have been associated with it. The old town grew up around the base of Castle Rock within the boundaries of the defensive King's Wall and, unable to spread outwards, grew upwards in a maze of tenements. However, during the 18th century new prosperity from the shipping trade resulted in the building of the New Town and the regular, spacious layout of the Georgian development makes a striking contrast with the old hotch-potch of streets. Princes Street is the main east-west thoroughfare with excellent shops on one side and Princes Street Gardens with their famous floral clock on the south side.

As befits such a splendid capital city there are numerous museums and art galleries packed with priceless treasures. Among these are the famous picture gallery in 16th-century Holyroodhouse, the present Royal Palace, and the fascinating and unusual Museum of Childhood.

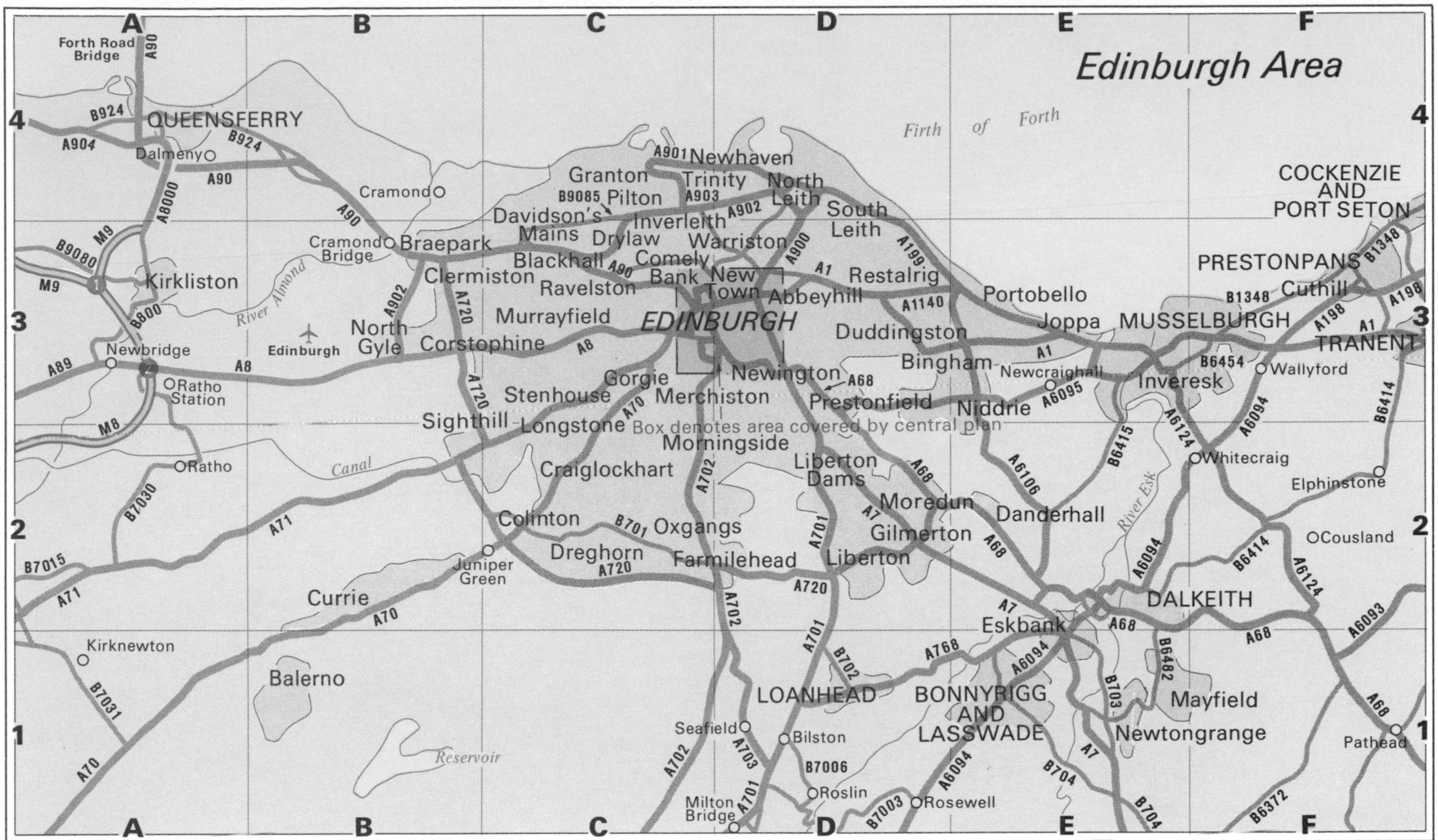

Map labels (partial): Forth Road Bridge, QUEENSFERRY, Dalmeny, Kirkliston, Newbridge, Ratho Station, Ratho, Kirknewton, Balerno, Currie, Juniper Green, Dreghorn, Colinton, Craiglockhart, Sighthill, Longstone, Stenhouse, Gorgie, Merchiston, Morningside, Cramond, Cramond Bridge, Braepark, Clermiston, Davidson's Mains, Drylaw, Ravelston, Blackhall, Comely Bank, North Gyle, Corstorphine, Murrayfield, EDINBURGH, Granton, Pilton, Trinity, Newhaven, North Leith, South Leith, Inverleith, Warriston, New Town, Abbeyhill, Restalrig, Duddingston, Newington, Prestonfield, Niddrie, Bingham, Newcraighall, Portobello, Joppa, MUSSELBURGH, Inveresk, Wallyford, COCKENZIE AND PORT SETON, PRESTONPANS, Cuthill, TRANENT, Oxgangs, Farmilehead, Liberton Dams, Liberton, Moredun, Gilmerton, Danderhall, Whitecraig, Elphinstone, Cousland, DALKEITH, Eskbank, Mayfield, Newtongrange, Pathead, LOANHEAD, BONNYRIGG AND LASSWADE, Seafield, Bilston, Milton Bridge, Roslin, Rosewell, Firth of Forth, River Almond, Canal, Reservoir, River Esk

Box denotes area covered by central plan

Street Index

Earl Grey Street	B2-C2
East Cross Causeway	F2
East Market Street	E5-E4-F4-F5
East Preston Street	F1
Eton Terrace	A5-A6
Fingal Place	D1-E1
Forrest Road	D3
Fountain Bridge	A2-B2-B3-C3
Frederick Street	C5
Forth Street	E6
Gardeners Crescent	B2-B3
George IV Bridge	D3-D4
George Square	E2
George Street	B5-C5-D5
Gillespie Crescent	B1-C1
Gilmore Park	A1-A2
Gilmore Place	A1-B1-B2-C2
Gladstone Terrace	E1
Glengyle Terrace	C1
Gloucester Lane	B6
Grass Market	D3
Great King Street	C6
Greenside Row	E6-F6
Grindley Street	B3-C3
Grove Street	A2-A3
Hanover Street	C6-D6-D5
Hay Market	A3
Heriot Row	B6-C6
High Riggs	C2-C3
High Street	D4-E4
Hill Street	C5
Holyrood Road	F4
Home Street	C2
Hope Park Terrace	F1
Hope Street	B4
Howe Street	C6
India Place	B6
India Street	B6
Jeffrey Street	E4
Johnston Terrace	C3-C4-D4
Kier Street	C3-D3
King's Stables Road	D4-C4-C3
Lady Lawson Street	C3
Lauriston Gardens	C2
Lauriston Place	C2-C3-D3
Lauriston Street	C2-C3
Lawn Market	D4
Leamington Terrace	A1-B1
Leith Street	E5-E6
Lennox Street	A6
Leven Street	C1-C2
Leven Terrace	C1-C2
Livingtone Place	E1
Lochrin Place	B2-C2
London Road	F6
Lonsdale Terrace	C2
Lothian Road	B3-B4
Lower Gilmore Place	B1-B2
Lutton Place	F1
Manor Place	A4
Marchmont Crescent	D1
Marchmont Road	D1
Market Street	D4-E4
Melville Drive	C2-C1-D1-E1-F1
Melville Street	A4-B4-B5
Melville Terrace	E1-F1
Moray Place	B5-B6
Morrison Street	A3-B3
New Street	F4-F5
Nicolson Street	E3-E2-F2
Niddry Street	E4
North Bridge	E4-E5
North West Circus Place	B6
Northumberland Street	C6-D6
Oxford Terrace	A6
Palmerston Place	A3-A4
Panmure Place	C2
Picardy Place	E6
Pleasance	F3-F4
Ponton Street	B2-C2
Potter Row	E2-E3
Princes Street	B4-C4-C5-D5-E5
Queen Street	B5-C5-C6-D6
Queensferry Road	A5-A6
Queensferry Street	A5-B5-B4
Ramsey Lane	D4
Randolph Crescent	A5-B5
Rankeillor Street	F2
Regent Road	E5-F5
Regent Terrace	F5
Richmond Lane	F2-F3
Richmond Place	E3-F3
Rose Street	B5-C5-D5
Rothesay Place	A4-A5
Roxbury Place	E3
Royal Circus	B6-C6
Royal Terrace	E6-F6
Rutland Square	B4
Rutland Street	B4
St Andrew Square	D5-D6
St Bernard's Crescent	A6-B6
St Giles Street	D4
St John Street	F4
St Leonards Hill	F2
St Leonards Lane	F2
St Leonard's Street	F1-F2
St Mary's Street	E4-F4
St Peter Place	A1
Sciennes	F1
Semples Street	B2-B3
Shandwick Place	B4
South Bridge	E3-E4
South Clerk Street	F1
South East Circus Place	C6
Spittal Street	C3
Stafford Street	A4-B4
Summerhall	F1
Sylvan Place	E1
The Mound	D4-D5
Tarvit Street	C2
Teviot Place	D3-E3
Thistle Street	C5-D5-D6
Torphichen Street	A3
Upper Dean Terrace	B6
Upper Gilmore Place	B1
Victoria Street	D4
Viewforth	A1-B1
Viewforth Terrace	A1
Walker Street	A4-A5
Warrender Park Terrace	C1-D1
Waterloo Place	E5
Waverley Bridge	D4-D5
Wemyss Place	B5-B6
West Approach Road	A2-A3-B3
West Cross-Causeway	E2
West End	B4
West Maitland Street	A3-A4
West Port	C3
West Preston Street	F1
West Richmond Street	E3-F3
West Tollcross	B2
Whitehouse Loan	B1-C1
William Street	A4
York Place	D6-E6
Young Street	B5-C5

EDINBURGH
Holyrood Palace originated as a guest house for the Abbey of Holyrood in the 16th century, but most of the present building was built for Charles II. Mary Queen of Scots was one of its most famous inhabitants.

Glasgow

Although much of Glasgow is distinctly Victorian in character, its roots go back very many centuries. Best link with the past is the cathedral; founded in the 6th century, it has features from many succeeding centuries, including an exceptional 13th-century crypt. Nearby is Provand's Lordship, the city's oldest house. It dates from 1471 and is now a museum. Two much larger museums are to

be found a little out of the centre – the Art Gallery and Museum contains one of the finest collections of paintings in Britain, while the Hunterian Museum, attached to the University, covers geology, archaeology, ethnography and more general subjects. On Glasgow Green is People's Palace – a museum of city life. Most imposing of the Victorian buildings are the City Chambers and City Hall which was built in 1841 as a concert hall but now houses the Scottish National Orchestra.

Paisley is famous for the lovely fabric pattern to which it gives its name. It was taken from fabrics brought from the Near East in the early 19th century, and its manufacture, along with the production of thread, is still important.

Greenock has been an important port and shipbuilding centre since as early as the 16th century. Its most famous son is James Watt, the inventor of steam power, born here in 1736. The town has numerous memorials to the great man.

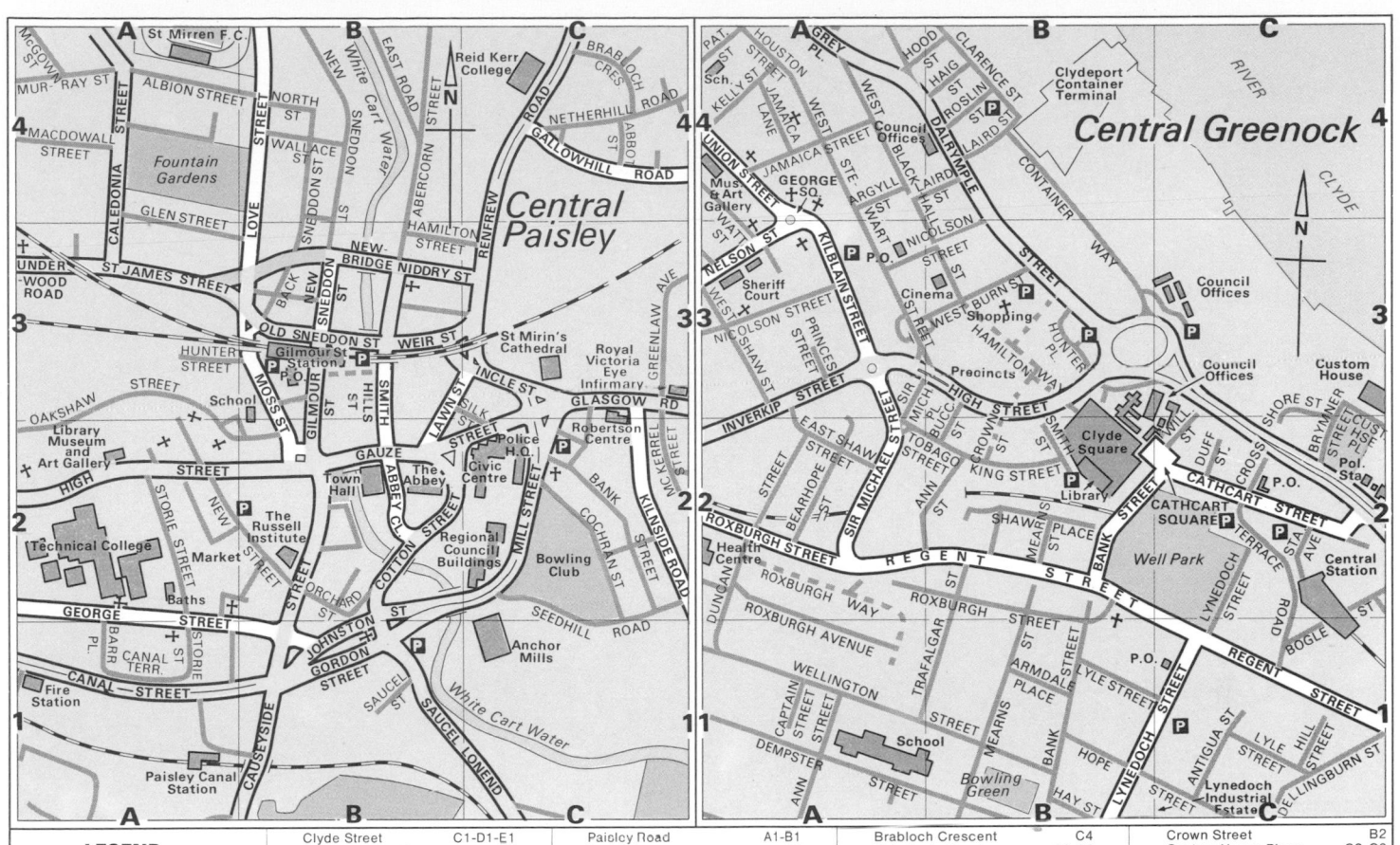

LEGEND

Town Plan
- AA recommended route
- Restricted roads
- Other roads
- Buildings of interest   Station ■
- Car parks   P
- Parks and open spaces
- One way streets →

Area Plan
- A roads
- B roads
- Locations   Garvock ○
- Urban area

Street Index with grid reference

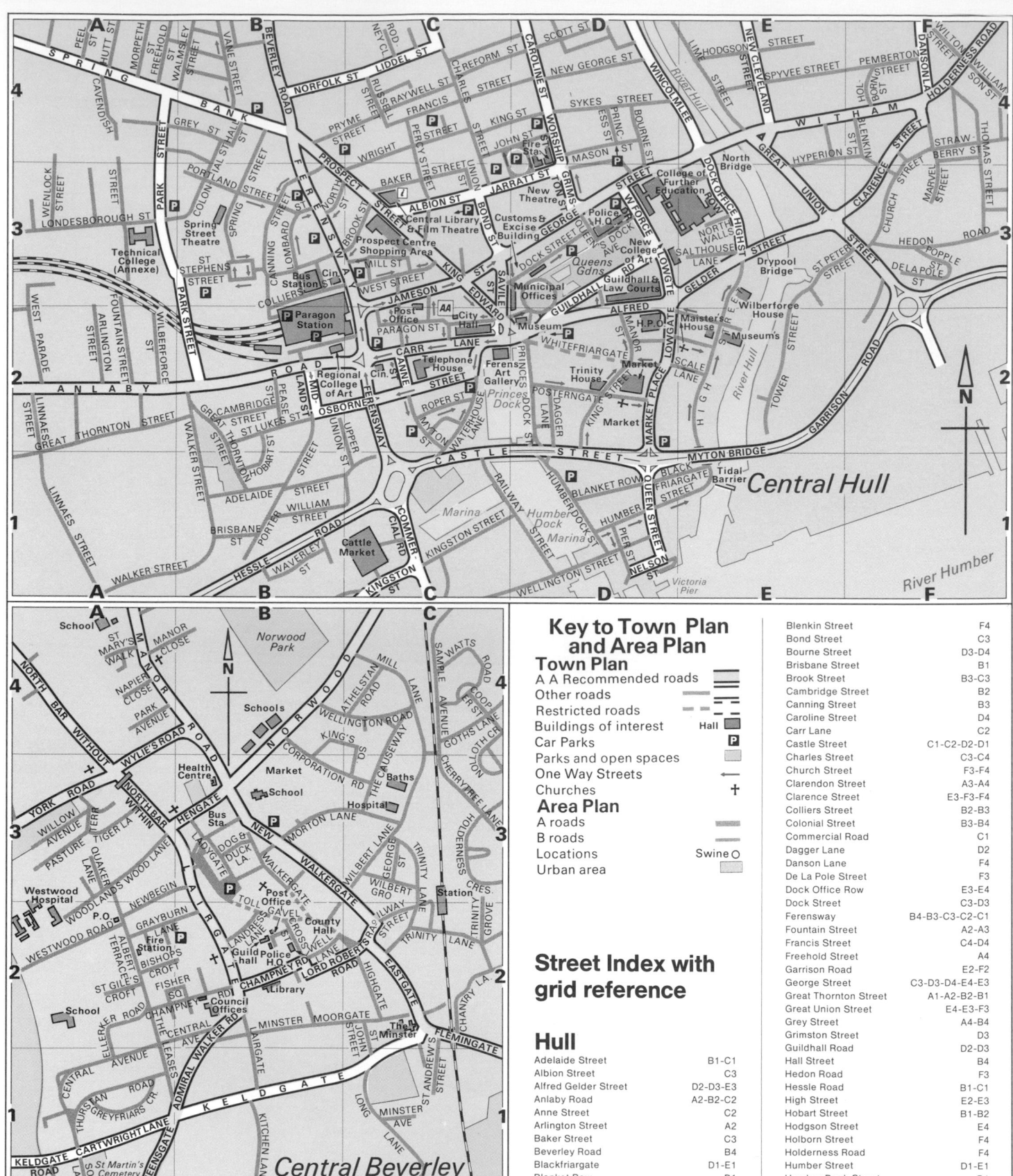

Key to Town Plan and Area Plan

Town Plan
A A Recommended roads	
Other roads	
Restricted roads	
Buildings of interest	Hall
Car Parks	P
Parks and open spaces	
One Way Streets	←
Churches	+

Area Plan
A roads	
B roads	
Locations	Swine ○
Urban area	

Street Index with grid reference

Hull

Adelaide Street	B1-C1
Albion Street	C3
Alfred Gelder Street	D2-D3-E3
Anlaby Road	A2-B2-C2
Anne Street	C2
Arlington Street	A2
Baker Street	C3
Beverley Road	B4
Blackfriargate	D1-E1
Blanket Row	D1

Blenkin Street	F4
Bond Street	C3
Bourne Street	D3-D4
Brisbane Street	B1
Brook Street	B3-C3
Cambridge Street	B2
Canning Street	B3
Caroline Street	D4
Carr Lane	C2
Castle Street	C1-C2-D2-D1
Charles Street	C3-C4
Church Street	F3-F4
Clarendon Street	A3-A4
Clarence Street	E3-F3-F4
Colliers Street	B2-B3
Colonial Street	B3-B4
Commercial Road	C1
Dagger Lane	D2
Danson Lane	F4
De La Pole Street	F3
Dock Office Row	E3-E4
Dock Street	C3-D3
Ferensway	B4-B3-C3-C2-C1
Fountain Street	A2-A3
Francis Street	C4-D4
Freehold Street	A4
Garrison Road	E2-F2
George Street	C3-D3-D4-E4-E3
Great Thornton Street	A1-A2-B2-B1
Great Union Street	E4-E3-F3
Grey Street	A4-B4
Grimston Street	D3
Guildhall Road	D2-D3
Hall Street	B4
Hedon Road	F3
Hessle Road	B1-C1
High Street	E2-E3
Hobart Street	B1-B2
Hodgson Street	E4
Holborn Street	F4
Holderness Road	F4
Humber Street	D1-E1
Humber Dock Street	D1

Hull

Officially Kingston-upon-Hull, this ancient port was specially laid out with new docks in 1293, on the decree of Edward I, and echoes of the town's past can be seen in the Town Docks Museum. The docks and the fishing industry are synonymous with Hull – it has Britain's busiest deep-sea fishing port – although flour-milling, vegetable oil extraction and petrochemical production are also important. The centre of Hull consists of broad streets and spacious squares and parks, such as Queen's Gardens, laid out on the site of what used to be Queen's Dock. The older part of the town which lies south-east of here between the docks and the River Hull is full of character, with a number of Georgian buildings and places of interest.

Beverley is one of England's most distinguished towns. Between its two principal buildings – the famous Minster and St Mary's Church – are medieval streets and pleasing market squares graced by redbrick Georgian houses built by the landed gentry of the East Riding during the town's heyday as a fashionable resort. The Minster's twin towers soar above the rooftops of the town as a constant reminder that here is one of the most beautiful pieces of Gothic architecture in Europe. The wealth of beauty and detail throughout is immense, but carving in both stone and wood is one of its most outstanding features.

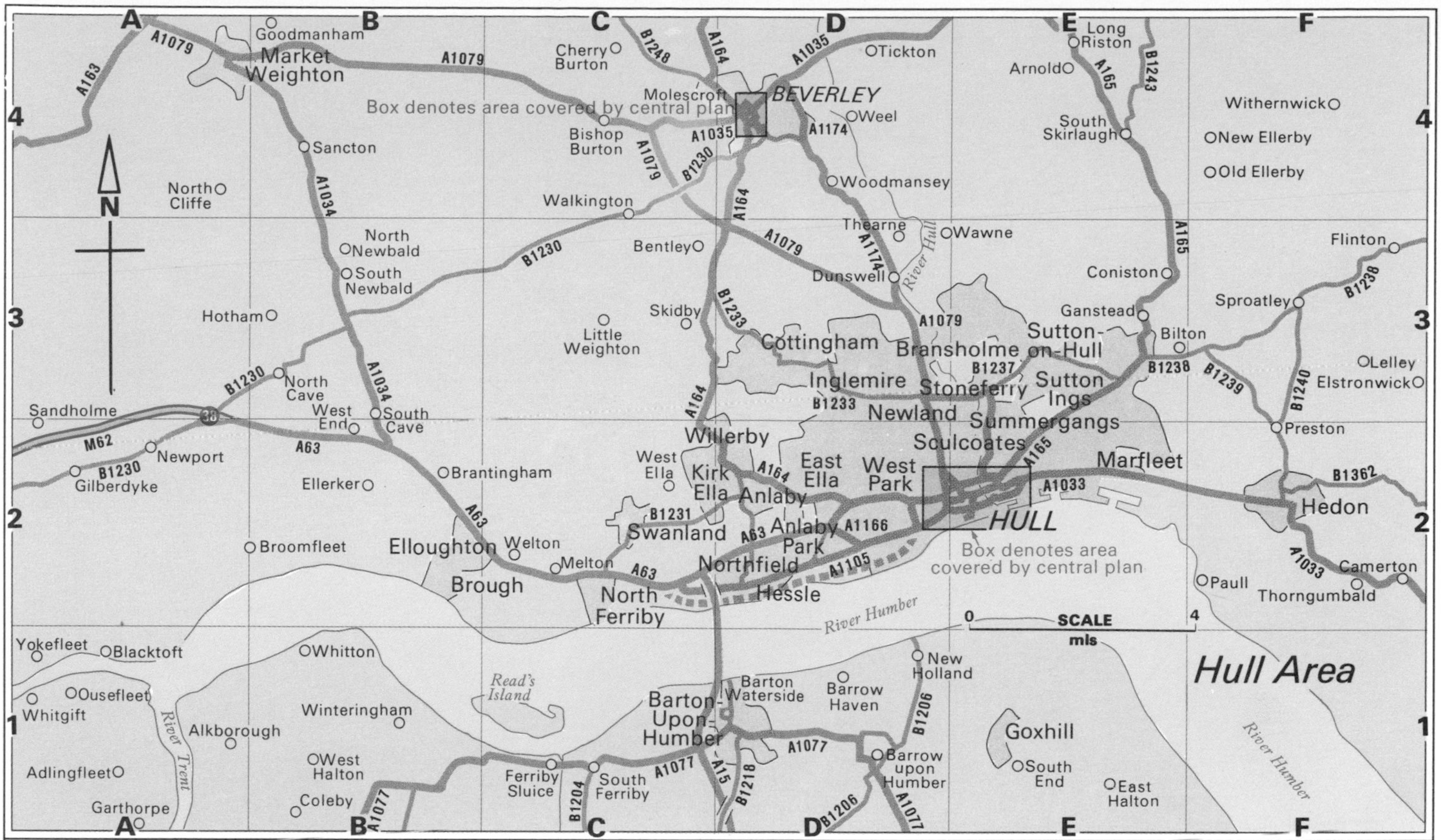

Hull Area

Box denotes area covered by central plan

Box denotes area covered by central plan

SCALE
0   4
mls

Hull Area

Hutt Street	A4	Princes Dock Street	D2	Witham	E4-F4	
Hyperion Street	E3-E4-F4	Prospect Place	B4-B3-C3	Worship Street	D3-D4	
Jameson Street	C2-C3	Pryme Street	B4-C4	Wright Street	C3-C4	
Jarrett Street	C3-D3	Queen Street	D1			
John Street	C4-D4	Queens Dock Avenue	D3			
King Street	C4-D4	Railway Street	C1-D1			
King Street	D2	Raywell Street	C4			
King Edward Street	C3-C2-D2	Reform Street	C4-D4			
Kingston Street	C1-D1	Rodney Close	C4			
Liddel Street	C4	Roper Street	C2			
Lime Street	D4-E4	Russell Street	C4			
Lombard Street	B3	St Lukes Street	B2			
Linnacs Street	A1-A2	St Peter Street	E3-F3			
Londesborough Street	A3	St Stephens Street	B3			
Lowgate	D2-D3	Salthouse Lane	E3			

Beverley

Manor Street	D2	Saville Street	C2-C3	Admiral Walker Road	A1-B1-B2	
Market Place	D2	Scale Lane	D2-E2	Albert Terrace	A2	
Marvel Street	F3-F4	Scott Street	D4	Athelston Road	C4	
Mason Street	D4	Spring Bank	A4-B4	Bishops Croft	A2-B2	
Midland Street	B2	Spring Street	B3-B4	Cartwright Lane	A1	
Mill Street	C3	Spyvee Street	E4-F4	Central Avenue	A1-A2-B2	
Morpeth Street	A4	Strawberry Street	F4	Champney Road	A2-B2	
Myton Bridge	E1-E2	Sykes Street	D4	Chantry Lane	C2	
Myton Street	C2	Thomas Street	F3-F4	Cherrytree Lane	C3-C4	
Nelson Street	D1	Tower Street	E2-E3	Cooper Street	C4	
New Cleveland Street	E4	Union Street	C3	Corporation Road	B4-B3-C3	
New George Street	D4	Upper Union Street	B2-C2-C1	Cross Street	C2	
Norfolk Street	B4-C4	Vane Street	B4	Dog and Duck Lane	B3	
North Street	B3	Walker Street	A1-B1-B2	Eastgate	C2	
North Walls	E3	Walmesley Street	B4	Ellerker Road	A1-A2	
Osborne Street	B2-C2	Waterhouse Lane	C1-C2	Flemingate	C1-C2	
Paragon Street	C2	Waverley Street	B1	Fisher Square	A2-B2	
Park Street	B2-B3-A3-A4	Wellington Street	C1-D1	George Street	C3	
Pease Street	B2	Wenlock Street	A3-A4	Goths Lane	C4	
Peel Street	A4	West Parade	A2-A3	Grayburn Lane	A2-B2	
Pemberton Street	F4	West Street	C3	Greyfriars Crescent	A1	
Percy Street	C3-C4	Whitefriar Gate	D2	Hengate	A3-B3	
Pier Street	D1	Wilberforce Drive	D3	Highgate	C2	
Popple Street	F3	Wilberforce Street	A2	Holderness Crescent	C3	
Porter Street	B1-B2	William Street	B1-C1	Keldgate	B1-C1	
Portland Street	B3	Williamson Street	F4	Keldgate Road	A1	
Posterngate	D2	Wilton Street	F4	Kings Square	B3-B4-C4-C3	
Princess Street	D4	Wincolmlee	D4-E4	Kitchen Lane	B1	

Ladygate	B3	
Lairgate	B1-B2-B3-A3	
Landress Lane	B2	
Long Lane	C1	
Lord Roberts Road	B2-C2	
Manor Close	A4-B4	
Manor Road	A4-B4-B3	

Mill Lane	C3-C4
Minster Avenue	C1
Minster Moorgate	B2-C2
Morton Lane	B3-C3
Napier Close	A4
New Walkergate	B3-C3-C2
Newbegin	A2-A3-B3
Nolloth Crescent	C3-C4
North Bar Within	A3
North Bar Without	A3-A4
Norwood	B3-B4-C4
Park Avenue	A4
Pasture Terrace	A3
Quaker Lane	A3
Queensgate	A1-B1
Railway Street	C2
St Andrew's Street	C1-C2
St Gile's Croft	A2
St John Street	C1-C2
St Mary's Walk	A4
Sample Avenue	C4
Sole Lane	A1
The Causeway	C3-C4
The Leases	A1-A2
Thurstan Road	A1
Tiger Lane	A3
Toll Gavel	B2-B3
Trinity Grove	C2-C3
Trinity Lane	C2-C3
Walkergate	B2-B3
Watts Road	C4
Well Lane	B2
Wellington Road	B4-C4
Westwood Road	A2
Wilbert Grove	C3
Wilbert Grove	C3
Wilbert Lane	B2-B3-C3
Willow Avenue	A3
Woodlands Wood Lane	A2-A3
Wylie's Road	A3-A4-B4
York Road	A3

HULL
Schemes to cross the Humber estuary were first discussed over 100 years ago, but it was not until 1981 that the mammoth project was sucessfully completed. At 4626ft, the Humber Bridge has the longest main span in the world.

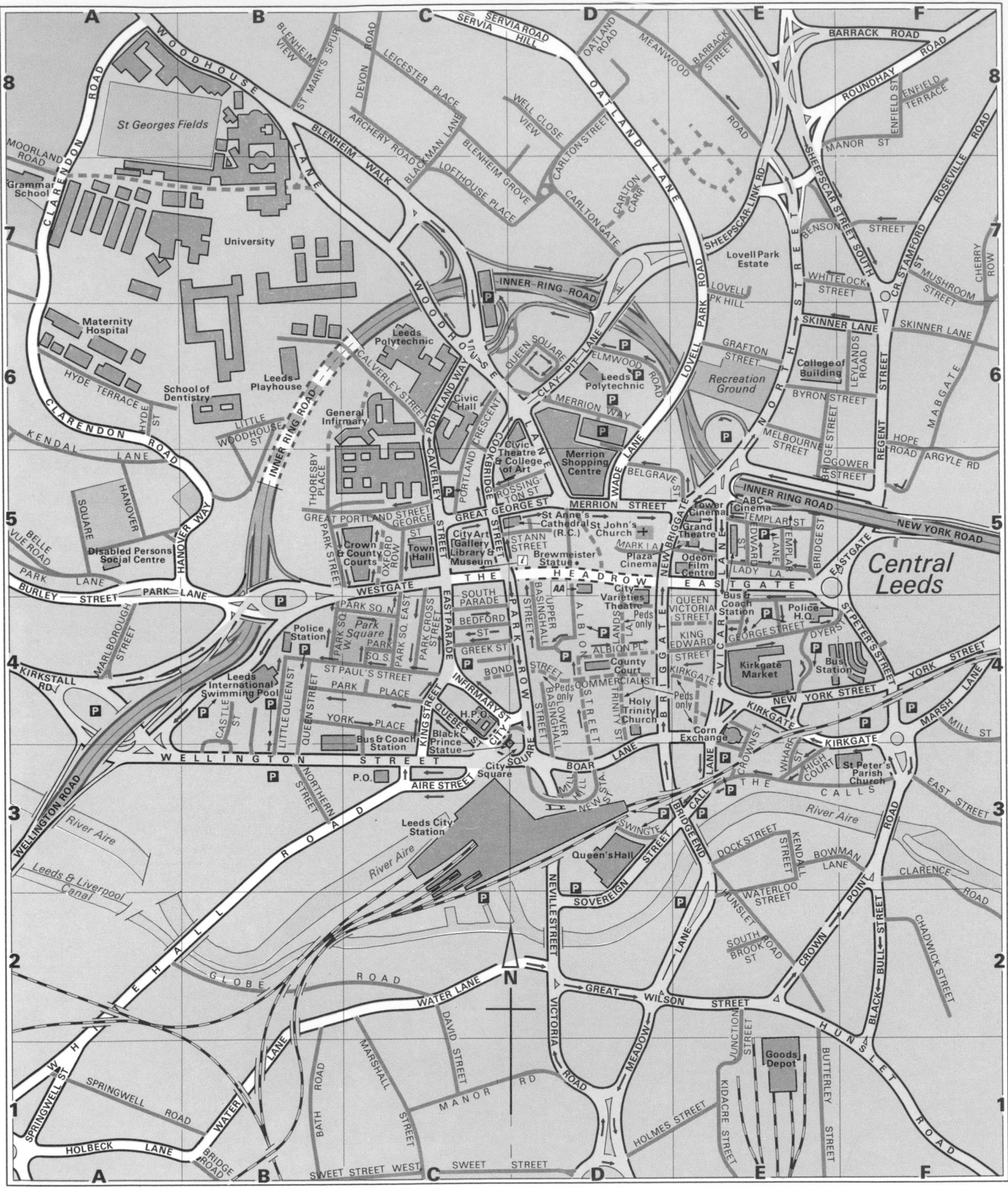

Leeds

In the centre of Leeds is its town hall – a monumental piece of architecture with a 225ft clock-tower. It was opened by Queen Victoria in 1858, and has been a kind of mascot for the city ever since. It exudes civic pride; such buildings could only have been created in the heyday of Victorian prosperity and confidence. Leeds' staple industry has always been the wool trade, but it only became a boom town towards the end of the 18th century, when textile mills were introduced. Today, the wool trade and ready-made clothing (Mr Hepworth and Mr Burton began their work here) are still important, though industries like paper, leather, furniture and electrical equipment are prominent.

Across Calverley Street from the town hall is the City Art Gallery, Library and Museum. Its collections include sculpture by Henry Moore, who was a student at Leeds School of Art. Nearby is the Headrow, Leeds' foremost shopping thoroughfare. On it is the City Varieties Theatre, venue for many years of the famous television programme 'The Good Old Days'. Off the Headrow are several shopping arcades, of which Leeds has many handsome examples. Leeds has a good number of interesting churches; perhaps the finest is St John's, unusual in that it dates from 1634, a time when few churches were built.

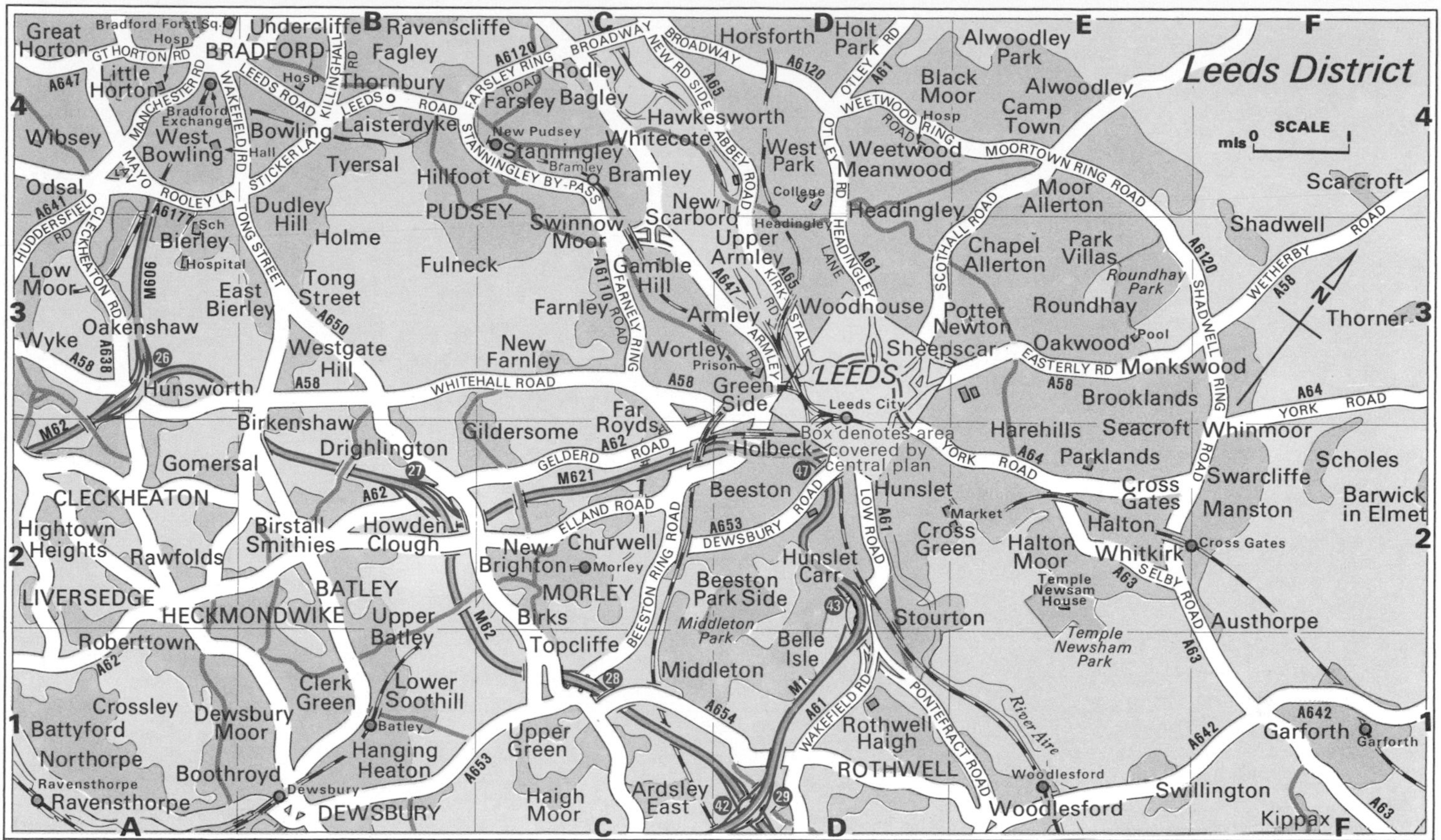

Leeds District

SCALE mls 0 1

LEGEND

Town Plan
- AA Recommended roads
- Other roads
- Restricted roads
- Buildings of interset — Museum
- AA Service Centre — AA
- Parks and open spaces
- Car Parks — P
- Churches — †
- One way streets

District Plan
- A roads
- B roads
- Stations — Kirkgate
- Urban area
- Buildings of interest — Hospital

Street Index with Grid Reference

Leeds

LEEDS
Offices now occupy the handsome twin-towered Civic Hall which stands in Calverley Street in front of the new buildings of Leeds Polytechnic. This area of the city – the commercial centre – has been extensively redeveloped

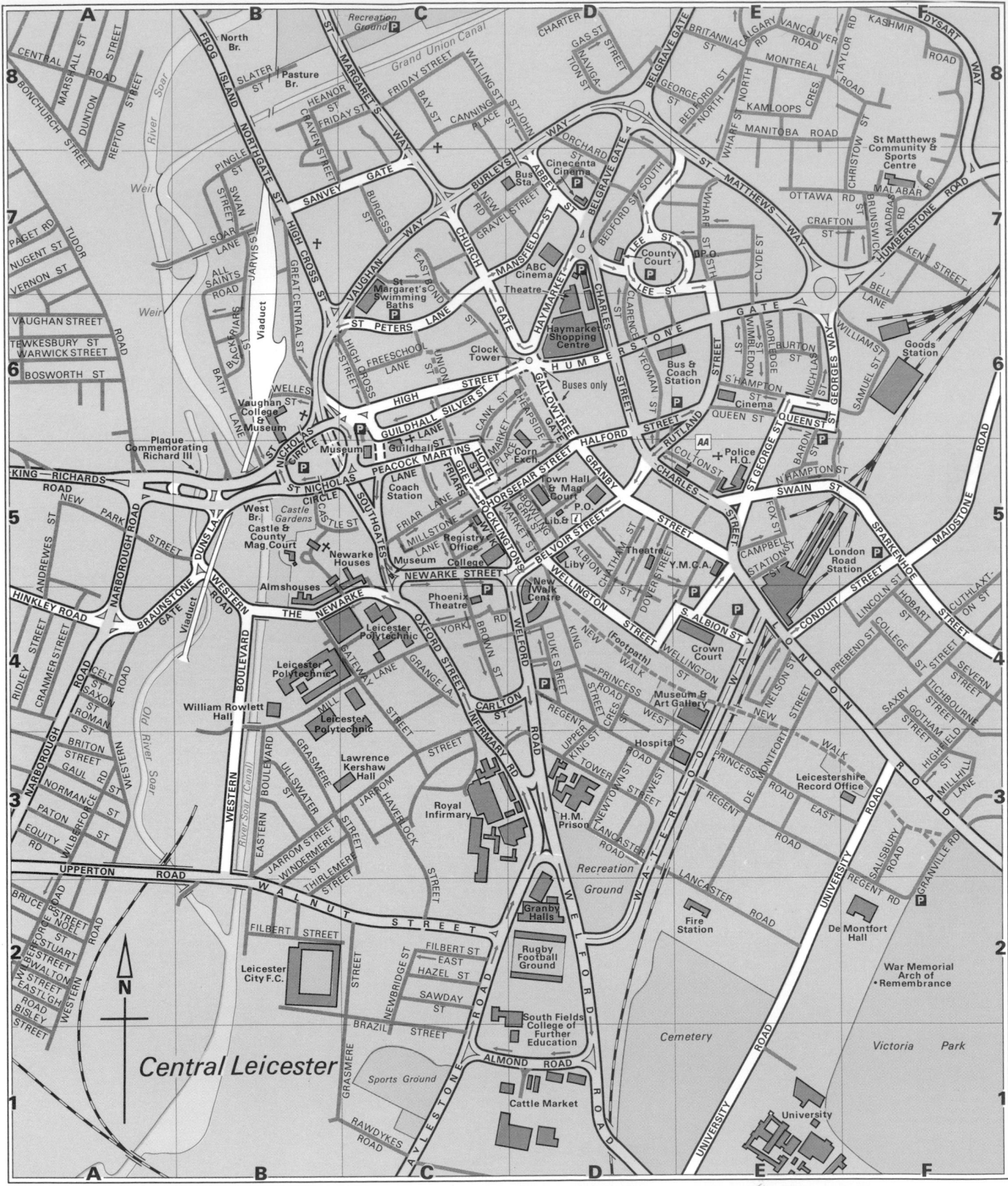

Leicester

A regional capital in Roman times, Leicester has retained many buildings from its eventful and distinguished past. Today the city is a thriving modern place, a centre for industry and commerce, serving much of the Midlands. Among the most outstanding monuments from the past is the Jewry Wall, a great bastion of Roman masonry. Close by are remains of the Roman baths and

several other contemporary buildings. Attached is a museum covering all periods from prehistoric times to 1500. Numerous other museums include the Wygston's House Museum of Costume, with displays covering the period 1769 to 1924; Newarke House, with collections showing changing social conditions in Leicester through four hundred years; and Leicestersh.. e Museum and Art Gallery, with collections of drawings, paintings, ceramics, geology and natural history.

The medieval Guildhall has many features of interest, including a great hall, library and police cells. Leicester's castle, although remodelled in the 17th century, retains a 12th-century great hall. The Church of St Mary de Castro, across the road from the castle, has features going back at least as far as Norman times; while St Nicholas's Church is even older, with Roman and Saxon foundations. St Martin's Cathedral dates mainly from the 13th to 15th centuries and has a notable Bishop's throne.

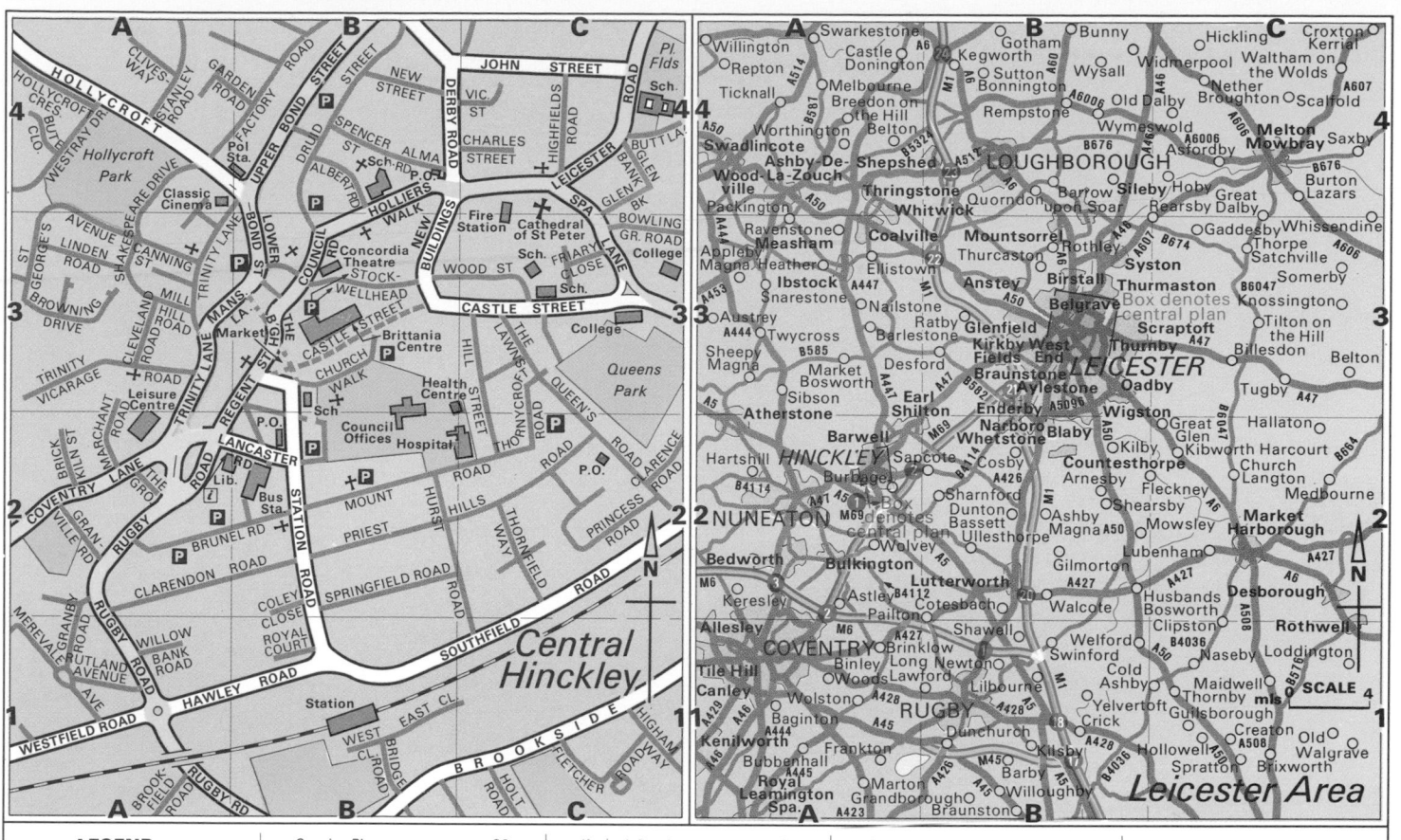

Central Hinckley

Leicester Area

LEGEND

Town Plan

AA Recommended route
Restricted roads
Other roads
Buildings of interest
Car parks   P
Parks and open spaces
One way streets

Area Plan

A roads
B roads
Locations   Creaton○
Urban area

Street Index with Grid Reference

Leicester

Abbey Street	D7
Albion Street	D4-D5
All Saints Road	B7
Almond Road	C1-D1
Andrewes Street	A4-A5
Aylestone Road	C1-C2
Baron Street	E5-E6
Bath Lane	B5-B6
Bay Street	C8
Bedford Street North	E8
Bedford Street South	D7
Belgrave Gate	D7-D8-E8
Bell Lane	F6-F7
Belvoir Street	D5
Bisley Street	A1-A2
Blackfriars Street	B6
Bonchurch Street	A7-A8
Bosworth Street	A6
Bowling Green Street	D5
Braunstone Gate	A4-B4-B5
Brazil Street	C1-C2
Britannia Street	E8
Briton Street	A3
Brown Street	C4
Bruce Street	A2
Brunswick Street	F7
Burgess Street	C7
Burleys Way	C7-D7-D8
Burton Street	E6
Calgary Road	E8
Campbell Street	E5
Cank Street	C6-D6
Canning Place	C8
Carlton Street	C4-D4
Castle Street	B5-C5
Celt Street	A4
Central Road	A8
Charles Street	D7-D6-D5-E5
Charter Street	D8
Chatham Street	D4-D5
Cheapside	D5-D6
Christow Street	F7-F8
Church Gate	C7-C6-D6
Clarence Street	D6-D7
Clyde Street	E6-E7
College Street	F4
Colton Street	D5-E5
Conduit Street	E4-F4-F5
Crafton Street	E7-F7
Cranmer Street	A4
Craven Street	B7-B8
Crescent Street	D4
Cuthlaxton Street	F4-F5
De Montfort Street	E3-E4
Dover Street	D4-D5
Duke Street	D4
Dunns Lane	B5
Dunton Street	A8
Dysart Way	F8
East Bond Street	C6-C7
Eastern Boulevard	B3-B4
Eastleigh Road	A2
Equity Road	A3
Filbert Street	B2-C2
Filbert Street East	C2
Fox Street	E5
Freeschool Lane	C6
Friar Lane	C5
Friday Street	B8-C8
Frog Island	B8
Gallowtree Gate	D6
Gas Street	E5
Gateway Street	B4-C4-C3
Gaul Street	A3
George Street	D8-E8
Gotham Street	F3-F4
Granby Street	D5-E5
Grange Lane	C5
Granville Road	F2-F3
Grasmere Street	B4-B3-C3-C2-C1-B1
Gravel Street	C7-D7
Great Central Street	B6-B7
Greyfriars	C5
Guildhall Lane	C6
Halford Street	D5-D6-E6
Haverlock Street	C2-C3
Haymarket	D6-D7
Hazel Street	C2
Heanor Street	B8-C8
High Cross Street	B7-B6-C6
Highfield Street	F3
High Street	C6-D6
Hinkley Road	A4
Hobart Street	F4
Horsefair Street	C5-D5
Hotel Street	C5
Humberstone Gate	D6-E6
Humberstone Road	F7
Infirmary Road	C4-C3-D3
Jarrom Street	B3-C3
Jarvis Street	B7
Kamloops Crescent	E8
Kashmir Road	F8
Kent Street	F7
King Richards Road	F7
King Street	D4
Lancaster Road	D3-E3-F2
Lee Street	D6-D7-E7
Lincoln Street	F4-F5
London Road	E5-E4-F4-F3
Madras Road	F7
Maidstone Road	F5-F6
Malabar Road	F7
Manitoba Road	E8
Mansfield Street	C7-D7
Market Place	C5-C6-D6
Market Street	D5
Marshall Street	A8
Morledge Street	E6
Montreal Road	E8-F8
Mill Hill Lane	F3
Mill Lane	B4-C4
Millstone Lane	C5
Narborough Road	A3-A4-A5
Navigation Street	D8
Nelson Street	E4
Newarke Street	C5
New Bridge Street	C2
New Park Street	A5-B5
New Road	C7
Newtown Street	D5
New Walk	D4-E4-E3-F3
Nicholas Street	E6
Noel Street	A2
Northampton Street	E5
Northgate Street	B7-B8
Norman Street	A3
Nugent Street	A8
Orchard Street	D7-D8
Ottawa Road	E7-F7
Oxford Street	C4
Paget Road	A7
Paton Street	A3
Peacock Lane	C5
Pingle Street	B7
Pocklingtons Walk	C5-D5
Prebend Street	E4-F4
Princess Road East	E3-F3
Princess Road West	D4
Queen Street	E6
Rawdykes Road	B1-C1
Regent Road	D4-D3-E3-F3-F2
Repton Street	A7-A8
Ridley Street	A4
Roman Street	A4
Rutland Street	D5-E5-E6
St George Street	E5-E6
St Georges Way	E6-E6
St John Street	E5
St Margaret's Way	B8-C8-C7
St Martins	C5
St Mathews Way	E6-E7
St Nicholas Circle	B6-B5-C5
St Peters Lane	C6
Salisbury Road	F2-F3
Samuel Stuart	F6
Sanvey Gate	B7-C7
Sawday Street	C2
Saxby Street	F4
Saxon Street	A4
Severn Street	F4
Silver Street	C6
Slater Street	B8
Soar Lane	B7
South Albion Street	E4
Southampton Street	E6
Southgates	C5
Sparkenhoe Street	F4-F5
Station Street	E5
Stuart Street	A3
Swain Street	E5-F5
Swan Street	B7
The Newarke	B4-C4
Taylor Road	E8-F8
Towkesbury Street	A6
Thirlemere Street	B2-B3-C3
Tichbourne Street	F3-F4
Tower Street	D3
Tudor Road	A6-A7-A8
Ullswater Street	B3
Union Street	C6
University Road	E1-E2-E3-F3
Upper King Street	D3-D4
Upperton Road	A3-B3-B2
Vancouver Road	E8
Vaughan Way	C6-C7
Vaughan Street	A6
Vernon Street	A6-A7
Walnut Street	B3-B2-C2
Walton Street	A3
Warwick Street	A6
Waterloo Way	D2-D3-E3-E4
Watling Street	C8
Welford Road	D1-D2-D3-D4
Welles Street	B6
Wellington Street	D4-E4-D5
Western Boulevard	B4
Western Road	A1-A2-A3-A4-B4-B5
West Street	D3-E3-E4
Wharf Street North	E7-E8
Wharf Street South	E7
Wilberforce Road	A2-A3
William Street	F6
Wimbledon Street	E6
Windermere Street	B2-B3-B3
Yeoman Street	D6
York Road	C4

Hinkley

Albert Road	B4
Alma Road	B4
Bowling Green Road	C3
Brick Kiln Street	A2
Bridge Road	B1
Brookfield Road	A1
Brookside	B1-C1
Browning Drive	A3
Brunel Road	A2-B2
Bute Close	A4
Butt Lane	C4
Canning Street	A3
Castle Street	B3-C3
Charles Street	C4
Church Walk	B3
Clarence Road	C2
Clarendon Road	A2-B2
Cleveland Road	A3
Clivesway	A4
Coley Close	B2
Council Road	B3
Coventry Lane	A2
Derby Road	B4
Druid Street	B3-B4
East Close	B1-C1
Factory Road	A4-B4
Fletcher Road	C1
Friary Close	C3
Garden Road	A4-B4
Glen Bank	C4
Granby Road	A1-A2
Granville Road	A2
Hawley Road	A1-B1
Higham Way	C1
Highfields Road	C4
Hill Street	C2-C3
Holliers Walk	B3-B4
Hollycroft	A4
Hollycroft Crescent	A4
Holt Road	C1
Hurst Road	B2-C2
John Street	C4
Lancaster Road	A2-B2
Leicester Road	C4
Linden Road	A3
Lower Bond Street	B3-B4
Mansion Lane	A3-B3
Marchant Road	A2-A3
Merevale Avenue	A1
Mill Hill Road	A3
Mount Road	B2-C2
New Buildings	B3-B4
New Street	B4
Priest Hills Road	B2-C2
Princess Road	C2
Queens Road	C2-C3
Regent Street	A2-A3-B3
Royal Court	B1
Rugby Road	A2-A1-B1
Rutland Avenue	A1
St George's Avenue	A3-A4
Shakespeare Drive	A3-A4
Southfield Road	B1-C1-C2
Spa Lane	C3-C4
Spencer Street	B4
Springfield Road	B2
Stanley Road	A4
Station Road	B1-B2
Stockwellhead	B3
The Borough	B3
The Grove	A2
The Lawns	C3
Thornfield Way	C2
Thornycroft Road	B3
Trinity Lane	A2-A3-A4-B4
Trinity Vicarage Road	A3
Upper Bond Street	B4
Victoria Street	C4
West Close	B1
Westray Drive	A4
Westfield Road	A1
Willow Bank Road	A1
Wood Street	B3-C3

Liverpool

Although its dock area has been much reduced, Liverpool was at one time second only to London in pre-eminence as a port. Formerly the centrepiece of the docks area are three monumental buildings – the Dock Board Offices, built in 1907 with a huge copper-covered dome; the Cunard Building, dating from 1912 and decorated with an abundance of ornamental carving; and best-known of all, the world-famous Royal Liver Building, with the two 'liver birds' crowning its twin cupolas.

Some of the city's best industrial buildings have fallen into disuse in recent years, and have been preserved as monuments of the industrial age. One has become a maritime museum housing full-sized craft and a workshop where maritime crafts are demonstrated. Other museums and galleries include the Walker Art Gallery, with excellent collections of European painting and sculpture; Liverpool City Libraries, one of the oldest and largest public libraries in Britain, with a vast collection of books and manuscripts; and Bluecoat Chambers, a Queen Anne building now used as a gallery and concert hall. Liverpool has two outstanding cathedrals: the Roman Catholic, completed in 1967 in an uncompromising controversial style; and the Protestant, constructed in the great tradition of Gothic architecture, but begun in 1904 and only recently completed.

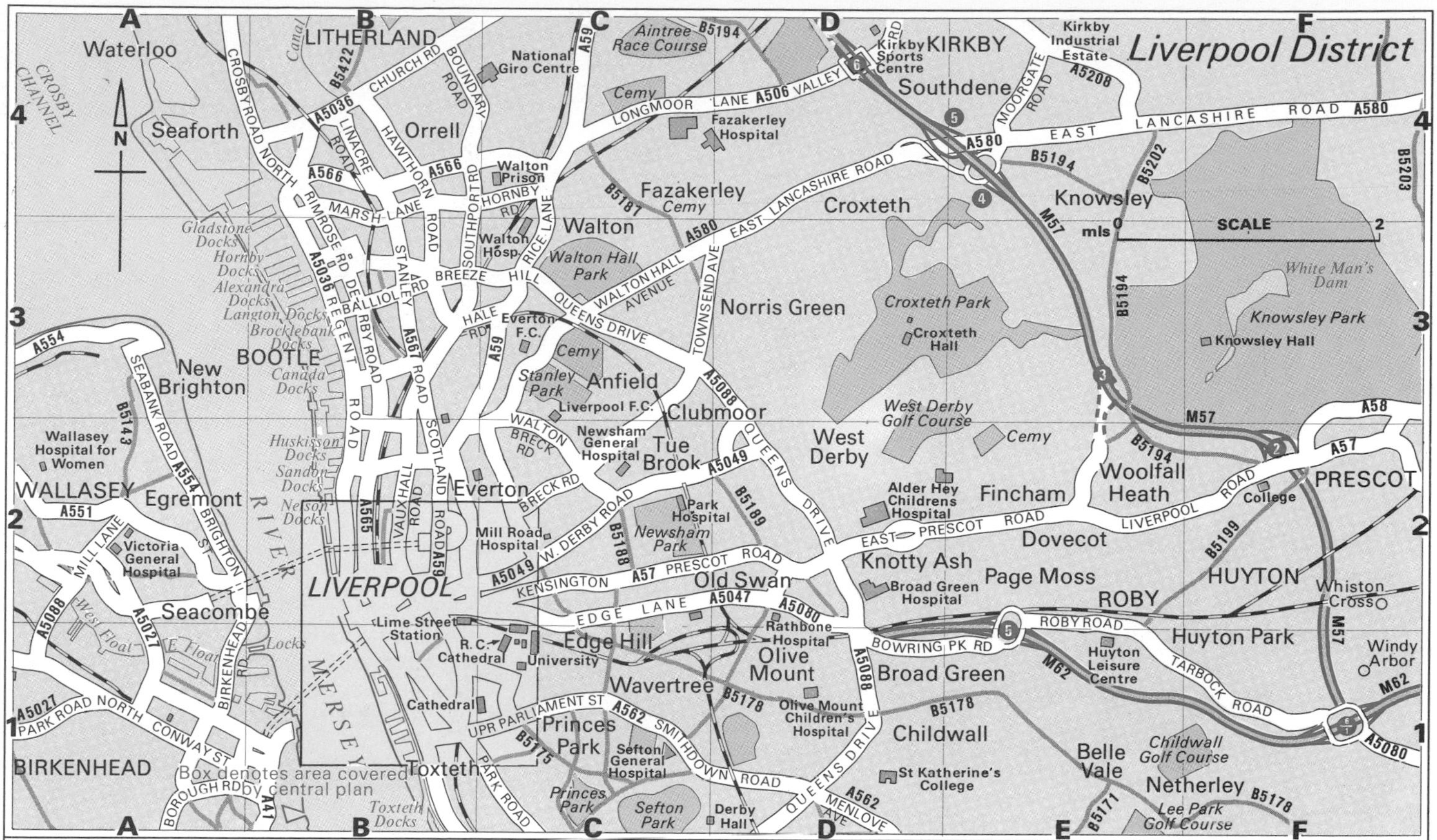

Liverpool District

(Map of Liverpool District showing areas including Waterloo, Seaforth, Litherland, Orrell, Kirkby, Southdene, Fazakerley, Walton, Croxteth, Norris Green, Knowsley Park, West Derby, Bootle, New Brighton, Wallasey, Egremont, Seacombe, Anfield, Clubmoor, Tue Brook, Everton, Old Swan, Knotty Ash, Page Moss, Dovecot, Huyton, Prescot, Birkenhead, Toxteth, Edge Hill, Wavertree, Olive Mount, Broad Green, Childwall, Belle Vale, Netherley, etc.)

Box denotes area covered by central plan

SCALE — mls 0 ... 2

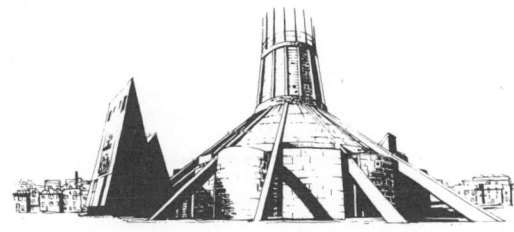

LIVERPOOL
The Metropolitan Cathedral of Christ the King is one of Liverpool's most striking landmarks. Crowning the conical roof is a tower of stained glass which throws a pool of coloured light on to the altar below.

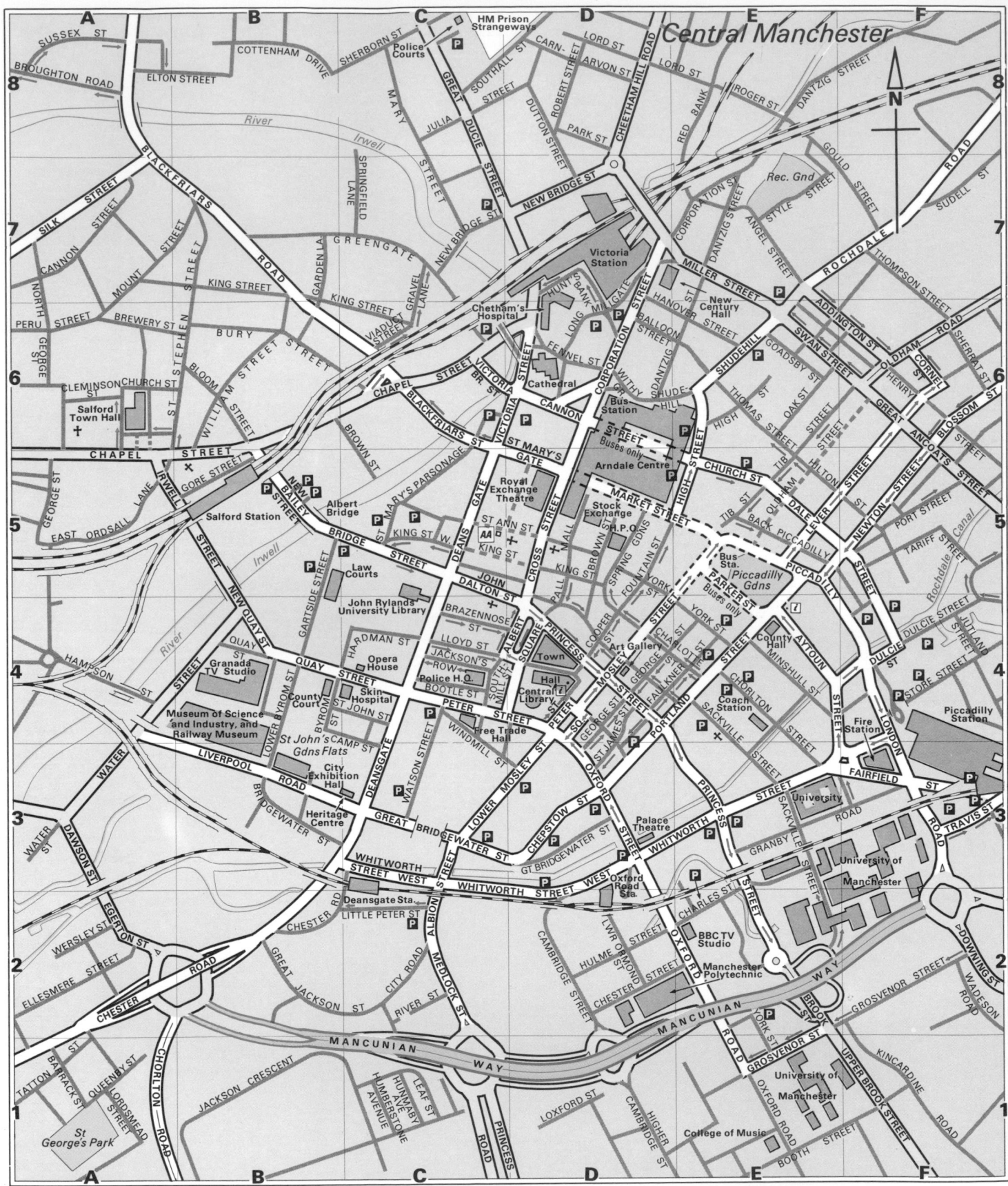

Manchester

The gigantic conurbation called Greater Manchester covers a staggering 60 square miles, reinforcing Manchester's claim to be Britain's second city. Commerce and industry are vital aspects of the city's character, but it is also an important cultural centre – the Halle Orchestra has its home at the Free Trade Hall (a venue for many concerts besides classical music), there are several theatres, a library (the John Rylands) which houses one of the most important collections of books in the world, and a number of museums and galleries, including the Whitworth Gallery with its lovely watercolours.

Like many great cities it suffered badly during the bombing raids of World War II, but some older buildings remain, including the town hall, a huge building designed in Gothic style by Alfred Waterhouse and opened in 1877. Manchester Cathedral dates mainly from the 15th century and is noted for its fine tower and outstanding carved woodwork. Nearby is Chetham's Hospital, also 15th-century and now housing a music school. Much new development has taken place, and more is planned. Shopping precincts cater for the vast population, and huge hotels have provided services up to international standards. On the edge of the city is the Belle Vue centre, a large entertainments complex including concert and exhibition facilities, and a speedway stadium.

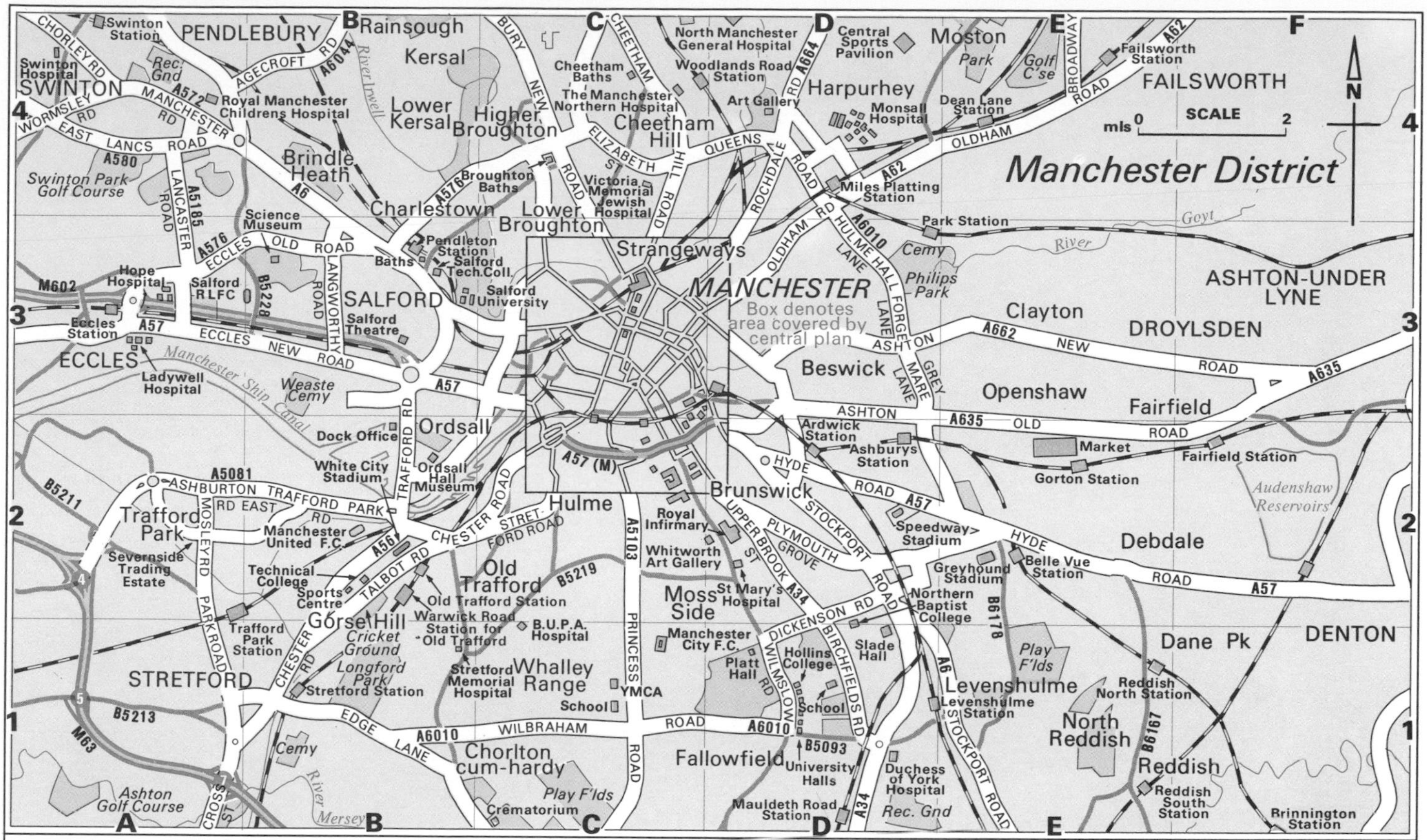

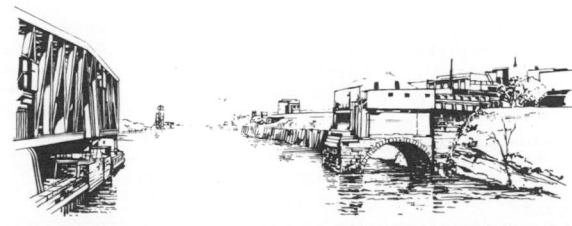

Key to Town Plan and Area Plan

Town Plan

- AA Recommended roads
- Other roads
- Restricted roads
- Buildings of interest (Baths)
- Car parks (P)
- Parks and open spaces
- Churches
- AA Centre (AA)
- One Way Streets

District Plan

- A roads
- B roads

STREET INDEX -with grid reference

Manchester

Addington Street	E7-E6-F6
Albert Square	C4-D4
Albion Street	C2-C3
Angel Street	E7
Aytoun Street	E4-F4-F3-E3
Back Piccadilly	E5-F5-F4
Balloon Street	D6-E6
Barrack Street	A1
Blackfriars Road	A8-A7-B7-B6-C6
Blackfriars Street	C5-C6
Bloom Street	B6
Blossom Street	F6
Booth Street	E1-F1
Bootle Street	C4
Brazennose Street	C4-D4
Brewery Street	A6-B6
Bridge Street	B5-C5
Bridgewater Street	B3
Brook Street	E2
Broughton Road	A8
Brown Street	B6-C6-C5
Brown Street	D4-D5
Bury Street	B6-C6
Byrom Street	B4
Cambridge Street	D2
Camp Street	B4-C4-C3
Cannon Street	A7
Cannon Street	D6-D5-E5
Carnarvon Street	D8
Chapel Street	A6-A5-B5-B6-C6-D6
Charles Street	E2
Charlotte Street	D4-E4
Cheetham Hill Road	D7-D8
Chepstow Street	D3
Chester Road	A1-A2-B2-C2-C3
Chester Street	D2-E2
Chorlton Road	B2-A2-A1-B1
Chorlton Street	E3-E4
Church Street	A6-B6
Church Street	E5
Cleminson Street	A6
City Road	C2
Cooper Street	D4
Cornel Street	F6
Corporation Street	D6-D7-E7
Cottenham Drive	B8
Cross Street	D4-D5-D6
Dale Street	E5-F5-F4
Dantzig Street	D6-E6-E7-E8-F8
Dawson Street	A3
Deansgate	C3-C4-C5
Downing Street	F2
Dulcie Street	F4
Dutton Street	D7-D8
East Ordsall Lane	A5
Egerton Street	A2
Ellesmere Street	A2
Elton Street	A8-B2
Fairfield Street	F3
Faulkner Street	D4-E4
Fennel Street	D6
Fountain Street	D4-D5
Garden Lane	B6-B7
Gartside Street	B4-B5
George Street	A5
George Street	D3-D4-E4
Goadsby Street	E6
Gore Street	B5
Gould Street	E8-E7-F7
Granby Road	E3-F3
Gravel Lane	C6-C7
Great Ancoats Street	F5-F6
Great Bridgewater Street	C3-D3
Great Ducie Street	C8-C7-D7
Great Jackson Street	B2-C2
Greengate	B7-C7
Grosvenor Street	E1-E2-F2
Hampson Street	A4
Hanover Street	D7-D6-E6
Hardman Street	C4
Henry Street	F5-F6
High Street	E5-E6
Higher Cambridge Street	D1
Hilton Street	E5-F5
Hulme Street	D2
Humberstone Avenue	C1
Hunmaby Avenue	C1
Hunt's Bank	D6-D7
Irwell Street	A5-B5
Jackson Crescent	B1-C1
Jackson's Row	C4
John Dalton Street	C5-C4-D4-D5
Julia Street	C8-D8
Jutland Street	F4
Kincardine Road	F1-F2
King Street	A7-B7-B6-C6
King Street	C5-D5
King St West	C5
Leaf Street	C1
Lever Street	E5-F5-F6
Little Peter Street	B2-C2
Liverpool Road	A4-A3-B4-B3-C3
Lloyd Street	C4
London Road	F3-F4
Long Millgate	D6-D7
Lord Street	D8-E8
Lordsmead Street	A1
Lower Byrom Street	B3-B4
Lower Mosley Street	C3-D3-D4
Lower Ormond Street	D2
Loxford Street	D1
Mancunian Way	B2-B1-C2-C1-D1-D2-E2-F2
Market Street	D5-E5
Mary Street	C7-C8
Medlock Street	C2
Miller Street	D7-E7-E6
Minshull Street	E4
Mosley Street	D4-D5-E4-E5
Mount Street	A6-A7-B7
Newton Street	F5
New Bailey Street	B5
New Bridge Street	C7-D7
North George Street	A6-A7
New Quay Street	B4-B5
Oak Street	E6
Oldham Road	F6-F7
Oldham Street	E5-E6-F6
Oxford Road	D2-E2-E1
Oxford Street	D4-D3-D2
Pall Mall	D4-D5
Park Street	D8
Parker Street	E4-E5
Peru Street	A6
Peter Street	C4-D4
Piccadilly	E5-E4-F4
Port Street	F5
Portland Street	D3-D4-E4-E5
Princess Road	C1-D1
Princess Street	D4-E4-D3-E3-E2
Quay Street	B4-C4
Queensby Street	A1
Red Bank	E7-E8
River Street	C2
Robert Street	D8
Rochdale Road	E7-F7-F8
Roger Street	E8
St Ann Street	C5-D5
St Mary's Gate	C5-C6-D5-D6
St Mary's Parsonage	C5-C6
St James Street	D3-D4
St John Street	B4-C4
St Peter Square	D4
St Stephen Street	A6-B6-B7
Sackville Street	E2-E3-E4
Sherrat Street	F6
Sherborn Street	B8-C8
Shudehill	D6-E6
Silk Street	A7
Southall Street	C8-D8
Southmill Street	C4
Spring Gardens	D4-D5
Springfield Lane	C7-C8
Store Street	F4
Style Street	E7-E8
Sudell Street	F7-F8
Sussex Street	A8
Swan Street	E6-F6
Tatton Street	A1
Tariff Street	F5
Thomas Street	E5-E6
Thompson Street	F6-F7
Tib Street	E5-E6-F6
Travis Street	F3
Upper Brook Street	E2-E1-F1
Viaduct Street	C6
Victoria Bridge Street	C6-D6
Victoria Street	C6-D6
Wadeson Road	F2
Water Street	A3-A4-B4
Watson Street	C3-C4
Wersley Street	A2
Whitworth Street	D3-E3
Whitworth Street West	B3-C3-C2-D2-D3
William Street	B6
Windmill Street	C4-C3-D3
Withy Green	D6
York Street	D5-D4-E4

MANCHESTER
The Barton Swing Bridge carries the Bridgewater Canal over the Manchester Ship Canal, which links Manchester with the sea nearly 40 miles away. Completed in 1894, the canal is navigable by vessels up to 15,000 tons.

Newcastle

Six bridges span the Tyne at Newcastle; they all help to create a striking scene, but the most impressive is the High Level Bridge, built by Robert Stephenson in 1845-49 and consisting of two levels, one for the railway and one for the road. It is from the river that some of the best views of the city can be obtained. Grey Street is Newcastle's most handsome thoroughfare. It dates from the time, between 1835 and 1840, when much of this part of the city was replanned and rebuilt. Elegant façades curve up to Grey's Monument. Close to the Monument is the Eldon Centre, combining sports facilities and shopping centre to form an integrated complex which is one of the largest of its kind in Europe. Newcastle has many museums. The industrial background of the city is traced in the Museum of Science and Engineering, while the Laing Art Gallery and Museum covers painting, costumes and local domestic history. The Hancock Museum has an exceptional natural history collection and the John George Joicey Museum has period displays in a 17th-century almshouse. In Black Gate is one of Britain's most unusual museums – a collection of over 100 sets of bagpipes. Within the University precincts are three further museums. Of the city's open spaces, Town Moor is the largest. At nearly 1,000 acres it is big enough to feel genuinely wild.

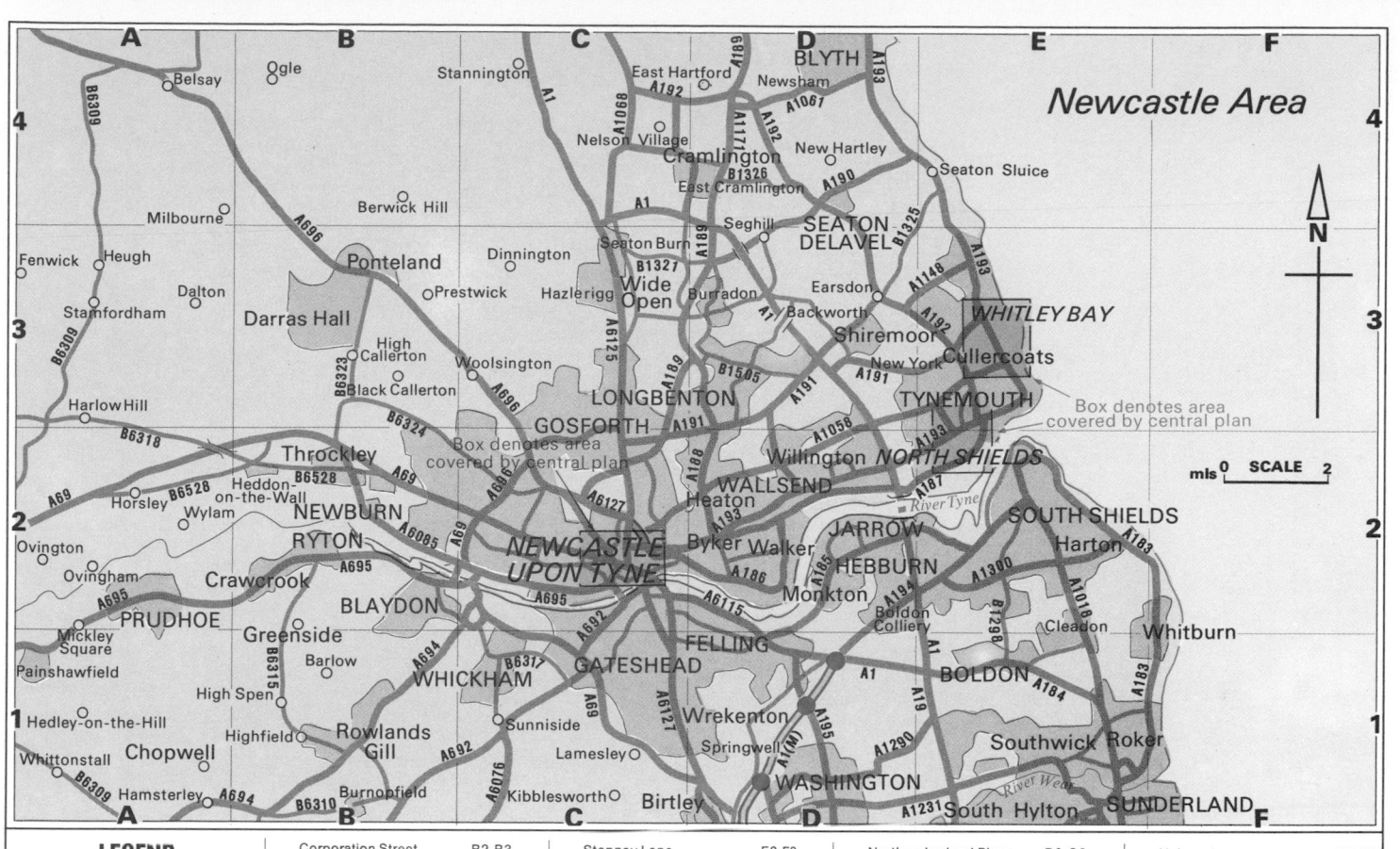

Newcastle Area

Box denotes area covered by central plan

mls 0 SCALE 2

LEGEND

Town Plan

AA recommended route
Restricted roads
Other roads
Buildings of interest — Hall
Car parks — P
Parks and open spaces
Metro stations — M
One way streets

Area Plan

A roads
B roads
Locations — Craghead○
Urban area

Street Index with Grid Reference

Newcastle

Abinger Street	A2
Argyle Street	E2
Avison Street	A3
Barrack Road	A4-B4-B3
Barras Bridge	D4
Bath Lane	B2-C2
Bigg Market Street	C2-D2
Blackett Street	C3-D3-D2
Blandford Street	B1-B2
Blenheim Street	B1-B2
Breamish Street	F2
Buckingham Street	A2-B2-B3
Byker Bridge	F2-F3
Byran Street	E3-E4
Central Motorway	E1-D1-D2-E2-E3-E4
Chester Street	E4
City Road	E1-E2-F2
Clarance Street	F2-F3
Clayton Street	C2
Clayton Street West	B1-C1-C2
Clothmarket	D2
College Street	D3-D4
Colliery Lane	B3
Collingwood Street	C1-D1
Cookson Close	A3
Copland Terrace	E3-F3
Coppice Way	F3
Corporation Street	B2-B3
Cotten Street	A2
Crawhill Road	F2
Croft Street	D2
Darn Crook	C2-C3
Dean Street	D1-D2
Derby Street	A3-A4
Diana Street	A2-A3-B3
Dinsdale Road	F4
Doncaster Road	F4
Douglas Terrace	A3-B3
Edward Place	A3
Ellison Place	D3-E3
Elswick Road	A2
Elswick Row	A2
Falconer Street	E3
Forth Street	C1-D1
Gallowgate	B3-C3
George Street	A1-B1
Gibson Street	F2
Gladstone Place	E4
Grainger Street	C1-C2-D2
Grantham Road	F4
Grey Street	D2
Great Markot	D1-D2
Harrison Place	E4
Haymarket	D3-D4
Helmsley Road	F4
High Bridge	D2
High Villa	A2
Hillgate	E1
Howard Street	F2
John Dobson Street	D3-D4
Leazes Lane	C3
Leazes Park Road	C3-C4
Leazes Terrace	C3-C4
Maple Terrace	A1
Market Street	D2
Marlborough Crescent	B1
Melbourne Street	E2-F2
Morden Street	C3
Moseley Street	D1-D2
Neville Street	C1
New Bridge Road	F2-F3
New Bridge Street	D3-E3-E2-F2
Newgate Street	C2-C3
New Mills	A4
Northumberland Street	D4-D3-E4
Nun Street	C2
Oakes Place	A2-B2-B3
Perry Street	C3-D3-D4
Pilgrim Street	D2
Pitt Street	B3
Portland Road	F3-F4
Pudding Chape	C1-C2
Quayside	D1-E1-F1-F2
Queen Victoria Road	C4
Rock Terrace	E3
Rosedale Terrace	F4
Rye Hill	A1-A2
St James Street	C3
St Mary's Place	D4
St Nicholas Square	D1-D2
St Thomas Street	C3-C4
Sandford Road	D4-E4
Sandhill	D1
Shield Street	E3-F3-F4
Sheildfield Lane	F3
Side	D1
Simpson Terrace	E3
South Shore Road	E1-F1
Stanhope Street	A3-B3
Stepney Lane	E2-F2
Stoddart Street	F3
Stone Street	A3
Stowell Street	B2-C2
Strawberry Place	B3-C3
Summerhill Grove	A2-B2-B1
Tindall Street	B3
Tower Street	E2
Union Street	F3
Vallum Way	A3
Victoria Square	E4
Walter Terrace	A4
Warwick Street	F4
Waterloo Street	B1-B2-C2
Wellington Street	B3
Westgate Road	A2-B2-C2-C1-D1
Westmorland Road	A1-B1
West Blandford Street	B1-B2
Worswick Street	D2
Wreatham Place	E3-F3

North Shields

Addison Street	B1
Albion Road	B3-C3
Albion Road West	A2-B2-B3
Alma Place	B3
Ayre's Terrace	B3
Bedford Street	B3-B2-C2
Belford Terrace	B4-C4
Borough Road	B2-B1-C1
Brightman Road	A3-B3
Brighton Grove	A3
Camden Street	C2-C3
Camp Terrace	B4
Campville	A4-B4
Cecil Street	B2
Charlotte Street	C2-C3
Chirton Green	A2
Chirton West View	A1-A2
Cleveland Avenue	B4
Cleveland Road	A4-B4
Cleveland Terrace	A3-A4
Clive Street	C1-C2
Coach Lane	A2-B2-B1
Collingwood View	A1-A2
Drummond Terrace	C3-C4
Fontbarn Terrace	C4
Grey Street	C3-C4
Grosvenor Place	A3-B3
Hawkey's Lane	A2-A3-A4
Hopper Street	A2
Howard Street	C2-C3
Howdon Road	B1-B1
Hylton Street	A1-B1
Jackson Street	C4
Laet Street	C1
Lansdowne Terrace	A3
Liddell Street	C2
Linskill Terrace	C3-C4
Lovaine Place	B2
Lovaine Terrace	B3
Military Road	C3-C4
Milton Terrace	A4
Nile Street	B3
Norfolk Street	C2-C3
North King Street	C3-C4

Northumberland Place	B3-C3
Park Crescent	C4
Preston Road	B3-B4
Prudhoe Street	D1-D2
Queen Street	C3
Rudyard Street	B2-C2-C1
Russell Street	B3
Sackville Street West	B2-C2
Saville Street	C2
Scorer Street	A2-A3
Seymour Street	B1
Sibthorne Street	C1-C2
Sidney Street	B2-B3
Spring Gardens	A2-A3
Spring Terrace	B3
Stanley Street	B1-B2
Stephenson Street	C2-C3
Stormont Street	A1-A2-B2
The Nook	A2
Trevor Terrace	B4-C4
Trinity Street	B1
Tyne Street	C2
Tynemouth Road	C3
Union Street	C2
Upper Elsdon Street	A1-B1
Vicarage Street	B1
Waldo Street	C1
Waterville Road	A1-B1
Waterville Terrace	B2
West Percy Road	A1-A2
West Percy Street	A2-B2-B3
William Street	B2-C2
Yeoman Street	C1-C2

Whitley Bay

Algernon Place	B2
Alma Place	B1
Alnwick Avenue	A3
Amble Avenue	A1-B1
Beach Avenue	A3-B3-B4
Beech Grove	A4
Belsay Avenue	A1-B1
Brook Street	B3-B4
Burfoot Crescent	B1
Burnside Road	A1-B1
Cambridge Avenue	B3-B4
Charles Avenue	B3-B4
Cheviot View	B2-C2
Chollerford Avenue	A1-B1
Clifton Terrace	B2-B3
Coquet Avenue	A4-B4
Countess Avenue	A4
Delaval Road	B2-C2-C1
Dilston Avenue	A2-B2
Duchess Avenue	A4
East Parade	B3-B4
Edwards Road	B2-C2
Egremont Place	B2
Esplanade	B2-B3-C3
Esplanade Place	B3-B2-C2
Etal Avenue	A2-B2
Felton Avenue	A2-B2
Gordon Square	C2
Grafton Road	C1
Grosvenor Drive	A3
Hawthorne Gardens	A4

Helena Avenue	B2-C2
Hill Heads Road	A2-A3-A2
Holly Avenue	A4-R4
Holystone Avenue	A1-A2
Jesmond Terrace	A2-B2
Kings Drive	A3
Lish Avenue	B1
Lovaine Avenue	A2
Marden Road	A2-A3-B3
Marden Road South	A1-A2
Margaret Road	C1
Marine Avenue	A4-B4
Marine Gardens	A4-B4
Mason Avenue	B3
Norham Road	A3
North Parade	B3
North View	B1
Ocean View	B3
Oxford Street	B3-B4
Park Avenue	B3-B4
Park Parade	A3-B3
Park Road	B4
Park View	A3-A4
Percy Avenue	A3-A4
Percy Gardens	A2
Percy Road	B2-C2-C3
Plessey Crescent	A2-B2-B1
Promenade	C1-C2-C3
Queens Drive	A2
Rockcliffe Street	C1-C2
Roxburgh Terrace	A3-B3
Shaftesbury Crescent	A1
Shorestone Avenue	A1-B1
South Parade	B3
Station Road	B2
Studley Gardens	A1-A2
The Broadway	A1
Trewit Road	B2
Victoria Avenue	B2-C2
Victoria Terrace	B2-B3
Warkworth Avenue	A3
Waters Street	C1
Whitley Road	B1-B2-B3
Windsor Crescent	C1
Windsor Terrace	C1
York Road	B3

Norwich

Fortunately the heart has not been ripped out of Norwich to make way for some bland precinct, so its ancient character has been preserved. Narrow alleys run between the streets – sometimes opening out into quiet courtyards, sometimes into thoroughfares packed with people, sometimes into lanes which seem quite deserted. It is a unique place, with something of interest on every corner.

The cathedral was founded in 1096 by the city's first bishop, Herbert de Losinga. Among its most notable features are the nave, with its huge pillars, the bishop's throne (a Saxon survival unique in Europe) and the cloisters with their matchless collection of roof bosses. Across the city is the great stone keep of the castle, set on a mound and dominating all around it. It dates from Norman times, but was refaced in 1834. The keep now forms part of Norwich Castle Museum –

an extensive and fascinating collection. Other museums are Bridewell Museum – collections relating to local crafts and industries within a 14th-century building – and Strangers' Hall, a genuinely 'old world' house, rambling and full of surprises, both in its tumble of rooms and in the things which they contain. Especially picturesque parts of the city are Elm Hill – a street of ancient houses; Tombland – with two gateways into the Cathedral Close; and Pull's Ferry – a watergate by the river.

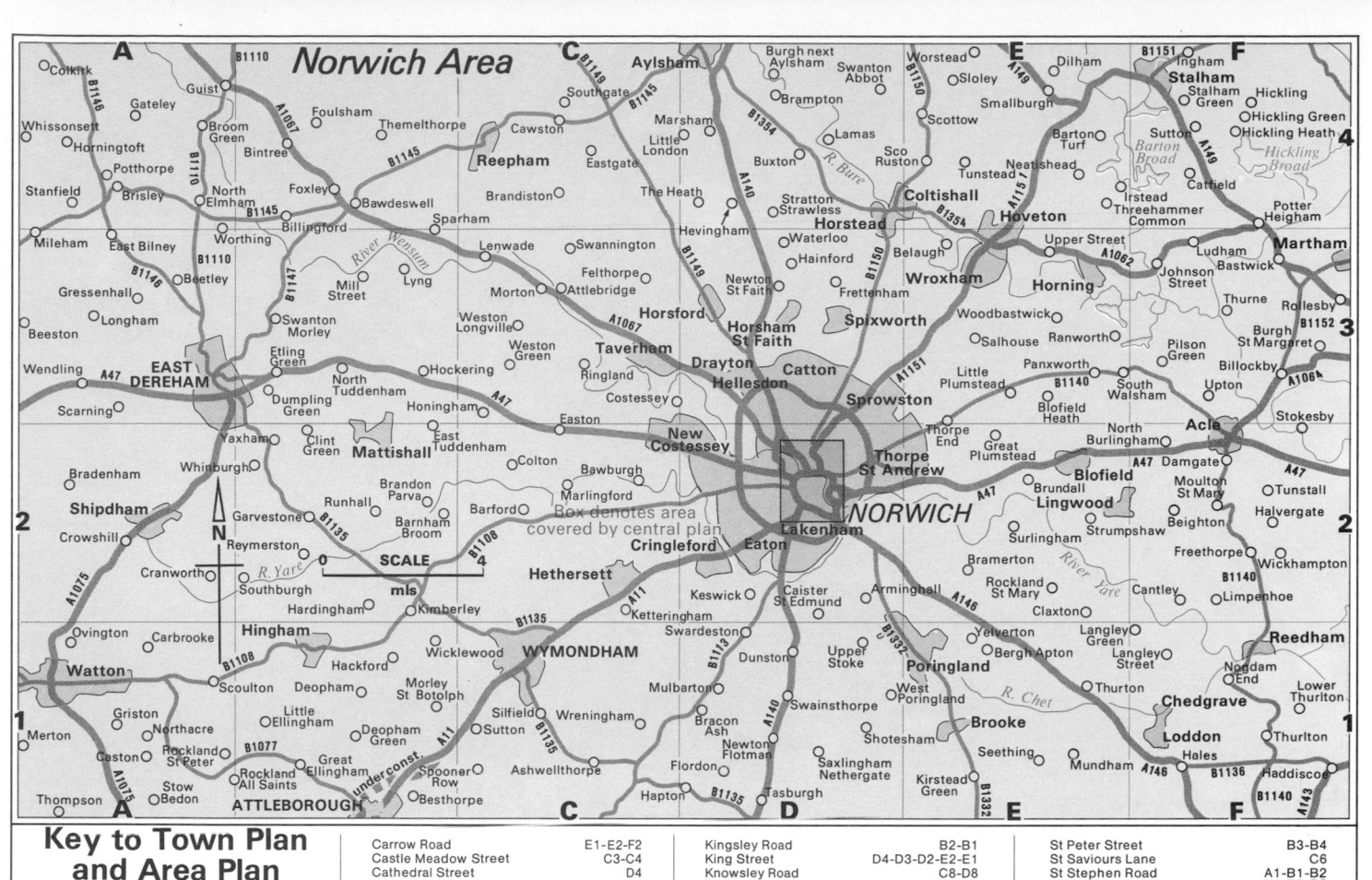

Key to Town Plan and Area Plan

Town Plan
AA Recommended roads
Restricted roads
Other roads
Buildings of interest — School
AA Service Centre — AA
Car Parks — P
Parks and open spaces
One Way Streets →

Area Plan
A roads
B roads
Locations — East Rushton
Urban area

Street Index with Grid Reference

Norwich

Street	Grid
Albany Road	C8
Albert Place	F5
All Saints Green	C2-C3
Alma Terrace	B7
Anchor Close	E6
Anchor Street	E7
Angel Road	B8
Argyle Street	D2-D1-E1
Ashby Street	C1
Aspland Road	E4
Aylesham Road	A8-B8
Baker Road	B7
Balfour Street	E7
Bank Plain	C4
Barn Road	A5
Barrack Street	D6-E6
Beaconsfield Road	C7-D7
Beatrice Road	F4
Bedford Street	C4
Bell Avenue	C3
Ber Street	C3-C2-D2-D1
Bethel Street	B4-B3
Bishopbridge Road	E5-E6
Bishopsgate	D5-E5
Blackfriars	C6-D6
Botolph Street	C6
Bracondale	D1-E1
Branford Road	D8
Brigg Street	C3
Britannia Road	F7-F6
Brunswick Road	A1
Bull Close	C8-C7-D7
Bull Close Road	C7-D7-D6
Buxton Road	B7-B8
Calvert Street	C6-C5
Camp Grove	F5
Cannell Green	E6
Carrow Hill	D1-E1

Street	Grid
Carrow Road	E1-E2-F2
Castle Meadow Street	C3-C4
Cathedral Street	D4
Cattle Market	C3-D3
Cedar Road	F3-F2
Chalkhill Road	E4
Chantry Road	B3
Chapelfield East	B3
Chapelfield North	A4-A3-B4-B3
Chapelfield Road	A3-B3-B2
Chapel Lodge	C2
Churchill Road	C8-D8
Charlton Road	D6
Chatham Street	B7-B6
City Road	D1
Clarence Road	F3-F2
Clarke Street	C7-C8
Cleveland Road	A4-B4
Colegate	B5-C5
Cowgate	C6-D6
Cow Hill	A4
Cozens Road	F2
Crome Road	D8-D7
Crooks Place	B2
Cross Street	B7-B6
Davey Place	C4
Derby Street	A6
Dereham Road	A5
Drayton Road	A8-B8
Duke Street	B6-B5-C5-C4
Eade Road	B8
Earlham Road	A4
Esdelle Street	B7-C7
Edward Street	C7-C6
Egyptian Road	E6-F6-F5
Ella Road	F4-F3
Elmhill	C5
Exchange Street	C4
Farmer Avenue	C3
Finklegate	D1
Fishergate	C5-C6-D6
Fishers Lane	B4
Florence Road	F4
Garden Street	D2
Gas Hill	E5-F5
Gertrude Road	E7-E8-F8
Gildencroft	B6
Gilman Road	F8
Golden Ball	C3
Golding Place	A5
Goldwell Road	C1
Grapes Hill	A5-A4
Greenhill Road	B7
Greyfriars Road	D4
Grove Avenue	A1-B1
Grove Road	A1-B1-C1-C2
Gurney Road	E6-F6-F7-F8
Guernsey Road	C7
Hall Road	D1
Hardy Road	F1-F2
Hassett Close	E7
Heathgate	E7-F7
Heath Road	C8-C7
Heigham Street	A6-A5
Hill House Road	F3-F4
Hollis Lane	C1-D1
Ipswich Road	A1
Jenkins Lane	B6
Kerrison Road	F2
Ketts Hill	E6-F6-F5
Kimberley Street	A3
Kings Lane	C1

Street	Grid
Kingsley Road	B2-B1
King Street	D4-D3-D2-E2-E1
Knowsley Road	C8-D8
Lavengrove Road	F8-F7 F7
London Street	C4
Long Row	B8-C8
Lothian Street	A5
Lower Clarence Road	E3-F3-F2
Lower Close	D4-E4
Magdalen Road	C7-C8
Magdalen Street	C7-C6-C5
Magpie Road	B7-C7
Malthouse Road	B2-B3
Mariners Lane	D1-D2
Market Avenue	C3-C4
Marlborough Road	C7-D7
Midland Street	A5-A6
Mons Avenue	F7
Morley Street	D7
Mountergate Street	D3-D4
Mousehold Avenue	D7-E7-E8-F8
Mousehold Street	D7-E7-E6-F6
Music House Lane	D2
Muspole Street	B5-C5
Newmarket Road	A1
New Mills Yard	B5
Norfolk Street	A2
Northcote Road	C8-D8
Oak Street	B6-B5
Old Barge Yard	D2-D3
Orchard Street	A5-A6
Palace Street	D5
Paragon Place	A4
Patteson Road	B8
Peacock Street	C6
Pitt Street	B6-C6
Pottergate	A4-B4
Prince of Wales Road	D4-E4-E3
Primrose Road	F4
Princes Street	C4-C5-D5
Quebec Road	F4-F5
Queens Road	B2-C2-C1
Queen Street	C4-D4
Recorder Road	E4
Red Lion Street	C3
Regina Road	B1
River Lane	D6
Riverside	E3-E2-E1
Riverside Road	E3-E4-E5
Romany Road	D8-E8
Ropemaker Row	A8
Rosary Road	E5-E4-F4-F3
Rosedale Crescent	F4
Rose Lane	D3-D4-E4
Rouen Road	C3-D3-D2
Rowington Road	B1
Rupert Street	A2-A3
St Andrew Street	C4
St Ann's Lane	D3
St Augustine Street	B7-B6
St Benedict Street	A5-B5-B4
St Crispins Road	B6-C6-D6
St Faiths Lane	D4
St George's Street	C6-C5-C4
St Giles Street	B4-C4
St James Close	E6
St John Street	D3
St Juliens Alley	D2-D3
St Leonards Road	E4-F4-F5
St Martin Road	A8-B8-A7-B7
St Mary's Road	B7
St Olaves Road	D8

Street	Grid
St Peter Street	B3-B4
St Saviours Lane	C6
St Stephen Road	A1-B1-B2
St Stephen Street	B2-B3-C3
St Stephen Square	B2
St Swithins Road	A5-B5
Sayer Street	A6
Shipstone Road	C8
Silver Road	D6-D7-D8
Silver Street	D7
Southwell Street	B1-C1
Spencer Street	D7-D8
Spitalfields	E6-F6
Sprowston Road	C8-D8
Stacy Road	C7
Starling Road	B7-C7
Stracey Road	F3
Surrey Street	C3-C2-C1-D1
Sussex Street	B6-B7
The Walk	C3-C4
Telegraph Lane West	F5-F4
Temple Road	C8
Theatre Street	B3-C3
Thorne Lane	C2-D2-D3
Thorpe Road	E3-F3
Timberhill Street	C3
Tombland	D5-D4
Trinity Street	A2-A1
Trory Street	A3
Union Street	A1-A2-A3
Upper Close	D4
Upper King Street	D4
Vauxhall Street	A3
Victoria Street	B2-B1
Walpole Street	A3
Waterloo Road	B7-B8-C8
Whitefriars	D6-D5
White Lion Street	C3
Willow Lane	A4-B4
Wingfield Road	B7
Wensum Street	C5-D5
Wessex Street	A2-B2
West Gardens	A3
Westle Gate	C3
Westwick Street	A5-B5-B4
Wodehouse Street	D7
Wood Street	B1

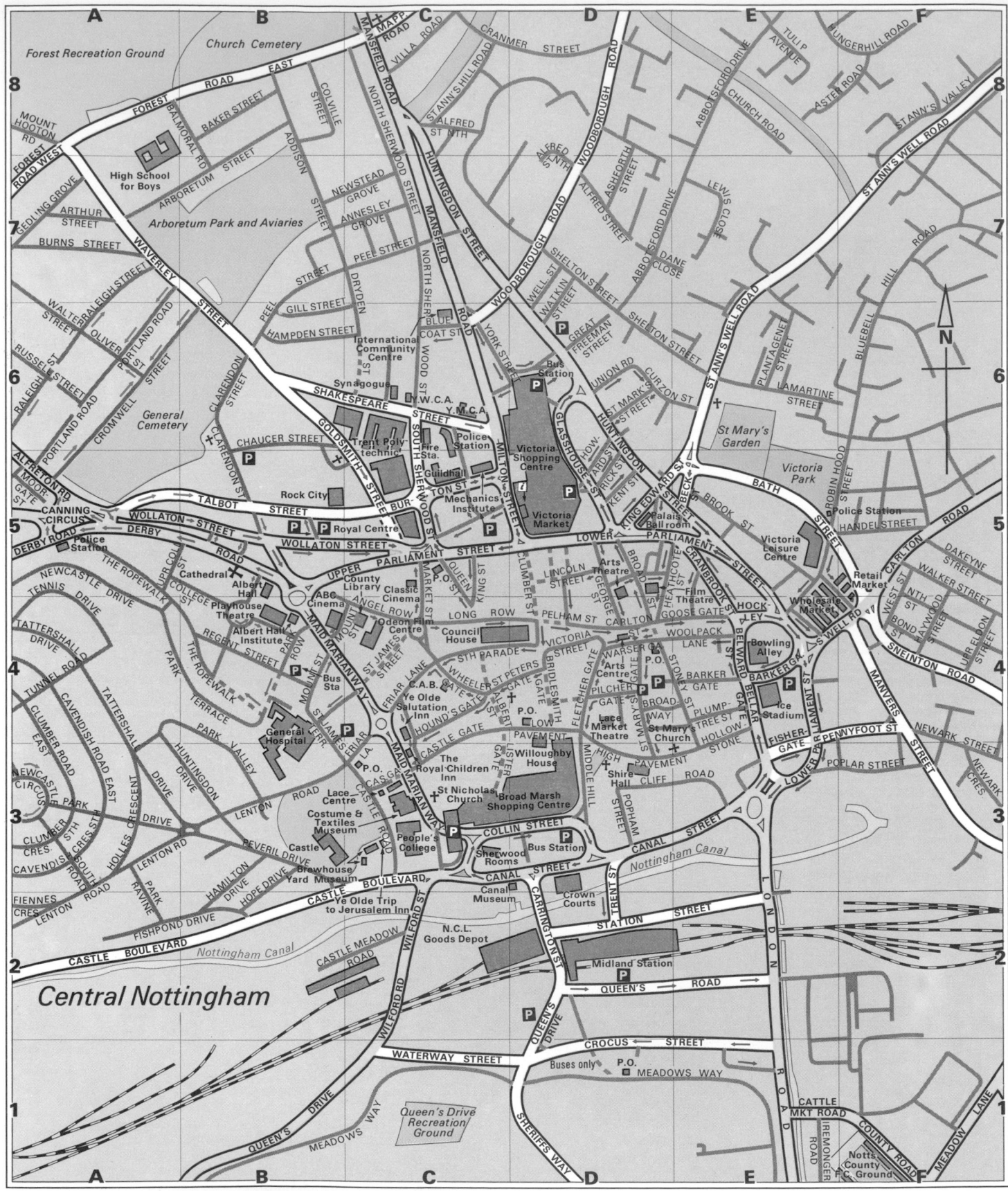

Nottingham

Hosiery and lace were the foundations upon which Nottingham's prosperity was built. The stockings came first – a knitting machine for these had been invented by a Nottinghamshire man as early as 1589 – but a machine called a 'tickler', which enabled simple patterns to be created in the stocking fabric, prompted the development of machine-made lace. The earliest fabric was produced in 1768, and an example from not much later than that is kept in the city's Castlegate Costume and Textile Museum. In fact, the entire history of lacemaking is beautifully explained in this converted row of Georgian terraces. The Industrial Museum at Wollaton Park has many other machines and exhibits tracing the development of the knitting industry, as well as displays on the other industries which have brought wealth to the city – tobacco, pharmaceuticals, engineering and printing. At Wollaton Hall is a natural history museum, while nearer the centre are the Canal Museum and the Brewhouse Yard Museum, a marvellous collection which shows items from daily life in the city up to the present day. Nottingham is not complete without mention of Robin Hood, the partly mythical figure whose statue is in the castle grounds. Although the castle itself has Norman foundations, the present structure is largely Victorian. It is now a museum.

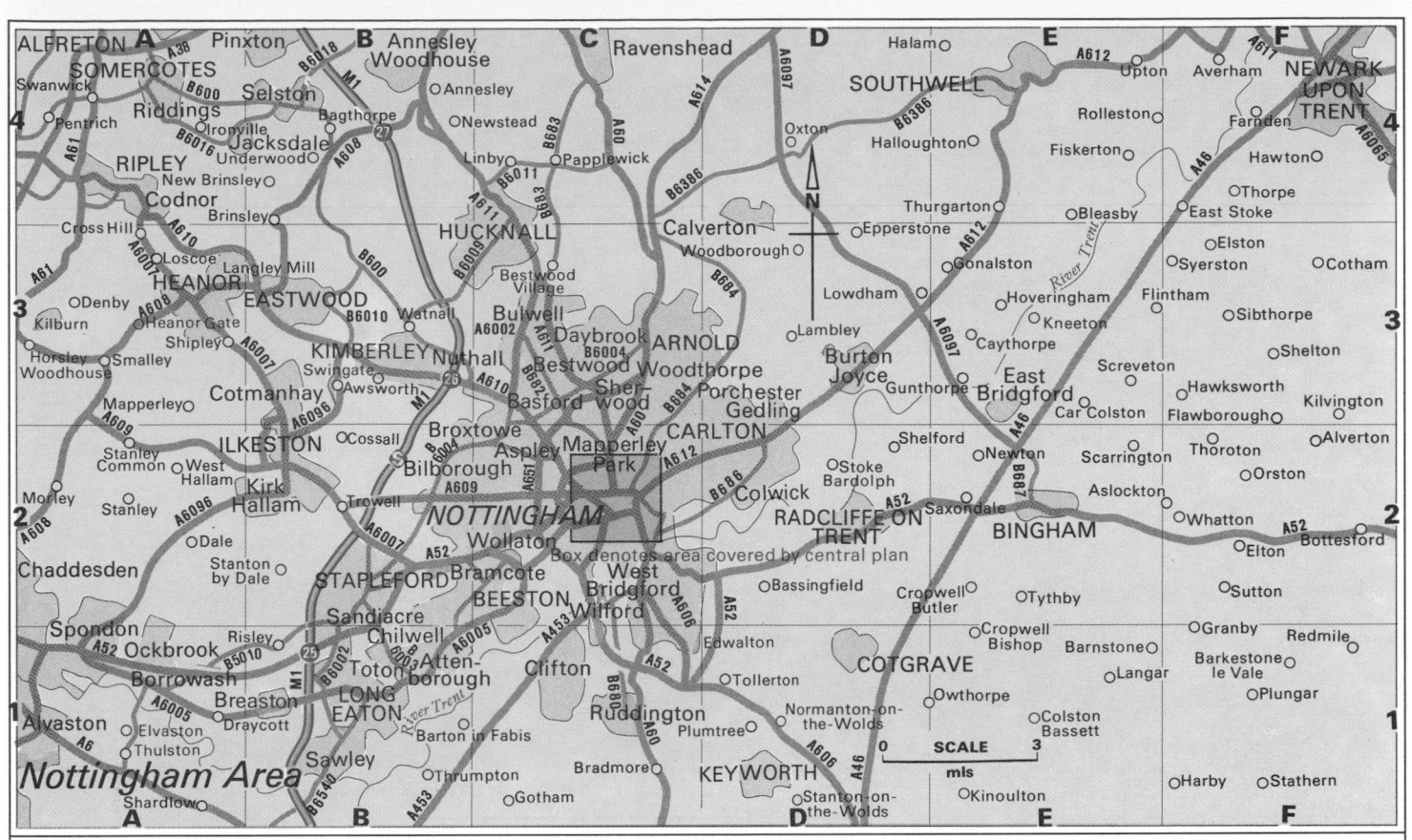

Key to Town Plan and Area Plan

Town Plan

AA Recommended roads	
Restricted roads	
Other roads	
Buildings of interest	Theatre ▪
Car Parks	P
Parks and open spaces	▪
Churches	†
One Way Streets	→

Area Plan

A roads	
B roads	
Locations	Bagthorpe○
Urban area	▪

Street Index with Grid Reference

Nottingham

Abbotsford Drive	D7-D7-E7-E8
Addison Street	B7-B8
Albert Street	C4
Alfred Street	D7
Alfred Street North	C8, D7-D8
Alfreton Road	A5-A6
Angel Road	B5-B4-C4
Annesley Grove	B7-C7
Ashford Street	D7-D8
Aster Road	E8-F8
Arboretum Street	A7-B7-B8
Arthur Street	A7
Baker Street	B8
Balmoral Road	A8-B8-B7
Barker Gate	E4
Bath Gate	E5-F5
Beck Street	E5
Bellar Gate	E4
Belward Street	E4
Bluebell Hill Road	F6-F7
Bluecoat Street	C6
Bond Street	F4
Bridlesmith Gate	D4
Broad Street	D4-D5
Broadway	D4-E4
Brook Street	E5
Burns Street	A7
Burton Street	C5

Canal Street	C3-D3-E3
Canning Circus	A5
Carlton Road	F5
Carlton Street	D4
Carrington Street	D2-D3
Castle Boulevard	A2-B2-B3-C3
Castle Gate	C3-C4
Castle Market Road	E1-F1
Castle Meadow Road	B2-C2
Castle Road	C3
Cavendish Crescent South	A3
Cavendish Road East	A3-A4
Chaucer Street	B5-B6
Church Road	E8
Clarendon Street	B5-B6
Cliff Road	D3-E3
Clumber Crescent South	A3
Clumber Road East	A3-A4
Clumber Street	D4-D5
College Street	A5-B5-B4
Collin Street	C3-D3
Colville Street	B8
County Road	F1
Cranbrook Street	E4-E5
Cranmer Street	C8-D8
Crocus Street	D1-E1
Cromwell Street	A5-B6-C6
Curzon Street	D6-E6
Dane Close	D7-E7
Dakeyne Street	F5
Derby Road	A5-B5
Dryden Street	C6-C7
Fieness Crescent	A2
Fishergate	E3-E4
Fishpond Drive	A2-B2
Fletcher Gate	D4
Forest Road East	A8-B8-C8
Forest Road West	A7-A8
Friar Lane	C3-C4
Gedling Grove	A7
George Street	D4-D5
Glasshouse Street	D5-D6
Gill Street	B6-C6
Goldsmith Street	B6-C6-C5
Goose Gate	D4-E4
Great Freeman Street	D6
Hamilton Drive	B2-B3
Hampden Street	B6-C6
Handel Street	E5-F5
Haywood Street	F4-F5
High Pavement	D4-D3-E3
Hockley	E4
Holles Crescent	A3
Hollowstone	E3-E4
Hope Drive	B2-B3
Hound's Gate	C4

Howard Street	D5-D6
Hungerhill Road	E8-F8
Huntingdon Drive	A4-A3-B3
Huntingdon Drive	C8-C7-D7-D6-D5-E5
Huskisson Street	C6
Iremonger Road	E1
Kent Street	D5
King Edward Street	D5-E5
King Street	C4-C5
Lamartine Street	E6-F6
Lenton Road	A2-A3-B3
Lewis Close	E7
Lincoln Street	D5
Lister Gate	C3-C4
London Road	E1-E2-E3
Long Row	C4-D4
Lower Parliament Street	D5-E5-E4-E3
Low Pavement	C4-D4
Maid Marion Way	B4-C4-C3
Mansfield Street	C6-C7-C8
Manvers Street	F3-F4
Mapperley Road	C8
Market Street	C4-C5
Meadow Lane	F1
Meadows Road	B1-C1-D1-E1
Middle Hill	D3-D4
Milton Street	C6-C5-D5
Moorgate Street	A5
Mount Hooton Road	A8
Mount Street	B4-C4
Newark Crescent	F3
Newark Street	F3-F4
Newcastle Circus	A3
Newcastle Drive	A4-A5
Newstead Grove	B7-C7
North Street	F4-F5
North Sherwood Street	C6-C7-C8
Oliver Street	A6
Park Drive	A3-B3
Park Ravine	A2-A3
Park Row	B4
Park Terrace	A4-B4
Park Valley	A4-B4-B3
Peel Street	B6-B7-C7
Pelham Street	D4
Pennyfoot Street	E4-F4
Peveril Drive	B3
Pilcher Gate	D4
Plantagenet Street	E6
Plumptree Street	E4
Popham Street	D3
Poplar Street	E3-F3
Portland Road	A5-A6-A7
Queen's Drive	B1-C1, D1-D2
Queen's Road	D2-E2
Queen Street	C4-C5

Releigh Street	A6-A7
Regent Street	B4
Rick Street	D5
Robin Hood Street	E5-F5-F6
Russell Street	A6
St Ann's Hill Road	C8
St Ann's Valley	F7-F8
St Ann's Well Road	E5-E6-E7-F7-F8
St James Street	C4
St James Terrace	B4-B3-C3
St Mark's Street	D6
St Peters Gate	C4-D4
Shakespeare Street	B6-C6
Shelton Street	D7-D6-E6
Sherriffs Way	D1
Sneinton Road	F4
South Parade	C4-D4
South Road	A3
South Sherwood Street	C5-C6
Southwell Road	E4-F4
Station Street	D2-E2
Stony Street	D4-E4
Talbot Street	A5-B5-C5
Tattershall Drive	A4-A3-B3
Tennis Drive	A4-A5-A4
The Robewalk	A5-A4-B4
Trent Street	D2-D3
Tulip Avenue	A8
Tunnel Road	A4
Union Road	D6
Upper College Street	A5-B5
Upper Eldon Street	F4
Upper Parliament Street	B5-C5-D5
Victoria Street	D4
Villa Road	C8
Walker Street	F4-F5
Walter Street	A6-A7
Warser Gate	D4
Waterway Street	C1-D1
Watkin Street	D6-D7
Waverely Street	A8-A7-B7-B6
Wellington Street	D6-D7
West Street	F4-F5
Wheeler Gate	C4
Wilford Road	C1-C2
Wilford Street	C2-C3
Wollaton Street	A5-B5-C5
Woodborough Road	C6-C7-D7-D8
Woolpack Lane	D4-E4
York Street	C6-D6

Oxford

From Carfax (at the centre of the city) round to Magdalen Bridge stretches High Street, one of England's best and most interesting thoroughfares. Shops rub shoulders with churches and colleges, alleyways lead to ancient inns and to a large covered market, and little streets lead to views of some of the finest architecture to be seen anywhere. Catte Street, beside St Mary's Church (whose lovely tower gives a panoramic view of Oxford), opens out into Radcliffe Square, dominated by the Radcliffe Camera, a great round structure built in 1749. Close by is the Bodleian Library, one of the finest collections of books and manuscripts in the world. All around are ancient college buildings. Close to Magdalen Bridge is Magdalen College, founded in 1448 and certainly not to be missed. Across the High Street are the Botanical Gardens, founded in 1621 and the oldest such foundation in England. Footpaths lead through Christ Church Meadow to Christ Church College and the cathedral. Tom Tower is the college's most notable feature; the cathedral is actually its chapel and is the smallest cathedral in England. Among much else not to be missed in Oxford is the Ashmolean Museum, whose vast collections of precious and beautiful objects from all over the world repay many hours of study; perhaps the loveliest treasure is the 9th-century Alfred Jewel.

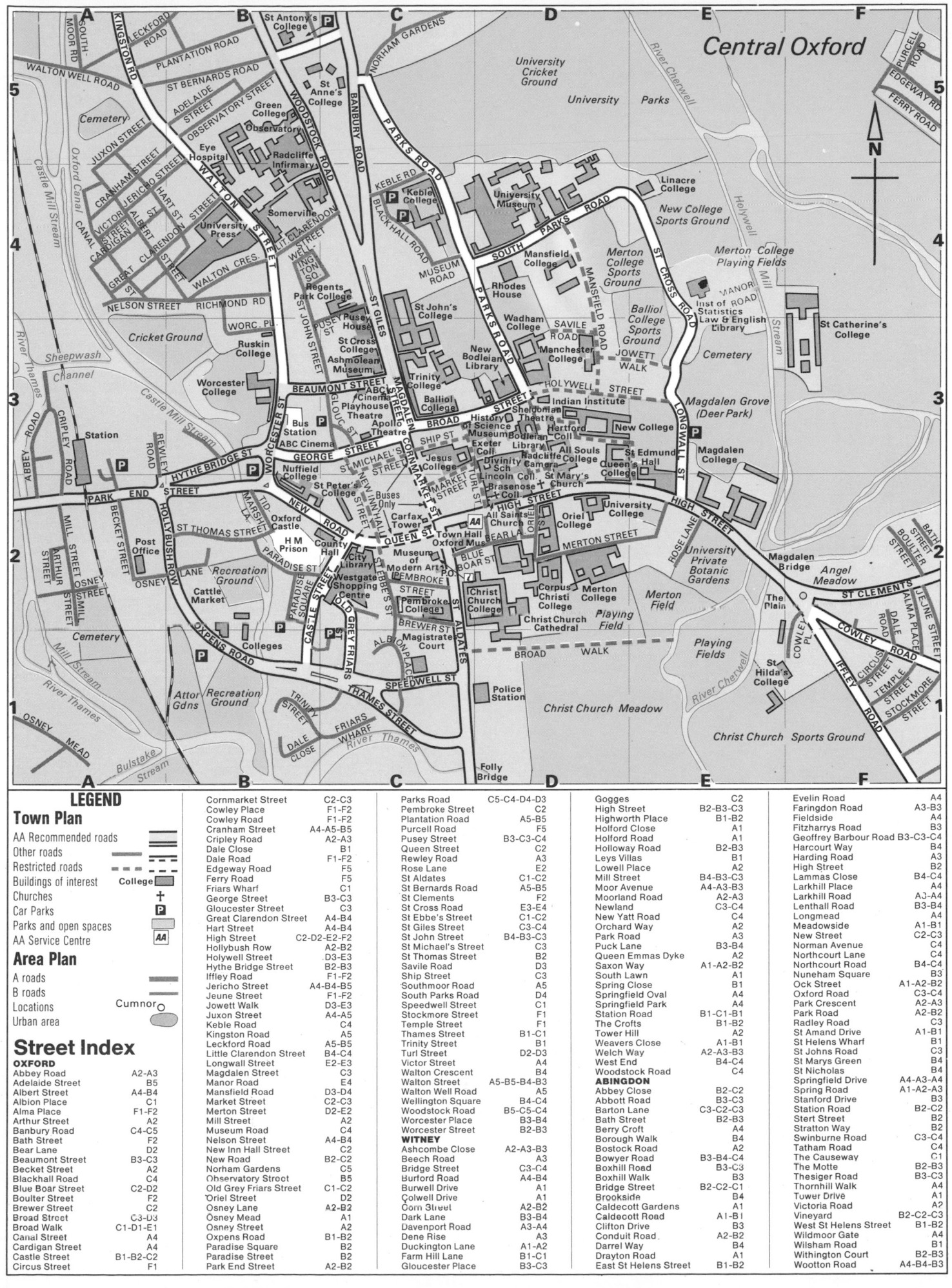

Central Oxford

LEGEND

Town Plan
- AA Recommended roads
- Other roads
- Restricted roads
- Buildings of interest — College
- Churches — †
- Car Parks — P
- Parks and open spaces
- AA Service Centre — AA

Area Plan
- A roads
- B roads
- Locations — Cumnor ○
- Urban area

Street Index

OXFORD

Abbey Road	A2-A3
Adelaide Street	B5
Albert Street	A4-B4
Albion Place	C1
Alma Place	F1-F2
Arthur Street	A2
Banbury Road	C4-C5
Bath Street	F2
Bear Lane	D2
Beaumont Street	B3-C3
Becket Street	A2
Blackhall Road	C4
Blue Boar Street	C2-D2
Boulter Street	F2
Brewer Street	C2
Broad Street	C3-D3
Broad Walk	C1-D1-E1
Canal Street	A4
Cardigan Street	A4
Castle Street	B1-B2-C2
Circus Street	F1
Cornmarket Street	C2-C3
Cowley Place	F1-F2
Cowley Road	F1-F2
Cranham Street	A4-A5-B5
Cripley Road	A2-A3
Dale Close	B1
Dale Road	F1-F2
Edgeway Road	F5
Ferry Road	F5
Friars Wharf	C1
George Street	B3-C3
Gloucester Street	C3
Great Clarendon Street	A4-B4
Hart Street	A4-B4
High Street	C2-D2-E2-F2
Hollybush Row	A2-B2
Holywell Street	D3-E3
Hythe Bridge Street	B2-B3
Iffley Road	F1-F2
Jericho Street	A4-B4-B5
Jeune Street	F1-F2
Jowett Walk	D3-E3
Juxon Street	A4-A5
Keble Road	C4
Kingston Road	A5
Leckford Road	A5-B5
Little Clarendon Street	B4-C4
Longwall Street	E2-E3
Magdalen Street	C3
Manor Road	E4
Mansfield Road	D3-D4
Market Street	C2-C3
Merton Street	D2-E2
Mill Street	A2
Museum Road	C4
Nelson Street	A4-B4
New Inn Hall Street	C2
New Road	B2-C2
Norham Gardens	C5
Observatory Street	B5
Old Grey Friars Street	C1-C2
Oriel Street	D2
Osney Lane	A2-B2
Osney Mead	A1
Osney Street	A2
Oxpens Road	B1-B2
Paradise Square	B2
Paradise Street	B2
Park End Street	A2-B2
Parks Road	C5-C4-D4-D3
Pembroke Street	C2
Plantation Road	A5-B5
Purcell Road	F5
Pusey Street	B3-C3-C4
Queen Street	C2
Rewley Road	A3
Rose Lane	E2
St Aldates	C1-C2
St Bernards Road	A5-B5
St Clements	F2
St Cross Road	E3-E4
St Ebbe's Street	C1-C2
St Giles Street	C3-C4
St John Street	B4-B3-C3
St Michael's Street	C3
St Thomas Street	B2
Savile Road	D3
Ship Street	C3
Southmoor Road	A5
South Parks Road	D4
Speedwell Street	C1
Stockmore Street	F1
Temple Street	F1
Thames Street	B1-C1
Trinity Street	B1
Turl Street	D2-D3
Victor Street	A4
Walton Crescent	B4
Walton Street	A5-B5-B4-B3
Walton Well Road	A5
Wellington Square	B4-C4
Woodstock Road	B5-C5-C4
Worcester Place	B3-B4
Worcester Street	B2-B3

WITNEY

Ashcombe Close	A2-A3-B3
Beech Road	A3
Bridge Street	C3-C4
Burford Road	A4-B4
Burwell Drive	A1
Colwell Drive	A1
Corn Street	A2-B2
Dark Lane	B3-B4
Davenport Road	A3-A4
Dene Rise	A3
Duckington Lane	A1-A2
Farm Hill Lane	B1-C1
Gloucester Place	B3-C3

Gogges	C2
High Street	B2-B3-C3
Highworth Place	B1-B2
Holford Close	A1
Holford Road	A1
Holloway Road	B2-B3
Leys Villas	B1
Lowell Place	A2
Mill Street	B4-B3-C3
Moor Avenue	A4-A3-B3
Moorland Road	A2-A3
Newland	C3-C4
New Yatt Road	C4
Orchard Way	A2
Park Road	A3
Puck Lane	B3-B4
Queen Emmas Dyke	A2
Saxon Way	A1-A2-B2
South Lawn	A1
Spring Close	B1
Springfield Oval	A4
Springfield Park	A4
Station Road	B1-C1-B1
The Crofts	B1-B2
Tower Hill	A2
Weavers Close	A1-B1
Welch Way	A2-A3-B3
West End	B4-C4
Woodstock Road	C4

ABINGDON

Abbey Close	B2-C2
Abbott Road	B3-C3
Barton Lane	C3-C2-C3
Bath Street	B2-B3
Berry Croft	A4
Borough Walk	B4
Bostock Road	A2
Bowyer Road	B3-B4-C4
Boxhill Road	B3-C3
Boxhill Walk	B3
Bridge Street	B2-C2-C1
Brookside	A4
Caldecott Gardens	A1
Caldecott Road	A1-B1
Clifton Drive	A1
Conduit Road	A2-B2
Darrel Way	B4
Drayton Road	A1
East St Helens Street	B1-B2

Evelin Road	A4
Faringdon Road	A3-B3
Fieldside	A4
Fitzharrys Road	B3
Geoffrey Barbour Road	B3-C3-C4
Harcourt Way	B4
Harding Road	B3
High Street	B2
Lammas Close	B4-C4
Larkhill Place	A4
Larkhill Road	A3-A4
Lenthall Road	B3-B4
Longmead	A4
Meadowside	A1-B1
New Street	C2-C3
Norman Avenue	C4
Northcourt Lane	C4
Northcourt Road	B4-C4
Nuneham Square	B3
Ock Street	A1-A2-B2
Oxford Road	C3-C4
Park Crescent	A2-A3
Park Road	A2-B2
Radley Road	C3
St Amand Drive	A1-B1
St Helens Wharf	B1
St Johns Road	C3
St Marys Green	B4
St Nicholas	B4
Springfield Drive	A4-A3-A4
Spring Road	A1-A2-A3
Stanford Drive	B3
Station Road	B2-C2
Stert Street	B2
Stratton Way	B2
Swinburne Road	C3-C4
Tatham Road	C4
The Causeway	C1
The Motte	B2-B3
Thesiger Road	B3-C3
Thornhill Walk	A4
Tower Drive	A1
Victoria Road	A2
Vineyard	B2-C2-C3
West St Helens Street	B1-B2
Wildmoor Gate	A4
Wilsham Road	B1
Withington Court	B2-B3
Wootton Road	A4-B4-B3

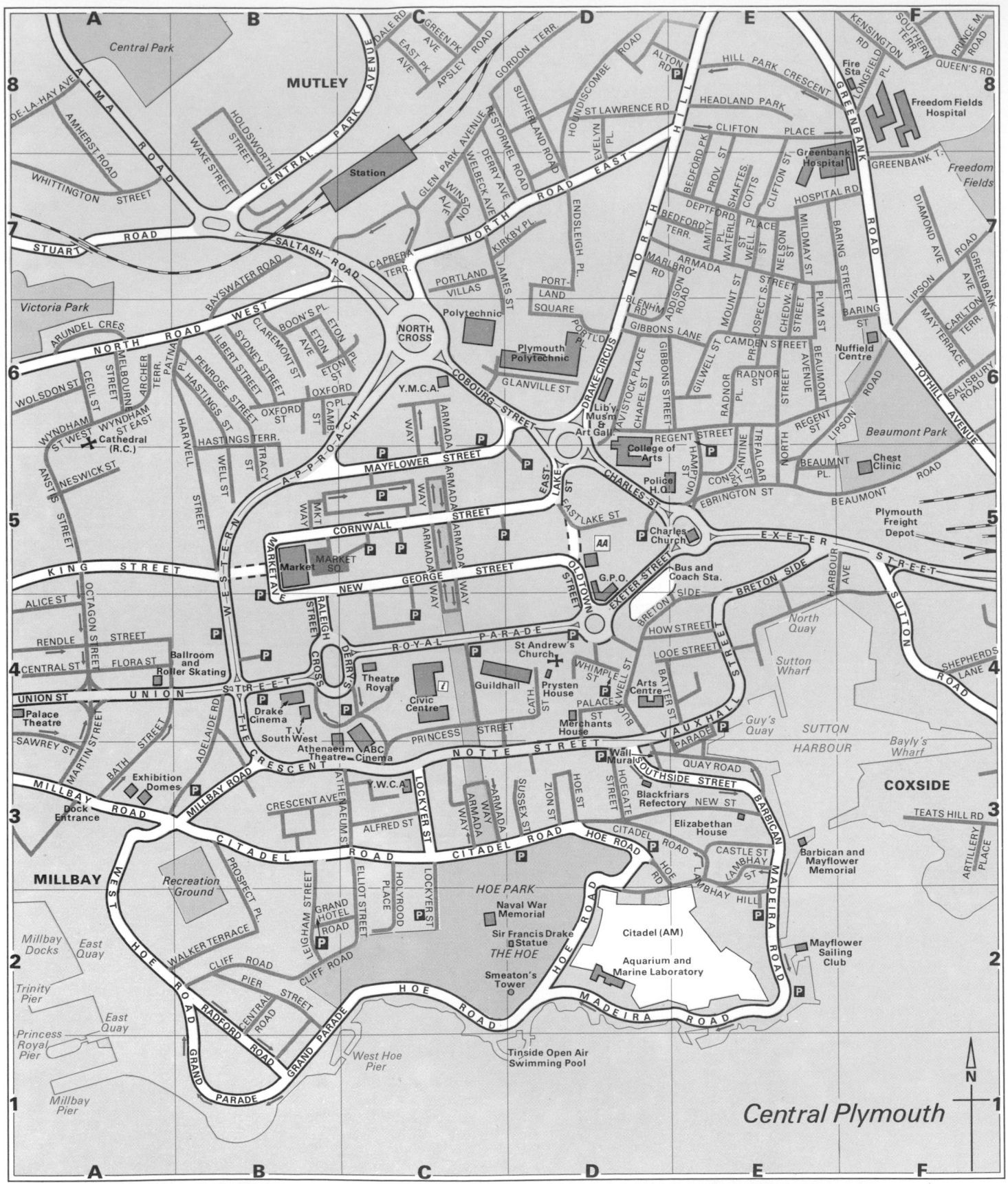

Plymouth

Ships, sailors and the sea permeate every aspect of Plymouth's life and history. Its superb natural harbour – Plymouth Sound – has ensured its importance as a port, yachting centre and naval base (latterly at Devonport) over many centuries. Sir Francis Drake is undoubtedly the city's most famous sailor. His statue stands on the Hoe – where he really did play bowls before tackling the

Spanish Armada. Also on the Hoe are Smeaton's Tower, which once formed the upper part of the third Eddystone Lighthouse, and the impressive Royal Naval War Memorial. Just east of the Hoe is the Royal Citadel, an imposing fortress built in 1666 by order of Charles II. North is Sutton Harbour, perhaps the most atmospheric part of Plymouth. Here fishing boats bob up and down in a harbour whose quays are lined with attractive old houses, inns and warehouses. One of the memorials on

Mayflower Quay just outside the harbour commemorates the sailing of the *Mayflower* from here in 1620. Plymouth's shopping centre is one of the finest of its kind, and was built after the old centre was badly damaged in World War II. Nearby is the 200ft-high tower of the impressive modern Civic Centre. Some buildings escaped destruction, including the Elizabethan House and the 500-year-old Prysten House. Next door is St Andrew's Church, with stained glass by John Piper.

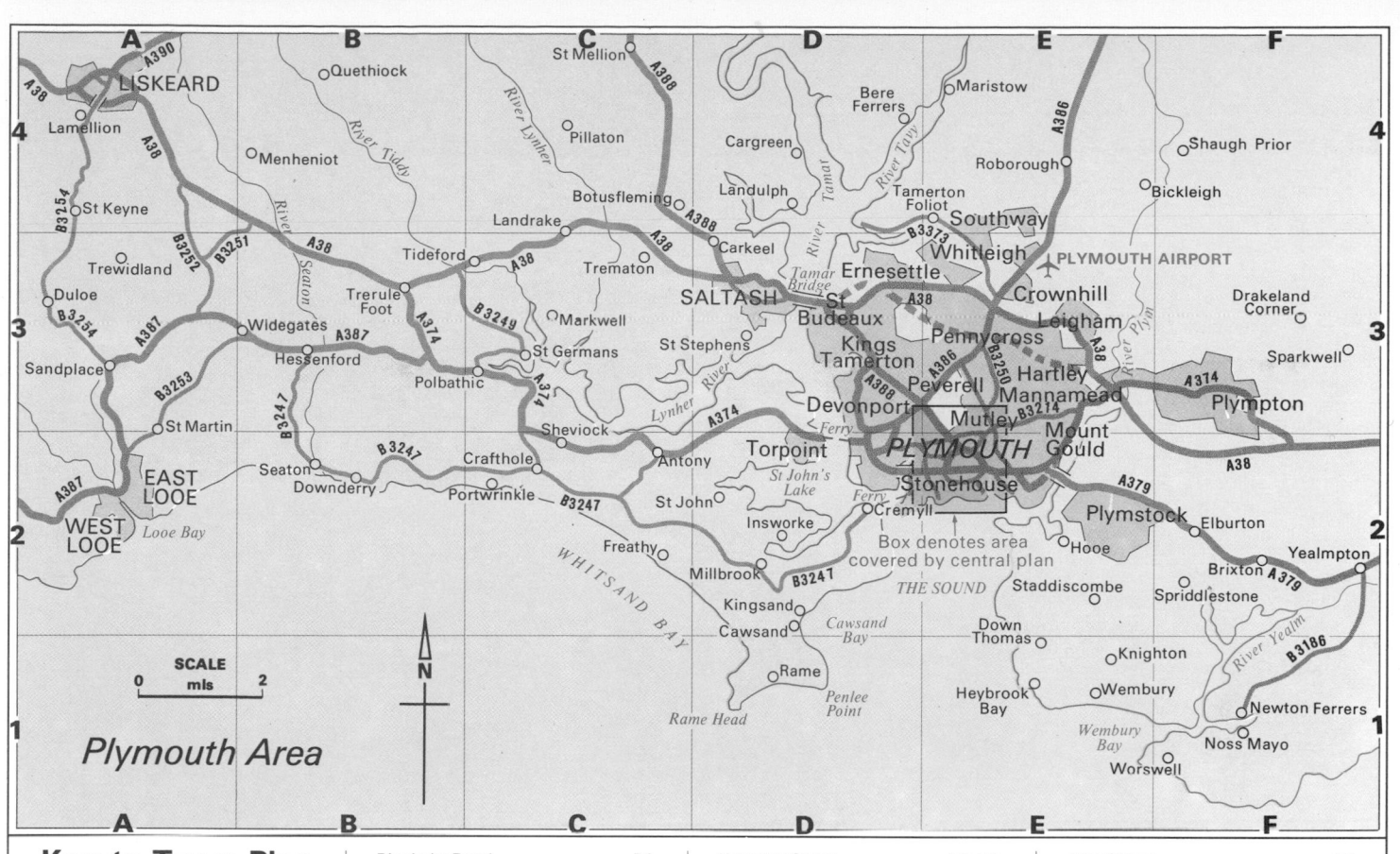

Key to Town Plan and Area Plan

Town Plan

AA Recommended roads ▬▬▬
Other roads ▬▬▬
Restricted roads ▬ ▬ ▬
Buildings of interest ▮
Car Parks P
Parks and open spaces ◢
One way streets ←

Area Plan

A roads ▬▬▬
B roads ▬▬▬
Locations Sandplace ○
Urban area ◢

Street Index with Grid Reference

Plymouth

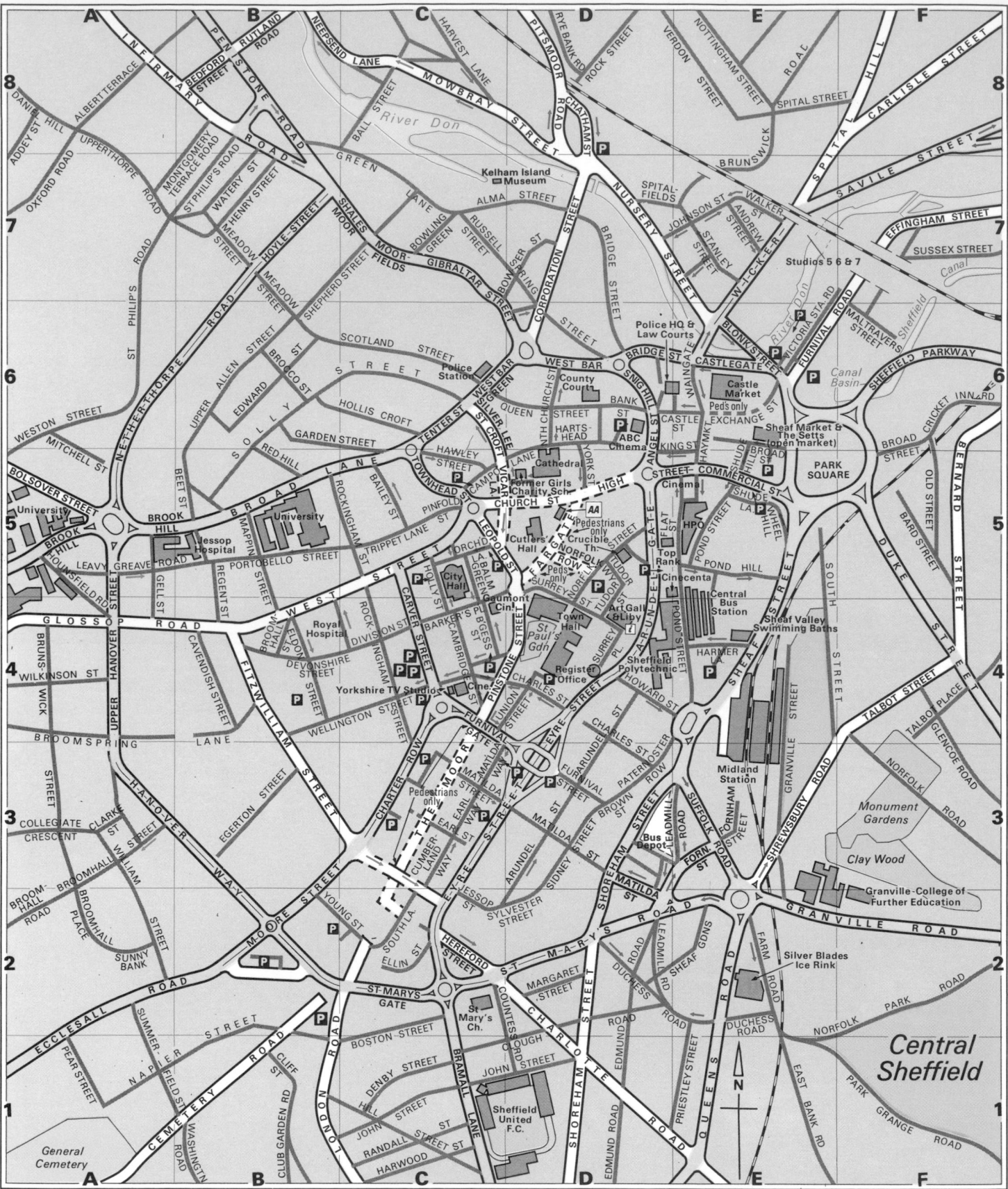

Sheffield

Cutlery – which has made the name of Sheffield famous throughout the world – has been manufactured here since at least as early as the time of Chaucer. The god of blacksmiths, Vulcan, is the symbol of the city's industry, and he crowns the town hall, which was opened in 1897 by Queen Victoria. At the centre of the industry, however, is Cutlers' Hall, the headquarters of the Company of Cutlers. This society was founded in 1624 and has the right to grant trade marks to articles of a sufficiently high standard. In the hall is the company's collection of silver, with examples of craftsmanship dating back every year to 1773. A really large collection of cutlery is kept in the city museum. Steel production, a vital component of the industry, was greatly improved when the crucible process was invented here in 1740. At Abbeydale Industrial Hamlet, 3½ miles south-west of the city centre, is a complete restored site open as a museum and showing 18th-century methods of steel production. Sheffield's centre, transformed since World War II, is one of the finest and most modern in Europe. There are no soot-grimed industrial eyesores here, for the city has stringent pollution controls and its buildings are carefully planned and set within excellent landscaping projects. Many parks are set in and around the city, and the Pennines are within easy reach.

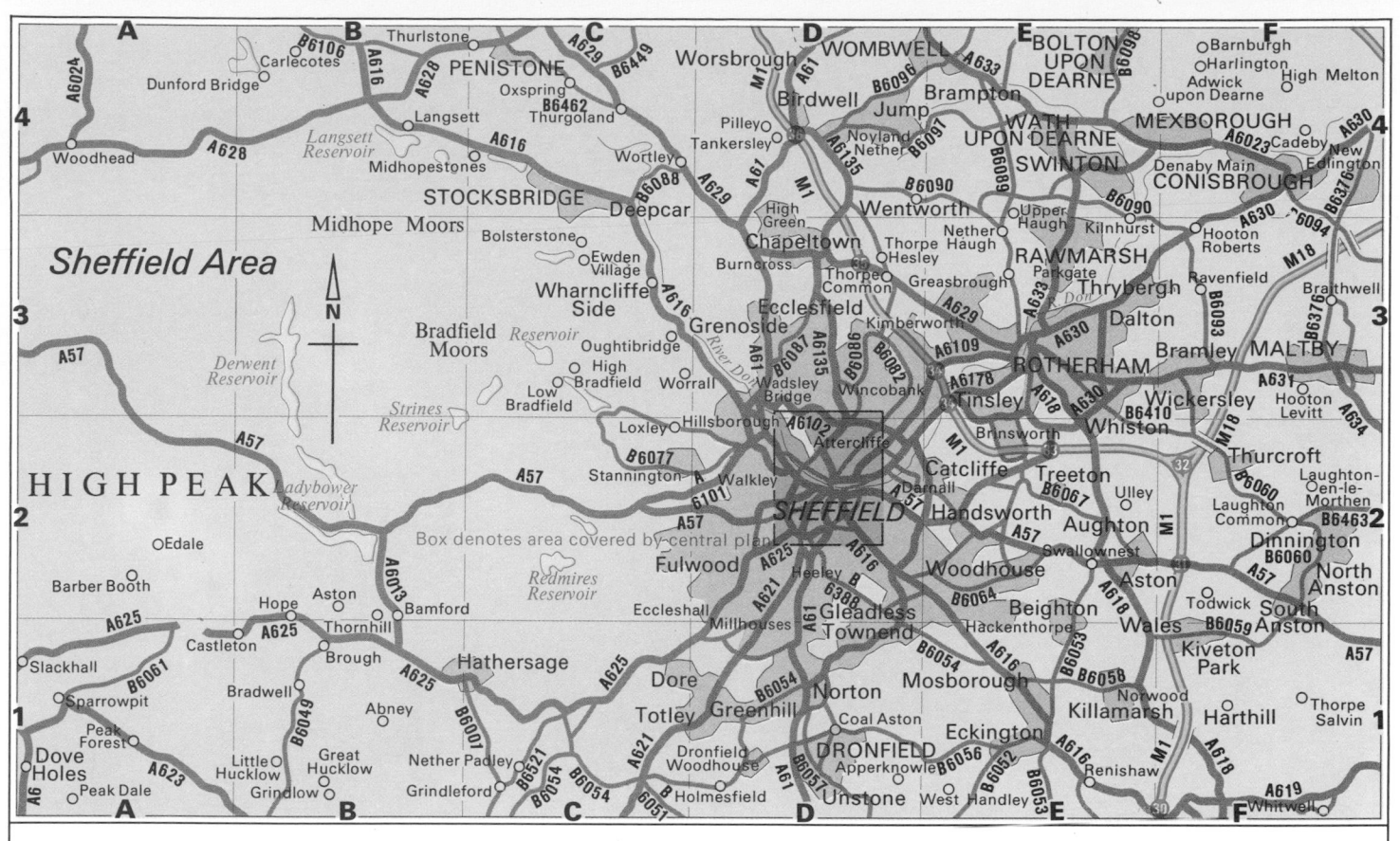

Sheffield Area

HIGH PEAK

Box denotes area covered by central plan

LEGEND

Town Plan
AA Recommended roads
Other roads
Restricted roads
Buildings of interest
One Way Streets
Car Parks
Parks and open spaces

Area Plan
A roads
B roads
Locations — Oakworth ○
Urban area

Street Index with grid reference

Sheffield

Addey Street	A7-A8
Albert Terrace	A8
Alma Street	C7-D7
Andrew Street	E7
Angel Street	D5-D6
Arundel Gate	D4-D5
Arundel Street	C2-D2-D3-D4
Bailey Street	C5
Ball Street	C8
Balm Green	C4-C5
Bank Street	D6
Bard Street	F5
Barker's Pool	C4-C5-D5
Bedford Street	B8
Beet Street	B5
Bernard Street	F4-F5-F6
Blonk Street	E6
Bolsover Street	A5
Boston Street	C1-C2
Bower Street	C7-D7
Bowling Green	C7
Bramall Lane	C1-C2
Bridge Street	D7-D6-E6
Broad Lane	B5-C5-D5
Broad Street	E6,F5-F6
Brocco Street	B6
Brook Hill	A5-B5
Broomhall Place	A2
Broomhall Road	A2
Broomhall Street	A2-A3,B4
Broomspring Lane	A4-B4
Brown Street	D3

Brunswick Street	A3-A4
Brunswick Road	F7-F8
Burgess Street	C4
Cambridge Street	C4
Campo Lane	C5-D5-D6
Carlisle Street	F8
Carver Street	C4-C5
Castle Street	D6-E6
Castlegate	E6
Cavendish Street	B4
Cemetery Road	A1-B1-B2
Charles Street	D3-D4
Charlotte Road	C2-D2-D1-E1
Charter Row	C3-C4
Chatham Street	D7-D8
Church Street	C5-D5
Clarke Street	A3
Cliff Street	B1
Clough Road	C1-D1-D2
Club Garden Road	C2
Collegiate Crescent	A3
Commercial Street	E5
Corporation Street	D6-D7
Countess Road	C2-D2-D1
Cricket Inn Road	F6
Cumberland Way	C3
Daniel Hill	A8
Denby Street	C1
Devonshire Street	B4-C4
Division Street	C4
Duchess Road	D2-E2
Duke Street	F4-F5
Earl Street	C3
Earl Way	C3
East Bank Road	E1-E2
Ecclesall Road	A1-A2-B2
Edmund Road	D1-D2
Edward Street	B6
Effingham Street	F7
Egerton Street	B3
Eldon Street	B4
Ellin Street	C3
Exchange Street	E6
Eyre Street	C2-C3-D3-D4
Fargate	D5
Farm Road	E2
Fitzwilliam Street	B4-B3-C3
Flat Street	E5
Fornham Street	E3
Furnival Gate	C3-C4-D3-D4
Furnival Road	E6-F6-F7
Furnival Street	D3
Garden Street	B6-C6-C5
Gell Street	A4-A5
Gibraltar Street	C7-C6-D6
Glencoe Road	F3-F4
Glossop Road	A4-B4
Granville Road	E2-F2
Granville Street	E3-E4
Green Lane	B8-C8-C7
Hanover Way	A3-B3-B2
Harmer Lane	E4
Hartshead	D6
Harwood Street	C1
Harvest Lane	C8

Hawley Street	C5
Haymarket	E5-E6
Henry Street	B7
Hereford Street	C2
High Street	D5-E5
Hollis Croft	B6-C6
Holly Street	C4-C5
Hounsfield Road	A4-A5
Howard Street	D4-E4
Hoyle Street	B7
Infirmary Road	A8-B8 B7
Jessop Street	C2
John Street	C1-D1
Johnson Street	D7-E7
King Street	D5-E5-E6
Leadmill Road	D2-D3-E3
Leavy Greave Road	A5-B5
Lee Croft	C5-C6
Leopold Street	C5-D5
London Road	C1-B1-B2-C2
Maltravers Street	F6
Mappin Street	B4-B5
Margaret Street	D2
Matilda Street	C3-D3-D2
Matilda Way	D2
Meadow Street	B6-B7
Mitchell Street	A5-A6
Montgomery Terrace Road	A7-B7-B8
Moorfields	C7
Moore Street	B2-B3-C3
Mowbray Street	C8-D8-D7
Napier Street	A1-B1-B2
Neepsend Lane	B8-C8
Netherthorpe Road	A5-A6-B6-B7
Norfolk Park Road	E1-E2-F2
Norfolk Road	F3-F4
Norfolk Row	D5
Norfolk Street	D4-D5
North Church Street	D6
Nottingham Street	E8
Nursery Street	D7-E7-E6
Old Street	F5-F6
Orchard Lane	C5
Oxford Road	A7-A8
Park Grange Road	E1-F1
Park Square	E5-E6-F6-F5
Paternoster Row	D3-D4-E4
Pear Street	A1
Penistone Road	B7-B8
Pinfold Street	C4
Pinstone Street	C4-D4-D5
Pitsmoor Road	D8
Pond Hill	E5
Pond Street	E4-E5
Portobello Street	B5-C5
Priestley Street	D1-E1-E2
Queen Street	C6-D6
Queen's Road	E1-E2
Randall Street	C1
Red Hill	B5-B6
Regent Street	B4-B5
Rock Street	D8
Rockingham Street	B5-C5-C4

Russell Street	C7
Rutland Road	B8
Rye Bank Road	D8
St Mary's Gate	C2
St Mary's Road	C2-D2-E2-E3
St Philip's Road	A6-A7-B7-B8
Savile Street	E7-F7-F8
Scotland Street	B6-C6
Shales Moor	B7-C7
Sheaf Gardens	D2-E2
Sheaf Street	E4-E5
Sheffield Parkway	F6
Shepherd Street	B6-B7-C7
Shoreham Street	D1-D2-D3-E3
Shrewsbury Road	E3-E4-F3-F4
Shude Lane	E5
Shude Hill	E5-E6
Sidney Street	D3
Silver Street	C6
Snig Hill	D6
Solly Street	B5-B6-C6
South Lane	C2
South Street	E4-E5
Spital Hill	E7-E8-F8
Spital Street	E8-F8
Spitalfields	D7-E7
Spring Street	D6-D7
Stanley Street	E7
Suffolk Road	E3
Summerfield Street	A2-A1-B1
Sunny Bank	A2
Surrey Place	D4
Surrey Street	D4-D5
Sussex Street	F7
Sylvester Street	C2-D2
Talbot Place	F4
Talbot Street	F4
Tenter Street	C6
The Moor	C3-C4
Townhead Street	C5
Trippet Lane	C5
Tudor Street	D4-D5
Tudor Way	D5
Union Street	C4-D4
Upper Allen Street	B6
Upper Hanover Street	A3-A4-A5
Upperthorpe Road	A7-A8
Verdon Street	D8-E8
Vicar Lane	C5-D5
Victoria Station Road	E6-E7-F7
Waingate	E6
Walker Street	E7
Washington Road	B1
Watery Street	B7-B8
Wellington Street	B4-C4
West Bar	D6
West Bar Green	C6-D6
West Street	B4-B5-C5
Weston Street	A5-A6
Wheel Hill	E5
Wicker	E6-E7
Wilkinson Street	A4
William Street	A2-A3
York Street	D5-D6
Young Street	B2-C2

199

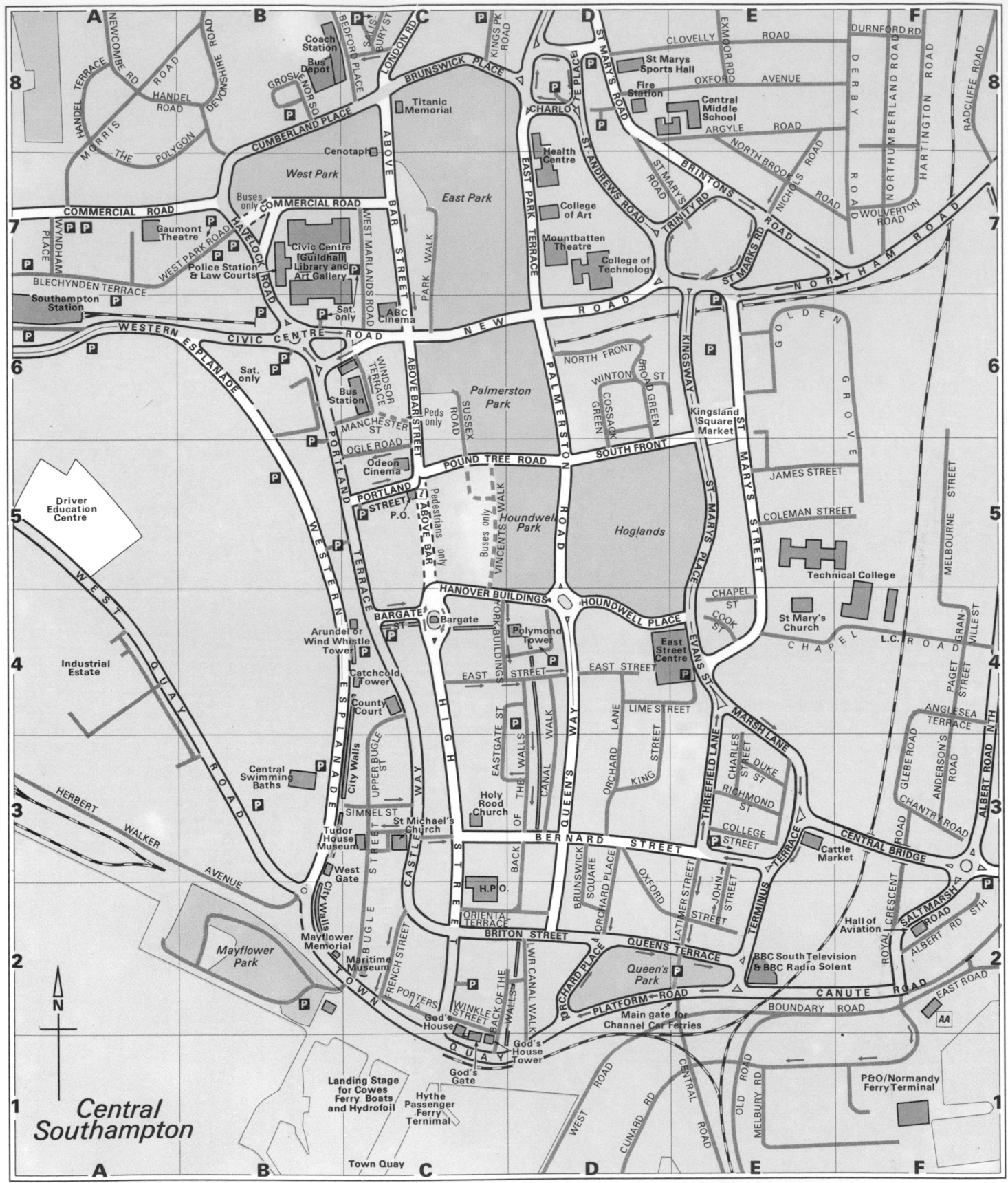

Southampton

In the days of the great ocean-going liners, Southampton was Britain's premier passenger port. Today container traffic is more important, but cruise liners still berth there. A unique double tide caused by the Solent waters, and protection from the open sea by the Isle of Wight, has meant that Southampton has always been a superb and important port. Like many great cities it was devastated by bombing raids during World War II. However, enough survives to make the city a fascinating place to explore. Outstanding are the town walls, which stand to their original height in some places, especially along Western Esplanade. The main landward entrance to the walled town was the Bargate – a superb medieval gateway with a Guildhall (now a museum) on its upper floor. The best place to appreciate old Southampton is in and around St Michael's Square. Here is St Michael's Church, oldest in the city and founded in 1070. Opposite is Tudor House Museum, a lovely gabled building housing much of interest. Down Bugle Street are old houses, with the town walls, pierced by the 13th-century West Gate, away to the right. At the corner of Bugle Street is the Wool House Maritime Museum, contained in a 14th-century warehouse. On the quayside is God's House Tower, part of the town's defences and now an archaeological museum.

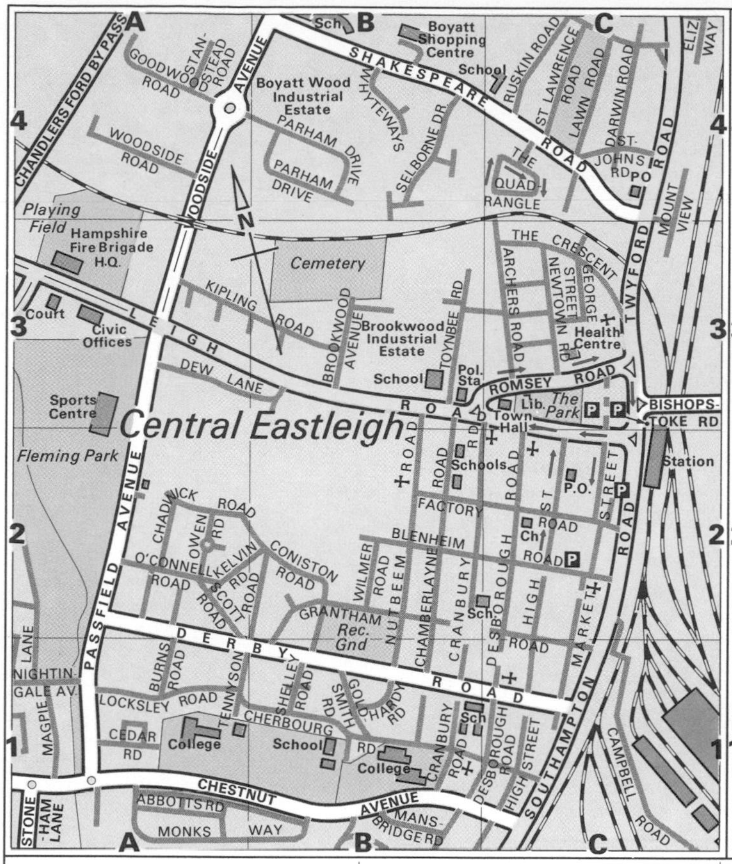

Key to Town Plan and Area Plan

Town Plan

A.A. Recommended roads	
Other roads	
Restricted roads	
Buildings of interest	Cinema
A A Service Centre	AA
Car Parks	P
Parks and open spaces	
One way streets	→

Area Plan

A roads	
B roads	
Locations	Ower O
Urban Area	

SOUTHAMPTON

Above Bar	C5
Above Bar Street	C5-C6-C7-C8
Albert Road North	F3-F4
Albert Road South	F2
Anderson's Road	F3-F4
Anglesea Terrace	F4
Argyle Road	E8-F8
Back of the Walls	C1-C2-D2-D3-D4
Bargate Street	C4
Bedford Place	B8-C8
Bernard Street	C3-D3-E3
Blechynden Terrace	A7
Boundary Road	E2-F2
Briton Street	C2-D2
Britons Road	D8-E8-E7
Broad Green	D6
Brunswick Place	C8-D8
Brunswick Square	D2-D3
Bugle Street	C2-C3
Canal Walk	D3-D4
Canute Road	E2-F2
Castle Way	C2-C3-C4
Central Bridge	E3-F3
Central Road	E1-E2
Chantry Road	F3
Chapel Road	E4-F4
Chapel Street	E4
Charles Street	E3
Charlotte Place	D8
Civic Centre Road	B6-C6
Clovelly Road	D8-E8-F8
Coleman Street	E5-F5
College Street	E3
Commercial Road	A7-B7-C7
Cook Street	E4
Cossack Green	D5-D6
Cumberland Place	B7-B8-C8
Cunard Road	D1-E1
Derby Road	F7-F8
Devonshire Road	B8
Duke Street	E3
Durnford Road	F8
East Road	F2
East Street	C4-D4
East Park Terrace	D6-D7-D8
Eastgate Street	D3-C3-C4-D4
Evans Street	E4
Exmoor Road	E8
French Street	C2
Glebe Road	F3-F4
Golden Grove	E6-F6-F5
Granville Street	F4
Grosvenor Square	B8
Handel Road	A8-B8
Handel Terrace	A8
Hanover Buildings	C5-C4-D4
Hartington Road	F7-F8
Havelock Road	B6-B7
Herbert Walker Avenue	A3-B3-B2
High Street	C1-C2-C3-C4
Houndwell Place	D4-E4
James Street	E5-F5
John Street	E2-E3
Kingsway	E6-E7
King Street	D3-D4
Kings Park Road	C8
Latimer Street	E2-E3
Lime Street	D4-E4
London Road	C8
Lower Canal Walk	D1-D2
Manchester Street	B6-C6
Marsh Lane	E3-E4
Melbourne Street	F4-F5-F6
Melbury Road	E1
Morris Road	A7-A8-B8
New Road	E6-D6-D7
Newcombe Road	A8
Nichols Road	E7-E8
North Brook Road	E8-E7-F7
North Front	D6
Northam Road	E6-E7-F7
Northumberland Road	F7-F8
Ogle Road	C5
Old Road	E1-E2
Orchard Lane	D3-D4
Orchard Place	D2-D3
Oriental Terrace	C2-D2
Oxford Avenue	D8-E8-F8
Oxford Street	D3-D2-E2
Paget Street	F4
Palmerston Road	D5-D6
Park Walk	C6-C7
Platform Road	D2-E2
Porters Lane	C2
Portland Street	C5
Portland Terrace	B6-B5-C5-C4
Pound Tree Road	C5-D5
Queens Terrace	D2-E2
Queen's Way	D2-D3-D4
Radcliffe Road	F7-F8
Richmond Street	E3
Royal Crescent Road	F2-F3
St Andrews Road	D7-D8
St Marks Road	E7
St Mary's Place	E4-E5
St Mary's Road	D8-D7-E7
St Mary's Street	E4-E5-E6
Salisbury Street	C8
Saltmarsh Road	F2-F3
Simnel Street	C3
South Front	D5-E5-E6-D6
Sussex Road	C5-C6
The Polygon	A8-A7-B7-B8
Terminus Terrace	E2-E3
Threefield Lane	E3-E4
Town Quay	B2-C2-C1-D1
Trinity Road	D7-E7
Upper Bugle Street	C3-C4
Vincents Walk	C5
West Marlands Road	C6-C7
West Road	D1-D2-E2
West Park Road	A7-B7
West Quay Road	A5-A4-B4-B3
Western Esplanade	B2-B3-B4-B5-B6-A6
Windsor Terrace	C6
Winkle Street	C1-C2
Winton Street	D6-E6
Wolverton Road	F7
Wyndham Place	A7
York Buildings	C4-D4

EASTLEIGH

Abbots Road	A1
Archers Road	C3
Blenheim Road	B2-C2
Brookwood Avenue	B3
Burns Road	A1
Campbell Road	C1
Cedar Road	A1
Chadwick Road	A2-B2
Chamberlayne Road	B1-B2-B3
Chandlers Ford By-pass	A4
Cherbourg Road	A1-B1-C1
Chestnut Avenue	A1-B1-C1
Coniston Road	B2
Cranbury Road	C1-C2-C3
Darwin Road	C4
Cranbury Road	C1-C2-C3
Darwin Road	C4
Derby Road	A2-A1-B1-C1
Desborough Road	B1-C1-C2
Dew Lane	A3-B3
Elizabeth Way	C4
Factory Road	B2-C2
George Street	C3
Goldsmith Road	B1
Goodwood Road	A4
Grantham Road	B1-B2-C2-C1
High Street	C1-C2
Kelvin Road	A2-B2
Kipling Road	A3-B3
Lawn Road	C4
Leigh Road	A3-B3-C3-C2
Locksley Road	A1
Magpie Lane	A1-A2
Mansbridge Road	B1
Market Street	C1-C2-C3
Monks Way	A1-B1
Mount View	C3-C4
Newtown Road	C3
Nightingale Avenue	A1
Nutbeem Road	B1-B2-B3
O'Connell Road	A2
Owen Road	A2
Parnham Drive	A4-B4
Passfield Avenue	A1-A2-A3
Romsey Road	B3-C3
Ruskin Road	C4
Stanstead Road	A4
Stoneham Lane	A1
St John's Road	C4
St Lawrence Road	C4
Scott Road	A2
Selborne Drive	B4
Shakespeare Road	B4-C4
Shelley Road	B1
Southampton Road	C1-C2
The Crescent	C3
The Quadrangle	C4
Tennyson Road	A1-A2-B2
Toynbee Road	B3
Twyford Road	C3-C4
Whyteways	B4
Wilmer Road	B2
Woodside Avenue	A3-A4
Woodside Road	A4

SOUTHAMPTON
Although liners still use Southampton's docks which handled all the great ocean-going passenger ships before the age of air travel replaced sea travel, the port is chiefly used by commercial traffic today.

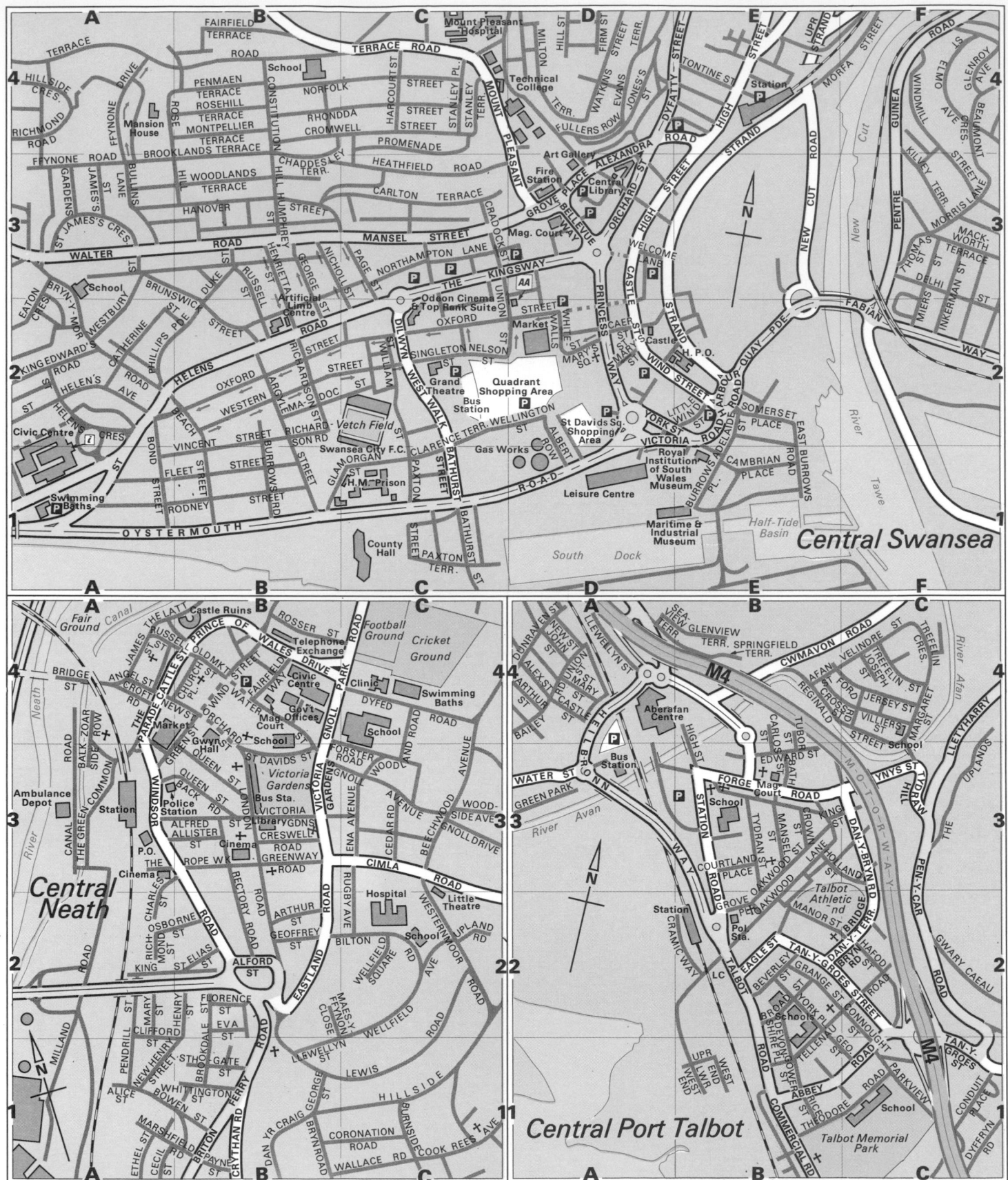

Central Swansea

Central Neath

Central Port Talbot

Swansea

Like nearly all the towns in the valleys and along the coast of Glamorgan, Swansea grew at an amazing speed during the Industrial Revolution. Ironworks, non-ferrous metal smelting works and mills and factories of every kind were built to produce the goods which were exported from the city's docks. There had been a settlement here from very early times – the city's name is derived from Sweyn's Ea – Ea means island, and Sweyn was a Viking pirate who had a base here. Heavy industry is still pre-eminent in the area, but commerce is of increasing importance and the university exerts a strong influence. Hundreds of acres of parkland and open space lie in and around the city, and just to the west is the Gower, one of the most beautiful areas of Wales. The history of Swansea is traced in the Maritime, Industrial and Royal Institution of South Wales Museums, while the Glynn Vivian Art Gallery contains notable paintings and porcelain.

Neath and **Port Talbot** are, like Swansea, dominated by heavy industry. Neath was once a Roman station, and later had a castle and an abbey, ruins of which can still be seen. Port Talbot has been an industrial centre since 1770, when a copper-smelting works was built. Steelworks and petrochemical works stretch for miles around Swansea Bay.

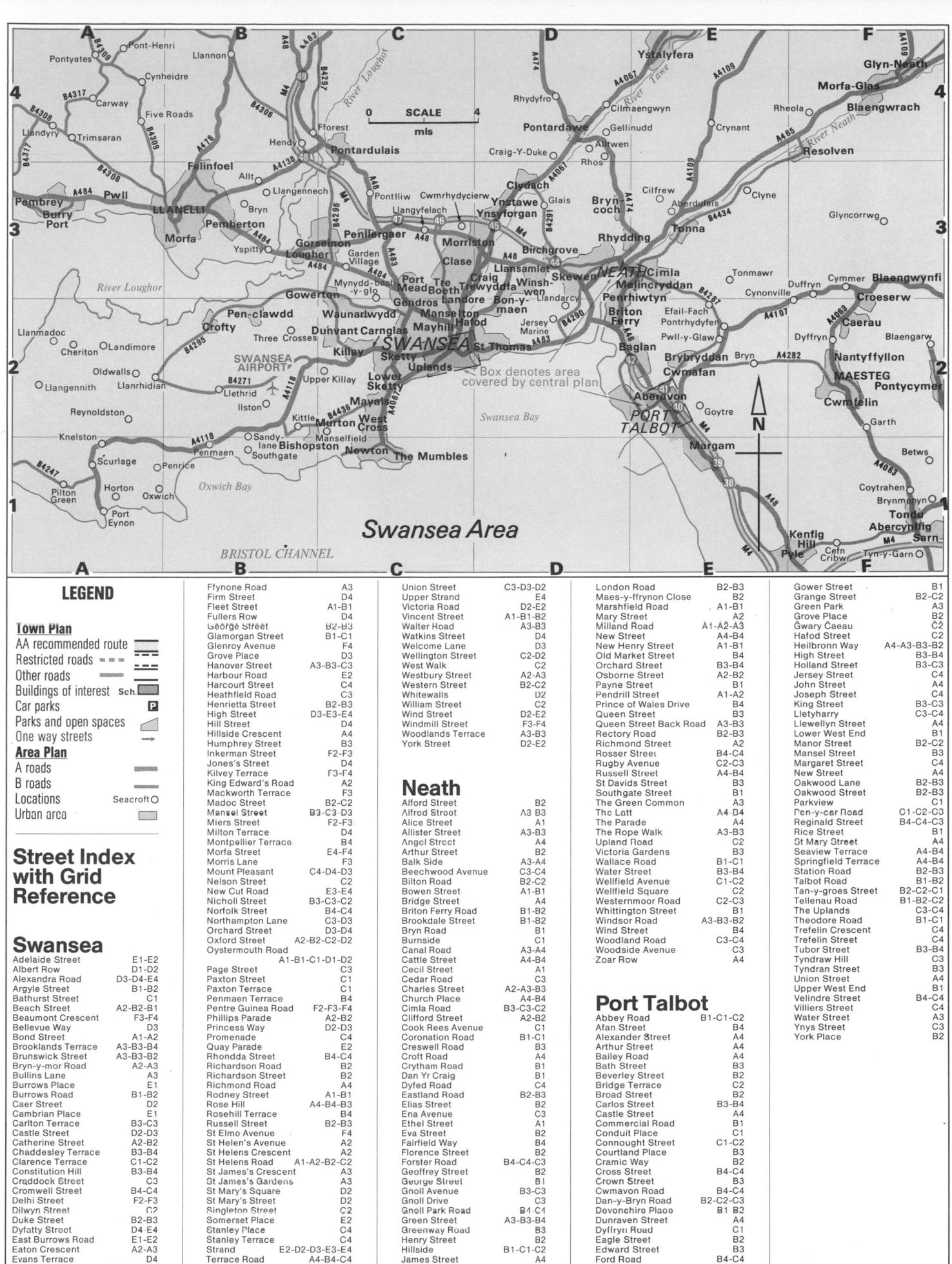

Swansea Area

BRISTOL CHANNEL

LEGEND

Town Plan

AA recommended route	
Restricted roads	
Other roads	
Buildings of interest	Sch.
Car parks	P
Parks and open spaces	
One way streets	

Area Plan

A roads	
B roads	
Locations	Seacroft○
Urban area	

Street Index with Grid Reference

Swansea

Adelaide Street	E1-E2
Albert Row	D1-D2
Alexandra Road	D3-D4-E4
Argyle Street	B1-B2
Bathurst Street	C1
Beach Street	A2-B2-B1
Beaumont Crescent	F3-F4
Bellevue Way	D3
Bond Street	A1-A2
Brooklands Terrace	A3-B3-B4
Brunswick Street	A3-B3-B2
Bryn-y-mor Road	A2-A3
Bullins Lane	A3
Burrows Place	E1
Burrows Road	B1-B2
Caer Street	D2
Cambrian Place	E1
Carlton Terrace	B3-C3
Castle Street	D2-D3
Catherine Street	A2-B2
Chaddesley Terrace	B3-B4
Clarence Terrace	C1-C2
Constitution Hill	B3-B4
Craddock Street	C3
Cromwell Street	B4-C4
Delhi Street	F2-F3
Dilwyn Street	C2
Duke Street	B2-B3
Dyfatty Street	D4-E4
East Burrows Road	E1-E2
Eaton Crescent	A2-A3
Evans Terrace	D4
Fabian Way	E2-E3-F3-F2
Fairfield Terrace	B4
Ffynone Drive	A3-A4
Ffynone Road	A3
Firm Street	D4
Fleet Street	A1-B1
Fullers Row	D4
George Street	B2-B3
Glamorgan Street	B1-C1
Glenroy Avenue	F4
Grove Place	D3
Hanover Street	A3-B3-C3
Harbour Road	E2
Harcourt Street	C4
Heathfield Road	C3
Henrietta Street	B2-B3
High Street	D3-E3-E4
Hill Street	D4
Hillside Crescent	A4
Humphrey Street	B3
Inkerman Street	F2-F3
Jones's Street	D4
Kilvey Terrace	F3-F4
King Edward's Road	A2
Mackworth Terrace	F3
Madoc Street	B2-C2
Mansel Street	B3-C3-D3
Miers Street	F2-F3
Milton Terrace	D4
Montpellier Terrace	B4
Morfa Street	E4-F4
Morris Lane	F3
Mount Pleasant	C4-D4-D3
Nelson Street	C2
New Cut Road	E3-E4
Nicholl Street	B3-C3-C2
Norfolk Street	B4-C4
Northampton Lane	C3-D3
Orchard Street	D3-D4
Oxford Street	A2-B2-C2-D2
Oystermouth Road	A1-B1-C1-D1-D2
Page Street	C3
Paxton Street	C1
Paxton Terrace	C1
Penmaen Terrace	B4
Pentre Guinea Road	F2-F3-F4
Phillips Parade	A2-B2
Princess Way	D2-D3
Promenade	C4
Quay Parade	E2
Rhondda Street	B4-C4
Richardson Road	B2
Richardson Street	B2
Richmond Road	A4
Rodney Street	A1-B1
Rose Hill	A4-B4-B3
Rosehill Terrace	B4
Russell Street	B2-B3
St Elmo Avenue	F4
St Helen's Avenue	A2
St Helens Crescent	A2
St Helens Road	A1-A2-B2-C2
St James's Crescent	A3
St James's Gardens	A3
St Mary's Square	D2
St Mary's Street	D2
Singleton Street	C2
Somerset Place	E2
Stanley Place	C4
Stanley Terrace	C4
Strand	E2-D2-D3-E3-E4
Terrace Road	A4-B4-C4
The Kingsway	C3-D3
Thomas Street	F3
Tontine Street	E4
Union Street	C3-D3-D2
Upper Strand	E4
Victoria Road	D2-E2
Vincent Street	A1-B1-B2
Walter Road	A3-B3
Watkins Street	D4
Welcome Lane	D3
Wellington Street	C2-D2
West Walk	C2
Westbury Street	A2-A3
Western Street	B2-C2
Whitewalls	D2
William Street	C2
Wind Street	D2-E2
Windmill Street	F3-F4
Woodlands Terrace	A3-B3
York Street	D2-E2

Neath

Alford Street	B2
Alfred Street	A3-B3
Alice Street	A1
Allister Street	A3-B3
Angel Street	A4
Arthur Street	B2
Balk Side	A3-A4
Beechwood Avenue	C3-C4
Bilton Road	B2-C2
Bowen Street	A1-B1
Bridge Street	A4
Briton Ferry Road	B1-B2
Brookdale Street	B1-B2
Bryn Road	B1
Burnside	C1
Canal Road	A3-A4
Cattle Street	A4-B4
Cecil Street	A1
Cedar Road	C3
Charles Street	A2-A3-B3
Church Place	A4-B4
Cimla Road	B3-C3-C2
Clifford Street	A2-B2
Cook Rees Avenue	C1
Coronation Road	B1-C1
Creswell Road	B3
Croft Road	A4
Crytham Road	B1
Dan Yr Craig	B1
Dyfed Road	C4
Eastland Road	B2-B3
Elias Street	B2
Ena Avenue	C3
Ethel Street	A1
Eva Street	B2
Fairfield Way	B4
Florence Street	B2
Forster Road	B4-C4-C3
Geoffrey Street	B2
George Street	B1
Gnoll Avenue	B3-C3
Gnoll Drive	C3
Gnoll Park Road	B4-C4
Green Street	A3-B3-B4
Greenway Road	B3
Henry Street	B2
Hillside	B1-C1-C2
James Street	A4
King Street	A2-B2
Lewis Road	B2-B1-C1-C2
Llewellyn Street	B1
London Road	B2-B3
Maes-y-ffrynon Close	B2
Marshfield Road	A1-B1
Mary Street	A2
Milland Road	A1-A2-A3
New Street	A4-B4
New Henry Street	A1-B1
Old Market Street	B4
Orchard Street	B3-B4
Osborne Street	A2-B2
Payne Street	B1
Pendrill Street	A1-A2
Prince of Wales Drive	B4
Queen Street	B3
Queen Street Back Road	A3-B3
Rectory Road	B2-B3
Richmond Street	A2
Rosser Street	B4-C4
Rugby Avenue	C2-C3
Russell Street	A4-B4
St Davids Street	B3
Southgate Street	B1
The Green Common	A3
The Lett	A4-B4
The Parade	A4
The Rope Walk	A3-B3
Upland Road	C2
Victoria Gardens	B3
Wallace Road	B1-C1
Water Street	B3-B4
Wellfield Avenue	C1-C2
Wellfield Square	C2
Westernmoor Road	C2-C3
Whittington Street	B1
Windsor Road	A3-B3-B2
Wind Street	B4
Woodland Road	C3-C4
Woodside Avenue	C3
Zoar Row	A4

Port Talbot

Abbey Road	B1-C1-C2
Afan Street	B4
Alexander Street	A4
Arthur Street	A4
Bailey Road	A4
Bath Street	B3
Beverley Street	B2
Bridge Terrace	C2
Broad Street	B2
Carlos Street	B3-B4
Castle Street	A4
Commercial Road	B1
Conduit Place	C1
Connought Street	C1-C2
Courtland Place	B3
Cramic Way	B2
Cross Street	B4-C4
Crown Street	B3
Cwmavon Road	B4-C4
Dan-y-Bryn Road	B2-C2-C3
Devonshire Place	B1-B2
Dunraven Street	A4
Dyffryn Road	C1
Eagle Street	B2
Edward Street	B3
Ford Road	B4-C4
Forge Road	B3
George Street	B2-B1-C1
Glenview Terrace	B4
Gower Street	B1
Grange Street	B2-C2
Green Park	A3
Grove Place	B2
Gwary Caeau	C2
Hafod Street	C2
Heilbronn Way	A4-A3-B3-B2
High Street	B3-B4
Holland Street	B3-C3
Jersey Street	C4
John Street	A4
Joseph Street	C4
King Street	B3-C3
Lletyharry	C3-C4
Llewellyn Street	A4
Lower West End	B1
Manor Street	B2-C2
Mansel Street	B3
Margaret Street	C4
New Street	A4
Oakwood Lane	B2-B3
Oakwood Street	B2-B3
Parkview	C1
Pen-y-car Road	C1-C2-C3
Reginald Street	B4-C4-C3
Rice Street	B1
St Mary Street	A4
Seaview Terrace	A4-B4
Springfield Terrace	A4-B4
Station Road	B2-B3
Talbot Road	B1-B2
Tan-y-groes Street	B2-C2-C1
Tellenau Road	B1-B2-C2
The Uplands	C3-C4
Theodore Road	B1-C1
Trefelin Crescent	C4
Trefelin Street	C4
Tubor Street	B3-B4
Tyndraw Hill	C3
Tyndran Street	B3
Union Street	A4
Upper West End	B1
Velindre Street	B4-C4
Villiers Street	C4
Water Street	A3
Ynys Street	C3
York Place	B2

Tourist Plans

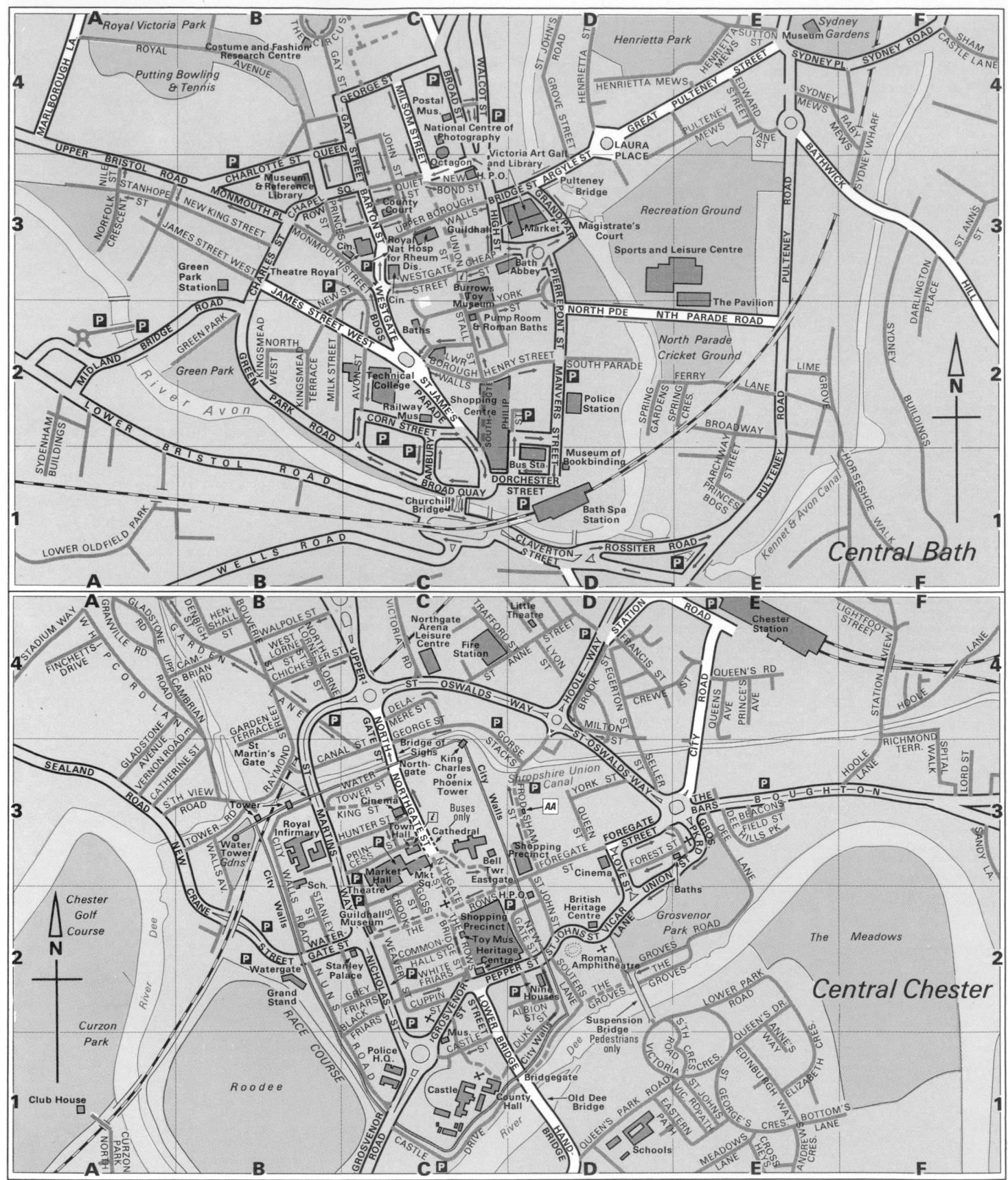

Central Bath

Central Chester

Bath

Here in this unique city are combined Britain's most impressive collection of Roman relics and the country's finest Georgian townscape of perfectly proportioned streets and crescents. Its attraction to Romans and fashionable 18th-century society alike was its mineral springs which can still be seen at the Roman baths. These are now the centre-piece of a Roman museum, where exhibits give a vivid impression of life 2000 years ago. The adjacent Pump Room, to which the waters were piped, was a focal point of social life in 18th- and 19th-century Bath. The city also has much to delight museum-lovers.

Chester

Chester is unique in being the only English city to have preserved the complete circuit of its Roman and medieval walls. On the west side, the top of the walls is now at pavement level, but on the other three sides the walk along the ramparts is remarkable. The view down the main street, the old Roman *Via Principalis*, reveals a dazzling display of the black and white timbered buildings for which Chester is famous. The Rows, a feature unique to the city and dating back to at least the 13th century, are covered galleries of shops raised to first-floor level. Chester's magnificent cathedral has beautifully carved choir stalls.

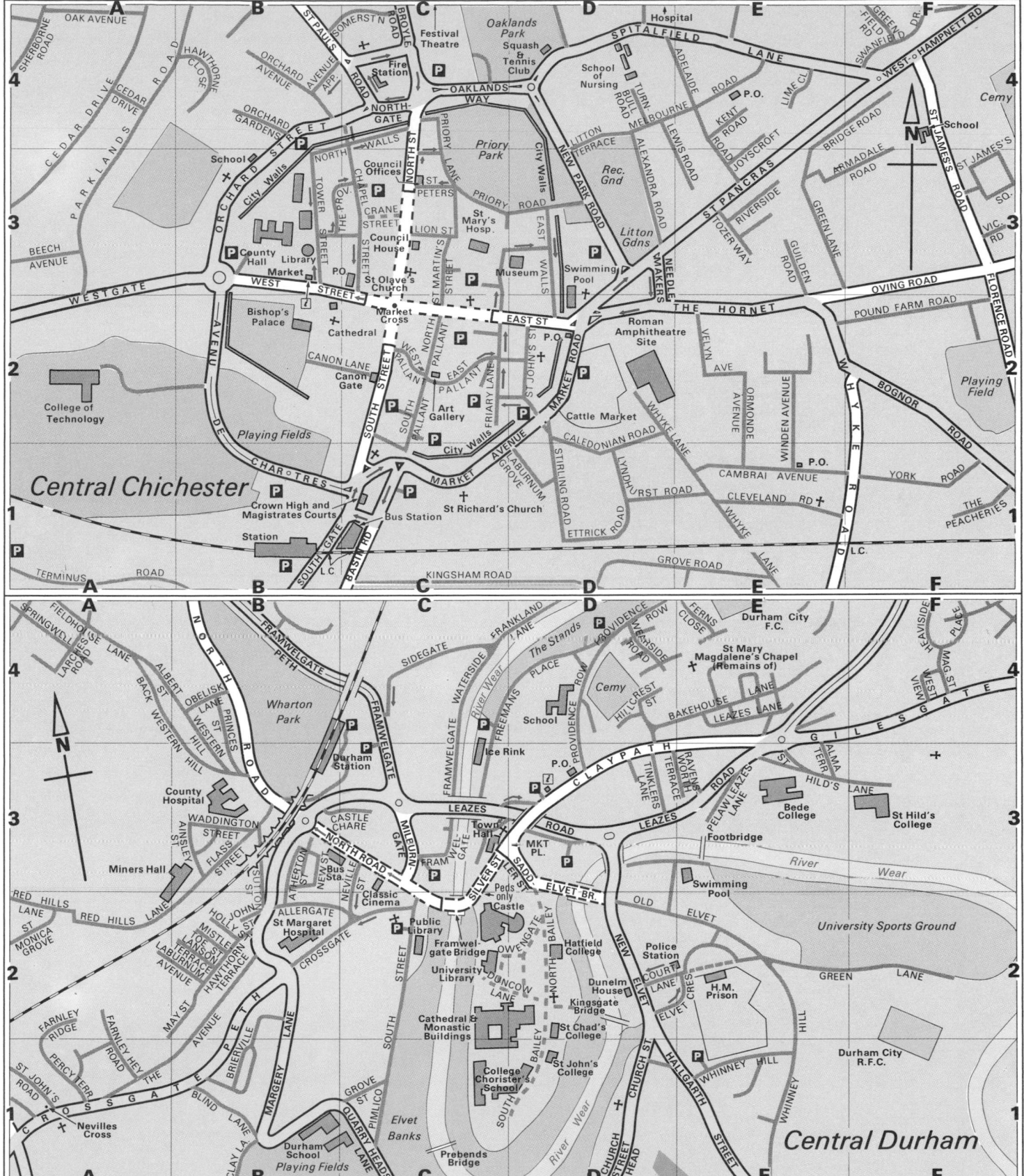

Chichester

The spire of Chichester Cathedral (which was consecrated in 1184), rises gracefully above the rooftops to the west of the city, which dates back to Roman times and is one of Britain's oldest. Notable among the 18th-century streets are the Pallants and the Pallant House, and at Fishbourne Priory nearby, visitors can admire the mosaics, formal garden and other remains of the largest Roman residence found in Britain. Chichester today gives pleasure to thousands with its Festival Theatre and its harbour – thronged with sailing enthusiasts throughout the summer.

Durham

Like sentinels, the castle and cathedral stand side by side high above the city, dramatically symbolising the military and religious power Durham wielded in the past – its origins dating from about 995. Today the city's university, the oldest in England after Oxford and Cambridge, occupies the castle and most of the buildings around peaceful Palace Green. The splendid Norman cathedral, on the other side of the Green, is one of the finest in Europe. The old city streets, known as vennels, ramble down the bluff to the wooded banks of the Wear. Here three historic bridges link the city's heart with the pleasant Georgian suburbs.

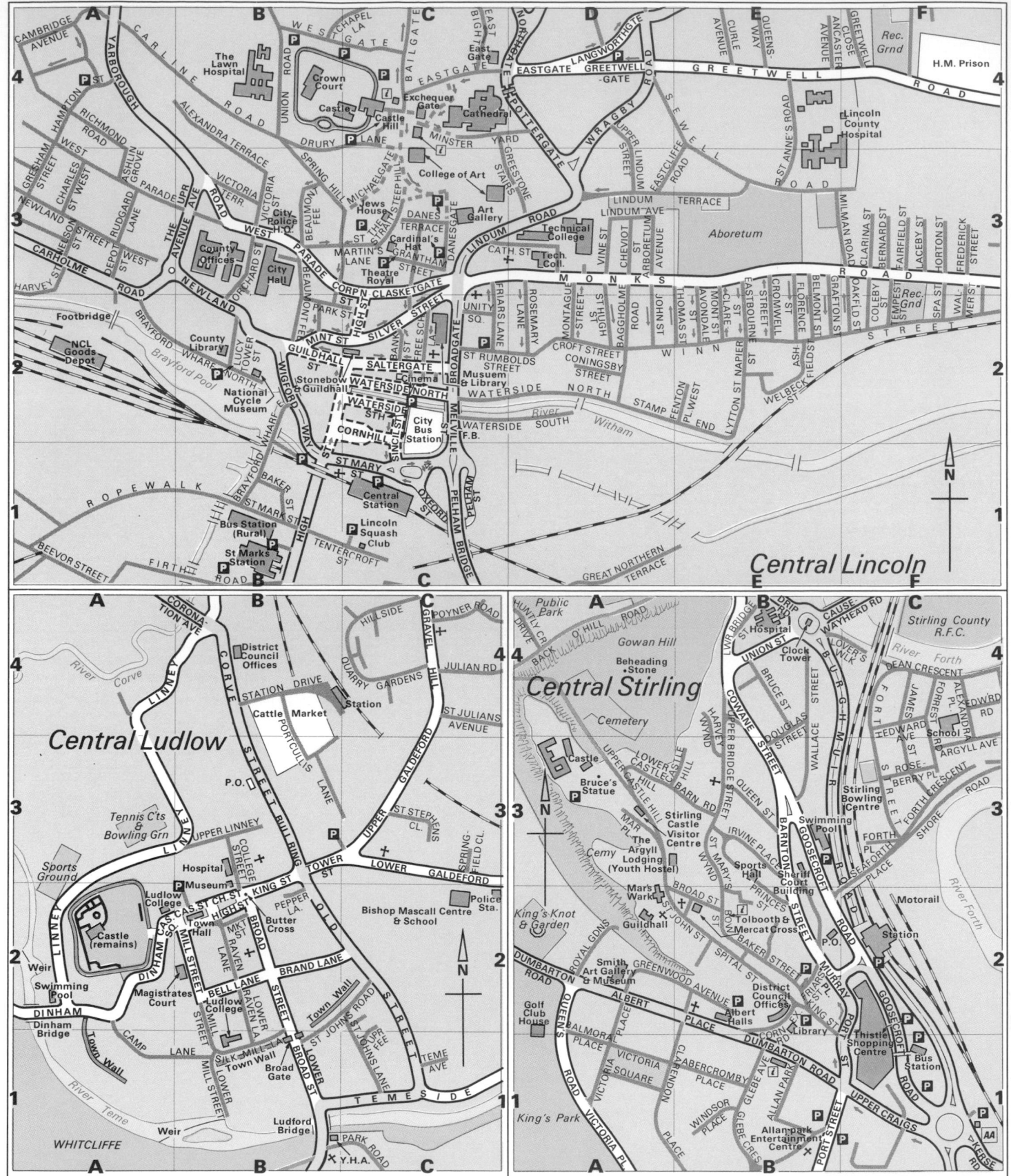

Central Lincoln

Central Ludlow

Central Stirling

Lincoln

Triple-spired Lincoln Cathedral (which houses a copy of Magna Carta) dominates the countryside for miles, while the cobbled streets of the medieval city struggle down the sides of the hill past old honey-coloured houses. Modern Lincoln owes much to engineering industries, but few winds of change have blown into the heart of the city, where the oldest inhabited house in England can be found.

Ludlow

The rivers Corve and Teme wash two sides of the steep hill on which Ludlow is built. Since the earliest times the town has been recognised as a strategic site, not least by the Normans. Their castle is now an impressive ruin crowning the hilltop. The town below is a charming mixture of wide Georgian streets, narrow medieval alleyways and leaning half-timbered Tudor buildings.

Stirling

Stirling lies close to Bannockburn, where Robert the Bruce inflicted an ignominious defeat on the armies of England in 1314, and twelve years later he held his first parliament in the town's Cambuskenneth Abbey, which can still be seen. The castle dates back to the 13th century and its Landmark Centre provides an exciting audio-visual display. There are fine views from the Wallace Memorial.

Salisbury

Salisbury is one of England's finest cities, thanks to its attractive site where the waters of the Avon and Nadder meet, its beautiful cathedral and its unspoilt centre. The people of the original settlement at Old Sarum, two miles to the north, moved down to the plain in 1220 and laid the first stone of the cathedral. Within 38 years it was completed and the result is a superb example of Early English architecture. The cloisters are the largest in England and the spire the tallest in Britain. All the houses within the Cathedral Close were built for cathedral officials, and although many have Georgian facades, most date back to the 13th century. One of the handsome mansions here is Mompesson House and, as it belongs to the National Trust, its equally fine interior can be viewed. The Museum of the Duke of Edinburgh's Royal Regiment is in another building. At one time, relations between the clergy and the citizens of Salisbury were not always harmonious, so the former built a protective wall around the Close.

The streets of the modern city follow the medieval grid pattern of squares, or 'chequers', and the tightly-packed houses provide a very pleasing townscape. Salisbury was granted its first charter in 1227 and flourished as a market and wool centre; there is still a twice-weekly market in the spacious square.

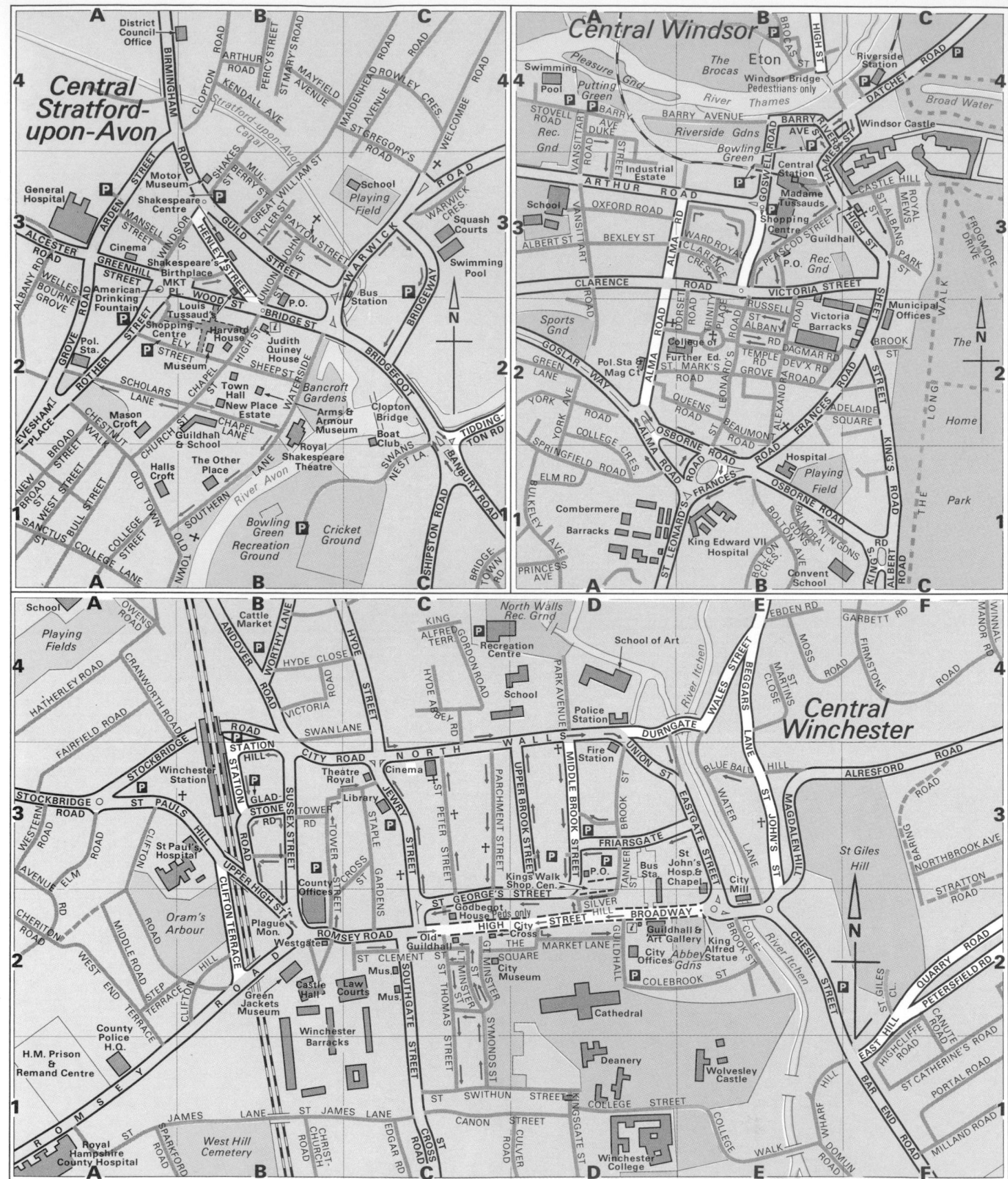

Stratford-upon-Avon

Second only to London as a tourist attraction, this charming old market town is a living memorial to William Shakespeare, England's most famous poet and playwright. His many plays are performed in the imposing Royal Shakespeare Theatre, built close to the River Avon. A wax work museum specialises in scenes from his works, and his childhood home in Henley Street is a fascinating museum.

Windsor

First built by the Normans to guard the approaches to London, the famous turreted castle towers over the Thames and dominates the town. Its State Apartments are magnificent, as is St George's Chapel, and Queen Mary's Dolls' House is an exquisite model house of the 1920s. The town itself, squeezed between the castle walls and the river, has several attractive streets graced with fine buildings.

Winchester

Tucked away unobtrusively in the heart of Winchester, once the capital of King Alfred's England, is the impressive cathedral. Nearby is Winchester College – one of the oldest and most famous public schools in England. The streets of the city are lined with charming old buildings of different periods, including the former Guildhall and the old Butter Cross, while an imposing statue of King Alfred dominates the Broadway.

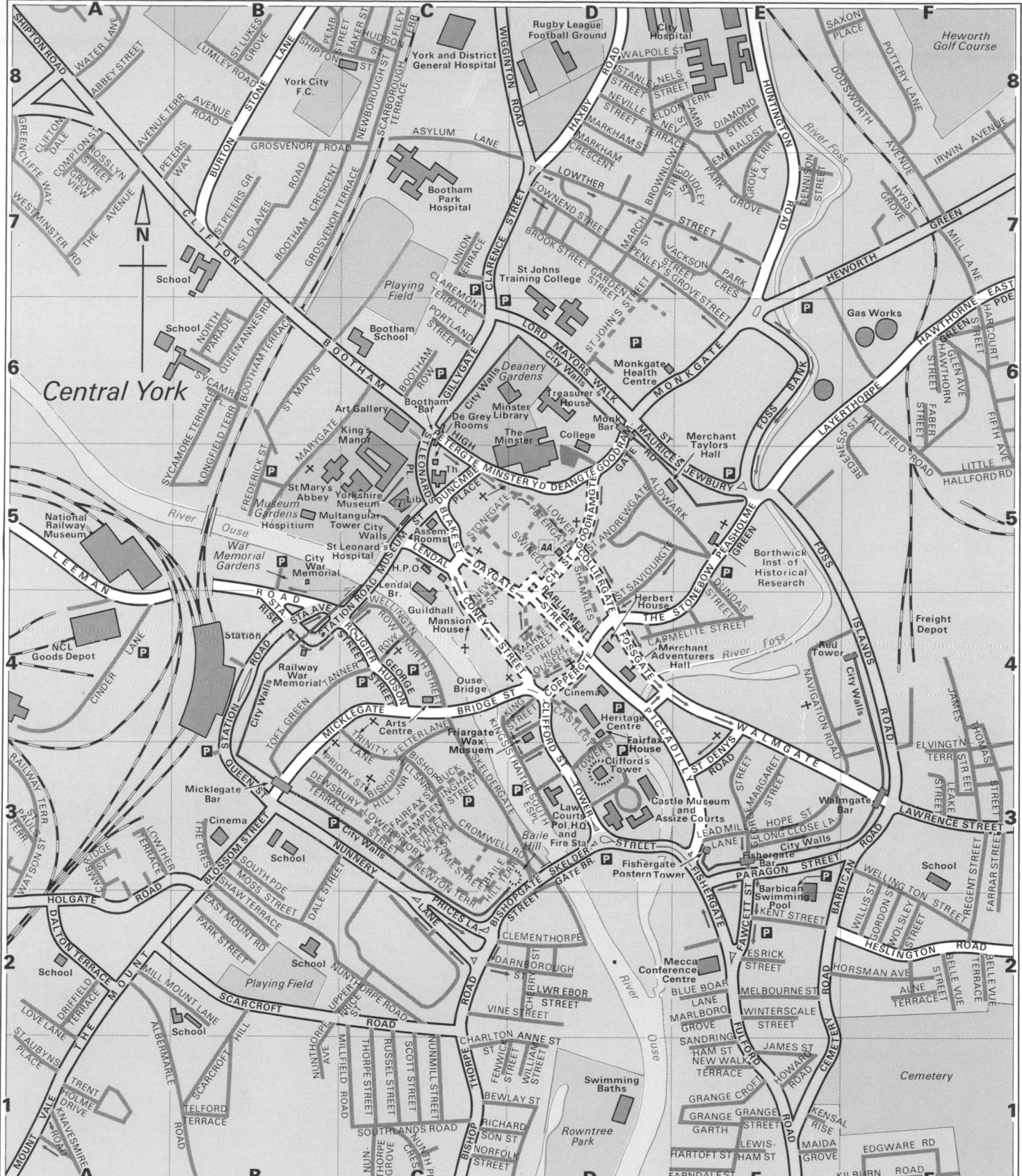

York

Without doubt the city's outstanding glory is York Minster, considered to be one of the greatest cathedral churches in Europe. It is especially famous for its beautiful windows which contain more than half the medieval stained glass in England.

Great walls enclose the historic city centre and their three mile circuit offers magnificent views of the Minster, York's numerous fine buildings, churches and the River Ouse. The ancient streets consist of a maze of fascinating lanes and alleys, some of them so narrow that the overhanging upper storeys of the houses almost touch. The most famous of these picturesque streets is The Shambles – one-time butchers' quarter of the city, but now taken over by antique and tourist-trade shops. York flourished throughout Tudor, Georgian and Victorian times, and handsome buildings from these periods also feature throughout the city.

The interesting Heritage Centre interprets the social and architectural history of the city and the Castle Museum gives a fascinating picture of York as it used to be. Other places of exceptional note in this city of riches include the Merchant Adventurer's Hall; the Treasurer's House, now owned by the National Trust and filled with fine paintings and furniture; the superb National Railway Museum, and the Jorvik Viking Centre where there is an exciting restoration of the original Viking settlement.

Key to Inner London Maps

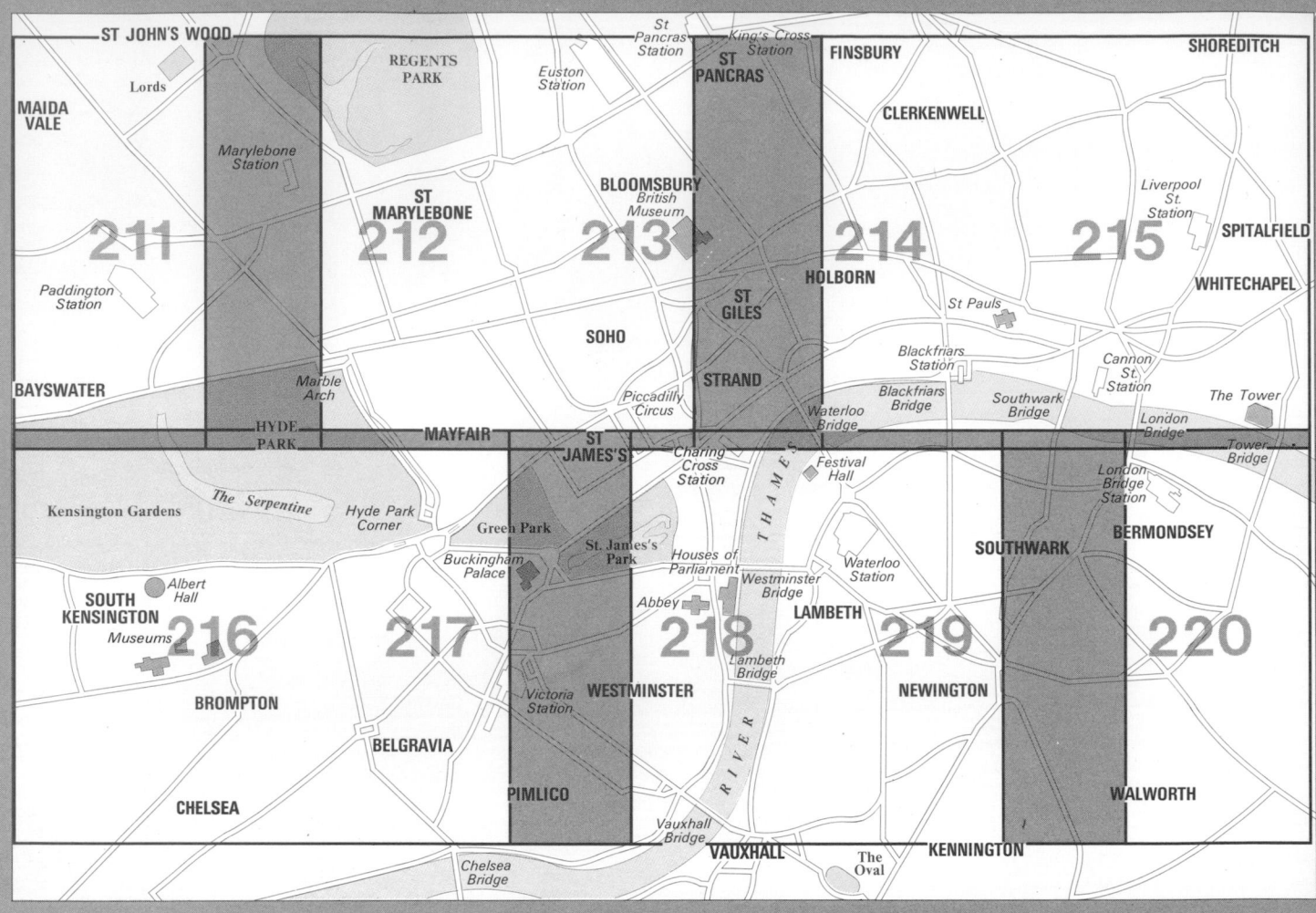

Legend

Motorway	≡≡≡	Hospital	Ⓗ
One-way street	←	Post office	P.O
No vehicular access	⊢⊣	Church or religious centre	†
Traffic roundabout	○	Water feature	*Thames*
Banned turn	⤳	Park or open space	◯
Parking	Ⓟ	Place of interest	*Museum*
Garage parking	Ⓖ	A.A. Centre	**AA**
British Rail Station	*Euston Station*	District name	**STRAND**
London Transport Station	*Holborn* ⊖	Overlap extent and number of continuing page	**218**
Police station	POL		

Scale: seven inches to one mile

The London Street Index

This map employs an arbitrary system of grid reference. Pages are identified by numbers and divided into twelve squares. Each square contains a blue letter; all references give the page number first, followed by the letter of the square in which a particular street can be found. Reference for Exhibition Road is *216*E, meaning that the relevant map is on page *216* and that the street appears in the square designated E.

Abbey Orchard St SW1 *218* E
Abbey St SE1 *220* F
Abbots Lane SE1 *220* B
Abchurch Lane EC4 *215* L
Abercorn Pl NW8 *211* A
Aberdeen Pl NW8 *211* E
Abingdon St SW1 *218* F
Acton St WC1 *214* A
Adam St WC2 *213* M
Adam's Row W1 *212* M
Addington St SE1 *219* D
Addle St EC2 *215* G
Adelaide St WC2 *213* L
Adeline Pl WC1 *213* H
Adpar St WC2 *211* E
Agar St WC2 *213* M
Agdon St EC1 *214* C
Albany Rd SE5 *220* M
Albany St NW1 *212* C
Albermale St W1 *213* K
Albert Embankment SE1/SE11 *218* M
Albert Pl W8 *216* D
Alberta St SE17 *219* L
Albion Pl EC1 *214* F
Albion St W2 *211* M
Aldbridge St SE17 *220* L
Aldermanbury EC2 *215* G
Alderney St SW1 *217* L
Aldersgate St EC1 *215* D
Aldford St W1 *212* L
Aldgate EC3 *215* J
Aldgate High St EC3 *215* J
Aldwych WC2 *214* K
Alexander Pl SW7 *216* J
Alfred Pl WC1 *213* E
Alice St SE *220* E
Alie St E1 *215* J
Allington St SW1 *217* E
Allsop Pl NW1 *212* E
Alsace Rd SE17 *220* L
Alscot Rd SE1 *220* J
Alvey St SE17 *220* L
Ambergate St SE17 *219* L
Ambrosden Av SW1 *218* G
Amelia St SE17 *219* L
Ampton St WC1 *214* A
Amwell St EC1 *214* B
Angel St EC1 *215* G
Appold St EC2 *215* F
Aquinas St SE1 *219* A
Arch St SE1 *291* J
Archer St W1 *213* L
Argyle St WC1 *213* C
Argyle Sq WC1 *213* C
Argyll St W1 *213* G
Arlington St SW1 *217* C
Arlington Way EC1 *214* C
Arne St WC2 *213* J
Arnold Circus E2 *215* C
Arthur St EC4 *215* L
Artillery Ln E1 *215* J
Artillery Row SW1 *218* D
Arundel St WC2 *214* L
Ashbridge St NW8 *211* F
Ashburn Gdns SW7 *216* G
Ashburn Mews SW7 *216* G
Ashburn Pl SW7 *216* G
Ashby St EC1 *214* C
Ashley Pl SW1 *217* J
Ashmill St NW1 *211* F
Ashworth Rd W9 *211* A
Astell St SW3 *216* M
Atterbury St SW1 *218* H
Attneave St WC1 *214* B
Augustus St NW1 *213* A
Aulton Pl SE11 *219* K
Austin St E2 *215* C
Austral St SE11 *219* H
Aveline St SE11 *219* K
Ave Maria Lane EC4 *214* J
Avery Row W1 *212* M
Avonmouth St SE11 *219* F
Aybrook St W1 *212* H
Aylesbury Rd SE17 *220* L
Aylesbury St EC1 *214* F
Aylesford St SW1 *218* L

Baches St N1 *215* B
Back Hill EC1 *214* E
Bacon St E2 *215* F
Bagshot St SE17 *220* M
Baker St W1 NW1 *212* E
Baker's Row EC1 *214* E
Balcombe St NW1 *212* D
Balderton St W1 *212* M
Baldwin's Gdns EC1 *214* E
Balfour St SE17 *220* G
Baltic St EC1 *215* D
Bankend SE1 *220* A
Bankside SE1 *214* M
Banner St EC1 *215* D
Barbican EC2 *215* D
Barnham St SE1 *220* C
Baron's Pl SE1 *219* E
Barrett St W1 *212* J
Barrie St W2 *211* L
Barter St WC1 *213* J
Bartholomew Cl EC1 *215* G
Bartholomew Ln EC2 *215* H
Bartholomew St SE1 *220* H
Basil St SW3 *216* F
Basinghall Av EC2 *215* G
Basinghall St EC2 *215* G
Bastwick St EC1 *215* D
Bateman's Row EC2 *215* C
Bath St EC1 *215* A
Bath Ter SE1 *219* F
Battle Bridge Ln SE1 *220* B
Bayley St WC1 *213* H
Bayliss Rd SE1 *219* D
Bayswater Rd W2 *211* K
Beaconsfield Rd SE17 *220* L
Beak St W1 *213* K
Bear Ln SE1 *219* B
Beauchamp Pl SW3 *216* F
Beaufort Gdns SW3 *216* F
Beaumont St W1 *212* F
Beckway St SE17 *220* L
Bedford Av WC1 *213* H
Bedfordbury WC2 *213* L
Bedford Pl WC1 *213* F
Bedford Row WC1 *214* E
Bedford Sq WC1 *213* H
Bedford St WC2 *213* M
Bedford Way WC1 *213* E
Beech St EC2 *215* D
Beeston Pl SW1 *217* E
Belgrave Pl SW1 *217* D
Belgrave Rd SW1 *217* J
Belgrave Sq SW1 *217* D
Belgrove St WC *213* C
Bell Ln E1 *215* J
Bell St NW1 *211* F
Bell Yd WC2 *214* H
Belvedere Rd SE1 *218* C
Benjamin St EC1 *214* F
Bentinck St W1 *212* J
Berkeley Sq W1 *212* M
Bermondsey St SE1 *220* B
Bernard St WC1 *213* F
Berners Mews W1 *213* G
Berners St W1 *213* G
Berry St EC1 *214* F
Berryfield Rd SE17 *219* L
Berwick St W1 *213* G
Bessborough Gdns SW1 *218* L
Bessborough Pl SW1 *218* L
Bessborough St SW1 *218* L
Bethnal Gn Rd E1 *218* F
Bevenden St N1 *215* B
Bevis Marks EC3 *215* J
Bickenhall St W1 *212* E
Bidborough St WC1 *213* B
Billiter St EC3 *215* J
Bina Gdns SW5 *216* G
Binney St W1 *212* M
Birchin Ln EC3 *215* L
Bird St W1 *212* J
Birdcage Walk SW1 *218* D
Birkenhead St WC1 *213* C
Bishop's Br Rd W2 *211* G
Bishopsgate EC2 *215* J
Bishop's Ter SE11 *219* G
Blackfriars Br SE1 *214* M
Blackfriars Rd SE1 *219* B
Black Prince Rd SE11 *218* J
Blackwood St SE17 *220* K
Blandford St W1 *212* H
Blomfield Rd W9 *211* D
Blomfield St EC2 *215* H
Blomfield Villas W2 *211* G
Bloomfield Ter SW1 *217* K
Bloomsbury Sq WC1 *213* J
Bloomsbury St WC1 *213* H
Bloomsbury Way WC1 *213* J
Bolsover St W1 *212* F
Boltons The SW10 *216* K
Bolton Gdns SW5 *216* K
Bolton St W1 *217* B
Bonhill St EC2 *215* E
Boot St N1 *215* B
Borough High St SE1 *220* D
Borough Rd SE1 *219* E
Borrett Close SE17 *219* M
Boscobel St NW8 *211* E
Boss St SE1 *220* C
Boston Pl NW1 *212* D
Boswell St WC1 *213* F
Botolph Ln EC3 *215* L
Boundary St E2 *215* C
Bourdon St W1 *212* M
Bourne St SW1 *217* G
Bourne Ter W2 *211* D
Bouverie St EC4 *214* H
Bow Ln EC4 *215* K
Bow St WC2 *213* J
Bowden St SE11 *219* K
Bowling Gn Ln EC1 *214* E
Bowling Gn Walk N1 *215* B
Boyfield St SE1 *219* E
Brad St SE1 *219* A
Braganza St SE17 *219* L
Brandon St SE17 *220* G
Bray Pl SW3 *216* J
Bread St EC4 *215* K
Bream's Buildings EC4 *214* H
Brechin Pl SW7 *216* K
Brandon St W1 *212* G
Bressenden Pl SW1 *217* F
Brewer St W1 *213* K
Brick Ln E1 E2 *215* C
Brick St W1 *217* B
Bridge St SW1 *218* F
Bridle Ln W1 *213* K
Briset St EC1 *214* F
Bristol Gdns W9 *211* D
Britannia St WC1 *214* A
Britannia Walk N1 *215* A
Britten Ct SW3 *216* M
Britton St EC1 *214* F
Broad Ct WC2 *213* J
Broadley St NW8 *211* E
Broadley Ter NW1 *211* F
Broad Sanctuary SW1 *218* E
Broadway SW1 *218* E
Broadwick St W1 *213* K
Brockham St SE1 *220* D
Brompton Pl SW3 *216* F
Brompton Rd SW3 *216* F
Brompton Sq SW3 *216* F
Brook Dr SE11 *219* G
Brook St W1 *212* M
Brook St W2 *211* L
Brooke St EC1 *214* H
Brook's Mews W1 *212* M
Brown St W1 *212* G
Browning St SE17 *219* M
Brownlow Mews WC1 *214* E
Brune St E1 *215* J
Brunswick Ct SE1 *220* F
Brunswick Pl N1 *215* B
Brunswick Sq WC1 *213* F
Brushfield St E1 *215* F
Bruton Ln W1 *212* M
Bruton Pl W1 *212* M
Bruton St W1 *212* M
Bryanston Pl W1 *212* G
Bryanston Sq W1 *212* H
Bryanston St W1 *212* L
Buckingham Gate SW1 *217* F
Buckingham Palace Rd SW1 *217* H
Bucknall St WC2 *213* H
Bulstrode St W1 *212* J
Bunhill Row EC1 *215* D
Burlington Gdns W1 *213* K
Burne St NW1 *211* F
Burnsall St SW3 *216* M
Burton St WC1 *213* B
Bury Pl WC1 *213* J
Bury St EC3 *215* J
Bury St SW1 *218* A
Bury Walk SW3 *216* H
Bush Ln EC4 *215* L
Bute St SW7 *216* H
Byng Pl WC1 *213* B
Byward St EC3 *215* M
Bywater St SW3 *216* M

Cabbell St NW1 *211* J
Cadiz St SE5 *220* K
Cadogan Gdns SW3 *217* G
Cadogan Ln SW1 *217* G
Cadogan Pl SW1 *217* D
Cadogan Sq SW1 *217* G
Cadogan St SW3 *216* J
Calmington Rd SE5 *220* M
Calthorpe St WC1 *214* E
Calvert Av E2 *215* C
Calvin St E1 *215* F
Cambridge Sq W2 *211* J
Cambridge St SW1 *217* L
Camlet St E2 *215* C
Camomile St EC3 *215* H
Canning Pl W8 *216* D
Cannon Row SW1 *218* F
Cannon St EC4 *215* K
Canterbury Pl SE17 *219* H
Capland St NW8 *211* E
Capper St WC1 *213* D
Carburton St W1 *213* D
Cardigan St SE11 *219* K
Cardington St NW11 *213* A
Carey St WC2 *214* H
Carlisle Ln SE1 *219* D
Carlisle Pl SW1 *217* J
Carlos Pl W1 *212* M
Carlton Gdns SW1 *218* B
Carlton House Ter SW1 *218* B
Carlyle Sq SW3 *216* L
Carmelite St EC4 *214* M
Carnaby St W1 *213* K
Caroline Ter SW1 *217* G
Carriage Rd, The SW1 *216* F
Carter Ln EC4 *214* M
Carter Pl SE17 *219* H
Carter St SE17 *219* L
Carting Ln WC2 *214* K
Cartwright Gdns WC1 *213* B
Castellain Rd W9 *211* D
Castle Ln SW1 *217* F
Catesby St SE17 *220* H
Catherine Pl SW1 *217* F
Catherine St WC2 *214* K
Causton St SW1 *218* H
Cavendish Pl W1 *212* J
Caxton St SW1 *218* D
Cayton St EC1 *215* A
Central Markets EC1 *214* J
Central St EC1 *215* A
Chadwick St SW1 *218* H
Chagford St NW1 *212* E
Chalton St NW1 *213* B
Chambord St E2 *215* C
Chancery Ln WC2 *214* H
Chandos Pl WC2 *213* M
Chandos St W1 *212* J
Chapel St NW1 *211* J
Chapel St SW1 *217* E
Chapter Rd SE17 *219* L
Chapter St SW1 *218* H
Charing Cross SW1 *218* B
Charing Cross Rd WC2 *213* H
Charles Sq N1 *215* B
Charles St W1 *217* B
Charles II St SW1 *218* B
Charleston St SE17 *220* G
Charlotte Rd EC2 *215* B
Charlotte St W1 *213* D
Charlwood St SW1 *218* K
Chart St N1 *215* B
Charthouse Sq EC1 *214* F
Charterhouse St EC1 *214* J
Chatham St SE17 *220* H
Cheapside EC2 *215* G
Chelsea Br Rd SW1 *217* K
Chelsea Manor St SW3 *216* M
Chelsea Sq SW3 *216* L
Cheltenham Ter SW3 *217* K
Chenies St WC1 *213* E
Chequer St EC1 *215* D
Chesham Pl SW1 *217* D
Chesham St SW1 *217* G
Chester Cl W1 *212* G
Chester Ct W1 *212* G
Chester Gate W1 *212* G
Chester Rd NW1 *212* C
Chester Row SW1 *217* G
Chester Sq SW1 *217* H
Chester St SW1 *217* E
Chester Ter NW1 *212* C
Chester Way SE11 *219* G
Chesterfield Hill W1 *217* B
Cheval Pl SW7 *216* F
Chicheley St SE1 *218* C
Chichester Rd W2 *211* D
Chichester St SW1 *218* K
Chiltern St W1 *212* E
Chilworth St W2 *211* G
Chiswell St EC1 *215* D
Chitty St W1 *213* D
Church St NW8 W2 *211* E
Church Yard Row SE11 *219* H
Churchill Gdns Rd SW1 *217* M
Churchway NW1 *213* B
Churton St SW1 *218* G
Circus Rd NW8 *211* B
City Rd EC1 *215* A
Clabon Mews SW1 *216* J
Clarence Gdns NW1 *213* A
Clarendon Gdns W9 *211* D
Clarendon Pl W2 *211* M
Clarendon St SW1 *217* L
Clarendon Ter W9 *211* E
Clareville Gv SW7 *216* G
Clareville St SW7 *216* G
Clarges St W1 *217* B
Claverton St SW1 *218* K
Cleaver Sq SE11 *219* K
Cleaver St SE11 *219* K
Clere St EC2 *215* E
Clerkenwell Cl EC1 *214* F
Clerkenwell Gn EC1 *214* F
Clerkenwell Rd EC1 *214* E
Cleveland Gdns W2 *211* G
Cleveland Row SW1 *218* A
Cleveland Sq W2 *211* G
Cleveland St W1 *213* D
Cleveland Ter W2 *211* G
Clifford St W1 *213* K
Clifton Gdns W9 *211* D
Clifton Pl W2 *211* L
Clifton Rd W9 *211* D
Clifton Sq EC2 *215* E
Clifton Villas W9 *211* D
Clink St SE1 *220* A
Clipstone St W1 *213* D
Cliveden Pl SW1 *217* G
Cloak Ln EC4 *215* K
Cloth Fair EC1 *214* J
Club Row E1/2 *215* C
Cobb St E1 *215* J
Cobourg St NW1 *213* A
Cock Ln EC1 *214* J
Cockspur St SW1 *218* B
Coin St SE1 *219* A
Colbeck Mews SW7 *216* G
Cole St SE1 *220* D
Coleman St EC2 *215* G
Coley St WC1 *214* E
Collingham Rd SW5 *216* G
Columbia Rd E2 *215* C
Commercial St E1 *215* F
Compton St EC1 *214* F
Concert Hall Approach SE1 *219* A
Conduit St W1 *213* K
Congreve St SE17 *220* H
Connaught Pl W2 *212* K
Connaught Sq W2 *212* G
Connaught St W2 *211* J
Constitution Hill SW1 *217* E
Content St SE17 *204* G
Conway St W1 *213* D
Cooper's Rd SE1 *220* M
Cooper's Row EC3 *215* M
Copperfield St SE1 *219* B
Copthall Av EC2 *215* H
Copthall Cl EC2 *215* H
Coptic St WC1 *213* H
Coral St SE1 *219* D
Coram St WC1 *213* E
Cork St W1 *213* K
Cornhill EC3 *215* H
Cornwall Gdns SW7 *216* G
Cornwall Rd SE1 *219* A
Coronet St N1 *215* B
Corporation Row EC1 *214* F
Corsham St N1 *215* B
Cosser St SE1 *219* D
Cosway St NW1 *211* F
Cotham St SE17 *220* G
Cottesmore Gdns SW8 *216* D
Cottington Cl SE11 *219* H
Cottington St SE11 *219* L
Coulson St SW3 *216* M
County St SE1 *220* G
Courtenay St SE11 *219* K
Courtfield Gdns SW5 *216* G
Courtfield Rd SW7 *216* G
Covent Gdn WC2 *213* M
Coventry St W1 *213* L
Cowcross St EC1 *214* F
Cowper St EC2 *215* B
Coxsons Way SE1 *220* F
Cramer St W1 *212* J
Crampton St SE17 *219* H
Cranbourn St WC2 *213* L
Cranley Gdns SW7 *216* L
Cranley Mews SW7 *216* K
Cranley Pl SW7 *216* H
Cranwood St EC1 *215* B
Craven Hill W2 *211* K
Craven Hill Gdns W2 *211* K

Principal Airports

Heathrow Airport, London *tel* 01-759 4321

The world's busiest International Airport, Heathrow lies just 16 miles west of the capital. Access to the passenger terminals 1, 2 and 3 is via the Heathrow tunnel, which links the central area with the M4 or the A4 Bath Road. Terminal 4 is accessible from the A30 or M25 junction 14. Heathrow central station is connected to the capital's underground network, linking the airport with central London in about 45 minutes.

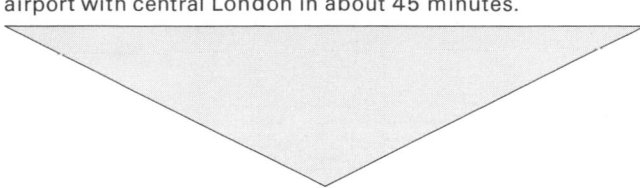

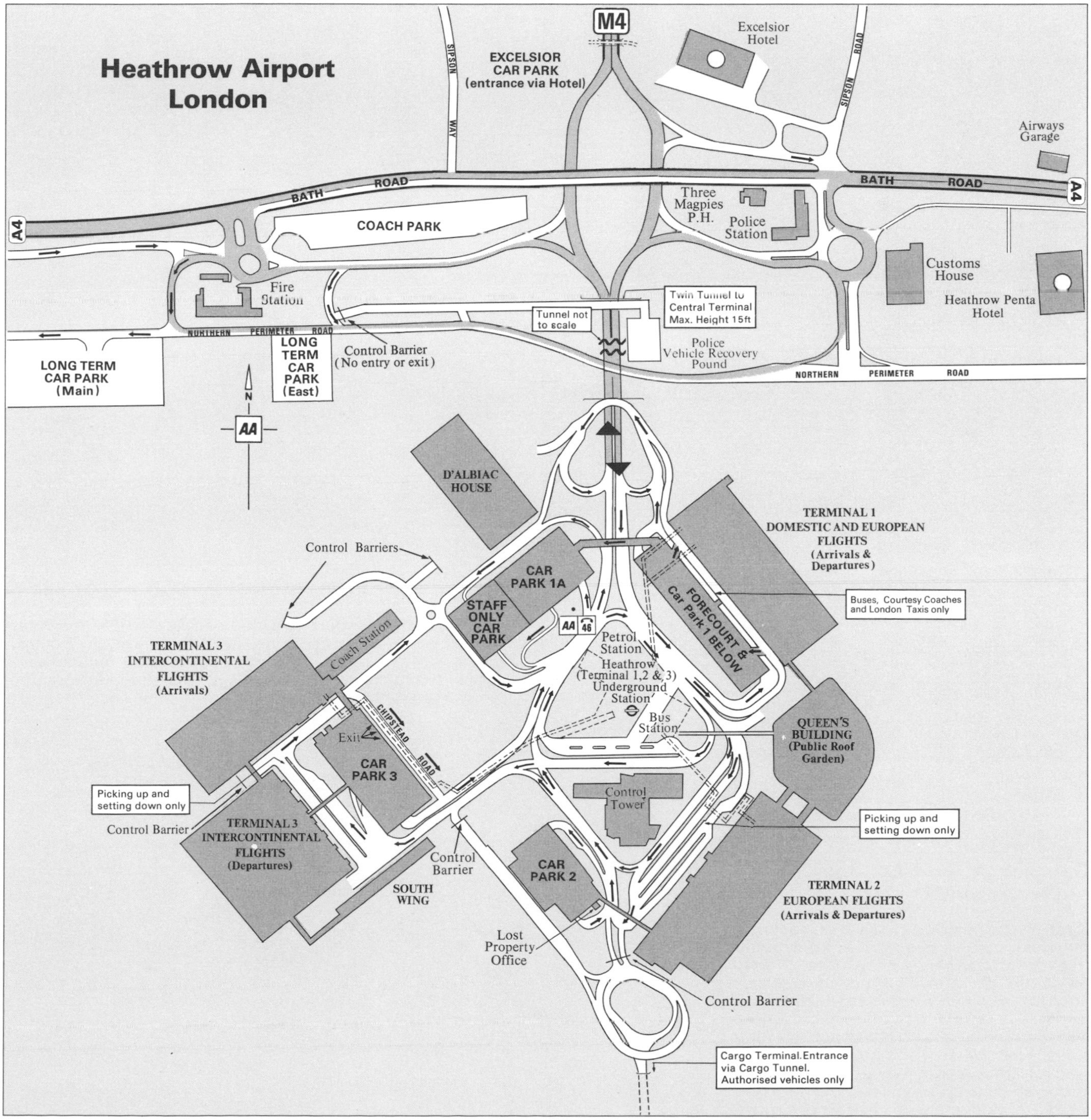

Heathrow Airport
London

Luton International Airport

Luton Map

VAUXHALL WAY
A505
EATON GREEN ROAD
CAR PARK 9
Petrol Station
INDUSTRIAL AREA
CENTRAL CAR STORAGE
Hangars
COVERED CAR PARK
Luton Flying Club
AIRPORT WAY
PERCIVAL WAY
FREIGHT WAY
Control Tower
24 hour petrol & Maintenance
Hangars
CAR PARK 7
CAR PARK 1 (Short Term)
Terminal Building
Hangars
CAR PARK 2
RUNWAY
GRASS
A505
AIRPORT WAY
Spectators Buffet & Bar
SPECTATORS CAR PARK
N
AA
CAR PARK 8
Fire Station
EAST TAXIWAY
EAST TAXIWAY
INDUSTRIAL PARK
EAST-WEST CONCRETE RUNWAY

Luton International Airport *tel* Luton 36061

Mainly used by package-holiday tour operators, Luton Airport lies some 2 miles east of the centre of Luton and close to the M1 motorway. Access from the north or south on the M1 is via junction 10 (3½ miles). Luton is on the main railway line from London and journey time is just 28 minutes by fast train from St Pancras station

Manchester International Airport

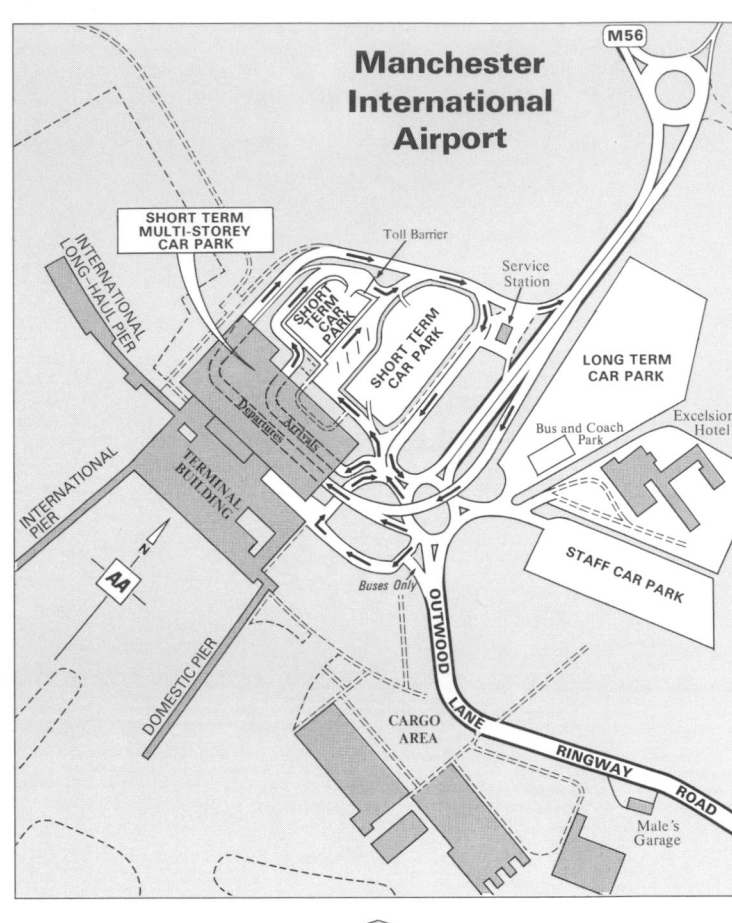

M56
SHORT TERM MULTI-STOREY CAR PARK
Toll Barrier
Service Station
INTERNATIONAL LONG-HAUL PIER
INTERNATIONAL PIER
SHORT TERM CAR PARK
SHORT TERM CAR PARK
LONG TERM CAR PARK
Bus and Coach Park
Excelsior Hotel
Departures
Arrivals
TERMINAL BUILDING
DOMESTIC PIER
N
AA
Buses Only
STAFF CAR PARK
OUTWOOD LANE
CARGO AREA
RINGWAY ROAD
Male's Garage

Manchester International Airport *tel* 061-437 5233

The largest UK airport outside London, Manchester International Airport lies just 9 miles south of Manchester city centre. Access to the airport is via junction 5 on the M56 motorway, which is connected to the extensive national motorway network. The nearest railway station is Heald Green about 2 miles from the airport.

Gatwick Airport London

A217
A23
Post House Hotel
Airport Service Station
Gatwick Penta Hotel
Gatwick Moat House Hotel
LONDON ROAD
Mole
River
ROAD NORTH
Construction Under
PERIMETER ROAD
SITE FOR NEW NORTH TERMINAL (OPEN 1987)
Perimeter road to be closed upon completion of new perimeter road
PERIMETER ROAD
Police Station
Control Barrier
General Aviation Terminal
A23
AIRPORT WAY
Barrier (Maintenance Vehicles only)
Cyclists only
Permit Holders Only
Road restricted to authorised vehicles
M23 SPUR
Petrol Station
BAA STAFF CAR PARK
SATELLITE
Spectator Area
Terminal Building
Gatwick Airport Station
3
2
1
Terminal Entrance
Gatwick Hilton Hotel
AA 63
STAFF CAR PARK
COACH PARK
Entrance and Exit
BAA Head Office
PIER 2
PIER 1
Cargo Terminal No2
MULTI-STOREY CAR PARKS
LONG TERM CAR PARK
N
AA

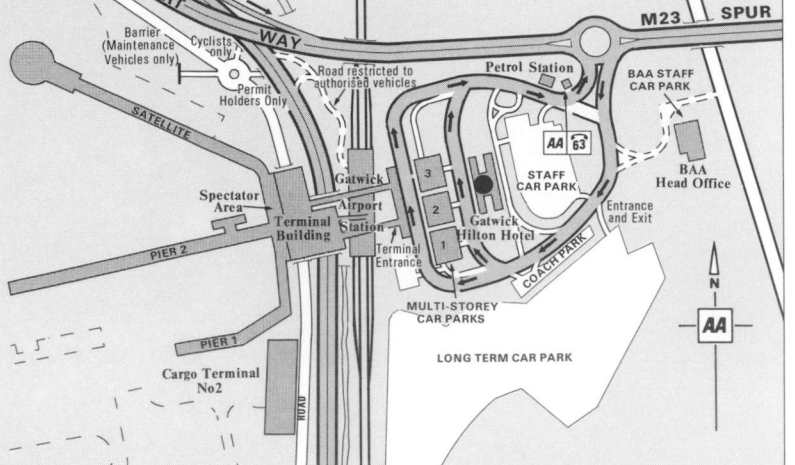

Gatwick Airport London
tel Crawley 28822

Most of the major airlines operate from Gatwick. It is also open to aircraft diverted from Heathrow, as well as the charter services of other airline companies. Access to Gatwick Airport is available from the M23 and A23 roads. There are ample parking facilities for both short and long stays. Fast rail services connect Gatwick Airport station with London (Victoria) in about 40 minutes and a fast coach service via M25 connects with Heathrow airport.

Index to Atlas

The towns and villages shown on the main maps of this atlas are listed alphabetically in the index. To find a place in the atlas, use the reference numbers given with each placename. The relevant page number is given with the National Grid reference number, so that the place can be quickly and accurately pinpointed. The National Grid system is explained on page XIII.

Ardnarff 228 Barrow Gurney

Ardnarff 101 NG 8935
Ardnastang 95 NM 8061
Ardo 105 NJ 8538
Ardoch 92 NO 0937
Ardorlich 90 NN 6322
Ardoyne 104 NJ 6527
Ardpatrick 81 NR 7560
Ardpeaton 90 NS 2185
Ardrishaig 89 NR 8585
Ardroil 109 NB 0432
Ardrossan 82 NS 2342
Ardshealach 95 NM 6967
Ardsley 59 SE 3805
Ardsley East 59 SE 3024
Ardslignish 95 NM 5661
Ardtalnaig 91 NN 7039
Ardullie 102 NH 5963
Ardvasar 95 NG 6303
Ardwell 68 NX 1045
Areley Kings 41 SO 8070
Argoed Mill 27 SN 9962
Aridhglas 88 NM 3123
Arinacrinachd 101 NG 7458
Arinagour 94 NM 2257
Arisaig 95 NM 6586
Arivruach 109 NB 2417
Arkendale 66 SE 3860
Arkesden 35 TL 4834
Arkholme 64 SD 5871
Arkley 21 TQ 2296
Arksey 60 SE 5706
Arkwright Town 53 SK 4270
Arlecdon 62 NY 0419
Arlesey 35 TL 1936
Arleston 41 SJ 6410
Arley (Ches.) 51 SJ 6780
Arley (Warw.) 43 SP 2890
Arlingham 32 SO 7010
Arlington (Devon) 6 SS 6140
Arlington (Glos.) 32 SP 1006
Arlington (E Susx) 13 TQ 5407
Armadale (Highld.) 111 NC 7864
Armadale (Lothian) 84 NS 9368
Armathwaite 71 NY 5046
Arminghall 47 TG 2504
Armitage 42 SK 0816
Armscote 33 SP 2444
Armthorpe 60 SE 6105
Arnabost 94 NM 2159
Arncliffe 65 SD 9371
Arncliffe Cote 65 SD 9470
Arncott 34 SP 6117
Arncroach 93 NO 5105
Arnesby 43 SP 6192
Arngask 92 NO 1310
Arnisdale 101 NG 8411
Arniston Engine 85 NT 3462
Arnol 109 NB 3148
Arnprior 90 NS 6194
Arnside 63 SD 4578
Arrad Foot 62 SD 3080
Arram 61 TA 0344
Arrathorne 65 SE 2093
Arreton 11 SZ 5386
Arrington 35 TL 3250
Arrochar 90 NN 2904
Arrow 32 SP 0856
Artafallie 102 NH 6249
Arthington 59 SE 2644
Arthingworth 44 SP 7581
Arthog 39 SH 6414
Arthrath 105 NJ 9636
Artrochie 105 NK 0032
Arundel 12 TQ 0107
Aryhoulan 96 NN 0168
Asby 62 NY 0620
Ascog 82 NS 1063
Ascot 20 SU 9168
Ascott-under-Wychwood 33 SP 2918
Asenby 66 SE 3975
Asfordby 44 SK 7018
Asfordby Hill 44 SK 7219
Asgarby (Lincs.) 55 TF 1145
Asgarby (Lincs.) 55 TF 3366
Ash (Kent) 21 TQ 5964
Ash (Kent) 15 TR 2958
Ash (Somer.) 8 ST 4720
Ash Bullayne 7 SS 7704
Ash Magna 51 SJ 5739
Ash Mill 7 SS 7823
Ash Priors 16 ST 1429
Ash Thomas 8 ST 0010
Ashampstead 19 SU 5676
Ashbocking 37 TM 1654
Ashbourne 52 SK 1846
Ashbrittle 8 ST 0521
Ashburton 5 SX 7569
Ashbury (Devon.) 6 SX 5097
Ashbury (Oxon.) 18 SU 2685
Ashby Folville 44 SK 7012
Ashby Magna 43 SP 5690
Ashby Parva 43 SP 5288
Ashby St. Ledgers 43 SP 5768
Ashby St. Mary 47 TG 3202
Ashby by Partney 55 TF 4266
Ashby cum Fenby 61 TA 2500
Ashby de la Launde 54 TF 0455
Ashby-de-la-Zouch 43 SK 3516
Ashchurch 32 SO 9233
Ashcombe 8 SX 9179
Ashcott 17 ST 4336
Ashdon 36 TL 5842
Asheldham 23 TL 9701
Ashen 36 TL 7442
Ashendon 34 SP 7014
Ashfield (Central) 91 NN 7803
Ashfield (Suff.) 37 TM 2062
Ashfield Green 37 TM 2673
Ashford (Derby.) 52 SK 1969
Ashford (Devon.) 6 SS 5335
Ashford (Kent) 15 TR 0142
Ashford (Surrey) 20 TQ 0671
Ashford Bowdler 40 SO 5170
Ashford Carbonel 40 SO 5270
Ashford Hill 19 SU 5562
Ashgill 84 NS 7849
Ashill (Devon) 8 ST 0811
Ashill (Norf.) 46 TF 8804
Ashill (Somer.) 8 ST 3217
Ashingdon 22 TQ 8693
Ashington (Northum.) 79 NZ 2687
Ashington (W Susx) 12 TQ 1315
Ashkirk 77 NT 4722
Ashleworth 32 SO 8125
Ashley (Cambs.) 36 TL 6961
Ashley (Ches.) 51 SJ 7784
Ashley (Devon.) 7 SS 6411
Ashley (Glos.) 18 ST 9394
Ashley (Hants.) 11 SU 3831
Ashley (Northants.) 44 SP 7991
Ashley (Staffs.) 51 SJ 7536
Ashley Green 34 SP 9705
Ashley Heath 10 SU 1105
Ashmansworth 19 SU 4156
Ashmansworthy 6 SS 3317
Ashmore 10 ST 9117
Ashorne 33 SP 3057
Ashover 53 SK 3463
Ashow 44 SP 3170
Ashperton 31 SO 6441
Ashprington 5 SX 8157
Ashreigney 6 SS 6213
Ashtead 21 TQ 1858
Ashton (Ches.) 50 SJ 5069
Ashton (Corn.) 2 SW 6028
Ashton (Devon.) 5 SX 8584
Ashton (Here & W) 30 SO 5164
Ashton (Northants.) 34 SP 7649
Ashton (Northants.) 45 TL 0588
Ashton Common 18 ST 8958
Ashton Keynes 18 SU 0494
Ashton under Hill 32 SO 9938
Ashton upon Mersey 51 SJ 7792
Ashton-in-Makerfield 57 SJ 5799
Ashton-under-Lyne 51 SJ 9399
Ashurst (Hants.) 11 SU 3310
Ashurst (Kent) 13 TQ 5038
Ashurst (W Susx) 12 TQ 1716
Ashurstwood 13 TQ 4236
Ashwater 6 SX 3895
Ashwell (Herts.) 35 TL 2639
Ashwell (Leic.) 44 SK 8613
Ashwellthorpe 47 TM 1397
Ashwick 17 ST 6447
Ashwicken 46 TF 7018
Askam in Furness 64 SD 2177
Askern 60 SE 5613
Askerswell 9 SY 5292
Askett 34 SP 8105
Askham (Cumbr.) 63 NY 5123
Askham (Notts.) 54 SK 7374
Askham Bryan 60 SE 5548
Askham Richard 60 SE 5347
Askrigg 65 SD 9491
Askwith 59 SE 1648
Aslackby 45 TF 0830
Aslacton 47 TM 1591
Aslockton 54 SK 7440
Aspatria 70 NY 1442
Aspenden 35 TL 3528
Aspley Guise 34 SP 9436
Aspull 58 SD 6108
Asselby 60 SE 7127
Assington 36 TL 9338
Astbury 51 SJ 8461
Astcote 34 SP 6753
Asterley 40 SJ 3707
Asterton 40 SO 3991
Asthall 33 SP 2811
Asthall Leigh 33 SP 3012
Astley (Here & W) 41 SO 7867
Astley (Salop) 40 SJ 5218
Astley (Warw.) 43 SP 3189
Astley Abbots 41 SO 7096
Astley Cross 41 SO 8069
Astley Green 58 SJ 7099
Aston (Berks.) 20 SU 7884
Aston (Ches.) 51 SJ 5578
Aston (Ches.) 51 SJ 6046
Aston (Derby.) 52 SK 1883
Aston (Here & W) 40 SO 4571
Aston (Herts.) 35 TL 2722
Aston (Oxon.) 33 SP 3302
Aston (S Yorks.) 53 SK 4685
Aston (Salop) 40 SJ 5228
Aston (Salop) 41 SJ 6109
Aston (Staffs.) 41 SJ 7540
Aston (Staffs.) 41 SJ 9131
Aston (W Mids) 42 SP 0789
Aston Abbotts 34 SP 8420
Aston Botterell 41 SO 6284
Aston Cantlow 32 SP 1359
Aston Clinton 34 SP 8812
Aston Crews 32 SO 6723
Aston End 35 TL 2724
Aston Eyre 41 SO 6594
Aston Flamville 43 SP 4692
Aston Ingham 29 SO 6823
Aston Magna 33 SP 1935
Aston Rogers 40 SJ 3406
Aston Rowant 20 SU 7299
Aston Sandford 34 SP 7507
Aston Somerville 32 SP 0438
Aston Subedge 32 SP 1341
Aston Tirrold 19 SU 5586
Aston Upthorpe 19 SU 5586
Aston juxta Mondrum 51 SJ 6556
Aston le Walls 33 SP 4950
Aston on Clun 40 SO 3981
Aston-on-Trent 43 SK 4129
Astwick 35 TL 2138
Astwood 34 SP 9547
Astwood Bank 32 SP 0362
Aswarby (Lincs.) 54 TF 0639
Aswardby (Lincs.) 54 TF 3770
Atcham 40 SJ 5408
Athelington 37 TM 2170
Athelney 17 ST 3428
Athelstaneford 86 NT 5377
Atherington 6 SS 5923
Atherstone 43 SP 3097
Atherstone on Stour 33 SP 2050
Atherton 58 SD 6703
Atlow 53 SK 2248
Attenborough 53 SK 5134
Attleborough (Norf.) 47 TM 0495
Attleborough (Warw.) 43 SP 3790
Attlebridge 47 TG 1216
Atwick 67 TA 1850
Atworth 18 ST 8565
Aubourn 54 SK 9262
Auchagallon 81 NR 8934
Auchamie 104 NJ 6341
Auchattie 99 NO 6994
Auchenblae 99 NO 7278
Auchenbowie 84 NS 7988
Auchencairn (Dumf & G) 69 NX 7951
Auchencarroch 90 NS 4182
Auchencrow 87 NT 8560
Auchendinny 85 NT 2561
Auchengray 85 NS 9953
Auchenhalrig 104 NJ 3661
Auchenheath 84 NS 8043
Auchentiber 82 NS 3647
Auchgourish 103 NH 9315
Auchindrain 89 NN 0303
Auchindrean 106 NH 1980
Auchininna 105 NJ 6446
Auchinleck (Strath.) 75 NS 5422
Auchinloch 84 NS 6670
Auchintore 96 NN 0972
Auchleuchries 105 NK 0136
Auchleven 104 NJ 6224
Auchlochan 84 NS 8037
Auchmacoy 105 NJ 9930
Auchmantle 68 NX 1762
Auchmillan 75 NS 5129
Auchmithie 99 NO 6744
Auchmuirbridge 92 NO 2101
Auchnacree 98 NO 4663
Auchnagatt 105 NJ 9341
Auchronie 98 NO 4480
Auchterarder 91 NN 9312
Auchterderran 92 NT 2195
Auchterhouse 93 NO 3337
Auchtermuchty 92 NO 2311
Auchterneed 102 NH 4959
Auchtertool 92 NT 2190
Auchtoo 90 NN 5620
Auckengill 112 ND 3764
Auckley 60 SE 6501
Audenshaw 58 SJ 9196
Audlem 51 SJ 6543
Audley 51 SJ 7950
Aughton (Humbs.) 60 SE 7038
Aughton (Lancs.) 57 SD 3804
Aughton (Lancs.) 64 SD 5467
Aughton (S Yorks.) 53 SK 4586
Aughton Park 57 SD 4106
Auldearn 103 NH 9155
Aulden 30 SO 4654
Auldhame 86 NT 5984
Auldhouse 84 NS 6250
Ault-a-chrinn 101 NG 9420
Aultbea 106 NG 8789
Aultgrishan 106 NG 7485
Aultiphurst 111 NC 8065
Aultmore (Grampn.) 104 NJ 4053
Aultnagoire 102 NH 5423
Aulton 104 NJ 6028
Aundorach 103 NH 9716
Aunsby 54 TF 0438
Auquhorthies 105 NJ 8329
Aust 29 ST 5789
Austerfield 53 SK 6594
Austonley 59 SE 1207
Austrey 43 SK 2906
Austwick 65 SD 7668
Authorpe 55 TF 4080
Authorpe Row 55 TF 5373
Avebury 18 SU 0969
Aveley 21 TQ 5680
Avening 18 ST 8797
Averham 54 SK 7654
Aveton Gifford 5 SX 6947
Avielochan 103 NH 9016
Aviemore 103 NH 8912
Avington 19 SU 3767
Avoch 103 NH 6955
Avon 9 SZ 1498
Avon Dassett 33 SP 4150
Avonbridge 84 NS 9072
Avonmouth 29 ST 5177
Avonwick 5 SX 7158
Awbridge 11 SU 3323
Awkley 29 ST 5885
Awliscombe 8 ST 1301
Awre 32 SO 7008
Awsworth 53 SK 4843
Axbridge 17 ST 4254
Axford (Hants.) 19 SU 6043
Axford (Wilts.) 18 SU 2369
Axminster 8 SY 2998
Axmouth 8 SY 2591
Aylburton 29 SO 6101
Ayle 71 NY 7149
Aylesbeare 8 SY 0391
Aylesbury 34 SP 8213
Aylesby 61 TA 2007
Aylesford 14 TQ 7359
Aylesham 15 TR 2352
Aylestone 43 SK 5701
Aylmerton 47 TG 1839
Aylsham 47 TG 1926
Aylton 31 SO 6537
Aymestrey 30 SO 4265
Aynho 33 SP 5133
Ayot St. Lawrence 35 TL 1916
Ayot St. Peter 35 TL 2115
Ayr 75 NS 3321
Aysgarth 65 SE 0088
Ayside 62 SD 3983
Ayston 44 SK 8601
Aythorpe Roding 22 TL 5815
Ayton (Berwick.) 87 NT 9260
Ayton (N Yorks.) 67 SE 9884
Azerley 66 SE 2574

B

Babbinswood 40 SJ 3329
Babcary 17 ST 5628
Babel 27 SN 8235
Babell 50 SJ 1574
Babeny 5 SX 6774
Babraham 35 TL 5150
Babworth 53 SK 6880
Back 109 NB 4840
Back of Keppoch 95 NM 6587
Backaland 113 HY 5630
Backbarrow 62 SD 3584
Backford 50 SJ 3971
Backhill of Clackriach 105 NJ 9347
Backies 108 NC 8302
Backmuir of New Gilston 93 NO 4308
Backwell 29 ST 4868
Backworth 79 NZ 2972
Bacon End 22 TL 6018
Baconsthorpe 47 TG 1237
Bacton (Here & W) 30 SO 3732
Bacton (Norf.) 47 TG 3434
Bacton (Suff.) 37 TM 0466
Bacup 58 SD 8622
Badachro 106 NG 7873
Badavanich 102 NH 1258
Badbury 18 SU 1980
Badby 33 SP 5559
Badcall (Highld.) 110 NC 1541
Badcall (Highld.) 110 NC 2355
Badcaul 106 NH 0191
Baddeley Green 51 SJ 9250
Baddesley Ensor 42 SP 2798
Baddidarach 110 NC 0923
Badenscoth 105 NJ 7038
Badenyon 104 NJ 3419
Badger 41 SO 7699
Badgers Mount 21 TQ 4962
Badgeworth (Glos.) 32 SO 9019
Badgworth (Somer.) 17 ST 3952
Badingham 37 TM 3067
Badlesmere 15 TR 0154
Badluarach 106 NG 9994
Badminton 18 ST 8082
Badrallach 106 NH 0691
Badsey 32 SP 0743
Badsworth 60 SE 4614
Badwell Ash 36 TL 9969
Bagby 66 SE 4680
Bagendon 32 SP 0006
Bagillt 50 SJ 2175
Baginton 43 SP 3474
Baglan 24 SS 7493
Bagley 40 SJ 4027
Bagnall 51 SJ 9250
Bagshot (Surrey) 20 SU 9163
Bagshot (Wilts.) 19 SU 3165
Bagthorpe (Norf.) 46 TF 7932
Bagthorpe (Notts.) 53 SK 4751
Bagworth 43 SK 4408
Bagwy Llydiart 29 SO 4427
Baildon 59 SE 1539
Baile Mor 88 NM 2824
Bailebeag 102 NH 5018
Baillieston 84 NS 6764
Bainbridge 66 SD 9390
Bainton (Cambs.) 45 TF 0906
Bairnkine 78 NT 6515
Baker Street 22 TQ 6381
Baker's End 35 TL 3917
Bakewell 53 SK 2168
Bala 49 SH 9236
Balallan 109 NB 2720
Balbeg 102 NH 4924
Balbeggie 92 NO 1629
Balbithan 105 NJ 7917
Balblair 103 NH 7066
Balchladich 110 NC 0330
Balchraggan 102 NH 5343
Balchrick 110 NC 1960
Balcombe 13 TQ 3130
Balcurvie 93 NO 3400
Baldersby 66 SE 3578
Balderstone 58 SD 6332
Balderton 54 SK 8151
Baldhu 2 SW 7743
Baldinnie 93 NO 4311
Baldock 35 TL 2434
Baldrine 56 SC 4281
Baldwin 56 SC 3581
Baldwin's Gate 51 SJ 7939
Baldwinholme 70 NY 3351
Bale 46 TG 0136
Balemartine 94 NL 9841
Balephuil 94 NL 9640
Balerno 85 NT 1666
Balfield 99 NO 5468
Balfour 113 HY 4716
Balfron 84 NS 5488
Balgarva 109 NF 7647
Balgaveny 105 NJ 6640
Balgavies 99 NO 5351
Balgedie 92 NO 1603
Balgove 105 NJ 8133
Balgowan 97 NN 6394
Balgown 100 NG 3868
Balgray 93 NO 4138
Balgrochan 84 NS 6278
Balhalgardy 105 NJ 7623
Balhary 98 NO 2646
Baligill 111 NC 8566
Balintore (Highld.) 108 NH 8675
Balintore (Tays.) 98 NO 2859
Balintraid 108 NH 7370
Balivanich 109 NF 7755
Balkeerie 98 NO 3244
Balkholme 60 SE 7828
Ball 40 SJ 3026
Ball Hill 19 SU 4263
Ballabeg 56 SC 2470
Ballacannell 56 SC 4382
Ballacarnane Beg 56 SC 3088
Ballachulish 96 NN 0758
Ballajora 56 SC 4790
Ballamodha 56 SC 2773
Ballantrae 68 NX 0882
Ballasalla (I. of M.) 56 SC 2870
Ballater 98 NO 3695
Ballaugh 56 SC 3493
Ballchraggan 108 NH 7775
Ballechin 97 NN 9353
Ballencrieff 86 NT 4878
Ballevullin 94 NL 9546
Balliekine 81 NR 8739
Ballig 56 SC 2882
Ballinaby 80 NR 2267
Ballindean 93 NO 2529
Ballinger Common 34 SP 9103
Ballingham 31 SO 5731
Ballingry 92 NT 1797
Ballinluig 98 NN 9852
Ballintuim 98 NO 1054
Balloch (Highld.) 103 NH 7346
Balloch (Strath.) 90 NS 3981
Balloch (Tays.) 91 NN 8419
Balloch (Tays.) 98 NO 3557
Ballochan 99 NO 5290
Balls Cross 12 SU 9826
Ballsalla (I. of M.) 56 SC 3497
Ballygown 94 NM 4343
Ballygrant 80 NR 3966
Ballymichael 81 NR 9231
Balmacara 101 NG 8028
Balmaclellan 69 NX 6578
Balmacneil 98 NN 9850
Balmae 69 NX 6845
Balmaha 90 NS 4290
Balmalcolm 93 NO 3108
Balmedie 105 NJ 9617
Balmerino 93 NO 3525
Balmerlawn 11 SU 3003
Balmore 84 NS 6073
Balmullo 93 NO 4220
Balmungie 103 NH 7359
Balnacra 101 NG 9746
Balnaguard 97 NN 9451
Balnaguisich 108 NH 6771
Balnahard 88 NM 4534
Balnain 102 NH 4430
Balnakeil 110 NC 3968
Balnaknock 100 NG 4162
Balnapaling 103 NH 7969
Balquhidder 90 NN 5320
Balsall Common 42 SP 2377
Balscote 33 SP 3841
Balsham 36 TL 5850
Baltasound (Unst) 113 HP 6208
Balterley 51 SJ 7550
Balthangie 105 NJ 8351
Baltonsborough 17 ST 5434
Balvaird 102 NH 5452
Balvicar 89 NM 7616
Bamburgh 87 NU 1834
Bamford 53 SK 2083
Bampton (Cumbr.) 63 NY 5118
Bampton (Devon.) 8 SS 9522
Bampton (Oxon.) 33 SP 3103
Banavie 96 NN 1177
Banbury 33 SP 4540
Banc-y-ffordd 26 SN 4037
Banchory 99 NO 6995
Banchory-Devenick 99 NJ 9101
Bancyfelin 25 SN 3218
Banff 105 NJ 6863
Bangor 48 SH 5872
Bangor-is-y-coed 50 SJ 3945
Banham 47 TM 0688
Bank 11 SU 2807
Bank Newton 65 SD 9152
Bank Street 31 SO 6362
Bankend (Dumf & G) 70 NY 0268
Bankend (Strath.) 84 NS 8033
Bankfoot 92 NO 0635
Bankglen 76 NS 5912
Bankhead (Grampn.) 104 NJ 6608
Bankhead (Grampn.) 105 NJ 8910
Banks (Cumbr.) 71 NY 5664
Banks (Lancs.) 57 SD 3820
Banks (Orkneys) 113 HY 4331
Bankshill 70 NY 1981
Banningham 47 TG 2129
Bannister Green 22 TL 6920
Bannockburn 91 NS 8190
Banstead 21 TQ 2559
Bantham 5 SX 6643
Banton 84 NS 7479
Banwell 17 ST 3959
Bapchild 15 TQ 9363
Bar Hill 35 TL 3864
Barassie 82 NS 3232
Baravullin 89 NM 9040
Barbaraville 108 NH 7471
Barber Booth 52 SK 1184
Barbon 63 SD 6282
Barbrook 7 SS 7147
Barby 43 SP 5470
Barcaldine 96 NM 9743
Barcheston 33 SP 2639
Barcombe 13 TQ 4214
Barcombe Cross 13 TQ 4216
Barden 65 SE 1493
Bardfield Saling 22 TL 6826
Bardney 55 TF 1169
Bardon Mill 71 NY 7764
Bardowie 84 NS 5873
Bardrainney 82 NS 3372
Bardsea 64 SD 3074
Bardsey 59 SE 3643
Bardsley 58 SD 9201
Bardwell 36 TL 9473
Barewood 30 SO 3856
Barford (Norf.) 47 TG 1107
Barford (Warw.) 33 SP 2660
Barford St. Martin 10 SU 0531
Barford St. Michael 33 SP 4332
Barfreston 15 TR 2650
Bargoed 28 SO 1500
Bargrennan 68 NX 3476
Barham (Cambs.) 45 TL 1375
Barham (Kent) 15 TR 2050
Barham (Suff.) 37 TM 1451
Barholm 45 TF 0811
Barkby 43 SK 6310
Barkestone-le-Vale 54 SK 7734
Barkham 20 SU 7866
Barking (Gtr London) 21 TQ 4785
Barking (Suff.) 37 TM 0653
Barkingside 21 TQ 4489
Barkisland 59 SE 0419
Barkston (Lincs.) 54 SK 9241
Barkston (N Yorks.) 60 SE 4936
Barkway 35 TL 3835
Barlaston 51 SJ 8938
Barlavington 12 SU 9716
Barlborough 53 SK 4777
Barlby 60 SE 6334
Barlestone 43 SK 4205
Barley (Herts.) 35 TL 4038
Barley (Lancs.) 58 SD 8240
Barleythorpe 44 SK 8409
Barling 23 TQ 9289
Barlow (Derby.) 53 SK 3474
Barlow (N Yorks.) 60 SE 6428
Barlow (Tyne and Wear) 72 NZ 1560
Barmby Moor 60 SE 7748
Barmby on the Marsh 60 SE 6828
Barmer 46 TF 8133
Barmouth 38 SH 6115
Barmpton 72 NZ 3118
Barmston 67 TA 1659
Barnack 45 TF 0705
Barnacle 43 SP 3884
Barnard Castle 72 NZ 0516
Barnard Gate 33 SP 4010
Barnardiston 36 TL 7148
Barnburgh 60 SE 4803
Barnby 47 TM 4789
Barnby Dun 60 SE 6109
Barnby Moor 53 SK 6684
Barnby in the Willows 54 SK 8552
Barnes 21 TQ 2276
Barnet 21 TQ 2496
Barnetby le Wold 61 TA 0509
Barney 46 TF 9932
Barnham (Suff.) 36 TL 8779
Barnham (W Susx) 12 SU 9604
Barnham Broom 47 TG 0807
Barnhead 99 NO 6657
Barnhill 104 NJ 1457
Barnhills 68 NW 9871
Barningham (Durham) 72 NZ 0810
Barningham (Suff.) 36 TL 9676
Barnoldby le Beck 61 TA 2303
Barnoldswick 58 SD 8746
Barns Green 12 TQ 1227
Barnsley (Glos.) 32 SP 0705
Barnsley (S Yorks.) 59 SE 3406
Barnstaple 6 SS 5533
Barnston (Essex) 22 TL 6519
Barnston (Mers.) 50 SJ 2783
Barnt Green 41 SP 0073
Barnton 51 SJ 6374
Barnwell All Saints 45 TL 0584
Barnwood 32 SO 8518
Barr 75 NX 2794
Barrachan 68 NX 3649
Barrack (Grampn) 105 NJ 8942
Barrapoll 94 NL 9542
Barras (Grampn.) 99 NO 8580
Barrasford 78 NY 9273
Barregarrow 57 SC 3288
Barrhead 82 NS 5058
Barrhill (Strath.) 68 NX 2382
Barrington (Cambs.) 35 TL 3949
Barrington (Somer.) 9 ST 3918
Barripper 2 SW 6338
Barrmill 82 NS 3651
Barrock 112 ND 2571
Barrow (Lancs.) 58 SD 7338
Barrow (Leic.) 44 SK 8815
Barrow (Salop) 41 SJ 6500
Barrow (Somer.) 17 ST 7231
Barrow (Suff.) 36 TL 7663
Barrow Gurney 29 ST 5267

Barrow Street 229 Bletchley (Salop)

Barrow Street 10 ST 8330
Barrow upon Humber 61 TA 0721
Barrow upon Soar 43 SK 5717
Barrow upon Trent 43 SK 3528
Barrow-in-Furness 64 SD 1969
Barrowby 54 SK 8736
Barrowden 44 SK 9400
Barrowford 58 SD 8538
Barry (S Glam.) 28 ST 1168
Barry (Tays) 93 NO 5334
Barry Island 28 ST 1166
Barsby 43 SK 6911
Barsham 47 TM 3989
Barston 42 SP 2078
Bartestree 31 SO 5641
Barthol Chapel 105 NJ 8134
Barthomley 32 SJ 7652
Bartley 11 SU 3012
Bartlow 36 TL 5845
Barton (Cambs.) 35 TL 4055
Barton (Ches.) 50 SJ 4454
Barton (Devon.) 8 SX 9067
Barton (Glos.) 32 SP 0925
Barton (Lancs.) 57 SD 5136
Barton (N Yorks.) 66 NZ 2208
Barton (Warw.) 32 SP 1051
Barton Bendish 46 TF 7105
Barton Hartshorn 34 SP 6431
Barton Mills 36 TL 7273
Barton Seagrave 44 SP 8877
Barton St. David 17 ST 5431
Barton Stacey 19 SU 4340
Barton Turf 47 TG 3522
Barton in Fabis 53 SK 5232
Barton in the Beans 43 SK 3906
Barton in the Clay 35 TL 0831
Barton on Sea 11 SZ 2493
Barton-Upon-Humber 61 TA 0222
Barton-le-Street 66 SE 7274
Barton-le-Willows 66 SE 7163
Barton-on-the-Heath 33 SP 2532
Barton-under-Needlewood 42 SK 1818
Barvas 109 NB 3649
Barway 45 TL 5475
Barwell 43 SP 4496
Barwick (Som.) 9 ST 5513
Barwick in Elmet 59 SE 3937
Baschurch 40 SJ 4222
Bascote 33 SP 4063
Basford Green 51 SJ 9951
Bashall Eaves 58 SD 6943
Bashley 11 SZ 2496
Basildon (Berks.) 19 SU 6078
Basildon (Essex) 22 TQ 7189
Basingstoke 19 SU 6351
Baslow 53 SK 2572
Bason Bridge 17 ST 3445
Bassaleg 29 ST 2786
Bassenthwaite 62 NY 2332
Bassett 11 SU 4116
Bassingbourn 35 TL 3344
Bassingfield 53 SK 6137
Bassingham 54 SK 9059
Bassingthorpe 44 SK 9628
Basta 113 HU 5295
Baston 45 TF 1114
Bastwick 47 TG 4217
Batcombe (Dorset.) 9 ST 6104
Batcombe (Somer.) 17 ST 6838
Bate Heath 51 SJ 6879
Bath 18 ST 7464
Bathampton 18 ST 7765
Bathealton 8 ST 0724
Batheaston 18 ST 7767
Bathford 18 ST 7866
Bathgate 85 NS 9768
Bathley 54 SK 7759
Bathpool (Corn.) 4 SX 2874
Batley 59 SE 2424
Batsford 33 SP 1834
Battersea 21 TQ 2876
Battisford 37 TM 0554
Battisford Tye 36 TM 0254
Battle (E Susx.) 14 TQ 7416
Battlefield 40 SJ 5117
Battlesbridge 22 TQ 7794
Battlesden 34 SP 9628
Battleton 16 SS 9127
Battramsley 11 SZ 3099
Baughurst 19 SU 5859
Baulking 19 SU 3190
Baumber 55 TF 2174
Baunton 32 SP 0204
Baverstock 10 SU 0231
Bawburgh 47 TG 1508
Bawdeswell 47 TG 0420
Bawdrip 17 ST 3339
Bawdsey 37 TM 3440
Bawtry 53 SK 6592
Baxenden 58 SD 7726
Baxterley 43 SP 2796
Bayble 109 NB 5231
Baydon 19 SU 2877
Bayford (Herts.) 35 TL 3108
Bayhead 109 NF 7468
Bayles 71 NY 7044
Baylham 37 TM 1051
Bayston Hill 40 SJ 4809
Bayton 41 SO 6973
Beachampton 34 SP 7737
Beachley 29 ST 5591
Beacon 8 ST 1705
Beacon End 23 TL 9524
Beacon Hill (Dorset) 10 SY 9794
Beacon's Bottom 20 SU 7895
Beaconsfield 20 SU 9490
Beadlam 66 SE 6584
Beadnell 87 NU 2329
Beaford 6 SS 5514
Beal (N Yorks.) 60 SE 5325
Beal (Northum.) 87 NU 0642
Bealings 37 TM 2348
Beaminster 9 ST 4801
Beamish 72 NZ 2253
Beamsley 65 SE 0752
Bean 21 TQ 5872
Beanacre 18 ST 9066
Beanley 79 NU 0818
Beare Green 12 TQ 1842
Bearley 33 SP 1760
Bearpark 72 NZ 2343
Bearsbridge 71 NY 7857
Bearsden 84 NS 5471
Bearsted 14 TQ 8055
Bearwood 10 SZ 0496
Beattock 77 NT 0702
Beauchamp Roding 22 TL 5809
Beauchief 53 SK 3381
Beaufort 28 SO 1611
Beaulieu 11 SU 3801
Beauly 102 NH 5246
Beaumaris 48 SH 6076
Beaumont (Cumbr.) 70 NY 3459
Beaumont (Essex) 23 TM 1725
Beausale 42 SP 2470
Beaworthy 6 SX 4699
Beazley End 22 TL 7428
Bebington 50 SJ 3384
Bebside 79 NZ 2881
Beccles 47 TM 4290
Becconsall 57 SD 4422
Beck Row 36 TL 6977
Beck Side 62 SD 2382
Beckbury 41 SJ 7601
Beckenham 21 TQ 3769
Beckermet 62 NY 0206
Beckfoot (Cumbr.) 70 NY 0949
Beckford 32 SO 9735
Beckhampton 18 SU 0868
Beckingham (Lincs.) 54 SK 8753
Beckingham (Notts.) 54 SK 7790
Beckington 18 ST 7951
Beckley (E Susx.) 14 TQ 8423
Beckley (Oxon) 33 SP 5611
Beckton 21 TQ 4381
Beckwithshaw 66 SE 2653
Becontree 21 TQ 4886
Bedale 66 SE 2688
Bedburn 72 NZ 1031
Beddau 28 ST 0585
Beddgelert 48 SH 5848
Beddingham 13 TQ 4408
Beddington 21 TQ 3165
Bedfield 37 TM 2266
Bedford 35 TL 0449
Bedhampton 12 SU 6906
Bedingfield 37 TM 1768
Bedlington 79 NZ 2581
Bedlinog 28 SO 0901
Bedmond 35 TL 0903
Bednall 41 SJ 9517
Bedrule 78 NT 6017
Bedstone 40 SO 3675
Bedwas 28 ST 1689
Bedworth 43 SP 3587
Beeby 43 SK 6608
Beech (Hants.) 11 SU 6938
Beech (Staffs.) 51 SJ 8538
Beech Hill 19 SU 6964
Beechingstoke 18 SU 0859
Beedon 19 SU 4877
Beeford 67 TA 1254
Beeley 53 SK 2667
Beelsby 61 TA 2001
Beenham 19 SU 5868
Beer (Devon) 8 SY 2289
Beer Hackett 9 ST 5911
Beercrocombe 8 ST 3220
Beesby 55 TF 4680
Beeson 5 SX 8140
Beeston (Beds.) 35 TL 1648
Beeston (Ches.) 50 SJ 5358
Beeston (Norf.) 46 TF 9015
Beeston (Notts.) 53 SK 5336
Beeston (W Yorks.) 59 SE 2930
Beeston Regis 47 TG 1742
Beeswing 69 NX 8969
Beetham 63 SD 4979
Beetley 46 TF 9718
Begbroke 33 SP 4613
Begelly 24 SN 1107
Beguildy 40 SO 1979
Beighton (Norf.) 47 TG 3808
Beighton (S Yorks.) 53 SK 4483
Beith 82 NS 3454
Bekesbourne 15 TR 1955
Belaugh 47 TG 2818
Belbroughton 41 SO 9177
Belchamp Otten 36 TL 8041
Belchamp St. Paul 36 TL 7942
Belchamp Walter 36 TL 8240
Belchford 54 TF 2975
Belford 87 NU 1033
Belhelvie 105 NJ 9417
Bell Busk 65 SD 9056
Bellabeg 104 NJ 3513
Bellanoch 89 NR 7992
Bellaty 98 NO 2459
Belleau 55 TF 4078
Bellehiglash 104 NJ 1837
Bellerby 65 SE 1192
Belliehill 99 NO 5663
Bellingdon 34 SP 9405
Bellingham 78 NY 8383
Belloch 81 NR 6737
Bellochantuy 80 NR 6632
Bells Yew Green 13 TQ 6136
Bellsbank 75 NS 4804
Bellshill (Northum.) 87 NU 1230
Bellshill (Strath.) 84 NS 7360
Bellspool 85 NT 1635
Bellsquarry 85 NT 0465
Belmaduthy 103 NH 6556
Belmesthorpe 45 TF 0410
Belmont (Lancs.) 58 SD 6715
Belmont (Unst) 113 HP 5600
Belnacraig 104 NJ 3716
Belowda 3 SW 9661
Belper 53 SK 3447
Belsay 79 NZ 1078
Belses 78 NT 5725
Belsford 5 SX 7659
Belstead 37 TM 1341
Belston 75 NS 3820
Belstone 5 SX 6193
Belthorn 58 SD 7124
Beltoft 60 SE 8006
Belton (Humbs.) 60 SE 7806
Belton (Leic.) 43 SK 4420
Belton (Leic.) 44 SK 8101
Belton (Lincs.) 54 SK 9239
Belton (Norf.) 47 TG 4802
Belvedere 21 TQ 4978
Belvoir 54 SK 8133
Bembridge 11 SZ 6488
Bemersyde 86 NT 5933
Bempton 67 TA 1972
Benacre 47 TM 5184
Benenden 14 TQ 8033
Benholm 99 NO 8069
Benington (Herts.) 35 TL 3023
Benington (Lincs.) 55 TF 3946
Benllech 48 SH 5182
Benmore (Central) 90 NN 4125
Bennacott 4 SX 2991
Bennecarrigan 74 NR 9423
Benniworth 55 TF 2081
Benover 14 TQ 7048
Benson 19 SU 6191
Benthall (Northum.) 87 NU 2328
Benthall (Salop) 41 SJ 6602
Bentham 32 SO 9116
Bentley (Hants.) 12 SU 7844
Bentley (Humbs.) 61 TA 0135
Bentley (S Yorks.) 60 SE 5605
Bentley (Warw.) 43 SP 2895
Bentley Heath 42 SP 1676
Bentpath 77 NY 3190
Bentworth 19 SU 6640
Benvie 93 NO 3231
Benwick 45 TL 3490
Beoley 42 SP 0669
Beoraidbeg 95 NM 6793
Bepton 12 SU 8518
Berden 35 TL 4629
Bere Alston 4 SX 4466
Bere Ferrers 5 SX 4563
Bere Regis 10 SY 8494
Berea 24 SM 7929
Berepper 2 SW 6522
Bergh Apton 47 TG 3000
Berinsfield 19 SU 5696
Berkeley 29 ST 6899
Berkhamsted 34 SP 9907
Berkley 18 ST 8049
Berkswell 42 SP 2479
Bermondsey 21 TQ 3579
Bernisdale 100 NG 4050
Berrick Salome 19 SU 6293
Berriew 40 SJ 1801
Berrington (Northum.) 87 NU 0043
Berrington (Salop) 40 SJ 5206
Berrow 17 ST 2952
Berrow Green 32 SO 7458
Berry Hill 29 SO 5712
Berry Pomeroy 5 SX 8261
Berryhillock 104 NJ 5060
Berrynarbor 6 SS 5546
Bersham 50 SJ 3048
Bersted 12 SU 9300
Berwick 13 TQ 5105
Berwick Bassett 15 SU 0973
Berwick Hill 79 NZ 1775
Berwick St. James 10 SU 0739
Berwick St. John 10 ST 9421
Berwick St. Leonard 10 ST 9233
Berwick-upon-Tweed 87 NT 9953
Besford 32 SO 9144
Bessacarr 60 SE 6101
Bessels Leigh 33 SP 4501
Bessingham 47 TG 1636
Besthorpe (Norf.) 47 TM 0695
Besthorpe (Notts.) 54 SK 8264
Beswick 61 TA 0148
Betchworth 21 TQ 2149
Bethel (Gwynedd) 48 SH 5265
Bethersden 15 TQ 9240
Bethesda (Dyfed) 24 SN 0918
Bethesda (Gwyn.) 48 SH 6266
Bethlehem 25 SN 6825
Bethnal Green 21 TQ 3583
Betley 51 SJ 7548
Betsham 22 TQ 6071
Betteshanger 15 TR 3152
Bettiscombe 9 SY 3999
Bettisfield 50 SJ 4535
Betton (Salop) 51 SJ 6836
Bettws Bledrws 26 SN 5952
Bettws Cedewain 40 SO 1296
Bettws Evan 26 SN 3047
Bettws Gwerfil Goch 49 SJ 0346
Bettws Malpas 29 ST 3090
Bettws-Newydd 29 SO 3606
Bettyhill 111 NC 7061
Betws (Dyfed) 25 SN 6311
Betws (Mid Glam.) 28 SS 9086
Betws Garmon 48 SH 5357
Betws-y-coed 49 SH 7956
Betws-yn-Rhos 49 SH 9073
Beulah (Dyfed) 26 SN 2846
Beulah (Powys) 27 SN 9251
Bevendean 13 TQ 3406
Bevercotes 53 SK 6972
Beverley 61 TA 0339
Beverston 18 ST 8693
Bevington 29 ST 6596
Bewaldeth 62 NY 2134
Bewcastle 71 NY 5674
Bewdley 41 SO 7875
Bewerley 65 SE 1564
Bewholme 67 TA 1650
Bexhill 14 TQ 7407
Bexley 21 TQ 4973
Bexwell 46 TF 6303
Beyton 36 TL 9363
Bibury 32 SP 1106
Bicester 33 SP 5822
Bickenhall 8 ST 2818
Bickenhill 42 SP 1882
Bicker 55 TF 2237
Bickerstaffe 57 SD 4404
Bickerton (Ches.) 50 SJ 5052
Bickerton (N Yorks.) 66 SE 4450
Bickington (Devon.) 6 SS 5332
Bickington (Devon.) 5 SX 7972
Bickleigh (Devon.) 8 SS 9407
Bickleigh (Devon.) 5 SX 5262
Bickleton 6 SS 5031
Bickley (Gtr. London) 21 TQ 4268
Bickley Moss 50 SJ 5448
Bicknacre 22 TL 7802
Bicknoller 16 ST 1039
Bicknor 14 TQ 8658
Bickton 10 SU 1412
Bicton (Salop) 40 SJ 4415
Bicton (Salop) 40 SO 2882
Bidborough 13 TQ 5643
Biddenden 14 TQ 8538
Biddenham 34 TL 0250
Biddestone 18 ST 8673
Biddisham 17 ST 3853
Biddlesden 34 SP 6340
Biddlestone 78 NT 9508
Biddulph 51 SJ 8857
Biddulph Moor 51 SJ 9057
Bideford 6 SS 4526
Bidford-on-Avon 32 SP 1052
Bielby 60 SE 7843
Bieldside 99 NJ 8702
Bierley 11 SZ 5077
Bierton 34 SP 8415
Bigbury 5 SX 6646
Bigbury-on-Sea 5 SX 6544
Bigby 61 TA 0507
Biggar (Cumbr.) 64 SD 1966
Biggar (Strath.) 85 NT 0437
Biggin (Derby.) 52 SK 1559
Biggin (Derby.) 53 SK 2548
Biggin (N. Yorks.) 60 SE 5434
Biggin Hill 21 TQ 4159
Biggleswade 35 TL 1944
Bighouse 111 NC 8964
Bighton 11 SU 6134
Bignor 12 SU 9814
Bilberry 4 SX 0159
Bilborough 53 SK 5241
Bilbrook (Staffs.) 41 SJ 8703
Bilbrough 60 SE 5246
Bilbster 112 ND 2852
Bildeston 36 TL 9949
Billericay 22 TQ 6794
Billesdon 44 SK 7103
Billesley 32 SP 1456
Billingborough 55 TF 1134
Billinge 57 SD 5300
Billingford (Norf.) 46 TG 0120
Billingford (Norf.) 37 TM 1678
Billingham 73 NZ 4624
Billinghay 54 TF 1554
Billingley 59 SE 4304
Billingshurst 12 TQ 0825
Billingsley 41 SO 7085
Billington (Beds.) 34 SP 9422
Billington (Lancs.) 58 SD 7235
Billockby 47 TG 4213
Billy Row 72 NZ 1637
Bilsborrow 57 SD 5140
Bilsby 55 TF 4776
Bilsington 15 TR 0434
Bilsthorpe 53 SK 6560
Bilston (Lothian) 85 NT 2664
Bilston (W Mids) 41 SO 9496
Bilstone 43 SK 3606
Bilting 15 TR 0549
Bilton (Humbs.) 61 TA 1532
Bilton (N Yorks.) 66 SE 4750
Bilton (Northum.) 79 NU 2210
Bilton (Warw.) 43 SP 4873
Binbrook 55 TF 2093
Bincombe 9 SY 6884
Binegar 17 ST 6149
Binfield 20 SU 8471
Binfield Heath 20 SU 7478
Bingfield 79 NY 9772
Bingham 54 SK 7039
Bingham's Melcombe 9 ST 7701
Bingley 59 SE 1039
Binham 46 TF 9839
Binley (Hants.) 19 SU 4153
Binley (W Mids) 43 SP 3778
Binniehill 84 NS 8572
Binstead (Hants.) 12 SU 7741
Binstead (I. of W.) 11 SZ 5792
Binton 32 SP 1454
Bintree 46 TG 0123
Binweston 40 SJ 3004
Birch (Essex) 23 TL 9419
Birch (Gtr. Mches.) 58 SD 8507
Birch Green 23 TL 9418
Birch Vale 52 SK 0286
Bircham Newton 46 TF 7633
Bircham Tofts 46 TF 7732
Birchanger 22 TL 5122
Bircher 30 SO 4765
Birchgrove (S Glam.) 28 ST 1679
Birchgrove (W Glam.) 25 SS 7098
Birchington 15 TR 3069
Birchover 53 SK 2462
Bircotes 53 SK 6391
Bird End 42 SP 0193
Birdbrook 36 TL 7041
Birdham 12 SU 8200
Birdingbury 43 SP 4368
Birdlip 32 SO 9214
Birdsgreen 41 SO 7685
Birdston 84 NS 6575
Birdwell 59 SE 3401
Birdwood 32 SO 7318
Birgham 87 NT 7939
Birkenhead 50 SJ 3188
Birkenhills 105 NJ 7445
Birkenshaw (Strath.) 84 NS 6962
Birkenshaw (W Yorks.) 59 SE 2028
Birkhall 98 NO 3493
Birkhill Feus 93 NO 3433
Birkin 60 SE 5226
Birley 30 SO 4553
Birling (Kent) 14 TQ 6860
Birling (Northum.) 79 NU 2406
Birlingham 32 SO 9343
Birmingham 42 SP 0787
Birnam 98 NO 0341
Birness 105 NJ 9933
Birse 99 NO 5596
Birsemore 99 NO 5297
Birstall 43 SK 5809
Birstall Smithies 59 SE 2226
Birstwith 66 SE 2459
Birtley (Here & W) 40 SO 3669
Birtley (Northum.) 78 NY 8778
Birtley (Tyne and Wear) 72 NZ 2755
Birts Street 32 SO 7836
Bisbrooke 44 SP 8899
Bishampton 32 SO 9851
Bishop Auckland 72 NZ 2029
Bishop Burton 61 SE 9839
Bishop Middleham 72 NZ 3231
Bishop Monkton 66 SE 3266
Bishop Norton 54 SK 9892
Bishop Sutton 17 ST 5859
Bishop Thornton 66 SE 2663
Bishop Wilton 67 SE 7955
Bishop's Castle 40 SO 3288
Bishop's Caundle 9 ST 6912
Bishop's Cleeve 32 SO 9527
Bishop's Frome 31 SO 6648
Bishop's Itchington 33 SP 3857
Bishop's Nympton 7 SS 7523
Bishop's Offley 41 SJ 7729
Bishop's Stortford 22 TL 4821
Bishop's Sutton 11 SU 6031
Bishop's Tachbrook 33 SP 3161
Bishop's Tawton 6 SS 5630
Bishop's Waltham 11 SU 5517
Bishop's Wood (Staffs.) 41 SJ 8309
Bishop's Caundle 9 ST 6913
Bishopbriggs 84 NS 6070
Bishops Cannings 18 SU 0364
Bishops Lydeard 16 ST 1629
Bishopsbourne 15 TR 1852
Bishopsteignton 8 SX 9173
Bishopstoke 11 SU 4619
Bishopston (W. Glam.) 15 SS 5889
Bishopstone (Bucks.) 34 SP 8010
Bishopstone (E Susx) 13 TQ 4701
Bishopstone (Here & W) 30 SO 4143
Bishopstone (Wilts.) 10 SU 0625
Bishopstone (Wilts.) 18 SU 2483
Bishopswood (Somer.) 8 ST 2512
Bishopsworth 29 ST 5768
Bishopthorpe 60 SE 5947
Bishopton (Durham) 72 NZ 3621
Bishopton (Strath.) 82 NS 4371
Bishton 29 ST 3887
Bisley (Glos.) 32 SO 9005
Bisley (Surrey) 20 SU 9559
Bispham 57 SD 3139
Bissoe 2 SW 7741
Bisterne Close 11 SU 2202
Bitchfield 44 SK 9828
Bittadon 6 SS 5441
Bittaford 5 SX 6557
Bittering 46 TF 9317
Bitterley 40 SO 5577
Bitterne 11 SU 4513
Bitteswell 43 SP 5385
Bitton 29 ST 6769
Bix 20 SU 7285
Blaby 43 SP 5697
Black Bourton 33 SP 2804
Black Callerton 72 NZ 1769
Black Crofts 89 NM 9234
Black Dog (Devon) 7 SS 8009
Black Notley 22 TL 7620
Black Torrington 6 SS 4605
Blackacre 77 NY 0490
Blackadder 87 NT 8452
Blackawton 5 SX 8050
Blackborough 8 ST 0909
Blackborough End 46 TF 6614
Blackboys 13 TQ 5220
Blackbrook (Staffs.) 51 SJ 7639
Blackburn (Grampn.) 105 NJ 8212
Blackburn (Lancs.) 58 SD 6827
Blackburn (Lothian) 85 NS 9865
Blackden Heath 51 SJ 7871
Blackdog (Grampn.) 105 NJ 9514
Blackfield 11 SU 4402
Blackford (Cumbr.) 70 NY 3962
Blackford (Somer.) 17 ST 4147
Blackford (Somer.) 17 ST 6526
Blackford (Tays.) 91 NN 8908
Blackfordby 43 SK 3318
Blackgang 11 SZ 4876
Blackhall Colliery 73 NZ 4539
Blackhaugh 86 NT 4238
Blackheath (Essex) 23 TM 0021
Blackheath (Surrey) 20 TQ 0346
Blackhill (Grampn.) 105 NK 0843
Blackland 18 SU 0168
Blackley 58 SD 8503
Blacklunans 98 NO 1560
Blackmill 28 SS 9386
Blackmoor 12 SU 7833
Blackmoor Gate 7 SS 6443
Blackmore 22 TL 6001
Blackmore End 36 TL 7430
Blackness 85 NT 0579
Blacknest 12 SU 7941
Blacko 58 SD 8541
Blackpill 25 SS 6290
Blackpool (Lancs.) 57 SD 3035
Blackpool Gate 71 NY 5377
Blackridge 84 NS 8967
Blackrock (Gwent) 28 SO 2112
Blackrock (Islay) 80 NR 3063
Blackrod 58 SD 6110
Blackshaw 70 NY 0465
Blackstone 13 TQ 2416
Blackthorn 34 SP 6219
Blackthorpe 36 TL 9063
Blacktoft 60 SE 8424
Blacktop 105 NJ 8604
Blackwater (Corn.) 2 SW 7346
Blackwater (Hants.) 20 SU 8559
Blackwater (I. of W.) 11 SZ 5086
Blackwater (Suff.) 37 TM 5077
Blackwaterfoot 74 NR 8928
Blackwell (Derby.) 52 SK 1272
Blackwell (Here & W) 41 SO 9972
Blackwood (Gwent) 28 ST 1797
Blackwood (Strath.) 84 NS 7943
Blackwood Hill 51 SJ 9255
Blacon 50 SJ 3767
Bladnoch 68 NX 4254
Bladon 33 SP 4414
Blaenannerch 26 SN 2449
Blaenau Ffestiniog 49 SH 7045
Blaenavon 29 SO 2509
Blaenawey 29 SO 2919
Blaengarw 28 SS 9092
Blaengwrach 28 SN 8605
Blaengwynfi 28 SS 8996
Blaenplwyf 26 SN 5775
Blaenporth 26 SN 2648
Blaenrhondda 28 SS 9299
Blaenwaun 25 SN 2327
Blagdon (Avon) 17 ST 5059
Blagdon (Devon) 5 SX 8561
Blagdon Hill (Somerset) 8 ST 2118
Blaich 96 NN 0476
Blaina 28 SO 2008
Blair Atholl 97 NN 8765
Blair Drummond 91 NS 7398
Blairgowrie 98 NO 1745
Blairhall 85 NT 0089
Blairingone 91 NS 9896
Blairlogie 91 NS 8396
Blairskaith 84 NS 5975
Blaisdon 32 SO 7016
Blakebrook 41 SO 8077
Blakedown 41 SO 8778
Blakelaw 87 NT 7730
Blakemere 30 SO 3641
Blakeney (Glos.) 29 SO 6707
Blakeney (Norf.) 46 TG 0243
Blakenhall (Ches.) 51 SJ 7247
Blakenhall (W Mids) 41 SO 9297
Blakeshall 41 SO 8381
Blakesley 34 SP 6250
Blanchland 72 NY 9650
Bland Hill 65 SE 2053
Blandford Forum 10 ST 8806
Blandford St. Mary 10 ST 8805
Blanefield 84 NS 5579
Blankney 54 TF 0660
Blantyre 84 NS 6857
Blar a' Chaorainn 96 NN 1068
Blarghour 89 NM 9913
Blarmachfoldach 96 NN 0969
Blashford 10 SU 1406
Blaston 44 SP 8095
Blatherwycke 44 SP 9795
Blawith 62 SD 2888
Blaxhall 37 TM 3657
Blaxton 60 SE 6600
Blaydon 72 NZ 1863
Bleadon 17 ST 3456
Blean 15 TR 1260
Bleasby 54 SK 7049
Blebocraigs 93 NO 4214
Bleddfa 40 SO 2068
Bledington 33 SP 2422
Bledlow 34 SP 7802
Bledlow Ridge 20 SU 7998
Blegbie 86 NT 4861
Blencarn 63 NY 6331
Blencogo 70 NY 1947
Blencow 63 NY 4532
Blendworth 12 SU 7113
Blennerhasset 70 NY 1741
Bletchingdon 33 SP 5017
Bletchingley 21 TQ 3250
Bletchley (Bucks.) 34 SP 8733
Bletchley (Salop) 51 SJ 6233

Bletherston 230 Broadwoodwidger

Bletherston 24 SN 0721
Bletsoe 34 TL 0258
Blewbury 19 SU 5385
Blickling 47 TG 1728
Blidworth 53 SK 5855
Blindcrake 62 NY 1434
Blindley Heath 21 TQ 3645
Blisland 4 SX 0973
Bliss Gate 41 SO 7472
Blissford 10 SU 1713
Blisworth 34 SP 7253
Blo Norton 36 TM 0179
Blockley 32 SP 1634
Blofield 47 TG 3309
Blore 52 SK 1349
Bloxham 33 SP 4235
Bloxwich 42 SJ 9902
Bloxworth 10 SY 8894
Blubberhouses 65 SE 1655
Blue Anchor (Somer.) 16 ST 0343
Blue Bell Hill 14 TQ 7462
Blunderston 47 TM 5197
Blunham 35 TL 1551
Blunsdon St. Andrew 18 SU 1389
Bluntisham 45 TL 3674
Blyborough 54 SK 9394
Blyford 37 TM 4276
Blymhill 41 SJ 8112
Blyth (Northum.) 79 NZ 3181
Blyth (Notts.) 53 SK 6287
Blyth Bridge 85 NT 1345
Blythburgh 37 TM 4575
Blythe Bridge 51 SJ 9541
Blyton 54 SK 8594
Bo'Ness 85 NS 9981
Boarhills 93 NO 5614
Boarhunt 11 SU 6008
Boarshead 13 TQ 5332
Boarstall 34 SP 6214
Boasley Cross 5 SX 5093
Boat of Garten 103 NH 9419
Boath 108 NH 5773
Bobbing 14 TQ 8865
Bobbington 41 SO 8090
Bobbingworth 22 TL 5305
Bocaddon 4 SX 1758
Bocking 22 TL 7623
Bocking Churchstreet 22 TL 7525
Boconnoc 4 SX 1460
Boddam (Grampn.) 105 NK 1342
Boddam (Shetld.) 113 HU 3915
Boddington 32 SO 8925
Bodedern 48 SH 3380
Bodelwyddan 49 SJ 0075
Bodenham (Here & W) 31 SO 5251
Bodenham (Wilts.) 10 SU 1626
Bodewryd 48 SH 3990
Bodfari 49 SJ 0970
Bodffordd 48 SH 4276
Bodfuan 48 SH 3237
Bodham Street 47 TG 1240
Bodiam 14 TQ 7826
Bodicote 33 SP 4537
Bodieve 3 SW 9973
Bodle Street Green 13 TQ 6514
Bodmin 4 SX 0767
Bodney 46 TL 8398
Bodorgan 48 SH 3867
Bog, The 40 SO 3597
Bogbrae 105 NK 0335
Bogend 82 NS 3932
Bogmoor 104 NJ 3562
Bogniebrae 104 NJ 5945
Bognor Regis 12 SZ 9399
Bograxie 105 NJ 7119
Bogside 84 NS 8353
Bogton 105 NJ 6751
Bogue 69 NX 6481
Bohortha 3 SW 8632
Bohuntine 96 NN 2882
Bojewyan 2 SW 3934
Bolam 72 NZ 1922
Bold Heath 50 SJ 5389
Boldon 72 NZ 3661
Boldon Colliery 72 NZ 3462
Boldre 11 SZ 3198
Boldron 72 NZ 0314
Bole 54 SK 7987
Bolehill 53 SK 2955
Boleside 86 NT 4933
Bolham Water 8 ST 1612
Bolingey 2 SW 7653
Bollington (Ches.) 51 SJ 7286
Bollington (Ches.) 51 SJ 9377
Bolney 13 TQ 2622
Bolnhurst 35 TL 0859
Bolshan 99 NO 6252
Bolsover 53 SK 4770
Bolsterstone 59 SK 2696
Bolstone 31 SO 5532
Boltby 66 SE 4886
Bolton (Cumbr.) 63 NY 6323
Bolton (Gtr Mches.) 58 SD 7108
Bolton (Humbs.) 61 SE 7752
Bolton (Lothian) 86 NT 5070
Bolton (Northum.) 79 NU 1013
Bolton Abbey 65 SE 0754
Bolton Percy 60 SE 5341
Bolton Upon Dearne 60 SE 4502
Bolton by Bowland 58 SD 7849
Bolton le Sands 64 SD 4867
Bolton-on-Swale 66 SE 2599
Boltonfellend 71 NY 4768
Boltongate 70 NY 2340
Bolventor 4 SX 1876
Bomere Heath 40 SJ 4719
Bonar-Bridge 108 NH 6191
Bonawe 89 NN 0133
Bonby 61 TA 0015
Boncath 26 SN 2038
Bonchester Bridge 78 NT 5811
Bondleigh 7 SS 6504
Bonehill 42 SK 1902
Bonhill 90 NS 3980
Boningale 41 SJ 8102
Bonjedward 78 NT 6523
Bonkle 84 NS 8356
Bonnington (Kent) 15 TR 0536
Bonnington (Lothian) 85 NT 1269
Bonnington Smiddy 93 NO 5739
Bonnybank 93 NO 3503
Bonnybridge 84 NS 8280
Bonnykelly 105 NJ 8553
Bonnyrigg 85 NT 3065
Bonnyton (Tays.) 93 NO 3338
Bonnyton (Tays.) 99 NO 6655
Bonsall 53 SK 2758
Bont 29 SO 3819
Bont Newydd (Gwyn.) 39 SH 7720
Bont-Dolgadfan 39 SH 8800
Bontddu 39 SH 6618
Bontgoch Elerch 39 SN 6886
Bontnewydd (Gwyn.) 48 SH 4859
Bontuchel 49 SJ 0857
Bonvilston 28 ST 0674
Booker 20 SU 8491
Booley 41 SJ 5725
Boosbeck 73 NZ 6516
Boot 62 NY 1701
Boothby Graffoe 54 SK 9859
Boothby Pagnell 54 SK 9730
Boothstown 58 SD 7200
Bootle (Cumbr.) 62 SD 1088
Bootle (Mers.) 50 SJ 3394
Boquhan 84 NS 5387
Boraston 41 SO 6170
Borden (Kent) 14 TQ 8863
Bordley 65 SD 9465
Bordon 12 SU 7935
Boreham (Essex) 22 TL 7509
Boreham (Wilts.) 18 ST 8944
Boreham Street 13 TQ 6611
Borehamwood 21 TQ 1996
Boreland (Dumf & G) 77 NY 1790
Boreraig 100 NG 1853
Borgie 111 NC 6759
Borgue (Dumf & G) 69 NX 6248
Borgue (Highld.) 112 ND 1325
Borley 36 TL 8442
Bornesketaig 100 NG 3771
Borness 69 NX 6145
Borough Green 21 TQ 6057
Boroughbridge 66 SE 3966
Borras Head 50 SJ 3653
Borrowash 53 SK 4134
Borrowby 66 SE 4289
Borrowdale (Cumbr.) 62 NY 2514
Borth 38 SN 6089
Borthwickbrae 77 NT 4113
Borthwickshiels 77 NT 4315
Borve (Barra) 109 NF 6501
Borve (I. O. Lewis) 109 NB 4055
Borve (Island of Skye) 100 NG 4448
Borwick 64 SD 5273
Bosavern 2 SW 3730
Bosbury 31 SO 6943
Boscastle 4 SX 0990
Boscombe (Dorset) 10 SZ 1191
Boscombe (Wilts.) 11 SU 2038
Boscoppa 4 SX 0353
Bosham 12 SU 8004
Bosherton 24 SR 9694
Boskednan 2 SW 4434
Bosley 51 SJ 9165
Bossall 66 SE 7160
Bossiney 4 SX 0688
Bossingham 15 TR 1549
Bostock Green 51 SJ 6769
Boston 55 TF 3244
Boston Spa 59 SE 4245
Botallack 2 SW 3632
Botcheston 43 SK 4804
Botesdale 37 TM 0475
Bothal 79 NZ 2386
Bothamsall 53 SK 6773
Bothel 62 NY 1838
Bothenhampton 9 SY 4791
Botley (Bucks.) 34 SP 9802
Botley (Hants.) 11 SU 5112
Botley (Oxon.) 33 SP 4806
Botolphs 12 TQ 1909
Bottacks 102 NH 4860
Bottesford (Humbs.) 60 SE 9107
Bottesford (Leic.) 54 SK 8038
Bottisham 36 TL 5460
Bottomcraig 93 NO 3724
Bottoms 58 SD 9321
Botusfleming 4 SX 4061
Botwnnog 48 SH 2631
Boughrood 30 SO 1239
Boughspring 29 ST 5597
Boughton (Norf.) 46 TF 7002
Boughton (Northants.) 44 SP 7565
Boughton (Notts.) 53 SK 6768
Boughton Aluph 15 TR 0348
Boughton Green 14 TQ 7651
Boughton Lees 15 TR 0247
Boughton Malherbe 14 TQ 8849
Boughton Street 15 TR 0559
Boulby 73 NZ 7519
Bouldon 40 SO 5485
Boulmer 79 NU 2614
Boultham 54 SK 9568
Bourn 35 TL 3256
Bourne (Lincs.) 45 TF 0920
Bourne End (Beds.) 34 SP 9644
Bourne End (Bucks.) 20 SU 8987
Bourne End (Herts.) 34 TL 0206
Bournebridge 21 TQ 5194
Bournemouth 10 SZ 0991
Bournes Green 32 SO 9104
Bournheath 41 SO 9474
Bournmoor 72 NZ 3051
Bournville 42 SP 0480
Bourton (Avon) 17 ST 3864
Bourton (Dorset) 17 ST 7630
Bourton (Oxon.) 18 SU 2387
Bourton (Salop) 41 SO 5996
Bourton on Dunsmore 43 SP 4370
Bourton-on-the-Hill 32 SP 1732
Bourton-on-the-Water 32 SP 1620
Bousd 94 NM 2563
Boveney 20 SU 9377
Boverton 28 SS 9868
Bovey Tracey 5 SX 8178
Bovingdon 35 TL 0103
Bovington Camp 10 SY 8389
Bow (Burray) (Ork) 113 ND 4897
Bow (Devon.) 7 SS 7201
Bow (Flotta) (Ork) 113 ND 3693
Bow Brickhill 34 SP 9034
Bow Street 38 SN 6284
Bow of Fife 93 NO 3112
Bowbank 63 NY 9423
Bowburn 72 NZ 3038
Bowcombe 11 SZ 4786
Bowd 8 SY 1190
Bowden (Borders) 86 NT 5530
Bowden (Devon.) 5 SX 8448
Bowden Hill 18 ST 9367
Bowdon 51 SJ 7586
Bower 112 ND 2463
Bowerchalke 10 SU 0122
Bowermadden 112 ND 2364
Bowers Gifford 22 TQ 7588
Bowershall 92 NT 0991
Bowertower 112 ND 2362
Bowes 72 NY 9913
Bowhill 77 NT 4227
Bowley 31 SO 5352
Bowlhead Green 12 SU 9138
Bowling 82 NS 4473
Bowling Bank 50 SJ 3948
Bowling Green 32 SO 8151
Bowmanstead 62 SD 3096
Bowmore 80 NR 3159
Bowness-on-Solway 70 NY 2262
Bowness-on-Windermere 62 SD 4097
Bowsden 87 NT 9941
Bowthorpe 47 TG 1709
Box (Glos.) 32 SO 8600
Box (Wilts.) 18 ST 8268
Boxbush (Glos.) 32 SO 7412
Boxford (Berks.) 19 SU 4271
Boxford (Suff.) 36 TL 9640
Boxgrove 12 SU 9007
Boxley 14 TQ 7759
Boxted (Suff) 36 TL 8251
Boxworth 35 TL 3464
Boyden Gate 15 TR 2264
Boylestone 52 SK 1835
Boyndie 104 NJ 6463
Boyndlie 105 NJ 9162
Boynton 67 TA 1368
Boysack 99 NO 6249
Boyton (Corn.) 4 SX 3192
Boyton (Suff.) 37 TM 3747
Boyton (Wilts.) 10 ST 9539
Bozeat 34 SP 9059
Braaid 56 SC 3176
Brabling Green 37 TM 2964
Brabourne 15 TR 1041
Brabourne Lees 15 TR 0840
Brabstermire 112 ND 3169
Bracadale 100 NG 3538
Braceborough 45 TF 0713
Bracebridge Heath 54 SK 9767
Braceby 54 TF 0135
Bracewell 58 SD 8648
Brackenfield 53 SK 3759
Bracklesham 12 SZ 8196
Brackletter 96 NN 1882
Brackley (Northants.) 33 SP 5837
Brackley (Strath.) 81 NR 7941
Bracknell 20 SU 8769
Braco 91 NN 8309
Bracobrae 104 NJ 5053
Bracon Ash 47 TM 1899
Bracora 95 NM 7192
Bracorina 95 NM 7292
Bradbourne 53 SK 2052
Bradbury 72 NZ 3128
Bradda 56 SC 1970
Bradden 33 SP 6448
Braddock 4 SX 1662
Bradenham 20 SU 8297
Bradenstoke 18 SU 0079
Bradfield (Berks.) 19 SU 6072
Bradfield (Essex) 23 TM 1430
Bradfield (Norf.) 47 TG 2633
Bradfield (S Yorks.) 53 SK 2692
Bradfield Combust 36 TL 8957
Bradfield Green 51 SJ 6859
Bradfield St. Clare 36 TL 9057
Bradfield St. George 36 TL 9160
Bradford (Devon.) 6 SS 4207
Bradford (Northum.) 87 NU 1532
Bradford (W Yorks.) 59 SE 1633
Bradford Abbas 9 ST 5814
Bradford Leigh 18 ST 8362
Bradford Peverell 9 SY 6592
Bradford on Avon 18 ST 8260
Bradford-on-Tone 8 ST 1722
Brading 11 SZ 6087
Bradley (Derby.) 53 SK 2145
Bradley (Hants.) 19 SU 6341
Bradley (Here & W) 32 SO 9860
Bradley (Humbs.) 61 TA 2406
Bradley (N Yorks.) 65 SE 0380
Bradley (Staffs.) 41 SJ 8717
Bradley Green 32 SO 9861
Bradley in the Moors 52 SK 0541
Bradmore 53 SK 5831
Bradninch 8 SS 9903
Bradnop 52 SK 0155
Bradpole 9 SY 4794
Bradshaw (Gtr. Mches.) 58 SD 7312
Bradstone 4 SX 3880
Bradwell (Bucks.) 34 SP 8339
Bradwell (Derby.) 52 SK 1781
Bradwell (Essex) 22 TL 8023
Bradwell (Norf.) 47 TG 5003
Bradwell Green 51 SJ 7563
Bradwell Grove 33 SP 2308
Bradwell Waterside 23 TL 9907
Bradwell-on-Sea 23 TM 0006
Bradworthy 6 SS 3213
Brae (Highld.) 106 NG 8185
Brae (Highld.) 103 NH 6662
Brae (Shetld.) 113 HU 3567
Brae of Achnahaird 110 NB 9913
Braedownie 98 NO 2875
Braefield 102 NH 4130
Braegrum 92 NO 0024
Braehead (Strath.) 84 NS 8134
Braehead (Strath.) 84 NS 9550
Braehead (Tays.) 99 NO 6852
Braehead (Wigtown.) 68 NX 4252
Braemar 98 NO 1592
Braemore 112 ND 0630
Braeside 82 NS 2375
Braeswick 113 HY 6037
Brafferton (Durham) 72 NZ 2921
Brafferton (N Yorks.) 66 SE 4370
Brafield-on-the-Green 34 SP 8158
Bragar 109 NB 2847
Bragbury End 35 TL 2621
Braidwood 84 NS 8448
Braigo 80 NR 2369
Brailes 33 SP 3139
Brailsford 53 SK 2541
Braintree 22 TL 7622
Braiseworth 37 TM 1371
Braishfield 11 SU 3725
Braithwaite 62 NY 2323
Braithwell 53 SK 5394
Bramber 12 TQ 1810
Bramcote (Notts.) 53 SK 5037
Bramdean 11 SU 6127
Bramerton 47 TG 2904
Bramfield (Herts.) 35 TL 2915
Bramfield (Suff.) 37 TM 4073
Bramford 37 TM 1246
Bramhall 51 SJ 8984
Bramham 59 SE 4242
Bramhope 59 SE 2543
Bramley (Hants.) 19 SU 6358
Bramley (S Yorks.) 53 SK 4892
Bramley (Surrey) 12 TQ 0044
Brampford Speke 8 SX 9298
Brampton (Cambs.) 45 TL 2170
Brampton (Cumbr.) 71 NY 5361
Brampton (Cumbr.) 63 NY 6723
Brampton (Lincs.) 54 SK 8479
Brampton (Norf.) 47 TG 2224
Brampton (S Yorks.) 59 SE 4101
Brampton (Suff.) 47 TM 4381
Brampton Abbotts 29 SO 6026
Brampton Ash 44 SP 7887
Brampton Bryan 40 SO 3672
Bramshall 52 SK 0633
Bramshaw 11 SU 2615
Bramshill 20 SU 7461
Bramshott 12 SU 8432
Bran End 22 TL 6525
Branault 95 NM 5369
Brancaster 46 TF 7743
Brancepeth 72 NZ 2238
Branchill 103 NJ 0852
Branderburgh 104 NJ 2371
Brandesburton 61 TA 1147
Brandeston 37 TM 2460
Brandiston 47 TG 1321
Brandon (Durham) 72 NZ 2439
Brandon (Lincs.) 54 SK 9048
Brandon (Northum.) 79 NU 0417
Brandon (Suff.) 46 TL 7886
Brandon (Warw.) 43 SP 4076
Brandon Bank 46 TL 6289
Brandon Creek 46 TL 6091
Brandon Parva 47 TG 0708
Brands Hatch 21 TQ 5764
Brandsby 66 SE 5872
Brane 2 SW 4028
Branscombe 8 SY 1988
Bransford 32 SO 7952
Bransgore 10 SZ 1897
Branston (Leic.) 44 SK 8029
Branston (Lincs.) 54 TF 0167
Branston (Staffs.) 42 SK 2221
Branstone 11 SZ 5583
Brant Broughton 54 SK 9154
Brantham 37 TM 1034
Branthwaite (Cumbr) 62 NY 0525
Brantingham 61 SE 9429
Branton (Northum.) 79 NU 0416
Branxholme 77 NT 4611
Branxton 87 NT 8937
Brassington 53 SK 2354
Brasted 21 TQ 4755
Brasted Chart 21 TQ 4653
Bratoft 55 TF 4765
Brattleby 54 SK 9480
Bratton 18 ST 9152
Bratton Clovelly 5 SX 4691
Bratton Fleming 7 SS 6437
Bratton Seymour 17 ST 6729
Braughing 35 TL 3925
Braunston (Leic.) 44 SK 8306
Braunston (Northants.) 43 SP 5366
Braunstone 43 SK 5502
Braunton 6 SS 4836
Brawby 67 SE 7378
Brawl 111 NC 8066
Brawlbin 112 ND 0757
Bray 20 SU 9079
Bray Shop 4 SX 3374
Braybrooke 44 SP 7684
Brayford 7 SS 6834
Brayton 60 SE 6030
Brazacott 4 SX 2691
Breachwood Green 35 TL 1522
Breaclete 109 NB 1537
Breadsall 53 SK 3639
Breadstone 32 SO 7101
Breadstone 32 SO 7000
Breage 2 SW 6128
Bream 29 SO 6005
Breamore 10 SU 1517
Brean 17 ST 2955
Brearton 66 SE 3260
Breasclete 109 NB 2135
Breaston 53 SK 4533
Brechfa 26 SN 5230
Brechin 99 NO 5960
Breckles 46 TL 9594
Breckrey 100 NG 5061
Brecon 28 SO 0428
Bredbury 51 SJ 9292
Brede 14 TQ 8218
Bredenbury 31 SO 6058
Bredfield 37 TM 2653
Bredgar 14 TQ 8860
Bredhurst 14 TQ 7962
Bredon 32 SO 9236
Bredon's Norton 32 SO 9339
Bredwardine 30 SO 3344
Breedon on the Hill 43 SK 4022
Breich 85 NS 9560
Breighton 60 SE 7033
Breinton 30 SO 4739
Bremhill 18 ST 9873
Brenchley 14 TQ 6741
Brendon (Devon) 7 SS 7648
Brenish 109 NA 9926
Brent 21 TQ 2084
Brent Eleigh 36 TL 9447
Brent Knoll 17 ST 3350
Brent Pelham 35 TL 4330
Brentford 21 TQ 1778
Brentwood 22 TQ 5993
Brenzett 15 TR 0027
Brereton 42 SK 0516
Brereton Green 51 SJ 7764
Brereton Heath 51 SJ 8064
Bressingham 47 TM 0780
Bretby 43 SK 2923
Bretford 43 SP 4277
Bretforton 32 SP 0943
Bretherton 57 SD 4720
Brettenham (Norf) 46 TL 9383
Brettenham (Suff.) 36 TL 9653
Bretton 50 SJ 3563
Brewham 17 ST 7136
Brewood 41 SJ 8808
Briantspuddle 10 SY 8193
Bricket Wood 35 TL 1301
Bricklehampton 32 SO 9842
Bride 56 NX 4501
Bridekirk 62 NY 1133
Bridell 26 SN 1742
Bridestowe 5 SX 5189
Brideswell 104 NJ 5739
Bridford 5 SX 8186
Bridge 15 TR 1854
Bridge End (Lincs.) 55 TF 1436
Bridge Green 35 TL 4636
Bridge Sollers 30 SO 4142
Bridge Street 36 TL 8749
Bridge Trafford 50 SJ 4471
Bridge of Alford 104 NJ 5617
Bridge of Allan 91 NS 7897
Bridge of Avon 104 NJ 1835
Bridge of Cally 98 NO 1351
Bridge of Canny 99 NO 6597
Bridge of Dee 69 NX 7360
Bridge of Don 105 NJ 9409
Bridge of Dye 99 NO 6585
Bridge of Earn 92 NO 1318
Bridge of Feugh 99 NO 7094
Bridge of Gairn 98 NO 3597
Bridge of Gaur 97 NN 5056
Bridge of Muchalls 99 NO 8991
Bridge of Orchy 90 NN 2939
Bridge of Weir 82 NS 3865
Bridgefoot 62 NY 0529
Bridgemary 11 SU 5702
Bridgend (Borders) 86 NT 5235
Bridgend (Dumf & G) 77 NT 0708
Bridgend (Fife.) 93 NO 3911
Bridgend (Grampn.) 104 NJ 3731
Bridgend (Islay) 80 NR 3362
Bridgend (Lothian) 85 NT 0475
Bridgend (Mid Glam.) 28 SS 9079
Bridgend (Strath.) 89 NR 8592
Bridgend (Strath.) 84 NS 6970
Bridgend (Tays.) 92 NO 1224
Bridgend (Tays.) 99 NO 5368
Bridgend of Lintrathen 98 NO 2854
Bridgerule 6 SS 2803
Bridges 40 SO 3996
Bridgetown (Somer.) 16 SS 9233
Bridgeyate 29 ST 6873
Bridgham 46 TL 9686
Bridgnorth 41 SO 7193
Bridgtown 41 SJ 9808
Bridgwater 17 ST 3037
Bridlington 67 TA 1766
Bridport 9 SY 4692
Bridstow 29 SO 5824
Brierfield 58 SD 8436
Brierley (Glos.) 29 SO 6215
Brierley (Here & W) 30 SO 4956
Brierley (S Yorks.) 59 SE 4011
Brierley Hill 41 SO 9187
Brig o'Turk 90 NN 5306
Brigg 61 TA 0007
Briggate 47 TG 3127
Brigham (Cumbr.) 62 NY 0830
Brigham (Humbs.) 67 TA 0753
Brighouse 59 SE 1423
Brighstone 11 SZ 4282
Brightgate 53 SK 2659
Brighthampton 33 SP 3803
Brightling 13 TQ 6821
Brightlingsea 23 TM 0816
Brighton (Corn.) 3 SW 9054
Brighton (E Susx) 13 TQ 3105
Brightons 84 NS 9277
Brightwalton 19 SU 4278
Brightwell (Oxon.) 19 SU 5790
Brightwell (Suff.) 37 TM 2543
Brightwell Baldwin 19 SU 6594
Brignall 72 NZ 0712
Brigsley 61 TA 2501
Brigsteer 63 SD 4889
Brigstock 44 SP 9485
Brill 34 SP 6513
Brilley 30 SO 2549
Brimfield 40 SO 5267
Brimington 53 SK 4073
Brimpsfield 32 SO 9312
Brimpton 19 SU 5564
Brind 60 SE 7430
Brindister 113 HU 2857
Brindle 57 SD 5924
Brindley Ford 51 SJ 8754
Brindley Heath 41 SJ 9914
Brineton 41 SJ 8013
Bringhurst 44 SP 8492
Brington 45 TL 0875
Briningham 46 TG 0334
Brinkhill 55 TF 3773
Brinkley 36 TL 6254
Brinklow 43 SP 4379
Brinkworth 18 SU 0184
Brinscall 58 SD 6321
Brinsley 53 SK 4548
Brinsop 30 SO 4344
Brinsworth 53 SK 4190
Brinton 46 TG 0335
Brinyan 113 HY 4327
Brisley 46 TF 9421
Brislington 29 ST 6170
Bristol 29 ST 5872
Briston 47 TG 0632
Britannia 58 SD 8821
Britford British Legion Village 14 TQ 7257
Briton Ferry 28 SS 7394
Britwell Salome 19 SU 6792
Brixham 5 SX 9255
Brixton 5 SX 5452
Brixton Deverill 10 ST 8638
Brixworth 44 SP 7470
Brize Norton 33 SP 2907
Broad Blunsdon 18 SU 1490
Broad Campden 32 SP 1537
Broad Chalke 10 SU 0325
Broad Green (Here & W) 32 SO 7656
Broad Haven 24 SM 8613
Broad Hill (Cambs.) 36 TL 5976
Broad Hinton 18 SU 1076
Broad Laying 19 SU 4362
Broad Marston 32 SP 1346
Broad Oak (Cumbr.) 62 SD 1194
Broad Oak (E Susx) 14 TQ 8320
Broad Oak (Here & W) 29 SO 4721
Broad Street (Kent) 14 TQ 8356
Broad Town 18 SU 0977
Broadbottom 51 SJ 9993
Broadbridge 12 SU 8105
Broadbridge Heath 12 TQ 1431
Broadclyst 8 SX 9897
Broadford 100 NG 6423
Broadhaugh 77 NT 4509
Broadheath (Gtr Mches.) 51 SJ 7689
Broadheath (Here & W) 31 SO 6665
Broadheath (Here & W) 32 SO 8156
Broadhembury 8 ST 1004
Broadhempston 5 SX 8066
Broadley (Grampn.) 104 NJ 4161
Broadley (Gtr Mches.) 58 SD 8716
Broadley Common 35 TL 4207
Broadmayne 9 SY 7286
Broadmeadows 86 NT 4130
Broadmere 19 SU 6247
Broadoak (Dorset) 9 SY 4496
Broadoak (E Susx) 13 TQ 6022
Broadoak (Kent) 15 TR 1661
Broadrashes 104 NJ 4354
Broadstairs 15 TR 3967
Broadstone (Dorset) 10 SZ 0095
Broadstone (Salop) 40 SO 5389
Broadwas 32 SO 7555
Broadwater 12 TQ 1504
Broadway (Here & W) 32 SP 0937
Broadway (Somer.) 8 ST 3215
Broadwell (Glos.) 33 SP 2027
Broadwell (Oxon.) 33 SP 2503
Broadwell (Warw.) 33 SP 4565
Broadwell Lane End 29 SO 5811
Broadwey 9 SY 6683
Broadwindsor 9 ST 4302
Broadwood-Kelly 6 SS 6105
Broadwoodwidger 4 SX 4089

C

Careby 232 Clare

Careby 44 TF 0216
Careston 99 NO 5260
Carew 24 SN 0403
Carew Cheriton 24 SN 0402
Carew Newton 24 SN 0404
Carey 31 SO 5631
Carfrae 86 NT 5769
Cargen 70 NX 9672
Cargenbridge 69 NX 9474
Cargill 92 NO 1536
Cargo 70 NY 3659
Cargreen 4 SX 4262
Carham 87 NT 7938
Carhampton 16 ST 0042
Carharrack 2 SW 7241
Carie (Tays.) 97 NN 6157
Carie (Tays.) 90 NN 6437
Carinish 109 NF 8159
Carisbrooke 11 SZ 4888
Cark 64 SD 3676
Carland Cross 2 SW 8454
Carlby 45 TF 0414
Carlecotes 59 SE 1703
Carleton (Cumbr.) 70 NY 4253
Carleton (Lancs.) 57 SD 3339
Carleton (N Yorks.) 58 SD 9749
Carleton Forehoe 47 TG 0805
Carleton Rode 47 TM 1192
Carlingcott 17 ST 6958
Carlisle 70 NY 3955
Carlops 85 NT 1656
Carloway 109 NB 2042
Carlton (Beds.) 34 SP 9555
Carlton (Cambs.) 36 TL 6453
Carlton (Cleve.) 72 NZ 3921
Carlton (Leic.) 43 SK 3905
Carlton (N Yorks.) 66 NZ 5004
Carlton (N Yorks.) 65 SE 0684
Carlton (N Yorks.) 66 SE 6086
Carlton (N Yorks.) 60 SE 6423
Carlton (Notts.) 53 SK 6141
Carlton (S Yorks.) 59 SE 3610
Carlton (Suff.) 37 TM 3864
Carlton (W Yorks.) 59 SE 3327
Carlton Colville 47 TM 5190
Carlton Curlieu 43 SP 6997
Carlton Husthwaite 66 SE 4976
Carlton Miniott 66 SE 3980
Carlton Scroop 54 SK 9445
Carlton in Lindrick 53 SK 5984
Carlton-le-Moorland 54 SK 9058
Carlton-on-Trent 54 SK 7963
Carluke 84 NS 8450
Carmacoup 76 NS 7927
Carmarthen 25 SN 4120
Carmel (Clwyd) 50 SJ 1676
Carmel (Dyfed) 25 SN 5816
Carmel (Gwyn.) 48 SH 3882
Carmel (Gwyn.) 48 SH 4954
Carmunnock 84 NS 5957
Carmyle 84 NS 6461
Carmyllie 99 NO 5542
Carn Brea 2 SW 6941
Carnaby 67 TA 1465
Carnach (Harris) 109 NG 2297
Carnbee 93 NO 5306
Carnbo 92 NO 0503
Carne 3 SW 9138
Carnell 82 NS 4632
Carnforth 64 SD 4970
Carnhell Green 2 SW 6137
Carnie 105 NJ 8105
Carno 39 SN 9696
Carnock 85 NT 0489
Carnon Downs 2 SW 7940
Carnousie 105 NJ 6650
Carnoustie 93 NO 5634
Carnwath 85 NS 9746
Carnyorth 2 SW 3733
Carperby 65 SE 0089
Carr Shield 71 NY 8047
Carr Vale 53 SK 4669
Carradale 81 NR 8138
Carrbridge 103 NH 9022
Carreglefn 48 SH 3889
Carrick (Fife.) 93 NO 4422
Carrick (Strath.) 89 NS 1995
Carriden 85 NT 0181
Carrine 74 NR 6709
Carrington (Gtr Mches.) 51 SJ 7492
Carrington (Lincs.) 55 TF 3155
Carrington (Lothian) 85 NT 3160
Carrog 50 SJ 1043
Carron (Central) 84 NS 8882
Carron (Grampn.) 104 NJ 2241
Carronbridge (Dumf & G) 76 NX 8697
Carrutherstown 70 NY 1071
Carrville 72 NZ 3043
Carsaig 88 NM 5421
Carseriggen 68 NX 3167
Carsethorn 70 NX 9959
Carshalton 21 TQ 2764
Carsington 53 SK 2553
Carskiey 74 NR 6508
Carsluith 69 NX 4854
Carsphairn 75 NX 5693
Carstairs 84 NS 9345
Carstairs Junction 84 NS 9545
Carswell Marsh 19 SU 3198
Carter's Clay 11 SU 3024
Carterton 33 SP 2706
Carthew 4 SX 0055
Carthorpe 66 SE 3083
Cartington 79 NU 0304
Cartland 84 NS 8646
Cartmel 62 SD 3778
Cartmel Fell 62 SD 4188
Carway 25 SN 4606
Cashmoor 10 ST 9813
Cassington 33 SP 4510
Casswell's Bridge 45 TF 1627
Castell-y-bwch 29 ST 2792
Casterton 63 SD 6279
Castle Acre 46 TF 8115
Castle Ashby 34 SP 8659
Castle Bank 41 SJ 9021
Castle Bolton 65 SE 0391
Castle Bromwich 42 SP 1489
Castle Bytham 44 SK 9818
Castle Caereinion 40 SJ 1605
Castle Camps 36 TL 6343
Castle Carrock 71 NY 5455
Castle Cary (Somer.) 17 ST 6332
Castle Combe 18 ST 8477
Castle Donington 43 SK 4427
Castle Douglas 69 NX 7662
Castle Eaton 18 SU 1495
Castle Eden 72 NZ 4338
Castle Frome 31 SO 6645
Castle Green (Cumbr.) 63 SD 5292
Castle Gresley 43 SK 2718
Castle Heaton 87 NT 9041
Castle Hedingham 36 TL 7835
Castle Hill (Suff.) 37 TM 1646
Castle Kennedy 68 NX 1059
Castle Morris 24 SM 9031
Castle Pulverbatch 40 SJ 4202
Castle Rising 46 TF 6624
Castle Stuart 103 NH 7449
Castlebay 109 NL 6698
Castlebythe 24 SN 0229
Castlecary (Strath.) 84 NS 7878
Castlecraig (Borders) 85 NT 1344
Castlecraig (Highld.) 103 NH 8369
Castleford 59 SE 4225
Castlehill (Strath.) 84 NS 8452
Castlemartin 24 SR 9198
Castlemorton 32 SO 7937
Castleside 72 NZ 0748
Castlethorpe 34 SP 7944
Castleton (Borders) 78 NY 5190
Castleton (Derby.) 52 SK 1582
Castleton (Gwent) 28 ST 2583
Castleton (N Yorks.) 66 NZ 6808
Castletown (Highld.) 112 ND 1967
Castletown (I. of M.) 56 SC 2667
Castletown (Tyne and Wear) 72 NZ 3558
Caston 46 TL 9598
Castor 45 TL 1298
Catacol 81 NR 9149
Catbrain 29 ST 5580
Catcliffe 53 SK 4288
Catcott 17 ST 3939
Caterham 21 TQ 3455
Catesby 33 SP 5159
Catfield 47 TG 3821
Catford 21 TQ 3872
Catforth 57 SD 4735
Cathcart 84 NS 5960
Cathedine 28 SO 1425
Catherington 11 SU 6914
Catherton 41 SO 6578
Catlodge 97 NN 6392
Catmore 19 SU 4580
Caton 64 SD 5364
Cator Court 5 SX 6877
Catrine 75 NS 5225
Catsfield 14 TQ 7213
Catshill 41 SO 9674
Cattal 66 SE 4454
Cattawade 37 TM 1033
Catterall 57 SD 4942
Catterick 66 SE 2397
Catterick Bridge 66 SE 2299
Catterick Camp 65 SE 1897
Catterlen 63 NY 4833
Catterline 99 NO 8678
Catterton 60 SE 5045
Catthorpe 43 SP 5578
Cattistock 9 SY 5999
Catton (N Yorks) 66 SE 3778
Catton (Norf.) 47 TG 2312
Catton (Northum.) 71 NY 8257
Catwick 61 TA 1245
Catworth 45 TL 0873
Caulcott 33 SP 5024
Cauldcotts 99 NO 6547
Cauldhame 91 NS 6494
Cauldon 52 SK 0749
Cauldside 71 NY 4480
Cauldwell 42 SK 2517
Caunsall 41 SO 8481
Caunton 54 SK 7460
Causewayhead 91 NS 8195
Causey Park 79 NZ 1794
Causeyend 105 NJ 9419
Cautley 63 SD 6994
Cavendish 36 TL 8046
Cavenham 36 TL 7669
Caversfield 33 SP 5824
Caversham 20 SU 7274
Caverswall 51 SJ 9442
Cawdor 103 NH 8450
Cawood 60 SE 5737
Cawsand 4 SX 4350
Cawston (Norb.) 47 TG 1324
Cawthorne 59 SE 2807
Cawton 66 SE 6476
Caxton 35 TL 3058
Caxton End 35 TL 3157
Caynham 40 SO 5473
Caythorpe (Lincs.) 54 SK 9348
Caythorpe (Notts.) 53 SK 6845
Cayton 67 TA 0583
Cefn Coch (Powys) 40 SJ 1026
Cefn Cribwr 28 SS 8582
Cefn Cross 28 SS 8682
Cefn-Einion 40 SO 2886
Cefn-brith 49 SH 9350
Cefn-coed-y-cymmer 28 SO 0307
Cefn-ddwysarn 49 SH 9638
Cefn-mawr (Clywd) 50 SJ 2842
Cefn-y-bedd 50 SJ 3156
Cefn-y-pant 24 SN 1925
Ceidio 48 SH 4085
Ceidio Fawr 48 SH 2638
Ceint 48 SH 4874
Cellan 27 SN 6149
Cellarhead (Staffs.) 51 SJ 9547
Cemaes 48 SH 3793
Cemmaes 39 SH 8306
Cemmaes Road 39 SH 8204
Cenarth 26 SN 2641
Cennin 48 SH 4645
Ceres 93 NO 4011
Cerne Abbas 9 ST 6601
Cerney Wick 18 SU 0796
Cerrigceinwen 48 SH 4273
Cerrigydrudion 49 SH 9548
Cessford 78 NT 7323
Chaceley 32 SO 8530
Chacewater 2 SW 7444
Chackmore 34 SP 6835
Chacombe 33 SP 4943
Chad Valley 42 SP 0385
Chadderton 58 SD 9005
Chaddesden 53 SK 3737
Chaddesley Corbett 41 SO 8973
Chaddleworth 19 SU 4177
Chadlington 33 SP 3221
Chadshunt 33 SP 3453
Chadwell St. Mary 22 TQ 6478
Chadwick End 42 SP 2073
Chaffcombe 8 ST 3510
Chagford 5 SX 7087
Chailey 13 TQ 3919
Chainhurst 14 TQ 7347
Chalbury Common 10 SU 0206
Chaldon 21 TQ 3155
Chaldon Herring or East Chaldon 10 SY 7983
Chale 11 SZ 4877
Chale Green 11 SZ 4880
Chalfont St. Giles 20 SU 9993
Chalfont St. Peter 20 SU 9990
Chalford 32 SO 8902
Chalgrove 19 SU 6396
Chalk 22 TQ 6772
Challacombe 7 SS 6941
Challoch 68 NX 3867
Challock Lees 15 TR 0050
Chalton (Beds.) 35 TL 0326
Chalton (Hants.) 12 SU 7316
Chalvington 13 TQ 5109
Chandler's Cross 20 TQ 0698
Chandler's Ford 11 SU 4320
Chantry (Somer.) 18 ST 7146
Chantry (Suff.) 37 TM 1443
Chapel 92 NT 2593
Chapel Allerton (Somer.) 17 ST 4050
Chapel Allerton (W Yorks.) 59 SE 3037
Chapel Amble 3 SW 9975
Chapel Brampton 44 SP 7266
Chapel Chorlton 51 SJ 8037
Chapel Haddlesey 60 SE 5826
Chapel Hill (Grampn.) 105 NK 0635
Chapel Hill (Gwent) 29 SO 5200
Chapel Hill (Lincs.) 55 TF 2054
Chapel Hill (Tays.) 92 NO 2021
Chapel Lawn 40 SO 3176
Chapel Le Dale 65 SD 7377
Chapel Row 19 SU 5669
Chapel St. Leonards 55 TF 5572
Chapel Stile 62 NY 3205
Chapel-en-le-Frith 52 SK 0580
Chapelend Way 36 TL 7039
Chapelgate 45 TF 4124
Chapelhall 84 NS 7826
Chapelhill (Highld.) 108 NH 8273
Chapelhill (Tays.) 92 NO 0030
Chapelknowe 70 NY 3173
Chapelton (Devon.) 6 SS 5826
Chapelton (Strath.) 84 NS 6848
Chapelton (Tays.) 99 NO 6247
Chapeltown (Grampn.) 104 NJ 2421
Chapeltown (Lancs.) 58 SD 7315
Chapeltown (S Yorks.) 59 SK 3596
Chapmanslade 18 ST 8247
Chappel 23 TL 8928
Chard 8 ST 3208
Chardstock 8 ST 3004
Charfield 29 ST 7292
Charing 15 TQ 9549
Charing Heath 15 TQ 9148
Charingworth 33 SP 1939
Charlbury 33 SP 3519
Charlcombe 29 ST 7467
Charlecote 33 SP 2656
Charles 7 SS 6832
Charles Tye 36 TM 0252
Charleston 98 NO 3845
Charlestown (Corn.) 4 SX 0351
Charlestown (Dorset) 9 SY 6579
Charlestown (Fife.) 85 NT 0683
Charlestown (Grampn.) 99 NJ 9300
Charlestown (Highld.) 106 NG 8174
Charlestown (Highld.) 103 NH 6448
Charlestown of Aberlour 104 NJ 2642
Charlesworth 52 SK 0092
Charlinch 16 ST 2337
Charlton (Gtr London) 21 TQ 4278
Charlton (Here & W) 32 SP 0045
Charlton (Northants.) 33 SP 5236
Charlton (W Susx.) 12 SU 8812
Charlton (Wilts.) 10 ST 9021
Charlton (Wilts.) 18 ST 9688
Charlton (Wilts.) 18 SU 1155
Charlton (Wilts.) 10 SU 1723
Charlton Abbots 32 SP 0324
Charlton Adam 17 ST 5328
Charlton Horethorne 9 ST 6623
Charlton Kings 32 SO 9620
Charlton Mackrell 17 ST 5228
Charlton Marshall 10 ST 8903
Charlton Musgrove 17 ST 7229
Charlton-on-Otmoor 33 SP 5615
Charlwood 13 TQ 2441
Charminster 9 SY 6792
Charmouth 9 SY 3693
Charndon 34 SP 6724
Charney Bassett 19 SU 3894
Charnock Richard 57 SD 5415
Charsfield 37 TM 2556
Chart Sutton 14 TQ 8049
Charter Alley 19 SU 5957
Charterhouse 17 ST 4955
Chartershall 91 NS 7990
Charterville Allotments 33 SP 3110
Chartham 15 TR 1054
Chartham Hatch 15 TR 1056
Chartridge 34 SP 9303
Charwelton 33 SP 5455
Chase Terrace 42 SK 0409
Chasetown 42 SK 0408
Chastleton 33 SP 2429
Chatburn 58 SD 7644
Chatcull 51 SJ 7934
Chatham 14 TQ 7567
Chathill 87 NU 1826
Chattenden 22 TQ 7672
Chatteris 45 TL 3986
Chattisham 37 TM 0942
Chatton 87 NU 0528
Chawleigh 7 SS 7112
Chawston 35 TL 1556
Chawton 12 SU 7037
Cheadle (Gtd Mches.) 51 SJ 8788
Cheadle (Staffs.) 52 SK 0043
Cheadle Hulme 51 SJ 8686
Cheam 21 TQ 2463
Chearsley 34 SP 7110
Chebsey 41 SJ 8528
Checkendon 19 SU 6682
Checkley (Ches.) 51 SJ 7245
Checkley (Staffs.) 52 SK 0237
Chedburgh 36 TL 7957
Cheddar 17 ST 4553
Cheddington 34 SP 9217
Cheddleton 51 SJ 9651
Cheddon Fitzpaine 16 ST 2327
Chedgrave 47 TM 3699
Chedington 9 ST 4805
Chediston 37 TM 3577
Chedworth 32 SP 0511
Chedzoy 17 ST 3337
Cheetham Hill 58 SD 8401
Cheldon 7 SS 7313
Chelford 51 SJ 8174
Chellaston 53 SK 3830
Chellington 34 SP 9656
Chelmarsh 41 SO 7187
Chelmondiston 37 TM 2037
Chelmorton 52 SK 1169
Chelmsford 22 TL 7006
Chelsfield 21 TQ 4864
Chelsworth 36 TL 9748
Cheltenham 32 SO 9422
Chelveston 44 SP 9969
Chelvey 29 ST 4668
Chelwood 17 ST 6361
Chelwood Gate 13 TQ 4130
Cheney Longville 40 SO 4184
Chenies 20 TQ 0198
Chepstow 29 ST 5393
Cherhill 18 SU 0370
Cherington (Warw.) 33 SP 2936
Cherington (Glos.) 18 ST 9098
Cheriton (Devon.) 7 SS 7346
Cheriton (Devon.) 8 ST 1001
Cheriton (Hants.) 11 SU 5828
Cheriton (W Glam.) 25 SS 4593
Cheriton Bishop 5 SX 7793
Cheriton Fitzpaine 7 SS 8606
Cherrington 41 SJ 6619
Cherry Burton 61 SE 9842
Cherry Hinton 35 TL 4857
Cherry Willingham 54 TF 0173
Chertsey 20 TQ 0466
Cheselbourne 9 SY 7699
Chesham 34 SP 9601
Chesham Bois 20 SU 9698
Cheshunt 35 TL 3502
Cheslyn Hay 41 SJ 9707
Chessington 21 TQ 1863
Chester 50 SJ 4066
Chester-le-Street 72 NZ 2751
Chesterblade 17 ST 6641
Chesterfield (Derby.) 53 SK 3871
Chesterfield (Staffs.) 42 SK 1005
Chesters (Borders) 78 NT 6210
Chesterton (Cambs.) 45 TL 1295
Chesterton (Oxon.) 33 SP 5621
Chesterton (Staffs.) 51 SJ 8249
Chesterton Green 33 SP 3558
Chestfield 15 TR 1365
Cheswardine 41 SJ 7129
Cheswick 87 NU 0346
Cheswick Green 42 SP 1275
Chetnole 9 ST 6008
Chettiscombe 8 SS 9614
Chettisham 45 TL 5483
Chettle 10 ST 9513
Chetton 41 SO 6690
Chetwode 34 SP 6429
Chetwynd Aston 41 SJ 7517
Cheveley 36 TL 6760
Chevening 21 TQ 4857
Chevington 36 TL 7860
Chevington Drift 79 NZ 2699
Chevithorne 8 SS 9715
Chew Magna 17 ST 5763
Chew Stoke 17 ST 5561
Chewton Mendip 17 ST 5952
Chicheley 34 SP 9046
Chichester 12 SU 8605
Chickerell 9 SY 6480
Chicklade 10 ST 9134
Chidden 11 SU 6517
Chiddingfold 12 SU 9635
Chiddingly 13 TQ 5414
Chiddingstone 13 TQ 5045
Chiddingstone Causeway 21 TQ 5147
Chideock 9 SY 4292
Chidham 12 SU 7803
Chieveley 19 SU 4773
Chignall Smealy 22 TL 6611
Chignall St. James 22 TL 6709
Chigwell 21 TQ 4493
Chigwell Row 21 TQ 4693
Chilbolton 11 SU 3939
Chilcomb (Hants.) 11 SU 5028
Chilcombe (Dorset) 9 SY 5291
Chilcompton 17 ST 6452
Chilcote 43 SK 2811
Child Okeford 10 ST 8312
Child's Ercall 41 SJ 6625
Childer Thornton 50 SJ 3677
Childrey 19 SU 3687
Childswickham 32 SP 0738
Childwall 50 SJ 4089
Chilfrome 9 SY 5898
Chilgrove 12 SU 8314
Chilham 15 TR 0753
Chillaton 4 SX 4381
Chillenden 15 TR 2753
Chillerton 11 SZ 4883
Chillesford 37 TM 3852
Chillingham 87 NU 0625
Chillington (Devon.) 5 SX 7942
Chillington (Somer.) 9 ST 3811
Chilmark 10 ST 9632
Chilson 33 SP 3119
Chilsworthy (Corn.) 4 SX 4172
Chilsworthy (Devon.) 6 SS 3206
Chilthorne Domer 9 ST 5219
Chilton (Bucks.) 34 SP 6811
Chilton (Durham) 72 NZ 3031
Chilton (Oxon.) 19 SU 4885
Chilton Cantelo 9 ST 5621
Chilton Foliat 19 SU 3170
Chilton Polden 17 ST 3739
Chilton Street 36 TL 7547
Chilton Trinity 11 ST 2939
Chilworth (Hants) 11 SU 4018
Chimney 33 SP 3500
Chineham 19 SU 6554
Chingford 21 TQ 3893
Chinley 52 SK 0382
Chinnor 20 SP 7500
Chipnall 51 SJ 7231
Chippenham (Cambs.) 36 TL 6669
Chippenham (Wilts.) 18 ST 9173
Chipperfield 35 TL 0401
Chipping (Herts.) 35 TL 3532
Chipping (Lancs.) 58 SD 6243
Chipping Campden 32 SP 1539
Chipping Hill 22 TL 8215
Chipping Norton 32 SP 3127
Chipping Ongar 22 TL 5502
Chipping Sodbury 29 ST 7282
Chipping Warden 33 SP 4948
Chipstable 16 ST 0427
Chipstead (Kent) 21 TQ 5056
Chipstead (Surrey) 21 TQ 2756
Chirbury 40 SO 2598
Chirk 50 SJ 2937
Chirmorie 68 NX 2076
Chirnside 87 NT 8756
Chirnsidebridge 87 NT 8556
Chirton 18 SU 0757
Chisbury 18 SU 2766
Chiselborough 9 ST 4614
Chiseldon 18 SU 1879
Chislehampton 19 SU 5999
Chislehurst 21 TQ 4470
Chislet 15 TR 2264
Chiswellgreen 35 TL 1303
Chiswick 21 TQ 2077
Chisworth 52 SJ 9991
Chithurst 12 SU 8423
Chittering 45 TL 4970
Chitterne 18 ST 9843
Chittlehamholt 7 SS 6420
Chittlehampton 7 SS 6325
Chittoe 18 ST 9666
Chivelstone 5 SX 7838
Chobham 20 SU 9761
Cholderton 18 SU 2242
Cholesbury 34 SP 9307
Chollerford 78 NY 9170
Chollerton 78 NY 9372
Cholsey 19 SU 5886
Cholstrey 30 SO 4659
Choppington 79 NZ 2583
Chopwell 72 NZ 1158
Chorley (Ches.) 51 SJ 5650
Chorley (Lancs.) 57 SD 5817
Chorley (Salop) 41 SO 6983
Chorley (Staffs.) 42 SK 0711
Chorleywood 20 TQ 0396
Chorlton 51 SJ 7250
Chorlton Lane 50 SJ 4547
Chowley 50 SJ 4756
Chrishall 35 TL 4439
Christchurch (Cambs.) 45 TL 4996
Christchurch (Dorset) 11 SZ 1593
Christchurch (Glos.) 29 SO 5713
Christian Malford 18 ST 9678
Christleton 50 SJ 4365
Christmas Common 20 SU 7193
Christon 17 ST 3956
Christon Bank 79 NU 2122
Christow 5 SX 8385
Chudleigh 5 SX 8679
Chudleigh Knighton 5 SX 8477
Chulmleigh 7 SS 6814
Chunal 52 SK 0391
Church 58 SD 7428
Church Brampton 44 SP 7165
Church Broughton 53 SK 2033
Church Crookham 20 SU 8152
Church Eaton 41 SJ 8417
Church End (Beds.) 34 SP 9921
Church End (Beds.) 35 TL 1937
Church End (Cambs.) 45 TF 3909
Church End (Cambs.) 35 TL 4857
Church End (Essex) 36 TL 5841
Church End (Hants.) 19 SU 6756
Church End (Warw.) 43 SP 2892
Church End (Wilts.) 18 SU 0278
Church Fenton 60 SE 5136
Church Gresley 43 SK 2918
Church Hanborough 33 SP 4212
Church Knowle 10 SY 9481
Church Langton 44 SP 7293
Church Lawford 43 SP 4476
Church Lawton 51 SJ 8255
Church Leigh 52 SK 0235
Church Lench 32 SP 0251
Church Minshull 51 SJ 6660
Church Norton 12 SZ 8695
Church Preen 40 SO 5398
Church Pulverbatch 40 SJ 4303
Church Stoke 40 SO 2694
Church Stowe (Northants.) 34 SP 6357
Church Street 22 TQ 7174
Church Stretton 40 SO 4593
Church Warsop 53 SK 5668
Churcham 32 SO 7618
Churchdown 32 SO 8819
Churchend (Essex) 22 TL 6323
Churchend (Essex) 23 TR 0092
Churchill (Avon) 17 ST 4359
Churchill (Here & W) 41 SO 8779
Churchill (Oxon.) 33 SP 2824
Churchingford 8 ST 2112
Churchover 43 SP 5080
Churchstanton 8 ST 1914
Churchstow (Devon.) 5 SX 7145
Churchtown (I. of M.) 56 SC 4294
Churchtown (Lancs.) 57 SD 4842
Churchtown (Mers.) 57 SD 3618
Churt 12 SU 8538
Churton 50 SJ 4156
Churwell 59 SE 2729
Chwilog 48 SH 4338
Chyandour 2 SW 4731
Cilan Uchaf 38 SH 2923
Cilcain 50 SJ 1765
Cilcennin 26 SN 5160
Cilfor 48 SH 6237
Cilfrew 28 SN 7600
Cilfynydd 28 ST 0892
Cilgerran 26 SN 1943
Cilgwyn 25 SN 7430
Ciliau-Aeron 26 SN 5058
Cilmalieu 95 NM 8955
Cilmery 27 SO 0051
Cilrhedyn 26 SN 2734
Ciltalgarth 49 SH 8840
Cilycwm 27 SN 7540
Cinderford 29 SO 6513
Cirencester 32 SP 0201
City Dulas 48 SH 4687
Clachaig 89 NS 1181
Clachan (Lismore Island) 95 NM 8543
Clachan (North Uist) 109 NF 8163
Clachan (Raasay) 100 NG 5436
Clachan (Strath.) 89 NM 7819
Clachan (Strath.) 81 NR 7656
Clachan Mor 94 NL 9847
Clachan of Campsie 84 NS 6179
Clachan of Glendaruel 89 NR 9984
Clachan-Seil 89 NM 7718
Clachbreck 81 NR 7675
Clachtoll 110 NC 0427
Clackavoid 98 NO 1463
Clackmannan 91 NS 9191
Clacton-on-Sea 23 TM 1715
Cladich 89 NN 0921
Claggan 95 NM 7049
Claigan 100 NG 2354
Claines 32 SO 8559
Clandown 17 ST 6955
Clanfield (Hants.) 11 SU 6916
Clanfield (Oxon.) 33 SP 2801
Clannaborough Barton 7 SS 7402
Clanville 19 SU 3148
Claonaig 81 NR 8656
Claonel 108 NC 5604
Clapgate (Dorset) 10 SU 0102
Clapham (Beds.) 35 TL 0252
Clapham (Gtd London) 21 TQ 2875
Clapham (N Yorks.) 65 SD 7469
Clapham (W Susx) 12 TQ 0906
Clappers 87 NT 9455
Clappersgate 62 NY 3603
Clapton (Somer.) 9 ST 4106
Clapton-in-Gordano 29 ST 4774
Clapton-on-the-Hill (Glos.) 32 SP 1617
Clapworthy 7 SS 6724
Clarbeston 24 SN 0421
Clarbeston Road 24 SN 0121
Clarborough 54 SK 7383
Clardon 112 ND 1468
Clare 36 TL 7645

Clarebrand 233 Crank

Clarebrand 69 NX 7666
Clarencefield 70 NY 0968
Clarkston 84 NS 5757
Clashmore 108 NH 7489
Clashnessie 110 NC 0530
Clatt 104 NJ 5426
Clatter 39 SN 9994
Clatworthy 16 ST 0530
Claughton (Lancs.) 57 SD 5242
Claughton (Lancs.) 64 SD 5666
Claverdon 33 SP 1964
Claverham 29 ST 4566
Clavering 35 TL 4832
Claverley 41 SO 7993
Claverton 18 ST 7864
Clawdd-newydd 49 SJ 0852
Clawton 6 SX 3599
Claxby (Lincs.) 55 TF 1194
Claxby (Lincs.) 55 TF 4571
Claxton (N Yorks.) 66 SE 6960
Claxton (Norf.) 47 TG 3303
Clay Common 47 TM 4781
Clay Coton 43 SP 5977
Clay Cross 53 SK 3963
Claybrooke Magna 43 SP 4988
Claydon (Oxon.) 33 SP 4550
Claydon (Suff.) 37 TM 1350
Claygate (Surrey) 21 TQ 1563
Claygate Cross 14 TQ 6155
Clayhanger (Devon.) 8 ST 0223
Clayhanger (W Mids.) 42 SK 0404
Clayhidon 8 ST 1615
Claypole 54 SK 8449
Clayton (S Yorks.) 60 SE 4507
Clayton (Staffs.) 51 SJ 8443
Clayton (W Susx.) 13 TQ 3014
Clayton (W Yorks.) 59 SE 1131
Clayton West 59 SE 2511
Clayton-le-Moors 58 SD 7431
Clayton-le-Woods 57 SD 5722
Clayworth 54 SK 7288
Cleadale 95 NM 4789
Cleadon 72 NZ 3862
Clearwell 29 SO 5708
Cleasby 72 NZ 2713
Cleat 113 ND 4585
Cleatlam 72 NZ 1118
Cleator 62 NY 0113
Cleator Moor 62 NY 0214
Cleckheaton 59 SE 1825
Clee St. Margaret 40 SO 5684
Cleedownton 41 SO 5880
Cleehill 41 SO 5975
Cleethorpes 61 TA 3008
Cleeton St. Mary 41 SO 6178
Cleeve 29 ST 4566
Cleeve Hill 32 SO 9827
Cleeve Prior 32 SP 0849
Clehonger 30 SO 4637
Cleish 92 NT 0998
Cleland 84 NS 7958
Clench Common 18 SU 1765
Clenchwarton 46 TF 5820
Clent 41 SO 9179
Cleobury Mortimer 41 SO 6775
Cleobury North 41 SO 6187
Cleongart 80 NR 6734
Clephanton 103 NH 8450
Clerklands 78 NT 5024
Clestran 113 HY 3107
Clevancy 18 SU 0475
Clevedon 29 ST 4071
Cleveleys 57 SD 3142
Cleverton 18 ST 9785
Clewer 17 ST 4350
Cley next the Sea 47 TG 0444
Cliburn 63 NY 5824
Cliddesden 19 SU 6349
Cliff End 14 TQ 8813
Cliffe (Kent) 22 TQ 7376
Cliffe (N Yorks.) 60 SE 6631
Cliffe Woods 22 TQ 7373
Clifford (Here & W) 30 SO 2445
Clifford (W Yorks.) 59 SE 4244
Clifford Chambers 33 SP 1952
Clifford's Mesne 29 SO 7023
Cliffsend 15 TR 3464
Clifton (Avon) 29 ST 5673
Clifton (Beds.) 35 TL 1739
Clifton (Central) 90 NN 3230
Clifton (Cumbr.) 62 NY 0429
Clifton (Cumbr.) 63 NY 5326
Clifton (Derby.) 52 SK 1644
Clifton (Here & W) 32 SO 8446
Clifton (Lancs.) 57 SD 4630
Clifton (Notts.) 53 SK 5434
Clifton (Oxon.) 33 SP 4831
Clifton Campville 42 SK 2510
Clifton Hampden 19 SU 5495
Clifton Reynes 34 SP 9051
Clifton upon Dunsmore 43 SP 5276
Clifton upon Teme 32 SO 7161
Climping 12 TQ 0002
Clint 66 SE 2559
Clint Green 46 TG 0210
Clinterty 105 NJ 8311
Clintmains 86 NT 6132
Clippesby 47 TG 4214
Clipsham 44 SK 9616
Clipston (Northants.) 44 SP 7181
Clipston (Notts.) 53 SK 6333
Clipstone 53 SK 6064
Clitheroe 58 SD 7441
Clive 40 SJ 5124
Clocaenog 49 SJ 0854
Clochan 104 NJ 4060
Clock Face 50 SJ 5291
Clodock 29 SO 3227
Clola 105 NK 0043
Clophill 35 TL 0838
Clopton (Northants.) 35 TL 0680
Clopton Green 36 TL 7654
Close Clark 56 SC 2775
Closeburn 76 NX 8992
Clothall 35 TL 2732
Clotton 50 SJ 5263
Clough Foot 58 SD 9123
Cloughton 67 TA 0094
Cloughton Newlands 67 TA 0096
Clousta 113 HU 3167
Clova (Tays.) 98 NO 3273
Clovelly 6 SS 3124
Clovenfords 86 NT 4436
Clovenstone 105 NJ 7717
Cluvulin 96 NN 0063
Clowne 53 SK 4975
Clows Top 41 SO 7171
Clun 40 SO 3081
Clunas 103 NH 8846
Clunbury 40 SO 3780
Clunes 96 NN 2088
Clungunford 40 SO 3978
Clunie (Grampn.) 104 NJ 6350
Clunie (Tays.) 98 NO 1043
Clunton 40 SO 3381
Cluny 92 NT 2495
Clutton (Avon) 17 ST 6159
Clutton (Ches.) 50 SJ 4654
Clydach (Gwent) 28 SO 2213
Clydach (W Glam.) 25 SN 6801
Clydach Vale 28 SS 9793
Clydebank 84 NS 5069
Clydey 26 SN 2535
Clyffe Pypard 18 SU 0776
Clynder 90 NS 2484
Clynderwen 24 SN 1219
Clynelish 108 NC 8905
Clynnog-fawr 48 SH 4149
Clyro 30 SO 2143
Clyst Honiton 8 SX 9893
Clyst Hydon 8 ST 0301
Clyst St. George 8 SX 9888
Clyst St. Lawrence 8 ST 0200
Clyst St. Mary 8 SX 9890
Cnwch Coch 27 SN 6775
Coad's Green 4 SX 2976
Coal Aston 53 SK 3679
Coalbrookdale 41 SJ 6604
Coalburn 84 NS 8034
Coalcleugh 71 NY 8045
Coaley 32 SO 7701
Coalpit Heath 29 ST 6780
Coalport 41 SJ 6902
Coalsnaughton 91 NS 9195
Coaltown of Balgonie 93 NT 2999
Coaltown of Wemyss 93 NT 3295
Coalville 43 SK 4214
Coast 106 NG 9290
Coatbridge 84 NS 7265
Coatdyke 84 NS 7464
Coate (Wilts.) 18 SU 0361
Coate (Wilts.) 18 SU 1782
Coates (Cambs.) 45 TL 3097
Coates (Glos.) 32 SO 9700
Coatham 73 NZ 5925
Coatham Mundeville 72 NZ 2919
Cobbaton 6 SS 6127
Coberley 32 SO 9615
Cobham (Kent) 14 TQ 6768
Cobham (Surrey) 20 TQ 1060
Cobnash 30 SO 4560
Cock Bridge 104 NJ 2509
Cock Clarks 22 TL 8102
Cockayne 66 SE 6298
Cockayne Hatley 35 TL 2549
Cockburnspath 87 NT 7770
Cockenzie and Port Seton 85 NT 4075
Cockerham 64 SD 4651
Cockerington 55 TF 3789
Cockermouth 62 NY 1230
Cockernhoe Green 35 TL 1223
Cockfield (Durham) 72 NZ 1224
Cockfield (Suff.) 36 TL 9054
Cockfosters 21 TQ 2896
Cocking 12 SU 8717
Cockington 5 SX 8964
Cocklake 17 ST 4349
Cockley Cley 46 TF 7904
Cockpole Green 20 SU 7981
Cockshutt 40 SJ 4329
Cockthorpe 46 TF 9842
Cockwood 8 SX 9780
Codda 4 SX 1777
Coddenham 37 TM 1354
Coddington (Ches.) 50 SJ 4455
Coddington (Here & W) 32 SO 7142
Coddington (Notts.) 54 SK 8354
Codford St. Mary 10 ST 9739
Codford St. Peter 18 ST 9640
Codicote 35 TL 2118
Codnor 53 SK 4149
Codrington 29 ST 7278
Codsall 41 SJ 8603
Codsall Wood 41 SJ 8405
Coed-y-paen 29 ST 3398
Coedana 48 SH 4381
Coedely 28 ST 0285
Coedkernew 29 ST 2783
Coedpoeth 50 SJ 2850
Coelbren 28 SN 8411
Coffinswell 5 SX 8868
Cofton Hackett 42 SP 0075
Cogenhoe 34 SP 8360
Coggeshall 22 TL 8522
Coillaig 89 NN 0120
Coille Mhorgil 96 NH 1001
Coity 28 SS 9281
Coker 9 ST 5312
Colaboll 108 NC 5610
Colan 3 SW 8661
Colaton Raleigh 8 SY 0787
Colby (Cumbr.) 63 NY 6620
Colby (I. of M.) 56 SC 2370
Colby (Norf.) 47 TG 2131
Colchester 23 TM 0025
Cold Ash 19 SU 5169
Cold Ashby 43 SP 6576
Cold Ashton 29 ST 7472
Cold Aston 32 SP 1219
Cold Brayfield 34 SP 9252
Cold Hanworth 54 TF 0383
Cold Hesledon 72 NZ 4147
Cold Higham 34 SP 6653
Cold Kirby 66 SE 5384
Cold Newton 44 SK 7106
Cold Norton 22 TL 8500
Cold Overton 44 SK 8110
Coldbackie 111 NC 6160
Coldblow 21 TQ 5173
Coldean 13 TQ 3408
Coldeast 5 SX 8274
Colden Common 11 SU 4822
Coldfair Green 37 TM 4361
Coldharbour (Surrey) 12 TQ 1443
Coldingham 87 NT 9065
Coldrain 92 NO 0700
Coldred 15 TR 2747
Coldridge 7 SS 6907
Coldstream 87 NT 8539
Coldwaltham 12 TQ 0216
Coldwells 105 NK 1039
Cole 17 ST 6633
Colebatch 40 SO 3187
Colebrook 8 ST 0006
Colebrooke 7 SX 7799
Coleby (Humbs.) 60 SE 8919
Coleby (Lincs.) 54 SK 9760
Coleford (Devon.) 7 SS 7701
Coleford (Glos.) 29 SO 5710
Coleford (Somer.) 17 ST 6848
Colehill 10 SU 0300
Coleman's Hatch 13 TQ 4533
Colemere 50 SJ 4232
Colenden 92 NO 1029
Coleorton 43 SK 3917
Colerne 18 ST 8171
Colesbourne 32 SO 9913
Colesden 35 TL 1255
Coleshill (Bucks.) 20 SU 9495
Coleshill (Oxon.) 18 SU 2393
Coleshill (Warw.) 42 SP 1989
Colgate 13 TQ 2332
Colgrain 90 NS 3280
Colinsburgh 93 NO 4703
Colinton 85 NT 2169
Colintraive 81 NS 0374
Colkirk 46 TF 9126
Collace 92 NO 2032
Collafirth (Shetld.) 113 HU 3482
Collaton St. Mary 5 SX 8660
College Town 20 SU 8561
Collessie 93 NO 2813
Collier Row 21 TQ 4991
Collier Street 14 TQ 7145
Collier's End 35 TL 3720
Colliery Row 72 NZ 3449
Collieston 105 NK 0328
Collin 70 NY 0276
Collingbourne Ducis 18 SU 2453
Collingbourne Kinston 18 SU 2355
Collingham (Notts.) 54 SK 8261
Collingham (W. Yorks.) 59 SE 3845
Collington 31 SO 6460
Collingtree 34 SP 7555
Colliston 99 NO 6045
Collynie 105 NJ 8436
Collyweston 44 SK 9903
Colmonell 68 NX 1586
Colmworth 35 TL 1058
Coln Rogers 32 SP 0809
Coln St. Aldwyns 32 SP 1405
Coln St. Dennis 32 SP 0810
Colnabaichin 104 NJ 2908
Colnbrook 20 TQ 0277
Colne (Cambs.) 45 TL 3776
Colne (Lancs.) 58 SD 8839
Colne Engaine 36 TL 8530
Colney 47 TG 1808
Colney Heath 35 TL 2005
Colney Street 35 TL 1502
Colp 105 NJ 7448
Colpy 104 NJ 6432
Colsterdale 65 SE 1280
Colsterworth 44 SK 9224
Colston Bassett 53 SK 7033
Coltfield 103 NJ 1163
Coltishall 47 TG 2619
Colton (Cumbr.) 62 SD 3186
Colton (N. Yorks.) 60 SE 5444
Colton (Norf.) 47 TG 1009
Colton (Staffs.) 42 SK 0520
Colvend 69 NX 8654
Colwall Green 32 SO 7541
Colwall Stone 32 SO 7542
Colwell 78 NY 9575
Colwich 42 SK 0121
Colwinston 28 SS 9475
Colworth 12 SU 9102
Colwyn Bay 49 SH 8478
Colyford 8 SY 2492
Colyton 8 SY 2493
Combe (Berks.) 19 SU 3760
Combe (Here & W) 30 SO 3463
Combe (Oxon.) 33 SP 4115
Combe Florey 16 ST 1531
Combe Hay 18 ST 7359
Combe Martin 6 SS 5846
Combe Moor 30 SO 3663
Combe Raleigh 8 ST 1502
Combe St. Nicholas 8 ST 3011
Combeinteignhead 8 SX 9071
Comberbach 51 SJ 6477
Comberton 35 TL 3856
Combrook 33 SP 3051
Combs (Derby.) 52 SK 0478
Combs (Suff.) 37 TM 0456
Combs Ford 37 TM 0457
Combwich 16 ST 2542
Comers 105 NJ 6707
Commins Coch 39 SH 8403
Common Edge 57 SD 3232
Common Moor 4 SX 2369
Common Side 53 SK 3375
Common, The 11 SU 2432
Commondale 73 NZ 6610
Compstall 51 SJ 9690
Compton (Berks.) 19 SU 5279
Compton (Devon.) 5 SX 8664
Compton (Hants.) 11 SU 4625
Compton (Surrey) 20 SU 9547
Compton (W. Susx.) 12 SU 7714
Compton (Wilts.) 18 SU 1352
Compton Abbas 10 ST 8718
Compton Abdale 32 SP 0516
Compton Bassett 18 SU 0372
Compton Beauchamp 19 SU 2887
Compton Bishop 17 ST 3955
Compton Chamberlayne 10 SU 0229
Compton Dando 17 ST 6464
Compton Dundon 17 ST 4933
Compton Martin 17 ST 5456
Compton Pauncefoot 17 ST 6425
Compton Valence 9 SY 5993
Comrie (Tays.) 91 NN 7722
Conchra 89 NS 0288
Concraigie 98 NO 1044
Conderton 32 SO 9637
Condicote 32 SP 1528
Condorrat 84 NS 7373
Condover 40 SJ 4906
Coney Weston 36 TL 9578
Coneyhurst Common 12 TQ 1024
Coneysthorpe 66 SE 7171
Congerstone 43 SK 3605
Congham 46 TF 7123
Congleton 51 SJ 8562
Congresbury 17 ST 4363
Congsby 55 TF 2258
Conington (Cambs.) 45 TL 1785
Conington (Cambs.) 45 TL 3266
Conisbrough 60 SK 5098
Conisholme 55 TF 3995
Coniston (Cumbr.) 62 SD 3097
Coniston (Humbs.) 61 TA 1535
Coniston Cold 65 SD 9054
Conistone 65 SD 9867
Connah's Quay 50 SJ 2869
Connel 89 NM 9134
Connor Downs 2 SW 5939
Conon Bridge 102 NH 5455
Cononley 59 SD 9846
Consall 51 SJ 9748
Consett 72 NZ 1150
Constable Burton 65 SE 1690
Constantine 2 SW 7229
Contin 102 NH 4555
Conwy 49 SH 7777
Conyer 15 TQ 9664
Cookbury 6 SS 4005
Cookham 20 SU 8985
Cookham Dean 20 SU 8785
Cookham Rise 20 SU 8884
Cookhill 32 SP 0558
Cookley (Here & W) 41 SO 8480
Cookley (Suff.) 37 TM 3475
Cookley Green 19 SU 6990
Cookney 99 NO 8793
Cooksbridge 13 TQ 4013
Cooksmill Green 22 TL 6306
Coolham 12 TQ 1222
Cooling 22 TQ 7575
Coombe (Corn.) 6 SS 2011
Coombe (Corn.) 3 SW 9551
Coombe Bissett 10 SU 1026
Coombe Hill 32 SO 8827
Coombe Keynes 10 SY 8484
Coombes 12 TQ 1908
Coopersale Common 35 TL 4702
Copdock 37 TM 1141
Copford Green 23 TL 9222
Copister 113 HU 4878
Cople 35 TL 1048
Copley 72 NZ 0825
Coplow Dale 52 SK 1679
Copmanthorpe 60 SE 5646
Coppathorne 6 SS 2000
Coppenhall 41 SJ 9019
Coppingford 45 TL 1680
Copplestone 7 SS 7702
Coppull 57 SD 5613
Copsale 12 TQ 1724
Copster Green 58 SD 6734
Copt Heath 42 SP 1778
Copt Hewick 66 SE 3371
Copt Oak 43 SK 4812
Copthorne 13 TQ 3139
Copythorne 11 SU 3014
Corbridge 72 NY 9964
Corby 44 SP 8988
Corby Glen 44 SK 9925
Coreley 41 SO 6173
Corfe 8 ST 2319
Corfe Castle 10 SY 9681
Corfe Mullen 10 SY 9798
Corfton 40 SO 4985
Corgarff 104 NJ 2708
Corhampton 11 SU 6120
Corley 43 SP 3085
Corley Ash 43 SP 2986
Corley Moor 43 SP 2884
Cornelly 28 SS 8281
Corney 62 SD 1191
Cornforth 72 NZ 3034
Cornhill 104 NJ 5858
Cornhill-on-Tweed 87 NT 8639
Cornholme (W Yorks.) 58 SD 9025
Cornish Hall End 36 TL 6836
Cornquoy 113 ND 5299
Cornriggs 71 NY 8441
Cornsay 72 NZ 1443
Cornwell 33 SP 2727
Cornwood 5 SX 6059
Cornworthy 5 SX 8255
Corpach 96 NN 0976
Corpusty 47 TG 1100
Corran (Highld.) 101 NM 8509
Corran (Highld.) 96 NN 0263
Corrany 56 SC 4589
Corrie 81 NS 0243
Corrie Common 70 NY 2085
Corriegour 96 NN 2895
Corriemoillie 102 NH 3663
Corrimony 102 NH 3830
Corringham (Essex) 22 TQ 7183
Corringham (Lincs.) 54 SK 8691
Corris Uchaf 39 SH 7408
Corrow 89 NN 1800
Corry 101 NG 6424
Corry of Ardnagrask 102 NH 5048
Corrynachenchy 95 NM 6542
Corscombe 9 ST 5105
Corse 104 NJ 6040
Corse of Kinnoir 104 NJ 5443
Corsham 18 ST 8669
Corsindae 105 NJ 6808
Corsley 18 ST 8246
Corsley Heath 18 ST 8245
Corsock 69 NX 7576
Corston (Avon) 29 ST 6965
Corston (Wilts.) 18 ST 9284
Corstorphine 85 NT 1972
Cortachy 98 NO 3959
Corton (Suff.) 47 TM 5497
Corton (Wilts.) 10 ST 9340
Corton Denham 9 ST 6322
Corwen 49 SJ 0743
Coryton (Devon.) 5 SX 4583
Coryton (Essex) 22 TQ 7482
Cosby 43 SP 5495
Coseley 41 SO 9494
Cosgrove 34 SP 7942
Cosham 11 SU 6605
Cosheston 24 SN 0003
Cossall 53 SK 4842
Cossington (Leics.) 43 SK 6013
Cossington (Somer.) 17 ST 3540
Costessey 47 TG 1712
Costock 43 SK 5726
Coston 44 SK 8422
Cot-town (Grampn.) 105 NJ 8140
Cot-town (Grampn.) 104 NJ 5026
Cotebrook 51 SJ 5765
Cotehill 71 NY 4750
Cotes (Cumbr.) 63 SD 4886
Cotes (Leic.) 43 SK 5520
Cotes (Staffs.) 51 SJ 8434
Cotesbach 43 SP 5382
Cotgrave 53 SK 6435
Cothall 105 NJ 8716
Cotham 54 SK 7947
Cothelstone 16 ST 1831
Cotherstone 72 NZ 0119
Cothill 19 SU 4699
Cotleigh 8 ST 2002
Coton (Cambs.) 35 TL 4158
Coton (Northants.) 43 SP 6771
Coton (Staffs.) 51 SJ 9832
Coton Clanford 41 SJ 8723
Coton in the Elms 42 SK 2415
Cott 5 SX 7861
Cottam (Lancs.) 57 SD 4932
Cottam (Notts.) 54 SK 8179
Cottartown 103 NJ 0331
Cottenham 45 TL 4507
Cotterdale 65 SD 8393
Cottered 35 TL 3129
Cotterstock 45 TL 0490
Cottesbrooke 44 SP 7073
Cottesmore 44 SK 9013
Cottingham (Humbs.) 61 TA 0532
Cottingham (Northants.) 44 SP 8490
Cottisford 33 SP 5831
Cotton 37 TM 0667
Cotton End 35 TL 0845
Cottown (Grampn.) 105 NJ 7715
Cotwalton 51 SJ 9234
Coughton (Warw.) 32 SP 0760
Coulags 101 NG 9645
Coull 99 NJ 5102
Coulport 90 NS 2087
Coulsdon 21 TQ 3059
Coulter 85 NT 0233
Coulton 66 SE 6374
Cound 40 SJ 5504
Coundon 72 NZ 2329
Coundon Grange 72 NZ 2327
Countersett 65 SD 9287
Countesthorpe 43 SP 5895
Countess Wear 8 SX 9489
Countisbury 7 SS 7449
Coupar Angus 92 NO 2139
Coupland 87 NT 9331
Cour 81 NR 8248
Court Henry 25 SN 5522
Courteenhall 34 SP 7653
Courtsend 23 TR 0293
Courtway 16 ST 2033
Cousland 85 NT 3768
Cousley Wood 13 TQ 6533
Cove (Devon.) 8 SS 9519
Cove (Hants.) 20 SU 8555
Cove (Highld.) 106 NG 8190
Cove (Strath.) 90 NS 2281
Cove Bay (Grampn.) 99 NJ 9501
Covehithe 47 TM 5281
Coven 41 SJ 9006
Coveney 45 TL 4882
Covenham St. Bartholomew 61 TF 3395
Covenham St. Mary 55 TF 3394
Coventry 43 SP 3379
Coverack 2 SW 7818
Coverham 65 SE 1086
Covington 45 TL 0570
Cowan Bridge 64 SD 6476
Cowbeech 13 TQ 6114
Cowbit 45 TF 2618
Cowbridge 28 SS 9974
Cowden 13 TQ 4640
Cowdenbeath 92 NT 1692
Cowes 11 SZ 4995
Cowesby 66 SE 4689
Cowfold 13 TQ 2122
Cowick 60 SE 6521
Cowie 84 NS 8389
Cowley (Devon.) 8 SX 9095
Cowley (Glos.) 32 SO 9614
Cowley (Gtr London) 20 TQ 0582
Cowley (Oxon.) 33 SP 5404
Cowlinge 36 TL 7154
Cowpen Bewley 73 NZ 4824
Cowplain 11 SU 7011
Cowshill 71 NY 8540
Cowstrandburn 92 NT 0390
Cox Common 47 TM 4082
Coxbank 51 SJ 6541
Coxbench 53 SK 3743
Coxheath 14 TQ 7451
Coxhoe 72 NZ 3235
Coxley 17 ST 5343
Coxwold 66 SE 5377
Coychurch 28 SS 9379
Coylton 75 NS 4119
Coylumbridge 103 NH 9110
Coynach 104 NJ 4405
Crabadon 5 SX 7655
Crabbs Cross 32 SP 0464
Crabtree 13 TQ 2225
Crabtree Green 50 SJ 3344
Crackenthorpe 63 NY 6622
Crackington Haven 6 SX 1496
Crackleybank 41 SJ 7611
Crackpot 65 SD 9796
Cracoe 65 SD 9760
Cradley 32 SO 7347
Crafthole 4 SX 3654
Cragabus 80 NR 3345
Cragg 59 SE 0023
Craggan (Strath.) 90 NS 2699
Craghead 72 NZ 2150
Crai 28 SN 8924
Craibstone (Grampn.) 105 NJ 8611
Craichie 99 NO 5047
Craig (Dumf & G) 69 NX 6875
Craig (Highld.) 101 NH 0349
Craig Penllyn 28 SS 9777
Craig-y-nos 28 SN 8315
Craigcefnparc 25 SN 6703
Craigdallie 92 NO 2428
Craigdam 105 NJ 8430
Craigearn 105 NJ 7214
Craigellachie (Grampn.) 104 NJ 2844
Craigend 92 NO 1120
Craigendoran 90 NS 3181
Craiggiecat 99 NO 8592
Craighat 90 NS 4984
Craighouse 80 NR 5267
Craigie (Grampn.) 105 NJ 9119
Craigie (Strath.) 82 NS 4232
Craigie (Tays.) 98 NO 1143
Craiglockhart 85 NT 2270
Craigmillar 85 NT 2871
Craignant 50 SJ 2535
Craigneuk (Strath.) 84 NS 7656
Craigneuk (Strath.) 84 NS 7764
Craignure 89 NM 7236
Craigo 99 NO 6864
Craigow 92 NO 0806
Craigrothie 93 NO 3710
Craigruie 90 NN 5020
Craigton (Grampn.) 99 NJ 8301
Craigton (Tays.) 98 NO 3250
Craigton (Tays.) 93 NO 5138
Craigtown 111 NC 8856
Craik 77 NT 3408
Crail 93 NO 6107
Crailing 78 NT 6824
Crailinghall 78 NT 6921
Crakehall 66 SE 2490
Crambe 66 SE 7364
Cramlington 79 NZ 2776
Cramond 85 NT 1876
Cramond Bridge 85 NT 1775
Cranage 51 SJ 7568
Cranberry 51 SJ 8236
Cranborne 10 SU 0513
Cranbourne 20 SU 9272
Cranbrook 14 TQ 7735
Cranbrook Common 14 TQ 7938
Cranfield 34 SP 9542
Cranford 20 TQ 1077
Cranford St. Andrew 44 SP 9277
Cranford St. John 44 SP 9276
Cranham (Essex) 21 TQ 5787
Cranham (Glos.) 32 SO 8912
Crank 50 SJ 5099

Cranleigh 234 Dolwen (Powys)

Cranleigh 12 TQ 0638
Cranmore (I. of W.) 11 SZ 3990
Cranmore (Somer.) 17 ST 6843
Cranna 104 NJ 6352
Crannach 104 NJ 4954
Cranoe 44 SP 7695
Cransford 37 TM 3164
Cranshaws 86 NT 6961
Cranstal 56 NX 4602
Crantock 2 SW 7860
Cranwell 54 TF 0349
Cranwich 46 TL 7795
Cranworth 46 TF 9804
Crapstone 5 SX 5067
Crarae 89 NR 9897
Craster 79 NU 2519
Cratfield 37 TM 3175
Crathes 99 NO 7596
Crathie (Grampn.) 98 NO 2695
Crathie (Highld.) 97 NN 5893
Crathorne 66 NZ 4407
Craven Arms 40 SO 4382
Crawcrook 72 NZ 1363
Crawford 76 NS 9520
Crawfordjohn 76 NS 8823
Crawick 76 NS 7710
Crawley (Hants.) 11 SU 4234
Crawley (Oxon.) 33 SP 3312
Crawley (W Susx.) 13 TQ 2636
Crawley Down 13 TQ 3437
Crawleyside 72 NY 9940
Crawshawbooth 58 SD 8125
Crawton 99 NO 8779
Cray (N Yorks.) 65 SD 9479
Cray's Pond 19 SU 6380
Crayford 21 TQ 5175
Crayke 66 SE 5670
Crays Hill 22 TQ 7192
Creacombe 7 SS 8119
Creagorry 109 NF 7948
Creaton 44 SP 7071
Credenhill 30 SO 4543
Crediton 7 SS 8300
Creech St. Michael 17 ST 2725
Creed 3 SW 9347
Creedy Park 7 SS 8302
Creekmouth 21 TQ 4581
Creeting St. Mary 37 TM 0956
Creeton 44 TF 0120
Creetown 69 NX 4758
Creggans 89 NN 0802
Cregneish 56 SC 1967
Cregrina 30 SO 1252
Creich (Fife.) 93 NO 3221
Creigiau 28 ST 0881
Cressage 41 SJ 5904
Cresselly 24 SN 0606
Cressing 22 TL 7920
Cresswell (Dyfed) 24 SN 0506
Cresswell (Northum.) 79 NZ 2993
Cresswell (Staffs.) 51 SJ 9739
Creswell (Derby.) 53 SK 5274
Cretingham 37 TM 2260
Crew Green 40 SJ 3215
Crewe (Ches.) 50 SJ 4253
Crewe (Ches.) 51 SJ 7055
Crewkerne 9 ST 4409
Crianlarich 90 NN 3825
Cribyn 26 SN 5251
Criccieth 48 SH 4938
Crich 53 SK 3554
Crichie 105 NJ 9544
Crichton 85 NT 3862
Crick (Northants.) 43 SP 5872
Crickadarn 27 SO 0942
Cricket St. Thomas 9 ST 3708
Crickheath 40 SJ 2923
Crickhowell 28 SO 2118
Cricklade 18 SU 0993
Cridling Stubbs 60 SE 5221
Crieff 91 NN 8621
Criggion 40 SJ 2915
Crigglestone 59 SE 3116
Crimond 105 NK 0556
Crimplesham 46 TF 6503
Crinaglack 102 NH 4240
Crinan 89 NR 7894
Cringleford 47 TG 1905
Crinow 24 SN 1214
Cripp's Corner 14 TQ 7821
Cripplesease 2 SW 5036
Croachy 103 NH 6527
Crockenhill 21 TQ 5067
Crockernwell 5 SX 7592
Crockerton 18 ST 8642
Crocketford or Ninemile Bar 69 NX 8272
Crockey Hill 60 SE 6246
Crockham Hill 21 TQ 4450
Crockleford Heath 23 TM 0426
Croes-y-mwyalch 29 ST 3092
Croeserw 28 SS 8695
Croesgoch 24 SM 8330
Croesyceiliog (Gwent) 25 SN 4016
Croesyceiliog (Gwent) 29 ST 3196
Croft (Ches.) 51 SJ 6393
Croft (Leic.) 43 SP 5195
Croft (Lincs.) 55 TF 5162
Croft-on-Tees 66 NZ 2909
Croftamie 90 NS 4786
Crofton (W. Yorks.) 59 SE 3717
Crofty 25 SS 5295
Crogen 49 SJ 0237
Croggan 89 NM 7027
Croglin 71 NY 5747
Croick 106 NH 4591
Cromarty 103 NH 7867
Cromdale 103 NJ 0728
Cromer (Herts.) 35 TL 2928
Cromer (Norf.) 47 TG 2142
Cromford 53 SK 2956
Cromhall 29 ST 6990
Cromhall Common 29 ST 6989
Cromore 109 NB 4021
Cromra 97 NN 5489
Cromwell 54 SK 7961
Cronberry 76 NS 6022
Crondall 20 SU 7948
Cronk, The 56 SC 3495
Cronk-y-Voddy 56 SC 3086
Cronton 50 SJ 4988
Crook (Cumbr.) 63 SD 4694
Crook (Durham) 72 NZ 1635
Crook of Devon 92 NO 0300
Crookham (Berks.) 19 SU 5364
Crookham (Northum.) 87 NT 9138
Crookham Village 20 SU 7952
Crookhouse 86 NT 7627
Crooklands 63 SD 5383
Cropredy 33 SP 4646
Cropston 43 SK 5511
Cropthorne 32 SO 9944
Cropton 67 SE 7589
Cropwell Bishop 53 SK 6835
Cropwell Butler 53 SK 6837
Crosby (Cumbr.) 62 NY 0738
Crosby (I. of M.) 56 SC 3279
Crosby (Mers.) 50 SJ 3099
Crosby Garrett 65 NY 7309
Crosby Ravensworth 63 NY 6214
Croscombe 17 ST 5844
Cross (Somerset) 17 ST 4154
Cross Ash 29 SO 4019
Cross Green (Devon.) 4 SX 3888
Cross Green (Suff.) 36 TL 9952
Cross Hands 25 SN 5612
Cross Houses (Salop) 40 SJ 5307
Cross Inn (Dyfed) 26 SN 3957
Cross Inn (Dyfed) 26 SN 5464
Cross Inn (Mid Glam.) 28 ST 0583
Cross Lanes (Clwyd) 50 SJ 3746
Cross Lanes (N Yorks.) 66 SE 5264
Cross Street 37 TM 1876
Cross in Hand 13 TQ 5621
Cross of Jackston 105 NJ 7432
Crossaig 81 NR 8351
Crossapoll 94 NL 9943
Crossbost 109 NB 3924
Crosscanonby 62 NY 0739
Crossdale Street 47 TG 2239
Crossens 57 SD 3719
Crossford (Fife.) 85 NT 0686
Crossford (Strath.) 84 NS 8246
Crossgates (Fife.) 85 NT 1488
Crossgates (Powys) 27 SO 0865
Crossgill 64 SD 5562
Crosshill (Fife.) 92 NT 1796
Crosshill (Strath.) 75 NS 3206
Crosshouse (Strath.) 82 NS 3938
Crossings 71 NY 5177
Crosskeys (Gwent) 28 ST 2292
Crosskirk 112 ND 0370
Crosslanes (Salop.) 40 SJ 3218
Crosslee 77 NT 3018
Crossmichael 69 NX 7267
Crossmoor 57 SD 4438
Crossroads 99 NO 7594
Crossway (Gwent) 29 SO 4419
Crossway Green 41 SO 8368
Crosswell 26 SN 1236
Crosthwaite 63 SD 4491
Croston 57 SD 4818
Crostwick 47 TG 2515
Crostwight 47 TG 3329
Crouch Hill 9 ST 7010
Croughton 33 SP 5433
Crovie 105 NJ 8065
Crow Hill 29 SO 6326
Crowan 2 SW 6434
Crowborough 13 TQ 5130
Crowcombe 16 ST 1336
Crowfield (Northants.) 34 SP 6141
Crowfield (Suff.) 37 TM 1557
Crowhurst (E Susx) 14 TQ 7512
Crowhurst (Surrey) 21 TQ 3947
Crowland 45 TF 2310
Crowlas 2 SW 5133
Crowle (Here & W) 32 SO 9256
Crowle (Humbs.) 60 SE 7713
Crowmarsh Gifford 19 SU 6189
Crownhill 5 SX 4857
Crownthorpe 47 TG 0803
Crowthorne 20 SU 8464
Crowton 51 SJ 5774
Croxall 42 SK 1913
Croxdale 72 NZ 2636
Croxden 52 SK 0639
Croxley Green 20 TQ 0795
Croxton (Cambs.) 35 TL 2459
Croxton (Humbs.) 61 TA 0912
Croxton (Norf.) 46 TL 8786
Croxton (Staffs.) 51 SJ 7832
Croxton Kerrial 44 SK 8329
Croy (Highld.) 103 NH 7949
Croy (Strath.) 84 NS 7275
Croyde 6 SS 4439
Croydon (Cambs.) 35 TL 3149
Croydon (Gtr London) 21 TQ 3365
Cruckmeole 40 SJ 4309
Cruckton 40 SJ 4210
Cruden Bay 105 NK 0936
Crudgington 41 SJ 6317
Crudwell 18 ST 9592
Crug 40 SO 1872
Crugmeer 3 SW 9076
Crulivig 109 NB 1733
Crumlin 28 ST 2198
Crundale (Dyfed) 24 SM 9718
Crundale (Kent) 15 TR 0749
Crunwear 24 SN 1810
Cruwys Morchard 7 SS 8712
Crux Easton 19 SU 4256
Crwbin 25 SN 4713
Crymmych 26 SN 1833
Crynant 28 SN 7095
Crystal Palace 21 TQ 3470
Cuaig 101 NG 7057
Cubbington 43 SP 3368
Cubert 2 SW 7857
Cublington 34 SP 8422
Cuckfield 13 TQ 3024
Cucklington 17 ST 7527
Cuckney 53 SK 5671
Cuddesdon 33 SP 5902
Cuddington (Bucks.) 34 SP 7311
Cuddington (Ches.) 51 SJ 5971
Cuddington Heath 50 SJ 4646
Cuddy Hill 57 SD 4937
Cudham 21 TQ 4459
Cudliptown 5 SX 5278
Cudworth (S Yorks.) 59 SE 3808
Cudworth (Somer.) 8 ST 3810
Cuffley 35 TL 3002
Culbo 103 NH 6360
Culbokie 102 NH 6059
Culburnie 102 NH 4941
Culcabock 103 NH 6844
Culcharry 103 NH 8650
Culcheth 51 SJ 6594
Culdrain 104 NJ 5133
Culduie 101 NG 7140
Culford 36 TL 8370
Culgaith 63 NY 6129
Culham 19 SU 5095
Culkein 110 NC 0333
Culkerton 18 ST 9296
Cullachie 103 NH 9720
Cullen 104 NJ 5166
Cullercoats 79 NZ 3571
Cullerlie 99 NJ 7603
Cullicudden 103 NH 6564
Cullingworth 59 SE 0636
Cullipool 89 NM 7313
Cullivoe 113 HP 5402
Culloch 91 NN 7818
Cullompton 8 ST 0207
Culmaily 108 NH 8099
Culmington 40 SO 4982
Culmstock 8 ST 1013
Culnacraig 106 NC 0603
Culrain 108 NH 5794
Culross 85 NS 9885
Culroy 75 NS 3114
Culsh (Grampn.) 105 NJ 8848
Culswick 113 HU 2745
Cultercullen 105 NJ 9124
Cults (Grampn.) 104 NJ 5331
Culverstone Green 14 TQ 6363
Culverthorpe 54 TF 0240
Culworth 33 SP 5447
Cumbernauld 84 NS 7676
Cumberworth 55 TF 5073
Cuminestown 105 NJ 8050
Cummersdale 70 NY 3952
Cummertrees 70 NY 1366
Cummingstown 103 NJ 1368
Cumnock 75 NS 5619
Cumnor 33 SP 4604
Cumrew 71 NY 5550
Cumwhinton 71 NY 4552
Cumwhitton 71 NY 5052
Cundall (N Yorks.) 66 SE 4272
Cunninghamhead 82 NS 3741
Cupar 93 NO 3714
Cupar Muir 93 NO 3613
Curbar 53 SK 2574
Curbridge (Hants.) 11 SU 5211
Curbridge (Oxon.) 33 SP 3208
Curdridge 11 SU 5313
Curdworth 42 SP 1892
Curland 8 ST 2716
Currie 85 NT 1867
Curry Mallet 8 ST 3221
Curry Rivel 9 ST 3824
Curtisden Green 14 TQ 7440
Cury 2 SW 6721
Cushnie 105 NJ 7962
Cushuish 16 ST 1930
Cusop 30 SO 2341
Cutiau 38 SH 6317
Cutnall Green 41 SO 8768
Cutsdean 32 SP 0830
Cutthorpe 53 SK 3473
Cuxham 19 SU 6695
Cuxton 14 TQ 7166
Cuxwold 61 TA 1701
Cwm (Clwyd) 49 SJ 0677
Cwm (Gwent) 28 SO 1805
Cwm (W Glam.) 25 SS 6895
Cwm Irfon 27 SN 8549
Cwm-Cewydd 39 SH 8713
Cwm-Llinau 39 SH 8407
Cwm-y-glo 48 SH 5562
Cwmafan 28 SS 7892
Cwmaman 28 SS 9999
Cwmbach (Dyfed) 25 SN 2525
Cwmbach (Mid Glam.) 28 SO 0201
Cwmbelan 39 SN 9481
Cwmbran 29 ST 2894
Cwmcarn 28 ST 2293
Cwmcarvan 29 SO 4707
Cwmcoy 26 SN 2941
Cwmdare 28 SN 9803
Cwmdu (Dyfed) 27 SN 6330
Cwmdu (Powys) 28 SO 1823
Cwmduad 26 SN 3731
Cwmfelin Boeth 24 SN 1919
Cwmfelin Mynach 24 SN 2324
Cwmffrwd 25 SN 4217
Cwmgwrach 28 SN 8605
Cwmisfael 25 SN 4915
Cwmllynfell 25 SN 7413
Cwmparc 28 SS 9496
Cwmpengraig 26 SN 3436
Cwmsychpant 26 SN 4746
Cwmtillery 28 SO 2105
Cwmyoy 29 SO 2923
Cwmystwyth 27 SN 7873
Cwrt-newydd 26 SN 4847
Cwrt-y-gollen 28 SO 2317
Cyffylliog 49 SJ 0557
Cymmer (Mid Glam.) 28 ST 0290
Cymmer (W Glam.) 28 SS 8696
Cynghordy 27 SN 8139
Cynwyd 49 SJ 0541
Cynwyl Elfed 25 SN 3727

D

Dacre (Cumbr.) 63 NY 4526
Dacre (N Yorks.) 65 SE 1960
Dacre Banks 65 SE 1961
Daddry Shield 63 NY 8937
Dadford 34 SP 6638
Dadlington 43 SP 4098
Dafen 25 SN 5201
Daffy Green 46 TF 9609
Dagenham 21 TQ 5084
Daglingworth 32 SO 9905
Dagnall 34 SP 9916
Dailly 75 NS 2701
Dairsie or Osnaburgh 93 NO 4117
Dalavich 89 NM 9612
Dalbeattie 69 NX 8361
Dalblair 76 NS 6419
Dalbog 99 NO 5871
Dalby 56 SC 2178
Dalcapon 98 NN 9755
Dalchalloch 97 NN 7264
Dalchenna 89 NN 0706
Dalchreichart 102 NH 2912
Dalcross 103 NH 7748
Dalderby 55 TF 2465
Dale (Derby.) 53 SK 4338
Dale (Dyfed) 24 SM 8005
Dale (Shetld.) 113 HU 1852
Dalelia 95 NM 7369
Dalgarven 82 NS 2945
Dalginross 91 NN 7721
Dalguise 98 NN 9947
Dalhalvaig 111 NC 8954
Dalham 36 TL 7261
Daliburgh 109 NF 7421
Dalkeith 85 NT 3367
Dall 97 NN 5956
Dallas 103 NJ 1252
Dalleagles 75 NS 5710
Dallinghoo 37 TM 2654
Dallington 13 TQ 6519
Dalmally 89 NN 1527
Dalmary 90 NS 5195
Dalmellington 75 NS 4705
Dalmeny 85 NT 1477
Dalmore (Highld.) 103 NH 6668
Dalnabreck 95 NM 7069
Dalnavie 108 NH 6483
Dalnawillan Lodge 112 ND 0341
Dalness 96 NN 1751
Dalqueich 92 NO 0704
Dalry 82 NS 2949
Dalrymple 75 NS 3514
Dalserf 84 NS 7950
Dalston 70 NY 3750
Dalswinton 69 NX 9385
Dalton (Dumf & G) 70 NY 1173
Dalton (Lancs.) 57 SD 4907
Dalton (N Yorks.) 65 NZ 1108
Dalton (N Yorks.) 66 SE 4376
Dalton (N Yorks.) 53 SK 4593
Dalton (Northum.) 71 NY 9158
Dalton (Northum.) 79 NZ 1172
Dalton Piercy 73 NZ 4631
Dalton in Furness 64 SD 2374
Dalton-le-Dale 72 NZ 4047
Dalton-on-Tees 66 NZ 2908
Dalveich 90 NN 6124
Dalwhinnie 97 NN 6384
Dalwood 8 ST 2400
Damerham 10 SU 1015
Damgate 47 TG 4009
Damnaglaur 68 NX 1235
Danbury 22 TL 7805
Danby 66 NZ 7009
Danby Wiske 66 SE 3398
Dandaleith 104 NJ 2845
Danderhall 85 NT 3069
Dane End 35 TL 3321
Dane Hills 43 SK 5605
Danebridge 51 SJ 9665
Danehill 13 TQ 4027
Daren-felen 28 SO 2212
Darenth 21 TQ 5671
Daresbury 51 SJ 5782
Darfield 59 SE 4104
Dargate 15 TR 0861
Darite 4 SX 2569
Darlaston 41 SO 9796
Darley Dale 53 SK 2762
Darlingscott 33 SP 2324
Darlington 72 NZ 2914
Darliston 51 SJ 5833
Darlochan 74 NR 6723
Darlton 54 SK 7773
Darowen 39 SH 8302
Darras Hall 79 NZ 1571
Darrington 60 SE 4919
Darsham 37 TM 4170
Dartford 21 TQ 5474
Dartington 5 SX 7862
Dartmeet 5 SX 6773
Dartmouth 5 SX 8751
Darton 59 SE 3110
Darvel 84 NS 5637
Darwen 58 SD 6922
Datchet 20 SU 9876
Datchworth 35 TL 2619
Dauntsey 18 ST 9882
Davenham 51 SJ 6570
Daventry 33 SP 5762
Davidstow 4 SX 1587
Davington 77 NT 2302
Daviot (Grampn.) 105 NJ 7528
Daviot (Highld.) 103 NH 7139
Davoch of Grange 104 NJ 4951
Dawley 41 SJ 6807
Dawlish 8 SX 9676
Dawlish Warren 8 SX 9778
Dawn 49 SH 8672
Dawsmere 55 TF 4430
Daylesford 33 SP 2425
Deal 15 TR 3752
Dean (Cumbr.) 62 NY 0725
Dean (Devon) 5 SX 7364
Dean (Hants.) 11 SU 5619
Dean (Somer.) 17 ST 6743
Dean Prior 5 SX 7363
Dean Row 51 SJ 8781
Deanburnhaugh 77 NT 3911
Deane 19 SU 5450
Deanland 10 ST 9918
Deanscale 62 NY 0926
Deanshanger 34 SP 7639
Deanston 91 NN 7101
Dearham 62 NY 0736
Debach 37 TM 2454
Debden 36 TL 5533
Debden Cross 36 TL 5832
Debenham 37 TM 1763
Dechmont 85 NT 0370
Deddington 33 SP 4631
Dedham 37 TM 0533
Deene 44 SP 9492
Deenethorpe 44 SP 9592
Deepcar 59 SK 2897
Deepcut 20 SU 9057
Deepdale (Cumbr.) 65 SD 7284
Deeping Gate 45 TF 1509
Deeping St. James 45 TF 1609
Deeping St. Nicholas 45 TF 2115
Deerhurst 32 SO 8729
Defford 32 SO 9143
Defynnog 28 SN 9227
Deganwy 49 SH 7779
Deighton (N Yorks.) 66 NZ 3801
Deighton (N Yorks.) 60 SE 6244
Deiniolen 48 SH 5863
Delabole 4 SX 0683
Delamere 51 SJ 5668
Dell 109 NB 4861
Delliefure 103 NJ 0731
Delph 59 SD 9807
Dembleby 54 TF 0437
Den, The 82 NS 3251
Denaby 60 SK 4899
Denbigh 49 SJ 0566
Denbury 5 SX 8268
Denby 53 SK 3946
Denby Dale 59 SE 2208
Denchworth 19 SU 3891
Denend 104 NJ 6038
Denford 44 SP 9976
Dengie 23 TL 9801
Denham (Bucks.) 20 TQ 0386
Denham (Suff.) 36 TL 7561
Denham (Suff.) 37 TM 1974
Denham Green 20 TQ 0388
Denhead (Fife.) 93 NO 4613
Denhead (Grampn.) 105 NJ 9952
Denhead of Arbirlot 99 NO 5543
Denhead of Gray 93 NO 3431
Denholm 78 NT 5718
Denholme 59 SE 0633
Denmead 11 SU 6511
Dennington 37 TM 2866
Denny 84 NS 8182
Dennyloanhead 84 NS 8180
Denshaw 58 SD 9710
Denside 99 NO 8095
Densole 15 TR 2141
Denston 36 TL 7652
Denstone 52 SK 0940
Dent 65 SD 7087
Denton (Cambs.) 45 TL 1487
Denton (Durham) 72 NZ 2118
Denton (E Susx.) 13 TQ 4502
Denton (Gtr. Mches.) 51 SJ 9295
Denton (Kent) 15 TR 2146
Denton (Lincs.) 54 SK 8632
Denton (N Yorks.) 59 SE 1448
Denton (Norf.) 47 TM 2887
Denton (Northants.) 34 SP 8357
Denton (Oxon.) 33 SP 5902
Denver 46 TF 6101
Denwick (Northum.) 79 NU 2014
Deopham 47 TG 0400
Deopham Green 47 TM 0499
Depden Green 36 TL 7756
Deptford (Gtr London) 21 TQ 3676
Deptford (Wilts.) 10 SU 0038
Derby 53 SK 3435
Derbyhaven 56 SC 2867
Deri 28 SO 1202
Derringstone 15 TR 2049
Derrington 41 SJ 8822
Derry Hill 18 ST 9670
Derrythorpe 60 SE 8208
Dersingham 46 TF 6830
Dervaig 94 NM 4351
Derwen 49 SJ 0650
Desborough 44 SP 8083
Desford 43 SK 4703
Detchant 87 NU 0836
Detling 14 TQ 7958
Deuddwr 40 SJ 2317
Devauden 29 ST 4899
Devil's Bridge 27 SN 7477
Devizes 18 SU 0061
Devonport 5 SX 4554
Devonside 91 NS 9296
Devoran 2 SW 7939
Dewlish 10 SY 7798
Dewsbury 59 SE 2422
Dhoon 56 SC 4586
Dhoor 56 SC 4396
Dhowin 56 NX 4101
Dial Post 12 TQ 1519
Dibden 11 SU 4108
Dibden Purlieu 11 SU 4106
Dickleburgh 47 TM 1682
Didbrook 32 SP 0531
Didcot 19 SU 5290
Diddington 45 TL 1965
Diddlebury 40 SO 5085
Didley 30 SO 4432
Didmarton 18 ST 8287
Didsbury 51 SJ 8490
Didworthy 5 SX 6862
Digby 54 TF 0754
Diggle 59 SE 0008
Dihewyd 26 SN 4855
Dilham 47 TG 3325
Dilhorne 51 SJ 9743
Dilston 72 NY 9763
Dilton Marsh 18 ST 8449
Dilwyn 30 SO 4154
Dinas (Dyfed) 24 SN 0139
Dinas (Dyfed) 26 SN 2730
Dinas (Gwyn.) 48 SH 2736
Dinas Powis 28 ST 1571
Dinas-Mawddwy 39 SH 8514
Dinchope 49 SO 4583
Dinder 17 ST 5744
Dinedor 31 SO 5336
Dingley 44 SP 7687
Dingwall 102 NH 5458
Dinnet 98 NO 4698
Dinnington (S Yorks.) 53 SK 5386
Dinnington (Somer.) 9 ST 4012
Dinnington (Tyne and Wear) 79 NZ 2073
Dinorwic 48 SH 5961
Dinton 10 SU 0131
Dinwoodie Mains 77 NY 1090
Dinworthy 6 SS 3015
Dippen 81 NR 7937
Dippin 74 NS 0422
Dipple (Grampn.) 104 NJ 3258
Dipple (Strath.) 75 NS 2002
Diptford 5 SX 7256
Dipton 72 NZ 1554
Dirleton 86 NT 5183
Discoed 30 SO 2764
Diseworth 43 SK 4524
Dishforth 66 SE 3873
Disley 51 SJ 9784
Diss 37 TM 1179
Distington 62 NY 0023
Ditcheat 17 ST 6236
Ditchingham 47 TM 3391
Ditchling 13 TQ 3215
Dittisham 5 SX 8655
Ditton (Ches.) 50 SJ 4986
Ditton (Kent) 14 TQ 7158
Ditton Green 36 TL 6658
Ditton Priors 41 SO 6089
Dixton (Glos.) 32 SO 9830
Dixton (Gwent) 29 SO 5114
Dobwalls 4 SX 2165
Doccombe 5 SX 7786
Dochgarroch 102 NH 6140
Docking 46 TF 7637
Docklow 31 SO 5657
Dockray 62 NY 3921
Doddinghurst 21 TQ 5998
Doddington (Cambs.) 45 TL 4090
Doddington (Kent) 15 TQ 9357
Doddington (Lincs.) 54 SK 9070
Doddington (Northum.) 87 NU 0032
Doddington (Salop) 41 SO 6176
Doddiscombsleigh 5 SX 8586
Dodford (Here & W) 41 SO 9273
Dodford (Northants.) 34 SP 6160
Dodington (Avon) 29 ST 7480
Dodleston 50 SJ 3661
Dodworth 59 SE 3105
Doe Lea 53 SK 4566
Dog Village 8 SX 9896
Dogdyke 55 TF 2055
Dogmersfield 20 SU 7852
Dol-for (Powys) 39 SH 8006
Dolanog 39 SJ 0612
Dolau (Powys) 40 SO 1367
Dolbenmaen 48 SH 5043
Dolfach 27 SN 9077
Dolfor (Powys) 40 SO 1087
Dolgarrog 49 SH 7766
Dolgellau 39 SH 7217
Doll 108 NC 8803
Dollar 91 NS 9697
Dolphinholme 64 SD 5153
Dolphinton 85 NT 1046
Dolton 6 SS 5712
Dolwen (Clwyd) 49 SH 8874
Dolwen (Powys) 39 SH 9707

Edgton 236 Fodderletter

Edgton 40 SO 3885
Edgware 21 TQ 2091
Edgworth 58 SD 7416
Edinample 90 NN 6022
Edinbane 100 NG 3451
Edinburgh 85 NT 2674
Edingale 42 SK 2112
Edingley 53 SK 6655
Edingthorpe 47 TG 3132
Edington (Somer.) 17 ST 3939
Edington (Wilts.) 18 ST 9252
Edith Weston 44 SK 9205
Edithmead 17 ST 3249
Edlesborough 34 SP 9719
Edlingham 79 NU 1108
Edlington 55 TF 2371
Edmondbyers 72 NZ 0150
Edmondsham 10 SU 0611
Edmondsley 72 NZ 2348
Edmondthorpe 44 SK 8517
Edmonton 21 TQ 3493
Ednam 86 NT 7337
Edradynate 97 NN 8852
Edrom 87 NT 8255
Edstaston 50 SJ 5131
Edstone 33 SP 1761
Edwalton 53 SK 5935
Edwardstone 36 TL 9442
Edwinsford 27 SN 6334
Edwinstowe 53 SK 6266
Edworth 35 TL 2241
Edwyn Ralph 31 SO 6457
Edzell 99 NO 5968
Efail Isaf 28 ST 0884
Efailnewydd 48 SH 3536
Efenechtyd 50 SJ 1155
Effingham 20 TQ 1253
Efford 7 SS 8901
Egerton (Gtr Mches.) 58 SD 7014
Egerton (Kent) 14 TQ 9047
Eggington 34 SP 9525
Egginton 52 SK 2628
Egglescliffe 72 NZ 4213
Eggleston 72 NZ 0023
Egham 20 TQ 0171
Egleton 44 SK 8707
Eglingham 79 NU 1019
Egloshayle 4 SX 0071
Egloskerry 4 SX 2786
Eglwys-Brewis 28 ST 0168
Eglwysbach 49 SH 8070
Eglwyswrw 26 SN 1438
Egmanton 54 SK 7368
Egremont 62 NY 0110
Egton 67 NZ 8006
Egton Bridge 67 NZ 8005
Egypt 105 NJ 9166
Eilanreach 101 NG 8017
Eilean Darach 106 NH 1087
Elan Village 27 SN 9365
Elberton (Avon) 29 ST 6088
Elburton (Devon.) 5 SX 5353
Elcombe 18 SU 1280
Eldernell 45 TL 3298
Eldersfield 32 SO 7931
Elderslie 82 NS 4462
Eldroth 65 SD 7665
Eldwick 59 SE 1240
Elford (Northum.) 87 NU 1830
Elford (Staffs.) 42 SK 1810
Elgin 104 NJ 2162
Elgol 100 NG 5214
Elham 15 TR 1744
Elie 93 NO 4900
Elim 48 SH 3584
Eling 11 SU 3612
Elishader 100 NG 5065
Elishaw 78 NY 8694
Elkesley 53 SK 6875
Elkstone 32 SO 9612
Elland 59 SE 1020
Ellastone 52 SK 1143
Ellemford 86 NT 7360
Ellen's Green 12 TQ 1035
Ellenhall 41 SJ 8426
Ellerbeck (N Yorks.) 66 SE 4396
Ellerby (Humbs.) 61 TA 1637
Ellerby (N Yorks.) 73 NZ 7914
Ellerdine Heath 41 SJ 6121
Ellerker 60 SE 9229
Ellerton (Humbs.) 60 SE 7039
Ellerton (Salop) 41 SJ 7126
Ellesborough 34 SP 8306
Ellesmere 50 SJ 3934
Ellesmere Port 50 SJ 4077
Ellingham (Norf.) 47 TM 3592
Ellingham (Northum.) 87 NU 1725
Ellingstring 65 SE 1783
Ellington (Northum.) 79 NZ 2792
Ellisfield 19 SU 6345
Ellistown 43 SK 4311
Ellon 105 NJ 9530
Ellough 47 TM 4486
Elloughton 61 SE 9428
Ellwood 29 SO 5808
Elm 45 TF 4607
Elm Park 21 TQ 5385
Elmbridge 41 SO 8967
Elmdon (Essex) 35 TL 4639
Elmdon (W Mids) 42 SP 1783
Elmdon Heath 42 SP 1580
Elmesthorpe 43 SP 4696
Elmhurst 42 SK 1112
Elmley Castle 32 SO 9841
Elmley Lovett 41 SO 8669
Elmore 32 SO 7715
Elmore Back 32 SO 7716
Elmscott 6 SS 2321
Elmsett 37 TM 0546
Elmstead Market 23 TM 0624
Elmsted Court 15 TR 1145
Elmstone 15 TR 2660
Elmstone Hardwicke 32 SO 9226
Elmswell 36 TL 9964
Elmton 53 SK 5073
Elphin 110 NC 2111
Elphinstone 85 NT 3970
Elrick 105 NJ 8206
Elrig 68 NX 3247
Elsdon (Northumb.) 78 NY 9393
Elsecar 59 SE 3800
Elsenham 22 TL 5425
Elsfield 33 SP 5409
Elsham 61 TA 0312
Elsing 47 TG 0516
Elslack 58 SD 9349
Elsrickle 85 NT 0643
Elstead (Surrey) 12 SU 9043
Elsted (W Susx.) 12 SU 8119
Elston (Notts) 54 SK 7548
Elstone 7 SS 6716
Elstow 35 TL 0547
Elstree 21 TQ 1895
Elstronwick 61 TA 2232
Elswick 57 SD 4138
Elsworth 35 TL 3163
Elterwater 62 NY 3204
Eltham 21 TQ 4274
Eltisley 35 TL 2759
Elton (Cambs.) 45 TL 0893
Elton (Ches.) 50 SJ 4575
Elton (Clev.) 72 NZ 4017
Elton (Derby) 53 SK 2261
Elton (Glos.) 29 SO 6914
Elton (Here & W) 40 SO 4571
Elton (Notts.) 54 SK 7638
Elvanfoot 76 NS 9517
Elvaston 53 SK 4132
Elveden 36 TL 8279
Elvingston 86 NT 4674
Elvington (Kent) 15 TR 2750
Elvington (N Yorks.) 60 SE 6947
Elwick (Cleve.) 73 NZ 4532
Elwick (Northum.) 87 NU 1136
Elworth 51 SJ 7361
Elworthy 16 ST 0835
Ely (Cambs.) 45 TL 5380
Ely (S Glam.) 28 ST 1476
Emberton 34 SP 8849
Embleton (Cumbr.) 62 NY 1630
Embleton (Northum.) 79 NU 2322
Embo 108 NH 8192
Emborough 17 ST 6151
Embsay 65 SE 0053
Emery Down 11 SU 2808
Emley 59 SE 2413
Emmer Green 20 SU 7177
Emmington 34 SP 7402
Emneth 45 TF 4807
Emneth Hungate 45 TF 5107
Empingham 44 SK 9408
Empshott 12 SU 7731
Emsworth 12 SU 7405
Enborne 19 SU 4365
Enchmarsh 40 SO 4996
End Moor 63 SD 5584
Enderby 43 SP 5399
Endon 51 SJ 9253
Enfield 21 TQ 3296
Enford 18 SU 1351
Engine Common 29 ST 6984
Englefield 19 SU 6272
Englefield Green 20 SU 9870
English Bicknor 29 SO 5815
English Frankton 40 SJ 4529
Englishcombe 17 ST 7162
Enham-Alamein 19 SU 3648
Enmore 16 ST 2335
Ennerdale Bridge 62 NY 0615
Enoch 76 NS 8801
Enochdhu 98 NO 0662
Ensbury 10 SZ 0896
Ensdon 40 SJ 4016
Ensis 6 SS 5626
Enstone 33 SP 3725
Enterkinfoot 76 NS 8504
Enville 40 SO 8286
Eoropie 109 NB 5156
Epperstone 53 SK 6548
Epping 35 TL 4602
Epping Green (Essex) 35 TL 4305
Epping Green (Herts.) 35 TL 2906
Epping Upland 35 TL 4404
Eppleby 72 NZ 1713
Epsom 21 TQ 2160
Epwell 33 SP 3540
Epworth 60 SE 7803
Erbistock 50 SJ 3541
Erbusaig 101 NG 7629
Erdington 42 SP 1291
Eredine 89 NM 9609
Eriboll 110 NC 4356
Ericstane 77 NT 0710
Eridge Green 13 TQ 5535
Erines 81 NR 8575
Eriswell 36 TL 7278
Erith 21 TQ 5177
Erlestoke 18 ST 9853
Ermington 5 SX 6353
Erpingham 47 TG 1831
Errogie 102 NH 5622
Errol 93 NO 2522
Ersary 109 NF 7100
Erskine 82 NS 4771
Ervie 68 NX 0067
Erwarton 37 TM 2234
Erwood 27 SO 0943
Eryholme 66 NZ 3208
Eryrys 50 SJ 2057
Escalls 2 SW 3627
Escrick 60 SE 6243
Esgairgeiliog 39 SH 7605
Esh 72 NZ 1944
Esh Winning 72 NZ 1942
Esher 20 TQ 1464
Eshott 79 NZ 2097
Eshton 65 SD 9356
Eskadale 102 NH 4539
Eskbank 85 NT 3266
Eskdale Green 62 NY 1400
Esprick 57 SD 4035
Essendine 44 TF 0412
Essendon 35 TL 2708
Essich 103 NH 6539
Essington 41 SJ 9603
Esslemont 105 NJ 9329
Eston 73 NZ 5518
Eswick 113 HU 4854
Etal 87 NT 9339
Etchilhampton 18 SU 0460
Etchingham 14 TQ 7126
Etchinghill (Kent) 15 TR 1639
Etchinghill (Staffs.) 42 SK 0218
Eton 20 SU 9678
Etteridge 97 NN 6892
Ettington 33 SP 2649
Etton (Humbs.) 61 SE 9743
Etton (Cambs.) 45 TF 1306
Ettrick 77 NT 2714
Ettrickbridge End 77 NT 3824
Etwall 53 SK 2732
Euston 36 TL 8978
Euxton 57 SD 5518
Evanton 102 NH 6066
Evedon 55 TF 0947
Evelix 108 NH 7690
Evenjobb 30 SO 2662
Evenley 33 SP 5834
Evenlode 33 SP 2229
Evenwood 72 NZ 1524
Evercreech 17 ST 6438
Everdon 33 SP 5957
Everingham 60 SE 8042
Everleigh 18 SU 1953
Everley 67 SE 9789
Eversholt 34 SP 9933
Evershot 9 ST 5704
Eversley 20 SU 7762
Eversley Cross 20 SU 7961
Everton (Beds.) 35 TL 2051
Everton (Hants) 11 SZ 2993
Everton (Notts.) 53 SK 6891
Evertown 70 NY 3576
Evesbatch 31 SO 6848
Evesham 32 SP 0344
Evington 43 SK 6203
Ewden Village 59 SK 2797
Ewell 21 TQ 2262
Ewell Minnis 15 TR 2643
Ewelme 19 SU 6491
Ewen 18 SU 0097
Ewenny 28 SS 9077
Ewerby 55 TF 1247
Ewesley 79 NZ 0592
Ewhurst (E Susx) 14 TQ 7924
Ewhurst (Surrey) 12 TQ 0940
Ewloe 50 SJ 3066
Eworthy 6 SX 4494
Ewshot 20 SU 8149
Ewyas Harold 29 SO 3828
Exbourne 6 SS 6002
Exbury 11 SU 4200
Exebridge 8 SS 9324
Exelby 66 SE 2986
Exeter 8 SX 9292
Exford 7 SS 8538
Exhall 32 SP 1055
Exminster 8 SX 9487
Exmouth 8 SY 0080
Exning 36 TL 6265
Exton (Devon) 8 SX 9886
Exton (Hants.) 11 SU 6121
Exton (Leic.) 44 SK 9211
Exton (Somer.) 16 SS 9233
Eyam 53 SK 2176
Eydon 33 SP 5450
Eye (Cambs.) 45 TF 2202
Eye (Here & W) 30 SO 4963
Eye (Suffolk) 37 TM 1473
Eyemouth 87 NT 9464
Eyeworth 35 TL 2545
Eyhorne Street 14 TQ 8354
Eyke 37 TM 3151
Eynesbury 35 TL 1859
Eynsford 21 TQ 5365
Eynsham 33 SP 4309
Eype 9 SY 4491
Eythorne 15 TR 2849
Eyton (Here & W) 30 SO 4761
Eyton (Salop) 40 SO 3687
Eyton upon the Weald Moors 41 SJ 6414

F

Faccombe 19 SU 3958
Faceby 66 NZ 4903
Faddiley 51 SJ 5752
Fadmoor 66 SE 6789
Faifley 82 NS 5073
Failand 29 ST 5272
Failford 75 NS 4526
Failsworth 58 SD 9002
Fair Oak (Hants.) 11 SU 4918
Fairbourne 38 SH 6113
Fairburn 60 SE 4727
Fairfield 41 SO 9475
Fairford 32 SP 1501
Fairlie 82 NS 2155
Fairlight 14 TQ 8612
Fairmile (Devon) 8 SY 0997
Fairmilehead 85 NT 2567
Fairoak (Staffs.) 51 SJ 7632
Fairseat 14 TQ 6261
Fairstead (Essex) 22 TL 7616
Fairstead (Norf.) 47 TG 2723
Fairwarp 13 TQ 4626
Fairy Cross 6 SS 4024
Fakenham 46 TF 9229
Fala 86 NT 4361
Fala Dam 86 NT 4261
Falahill 85 NT 3956
Faldingworth 54 TF 0684
Falfield 29 ST 6893
Falkenham 37 TM 2939
Falkirk 84 NS 8880
Falkland 92 NO 2507
Falla 78 NT 7013
Fallin 91 NS 8391
Falmer 13 TQ 3508
Falmouth 2 SW 8032
Falstone 78 NY 7287
Fanagmore 110 NC 1750
Fangdale Beck 66 SE 5694
Fangfoss 67 SE 7653
Fanmore 94 NM 4244
Fans 86 NT 6140
Far Cotton 34 SP 7458
Far Sawrey 63 SD 3795
Faraclett 113 HY 4433
Farcet 45 TL 2094
Farden 41 SO 5776
Fareham 11 SU 5806
Farewell 42 SK 0811
Faringdon 19 SU 2895
Farington 57 SD 5425
Farlam 71 NY 5558
Farleigh (Surrey) 21 TQ 3660
Farleigh Hungerford 18 ST 7957
Farleigh Wallop 19 SU 6246
Farlesthorpe 55 TF 4774
Farley (Salop) 40 SJ 3808
Farley (Staffs.) 52 SK 0644
Farley (Wilts.) 11 SU 2229
Farley Green 20 TQ 0645
Farley Hill 20 SU 7564
Farleys End 32 SO 7615
Farlington 66 SE 6167
Farlow 41 SO 6380
Farmborough 17 ST 6560
Farmcote 32 SP 0629
Farmers 27 SN 6444
Farmington 32 SP 1315
Farmoor 33 SP 4407
Farmtown 104 NJ 5051
Farnborough (Berks.) 19 SU 4381
Farnborough (Gtr London) 21 TQ 4464
Farnborough (Hants.) 20 SU 8753
Farnborough (Warw.) 33 SP 4349
Farncombe 20 SU 9745
Farndish 34 SP 9263
Farndon (Ches.) 50 SJ 4154
Farndon (Notts.) 54 SK 7651
Farnell 99 NO 6255
Farnham (Dorset) 10 ST 9514
Farnham (Essex) 35 TL 4724
Farnham (N Yorks.) 66 SE 3460
Farnham (Suff.) 37 TM 3660
Farnham (Surrey) 20 SU 8446
Farnham Common 20 SU 9584
Farnham Green 35 TL 4625
Farnham Royal 20 SU 9682
Farningham 21 TQ 5566
Farnley 59 SE 2147
Farnley Tyas 59 SE 1612
Farnsfield 53 SK 6456
Farnworth (Ches.) 50 SJ 5187
Farnworth (Gtr Mches.) 58 SD 7305
Farr (Highld.) 111 NC 7163
Farr (Highld.) 103 NH 6833
Farr (Highld.) 97 NH 8203
Farringdon 8 SY 0191
Farrington Gurney 17 ST 6255
Farsley 59 SE 2135
Farthinghoe 33 SP 5339
Farthingstone 34 SP 6155
Farway 8 SY 1895
Fasnacloich 96 NN 0247
Fasque 99 NO 6475
Fassfern 96 NN 0278
Fatfield 72 NZ 3053
Fattahead 105 NJ 6657
Faugh 71 NY 5154
Fauldhouse 84 NS 9260
Faulkbourne 22 TL 7917
Faulkland 18 ST 7354
Fauls 51 SJ 5933
Faversham 15 TR 0161
Favillar 104 NJ 2734
Fawfieldhead 52 SK 0763
Fawkham Green 21 TQ 5865
Fawler 33 SP 3717
Fawley (Berks.) 19 SU 3981
Fawley (Bucks.) 20 SU 7586
Fawley (Hants.) 11 SU 4503
Fawley Chapel 29 SO 5829
Faxfleet 60 SE 8624
Faygate 13 TQ 2134
Fazeley 42 SK 2001
Fearby 65 SE 1981
Fearnan 97 NN 7244
Fearnhead 51 SJ 6290
Fearnmore 101 NG 7260
Featherstone (Staffs.) 41 SJ 9305
Featherstone (W Yorks.) 59 SE 4222
Feckenham 32 SP 0061
Fedderate 105 NJ 8949
Feering 36 TL 8720
Feetham 65 SD 9898
Felbridge 13 TQ 3739
Felbrigg 47 TG 2039
Felcourt 13 TQ 3841
Felden 35 TL 0404
Felindre (Dyfed) 25 SN 7027
Felindre (Powys) 40 SO 1681
Felinfach 27 SO 0933
Felinfoel 25 SN 5202
Felingwm Uchaf 25 SN 5024
Felixkirk 66 SE 4684
Felixstowe 37 TM 3034
Felkington 87 NT 9444
Felling 72 NZ 2762
Felmersham 34 SP 9957
Felmingham 47 TG 2529
Felpham 12 SZ 9599
Felsham 36 TL 9457
Felsted 22 TL 6720
Feltham 20 TQ 1072
Felthorpe 47 TG 1618
Felton (Avon) 29 ST 5165
Felton (Here & W) 31 SO 5748
Felton (Northum.) 79 NU 1800
Felton Butler 40 SJ 3917
Feltwell 46 TL 7190
Feltwell Anchor 46 TL 6789
Fen Ditton 35 TL 4860
Fen Drayton 45 TL 3468
Fen End 42 SP 2274
Fence 58 SD 8237
Fendike Corner 55 TF 4560
Feniscowles 58 SD 6425
Feniton 8 SY 1199
Fenny Bentley 52 SK 1750
Fenny Bridges 8 SY 1198
Fenny Compton 33 SP 4152
Fenny Drayton 43 SP 3597
Fenny Stratford 34 SP 8834
Fenrother 79 NZ 1792
Fenstanton 45 TL 3168
Fenton (Cambs.) 45 TL 3279
Fenton (Lincs.) 54 SK 8476
Fenton (Lincs.) 54 SK 8750
Fenton (Staffs.) 51 SJ 8944
Fenton Town 87 NT 9733
Fenwick (Northum.) 87 NU 0639
Fenwick (Northum.) 79 NZ 0572
Fenwick (S Yorks.) 60 SE 5916
Fenwick (Strath.) 82 NS 4643
Feochaig 74 NR 7714
Feock 2 SW 8238
Feolin Ferry 80 NR 4469
Feriniquarrie 100 NG 1750
Fern 99 NO 4861
Ferndale 28 SS 9997
Ferndown 10 SU 0700
Ferness 103 NH 9645
Fernham 19 SU 2991
Fernhill Heath 32 SO 8659
Fernhurst 12 SU 9028
Fernie 93 NO 3115
Fernilea 100 NG 3732
Fernilee 52 SK 0178
Ferrensby 66 SE 3660
Ferring 12 TQ 0902
Ferrybridge 60 SE 4824
Ferryden 99 NO 7156
Ferryhill 72 NZ 2832
Ferryside 25 SN 3610
Fersfield 47 TM 0682
Feshiebridge 97 NH 8504
Fetcham 21 TQ 1555
Fetterangus 105 NJ 9850
Fettercairn 99 NO 6573
Fewcott 33 SP 5427
Fewston 65 SE 1954
Ffairfach 25 SN 6220
Ffestiniog 49 SH 7042
Fforest 25 SN 5804
Ffostrasol 26 SN 3747
Ffrith 50 SJ 2855
Ffrwdgrech 28 SO 0227
Ffynnonddrain 25 SN 4021
Ffynnongroew 50 SJ 1382
Fiddes 99 NO 8181
Fiddington (Glos.) 32 SO 9231
Fiddington (Somer.) 16 ST 2140
Fiddlers Hamlet 35 TL 4701
Field 52 SK 0233
Field Broughton 62 SD 3881
Field Dalling 46 TG 0039
Field Head 43 SK 4909
Fifehead Magdalen 10 ST 7721
Fifehead Neville 9 ST 7610
Fifield (Berks.) 20 SU 9076
Fifield (Oxon.) 33 SP 2318
Figheldean 18 SU 1547
Filby 47 TG 4613
Filey 67 TA 1180
Filgrave 34 SP 8748
Filkins 33 SP 2304
Filleigh (Devon.) 7 SS 6628
Filleigh (Devon.) 7 SS 7410
Fillingham 54 SK 9485
Fillongley 43 SP 2787
Filton 29 ST 6079
Fimber 67 SE 8960
Finavon 99 NO 4957
Fincham 46 TF 6806
Finchampstead 20 SU 7963
Finchdean 12 SU 7312
Finchingfield 36 TL 6832
Finchley 21 TQ 2890
Findern 53 SK 3030
Findhorn 103 NJ 0464
Findo Gask 91 NO 0020
Findochty 104 NJ 4667
Findon (Grampn.) 99 NO 9397
Findon (W. Susx) 12 TQ 1208
Findon Mains 102 NH 6060
Finedon 44 SP 9272
Fingal Street 37 TM 2169
Fingask 105 NJ 7827
Fingest 20 SU 7791
Finghall 65 SE 1889
Fingringhoe 23 TM 0220
Finmere 34 SP 6333
Finnart 97 NN 5157
Finningham 37 TM 0669
Finningley 104 SK 6699
Finnygaud 104 NJ 6054
Finsbay 109 NG 0786
Finsbury 21 TQ 3282
Finstall 41 SO 9869
Finsthwaite 62 SD 3687
Finstock 33 SP 3516
Finstown 113 HY 3514
Fintry (Central) 84 NS 6186
Fintry (Grampn.) 105 NJ 7554
Fionnphort (Island of Mull) 88 NM 2923
Fir Tree 72 NZ 1334
Firbeck 53 SK 5688
Firgrove 58 SD 9113
Firsby 55 TF 4563
Fishbourne (I of W) 11 SZ 5592
Fishbourne (W Susx) 12 SU 8304
Fishburn 72 NZ 3632
Fishcross 91 NS 8995
Fisher's Pond 11 SU 4820
Fisherford 105 NJ 6635
Fisherstreet 12 SU 9531
Fisherton (Highld.) 103 NH 7451
Fisherton (Strath.) 75 NS 2717
Fishguard 24 SM 9637
Fishlake 60 SE 6513
Fishpool 58 SD 8009
Fishtoft 55 TF 3642
Fishtoft Drove 55 TF 3148
Fishtown of Usan 99 NO 7254
Fishwick 87 NT 9151
Fiskavaig 100 NG 3234
Fiskerton (Lincs.) 54 TF 0472
Fiskerton (Notts.) 54 SK 7351
Fittleton 18 SU 1449
Fittleworth 12 TQ 0119
Fitton End 45 TF 4312
Fitz 40 SJ 4417
Fitzhead 16 ST 1228
Fitzwilliam 59 SE 4115
Five Ashes 13 TQ 5525
Five Oak Green 13 TQ 6445
Five Oaks (W. Sussex) 12 TQ 0928
Five Roads 25 SN 4905
Fivehead 8 ST 3522
Flackwell Heath 20 SU 8890
Fladbury 32 SO 9946
Fladdabister 113 HU 4332
Flagg 52 SK 1368
Flamborough 67 TA 2270
Flamstead 35 TL 0814
Flansham 12 SU 9601
Flasby 65 SD 9456
Flash 52 SK 0267
Flashader 100 NG 3553
Flatt, The 71 NY 5678
Flaunden 34 TL 0100
Flawborough 54 SK 7842
Flawith 66 SE 4865
Flax Bourton 29 ST 5069
Flaxby 66 SE 3957
Flaxley 29 SO 6915
Flaxpool 16 ST 1435
Flaxton 66 SE 6762
Fleckney 43 SP 6493
Flecknoe 33 SP 5163
Fleet (Hants.) 20 SU 8054
Fleet (Lincs.) 45 TF 3823
Fleet Hargate 45 TF 3925
Fleetham 79 NU 1928
Fleetwood 57 SD 3247
Flemingston 28 ST 0170
Flemington 84 NS 6559
Flempton 36 TL 8169
Fletching 13 TQ 4323
Flexford 20 SU 9350
Flimby 62 NY 0233
Flimwell 14 TQ 7131
Flint 50 SJ 2472
Flint Mountain 50 SJ 2369
Flintham 54 SK 7446
Flinton 61 TA 2136
Flitcham 46 TF 7226
Flitton 35 TL 0536
Flitwick 35 TL 0335
Flixborough 60 SE 8715
Flixton (Gtr Mches.) 51 SJ 7494
Flixton (N Yorks.) 67 TA 0479
Flixton (Suff.) 47 TM 3186
Flockton 59 SE 2314
Flodden 87 NT 9235
Flodigarry 100 NG 4671
Flookburgh 64 SD 3675
Flordon 47 TM 1897
Flore 34 SP 6460
Flotterton 79 NT 9902
Flowton 37 TM 0847
Flushing (Corn.) 2 SW 8034
Flushing (Grampn.) 105 NK 0546
Flyford Flavell 32 SO 9754
Fobbing 22 TQ 7183
Fochabers 104 NJ 3458
Fochriw 28 SO 1005
Fockerby 60 SE 8419
Fodderletter 104 NJ 1421

Foel 237 Gowdall

Foel 39 SH 9911
Foffarty 98 NO 4145
Foggathorpe 60 SE 7537
Fogo 87 NT 7749
Foindle 110 NC 1948
Folda 98 NO 1964
Fole 52 SK 0437
Foleshill 43 SP 3582
Folke 9 ST 6513
Folkestone 15 TR 2336
Folkingham 54 TF 0733
Folkington 13 TQ 5604
Folksworth 45 TL 1489
Folkton 67 TA 0579
Folla Rule 105 NJ 7333
Follifoot 66 SE 3452
Folly Gate 6 SX 5797
Fonthill Bishop 10 ST 9332
Fonthill Gifford 10 ST 9231
Fontmell Magna 10 ST 8616
Fontwell 12 SU 9407
Foolow 52 SK 1976
Foots Cray 21 TQ 4770
Forcett 72 NZ 1712
Ford (Bucks.) 34 SP 7709
Ford (Glos.) 32 SP 0829
Ford (Northum.) 87 NT 9437
Ford (Salop) 40 SJ 4113
Ford (Staffs.) 52 SK 0654
Ford (Strath.) 89 NM 8603
Ford (W Susx) 12 TQ 0003
Ford (Wilts.) 18 ST 8475
Ford End 22 TL 6716
Ford Street (Somer.) 8 ST 1518
Fordcombe 13 TQ 5240
Fordell 85 NT 1588
Forden 40 SJ 2201
Fordham (Cambs.) 36 TL 6370
Fordham (Essex) 23 TL 9228
Fordham (Norf.) 46 TL 6199
Fordingbridge 10 SU 1413
Fordon 67 TA 0475
Fordoun 99 NO 7475
Fordstreet (Essex) 23 TL 9227
Fordwells 33 SP 3013
Fordwich 15 TR 1859
Fordyce 104 NJ 5563
Foremark 43 SK 3326
Forest Gate 21 TQ 4085
Forest Green 12 TQ 1241
Forest Head 71 NY 5857
Forest Hill 33 SP 5807
Forest Mill 91 NS 9594
Forest Row 13 TQ 4235
Forest Town 53 SK 5662
Forestburn Gate 79 NZ 0696
Forestfield 84 NS 8566
Forestside 12 SU 7512
Forfar 98 NO 4550
Forgandenny 92 NO 0818
Forgie 104 NJ 3954
Formby 57 SD 2907
Forncett End 47 TM 1493
Forncett St. Mary 47 TM 1694
Forncett St. Peter 47 TM 1693
Forneth 98 NO 0945
Fornham All Saints 36 TL 8367
Fornham St. Martin 36 TL 8566
Forres 103 NJ 0358
Forsbrook 51 SJ 9641
Forse 112 ND 2234
Forsinard 111 NC 8842
Forstal, The 14 TQ 8946
Forston 9 SY 6695
Fort Augustus 102 NH 3709
Fort George 103 NH 7656
Fort William 96 NN 1074
Forter 98 NO 1864
Forteviot 92 NO 0517
Forth 84 NS 9453
Forthampton 32 SO 8532
Fortingall 97 NN 7447
Forton (Hants.) 19 SU 4243
Forton (Lancs.) 64 SD 4851
Forton (Salop) 40 SJ 4216
Forton (Somer.) 8 ST 3300
Forton (Staffs.) 41 SJ 7521
Fortree 105 NJ 9640
Fortrie 105 NJ 6645
Fortrose 103 NH 7256
Fortuneswell 9 SY 6873
Forty Hill 21 TQ 3398
Forward Green 37 TM 1059
Fosbury 19 SU 3157
Fosdyke 55 TF 3133
Foss 97 NN 7958
Foss-y-ffin 26 SN 4460
Fossebridge 32 SP 0811
Foster Street 35 TL 4909
Foston (Derby.) 52 SK 1831
Foston (Lincs.) 54 SK 8542
Foston on the Wolds 67 TA 1055
Fotherby 55 TF 3191
Fotheringhay 45 TL 0593
Foul Mile 13 TQ 6215
Foulden (Borders) 87 NT 9355
Foulden (Norf.) 46 TL 7699
Foulridge 58 SD 8942
Foulsham 47 TG 0324
Fountainhall 86 NT 4349
Four Ashes (Suffolk) 36 TM 0070
Four Crosses (Powys) 39 SJ 0508
Four Crosses (Powys) 40 SJ 2718
Four Crosses (Staffs.) 41 SJ 9509
Four Elms 21 TQ 4648
Four Forks 16 ST 2336
Four Gotes 45 TF 4516
Four Lanes 2 SW 6838
Four Marks 11 SU 6634
Four Mile Bridge 48 SH 2778
Four Oaks (E Susx) 14 TQ 8624
Four Oaks (W Mids) 42 SP 1198
Four Oaks (W Mids) 42 SP 2480
Four Throws 14 TQ 7729
Fourlanes End 51 SJ 8059
Fourstones 71 NY 8967
Fovant 10 SU 0028
Foveran 105 NJ 9824
Fowey 4 SX 1251
Fowlis 93 NO 3133
Fowlis Wester 91 NN 9223
Fowlmere 35 TL 4245
Fownhope 31 SO 5734
Fox Lane 20 SU 8557
Foxdale 56 SC 2878
Foxearth 36 TL 8344
Foxfield 62 SD 2085
Foxham 18 ST 9777
Foxhole (Corn.) 3 SW 9654
Foxholes (N Yorks.) 67 TA 0173
Foxley (Norf.) 47 TG 0321
Foxley (Wilts.) 18 ST 8985
Foxt 52 SK 0348
Foxton (Cambs.) 35 TL 4148
Foxton (Leic.) 44 SP 7090
Foxup 65 SD 8676
Foxwist Green 51 SJ 6268
Foy 29 SO 5928
Foyers 102 NH 4921
Fraddon 3 SW 9158
Fradley 42 SK 1513
Fradswell 51 SJ 9831
Fraisthorpe 67 TA 1561
Framfield 13 TQ 4920
Framingham Earl 47 TG 2702
Framingham Pigot 47 TG 2703
Framlingham 37 TM 2863
Frampton (Dorset) 9 SY 6294
Frampton (Lincs.) 55 TF 3239
Frampton Cotterell 29 ST 6582
Frampton Mansell 32 SO 9202
Frampton West End 55 TF 3041
Frampton on Severn 32 SO 7407
Framsden 37 TM 1959
Framwellgate Moor 72 NZ 2644
Franche 41 SO 8178
Frankby 50 SJ 2486
Frankley 41 SO 9980
Frankton 43 SP 4270
Frant 13 TQ 5835
Fraserburgh 105 NJ 9966
Frating Green 23 TM 0923
Fratton 11 SU 6600
Freathy 4 SX 3952
Freckenham 36 TL 6672
Freckleton 57 SD 4228
Freeby 44 SK 8020
Freeland 33 SP 4112
Freethorpe 47 TG 4105
Freethorpe Common 47 TG 4004
Freiston 55 TF 3743
Fremington (Devon) 6 SS 5132
Frenchay 29 ST 6377
Frenchbeer 5 SX 6785
Frensham 12 SU 8441
Freshfield 36 SD 2807
Freshwater 11 SZ 3487
Fressingfield 37 TM 2677
Freston 37 TM 1739
Freswick 112 ND 3667
Frettenham 47 TG 2417
Freuchie 93 NO 2806
Friar's Gate 13 TQ 4933
Friday Bridge 45 TF 4605
Fridaythorpe 67 SE 8759
Friern Barnet 21 TQ 2892
Friesthorpe 54 TF 0683
Frieth 20 SU 7990
Frilford 19 SU 4497
Frilsham 19 SU 5373
Frimley 20 SU 8758
Frindsbury 14 TQ 7369
Fring 46 TF 7334
Fringford 34 SP 6028
Frinsted 14 TQ 8957
Frinton-on-Sea 23 TM 2319
Friockheim 99 NO 5949
Frisby on the Wreake 43 SK 6917
Friskney 55 TF 4555
Friston (E Susx) 13 TV 5408
Friston (Suff.) 37 TM 4160
Fritchley 53 SK 3553
Frith Bank 55 TF 3147
Frith Common 41 SO 6969
Fritham 11 SU 2413
Frithelstock 6 SS 4619
Frithville 55 TF 3250
Frittenden 14 TQ 8141
Fritton (Norf.) 47 TG 4700
Fritton (Norf.) 47 TM 2293
Fritwell 33 SP 5229
Frizington 62 NY 0316
Frocester 32 SO 7803
Frodesley 40 SJ 5101
Frodsham 50 SJ 5177
Froggatt 53 SK 2476
Froghall 52 SK 0247
Frogmore (Hants) 20 SU 8360
Frolesworth 43 SP 5090
Frome 18 ST 7747
Frome St. Quintin 9 ST 5902
Fromes Hill 31 SO 6846
Fron (Gwyn.) 48 SH 3539
Fron (Powys) 40 SJ 2203
Fron (Powys) 30 SO 0865
Fron Cysyllte 50 SJ 2741
Fron-goch 49 SH 9039
Frosterley 72 NZ 0237
Froxfield 19 SU 2967
Froxfield Green 11 SU 7025
Fryerning 22 TL 6400
Fryton 66 SE 6875
Fulbeck 54 SK 9450
Fulbourn 35 TL 5256
Fulbrook 33 SP 2513
Fulford (N Yorks.) 60 SE 6149
Fulford (Somer.) 16 ST 2129
Fulford (Staffs.) 51 SJ 9438
Fulham 21 TQ 2576
Fulking 13 TQ 2411
Full Sutton 67 SE 7455
Fuller Street 22 TL 7415
Fuller's Moor 50 SJ 4953
Fullerton 11 SU 3739
Fulletby 55 TF 2973
Fullwood 82 NS 4450
Fulmer 20 SU 9985
Fulmodeston 46 TF 9931
Fulnetby 55 TF 0979
Fulstow 61 TF 3297
Fulwell 72 NZ 3959
Fulwood (Lancs.) 57 SD 5331
Fulwood (S Yorks.) 53 SK 3085
Funtington 12 SU 7908
Funtley 11 SU 5608
Funzie 113 HU 6689
Furnace (Strath.) 89 NN 0200
Furneux Pelham 35 TL 4327
Fyfett 8 ST 2314
Fyfield (Essex) 22 TL 5707
Fyfield (Glos.) 33 SP 2003
Fyfield (Hants.) 19 SU 2946
Fyfield (Oxon.) 19 SU 4298
Fyfield (Wilts.) 18 SU 1468
Fylingthorpe 67 NZ 9405
Fyvie 105 NJ 7037

G

Garvard 88 NR 3691
Garve 102 NH 3961
Garvestone 46 TG 0207
Gabroc Hill 82 NS 4551
Gaddesby 43 SK 6813
Gaer 28 SO 1721
Gaerwen 48 SH 4871
Gagingwell 33 SP 4025
Gainford 72 NZ 1716
Gainsborough 54 SK 8189
Gainsford End 36 TL 7235
Gairloch 106 NG 8076
Gairlochy 96 NN 1784
Gairney Bank 92 NT 1299
Galashiels 86 NT 4936
Galby 43 SK 6901
Galgate 64 SD 4855
Galhampton 17 ST 6329
Gallatown 93 NT 2994
Galley Common 43 SP 3192
Galleyend 22 TL 7103
Galleywood 22 TL 7002
Gallowfauld 98 NO 4342
Galltair 101 NG 8120
Galmisdale 95 NM 4784
Galmpton (Devon) 5 SX 6940
Galmpton (Devon) 5 SX 8856
Galphay 66 SE 2572
Galston 82 NS 5036
Galtrigill 100 NG 1854
Gamblesby 63 NY 6039
Gamlingay 35 TL 2452
Gamrie 105 NJ 7962
Gamston (Notts.) 53 SK 6037
Gamston (Notts.) 54 SK 7076
Ganavan 89 NM 8632
Ganllwyd 39 SH 7224
Gannochy 99 NO 5970
Ganstead 61 TA 1434
Ganthorpe 66 SE 6870
Ganton 67 SE 9877
Garbhallt (Strath.) 89 NS 0295
Garboldisham 46 TM 0081
Gardenstown 105 NJ 7964
Gare Hill 18 ST 7840
Garelochhead 90 NS 2491
Garford 19 SU 4296
Garforth 59 SE 4033
Gargrave 65 SD 9354
Gargunnock 91 NS 7094
Garinin 109 NB 1944
Garlieston 69 NX 4746
Garlogie 105 NJ 7805
Garmond 105 NJ 8052
Garmony 88 NM 6741
Garmouth 104 NJ 3364
Garn 48 SH 2734
Garn-Dolbenmaen 48 SH 4944
Garnant 25 SN 6813
Garnett Bridge 63 SD 5299
Garnkirk 84 NS 6768
Garrabost 109 NB 5133
Garraron 89 NM 8008
Garras 2 SW 7023
Garreg 48 SH 6141
Garreg Bank 40 SJ 2811
Garrick 91 NN 8412
Garrigill 71 NY 7441
Garros 100 NG 4963
Garrow 91 NN 8240
Garsdon 18 ST 9687
Garshall Green 51 SJ 9633
Garsington 33 SP 5802
Garstang 57 SD 4945
Garston 50 SJ 4083
Garswood 50 SJ 5599
Gartcosh 84 NS 6968
Garth (Clwyd) 50 SJ 2542
Garth (I. of M.) 56 SC 3177
Garth (Mid Glam.) 28 SS 8690
Garth (Powys) 27 SN 9549
Garthbrengy 27 SO 0433
Gartheli 27 SN 5956
Garthmyl 40 SO 1999
Garthorpe (Humbs.) 60 SE 8419
Garthorpe (Leic.) 44 SK 8320
Gartmore 90 NS 5297
Gartness (Central) 90 NS 5086
Gartness (Strath.) 84 NS 7864
Gartocharn 90 NS 4286
Garton 61 TA 2635
Garton-on-the-Wolds 67 SE 9859
Gartymore 112 ND 0114
Garvald 86 NT 5870
Garvan 96 NM 9777
Garvock 82 NS 2571
Garway 29 SO 4522
Garynahine 109 NB 2331
Gastard 18 ST 8868
Gasthorpe 46 TL 9780
Gatcombe 11 SZ 4885
Gate Burton 54 SK 8382
Gate Helmsley 66 SE 6955
Gatebeck 63 SD 5485
Gateforth 60 SE 5528
Gatehead 82 NS 3936
Gatehouse 78 NY 7988
Gatehouse of Fleet 69 NX 5956
Gatelawbridge 76 NX 9096
Gateley 46 TF 9624
Gatenby 66 SE 3287
Gateshead 72 NZ 2562
Gatesheath 50 SJ 4760
Gateside (Fife.) 92 NO 1809
Gateside (Strath.) 82 NS 3653
Gateside (Tays.) 98 NO 4344
Gathurst 57 SD 5307
Gatley 51 SJ 8387
Gattonside 86 NT 5435
Gatwick Airport - London 13 TQ 2841
Gauldry 93 NO 3723
Gaunt's Common 10 SU 0205
Gautby 55 TF 1772
Gavinton 87 NT 7652
Gawber 59 SE 3207
Gawcott 34 SP 6831
Gawsworth 51 SJ 8869
Gawthrop 63 SD 6987
Gawthwaite 62 SD 2784
Gay Street 12 TQ 0820
Gaydon 33 SP 3654
Gayfield 113 HY 4930
Gayhurst 34 SP 8446
Gayles 65 NZ 1207
Gayton (Mers.) 50 SJ 2680
Gayton (Norf.) 46 TF 7219
Gayton (Northants.) 34 SP 7054
Gayton (Staffs.) 41 SJ 9728
Gayton Thorpe 46 TF 7418
Gayton le Marsh 55 TF 4284
Gaywood 46 TF 6320
Gazeley 36 TL 7264
Geary 100 NG 2661
Gedding 36 TL 9457
Geddington 44 SP 8983
Gedintailor 100 NG 5235
Gedney 45 TF 4024
Gedney Broadgate 45 TF 4022
Gedney Drove End 45 TF 4629
Gedney Dyke 45 TF 4126
Gedney Hill 45 TF 3311
Geise 112 ND 1064
Geldeston 47 TM 3891
Gell 49 SH 8569
Gelli Gynan 50 SJ 1854
Gelligaer 28 ST 1397
Gellilydan 49 SH 6839
Gellioedd 49 SH 9344
Gelly 24 SN 0819
Gellyburn 92 NO 0939
Gellywen 25 SN 2723
Gelston 69 NX 7758
Genoch Mains 68 NX 1356
Gentleshaw 42 SK 0511
George Nympton 7 SS 7023
Georgeham 6 SS 4639
Georgetown (Strath.) 82 NS 4567
Georgia 2 SW 4836
Georth 113 HY 3626
Germansweek 4 SX 4394
Germoe 2 SW 5829
Gerrans 3 SW 8735
Gerrards Cross 20 TQ 0088
Gestingthorpe 36 TL 8138
Geuffordd 40 SJ 2114
Gibraltar 55 TF 5558
Gidea Park 21 TQ 5390
Gidleigh 5 SX 6788
Gifford 86 NT 5368
Giggleswick 65 SD 8163
Gilberdyke 60 SE 8329
Gilcrux 62 NY 1138
Gildersome 59 SE 2429
Gildingwells 53 SK 5585
Gileston 28 ST 0167
Gilfach 28 ST 1598
Gilfach Goch 28 SS 9890
Gilfachrheda 26 SN 4058
Gillamoor 66 SE 6890
Gilling East 66 SE 6176
Gilling West 65 NZ 1805
Gillingham (Dorset) 10 ST 8026
Gillingham (Kent) 14 TQ 7768
Gillingham (Norf.) 47 TM 4191
Gillow Heath 51 SJ 8858
Gills 112 ND 3172
Gilmerton (Lothian) 85 NT 2968
Gilmerton (Tays.) 91 NN 8823
Gilmorton 43 SP 5787
Gilsland 71 NY 6366
Gilsland Spa 71 NY 6367
Gilston 86 NT 4456
Gilwern 28 SO 2414
Gimingham 47 TG 2836
Gipping 37 TM 0763
Gipsey Bridge 55 TF 2850
Girlsta 113 HU 4351
Girsby 66 NZ 3508
Girthon 69 NX 6053
Girton (Cambs.) 35 TL 4262
Girton (Notts.) 54 SK 8266
Girvan 75 NX 1897
Gisburn 58 SD 8248
Gisleham 47 TM 5188
Gislingham 37 TM 0771
Gissing 47 TM 1485
Gittisham 8 SY 1398
Gladestry 30 SO 2355
Gladsmuir 86 NT 4573
Glais 25 SN 7000
Glaisdale 67 NZ 7705
Glamis 98 NO 3846
Glan-Conwy 49 SH 8352
Glan-Mule 40 SO 1690
Glan-y-don 50 SJ 1679
Glan-yr-afon (Gwyn.) 49 SJ 0242
Glan-yr-afon (Gwyn.) 49 SH 9141
Glanaber Terrace 49 SH 7547
Glanaman 25 SN 6713
Glandford 47 TG 0441
Glandwr (Dyfed) 24 SN 1928
Glangrwyne 28 SO 2316
Glanrhyd 20 SN 1442
Glanton 79 NU 0714
Glanton Pike 79 NU 0514
Glanvilles Wootton 9 ST 6708
Glapthorn 44 TL 0290
Glapwell 53 SK 4766
Glasbury 30 SO 1739
Glascote 42 SK 2203
Glascwm 30 SO 1553
Glasdrum 96 NN 0046
Glasfryn 49 SH 9150
Glasgow 84 NS 5865
Glasinfryn 48 SH 5868
Glaspwll 39 SN 7397
Glasserton 68 NX 4238
Glassford 84 NS 7247
Glasshouse Hill 32 SO 7020
Glasshouses 65 SE 1764
Glasslaw 105 NJ 8659
Glasslie 92 NO 2305
Glasson (Cumbr.) 70 NY 2560
Glasson (Lancs.) 64 SD 4455
Glassonby 63 NY 5738
Glasterlaw 99 NO 6051
Glaston 44 SK 8900
Glastonbury 17 ST 4938
Glatton 45 TL 1586
Glazebury 58 SJ 6796
Glazeley 41 SO 7088
Gleadless Townend 53 SK 3883
Gleadsmoss 51 SJ 8469
Gleaston 64 SD 2570
Glemsford 36 TL 8247
Glen Auldyn 56 SC 4393
Glen Parva 43 SP 5798
Glen Vine 56 SC 3378
Glenancross 95 NM 6691
Glenbarr 80 NR 6736
Glenbervie 99 NO 7680
Glenboig 84 NS 7268
Glenbreck 77 NT 0521
Glenbuck 76 NS 7429
Glenburn 82 NS 4761
Glencaple 70 NX 9968
Glencarse 92 NO 1922
Glencloy 81 NS 0036
Glencoe 96 NN 1058
Glencraig 92 NT 1795
Glendevon 91 NN 9804
Glendoick 92 NO 2022
Glenduckie 93 NO 2818
Glenegedale 80 NR 3351
Glenelg 101 NG 8119
Glenfarg 92 NO 1310
Glenfield 43 SK 5306
Glenfinart 89 NS 1987
Glenfinnan 95 NM 9080
Glenfoot 92 NO 1715
Glengarnock 82 NS 3252
Glengrasco 100 NG 4444
Glenkindie 104 NJ 4313
Glenlee 69 NX 6080
Glenluce 68 NX 1957
Glenmavis 84 NS 7567
Glenmaye 56 SC 2380
Glenmore (Skye) 100 NG 4340
Glenridding 62 NY 3817
Glenrothes 92 NO 2600
Glensaugh 99 NO 6778
Glensluain 89 NS 0999
Glentham 54 TF 0090
Glentress 85 NT 2839
Glentrool Village 68 NX 3578
Glentworth 54 SK 9488
Glespin 76 NS 8028
Gletness 113 HU 4651
Glewstone 29 SO 5522
Glinton 45 TF 1506
Glooston 44 SP 7596
Glossop 52 SK 0393
Gloster Hill 79 NU 2504
Gloucester 32 SO 8318
Gloup 113 HP 5004
Glusburn 59 SE 0344
Glympton 33 SP 4221
Glyn 49 SH 7457
Glyn Ceiriog 50 SJ 2038
Glyn-Cywarch 48 SH 6034
Glyn-Neath 28 SN 8806
Glynarthen 26 SN 3148
Glyncorrwg 28 SS 8799
Glynde 13 TQ 4509
Glyndebourne 13 TQ 4510
Glyndyfrdwy 50 SJ 1542
Glyntaff 28 ST 0889
Glynteg 26 SN 3637
Gnosall 41 SJ 8220
Gnosall Heath 41 SJ 8419
Goadby 44 SP 7598
Goadby Marwood 44 SK 7826
Goatacre 18 SU 0176
Goathill 9 ST 6717
Goathland 67 NZ 8301
Goathurst 16 ST 2534
Gobowen 50 SJ 3033
Godalming 12 SU 9743
Godmanchester 45 TL 2470
Godmanstone 9 SY 6697
Godmersham 15 TR 0650
Godney 17 ST 4842
Godolphin Cross 2 SW 6031
Godre'r-graig 25 SN 7507
Godshill (Hants.) 10 SU 1714
Godshill (I. of W.) 11 SZ 5281
Godstone 21 TQ 3551
Goetre 29 SO 3205
Goff's Oak 35 TL 3202
Gogar 85 NT 1672
Goginan 39 SN 6981
Golan 48 SH 5242
Golant 4 SX 1254
Golberdon 4 SX 3271
Golborne 51 SJ 6097
Golcar 59 SE 0915
Goldcliff 29 ST 3683
Golden Cross 13 TQ 5312
Golden Green 14 TQ 6348
Golden Grove 26 SN 5919
Golden Pot 12 SU 7143
Golden Valley 32 SO 9022
Goldenhill 51 SJ 8553
Golders Green 21 TQ 2488
Goldhanger 23 TL 9009
Golding 40 SJ 5403
Goldsborough (N Yorks.) 73 NZ 8314
Goldsborough (N Yorks.) 66 SE 3856
Goldsithney 2 SW 5430
Goldthorpe 60 SE 4604
Gollanfield 103 NH 8052
Golspie 108 NH 8399
Golval 111 NC 8962
Gomersal 59 SE 2026
Gomshall 20 TQ 0847
Gonalston 63 SK 6847
Good Easter 22 TL 6212
Gooderstone 46 TF 7602
Goodleigh 6 SS 5934
Goodmanham 60 SE 8842
Goodnestone (Kent) 15 TR 0461
Goodnestone (Kent) 15 TR 2554
Goodrich 29 SO 5719
Goodrington 5 SX 8958
Goodwick 24 SM 9438
Goodworth Clatford 19 SU 3642
Goodyers End 43 SP 3385
Goole 60 SE 7423
Goonbell 2 SW 7249
Goonhavern 2 SW 7953
Gooseham 6 SS 2316
Goosetrey 51 SJ 7769
Goosey 19 SU 3591
Goosnargh 57 SD 5536
Gordon 86 NT 6443
Gordonbush 108 NC 8409
Gordonstown (Grampn.) 104 NJ 5656
Gordonstown (Grampn.) 105 NJ 7138
Gorebridge 85 NT 3461
Gorefield 45 TF 4112
Goring 19 SU 6080
Goring-by-Sea 12 TQ 1102
Gorleston on Sea 47 TG 5203
Gorley 10 SU 1511
Gorrachie 105 NJ 7358
Gorran Haven 4 SX 0141
Gors 27 SN 6277
Gorsedd 50 SJ 1476
Gorseinon 25 SS 5998
Gorslas 25 SN 5713
Gorsley 29 SO 6826
Gorstan 102 NH 3862
Gorsty Common 30 SO 4537
Gorton 58 SJ 8996
Gosbeck 37 TM 1555
Gosberton 55 TF 2331
Gosfield 22 TL 7829
Gosforth (Cumbr.) 62 NY 0603
Gosforth (Tyne and Wear) 72 NZ 2467
Gosmore 35 TL 1927
Gosport 11 SZ 6199
Goswick 87 NU 0545
Gotham 53 SK 5330
Gotherington 32 SO 9629
Goudhurst 14 TQ 7337
Goulceby 55 TF 2579
Gourdas 105 NJ 7741
Gourdon 99 NO 8270
Gourock 82 NS 2477
Govan 84 NS 5464
Gowanhill 105 NK 0363
Gowdall 60 SE 6122

Gowerton 238 Haresfield

Gowerton 25 SS 5896
Gowkhall 85 NT 0589
Goxhill (Humbs.) 67 TA 1021
Goxhill (Humbs.) 61 TA 1844
Graffham (W Susx.) 12 SU 9216
Grafham (Cambs.) 45 TL 1669
Grafton (Here & W) 30 SO 4937
Grafton (Here & W) 31 SO 5761
Grafton (N Yorks.) 66 SE 4163
Grafton (Oxon.) 33 SP 2600
Grafton Flyford 32 SO 9655
Grafton Regis 34 SP 7546
Grafton Underwood 44 SP 9280
Grafty Green 14 TQ 8748
Graianrhyd 50 SJ 2156
Graig (Clwyd) 49 SJ 0872
Graig (Gwyn.) 49 SH 8071
Graig-fechan 50 SJ 1454
Grain 22 TQ 8876
Grainsby 61 TF 2799
Grainthorpe 61 TF 3896
Graizelound 60 SK 7798
Gramisdale 109 NF 8155
Grampound 3 SW 9348
Grampound Road 3 SW 9150
Granborough 34 SP 7625
Granby 54 SK 7536
Grandborough 43 SP 4866
Grandtully 97 NN 9152
Grange (Cumbr.) 62 NY 2517
Grange (Mers.) 50 SJ 2286
Grange (N Yorks.) 66 SE 5796
Grange Hill 21 TQ 4492
Grange Moor 59 SE 2216
Grange Villa 72 NZ 2352
Grange of Lindores 92 NO 2516
Grange-over-Sands 64 SD 4077
Grangemouth 84 NS 9281
Grangepans 85 NT 0282
Grangetown 73 NZ 5420
Granish 103 NH 8914
Gransmoor 67 TA 1259
Grantchester 35 TL 4355
Grantham 54 SK 9135
Grantley 66 SE 2369
Grantlodge 105 NJ 7017
Granton (Dumf & G) 77 NT 0709
Granton (Lothian) 85 NT 2277
Grantown-on-Spey 103 NJ 0327
Grantshouse 87 NT 8065
Grappenhall 51 SJ 6385
Grasby 61 TA 0804
Grasmere 62 NY 3307
Grasscroft 59 SD 9704
Grassendale 50 SJ 3985
Grassholme 63 NY 9221
Grassington 65 SE 0064
Grassmoor 53 SK 4067
Grassthorpe 54 SK 7967
Grateley 19 SU 2741
Gratwich 52 SK 0231
Graveley (Cambs.) 35 TL 2564
Graveley (Herts.) 35 TL 2328
Gravelly Hill 42 SP 1090
Graveney 15 TR 0562
Gravesend 22 TQ 6473
Gravir 109 NB 3715
Grayingham 61 SK 9395
Grayrigg 63 SD 5797
Grays 22 TQ 6177
Grayshott 12 SU 8735
Grayswood 12 SU 9234
Grazeley 19 SU 6966
Greasbrough 53 SK 4195
Greasby 50 SJ 2587
Great Abington 35 TL 5348
Great Addington 44 SP 9575
Great Alne 32 SP 1159
Great Altcar 57 SD 3206
Great Amwell 35 TL 3712
Great Asby 63 NY 6813
Great Ashfield 36 TL 9967
Great Ayton 73 NZ 5510
Great Baddow 22 TL 7204
Great Badminton 18 ST 8082
Great Bardfield 36 TL 6730
Great Barford 35 TL 1352
Great Barr 42 SP 0495
Great Barrington 33 SP 2013
Great Barrow 50 SJ 4668
Great Barton 36 TL 8967
Great Barugh 67 SE 7478
Great Bavington 79 NY 9880
Great Bedwyn 18 SU 2764
Great Bentley 23 TM 1121
Great Billing 34 SP 8162
Great Bircham 46 TF 7632
Great Blakenham 37 TM 1150
Great Bolas 41 SJ 6421
Great Bookham 21 TQ 1454
Great Bosullow 2 SW 4133
Great Bourton 33 SP 4545
Great Bowden 44 SP 7488
Great Bradley 36 TL 6753
Great Braxted 22 TL 8614
Great Bricett 37 TM 0350
Great Brickhill 34 SP 9030
Great Bridgeford 41 SJ 8827
Great Brington 43 SP 6665
Great Bromley 23 TM 0826
Great Broughton (Cumbr.) 62 NY 0731
Great Broughton (N. Yorks.) 66 NZ 5406
Great Budworth 51 SJ 6677
Great Burdon 72 NZ 3116
Great Burstead 22 TQ 6892
Great Busby 66 NZ 5105
Great Canfield 22 TL 5917
Great Carlton 55 TF 4185
Great Casterton 44 TF 0009
Great Chart 15 TQ 9842
Great Chatwell 41 SJ 7914
Great Chesterford 35 TL 5042
Great Cheverell 18 ST 9858
Great Chishill 35 TL 4238
Great Clacton 23 TM 1716
Great Coates 61 TA 2310
Great Comberton 32 SO 9542
Great Corby 71 NY 4754
Great Cornard 36 TL 8840
Great Coxwell 18 SU 2693
Great Cransley 44 SP 8376
Great Cressingham 46 TF 8501
Great Crosby 50 SJ 3199
Great Cubley 52 SK 1637
Great Dalby 44 SK 7414
Great Doddington 34 SP 8864
Great Driffield 67 TA 0257
Great Dunham 46 TF 8714
Great Dunmow 22 TL 6221
Great Durnford 10 SU 1338
Great Easton (Essex) 22 TL 6125
Great Easton (Leic.) 44 SP 8493
Great Eccleston 57 SD 4240
Great Edstone 66 SE 7084
Great Ellingham 46 TM 0196
Great Elm 18 ST 7449
Great Eversden 35 TL 3653
Great Finborough 36 TM 0157
Great Fransham 46 TF 8913
Great Gaddesden 34 TL 0211
Great Gidding 45 TL 1183
Great Givendale 67 SE 8153
Great Glemham 37 TM 3361
Great Glen 43 SP 6597
Great Gonerby 54 SK 9038
Great Gransden 35 TL 2756
Great Green (Norf.) 47 TM 2789
Great Green (Suff.) 36 TL 9155
Great Habton 67 SE 7576
Great Hale 55 TF 1443
Great Hallingbury 22 TL 5119
Great Hanwood 40 SJ 4309
Great Harrowden 44 SP 8871
Great Harwood 58 SD 7332
Great Haseley 34 SP 6401
Great Hatfield 61 TA 1842
Great Heck 60 SE 5920
Great Henny 36 TL 8738
Great Hinton 18 ST 9058
Great Hockham 46 TL 9592
Great Holland 23 TM 2119
Great Horkesley 36 TL 9731
Great Hormead 35 TL 4030
Great Horwood 34 SP 7731
Great Houghton (Northants.) 34 SP 7958
Great Houghton (S Yorks.) 59 SE 4206
Great Hucklow 52 SK 1777
Great Kelk 67 TA 1058
Great Kingshill 20 SU 8798
Great Langton 66 SE 2996
Great Leighs 22 TL 7317
Great Limber 61 TA 1308
Great Livermere 36 TL 8871
Great Longstone 53 SK 1971
Great Lumley 72 NZ 2949
Great Lyth 40 SJ 4507
Great Malvern 32 SO 7845
Great Maplestead 36 TL 8034
Great Marton 57 SD 3335
Great Massingham 46 TF 7922
Great Milton 34 SP 6302
Great Missenden 34 SP 8901
Great Mitton 58 SD 7138
Great Mongeham 15 TR 3451
Great Moulton 47 TM 1690
Great Musgrave 63 NY 7613
Great Ness 40 SJ 3918
Great Oakley (Essex) 23 TM 1927
Great Oakley (Northants.) 44 SP 8686
Great Offley 35 TL 1427
Great Ormside 63 NY 7017
Great Orton 70 NY 3254
Great Oxendon 44 SP 7383
Great Palgrave 46 TF 8312
Great Parndon 35 TL 4308
Great Paxton 35 TL 2164
Great Plumstead 47 TG 3010
Great Ponton 54 SK 9230
Great Postland 45 TF 2612
Great Preston 59 SE 4029
Great Raveley 45 TL 2581
Great Rissington 33 SP 1917
Great Rollright 33 SP 3231
Great Ryburgh 46 TF 9527
Great Ryle 79 NU 0212
Great Saling 22 TL 7025
Great Salkeld 63 NY 5536
Great Sampford 36 TL 6435
Great Sankey 51 SJ 5688
Great Saxham 36 TL 7862
Great Shefford 19 SU 3875
Great Shelford 35 TL 4652
Great Smeaton 66 NZ 3404
Great Snoring 46 TF 9434
Great Somerford 18 ST 9682
Great Soudley 41 SJ 7228
Great Stainton 72 NZ 3322
Great Stambridge 23 TQ 9092
Great Staughton 35 TL 1264
Great Steeping 55 TF 4364
Great Stonar 15 TR 3359
Great Strickland 63 NY 5522
Great Stukeley 35 TL 2275
Great Sturton 55 TF 2176
Great Swinburne 78 NY 9375
Great Tew 33 SP 3929
Great Tey 22 TL 8925
Great Torrington 6 SS 4919
Great Tosson 79 NU 0300
Great Totham (Essex) 22 TL 8511
Great Totham (Essex) 22 TL 8613
Great Wakering 23 TQ 9487
Great Waldingfield 36 TL 9143
Great Walsingham 46 TF 9437
Great Waltham 22 TL 6913
Great Warley 21 TQ 5890
Great Washbourne 32 SO 9834
Great Welnetham 36 TL 8759
Great Wenham 37 TM 0738
Great Whittington 79 NZ 0070
Great Wigborough 23 TL 9615
Great Wilbraham 35 TL 5557
Great Wishford 10 SU 0835
Great Witcombe 32 SO 9014
Great Witley 32 SO 7566
Great Wolford 33 SP 2434
Great Wratting 36 TL 6848
Great Wyrley 41 SJ 9907
Great Wytheford 41 SJ 5719
Great Yarmouth 47 TG 5207
Great Yeldham 36 TL 7638
Greatford 45 TF 0811
Greatham (Cleve.) 73 NZ 4927
Greatham (Hants.) 12 SU 7730
Greatham (W Susx) 12 TQ 0415
Greatstone-on-Sea 15 TR 0822
Greatworth 33 SP 5542
Green Hammerton 66 SE 4656
Green Hill (Wilts.) 18 SU 0686
Green Ore 17 ST 5749
Green Street (Herts.) 21 TQ 1998
Green Street Green (Gtr London) 21 TQ 4563
Green, The (Cumbr.) 62 SD 1784
Green, The (Wilts.) 10 ST 8731
Greenburn 84 NS 9360
Greendykes 87 NU 0628
Greenfield (Beds.) 35 TL 0534
Greenfield (Clwyd) 50 SJ 1977
Greenfield (Oxon.) 20 SU 7191
Greenford 21 TQ 1382
Greengairs 84 NS 7870
Greenham 19 SU 4865
Greenhaugh 78 NY 7987
Greenhead (Northum.) 71 NY 6665
Greenhill (Central) 84 NS 8278
Greenhill (Gtr London) 21 TQ 1688
Greenhill (S Yorks.) 53 SK 3481
Greenhithe 21 TQ 5974
Greenholm 84 NS 5637
Greenhow Hill 65 SE 1164
Greenigo 113 HY 4107
Greenland 112 ND 2367
Greenlaw 86 NT 7145
Greenloaning 91 NN 8307
Greenmount 58 SD 7714
Greenock 82 NS 2776
Greenodd 62 SD 3182
Greens Norton 34 SP 6649
Greenside 72 NZ 1362
Greenskairs 105 NJ 7863
Greenstead Green 22 TL 8227
Greensted 22 TL 5302
Greenwich 21 TQ 3877
Greet 32 SP 0230
Greete 41 SO 5770
Greetham (Leic.) 44 SK 9214
Greetham (Lincs.) 55 TF 3070
Greetland 59 SE 0821
Greinton 17 ST 4136
Grendon (Northants.) 34 SP 8760
Grendon (Warw.) 43 SP 2899
Grendon Common 42 SP 2799
Grendon Green 31 SO 5957
Grendon Underwood 34 SP 6720
Grenoside 53 SK 3394
Gresford 50 SJ 3454
Gresham 47 TG 1738
Greshornish 100 NG 3454
Gress 109 NB 4842
Gressenhall 46 TF 9615
Gressenhall Green 46 TF 9616
Gressingham 64 SD 5769
Greta Bridge 72 NZ 0813
Gretna 70 NY 3167
Gretna Green 70 NY 3268
Gretton (Glos.) 32 SP 0030
Gretton (Northants.) 44 SP 9094
Gretton (Salop) 40 SO 5195
Grewelthorpe 66 SE 2276
Greysouthen 62 NY 0729
Greystoke 62 NY 4330
Greystone 99 NO 5343
Greywell 20 SU 7151
Griff 43 SP 3588
Griffithstown 28 ST 2999
Grigghall 63 SD 4691
Grimeford Village 58 SD 6112
Grimethorpe 59 SE 4109
Grimley 32 SO 8360
Grimoldby 55 TF 3988
Grimsargh 57 SD 5834
Grimsby 61 TA 2810
Grimscote 34 SP 6553
Grimscott 6 SS 2606
Grimshader 109 NB 4026
Grimsthorpe 44 TF 0423
Grimston (Leic.) 43 SK 6821
Grimston (Norf.) 46 TF 7221
Grimstone 9 SY 6393
Grindale 67 TA 1371
Grindle 41 SJ 7403
Grindleford 53 SK 2477
Grindleton 58 SD 7545
Grindley Brook 50 SJ 5243
Grindlow 52 SK 1877
Grindon (Northum.) 87 NT 9144
Grindon (Staffs.) 52 SK 0854
Gringley on the Hill 54 SK 7390
Grinsdale 70 NY 3758
Grinshill 40 SJ 5223
Grinton 65 SE 0498
Gristhorpe 67 TA 0882
Griston 46 TL 9499
Grittenham 18 SU 0382
Grittleton 18 ST 8579
Grizebeck 62 SD 2384
Grizedale 62 SD 3394
Groby 43 SK 5207
Groes (Clwyd) 49 SJ 0064
Groes (W Glam.) 28 SS 7986
Groes-faen 28 ST 0780
Groesffordd Marli 49 SJ 0073
Groeslon (Gwyn.) 48 SH 4755
Grogport 81 NR 8044
Gronant 49 SJ 0883
Groombridge 13 TQ 5337
Grosebay 109 NG 1592
Grosmont (Gwent) 29 SO 4024
Grosmont (N Yorks.) 67 NZ 8205
Groton 36 TL 9641
Grove (Dorset) 9 SY 6972
Grove (Kent) 15 TR 2362
Grove (Notts.) 54 SK 7379
Grove (Oxon.) 19 SU 4090
Grove Park 21 TQ 4172
Grovesend 25 SN 5900
Gruids 108 NC 5604
Grula 100 NG 3826
Gruline 88 NM 5440
Grundisburgh 37 TM 2251
Gruting 113 HU 2748
Gualachulain 96 NN 1145
Guardbridge 93 NO 4519
Guarlford 32 SO 8145
Guay 98 NO 0049
Guestling Green 14 TQ 8513
Guestwick 47 TG 0627
Guide Post 79 NZ 2585
Guilden Morden 35 TL 2744
Guilden Sutton 50 SJ 4468
Guildford 20 TQ 0049
Guildtown 92 NO 1331
Guilsborough 43 SP 6773
Guilsfield 40 SJ 2111
Guisborough 73 NZ 6115
Guiseley 64 SE 1941
Guist 46 TF 9925
Guiting Power 32 SP 0924
Gullane 86 NT 4882
Gulval 2 SW 4831
Gumfreston 24 SN 1101
Gumley 43 SP 6890
Gunby (Lincs.) 44 SK 9021
Gundleton 11 SU 6133
Gunn 6 SS 6333
Gunnerside 65 SD 9598
Gunnerton 78 NY 9074
Gunness 60 SE 8411
Gunnislake 4 SX 4371
Gunnista 113 HU 5043
Gunthorpe (Norf.) 46 TG 0135
Gunthorpe (Notts.) 53 SK 6744
Gurnard 11 SZ 4795
Gurney Slade 17 ST 6249
Gurnos 28 SN 7709
Gussage All Saints 10 SU 0010
Gussage St. Michael 10 ST 9811
Guston 15 TR 3244
Gutcher 113 HU 5498
Guthrie 99 NO 5650
Guy's Head 45 TF 4825
Guy's Marsh 9 ST 8420
Guyhirn 45 TF 3903
Guyzance 79 NU 2103
Gwaenysgor 49 SJ 0780
Gwalchmai 48 SH 3975
Gwaun-Cae-Gurwen 25 SN 7011
Gwbert-on-Sea 26 SN 1650
Gweek 2 SW 7026
Gwehelog 29 SO 3804
Gwenddwr 27 SO 0643
Gwennap 2 SW 7340
Gwenter 2 SW 7418
Gwernaffield 50 SJ 2064
Gwernesney 29 SO 4101
Gwernogle 26 SN 5234
Gwernymynydd 50 SJ 2162
Gwespyr 50 SJ 1183
Gwinear 2 SW 5937
Gwithian 2 SW 5841
Gwyddelwern 49 SJ 0746
Gwyddgrug 26 SN 4635
Gwytherin 49 SH 8761

H

Habberley (Here & W) 41 SO 8077
Habberley (Salop) 40 SJ 3903
Habrough 61 TA 1514
Hacconby 45 TF 1025
Haceby 54 TF 0236
Hacheston 37 TM 3059
Hackenthorpe 53 SK 4183
Hacketts 35 TL 3208
Hackford 47 TG 0502
Hackforth 66 SE 2493
Hackleton 34 SP 8055
Hackness (N Yorks.) 67 SE 9690
Hackney 21 TQ 3585
Hackthorn 54 SK 9882
Hackthorpe 63 NY 5423
Hadden 87 NT 7836
Haddenham (Bucks.) 34 SP 7408
Haddenham (Cambs.) 45 TL 4675
Haddington (Lothian) 86 NT 5174
Haddiscoe 47 TM 4497
Haddon 45 TL 1392
Hademore 42 SK 1708
Hadfield 59 SK 0296
Hadham Cross 35 TL 4218
Hadham Ford 35 TL 4321
Hadleigh (Essex) 22 TQ 8087
Hadleigh (Suff.) 36 TM 0242
Hadley 41 SJ 6712
Hadley End 42 SK 1320
Hadlow 14 TQ 6349
Hadlow Down 13 TQ 5324
Hadnall 40 SJ 5120
Hadstock 36 TL 5645
Hadzor 32 SO 9162
Haffenden Quarter 14 TQ 8841
Hafod-Dinbych 49 SH 8953
Haggbeck 71 NY 4774
Hagley (Here & W) 31 SO 5641
Hagley (Here & W) 41 SO 9181
Hagworthingham 55 TF 3469
Haigh 58 SD 6108
Haighton Green 57 SD 5634
Hail Weston 35 TL 1662
Haile 62 NY 0308
Hailes 32 SP 0530
Hailey (Herts.) 35 TL 3710
Hailey (Oxon.) 33 SP 3512
Hailsham 13 TQ 5909
Hainault 21 TQ 4691
Hainford 47 TG 2218
Hainton 55 TF 1784
Haisthorpe 67 TA 1264
Halam 53 SK 6754
Halberton 8 ST 0012
Halcro 112 ND 2260
Hale (Ches.) 50 SJ 4682
Hale (Gtr Mches.) 51 SJ 7786
Hale (Hants.) 10 SU 1919
Hale Bank 50 SJ 4784
Hale Street 14 TQ 6749
Halebarns 51 SJ 7985
Hales (Norf.) 47 TM 3897
Hales (Staffs.) 51 SJ 7134
Hales Place 15 TR 1459
Halesowen 41 SO 9683
Halesworth 37 TM 3877
Halewood 50 SJ 4585
Halford (Salop) 40 SO 4383
Halford (Warw.) 33 SP 2545
Halfpenny Green 41 SO 8292
Halfway (Berks.) 16 SU 4068
Halfway (Dyfed) 27 SN 6430
Halfway House 40 SJ 3411
Halfway Houses 23 TQ 9373
Halifax 59 SE 0825
Halistra 100 NG 2459
Halket 82 NS 4252
Halkirk 112 ND 1359
Halkyn 50 SJ 2071
Hall Green (W. Mids) 42 SP 1181
Hall's Green 35 TL 2728
Halland 13 TQ 5016
Hallaton 44 SP 7896
Hallatrow 17 ST 6356
Hallbankgate 71 NY 5859
Hallen 29 ST 5479
Hallin 100 NG 2559
Halling 14 TQ 7063
Hallington (Northum.) 79 NY 9875
Halloughton 53 SK 6851
Hallow 32 SO 8258
Hallrule 78 NT 5914
Hallsands 5 SX 8138
Halltoft End 55 TF 3645
Hallworthy 4 SX 1787
Hallyne 85 NT 1940
Halmer End 51 SJ 7949
Halmore 29 SO 6902
Halmyre Mains 85 NT 1749
Halnaker 12 SU 9108
Halsall 57 SD 3710
Halse (Northants.) 33 SP 5640
Halse (Somer.) 16 ST 1327
Halsetown 2 SW 5038
Halsham 61 TA 2627
Halsinger 6 SS 5138
Halstead (Essex) 36 TL 8130
Halstead (Kent) 21 TQ 4961
Halstead (Leic.) 44 SK 7505
Halstock 9 ST 5308
Haltham 55 TF 2463
Halton (Bucks.) 34 SP 8710
Halton (Ches.) 50 SJ 5381
Halton (Clwyd) 50 SJ 3039
Halton (Lancs.) 64 SD 5065
Halton East 65 SE 0454
Halton Gill 65 SD 8876
Halton Holegate 55 TF 4165
Halton Lea Gate 71 NY 6558
Halton West 65 SD 8454
Haltwhistle 71 NY 7064
Halvergate 47 TG 4206
Halwell 5 SX 7753
Halwill 6 SX 4299
Halwill Junction 6 SS 4400
Ham (Glos.) 29 ST 6898
Ham (Gtr London) 21 TQ 1772
Ham (Highld.) 112 ND 2373
Ham (Kent) 15 TR 3354
Ham (Wilts.) 19 SU 3262
Ham Green (Here & W) 32 SP 0063
Ham Street (Somer.) 17 ST 5534
Hamble 11 SU 4806
Hambleden (Bucks.) 20 SU 7886
Hambledon (Hants.) 11 SU 6414
Hambledon (Surrey) 12 SU 9638
Hambleton (Lancs.) 57 SD 3742
Hambleton (N Yorks.) 60 SE 5430
Hambridge 9 ST 3921
Hambrook (Avon) 29 ST 6378
Hambrook (W Susx.) 12 SU 7806
Hameringham 55 TF 3167
Hamerton 45 TL 1379
Hamilton 84 NS 7255
Hammersmith 21 TQ 2279
Hammerwich 42 SK 0707
Hammoon 10 ST 8114
Hamnavoe (Shetld.) 113 HU 4971
Hamnavoe (West Burra) 113 HU 3635
Hampden 34 SP 8603
Hampden Park 13 TQ 6002
Hampden Row 34 SP 8402
Hampnett 32 SP 0915
Hampole 60 SE 5010
Hampreston 10 SZ 0598
Hampstead 21 TQ 2485
Hampstead Norris 19 SU 5276
Hampsthwaite 66 SE 2558
Hampton (Gtr London) 20 TQ 1369
Hampton (Salop) 41 SO 7486
Hampton Bishop 31 SO 5538
Hampton Heath 50 SJ 4949
Hampton Lovett 32 SO 8865
Hampton Lucy 33 SP 2557
Hampton Poyle 33 SP 5015
Hampton in Arden 42 SP 2081
Hampton on the Hill 33 SP 2564
Hamsey 13 TQ 4112
Hamstall Ridware 42 SK 1019
Hamstead (I. of W.) 11 SZ 4091
Hamstead (W Mids) 42 SP 0593
Hamstead Marshall 19 SU 4165
Hamsterley (Durham) 72 NZ 1131
Hamsterley (Durham) 72 NZ 1156
Hamstreet (Kent) 15 TR 0034
Hamworthy 10 SY 9990
Hanbury (Here & W) 32 SO 9663
Hanbury (Staffs.) 42 SK 1727
Hanchurch 51 SJ 8441
Handbridge 50 SJ 4164
Handcross 13 TQ 2630
Handforth 51 SJ 8883
Handley 50 SJ 4657
Handsacre 42 SK 0916
Handsworth (S Yorks.) 53 SK 4086
Handsworth (W Mids) 42 SP 0490
Hanford 51 SJ 8642
Hanging Langford 10 SU 0237
Hanham 17 ST 6372
Hankelow 51 SJ 6645
Hankerton 18 ST 9690
Hankham 13 TQ 6105
Hanley 51 SJ 8847
Hanley Castle 32 SO 8342
Hanley Swan 32 SO 8143
Hanley William 41 SO 6765
Hanlith 65 SD 9061
Hanmer 50 SJ 4540
Hannington (Hants.) 19 SU 5355
Hannington (Northants.) 44 SP 8171
Hannington (Wilts.) 18 SU 1793
Hannington Wick 18 SU 1795
Hanslope 34 SP 8046
Hanthorpe 45 TF 0824
Hanwell 33 SP 4343
Hanworth (Gtr London) 20 TQ 1271
Hanworth (Norf.) 47 TG 1935
Happendon 84 NS 8533
Happisburgh 47 TG 3731
Happisburgh Common 47 TG 3729
Hapsford 50 SJ 4774
Hapton (Lancs.) 58 SD 7931
Hapton (Norf.) 47 TM 1796
Harberton 5 SX 7758
Harbertonford 5 SX 7856
Harbledown 15 TR 1358
Harborne 42 SP 0384
Harborough Magna 43 SP 4779
Harbottle 78 NT 9304
Harbury 33 SP 3759
Harby (Leic.) 54 SK 7431
Harby (Notts.) 54 SK 8770
Harcombe (Devon) 8 SY 1590
Harden 59 SE 0838
Hardenhuish 18 ST 9074
Hardgate (Grampn.) 99 NJ 7801
Hardham 12 TQ 0317
Hardingham 46 TG 0403
Hardings Wood 51 SJ 8054
Hardingstone 34 SP 7657
Hardington 18 ST 7452
Hardington Mandeville 9 ST 5111
Hardington Marsh 9 ST 5009
Hardley 11 SU 4205
Hardley Street 47 TG 3801
Hardmead 34 SP 9347
Hardrow 65 SD 8691
Hardstoft 53 SK 4463
Hardway (Hants.) 11 SU 6101
Hardway (Somer.) 17 ST 7134
Hardwick (Bucks.) 34 SP 8019
Hardwick (Cambs.) 35 TL 3758
Hardwick (Norf.) 47 TM 2290
Hardwick (Northants.) 44 SP 8569
Hardwick (Oxon.) 33 SP 3706
Hardwick (Oxon.) 33 SP 5729
Hardwicke (Glos.) 32 SO 7912
Hardwicke (Glos.) 32 SO 9127
Hare Hatch 20 SU 8077
Hare Street 35 TL 3929
Hareby 55 TF 3365
Hareden 64 SD 6350
Harefield 20 TQ 0590
Harehope 79 NU 0920
Harescombe 32 SO 8410
Haresfield 32 SO 8110

Hockwold cum Wilton 240 Jurby West

Hockwold cum Wilton 46 TL 7288
Hockworthy 8 ST 0319
Hoddesdon 35 TL 3709
Hoddlesdon 58 SD 7122
Hodgeston 24 SS 0399
Hodnet 41 SJ 6128
Hodthorpe 53 SK 5476
Hoe (Norf.) 46 TF 9916
Hoe Gate 11 SU 6213
Hoggeston 34 SP 8025
Hoghton 58 SD 6125
Hognaston 53 SK 2350
Hogsthorpe 55 TF 5372
Holbeach 45 TF 3625
Holbeach Bank 45 TF 3627
Holbeach Drove 45 TF 3212
Holbeach Hurn 45 TF 3927
Holbeach St. Johns 45 TF 3418
Holbeach St. Marks 55 TF 3731
Holbeach St. Matthew 55 TF 4132
Holbeck 53 SK 5473
Holberrow Green 32 SP 0259
Holbeton 5 SX 6150
Holbrook (Derby) 53 SK 3645
Holbrook (Suff.) 37 TM 1636
Holburn 87 NU 0436
Holbury 11 SU 4303
Holcombe (Devon.) 8 SX 9574
Holcombe (Somer.) 17 ST 6649
Holcombe Rogus 8 ST 0519
Holcot 44 SP 7969
Holden 58 SD 7749
Holdenby 43 SP 6967
Holdgate 40 SO 5589
Holdingham 54 TF 0547
Holestane 76 NX 8799
Holford 16 ST 1541
Holker 65 SD 3577
Holkham 46 TF 8944
Hollacombe (Devon) 6 SS 3702
Holland (Stronsay) 113 HY 6622
Holland-on-Sea 23 TM 2016
Hollandstoun 113 HY 7553
Hollesley 37 TM 3544
Hollingbourne 14 TQ 8455
Hollington (Derby) 53 SK 2239
Hollington (E Susx.) 14 TQ 7911
Hollington (Staffs.) 52 SK 0538
Hollingworth 52 SK 0096
Hollins 58 SD 8108
Hollins Green 51 SJ 6990
Hollinsclough 52 SK 0666
Hollinswood 41 SJ 6909
Hollinwood 50 SJ 5236
Hollocombe 6 SS 6311
Holloway 53 SK 3256
Hollowell 43 SP 6972
Holly End 45 TF 4906
Hollybush (Gwent) 28 SO 1603
Hollybush (Here & W) 32 SO 7636
Hollybush (Strath.) 75 NS 3914
Hollym 61 TA 3425
Holmbury St. Mary 12 TQ 1144
Holme (Cambs.) 45 TL 1987
Holme (Cumbr.) 63 SD 5278
Holme (Notts.) 54 SK 8059
Holme (W Yorks.) 59 SE 1005
Holme Chapel 58 SD 8728
Holme Hale 46 TF 8807
Holme Lacy 31 SO 5535
Holme Marsh 30 SO 3354
Holme next the Sea 46 TF 7043
Holme on the Wolds 61 SE 9646
Holme upon Spalding Moor 60 SE 8138
Holmer Green 20 SU 9097
Holmes Chapel 51 SJ 7667
Holmesfield 53 SK 3277
Holmeswood 57 SD 4316
Holmewood 53 SK 4365
Holmfirth 59 SE 1408
Holmhead 75 NS 5620
Holmpton 61 TA 3623
Holmrook 62 SD 0799
Holne 5 SX 7069
Holnest 9 ST 6509
Holsworthy 6 SS 3403
Holsworthy Beacon 6 SS 3508
Holt (Clwyd) 50 SJ 4053
Holt (Dorset) 10 SU 0203
Holt (Here & W) 32 SO 8262
Holt (Norf.) 47 TG 0738
Holt (Wilts.) 18 ST 8661
Holt End 42 SP 0769
Holt Heath (Here & W) 32 SO 8163
Holtby 66 SE 6754
Holton (Oxon.) 33 SP 6006
Holton (Somer.) 17 ST 6826
Holton (Suff.) 37 TM 4077
Holton Heath 10 SY 9491
Holton St. Mary 37 TM 0537
Holton cum Beckering 55 TF 1181
Holton le Clay 61 TA 2802
Holton le Moor 61 TF 0797
Holwell (Herts.) 35 TL 1633
Holwell (Leic.) 44 SK 7323
Holwell (Oxon) 33 SP 2309
Holwick 63 NY 9026
Holy Cross 41 SO 9279
Holybourne 12 SU 7341
Holyhead 48 SH 2482
Holymoorside 53 SK 3369
Holyport 20 SU 8977
Holystone 78 NT 9502
Holytown 84 NS 7760
Holywell (Cambs.) 45 TL 3370
Holywell (Clwyd) 50 SJ 1875
Holywell (Corn.) 5 SW 7658
Holywell (Dorset) 9 ST 5904
Holywell Green 59 SE 0918
Holywell Lake 8 ST 1020
Holywell Row 36 TL 7077
Holywood 69 NX 9480
Hom Green 29 SO 5822
Homer 41 SJ 6101
Homersfield 47 TM 2885
Homington 10 SU 1226
Honey Hill 15 TR 1161
Honeyborough 24 SM 9506
Honeybourne 32 SP 1144
Honeychurch 6 SS 6202
Honiley 42 SP 2472
Honing 47 TG 3227
Honingham 47 TG 1011
Honington (Lincs.) 54 SK 9443
Honington (Suff.) 36 TL 9174
Honington (Warw.) 33 SP 2642
Honiton 8 ST 1600
Honley 59 SE 1311
Hoo (Kent) 22 TQ 7872
Hoo Green 37 TM 2559
Hooe (Devon.) 5 SX 5052
Hooe (E Susx) 13 TQ 6809
Hook (Dyfed) 24 SM 9811
Hook (Hants.) 20 SU 7254
Hook (Humbs.) 60 SE 7525
Hook (Surrey) 21 TQ 1764
Hook (Wilts.) 18 SU 0784
Hook Norton 33 SP 3533
Hooke (Dorset) 9 ST 5300
Hookgate 51 SJ 7435
Hookway 7 SX 8598
Hookwood 13 TQ 2643
Hoole 50 SJ 4367
Hooton 50 SJ 3679
Hooton Levitt 53 SK 5291
Hooton Pagnell 60 SE 4808
Hooton Roberts 60 SK 4897
Hop Pole 45 TF 1813
Hope (Clwyd) 50 SJ 3058
Hope (Derby.) 52 SK 1783
Hope (Devon.) 5 SX 6740
Hope (Powys) 40 SJ 2507
Hope (Salop) 40 SJ 3401
Hope Bagot 41 SO 5874
Hope Bowdler 40 SO 4792
Hope Mansell 29 SO 6219
Hope under Dinmore 30 SO 5052
Hopeman 104 NJ 1469
Hopesay 40 SO 3883
Hopton (Salop) 41 SJ 5926
Hopton (Staffs.) 41 SJ 9426
Hopton (Suff.) 36 TL 9979
Hopton Cangeford 40 SO 5480
Hopton Castle 40 SO 3678
Hopton Wafers 41 SO 6476
Hopton on Sea 47 TG 5200
Hopwas 42 SK 1705
Hopwood 42 SP 0375
Horam 13 TQ 5717
Horbling 55 TF 1135
Horbury 59 SE 2918
Horden 73 NZ 4441
Horderley 40 SO 4086
Hordle 11 SZ 2795
Hordley 40 SJ 3730
Horeb 26 SN 3942
Horham 37 TM 2172
Horkesley Heath 23 TL 9829
Horkstow 61 SE 9818
Horley (Oxon.) 33 SP 4143
Horley (Surrey) 13 TQ 2843
Horn Hill 20 TQ 0292
Hornblotton Green 17 ST 5833
Hornby (Lancs.) 64 SD 5868
Hornby (N Yorks.) 66 NZ 3605
Horncastle 55 TF 2669
Hornchurch 21 TQ 5487
Horncliffe 87 NT 9249
Horndean 11 SU 7013
Horndon on the Hill 22 TQ 6683
Horne 13 TQ 3344
Horning 47 TG 3417
Horninghold 44 SP 8097
Horninglow 42 SK 2324
Horningsea 35 TL 4962
Horningsham 18 ST 8241
Horningtoft 46 TF 9323
Hornsby 71 NY 5150
Hornsea 61 TA 2047
Hornsey 21 TQ 3089
Hornton 33 SP 3945
Horrabridge 5 SX 5169
Horringer 36 TL 8261
Horsebridge (E Susx) 13 TQ 5711
Horsebridge (Hants.) 11 SU 3430
Horsebrook 41 SJ 8810
Horsehay 41 SJ 6707
Horseheath 36 TL 6147
Horsehouse 65 SE 0481
Horsell 20 SU 9959
Horseman's Green 50 SJ 4441
Horseway 45 TL 4287
Horsey (Norf.) 47 TG 4523
Horsford 47 TG 1916
Horsforth 59 SE 2337
Horsham (Here & W) 32 SO 7357
Horsham (W Susx) 12 TQ 1730
Horsham St. Faith 47 TG 2114
Horsington (Lincs.) 55 TF 1868
Horsington (Somer.) 9 ST 7023
Horsley (Derby.) 53 SK 3744
Horsley (Glos.) 18 ST 8398
Horsley (Northum.) 78 NY 8496
Horsley (Northum.) 72 NZ 0966
Horsley Cross 23 TM 1227
Horsley Woodhouse 53 SK 3945
Horsleycross Street 23 TM 1228
Horsleyhill 78 NT 5319
Horsmonden 14 TQ 7040
Horspath 33 SP 5704
Horstead 47 TG 2619
Horsted Keynes 13 TQ 3828
Horton (Avon) 29 ST 7684
Horton (Berks.) 20 TQ 0175
Horton (Bucks.) 34 SP 9219
Horton (Dorset) 10 SU 0307
Horton (Northants.) 34 SP 8254
Horton (Northum.) 87 NU 0230
Horton (Staffs.) 51 SJ 9457
Horton (W Glam.) 25 SS 4785
Horton (Wilts.) 18 SU 0463
Horton Green 50 SJ 4549
Horton Heath (Hants.) 11 SU 4916
Horton Kirby 21 TQ 5668
Horton in Ribblesdale 65 SD 8172
Horwich 58 SD 6311
Horwood 6 SS 5027
Hose 44 SK 7329
Hosh 91 NN 8523
Hotham 60 SE 8934
Hothfield 15 TQ 9644
Hoton 43 SK 5722
Hough 51 SJ 7151
Hough Green 50 SJ 4885
Hough-on-the-Hill 54 SK 9246
Hougham 54 SK 8844
Hougharry 109 NF 7071
Houghton (Cambs.) 45 TL 2871
Houghton (Cumbr.) 70 NY 4159
Houghton (Dyfed) 24 SM 9807
Houghton (Hants.) 11 SU 3331
Houghton (W Susx) 12 TQ 0111
Houghton Conquest 35 TL 0441
Houghton Regis 34 TL 0224
Houghton St. Giles 46 TF 9235
Houghton le Spring 72 NZ 3450
Houghton on the Hill 43 SK 6703
Houll 113 HU 3792
Houlsyke 67 NZ 7308
Hound Green 20 SU 7259
Houndslow 86 NT 6347
Houndwood 87 NT 8464
Hounslow 20 TQ 1276
Housetter 113 HU 3784
Houston 82 NS 4067
Houstry 112 ND 1534
Hove 13 TQ 2805
Hoveringham 53 SK 6946
Hoversta 113 HU 4940
Hoveton 47 TG 3018
Hovingham 66 SE 6675
How 71 NY 5056
How Caple 31 SO 6030
Howden 60 SE 7428
Howden-le-Wear 72 NZ 1633
Howe (Cumbr.) 63 SD 4588
Howe (Highld.) 112 ND 3062
Howe (Norf.) 47 TM 2799
Howe Green 22 TL 7403
Howe Street (Essex) 22 TL 6914
Howe Street (Essex) 36 TL 6934
Howe of Teuchar 105 NJ 7947
Howe, The 56 SC 1967
Howell 27 TF 1346
Howey 30 SO 0558
Howgate 85 NT 2457
Howick 79 NU 2517
Howlaws 86 NT 7242
Howle 41 SJ 6823
Howlett End 36 TL 5834
Howmore 109 NF 7636
Hownam 78 NT 7719
Hownam Mains 78 NT 7820
Howsham (Humbs.) 61 TA 0404
Howsham (N Yorks.) 67 SE 7362
Howton 29 SO 4129
Howwood 82 NS 3960
Hoxne 37 TM 1877
Hoylake 50 SJ 2189
Hoyland Nether 59 SE 3600
Hoyland Swaine 59 SE 2604
Hubbert's Bridge 55 TF 2643
Huby (N. Yorks.) 66 SE 5665
Huby (N. Yorks.) 59 SE 2747
Hucclecote 32 SO 8717
Hucking 14 TQ 8358
Hucknall 53 SK 5349
Huddersfield 59 SE 1416
Huddington 32 SO 9457
Hudscott 7 SS 6525
Hudswell 65 NZ 1400
Huggate 67 SE 8855
Hugh Town 2 SV 9010
Hughenden Valley 20 SU 8695
Hughley 40 SO 5697
Hugmore 50 SJ 3752
Huish (Devon.) 6 SS 5311
Huish (Wilts.) 18 SU 1463
Huish Champflower 16 ST 0429
Huish Episcopi 17 ST 4226
Hulcott 34 SP 8516
Hulland 53 SK 2447
Hullavington 18 ST 8982
Hullbridge 22 TQ 8194
Hulme End 52 SK 1059
Hulme Walfield 51 SJ 8465
Hulver Street 47 TM 4686
Humber Court 31 SO 5356
Humberston 61 TA 3105
Humberstone 43 SK 6206
Humbie 86 NT 4562
Humbleton (Humbs.) 61 TA 2234
Humbleton (Northum.) 87 NT 9728
Hume 86 NT 7041
Humshaugh 78 NY 9171
Huna 112 ND 3573
Huncoat 58 SD 7730
Huncote 43 SP 5197
Hundalee 78 NT 6418
Hunderthwaite 72 NY 9821
Hundleby 55 TF 3966
Hundleton 24 SM 9600
Hundon 36 TL 7348
Hundred Acres 11 SU 5911
Hundred End 57 SD 4122
Hundred, The 31 SO 5264
Hungarton 43 SK 6807
Hungerford (Berks.) 19 SU 3368
Hungerford (Hants.) 10 SU 1612
Hungerford Newtown 19 SU 3571
Hunmanby 67 TA 0977
Hunningham 43 SP 3768
Hunsdon 35 TL 4114
Hunsingore 66 SE 4253
Hunsonby 63 NY 5835
Hunspow 112 ND 2172
Hunstanton 46 TF 6741
Hunstanworth 72 NY 9449
Hunston (Suff.) 36 TL 9768
Hunston (W Susx) 12 SU 8601
Hunstrete 17 ST 6462
Hunt End 32 SP 0364
Hunt's Cross 50 SJ 4385
Huntingdon (Cambs.) 45 TL 2371
Huntingfield 37 TM 3374
Huntington (Here & W) 30 SO 2553
Huntington (Lothian) 86 NT 4875
Huntington (N Yorks.) 66 SE 6156
Huntington (Staffs) 41 SJ 9713
Huntingtower 92 NO 0725
Huntley 32 SO 7219
Huntly 104 NJ 5339
Hunton (Kent) 14 TQ 7149
Hunton (N Yorks.) 65 SE 1892
Huntsham 8 ST 0020
Huntspill 17 ST 3045
Huntworth 17 ST 3134
Hunwick 72 NZ 1832
Hunworth 47 TG 0635
Hurdsfield 51 SJ 9274
Hurley (Berks.) 20 SU 8283
Hurley (Warw.) 42 SP 2495
Hurlford 82 NS 4536
Hurliness 113 ND 2888
Hurn 10 SZ 1296
Hursley 11 SU 4225
Hurst (Berks.) 20 SU 7972
Hurst (Gtr Mches.) 53 SD 9400
Hurst (N. Yorks) 65 NZ 0402
Hurst Green (E Susx) 14 TQ 7327
Hurst Green (Lancs.) 58 SD 6838
Hurst Green (Surrey) 21 TQ 3951
Hurstbourne Priors 19 SU 4346
Hurstbourne Tarrant 19 SU 3853
Hurstpierpoint 13 TQ 2816
Hurtiso 113 HY 5001
Hurworth-on-Tees 72 NZ 3010
Hury 72 NY 9619
Husbands Bosworth 43 SP 6484
Husborne Crawley 34 SP 9535
Husinish 109 NA 9812
Husthwaite 66 SE 5175
Huthwaite 53 SK 4659
Huttoft 55 TF 5176
Hutton (Avon) 17 ST 3458
Hutton (Borders) 87 NT 9053
Hutton (Cumbr.) 62 NY 4326
Hutton (Essex) 22 TQ 6394
Hutton (Lancs.) 57 SD 4926
Hutton (N Yorks.) 67 SE 7667
Hutton Bonville 66 NZ 3300
Hutton Buscel 67 SE 9784
Hutton Conyers 66 SE 3273
Hutton Cranswick 67 TA 0252
Hutton End 63 NY 4538
Hutton Henry 72 NZ 4236
Hutton Magna 72 NZ 1212
Hutton Roof (Cumbr.) 62 NY 3734
Hutton Roof (Cumbr.) 63 SD 5777
Hutton Rudby 66 NZ 4606
Hutton Sessay 66 SE 4776
Hutton Wandesley 66 SE 5050
Hutton-le-Hole 66 SE 7090
Huxley 50 SJ 5061
Huyton 50 SJ 4490
Hycemoor 62 SD 0989
Hyde (Glos.) 32 SO 8801
Hyde (Gtr. Mches.) 51 SJ 9294
Hyde Heath 34 SP 9300
Hydestile 12 SU 9740
Hynish 94 NL 9839
Hyssington 40 SO 3194
Hythe (Hants.) 11 SU 4207
Hythe (Kent) 15 TR 1635

I

Ibberton 10 ST 7807
Ible 53 SK 2457
Ibsley 10 SU 1509
Ibstock 43 SK 4010
Ibstone 20 SU 7593
Ibthorpe 19 SU 3753
Ibworth 19 SU 5654
Ickburgh 46 TL 8195
Ickenham 20 TQ 0786
Ickford 34 SP 6407
Ickham 15 TR 2258
Ickleford 35 TL 1831
Icklesham 14 TQ 8816
Ickleton 35 TL 4943
Icklingham 36 TL 7772
Ickwell Green 35 TL 1545
Icomb 33 SP 2122
Idbury 33 SP 2320
Iddesleigh 6 SS 5608
Ide 5 SX 8990
Ide Hill 21 TQ 4851
Ideford 5 SX 8977
Iden 14 TQ 9123
Iden Green (Kent) 14 TQ 8031
Idlicote 33 SP 2844
Idmiston 11 SU 1937
Idridgehay 53 SK 2849
Idrigil 100 NG 3863
Idstone 18 SU 2584
Ifield (W Susx) 13 TQ 2537
Ifold 12 TQ 0231
Iford 13 TQ 4007
Ifton Heath 50 SJ 3236
Ightfield 51 SJ 5938
Ightham 21 TQ 5956
Iken 37 TM 4155
Ilam 52 SK 1351
Ilchester 9 ST 5222
Ilderton 79 NU 0121
Ilford 21 TQ 4586
Ilfracombe 6 SS 5147
Ilkeston 53 SK 4642
Ilketshall St. Andrew 47 TM 3887
Ilketshall St. Margaret 47 TM 3485
Ilkley 59 SE 1147
Illey 41 SO 9881
Illingworth 59 SE 0728
Illogan 2 SW 6643
Illston on the Hill 44 SP 7099
Ilmer 34 SP 7605
Ilmington 33 SP 2143
Ilminster 8 ST 3614
Ilsington 5 SX 7876
Ilston 25 SS 5590
Ilton (N. Yorks.) 65 SE 1878
Ilton (Somer.) 8 ST 3517
Imachar 81 NR 8640
Immingham 61 TA 1714
Immingham Dock 61 TA 1816
Impington 35 TL 4463
Ince 50 SJ 4476
Ince Blundell 57 SD 3203
Ince-in-Makerfield 57 SD 5903
Inchbare 99 NO 6065
Inchberry 104 NJ 3155
Inchinnan 82 NS 4768
Inchlaggan 96 NH 1801
Inchnacardoch 102 NH 3710
Inchnadamph 110 NC 2522
Inchture 93 NO 2728
Inchyra 92 NO 1820
Indian Queens 3 SW 9158
Ingatestone 22 TQ 6499
Ingbirchworth 59 SE 2205
Ingestre 41 SJ 9724
Ingham (Lincs.) 54 SK 9483
Ingham (Norf.) 47 TG 3825
Ingham (Suff.) 36 TL 8570
Ingleby Arncliffe 66 NZ 4400
Ingleby Greenhow 66 NZ 5806
Inglesbatch 17 ST 7061
Inglesham 18 SU 2098
Ingleton (Durham) 72 NZ 1720
Ingleton (N Yorks.) 64 SD 6972
Inglewhite 57 SD 5439
Ingoe 79 NZ 0374
Ingoldisthorpe 46 TF 6832
Ingoldmells 55 TF 5668
Ingoldsby 44 TF 0030
Ingram 79 NU 0116
Ingrave 22 TQ 6292
Ings 63 SD 4498
Ingst 29 ST 5887
Ingworth 47 TG 1929
Inkberrow 32 SP 0157
Inkhorn 105 NJ 9239
Inkpen 19 SU 3564
Inkstack 112 ND 2570
Inn 96 NM 9956
Innellan 82 NS 1469
Innerleithen 85 NT 3336
Innerleven 93 NO 3700
Innermessan 68 NX 0863
Innerwick (Lothian) 86 NT 7273
Innerwick (Tays.) 97 NN 5947
Insch 104 NJ 6327
Insh 97 NH 8101
Inskip 57 SD 4537
Instow 6 SS 4730
Insworke 4 SX 4252
Inver (Grampn.) 98 NO 2393
Inver (Highld.) 108 NH 8682
Inverailort 95 NM 7681
Inveralligin 101 NG 8457
Inverallochy 105 NK 0464
Inveramsay 105 NJ 7424
Inveran 108 NH 5797
Inveraray 89 NN 0908
Inverarish 100 NG 5535
Inverarnan 90 NN 3118
Inverbervie 99 NO 8372
Invercreran 96 NN 0147
Inverdruie 103 NJ 9010
Inverebrie 105 NJ 9233
Inveresk 85 NT 3471
Inverey 98 NO 0889
Inverfarigaig 102 NH 5224
Invergarry 96 NH 3101
Invergeldie 91 NN 7427
Invergordon 103 NH 7168
Invergowrie 93 NO 3430
Inverhadden 97 NN 6757
Inverharroch 104 NJ 3831
Inverie 95 NG 7600
Inverinate 101 NG 9122
Inverkeilor 99 NO 6649
Inverkeithing 85 NT 1383
Inverkeithny 104 NJ 6246
Inverkip 82 NS 2071
Inverkirkaig 110 NC 0819
Inverlael 107 NH 1885
Inverlochlarig 90 NN 4318
Invermoriston 102 NH 4117
Invernaver 111 NC 7060
Inverness 103 NH 6645
Invernoaden 89 NS 1197
Inverquharity 98 NO 4057
Inverquhomery 105 NK 0246
Inverroy 96 NN 2581
Invershin 109 NH 5796
Inverugie 105 NK 0947
Inveruglas 90 NN 3109
Inverurie 105 NJ 7721
Invervar 97 NN 6648
Inwardleigh 6 SX 5599
Inworth 22 TL 8717
Iping 12 SU 8522
Ipplepen 5 SX 8366
Ipsden 19 SU 6385
Ipstones 52 SK 0249
Ipswich 37 TM 1744
Irby 50 SJ 2584
Irby in the Marsh 55 TF 4763
Irby upon Humber 61 TA 1904
Irchester 34 SP 9265
Ireby (Cumbr.) 62 NY 2338
Ireby (Lancs.) 64 SD 6575
Ireleth 64 SD 2277
Ireshopeburn 63 NY 8638
Irlam 51 SJ 7194
Irnham 44 TF 0226
Iron Acton 29 ST 6783
Iron Cross 32 SP 0552
Iron-Bridge 41 SJ 6703
Ironside 105 NJ 8852
Ironville 53 SK 4351
Irstead 47 TG 3620
Irthington 71 NY 4961
Irthlingborough 44 SP 9470
Irton 67 TA 0084
Irvine 82 NS 3239
Isauld 111 NC 9765
Isfield 13 TQ 4417
Isham 44 SP 8873
Isle Abbotts 8 ST 3520
Isle Brewers 8 ST 3621
Isle of Whithorn 69 NX 4736
Isleham 36 TL 6474
Isleornsay 101 NG 6912
Isleworth 21 TQ 1675
Isley Walton 43 SK 4225
Islington 21 TQ 3085
Islip (Northants.) 44 SP 9879
Islip (Oxon.) 33 SP 5214
Islivig 109 NA 9927
Itchen Abbas 11 SU 5332
Itchen Stoke 11 SU 5532
Itchingfield 12 TQ 1328
Itchington 29 ST 6586
Itteringham 47 TG 1430
Itton (Devon.) 7 SX 6898
Itton (Gwent) 29 ST 4896
Ivegill 70 NY 4143
Iver 20 TQ 0381
Iver Heath 20 TQ 0283
Iveston 72 NZ 1350
Ivinghoe 34 SP 9416
Ivinghoe Aston 34 SP 9518
Ivington 30 SO 4756
Ivington Green 30 SO 4656
Ivy Hatch 21 TQ 5854
Ivybridge 5 SX 6356
Ivychurch 15 TR 0227
Iwade 14 TQ 9067
Iwerne Courney or Shroton 10 ST 8512
Iwerne Minster 10 ST 8614
Ixworth 36 TL 9370
Ixworth Thorpe 36 TL 9172

J

Jack Hill 65 SE 1951
Jackstown 105 NJ 7531
Jackton 84 NS 5953
Jacobstow (Corn.) 6 SX 1995
Jacobstowe (Devon) 6 SS 5801
Jameston (Dyfed) 24 SS 0599
Jamestown (Dumf & G) 77 NY 2996
Jamestown (Highld.) 102 NH 4756
Jamestown (Strath.) 90 NS 3981
Janetstown 112 ND 1932
Jarrow 72 NZ 3265
Jawcraig 84 NS 8475
Jaywick 23 TM 1513
Jedburgh 78 NT 6520
Jeffreyston 24 SN 0906
Jemimaville 103 NH 7165
Jevington 13 TQ 5601
Johnby 62 NY 4333
Johnshaven 99 NO 7966
Johnston (Dyfed) 24 SM 9310
Johnstone (Strath.) 82 NS 4263
Johnstonebridge 77 NY 1091
Jordans 20 SU 9791
Jump 59 SE 3701
Juniper Green 85 NT 2068
Jurby East 56 SC 3899
Jurby West 56 SC 3598

Kaber 241 Kyre Park

K

Kaber 63 NY 7911
Kaimes (Lothian) 85 NT 2767
Kames (Strath.) 89 NM 8211
Kames (Strath.) 81 NR 9771
Kames (Strath.) 76 NS 6926
Kea 2 SW 8042
Keadby 60 SE 8311
Keal 55 TF 3763
Keal Cotes 55 TF 3661
Kearsley 58 SD 7504
Kearstwick 63 SD 6079
Kearton 65 SD 9999
Keasden 65 SD 7266
Keddington (Lincs.) 55 TF 3388
Kedington (Suff.) 36 TL 7046
Kedleston 53 SK 2941
Keelby 61 TA 1610
Keele 51 SJ 8045
Keeley Green 34 TL 0046
Keeston 24 SM 9019
Keevil 18 ST 9157
Kegworth 43 SK 4826
Kehelland 2 SW 6241
Keig 104 NJ 6119
Keigar 113 HY 5506
Keighley 59 SE 0641
Keilarsbrae 91 NS 8993
Keilhill 105 NJ 7259
Keillor 93 NO 2640
Keillour 91 NN 9725
Keils 80 NR 5268
Keinton Mandeville 17 ST 5430
Keir Mill 76 NX 8593
Keisby 44 TF 0328
Keiss 112 ND 3461
Keith 104 NJ 4350
Keithock 99 NO 6063
Kelbrook 58 SD 9044
Kelby 54 TF 0041
Keld (Cumbr.) 63 NY 5514
Keld (N Yorks.) 65 NY 8901
Kelfield 60 SE 5938
Kelham 54 SK 7755
Kellan 88 NM 5342
Kellas (Grampn.) 104 NJ 1654
Kellas (Tays.) 93 NO 4535
Kellaton 5 SX 8039
Kelleth 63 NY 6605
Kelling 47 TG 0942
Kellington 60 SE 5524
Kelloe 72 NZ 3435
Kelly 4 SX 3981
Kelly Bray 4 SX 3571
Kelmarsh 44 SP 7379
Kelmscot 18 SU 2499
Kelsale 37 TM 3865
Kelsall 50 SJ 5268
Kelshall 35 TL 3236
Kelso 86 NT 7333
Kelstern 55 TF 2590
Kelston 29 ST 6966
Keltneyburn (Tays.) 97 NN 7749
Kelty 92 NT 1494
Kelvedon 22 TL 8618
Kelvedon Hatch 21 TQ 5698
Kelynack 2 SW 3729
Kemback 93 NO 4115
Kemberton 41 SJ 7204
Kemble 18 ST 9897
Kemerton 32 SO 9437
Kemnay 105 NJ 7315
Kemp Town 13 TQ 3303
Kempley 29 SO 6729
Kempsey 32 SO 8549
Kempsford 18 SU 1596
Kempston 34 TL 0347
Kempston Hardwick 35 TL 0244
Kempton 40 SO 3582
Kemsing 21 TQ 5558
Kenardington 15 TQ 9732
Kenchester 30 SO 4343
Kencot 33 SP 2504
Kendal 63 SD 5192
Kenfig 28 SS 8081
Kenfig Hill 28 SS 8483
Kenilworth 43 SP 2872
Kenley (Gtr London) 21 TQ 3259
Kenley (Salop) 40 SJ 5600
Kenmore (Highld.) 101 NG 7557
Kenmore (Tays.) 97 NN 7745
Kenn (Avon) 29 ST 4168
Kenn (Devon.) 8 SX 9285
Kennacraig 81 NR 8262
Kennerleigh 7 SS 8107
Kennet 91 NS 9291
Kennethmont 104 NJ 5328
Kennett 36 TL 7068
Kennford 8 SX 9186
Kenninghall 47 TM 0386
Kennington (Kent) 15 TR 0245
Kennington (Oxon) 33 SP 5202
Kennoway 93 NO 3402
Kennyhill 36 TL 6680
Kennythorpe 67 SE 7865
Kenovay 94 NL 9946
Kensaleyre 100 NG 4251
Kensington and Chelsea 21 TQ 2778
Kensworth 34 TL 0318
Kensworth Common 35 TL 0317
Kent's Green 32 SO 7423
Kent's Oak 11 SU 3224
Kentallen 96 NN 0057
Kentford 36 TL 7066
Kentisbeare 8 ST 0608
Kentisbury 6 SS 6144
Kentmere 63 NY 4504
Kenton (Devon.) 8 SX 9583
Kenton (Suff.) 37 TM 1965
Kentra 95 NM 6568
Kents Bank 64 SD 3975
Kenwick 40 SJ 4230
Kenwyn 2 SW 8145
Kenyon 58 SJ 6295
Keoldale 110 NC 3866
Keppanach 96 NN 0262
Keppoch 101 NG 9621
Kepwick 66 SE 4690
Keresley 43 SP 3182
Kerne Bridge 29 SO 5819
Kerridge 51 SJ 9376
Kerris 2 SW 4427
Kerry 40 SO 1490
Kerry's Gate 30 SO 3933
Kerrycroy 82 NS 1061
Kersall 54 SK 7162
Kersey 36 TM 0044
Kershader 109 NB 3419
Kersoe 32 SO 9939
Kerswell 8 ST 0806
Kerswell Green 32 SO 8646
Kesgrave 37 TM 2245
Kessingland 47 TM 5286
Kestle Mill 2 SW 8459
Keston 21 TQ 4164
Keswick (Cumbr.) 62 NY 2723
Keswick (Norf.) 47 TG 2004
Keswick (Norf.) 47 TG 3533
Kettering 44 SP 8778
Ketteringham 47 TG 1503
Kettins 92 NO 2338
Kettlebaston 36 TL 9650
Kettlebridge 93 NO 3007
Kettlebrook 42 SK 2103
Kettleburgh 37 TM 2660
Kettleshulme 51 SJ 9879
Kettlestone 46 TF 9631
Kettlethorpe 54 SK 8475
Kettlewell 65 SD 9772
Ketton 44 SK 9704
Kew 21 TQ 1877
Kewstoke 17 ST 3363
Kexbrough 59 SE 3009
Kexby (Lincs.) 54 SK 8785
Kexby (N Yorks.) 66 SE 7050
Key Green 51 SJ 8963
Keyham 43 SK 6606
Keyhaven 11 SZ 3091
Keymer 13 TQ 3115
Keyningham 61 TA 2425
Keynsham 29 ST 6568
Keysoe 35 TL 0763
Keysoe Row 35 TL 0861
Keyston 44 TL 0475
Keyworth 53 SK 6130
Kibblesworth 72 NZ 2456
Kibworth Beauchamp 43 SP 6893
Kibworth Harcourt 43 SP 6894
Kidbrooke 21 TQ 4076
Kiddemore Green 41 SJ 8509
Kidderminster 41 SO 8376
Kiddington 33 SP 4122
Kidlington 33 SP 4913
Kidmore End 20 SU 6979
Kidsgrove 51 SJ 8354
Kidwelly 25 SN 4106
Kielder 78 NY 6293
Kiells 80 NR 4168
Kilbarchan 82 NS 4063
Kilbeg 95 NG 6506
Kilberry 81 NR 7164
Kilbirnie 82 NS 3154
Kilbride (S. Uist) 109 NF 7514
Kilbride (Skye) 100 NG 5820
Kilbride (Strath.) 89 NM 8525
Kilburn (Derby.) 53 SK 3845
Kilburn (N Yorks.) 66 SE 5179
Kilby 43 SP 6295
Kilcadzow 84 NS 8848
Kilchattan (Bute) 82 NS 1054
Kilchattan (Colonsay) 88 NR 3795
Kilchenzie 74 NR 6725
Kilchiaran 80 NR 2060
Kilchoan 95 NM 4963
Kilchoman 80 NR 2163
Kilchrenan 89 NN 0322
Kilconquhar 93 NO 4802
Kilcot 29 SO 6925
Kilcoy 102 NH 5751
Kilcreggan 90 NS 2380
Kildale 66 NZ 6009
Kildalloig 74 NR 7518
Kildonan (Highld.) 111 NC 9121
Kildonan (Island of Arran) 74 NS 0321
Kildonan Lodge 111 NC 9122
Kildrummy 104 NJ 4617
Kildwick 59 SE 0145
Kilfinan 81 NR 9378
Kilfinnan 96 NN 2795
Kilgetty 24 SN 1207
Kilgwrrwg Common 29 ST 4797
Kilham (Humbs.) 67 TA 0564
Kilham (Northumb.) 87 NT 8832
Kilkhampton 6 SS 2511
Killamarsh 53 SK 4680
Killay 25 SS 6092
Killchianaig 88 NR 6486
Killean 81 NR 6944
Killearn 90 NS 5286
Killerby 72 NZ 1919
Killichonan 97 NN 5458
Killichronan 95 NM 5441
Killiechanate 96 NN 2481
Killiecrankie 97 NN 9162
Killilan 101 NG 9430
Killimster 112 ND 3156
Killin 90 NN 5732
Killinghall 66 SE 2858
Killington 63 SD 6188
Killochyett 86 NT 4545
Kilmacolm 82 NS 3569
Kilmahumaig 89 NR 7893
Kilmaluag 100 NG 4374
Kilmany 93 NO 3821
Kilmarie 100 NG 5417
Kilmarnock 82 NS 4237
Kilmartin 89 NR 8398
Kilmaurs 82 NS 4141
Kilmelford 89 NM 8413
Kilmersdon 17 ST 6952
Kilmeston 11 SU 5825
Kilmichael Glassary 89 NR 8593
Kilmington (Devon.) 8 SY 2798
Kilmington (Wilts.) 17 ST 7736
Kilmorack 102 NH 4944
Kilmore (Island of Skye) 95 NG 6507
Kilmory (Highld.) 95 NM 5270
Kilmory (Island of Arran) 74 NR 9621
Kilmory (Strath.) 81 NR 7075
Kilmuir (Highld.) 103 NH 6749
Kilmuir (Highld.) 108 NH 7573
Kilmuir (Island of Skye) 100 NG 2547
Kilmun 89 NS 1781
Kiln Pit Hill 72 NZ 0454
Kilnave 80 NR 2871
Kilndown 13 TQ 7035
Kilnhurst 60 SK 4697
Kilninian 94 NM 3945
Kilninver 89 NM 8221
Kilnsea 61 TA 4015
Kilnsey 65 SD 9767
Kilnwick 61 SE 9949
Kiloran 88 NR 3996
Kilpatrick 74 NR 9027
Kilpeck 30 SO 4430
Kilphedir 112 NC 9818
Kilpin 60 SE 7726
Kilrenny 93 NO 5705
Kilsby 43 SP 5671
Kilspindie 92 NO 2225
Kilsyth 84 NS 7178
Kiltarlity 102 NH 5041
Kilton 16 ST 1644
Kilvaxter 100 NG 3869
Kilve 16 ST 1443
Kilvington 54 SK 8042
Kilwinning 82 NS 3043
Kimberley (Norf.) 47 TG 0704
Kimberley (Notts.) 53 SK 4944
Kimble 34 SP 8206
Kimble Wick 34 SP 8007
Kimblesworth 72 NZ 2547
Kimbolton (Cambs.) 45 TL 0967
Kimbolton (Here & W) 31 SO 5261
Kimcote 43 SP 5888
Kimmeridge 10 SY 9179
Kimmerston 87 NT 9535
Kimpton (Hants.) 19 SU 2746
Kimpton (Herts.) 35 TL 1718
Kinbrace 111 NC 8631
Kinbuck 91 NN 7905
Kincaple 93 NO 4518
Kincardine (Fife.) 84 NS 9387
Kincardine (Highld.) 108 NH 6089
Kincardine O'Neil 99 NO 5999
Kinclaven 92 NO 1538
Kincraig 103 NH 8305
Kincraigie 98 NN 9849
Kindallachan 98 NN 9950
Kineton (Glos.) 32 SP 0926
Kineton (Warw.) 33 SP 3351
Kinfauns 92 NO 1622
King Sterndale 52 SK 0972
King's Bromley 42 SK 1216
King's Cliffe 44 TL 0097
King's Coughton 32 SP 0858
King's Heath 42 SP 0781
King's Lynn 46 TF 6220
King's Norton (Leic.) 44 SK 6800
King's Norton (W Mids) 42 SP 0579
King's Nympton 7 SS 6819
King's Pyon 30 SO 4350
King's Somborne 11 SU 3631
King's Stag 9 ST 7210
King's Stanley 32 SO 8103
King's Sutton 33 SP 5036
King's Walden 35 TL 1623
Kingarth 81 NS 0956
Kingcoed 29 SO 4205
Kingham 33 SP 2523
Kingholm Quay 70 NX 9773
Kinghorn 85 NT 2686
Kinglassie 92 NT 2298
Kingoodie 93 NO 3329
Kings Caple 29 SO 5628
Kings Langley 35 TL 0702
Kings Meaburn 63 NY 6221
Kings Muir (Borders) 85 NT 2539
Kings Ripton 45 TL 2576
Kings Worthy 11 SU 4932
Kingsand 4 SX 4350
Kingsbarns 93 NO 5912
Kingsbridge (Devon.) 5 SX 7344
Kingsbridge (Somer.) 16 SS 9837
Kingsburgh 100 NG 3955
Kingsbury (Gtr London) 21 TQ 1989
Kingsbury (Warw.) 42 SP 2196
Kingsbury Episcopi 9 ST 4320
Kingsclere 19 SU 5258
Kingscote 18 ST 8196
Kingscott 6 SS 5318
Kingscross 74 NS 0428
Kingsdon 17 ST 5126
Kingsdown 15 TR 3748
Kingseat 92 NT 1290
Kingsey 34 SP 7406
Kingsfold 12 TQ 1636
Kingsford 41 SO 8281
Kingshall Street 36 TL 9161
Kingshouse 90 NN 5620
Kingskerswell 5 SX 8767
Kingskettle 93 NO 3008
Kingsland 30 SO 4461
Kingsley (Ches) 50 SJ 5474
Kingsley (Hants.) 12 SU 7838
Kingsley (Staffs.) 52 SK 0047
Kingsley Green 12 SU 8930
Kingsmuir (Fife) 93 NO 5409
Kingsmuir (Tays.) 98 NO 4840
Kingsnorth 15 TR 0039
Kingstanding 42 SP 0794
Kingsteignton 5 SX 8773
Kingsthorne 30 SO 4932
Kingsthorpe 34 SP 7563
Kingston (Cambs.) 35 TL 3455
Kingston (Devon.) 5 SX 6347
Kingston (Dorset) 9 ST 7509
Kingston (Dorset) 10 SY 9579
Kingston (Grampn.) 104 NJ 3365
Kingston (Hants.) 10 SU 1401
Kingston (I. of W.) 11 SZ 4781
Kingston (Kent) 15 TR 1951
Kingston (Lothian) 86 NT 5482
Kingston Bagpuize 19 SU 4098
Kingston Blount 20 SU 7399
Kingston Deverill 10 ST 8436
Kingston Lisle 19 SU 3287
Kingston Russell 9 SY 5891
Kingston Seymour 29 ST 3966
Kingston St. Mary 16 ST 2229
Kingston by Sea 13 TQ 2205
Kingston near Lewes 13 TQ 3908
Kingston on Soar 43 SK 5027
Kingston upon Hull 61 TA 0929
Kingston upon Thames 21 TQ 1869
Kingstone (Here & W) 30 SO 4235
Kingstone (Somer.) 8 ST 3713
Kingstone (Staffs.) 42 SK 0629
Kingstown 70 NY 3959
Kingswear 5 SX 8851
Kingswells 105 NJ 8606
Kingswinford 41 SO 8888
Kingswood (Avon) 29 ST 6473
Kingswood (Bucks) 34 SP 6819
Kingswood (Glos.) 29 ST 7491
Kingswood (Kent) 14 TQ 8351
Kingswood (Powys) 40 SJ 2402
Kingswood (Surrey) 21 TQ 2455
Kingswood (Warw.) 42 SP 1871
Kington (Here & W) 30 SO 2956
Kington (Here & W) 32 SO 9955
Kington Langley 18 ST 9276
Kington Magna 9 ST 7622
Kington St. Michael 18 ST 9077
Kingussie 97 NH 7500
Kingweston 17 ST 5230
Kinharrachie (Grampn.) 105 NJ 9231
Kinkell Bridge 91 NN 9316
Kinlet 41 SO 7280
Kinloch (Highld.) 110 NC 3434
Kinloch (Rhum) 94 NM 4099
Kinloch (Tays.) 98 NO 1444
Kinloch (Tays.) 98 NO 2644
Kinloch Hourn 95 NG 9407
Kinloch Rannoch 97 NN 6658
Kinlochard 90 NN 4502
Kinlochbervie 110 NC 2156
Kinlocheil 96 NM 9779
Kinlochewe 101 NH 0261
Kinlochleven 96 NN 1861
Kinloss 103 NJ 0661
Kinmuck 105 NJ 8119
Kinmundy 105 NJ 8817
Kinnadie 105 NJ 9643
Kinnaird 92 NO 2428
Kinneff 99 NO 8574
Kinnelhead 76 NT 0201
Kinnell 99 NO 6050
Kinnerley 40 SJ 3321
Kinnersley (Here & W) 30 SO 3449
Kinnersley (Here & W) 32 SO 8743
Kinnerton (Ches.) 50 SJ 3361
Kinnerton (Powys) 30 SO 2463
Kinnesswood 92 NO 1702
Kinninvie 72 NZ 0521
Kinnordy 98 NO 3654
Kinoulton 53 SK 6730
Kinross 92 NO 1102
Kinrossie 92 NO 1832
Kinsham (Here & W) 30 SO 3664
Kinsley 59 SE 4114
Kintbury 19 SU 3866
Kintessack 103 NJ 0060
Kintillo 92 NO 1317
Kintocher 104 NJ 5709
Kintore 105 NJ 7916
Kinveachy 103 NH 9118
Kinver 41 SO 8433
Kippax 59 SE 4130
Kippen 91 NS 6594
Kippford or Scaur 69 NX 8355
Kirby Bedon 47 TG 2705
Kirby Cane 47 TM 3794
Kirby Cross 23 TM 2120
Kirby Grindalythe 67 SE 9067
Kirby Hill (N Yorks.) 65 NZ 1306
Kirby Hill (N Yorks.) 66 SE 3868
Kirby Knowle 66 SE 4687
Kirby Misperton 67 SE 7779
Kirby Muxloe 43 SK 5104
Kirby Row 47 TM 3792
Kirby Sigston 66 SE 4194
Kirby Underdale 67 SE 8158
Kirby Wiske 66 SE 3784
Kirby le Soken 23 TM 2222
Kirdford 12 TQ 0226
Kirk 112 ND 2859
Kirk Bramwith 60 SE 6111
Kirk Connel (Dumf & G) 76 NS 7312
Kirk Deighton 66 SE 3950
Kirk Ella 61 TA 0129
Kirk Hallam 53 SK 4540
Kirk Hammerton 66 SE 4655
Kirk Ireton 53 SK 2650
Kirk Langley 53 SK 2838
Kirk Merrington 72 NZ 2631
Kirk Michael (I. of M.) 56 SC 3190
Kirk Sandall 60 SE 6007
Kirk Smeaton 60 SE 5116
Kirk Yetholm 87 NT 8227
Kirk of Shotts 84 NS 8462
Kirkabister 113 HU 4938
Kirkandrews upon Eden 70 NY 3558
Kirkbampton 70 NY 3056
Kirkbean 70 NX 9859
Kirkbride 70 NY 2356
Kirkbuddo 99 NO 5043
Kirkburn (Humbs.) 67 SE 9855
Kirkburton 59 SE 1912
Kirkby (Lincs.) 54 TF 0692
Kirkby (Mers.) 50 SJ 4098
Kirkby (N Yorks.) 66 NZ 5306
Kirkby Fleetham 66 SE 2984
Kirkby Green 54 TF 0857
Kirkby Lonsdale 63 SD 6178
Kirkby Malham 65 SD 8960
Kirkby Mallory 43 SK 4500
Kirkby Malzeard 66 SE 2374
Kirkby Overblow 59 SE 3249
Kirkby Stephen 65 NY 7708
Kirkby Thore 63 NY 6325
Kirkby Underwood 45 TF 0727
Kirkby in Ashfield 53 SK 5056
Kirkby la Thorpe 54 TF 0946
Kirkby on Bain 55 TF 2362
Kirkbymoorside 66 SE 6986
Kirkcaldy 93 NT 2791
Kirkcambeck 71 NY 5368
Kirkcarswell 69 NX 7549
Kirkcolm 68 NX 0268
Kirkconnel 76 NS 7312
Kirkconnel 70 NX 9868
Kirkcowan 68 NX 3260
Kirkcudbright 69 NX 6851
Kirkfieldbank 84 NS 8643
Kirkgunzeon 69 NX 8666
Kirkham (Lancs.) 57 SD 4231
Kirkham (N Yorks.) 67 SE 7365
Kirkhamgate 59 SE 2922
Kirkharle 79 NZ 0182
Kirkheaton (Northum.) 79 NZ 0177
Kirkheaton (W Yorks.) 59 SE 1817
Kirkhill (Highld.) 102 NH 5545
Kirkhill (Tays.) 99 NO 6860
Kirkhope (Borders) 77 NT 3823
Kirkhouse 85 NT 3233
Kirkibost (Island of Skye) 100 NG 5417
Kirkinch 98 NO 3144
Kirkinner 68 NX 4251
Kirkintilloch 84 NS 6573
Kirkland (Cumbr.) 62 NY 0718
Kirkland (Cumbr.) 63 NY 6432
Kirkland (Dumf & G) 76 NS 7214
Kirkland (Dumf & G) 76 NX 8090
Kirkleatham 73 NZ 5921
Kirklevington 66 NZ 4309
Kirkley 47 TM 5491
Kirkleyditch 51 SJ 8778
Kirklington (N Yorks.) 66 SE 3181
Kirklington (Notts.) 53 SK 6757
Kirklinton 70 NY 4366
Kirkliston 85 NT 1274
Kirkmaiden 68 NX 1236
Kirkmichael (Strath.) 75 NS 3408
Kirkmichael (Tays.) 98 NO 0860
Kirkmuirhill 84 NS 7943
Kirknewton (Lothian) 85 NT 1166
Kirknewton (Northum.) 87 NT 9130
Kirkoswald (Cumbr.) 71 NY 5541
Kirkoswald (Strath.) 75 NS 2407
Kirkpatrick Durham 69 NX 7870
Kirkpatrick-Fleming 70 NY 2770
Kirksanton 62 SD 1380
Kirkstall 59 SE 2635
Kirkstile (Dumf & G) 77 NY 3690
Kirkton (Borders) 78 NT 5413
Kirkton (Dumf & G) 70 NX 9781
Kirkton (Fife.) 93 NO 3625
Kirkton (Grampn.) 104 NJ 6112
Kirkton (Grampn.) 104 NJ 6425
Kirkton (Grampn.) 105 NJ 6950
Kirkton (Grampn.) 105 NJ 8243
Kirkton (Grampn.) 105 NK 1050
Kirkton (Highld.) 101 NG 9141
Kirkton (Highld.) 108 NH 7998
Kirkton (Tays.) 91 NN 9618
Kirkton (Tays.) 98 NO 4246
Kirkton Manor 85 NT 2137
Kirkton of Airlie 98 NO 3151
Kirkton of Auchterhouse 93 NO 3338
Kirkton of Barevan 103 NH 8347
Kirkton of Collace 92 NO 1931
Kirkton of Craig 99 NO 7055
Kirkton of Durris 99 NO 7796
Kirkton of Glenbuchat 104 NJ 3715
Kirkton of Glenisla 98 NO 2160
Kirkton of Kingoldrum 98 NO 3354
Kirkton of Largo 93 NO 4203
Kirkton of Lethendy 98 NO 1241
Kirkton of Logie Buchan 105 NJ 9829
Kirkton of Maryculter 99 NO 8599
Kirkton of Menmuir 99 NO 5364
Kirkton of Monikie 93 NO 5138
Kirkton of Rayne 105 NJ 6930
Kirkton of Skene 105 NJ 8007
Kirkton of Strathmartine 93 NO 3735
Kirkton of Tealing 93 NO 4037
Kirktown 105 NK 0952
Kirktown of Auchterless 105 NJ 7141
Kirktown of Bourtie 105 NJ 8024
Kirktown of Deskford 104 NJ 5061
Kirktown of Fetteresso 99 NO 8585
Kirkwall 113 HY 4410
Kirkwhelpington 79 NY 9984
Kirmington 61 TA 1011
Kirmond le Mire 55 TF 1892
Kirn 82 NS 1878
Kirriemuir 98 NO 3854
Kirstead Green 47 TM 2997
Kirtlebridge 70 NY 2372
Kirtling 36 TL 6857
Kirtling Green 36 TL 6855
Kirtlington 33 SP 4919
Kirtomy 111 NC 7463
Kirton (Highld.) 101 NG 8327
Kirton (Lincs.) 55 TF 3038
Kirton (Notts.) 63 SK 6869
Kirton (Suff.) 37 TM 2739
Kirton End 55 TF 2840
Kirton Holme 55 TF 2642
Kirton in Lindsey 61 SK 9398
Kislingbury 34 SP 6959
Kites Hardwick 43 SP 4668
Kittybrewster 105 NJ 9208
Kitwood 11 SU 6633
Kiveton Park 53 SK 4982
Knaith 54 SK 8284
Knap Corner 10 ST 8023
Knaphill 20 SU 9658
Knapp (Somer.) 17 ST 3025
Knapp (Tays.) 93 NO 2831
Knapton (N Yorks.) 66 SE 5652
Knapton (N Yorks.) 67 SE 8775
Knapton (Norf.) 47 TG 3034
Knapwell 35 TL 3362
Knaresborough 66 SE 3557
Knarsdale 71 NY 6753
Knaven 105 NJ 8943
Knayton 66 SE 4387
Knebworth 35 TL 2520
Kneesall 54 SK 7064
Kneesworth 35 TL 3444
Kneeton 54 SK 7146
Knelston 25 SS 4689
Knightacott 7 SS 6439
Knightcote 33 SP 3954
Knighton (Devon.) 5 SX 5249
Knighton (Leic.) 43 SK 6001
Knighton (Powys) 40 SO 2872
Knighton (Staffs.) 51 SJ 7240
Knighton (Staffs.) 41 SJ 7427
Knightwick 32 SO 7355
Knill 30 SO 2960
Knipton 54 SK 8231
Knitsley 72 NZ 1148
Kniveton 53 SK 2050
Knock (Cumbr.) 63 NY 6826
Knock (Grampn.) 104 NJ 5452
Knock (Island of Mull) 88 NM 5438
Knock (Isle of Lewis) 109 NB 4931
Knockally 112 ND 1428
Knockan 107 NC 2110
Knockando 104 NJ 1941
Knockbain (Highld.) 102 NH 6255
Knockbrex 69 NX 5849
Knockdee 112 ND 1761
Knockdolian 68 NX 1285
Knockenkelly 74 NS 0426
Knockentiber 82 NS 3939
Knockholt 21 TQ 4658
Knockholt Pound 21 TQ 4859
Knockin 40 SJ 3322
Knocknaha 74 NR 6817
Knockrome 80 NR 5571
Knocksharry 56 SC 2785
Knodishall 37 TM 4261
Knolls Green 51 SJ 8079
Knolton 50 SJ 3738
Knook 18 ST 9341
Knossington 44 SK 8008
Knott End-on-Sea 57 SD 3548
Knotting 34 TL 0063
Knottingley 60 SE 5023
Knotty Green 20 SU 9392
Knowbury 41 SO 5774
Knowe 68 NX 3171
Knowehead 76 NX 6090
Knowesgate 79 NY 9885
Knoweside 75 NS 2512
Knowl Hill 20 SU 8279
Knowle (Avon) 29 ST 6170
Knowle (Devon.) 6 SS 4938
Knowle (Devon.) 7 SS 7801
Knowle (W Mids) 42 SP 1876
Knowle Green 58 SD 6337
Knowlton 15 TR 2853
Knowsley 50 SJ 4395
Knowstone 7 SS 8223
Knucklas 40 SO 2574
Knutsford 51 SJ 7578
Knypersley 51 SJ 8856
Kyle of Lochalsh 101 NG 7627
Kyleakin 101 NG 7526
Kylerhea 101 NG 7820
Kylesku 110 NC 2334
Kylestrome 110 NC 2234
Kyloe 87 NU 0540
Kynnersley 41 SJ 6716
Kyre Park 31 SO 6263

L

Livingston 243 Lunsford's Cross

Livingston 85 NT 0568
Livingston Village 85 NT 0366
Lixwm 50 SJ 1671
Lizard 2 SW 6912
Llanaber 38 SH 6018
Llanaelhaearn 48 SH 3844
Llanafan 27 SN 6872
Llanafan-fechan 27 SN 9650
Llanallgo 48 SH 5085
Llanarmon 48 SH 4239
Llanarmon Dyffryn Ceiriog 50 SJ 1532
Llanarmon-yn-Ial 50 SJ 1856
Llanarth (Dyfed) 26 SN 4257
Llanarth (Gwent.) 29 SO 3711
Llanarthney 25 SN 5320
Llanasa 50 SJ 1081
Llanbabo 48 SH 3786
Llanbadarn Fawr 38 SN 6080
Llanbadarn Fynydd 27 SO 0977
Llanbadarn-y-garreg 30 SO 1148
Llanbadrig 48 SH 3794
Llanbeder 29 ST 3890
Llanbedr (Gwyn.) 38 SH 5826
Llanbedr (Powys) 30 SO 1346
Llanbedr (Powys) 28 SO 2320
Llanbedr-Dyffryn-Clwyd 50 SJ 1459
Llanbedr-y-cennin 49 SH 7659
Llanbedrgoch 48 SH 5180
Llanbedrog 48 SH 3231
Llanberis 48 SH 5760
Llanbister 40 SO 1073
Llanblethian 28 SS 9873
Llanboidy 24 SN 2123
Llanbradach 28 ST 1490
Llanbrynmair 39 SH 9002
Llancarfan 28 ST 0570
Llancayo 29 SO 3603
Llancynfelyn 39 SN 6492
Llandanwg 38 SH 5728
Llandawke 25 SN 2811
Llanddaniel Fab 48 SH 4970
Llanddarog 25 SN 5016
Llanddeiniol 26 SN 5672
Llanddeiniolen 48 SH 5465
Llandderfel 49 SH 9837
Llanddeusant (Dyfed) 28 SN 7724
Llanddeusant (Gwyn.) 48 SH 3485
Llanddew 27 SO 0530
Llanddewi 25 SS 4689
Llanddewi Brefi 27 SN 6655
Llanddewi Rhydderch 29 SO 3412
Llanddewi Velfrey 24 SN 1417
Llanddewi Ystradenni 40 SO 1068
Llanddewi'r Cwm 27 SO 0348
Llanddoget 49 SH 8063
Llanddona 48 SH 5779
Llanddowror 25 SN 2514
Llanddulas 49 SH 9078
Llanddyfnan 48 SH 5078
Llandebie 25 SN 6215
Llandefaelog 25 SN 4111
Llandefaelog Fach 27 SO 0332
Llandegai 48 SH 5970
Llandegfan 48 SH 5674
Llandegla 50 SJ 1952
Llandegley 30 SO 1363
Llandegveth 29 ST 3395
Llandeilo 25 SN 6322
Llandeilo Graban 27 SO 0944
Llandeilo'r Fan 27 SN 8943
Llandeloy 24 SM 8526
Llandenny 29 SO 4104
Llandevenny 29 ST 4186
Llandinabo 29 SO 5128
Llandinam 39 SO 0288
Llandissilio 24 SN 1221
Llandogo 29 SO 5204
Llandough (S Glam.) 28 SS 9972
Llandough (S Glam.) 28 ST 1673
Llandovery 27 SN 7634
Llandow 28 SS 9473
Llandre (Dyfed) 38 SN 6286
Llandrillo 49 SJ 0337
Llandrillo-yn-Rhos 49 SH 8380
Llandrindod Wells 27 SO 0561
Llandrinio 40 SJ 2917
Llandudno 49 SH 7782
Llandudno Junction 49 SH 7977
Llandwrog 48 SH 4556
Llandyfan 25 SN 6417
Llandyfriog 26 SN 3241
Llandyfrydog 48 SH 4485
Llandygwydd 26 SN 2443
Llandyrnog 50 SJ 1064
Llandyssil 40 SO 1995
Llandysul 26 SN 4140
Llanegryn 38 SH 5905
Llanegwad 25 SN 5121
Llaneilian 48 SH 4692
Llanelian-yn-Rhos 49 SH 8376
Llanelidan 50 SJ 1050
Llanelieu 30 SO 1834
Llanellen 29 SO 3010
Llanelli (Dyfed) 25 SN 5000
Llanelltyd 39 SH 7119
Llanelly (Gwent) 28 SO 2314
Llanelwedd 27 SO 0451
Llanenddwyn 38 SH 5823
Llanengan 38 SH 2927
Llanerchymedd 39 SH 4138
Llanerfyl 39 SJ 0309
Llanfachraeth 48 SH 3182
Llanfachreth 39 SH 7522
Llanfaelog 48 SH 3373
Llanfaes 48 SH 6077
Llanfaethlu 48 SH 3186
Llanfaglan 48 SH 4760
Llanfair (Gwyn.) 38 SH 5729
Llanfair Caereinion 40 SJ 1006
Llanfair Clydogau 27 SN 6251
Llanfair Dyffryn Clwyd 50 SJ 1355
Llanfair P. G. 48 SH 5371
Llanfair Talhaiarn 49 SH 9269
Llanfair Waterdine 40 SO 2476
Llanfair-Nant-Gwyn 26 SN 1637
Llanfair-yn-Neubwll 48 SH 3077
Llanfairfechan 49 SH 6874
Llanfairynghornwy 48 SH 3290
Llanfallteg 24 SN 1520
Llanfallteg West 24 SN 1519
Llanfaredd 27 SO 0651
Llanfechain 40 SJ 1820
Llanfechell 48 SH 3691
Llanfendigaid 38 SH 5605
Llanferres 50 SJ 1860
Llanfflewyn 48 SH 3689
Llanfihangel 39 SJ 0817
Llanfihangel Glyn Myfyr 49 SH 9849
Llanfihangel Nant Bran 27 SN 9434
Llanfihangel Rhydithon 40 SO 1466
Llanfihangel Rogiet 29 ST 4487
Llanfihangel ar-Arth 26 SN 4539
Llanfihangel-Tal-y-llyn 28 SO 1128
Llanfihangel-nant-Melan 30 SO 1758
Llanfihangel-uwch-Gwili 25 SN 4822
Llanfihangel-y-Creuddyn 27 SN 6676
Llanfihangel-y-pennant (Gwyn.) 48 SH 5245
Llanfihangel-y-pennant (Gwyn.) 39 SH 6708
Llanfihangel-y-traethau 48 SH 5935
Llanfilo 30 SO 1133
Llanfoist 29 SO 2813
Llanfor 49 SH 9336
Llanfrechfa 29 ST 3193
Llanfrothen 48 SH 6241
Llanfrynach 28 SO 0726
Llanfwrog (Clwyd) 50 SJ 1157
Llanfwrog (Gwyn.) 48 SH 3083
Llanfyllin 40 SJ 1419
Llanfynydd (Clwyd) 50 SJ 2756
Llanfynydd (Dyfed) 25 SN 5527
Llanfyrnach 26 SN 2231
Llangadfan 39 SJ 0010
Llangadog 25 SN 7028
Llangadwaladr (Clwyd) 40 SJ 1730
Llangadwaladr (Gwyn.) 48 SH 3869
Llangaffo 48 SH 4468
Llangain 25 SN 3815
Llangammarch Wells 27 SN 9347
Llangan 28 SS 9577
Llangarron 29 SO 5221
Llangathen 25 SN 5822
Llangattock 28 SO 2117
Llangattock Lingoed 29 SO 3620
Llangattock-Vibon-Avel 29 SO 4515
Llangedwyn 40 SJ 1824
Llangefni 48 SH 4575
Llangeinor 28 SS 9187
Llangeitho 27 SN 6159
Llangeler 26 SN 3739
Llangelynin 38 SH 5707
Llangendeirne 25 SN 4514
Llangennech 25 SN 5601
Llangennith 25 SS 4291
Llangenny 28 SO 2418
Llangernyw 49 SH 8767
Llangian 38 SH 2928
Llanglydwen 24 SN 1826
Llangoed 48 SH 6079
Llangoedmor 26 SN 2045
Llangollen 50 SJ 2141
Llangolman 24 SN 1127
Llangorse 28 SO 1327
Llangovan 29 SO 4505
Llangower 49 SH 9032
Llangranog 26 SN 3154
Llangristiolus 48 SH 4373
Llangrove 29 SO 5219
Llangua 29 SO 3926
Llangunllo 40 SO 2171
Llangunnor 25 SN 4219
Llangurig 39 SN 9080
Llangwm (Clwyd) 49 SH 9644
Llangwm (Dyfed) 24 SM 9909
Llangwm-isaf 29 SO 4200
Llangwnnadl 48 SH 2033
Llangwyfan 50 SJ 1266
Llangwyllog 48 SH 4379
Llangwyryfon 27 SN 5970
Llangybi (Dyfed) 27 SN 6053
Llangybi (Gwent) 29 ST 3796
Llangybi (Gwyn.) 48 SH 4240
Llangyfelach 25 SS 6499
Llangynhafal 50 SJ 1263
Llangynidr 28 SO 1519
Llangynin 25 SN 2519
Llangynog (Dyfed) 25 SN 3316
Llangynog (Powys) 39 SJ 0526
Llanharan 28 ST 0083
Llanharry 28 ST 0080
Llanhennock 29 ST 3592
Llanhilleth 28 SO 2100
Llanidloes 39 SN 9584
Llaniestyn 48 SH 2633
Llanigon 30 SO 2139
Llanilar 27 SN 6275
Llanilid 28 SS 9781
Llanishen (Gwent) 29 SO 4703
Llanishen (S Glam.) 28 ST 1781
Llanllechid 48 SH 6268
Llanlleonfel 27 SN 9350
Llanllowell 29 ST 3998
Llanllugan 39 SJ 0402
Llanllwch 25 SN 3818
Llanllwchaiarn 40 SO 1192
Llanllyfni 48 SH 4651
Llanmadoc 25 SS 4493
Llanmaes 28 SS 9869
Llanmartin 29 ST 3989
Llanmerewig 40 SO 1593
Llanmihangel 28 SS 9771
Llanmorlais 25 SS 5294
Llannefydd 49 SH 9770
Llannon 25 SN 5408
Llannor 48 SH 3537
Llanon 26 SN 5167
Llanpumsaint 25 SN 4129
Llanrhaeadr 49 SJ 0763
Llanrhaeadr-ym-Mochnant 40 SJ 1226
Llanrhidian 25 SS 4992
Llanrhos 49 SH 7880
Llanrhyddlad 48 SH 3389
Llanrhystud 26 SN 5369
Llanrian 24 SM 8131
Llanrothal 29 SO 4618
Llanrug 48 SH 5363
Llanrwst 49 SH 7961
Llansadurnen 25 SN 2810
Llansadwrn (Dyfed) 27 SN 6931
Llansadwrn (Gwyn.) 48 SH 5575
Llansaint 25 SN 3808
Llansannan 49 SH 9365
Llansannor 28 SS 9977
Llansantffraed 28 SO 1223
Llansantffraed-Cwmdeuddwr 27 SN 9667
Llansantffraed-in-Elvel 27 SO 0954
Llansantffraid 26 SN 5167
Llansantffraid Glan Conwy 49 SH 8075
Llansantffraid-ym-Mechain 40 SJ 2220
Llansawel 27 SN 6136
Llansilin 40 SJ 2028
Llansoy 29 SO 4402
Llanstadwell 24 SM 9505
Llansteffan (Dyfed) 25 SN 3511
Llanstephan (Powys) 30 SO 1142
Llanthony 29 SO 2827
Llantilio-Crossenny 29 SO 3914
Llantrisant (Gwent) 29 ST 3996
Llantrisant (Mid Glam.) 28 ST 0483
Llantrithyd 28 ST 0472
Llantwit Fardre 28 ST 0785
Llantwit Major 28 SS 9768
Llantysilio 50 SJ 1943
Llanuwchllyn 49 SH 8730
Llanvaches 29 ST 4391
Llanvair-Discoed 29 ST 4492
Llanvapley 29 SO 3614
Llanvetherine 29 SO 3617
Llanveynoe 30 SO 3031
Llanvihangel Crucorney 29 SO 3220
Llanvihangel Gobion 29 SO 3409
Llanvihangel-Ystern-Llewern 29 SO 4313
Llanwarne 29 SO 5028
Llanwddyn 39 SJ 0219
Llanwenog 26 SN 4945
Llanwern 29 ST 3688
Llanwinio 25 SN 2626
Llanwnda (Dyfed) 24 SM 9339
Llanwnda (Gwyn.) 48 SH 4758
Llanwnen 26 SN 5347
Llanwnog 39 SO 0293
Llanwrda 27 SN 7131
Llanwrin 39 SH 7803
Llanwrthwl 27 SN 9763
Llanwrtyd 27 SN 8647
Llanwrtyd Wells 27 SN 8746
Llanwyddelan 39 SJ 0801
Llanyblodwel 40 SJ 2322
Llanybri 25 SN 3312
Llanybyther 26 SN 5244
Llanycefn 24 SN 0923
Llanychaer Bridge 24 SM 9835
Llanycrwys 27 SN 6445
Llanymawddwy 39 SH 9019
Llanymynech 40 SJ 2620
Llanynghenedl 48 SH 3181
Llanynys 50 SJ 1062
Llanyre 27 SO 0462
Llanystumdwy 48 SH 4738
Llanywern 28 SO 1028
Llawhaden 24 SN 0717
Llawnt 40 SJ 2430
Llawryglyn 39 SN 9291
Llay 50 SJ 3255
Llechcynfarwy 48 SH 3881
Llechfaen 28 SO 0828
Llechryd (Dyfed) 26 SN 2243
Llechryd (Mid Glam.) 28 SO 1009
Llechrydau 50 SJ 2234
Lledrod (Clwyd) 40 SJ 2229
Lledrod (Dyfed) 27 SN 6470
Llidiadnenog 26 SN 5437
Llidiardau 38 SH 1929
Llithfaen 48 SH 3543
Llong 50 SJ 2562
Llowes 30 SO 1941
Llwydcoed 28 SN 9905
Llwydiarth 39 SJ 0315
Llwyn 40 SO 2880
Llwyncelyn 26 SN 4459
Llwyndafydd 26 SN 3755
Llwynderw 40 SJ 2004
Llwyndryrys 48 SH 3741
Llwyngwril 38 SH 5909
Llwynhendy 25 SS 5599
Llwynmawr 50 SJ 2236
Llwynypia 28 SS 9993
Llynclys 40 SJ 2924
Llynfaes 48 SH 4178
Llys-y-fran 24 SN 0424
Llysfaen 49 SH 8977
Llyswen (Powys) 30 SO 1337
Llysworney 28 SS 9674
Llywel 27 SN 8630
Loan 84 NS 9575
Loanend 87 NT 9450
Loanhead 85 NT 2765
Loans 82 NS 3431
Lochailort (Highld.) 95 NM 7682
Lochaline (Highld.) 95 NM 6744
Lochans 68 NX 0656
Locharbriggs 70 NX 9980
Lochawe (Strath.) 89 NN 1227
Lochboisdale (S. Uist) 109 NF 7820
Lochbuie (Strath.) 88 NM 6125
Lochcarron (Highld.) 101 NG 9039
Lochdonhead 89 NM 7333
Lochead 81 NR 7778
Lochearnhead 90 NN 5823
Lochee 93 NO 3631
Lochend (Highld.) 102 NH 5937
Locheport (N. Uist) 109 NF 8563
Lochfoot 69 NX 8973
Lochgair 89 NR 9290
Lochgarthside 102 NH 5219
Lochgelly 92 NT 1893
Lochgilphead 89 NR 8687
Lochgoilhead 90 NN 1901
Lochhill 104 NJ 2964
Lochinver 110 NC 0922
Lochlane 91 NN 8320
Lochluichart 102 NH 3262
Lochmaben 70 NY 0882
Lochnaw 68 NW 9962
Lochore 92 NT 1796
Lochranza (Island of Arran) 81 NR 9350
Lochside (Grampn.) 99 NO 7464
Lochside (Highland.) 111 NC 8735
Lochton 99 NO 7592
Lochwinnoch 82 NS 3558
Lochwood (Strath.) 84 NS 6966
Lockengate 4 SX 0361
Lockerbie 70 NY 1381
Lockeridge 18 SU 1467
Lockerley 11 SU 2925
Locking 17 ST 3659
Lockington (Humbs.) 67 SE 9947
Lockington (Leic.) 43 SK 4628
Lockleywood 41 SJ 6828
Lockmaddy 109 NF 9168
Locks Heath 11 SU 5207
Lockton 67 SE 8489
Loddington (Leic.) 44 SK 7802
Loddington (Northants.) 44 SP 8178
Loddiswell 5 SX 7148
Loddon 47 TM 3698
Lode 35 TL 5362
Loders 9 SY 4994
Lodsworth 12 SU 9223
Lofthouse (N Yorks.) 65 SE 1073
Lofthouse (W Yorks.) 59 SE 3325
Loftus 73 NZ 7118
Logan 75 NS 5820
Loggerheads 51 SJ 7336
Logie (Fife) 93 NO 4020
Logie (Grampn.) 105 NK 0356
Logie (Tays.) 99 NO 6963
Logie Coldstone 98 NJ 4304
Logie Hill 108 NH 7776
Logie Newton 105 NJ 6638
Logie Pert 99 NO 6664
Logierait 98 NN 9752
Login 24 SN 1623
Lolworth 35 TL 3664
Lonbain 101 NG 6853
Londesborough 60 SE 8645
London 21 TQ 3281
London Colney 35 TL 1603
Londonderry 66 SE 3087
Londonthorpe 54 SK 9537
Londubh 106 NG 8680
Long Ashton 29 ST 5470
Long Bennington 54 SK 8344
Long Bredy 9 SY 5690
Long Buckby 43 SP 6267
Long Clawson 44 SK 7227
Long Common 11 SU 5014
Long Compton (Staffs.) 41 SJ 8522
Long Compton (Warw.) 33 SP 2832
Long Crendon 34 SP 6908
Long Crichel 10 ST 9710
Long Ditton 21 TQ 1666
Long Drax 60 SE 6528
Long Duckmanton 53 SK 4371
Long Eaton 53 SK 4933
Long Hanborough 33 SP 4114
Long Hermiston 85 NT 1770
Long Itchington 33 SP 4165
Long Lawford 43 SP 4775
Long Load 9 ST 4623
Long Marston (Herts.) 34 SP 8915
Long Marston (N Yorks.) 66 SE 5051
Long Marston (Warw.) 32 SP 1548
Long Marton 63 NY 6624
Long Melford 36 TL 8646
Long Newnton (Glos.) 18 ST 9092
Long Preston 65 SD 8357
Long Riston 61 TA 1242
Long Stratton 47 TM 1992
Long Street (Bucks.) 34 SP 7946
Long Sutton (Hants.) 20 SU 7347
Long Sutton (Lincs.) 45 TF 4322
Long Sutton (Somer.) 9 ST 4625
Long Thurlow 37 TM 0168
Long Whatton 43 SK 4723
Long Wittenham 19 SU 5493
Longbenton 72 NZ 2668
Longborough 33 SP 1729
Longbridge (W Mids) 42 SP 0178
Longbridge (Warw.) 33 SP 2662
Longbridge Deverill 18 ST 8640
Longburton 9 ST 6412
Longcliffe 53 SK 2255
Longcot 18 SU 2790
Longcroft 84 NS 7979
Longden 40 SJ 4306
Longdon (Here & W) 32 SO 8336
Longdon (Staffs.) 42 SK 0714
Longdon upon Tern 41 SJ 6215
Longdown 5 SX 8691
Longdowns 2 SW 7434
Longfield 14 TQ 6069
Longford (Derby.) 53 SK 2137
Longford (Glos.) 32 SO 8320
Longford (Gtr London) 20 TQ 0576
Longford (Salop) 51 SJ 6433
Longford (Salop) 41 SJ 7218
Longford (W Mids.) 43 SP 3583
Longforgan 93 NO 3129
Longformacus 86 NT 6957
Longframlington 79 NU 1201
Longham (Dorset) 10 SZ 0697
Longham (Norf.) 46 TF 9415
Longhirst 79 NZ 2289
Longhope 29 SO 6819
Longhorsley 79 NZ 1494
Longhoughton 79 NU 2414
Longley Green 32 SO 7350
Longmanhill 105 NJ 7462
Longmoor Camp 12 SU 7930
Longmorn 104 NJ 2358
Longnewton (Bord) 86 NT 5827
Longnewton (Cleve.) 72 NZ 3816
Longney 32 SO 7612
Longniddry 86 NT 4476
Longnor (Salop) 40 SJ 4800
Longnor (Staffs.) 52 SK 0864
Longparish 19 SU 4344
Longridge (Lancs.) 58 SD 6037
Longridge (Lothian) 84 NS 9462
Longriggend 84 NS 8270
Longsdon 51 SJ 9554
Longside 105 NK 0347
Longslow 51 SJ 6535
Longstanton 45 TL 4066
Longstock 11 SU 3536
Longstone Wells 7 SS 7634
Longstowe 35 TL 3054
Longstreet (Wilts.) 18 SU 1451
Longthorpe 45 TL 1698
Longton (Lancs.) 57 SD 4725
Longton (Staffs.) 51 SJ 9043
Longtown (Cumbr.) 70 NY 3768
Longtown (Here & W) 29 SO 3228
Longville in the Dale 40 SO 5393
Longwick 34 SP 7805
Longwitton 79 NZ 0788
Longwood 41 SJ 6007
Longworth 19 SU 3899
Longyester 86 NT 5465
Lonmore 100 NG 2646
Loose 14 TQ 7552
Loosley Row 34 SP 8100
Lootcherbrae 104 NJ 6054
Lopcombe Corner 11 SU 2435
Lopen 9 ST 4214
Loppington 40 SJ 4629
Lorbottle 79 NU 0306
Lornty 98 NO 1746
Loscoe 53 SK 4247
Lossiemouth 104 NJ 2370
Lossit 80 NR 1856
Lostock Gralam 51 SJ 6976
Lostock Junction 57 SD 6708
Lostwithiel 4 SX 1059
Lothbeg 108 NC 9410
Lothersdale 58 SD 9545
Lothmore 111 NC 9611
Loudwater 20 SU 8990
Loughborough 43 SK 5319
Loughor 25 SS 5898
Loughton (Bucks.) 34 SP 8337
Loughton (Essex) 21 TQ 4296
Loughton (Salop) 41 SO 6183
Lound (Lincs.) 45 TF 0618
Lound (Notts.) 53 SK 6986
Lound (Suff.) 47 TM 5099
Lount 43 SK 3819
Louth 55 TF 3287
Love Clough 58 SD 8126
Lover 11 SU 2120
Loversall 60 SK 5798
Loves Green 22 TL 6404
Loveston 24 SN 0808
Lovington 17 ST 5931
Low Bradfield 53 SK 2691
Low Bradley 59 SE 0048
Low Braithwaite 70 NY 4242
Low Brunton 71 NY 9269
Low Burnham 60 SE 7702
Low Catton 66 SE 7053
Low Crosby 71 NY 4459
Low Dinsdale 72 NZ 3411
Low Eggborough 60 SE 5522
Low Gate 71 NY 9064
Low Ham 17 ST 4329
Low Hesket 71 NY 4646
Low Hesleyhurst 79 NZ 0997
Low Moor 58 SD 7241
Low Redford 72 NZ 0731
Low Row (Cumbr.) 71 NY 5863
Low Row (N Yorks.) 65 SD 9897
Low Santon 61 SE 9312
Low Street 47 TG 3424
Low Torry 85 NT 0086
Low Worsall 66 NZ 3909
Lowca 62 NX 9821
Lowdham 53 SK 6646
Lower Aisholt 16 ST 2035
Lower Assendon 20 SU 7484
Lower Beeding 13 TQ 2227
Lower Benefield 44 SP 9888
Lower Bentham 64 SD 6469
Lower Bentley 32 SO 9865
Lower Boddington 33 SP 4752
Lower Breakish 101 NG 6725
Lower Bullingham 30 SO 5038
Lower Cam 32 SO 7401
Lower Chapel 27 SO 0235
Lower Chute 19 SU 3153
Lower Cwmtwrch 26 SN 7710
Lower Darwen 58 SD 6824
Lower Down 40 SO 3384
Lower Dunsforth 66 SE 4464
Lower Farringdon 12 SU 7035
Lower Frankton 50 SJ 3732
Lower Froyle 12 SU 7544
Lower Gledfield 108 NH 5990
Lower Green 46 TF 9837
Lower Greenbank 64 SD 5254
Lower Halstow 14 TQ 8567
Lower Hardres 15 TR 1453
Lower Heyford 33 SP 4824
Lower Higham 22 TQ 7172
Lower Hordley 40 SJ 3929
Lower Killeyan 80 NR 2743
Lower Langford 17 ST 4660
Lower Largo 93 NO 4102
Lower Lemington 33 SP 2134
Lower Lye 40 SO 4067
Lower Maes-coed 30 SO 3431
Lower Mayland 23 TL 9101
Lower Moor 32 SO 9847
Lower Nazeing 35 TL 3906
Lower Penarth 28 ST 1869
Lower Penn 41 SO 8696
Lower Pennington 11 SZ 3193
Lower Peover 51 SJ 7474
Lower Quinton 33 SP 1847
Lower Shelton 34 SP 9942
Lower Shiplake 20 SU 7779
Lower Shuckburgh 33 SP 4862
Lower Slaughter 32 SP 1622
Lower Stanton St. Quintin 18 ST 9180
Lower Sundon 35 TL 0526
Lower Swanwick 11 SU 4909
Lower Swell 32 SP 1725
Lower Thurlton 47 TM 4299
Lower Tysoe 33 SP 3445
Lower Upham 11 SU 5219
Lower Vexford 16 ST 1135
Lower Weare 17 ST 4053
Lower Wield 19 SU 6340
Lower Winchendon 34 SP 7312
Lower Woodend 20 SU 8187
Lower Woodford 10 SU 1235
Lowesby 44 SK 7207
Lowestoft 47 TM 5493
Lowestoft End 47 TM 5394
Loweswater 62 NY 1421
Lowgill (Lancs.) 64 SD 6564
Lowick (Cumbr.) 62 SD 2985
Lowick (Northants.) 44 SP 9781
Lowick (Northum.) 87 NU 0139
Lownie Moor 99 NO 4848
Lowsonford 42 SP 1867
Lowthorpe 67 TA 0860
Lowton 58 SJ 6197
Lowton Common 58 SJ 6397
Loxbeare 8 SS 9116
Loxhill 12 TQ 0037
Loxhore 6 SS 6138
Loxley 33 SP 2553
Loxton 17 ST 3755
Loxwood 12 TQ 0431
Lubenham 44 SP 7087
Luccombe 16 SS 9144
Luccombe Village 11 SZ 5880
Lucker 87 NU 1530
Luckett 4 SX 3873
Luckington 18 ST 8383
Lucklawhill 93 NO 4222
Luckwell Bridge 16 SS 9038
Lucton 30 SO 4364
Ludborough 55 TF 2995
Ludchurch 24 SN 1411
Luddenden 59 SE 0425
Luddesdown 14 TQ 6766
Luddington 60 SE 8216
Ludford (Lincs.) 55 TF 1989
Ludford (Salop) 40 SO 5173
Ludgershall (Bucks.) 34 SP 6617
Ludgershall (Wilts.) 18 SU 2650
Ludgvan 2 SW 5033
Ludham 47 TG 3818
Ludlow 40 SO 5175
Ludwell 10 ST 9122
Ludworth 72 NZ 3641
Luffincott 4 SX 3394
Luffness 86 NT 4780
Lugar 75 NS 5821
Luggiebank 84 NS 7672
Lugton 82 NS 4152
Lugwardine 31 SO 5441
Luib 100 NG 5628
Lulham 30 SO 4041
Lullington (Derby.) 42 SK 2513
Lullington (Somer.) 18 ST 7851
Lulsgate Bottom 29 ST 5065
Lulsley 32 SO 7455
Lumb (W Yorks) 59 SE 0221
Lumby 60 SE 4830
Lumloch 84 NS 6369
Lumphanan 104 NJ 5804
Lumphinnans 92 NT 1692
Lumsden 104 NJ 4722
Lunan 99 NO 6851
Lunanhead 99 NO 4752
Luncarty 92 NO 0929
Lund (Humbs.) 61 SE 9648
Lund (N Yorks.) 60 SE 6532
Lundie (Tays.) 93 NO 2836
Lundin Links 93 NO 4002
Lunna 113 HU 4969
Lunning 113 HU 5066
Lunsford's Cross 14 TQ 7210

Lunt 244 Milltown of Campfield

Lunt 57 SD 3401
Luntley 30 SO 3955
Luppitt 8 ST 1606
Lupton 63 SD 5581
Lurgashall 12 SU 9326
Lurgmore 102 NH 5937
Lusby 55 TF 3367
Luss 90 NS 3592
Lusta 100 NG 2756
Lustleigh 5 SX 7881
Luston 30 SO 4863
Luthermuir 99 NO 6568
Luthrie 93 NO 3219
Luton (Beds.) 35 TL 0821
Luton (Devon) 8 SX 9076
Luton (Kent) 14 TQ 7766
Lutterworth 43 SP 5484
Lutton (Devon.) 5 SX 5959
Lutton (Lincs.) 45 TF 4325
Lutton (Northants.) 45 TL 1187
Luxborough 16 SS 9738
Luxulyan 4 SX 0458
Lybster 112 ND 2435
Lydbury North 40 SO 3486
Lydcott 7 SS 6936
Lydd 15 TR 0421
Lydd-on-Sea 15 TR 0819
Lydden 15 TR 2645
Lyddington 44 SP 8797
Lydeard St. Lawrence 16 ST 1232
Lydford (Devon.) 5 SX 5084
Lydford (Somer.) 17 ST 5731
Lydgate (W. Yorks) 58 SD 9225
Lydham 40 SO 3391
Lydiard Millicent 18 SU 0986
Lydiate 57 SD 3604
Lydlinch 9 ST 7413
Lydney 29 SO 6203
Lydstep 24 SS 0898
Lye 41 SO 9284
Lye Green 34 SP 9703
Lyford 19 SU 3994
Lymbridge Green 15 TR 1243
Lyme Regis 8 SY 3492
Lyminge 15 TR 1641
Lymington 11 SZ 3295
Lyminster 12 TQ 0204
Lymm 51 SJ 6786
Lymore 11 SZ 2992
Lympne 15 TR 1235
Lympsham 17 ST 3454
Lympstone 8 SX 9984
Lynchat 97 NH 7801
Lyndhurst 11 SU 2907
Lyndon 44 SK 9004
Lyne 20 TQ 0166
Lyne of Gorthleck 102 NH 5420
Lyne of Skene 105 NJ 7610
Lyneal 50 SJ 4433
Lynegar 112 ND 2357
Lyneham (Oxon.) 33 SP 2720
Lyneham (Wilts.) 18 SU 0179
Lynemouth 79 NZ 2991
Lyness 113 ND 3094
Lyng (Norf.) 47 TG 0617
Lyng (Somer.) 17 ST 3328
Lynmouth 7 SS 7249
Lynsted 15 TQ 9461
Lynton 7 SS 7149
Lyon's Gate 9 ST 6605
Lyonshall 30 SO 3356
Lytchett Matravers 10 SY 9495
Lytchett Minster 10 SY 9593
Lyth 112 ND 2763
Lytham 57 SD 3727
Lytham St. Anne's 57 SD 3427
Lythe 73 NZ 8413

M

Mabe Burnthouse 2 SW 7634
Mabie 69 NX 9570
Mablethorpe 55 TF 5085
Macclesfield 51 SJ 9173
Macduff 105 NJ 7064
Macharioch 74 NR 7309
Machen 28 ST 2189
Machrihanish 74 NR 6220
Machynlleth 39 SH 7401
Mackworth 53 SK 3137
Macmerry 86 NT 4372
Madderty 91 NN 9522
Maddiston 84 NS 9476
Madehurst 12 SU 9810
Madeley (Salop) 41 SJ 6904
Madeley (Staffs.) 51 SJ 7744
Madingley 35 TL 3960
Madley 30 SO 4138
Madresfield 32 SO 8047
Madron 2 SW 4532
Maenclochog 24 SN 0827
Maendy 28 ST 0176
Maentwrog 49 SH 6640
Maer 51 SJ 7938
Maerdy (Clwyd) 49 SJ 0144
Maerdy (Mid Glam.) 28 SS 9798
Maes-glas 29 ST 2985
Maes-y-cwmmer 28 ST 1794
Maesbrook 40 SJ 3121
Maesbury Marsh 40 SJ 3125
Maesgwynne 24 SN 2024
Maeshafn 50 SJ 2061
Maesllyn 26 SN 3644
Maesmynis 27 SO 0148
Maesteg 28 SS 8591
Maesybont 25 SN 5616
Magdalen Laver 22 TL 5108
Maggieknockater 104 NJ 3145
Magham Down 13 TQ 6111
Maghull 57 SD 3702
Magor 29 ST 4287
Maiden Bradley 17 ST 8038
Maiden Law 72 NZ 1749
Maiden Newton 9 SY 5997
Maidencombe 8 SX 9268
Maidenhead 20 SU 8881
Maidens 75 NS 2107
Maidenwell 3 SX 1470
Maidford 34 SP 6052
Maids' Moreton 34 SP 7035
Maidstone 14 TQ 7656
Maidwell 44 SP 7477
Mail 113 HU 4328
Mains 102 NH 4239
Mains of Ardestie 93 NO 5034
Mains of Balhall 99 NO 5163
Mains of Ballindarg 98 NO 4051
Mains of Dalvey 103 NJ 1132
Mains of Drum 99 NO 8099
Mains of Thornton 99 NO 6871
Mains of Throsk 91 NS 8690
Mainstone 40 SO 2687
Maisemore 32 SO 8121
Malborough 5 SX 7039
Malden 21 TQ 2166
Maldon 22 TL 8506
Malham 65 SD 9062
Mallaig 95 NM 6796
Malleny Mills 85 NT 1665
Mallwyd 39 SH 8612
Malmesbury 18 ST 9387
Malpas (Ches.) 50 SJ 4847
Malpas (Cornwall) 2 SW 8442
Maltby (Cleve.) 73 NZ 4613
Maltby (S Yorks.) 53 SK 5392
Maltby le Marsh 55 TF 4681
Maltman's Hill 14 TQ 9043
Malton 67 SE 7871
Malvern Link 32 SO 7848
Malvern Wells 32 SO 7742
Mamble 41 SO 6871
Manaccan 2 SW 7625
Manafon 40 SJ 1102
Manaton 5 SX 7481
Manby 55 TF 3986
Mancetter 43 SP 3196
Manchester 51 SJ 8397
Mancot 50 SJ 3267
Mandally 96 NH 2900
Manea 45 TL 4789
Manfield 72 NZ 2213
Mangotsfield 29 ST 6676
Manish (Harris) 109 NG 1089
Mankinholes 58 SD 9523
Manley 50 SJ 5071
Manmoel 28 SO 1703
Mannel 94 NL 9840
Manning's Heath 12 TQ 2028
Manningford Bohune 18 SU 1357
Manningford Bruce 18 SU 1359
Mannington 10 SU 0605
Manningtree 37 TM 1031
Mannofield 105 NJ 9104
Manorbier 24 SS 0698
Manorhill 86 NT 6632
Manorowen 24 SM 9336
Mansell Gamage 30 SO 3944
Mansell Lacy 30 SO 4245
Mansergh 63 SD 6082
Mansfield (Notts.) 53 SK 5361
Mansfield (Strath.) 76 NS 6214
Mansfield Woodhouse 53 SK 5363
Mansriggs 62 SD 2880
Manston (Dorset) 10 ST 8115
Manthorpe (Lincs.) 45 TF 0616
Manton (Humbs.) 61 SE 9302
Manton (Leic.) 44 SK 8704
Manton (Wilts.) 18 SU 1768
Manuden 35 TL 4926
Maple Cross 20 TQ 0392
Maplebeck 54 SK 7160
Mapledurham 19 SU 6776
Mapledurwell 19 SU 6851
Maplehurst 12 TQ 1924
Mapleton 51 SK 1748
Mapperley 53 SK 4343
Mapperton 9 SY 5099
Mappleborough Green 32 SP 0866
Mappleton 61 TA 2244
Mappowder 9 ST 7105
Marazion 2 SW 5130
Marbury 51 SJ 5545
March 45 TL 4197
Marcham 19 SU 4596
Marchamley 41 SJ 5929
Marchbankwood 77 NY 0899
Marchington 42 SK 1330
Marchington Woodlands 42 SK 1128
Marchwiel 50 SJ 3547
Marchwood 11 SU 3810
Marcross 28 SS 9269
Marden (Here & W) 30 SO 5247
Marden (Kent) 14 TQ 7444
Marden (Wilts.) 18 SU 0857
Mardy 29 SO 3016
Mare Green 17 ST 3326
Marefield 44 SK 7408
Mareham le Fen 55 TF 2761
Mareham on the Hill 55 TF 2867
Maresfield 13 TQ 4624
Marfleet 61 TA 1329
Margam 28 SS 7887
Margaret Marsh 10 ST 8218
Margaret Roding 22 TL 5912
Margaretting 22 TL 6601
Margate 15 TR 3670
Margnaheglish 81 NS 0331
Marham 46 TF 7110
Marhamchurch 6 SS 2203
Marholm 45 TF 1402
Marian-glas 48 SH 5084
Mariansleigh 7 SS 7422
Marishader 100 NG 4963
Maristow 5 SX 4764
Mark 17 ST 3747
Mark Causeway 17 ST 3547
Mark Cross 13 TQ 5831
Markbeech 13 TQ 4842
Markby 55 TF 4878
Market Bosworth 43 SK 4003
Market Deeping 45 TF 1310
Market Drayton 51 SJ 6734
Market Harborough 44 SP 7387
Market Lavington 18 SU 0154
Market Overton 44 SK 8816
Market Rasen 55 TF 1089
Market Stainton 55 TF 2279
Market Weighton 60 SE 8741
Market Weston 36 TL 9877
Markethill 92 NO 2239
Markfield 43 SK 4810
Markham 28 SO 1601
Markinch 93 NO 2901
Markington 66 SE 2864
Marks Tey 23 TL 9123
Marksbury 17 ST 6662
Markwell 4 SX 3658
Markyate 35 TL 0616
Marlborough 18 SU 1869
Marlcliff 32 SP 0950
Marldon 5 SX 8663
Marlesford 37 TM 3258
Marley Green 51 SJ 5745
Marlingford 47 TG 1208
Marloes 24 SM 7908
Marlow 20 SU 8587
Marlpit Hill 21 TQ 4447
Marnhull 10 ST 7718
Marnoch 104 NJ 5950
Marple 51 SJ 9588
Marr 60 SE 5105
Marrick 65 SE 0798
Marros 24 SN 2008
Marsden 59 SE 0411
Marsh 8 ST 2410
Marsh Baldon 19 SU 5699
Marsh Gibbon 34 SP 6423
Marsh Green (Devon.) 8 SY 0493
Marsh Green (Kent) 13 TQ 4344
Marsh Green (Salop) 41 SJ 6014
Marsh, The 40 SO 3197
Marshall's Heath 35 TL 1515
Marsham 47 TG 1924
Marshborough 15 TR 2958
Marshbrook 40 SO 4389
Marshchapel 61 TF 3598
Marshfield (Avon) 18 ST 7773
Marshfield (Gwent) 29 ST 2582
Marshgate 4 SX 1592
Marshside 57 SD 3419
Marshwood 9 SY 3899
Marske 65 NZ 1000
Marske-by-the-Sea 73 NZ 6322
Marston (Ches.) 51 SJ 6474
Marston (Here & W) 30 SO 3657
Marston (Lincs.) 54 SK 8943
Marston (Oxon.) 33 SP 5208
Marston (Staffs.) 41 SJ 8314
Marston (Staffs.) 41 SJ 9227
Marston (Warw.) 42 SP 2095
Marston (Wilts.) 18 ST 9656
Marston Green 42 SP 1685
Marston Magna 9 ST 5922
Marston Meysey 18 SU 1297
Marston Montgomery 52 SK 1338
Marston Moretaine 34 SP 9941
Marston St. Lawrence 33 SP 5342
Marston Trussell 43 SP 6986
Marston on Dove 42 SK 2329
Marstow 29 SO 5519
Marsworth 34 SP 9214
Marten 19 SU 2860
Marthall 51 SJ 8076
Martham 47 TG 4518
Martin (Hants.) 10 SU 0719
Martin (Lincs.) 55 TF 1259
Martin Dales 55 TF 1761
Martin Hussingtree 32 SO 8860
Martinhoe 7 SS 6648
Martinscroft 51 SJ 6589
Martinstown 9 SY 6488
Martlesham 37 TM 2547
Martletwy 24 SN 0310
Martley 32 SO 7559
Martock 9 ST 4619
Marton (Ches.) 51 SJ 8468
Marton (Cleve.) 73 NZ 5115
Marton (Lincs.) 54 SK 8381
Marton (N Yorks.) 66 SE 4162
Marton (N Yorks.) 66 SE 7383
Marton (Salop) 40 SJ 2802
Marton (Warw.) 43 SP 4069
Marwick 113 HY 2325
Marwood 6 SS 5437
Mary Tavy 5 SX 5079
Marybank 102 NH 4753
Maryburgh 102 NH 5456
Marygold 87 NT 8160
Maryhill 105 NJ 8245
Marykirk 99 NO 6865
Marylebone 57 SD 5807
Marypark 104 NJ 1938
Maryport (Cumbr.) 62 NY 0336
Maryport (Dumf & G) 68 NX 1434
Marystow 4 SX 4382
Maryton 99 NO 6856
Marywell (Grampn.) 99 NO 5896
Marywell (Tays.) 99 NO 6544
Masham 66 SE 2280
Mashbury 22 TL 6511
Mastrick 105 NJ 9007
Matching 22 TL 5212
Matching Green 22 TL 5311
Matching Tye 22 TL 5111
Matfen 79 NZ 0371
Matfield 13 TQ 6541
Mathern 29 ST 5291
Mathon 32 SO 7345
Mathry 24 SM 8832
Matlaske 47 TG 1534
Matlock 53 SK 3060
Matlock Bath 53 SK 2958
Matson 32 SO 8316
Matterdale End 62 NY 3923
Mattersey 53 SK 6889
Mattingley 20 SU 7357
Mattishall 47 TG 0510
Mattishall Burgh 47 TG 0511
Mauchline 75 NS 4927
Maud 105 NJ 9247
Maugersbury 33 SP 1925
Maughold 56 SC 4991
Maulden 35 TL 0538
Maulds Meaburn 63 NY 6216
Maunby 66 SE 3486
Maund Bryan 31 SO 5550
Mautby 47 TG 4712
Mavesyn Ridware 42 SK 0817
Mavis Enderby 55 TF 3666
Maw Green 42 SP 0197
Mawbray 70 NY 0846
Mawdesley 57 SD 4914
Mawgan 2 SW 7024
Mawla 2 SW 7045
Mawnan 2 SW 7827
Mawnan Smith 2 SW 7728
Maxey 45 TF 1208
Maxstoke 42 SP 2386
Maxton 86 NT 6129
Maxwellheugh 86 NT 7333
Maxwellston 75 NS 2600
Mayback 113 HY 5053
Maybole 75 NS 3009
Mayfield (E Susx) 13 TQ 5827
Mayfield (Lothian) 85 NT 3564
Mayfield (Staffs.) 52 SK 1545
Mayford 20 SU 9956
Maypole (Gwent.) 29 SO 4716
Maypole Green 47 TM 4195
Maywick 113 HU 3824
Meadle 34 SP 8005
Meadowtown 40 SJ 3101
Meal Bank 63 SD 5495
Mealsgate 70 NY 2141
Mearbeck 65 SD 8160
Meare 17 ST 4541
Mears Ashby 44 SP 8366
Measham 43 SK 3312
Meathop 63 SD 4380
Meaux 61 TA 0939
Meavy 5 SX 5467
Medbourne 44 SP 8093
Meddon 6 SS 2717
Medmenham 20 SU 8084
Medstead 11 SU 6537
Meer End 42 SP 2474
Meerbrook 51 SJ 9860
Meesden 35 TL 4432
Meeth 6 SS 5408
Meidrim 25 SN 2820
Meifod 40 SJ 1513
Meigle 98 NO 2844
Meikle Earnock 84 NS 7253
Meikle Strath 99 NO 6471
Meikle Tarty 105 NJ 9928
Meikle Wartle 105 NJ 7230
Meikleour 92 NO 1539
Meinciau 25 SN 4610
Meir 51 SJ 9342
Melbourn (Cambs.) 35 TL 3844
Melbourne (Derby.) 43 SK 3825
Melbourne (Humbs.) 60 SE 7543
Melbury Bubb 9 ST 5906
Melbury Osmond 9 ST 5707
Melbury Sampford 9 ST 5705
Melchbourne 44 TL 0265
Melcombe Bingham 9 ST 7602
Meldon (Devon) 5 SX 5592
Meldon (Northum.) 79 NZ 1284
Meldreth 35 TL 3746
Melfort 89 NM 8314
Meliden 49 SJ 0580
Melin Court 28 SN 8201
Melin-y-coed 49 SH 8160
Melin-y-ddol 39 SJ 0807
Melin-y-grug 39 SJ 0507
Melin-y-wig 49 SJ 0448
Melkinthorpe 63 NY 5525
Melkridge 71 NY 7363
Melksham 18 ST 9063
Melldalloch 81 NR 9375
Melling (Lancs.) 64 SD 5970
Melling (Mers.) 57 SD 3800
Mellis 37 TM 0974
Mellon Charles 106 NG 8491
Mellor (Gtr Mches.) 51 SJ 9888
Mellor (Lancs.) 58 SD 6530
Mellor Brook 58 SD 6331
Mells (Somer) 17 ST 7249
Melmerby (Cumbr.) 63 NY 6137
Melmerby (N Yorks.) 65 SE 0785
Melmerby (N Yorks.) 66 SE 3376
Melplash 9 SY 4797
Melrose 86 NT 5433
Melsonby 65 NZ 1908
Meltham 59 SE 0910
Melton (Suff.) 37 TM 2850
Melton Constable 47 TG 0433
Melton Mowbray 44 SK 7518
Melton Ross 61 TA 0610
Meltonby 67 SE 7952
Melvaig 106 NG 7486
Melverley 40 SJ 3316
Melvich 111 NC 8864
Membury 8 ST 2703
Memsie 105 NJ 9762
Memus 98 NO 4258
Menabilly 4 SX 0951
Menai Bridge 48 SH 5572
Mendham 47 TM 2783
Mendlesham 37 TM 1065
Mendlesham Green 37 TM 0963
Menheniot 4 SX 2862
Mennock 76 NS 8008
Menston 59 SE 1743
Menstrie 91 NS 8596
Mentmore 34 SP 9019
Meole Brace 40 SJ 4811
Meonstoke 11 SU 6119
Meopham 14 TQ 6466
Meopham Station 14 TQ 6467
Mepal 45 TL 4481
Meppershall 35 TL 1336
Mere (Ches.) 51 SJ 7281
Mere (Wilts.) 10 ST 8132
Mere Brow 57 SD 4118
Mere Green 42 SP 1298
Mereclough 58 SD 8730
Mereworth 14 TQ 6553
Mergie 99 NO 7988
Meriden 42 SP 2482
Merkadale 100 NG 3831
Merkland 75 NX 2491
Merlin's Bridge 24 SM 9414
Merrington 40 SJ 4621
Merriott 9 ST 4412
Merrivale 5 SX 5475
Merrymeet 4 SX 2766
Mersham 15 TR 0539
Merstham 21 TQ 2953
Merston 12 SU 8903
Merstone 11 SZ 5285
Merther 3 SW 8644
Merthyr 25 SN 3520
Merthyr Cynog 27 SN 9837
Merthyr Dyfan 28 ST 1169
Merthyr Mawr 28 SS 8877
Merthyr Tydfil 28 SO 0406
Merthyr Vale 28 ST 0899
Merton (Devon.) 6 SS 5212
Merton (Gtr London) 21 TQ 2569
Merton (Norf.) 46 TL 9098
Merton (Oxon.) 33 SP 5717
Mervinslaw 78 NT 6713
Meshaw 7 SS 7519
Messing 23 TL 8918
Messingham 60 SE 8904
Metfield 37 TM 2980
Metheringham 54 TF 0661
Methil 93 NT 3699
Methley 59 SE 3826
Methlick 105 NJ 8537
Methven 92 NO 0225
Methwold 46 TL 7394
Methwold Hythe 46 TL 7195
Mettingham 47 TM 3689
Mevagissey 4 SX 0144
Mexborough 60 SK 4799
Mey 112 ND 2872
Meysey Hampton 18 SU 1199
Miavaig 109 NB 0834
Michaelchurch 29 SO 5125
Michaelchurch Escley 30 SO 3134
Michaelchurch-on-Arrow 30 SO 2450
Michaelston-le-Pit 28 ST 1573
Michaelston-y-Fedw 28 ST 2484
Michaelstow 4 SX 0778
Micheldever 11 SU 5138
Michelmersh 11 SU 3426
Mickfield 37 TM 1361
Mickle Trafford 50 SJ 4469
Mickleby 73 NZ 8013
Micklefield 59 SE 4433
Mickleham 21 TQ 1753
Mickleover 53 SK 3034
Mickleton (Durham) 72 NY 9623
Mickleton (Glos.) 32 SP 1543
Mickley (N. Yorks.) 66 SE 2576
Mickley Square 72 NZ 0761
Mid Ardlaw 105 NJ 9464
Mid Beltie 99 NJ 6200
Mid Cairncross 99 NO 4979
Mid Sannox 81 NS 0145
Mid Thundergay 81 NR 8846
Mid Yell 113 HU 4991
Midbea 113 HY 4444
Middle Assendon 20 SU 7385
Middle Aston 33 SP 4726
Middle Barton 33 SP 4326
Middle Claydon 34 SP 7125
Middle Drums 99 NO 5957
Middle Littleton 32 SP 0747
Middle Maes-coed 30 SO 3334
Middle Rasen 54 TF 0889
Middle Town (Scilly Isles) 2 SV 8708
Middle Tysoe 33 SP 3344
Middle Wallop 11 SU 2937
Middle Winterslow 11 SU 2432
Middle Witchyburn 104 NJ 6356
Middle Woodford 10 SU 1136
Middlebie 70 NY 2176
Middleham 65 SE 1287
Middlehope 40 SO 4988
Middlemarsh 9 ST 6707
Middlesbrough 73 NZ 4920
Middlesmoor 65 SE 0974
Middlestone Moor 72 NZ 2532
Middlestown 59 SE 2617
Middleton (Cumbr.) 63 SD 6286
Middleton (Derby.) 53 SK 1963
Middleton (Derby.) 53 SK 2755
Middleton (Essex) 36 TL 8639
Middleton (Gtr Mches.) 58 SD 8606
Middleton (Here & W) 40 SO 5469
Middleton (Lancs.) 64 SD 4258
Middleton (Lothian) 85 NT 3657
Middleton (N Yorks.) 67 SE 7885
Middleton (N Yorks.—W Yorks.) 59 SE 1249
Middleton (Norf.) 46 TF 6616
Middleton (Northants.) 44 SP 8490
Middleton (Northum.) 79 NU 0024
Middleton (Northum.) 87 NU 1035
Middleton (Northum.) 79 NZ 0585
Middleton (Salop) 40 SJ 3128
Middleton (Salop) 40 SO 5377
Middleton (Suff.) 37 TM 4267
Middleton (Tays.) 98 NO 1206
Middleton (Tiree) 94 NL 9443
Middleton (W Yorks.) 59 SE 3027
Middleton (Warw.) 42 SP 1798
Middleton Cheney 33 SP 4941
Middleton Green 51 SJ 9935
Middleton Hall 79 NT 9825
Middleton Priors 41 SO 6290
Middleton Scriven 41 SO 6787
Middleton St. George 72 NZ 3412
Middleton Stoney 33 SP 5323
Middleton Tyas 66 NZ 2205
Middleton-in-Teesdale 72 NY 9425
Middleton-on-Sea 12 SU 9800
Middleton-on-the-Wolds 61 SE 9449
Middletown 40 SJ 3012
Middlewich 51 SJ 7066
Middlewood Green 37 TM 0961
Middleyard 82 NS 5132
Middlezoy 17 ST 3733
Middridge 72 NZ 2526
Midfield 111 NC 5864
Midge Hall 57 SD 5123
Midgeholme 71 NY 6458
Midgham 19 SU 5567
Midgley 59 SE 0226
Midhopestones 59 SK 2399
Midhurst 12 SU 8821
Midlem 86 NT 5227
Midsomer Norton 17 ST 6654
Midtown (Highld.) 106 NG 8285
Midtown (Highld.) 113 NC 5862
Midville 55 TF 3857
Migvie 104 NJ 4306
Milborne Port 9 ST 6718
Milborne St. Andrew 10 SY 8097
Milborne Wick 9 ST 6620
Milbourne (Northum.) 79 NZ 1175
Milburn (Cumbr.) 63 NY 6529
Milbury Heath 29 ST 6690
Milby 66 SE 4067
Milcombe 33 SP 4134
Milden 36 TL 9546
Mildenhall (Suff.) 36 TL 7074
Mildenhall (Wilts.) 18 SU 2069
Mile Elm 18 ST 9968
Mile End (Essex) 23 TL 9827
Milebrook 40 SO 3172
Milebush 14 TQ 7546
Mileham 46 TF 9119
Milesmark 85 NT 0688
Milfield 87 NT 9333
Milford (Derby.) 53 SK 3445
Milford (Staffs.) 41 SJ 9721
Milford (Surrey) 12 SU 9442
Milford Haven (Dyfed) 24 SM 9006
Milford on Sea 11 SZ 2891
Milkwall 29 SO 5809
Mill Bank 59 SE 0321
Mill End (Bucks.) 20 SU 7885
Mill End (Herts.) 35 TL 3332
Mill Green (Essex) 22 TL 6400
Mill Hill (Gtr London) 21 TQ 2292
Mill Lane 20 SU 7850
Mill Street (Norf.) 46 TG 0118
Mill of Kingoodie 105 NJ 8425
Milland 12 SU 8228
Milland Marsh 12 SU 8326
Millbreck 105 NK 0045
Millbridge 12 SU 8542
Millbrook (Beds.) 34 TL 0138
Millbrook (Corn.) 4 SX 4252
Millbrook (Hants.) 11 SU 4012
Millburn (Strath.) 75 NS 4429
Millcorner 14 TQ 8223
Miller's Dale 52 SK 1373
Millerhill 85 NT 3269
Millgreen (Salop) 41 SJ 6727
Millgrip 113 HY 6123
Millheugh 84 NS 7551
Millholme 63 SD 5690
Millhouse (Strath.) 81 NR 9570
Millikenpark 82 NS 4162
Millington 67 SE 8351
Millmeece 51 SJ 8333
Millom 62 SD 1780
Millport 82 NS 1655
Millthrop 63 SD 6691
Milltimber 99 NJ 8501
Millton of Auchriachan 104 NJ 1718
Milltown (Derby.) 53 SK 3561
Milltown (Dumf & G) 70 NY 3375
Milltown (Grampn.) 104 NJ 4616
Milltown of Aberdalgie 92 NO 0720
Milltown of Auchindown 104 NJ 3540
Milltown of Campfield 99 NJ 6400

N

O

Pontycymer 248 Ripponden

Pontycymer 28 SS 9091
Pontypool 29 SO 2701
Pontypridd 28 ST 0690
Pontywaun 28 ST 2293
Pooksgreen 11 SU 3710
Pool (Scilly Isles) 2 SV 8714
Pool (W Yorks.) 59 SE 2445
Pool Quay 40 SJ 2512
Pool Street 36 TL 7637
Pool o' Muckhart 91 NO 0001
Poole (Dorset) 10 SZ 0190
Poole Green 51 SJ 6355
Poole Keynes 18 ST 9995
Poolewe 106 NG 8580
Pooley Bridge 63 NY 4724
Poolhill 32 SO 7329
Popham 19 SU 5543
Poplar 21 TQ 3781
Porchfield 11 SZ 4491
Porin 102 NH 3155
Porkellis 2 SW 6933
Porlock 7 SS 8846
Port Ann 89 NR 9086
Port Appin 95 NM 9045
Port Askaig 80 NR 4369
Port Bannatyne 81 NS 0867
Port Carlisle 70 NY 2461
Port Charlott 80 NR 2558
Port Dinorwic 48 SH 5267
Port Driseach 81 NR 9973
Port Ellen 80 NR 3645
Port Elphinstone 105 NJ 7719
Port Erin 56 SC 1969
Port Glasgow 82 NS 3274
Port Henderson 106 NG 7573
Port Isaac 4 SW 9980
Port Logan 68 NX 0940
Port Mor 94 NM 4279
Port Mulgrave 73 NZ 7917
Port Quin 3 SW 9780
Port St. Mary 56 SC 2067
Port Sunlight 50 SJ 3483
Port Talbot 25 SS 7690
Port Wemyss 80 NR 1751
Port William 68 NX 3343
Port e Vullen 56 SC 4793
Port of Menteith 90 NN 5801
Port of Ness 109 NB 5363
Port-Eynon 25 SS 4685
Portavadie 81 NR 9369
Portbury 29 ST 4975
Portchester 11 SU 6105
Portencross 82 NS 1748
Portesham 9 SY 6085
Portfield Gate 24 SM 9115
Portgain 24 SM 8132
Portgate 4 SX 4185
Portgaverne 4 SX 0080
Portgordon 104 NJ 3964
Portgower 112 ND 0013
Porth (Mid Glam) 28 ST 0291
Porth Mellin 2 SW 6618
Porth Navas 2 SW 7428
Porthallow (Corn.) 2 SW 7923
Porthcawl 28 SS 8176
Porthcurno 2 SW 3822
Porthgain 24 SM 8132
Porthleven 2 SW 6225
Porthmadog 48 SH 5638
Porthmeor 2 SW 4337
Portholland 3 SW 9541
Porthoustock 2 SW 8021
Porthpean 4 SX 0350
Porthtowan 2 SW 6847
Porthyrhyd (Dyfed) 25 SN 5115
Porthyrhyd (Dyfed) 27 SN 7137
Portincaple 90 NS 2393
Portington 60 SE 7830
Portinnisherrich 89 NM 9711
Portishead 29 ST 4676
Portknockie 104 NJ 4868
Portlethen 99 NO 9396
Portloe 3 SW 9339
Portmahomack 108 NH 9184
Portmore (Hants.) 11 SZ 3397
Portnacroish 95 NM 9247
Portnaguiran 109 NB 5537
Portnahaven 80 NR 1652
Portnalong 100 NG 3434
Portnancon 110 NC 4260
Portneora 101 NG 7732
Portobello (Lothian) 85 NT 3073
Porton 10 SU 1836
Portpatrick 68 NX 0054
Portreath 2 SW 6545
Portree 100 NG 4843
Portscatho 3 SW 8735
Portsea 11 SU 6300
Portskerra 111 NC 8765
Portskewett 29 ST 4988
Portslade 13 TQ 2506
Portslade-by-Sea 13 TQ 2604
Portsmouth (Hants.) 11 SU 6501
Portsoy 104 NJ 5865
Portswood 11 SU 4314
Portuairk 95 NM 4468
Portway (Warw.) 42 SP 0872
Portwrinkle 4 SX 3553
Poslingford 36 TL 7648
Postbridge 5 SX 6579
Postcombe 34 SU 7099
Postling 15 TR 1439
Postwick 47 TG 2907
Potarch 99 NO 6097
Potsgrove 34 SP 9529
Pott Row 46 TF 7021
Pott Shrigley 51 SJ 9479
Potten End 34 TL 0108
Potter Heigham 47 TG 4119
Potter Street 35 TL 4608
Potter's Cross 41 SO 8484
Potterhanworth 54 TF 0566
Potterne 18 ST 9958
Potterne Wick 18 ST 9957
Potters Bar 35 TL 2501
Potterspury 34 SP 7543
Potto 66 NZ 4703
Potton 35 TL 2249
Poughill (Corn.) 6 SS 2207
Poughill (Devon.) 7 SS 8508
Poulshot 18 ST 9659
Poulton 32 SP 1001
Poulton-le-Fylde 57 SD 3439
Pound Bank 41 SO 7373
Pound Hill 13 TQ 2937
Poundon 34 SP 6425
Poundsgate 5 SX 7072
Poundstock 6 SX 2099
Powburn (Nothum.) 79 NU 0616
Powderham 8 SX 9784
Powerstock 9 SY 5196
Powfoot 70 NY 1465
Powick 32 SO 8351
Powmill 92 NT 0197
Poxwell 9 SY 7484
Poyle 20 TQ 0376
Poynings 13 TQ 2612
Poyntington 9 ST 6419
Poynton 51 SJ 9283
Poynton Green 40 SJ 5618
Poys Street 37 TM 3570
Poystreet Green 36 TL 9858
Praa Sands 2 SW 5828
Pratt's Bottom 21 TQ 4762
Praze-an-Beeble 2 SW 6336
Predannack Wollas 2 SW 6616
Prees 51 SJ 5533
Prees Green 51 SJ 5631
Prees Higher Heath 51 SJ 5636
Preesall 57 SD 3646
Preesgweene 50 SJ 3135
Pren-gwyn 26 SN 4244
Prendwick 79 NU 0012
Prenteg 48 SH 5841
Prenton 50 SJ 3184
Prescot (Mers.) 50 SJ 4692
Prescott (Salop) 40 SJ 4221
Pressen 87 NT 8335
Prestatyn 49 SJ 0682
Prestbury (Ches.) 51 SJ 8976
Presteigne 30 SO 3164
Presthope 41 SO 5897
Prestleigh 17 ST 6340
Preston (Borders) 87 NT 7957
Preston (Devon.) 5 SX 8574
Preston (Dorset) 9 SY 7082
Preston (E Susx) 13 TQ 3107
Preston (Glos.) 31 SO 6734
Preston (Glos.) 32 SP 0400
Preston (Herts.) 35 TL 1724
Preston (Humbs.) 61 TA 1830
Preston (Kent) 15 TR 0260
Preston (Kent) 15 TR 2561
Preston (Lancs.) 57 SD 5329
Preston (Leic.) 44 SK 8602
Preston (Lothian) 86 NT 5977
Preston (Suff.) 36 TL 9450
Preston (Wilts.) 18 SU 0377
Preston Bagot 33 SP 1766
Preston Bissett 34 SP 6530
Preston Brockhurst 40 SJ 5324
Preston Brook 51 SJ 5680
Preston Candover 19 SU 6041
Preston Capes 33 SP 5754
Preston Gubbals 40 SJ 4819
Preston Wynne 31 SO 5646
Preston on Stour 33 SP 2049
Preston on Wye 30 SO 3842
Preston upon the Weald Moors 41 SJ 6815
Preston-under-Scar 65 SE 0791
Prestonpans 85 NT 3874
Prestwich (Gtr. Mches.) 58 SD 8103
Prestwick (Northum.) 79 NZ 1872
Prestwick (Strath.) 75 NS 3525
Prestwood 20 SP 8700
Price Town 28 SS 9392
Prickwillow 46 TL 5982
Priddy 17 ST 5250
Priest Hutton 64 SD 5273
Priestweston 40 SO 2997
Primethorpe 43 SP 5293
Primrose Green 47 TG 0616
Primrose Hill (Cambs.) 45 TL 3889
Primrose Hill (Herts.) 35 TL 0803
Princes Risborough 34 SP 8003
Princethorpe 43 SP 4070
Princetown 5 SX 5873
Prior Muir 93 NO 5213
Priors Hardwick 33 SP 4756
Priors Marston 33 SP 4857
Priory Wood 30 SO 2545
Priston 17 ST 6960
Prittlewell 22 TQ 8787
Privett 11 SU 6726
Probus 3 SW 8947
Prudhoe 72 NZ 0962
Puckeridge 35 TL 3823
Puckington 8 ST 3718
Pucklechurch 29 ST 6976
Puddington (Ches.) 50 SJ 3273
Puddington (Devon) 7 SS 8310
Puddledock 47 TM 0592
Puddletown 9 SY 7594
Pudleston 31 SO 5659
Pudsey 59 SE 2232
Pulborough 12 TQ 0418
Puleston 41 SJ 7322
Pulford 50 SJ 3758
Pulham 9 ST 7008
Pulham Market 47 TM 1986
Pulham St. Mary 47 TM 2185
Pulloxhill 35 TL 0634
Pumpherston 85 NT 0669
Pumsaint 27 SN 6540
Puncheston 24 SN 0029
Puncknowle 9 SY 5388
Punnett's Town 13 TQ 6220
Purbrook 11 SU 6707
Purfleet 21 TQ 5578
Puriton 17 ST 3241
Purleigh 22 TL 8301
Purley (Berks.) 19 SU 6676
Purley (Gtr Lon.) 21 TQ 3161
Purlogue 40 SO 2877
Purls Bridge 45 TL 4787
Purse Caundle 9 ST 6917
Purslow 40 SO 3680
Purston Jaglin 59 SE 4319
Purton (Glos.) 29 SO 6605
Purton (Glos.) 29 SO 6904
Purton (Wilts.) 18 SU 0887
Purton Stoke 18 SU 0890
Pury End 34 SP 7045
Pusey 19 SU 3596
Putley 31 SO 6437
Putney 21 TQ 2274
Puttenham (Herts.) 34 SP 8814
Puttenham (Surrey) 20 SU 9347
Puxton 17 ST 4063
Pwll 25 SN 4801
Pwll-y-glaw 28 SS 7993
Pwllcrochan 24 SM 9202
Pwlldefaid 38 SH 1526
Pwllheli 48 SH 3735
Pwllmeyric 29 ST 5192
Pye Corner (Gwent) 29 ST 3485
Pye Green 41 SJ 9814
Pyecombe 13 TQ 2912
Pyle (I. of W.) 11 SZ 4879
Pyle (Mid Glam.) 28 SS 8282
Pylle 17 ST 6038
Pymore (Cambs.) 45 TL 4986
Pyrford 20 TQ 0458
Pyrton 19 SU 6895
Pytchley 44 SP 8574
Pyworthy 6 SS 3102

Q

Quabbs 40 SO 2080
Quadring 55 TF 2233
Quainton 34 SP 7420
Quarff 113 HU 4235
Quarley 18 SU 2743
Quarndon 53 SK 3340
Quarrier's Homes 82 NS 3666
Quarrington 54 TF 0544
Quarrington Hill 72 NZ 3337
Quarry Bank (W Mids.) 41 SO 9386
Quarrybank (Ches.) 50 SJ 5465
Quarrywood 104 NJ 1864
Quarter 84 NS 7251
Quatford 41 SO 7390
Quatt 41 SO 7588
Quebec 72 NZ 1743
Quedgeley 32 SO 8114
Queen Adelaide 46 TL 5681
Queen Camel 9 ST 5924
Queen Charlton 29 ST 6366
Queenborough 23 TQ 9172
Queensbury 59 SE 1030
Queensferry (Clwyd) 50 SJ 3168
Queensferry (Lothian) 85 NT 1278
Queenzieburn 84 NS 6977
Quendale 113 HU 3713
Quendon 35 TL 5130
Queniborough 43 SK 6412
Quenington 32 SP 1404
Quernmore 64 SD 5160
Quethiock 4 SX 3164
Quidenham 46 TM 0287
Quidhampton (Hants) 19 SU 5150
Quidhampton (Wilts.) 10 SU 1030
Quilquox 105 NJ 9038
Quine's Hill 56 SC 3473
Quinton 34 SP 7754
Quintrell Downs 2 SW 8460
Quoditch 6 SX 4097
Quoig 91 NN 8222
Quorndon 43 SK 5616
Quothquan 85 NS 9939

R

Raby 50 SJ 3179
Rachub 48 SH 6268
Rackenford 7 SS 8418
Rackham 12 TQ 0514
Rackheath 47 TG 2814
Racks 70 NY 0374
Rackwick (Hoy) 113 ND 1999
Radcliffe (Gtr Mches) 58 SD 7806
Radcliffe (Northum.) 79 NU 2602
Radcliffe on Trent 53 SK 6439
Radclive 34 SP 6734
Radcot 19 SU 2899
Radernie 93 NO 4609
Radford Semele 33 SP 3464
Radlett 20 TL 1600
Radley 19 SU 5398
Radnage 20 SU 7897
Radstock 17 ST 6854
Radstone 33 SP 5840
Radway 33 SP 3648
Radway Green 51 SJ 7754
Radwell 35 TL 2335
Radwinter 36 TL 6037
Radyr 28 ST 1380
Rafford 103 NJ 0656
Ragdale 43 SK 6619
Raglan 29 SO 4107
Ragnall 54 SK 8073
Rahane 90 NS 2386
Rainford 57 SD 4700
Rainham (Gtr London) 21 TQ 5282
Rainham (Kent) 14 TQ 8165
Rainhill 50 SJ 4990
Rainhill Stoops 50 SJ 5090
Rainow 51 SJ 9575
Rainton 66 SE 3775
Rainworth 53 SK 5958
Raisbeck 63 NY 6407
Rait 92 NO 2226
Raithby (Lincs.) 55 TF 3084
Raithby (Lincs.) 55 TF 3767
Rake 12 SU 8027
Ram Lane 15 TQ 9646
Ramasaig 100 NG 1644
Rame (Corn.) 2 SW 7233
Rame (Corn.) 4 SX 4249
Rampisham 9 ST 5502
Rampside 64 SD 2366
Rampton (Cambs.) 45 TL 4268
Rampton (Notts.) 54 SK 7978
Ramsbottom 58 SD 7916
Ramsbury 18 SU 2771
Ramscraigs 112 ND 1427
Ramsdean 12 SU 7021
Ramsdell 19 SU 5957
Ramsden (Oxon.) 33 SP 3515
Ramsden Bellhouse 22 TQ 7194
Ramsden Heath 22 TQ 7195
Ramsey (Cambs.) 45 TL 2885
Ramsey (Essex) 37 TM 2130
Ramsey (I. of M.) 56 SC 4594
Ramsey Forty Foot 45 TL 3187
Ramsey Mereside 45 TL 2889
Ramsey St. Mary's 45 TL 2588
Ramsgate 15 TR 3865
Ramsgill 65 SE 1170
Ramshorn 52 SK 0845
Ranby 53 SK 6480
Rand 55 TF 1078
Randwick 32 SO 8206
Ranfurly 82 NS 3865
Rangemore 42 SK 1822
Rangeworthy 29 ST 6886
Rankinston 75 NS 4514
Ranskill 53 SK 6587
Ranton 41 SJ 8524
Ranworth 47 TG 3514
Rascarrel 69 NX 7948
Raskelf 66 SE 4971
Rassau 28 SO 1411
Rastrick 59 SE 1321
Ratagan 101 NG 9220
Ratby 43 SK 5105
Ratcliffe Culey 43 SP 3299
Ratcliffe on the Wreake 43 SK 6314
Rathen 105 NK 0060
Rathillet 93 NO 3620
Rathmell 65 SD 8059
Ratho 85 NT 1370
Rathven 104 NJ 4465
Ratley (Warw.) 33 SP 3847
Ratlinghope 40 SO 4096
Rattar 112 ND 2672
Ratten Row 57 SD 4241
Rattery 5 SX 7361
Rattlesden 36 TL 9758
Rattray 98 NO 1745
Rauceby 54 TF 0146
Raughton Head 70 NY 3745
Raunds 44 SP 9972
Ravenfield 53 SK 4895
Ravenglass 62 SD 0896
Raveningham 47 TM 3996
Ravenscar 67 NZ 9801
Ravensdale 56 SC 3592
Ravensden 35 TL 0754
Ravenshead 53 SK 5654
Ravensmoor 51 SJ 6250
Ravensthorpe (Northants.) 43 SP 6670
Ravensthorpe (W Yorks.) 59 SE 2220
Ravenstone (Bucks.) 34 SP 8450
Ravenstone (Leic.) 43 SK 4013
Ravenstonedale 65 NY 7203
Ravenstruther 84 NS 9245
Ravensworth 65 NZ 1407
Raw 67 NZ 9305
Rawcliffe (Humbs.) 60 SE 6822
Rawcliffe (N Yorks.) 66 SE 5855
Rawcliffe Bridge 60 SE 6921
Rawdon 59 SE 2139
Rawmarsh 53 SK 4396
Rawreth 22 TQ 7793
Rawridge 8 ST 2006
Rawtenstall 58 SD 8122
Raydon 37 TM 0438
Raylees 78 NY 9291
Rayleigh 22 TQ 8090
Rayne 22 TL 7222
Reach 36 TL 5666
Read 58 SD 7634
Reading 20 SU 7272
Reading Street 14 TQ 9230
Reagill 63 NY 6017
Rearquhar 108 NH 7492
Rearsby 43 SK 6514
Rease Heath 51 SJ 6454
Reaster 112 ND 2565
Reawick 113 HU 3244
Reay 111 NC 9664
Reculver 15 TR 2269
Red Dial 70 NY 2545
Red Roses 24 SN 2012
Red Row 79 NZ 2599
Red Street 51 SJ 8251
Red Wharf Bay (Gwyn.) 48 SH 5281
Redberth 24 SN 0804
Redbourn 35 TL 1012
Redbourne 54 SK 9699
Redbridge 21 TQ 4389
Redbrook Street 15 TQ 9336
Redburn (Highld.) 102 NH 5767
Redburn (Highld.) 103 NH 9447
Redcar 73 NZ 6024
Redcastle (Highld.) 102 NH 5849
Redcastle (Tays.) 99 NO 6850
Redcliff Bay 29 ST 4475
Redding 84 NS 9178
Reddingmuirhead 84 NS 9177
Reddish 51 SJ 8993
Redditch 42 SP 0468
Rede 36 TL 8055
Redenhall 47 TM 2684
Redford 99 NO 5644
Redgrave 37 TM 0478
Redheugh 98 NO 4463
Redhill (Avon) 17 ST 4962
Redhill (Grampn.) 105 NJ 6837
Redhill (Grampn.) 99 NJ 7704
Redhill (Surrey) 21 TQ 2850
Redisham 47 TM 4084
Redland (Avon) 29 ST 5875
Redland (Orkney) 113 HY 3724
Redlingfield 37 TM 1871
Redlynch (Somer.) 17 ST 6933
Redlynch (Wilts.) 10 SU 2020
Redmarley D'Abitot 32 SO 7531
Redmarshall 72 NZ 3821
Redmile 54 SK 7935
Redmire 65 SE 0491
Redmoor 4 SX 0761
Rednal 40 SJ 3628
Redpath 86 NT 5835
Redpoint (Highld.) 101 NG 7368
Redruth 2 SW 6941
Redwick (Avon) 29 ST 5485
Redwick (Gwent) 29 ST 4184
Redworth 72 NZ 2423
Reed 35 TL 3636
Reedham 47 TG 4201
Reedness 60 SE 7922
Reepham (Lincs.) 54 TF 0373
Reepham (Norf.) 47 TG 1023
Reeth 65 SE 0499
Regaby 56 SC 4397
Reiff 110 NB 9614
Reigate 21 TQ 2550
Reighton 67 TA 1275
Reiss 112 ND 3354
Rejerrah 2 SW 8055
Relubbus 2 SW 5632
Relugas 103 NH 9948
Remenham 20 SU 7784
Remenham Hill 20 SU 7883
Rempstone 43 SK 5724
Rendcomb 32 SP 0109
Rendham 37 TM 3564
Renfrew 82 NS 4967
Renhold 35 TL 0953
Renishaw 53 SK 4477
Rennington 79 NU 2118
Renton 82 NS 3878
Renwick 71 NY 5943
Repps 47 TG 4116
Repton 43 SK 3026
Resipole 95 NM 7264
Resolis 103 NH 6765
Resolven 28 SN 8202
Reston 87 NT 8861
Reswallie 99 NO 5051
Retew 3 SW 9256
Retford 54 SK 7080
Rettendon 22 TQ 7698
Revesby 55 TF 2961
Rewe 8 SX 9499
Reydon 37 TM 4977
Reymerston 46 TG 0206
Reynalton 24 SN 0909
Reynoldston 25 SS 4890
Rhandirmwyn 27 SN 7843
Rhayader 27 SN 9668
Rhedyn 48 SH 3032
Rheindown 102 NH 5147
Rhemore 95 NM 5750
Rhes-y-cae 50 SJ 1870
Rhewl (Clwyd) 50 SJ 1060
Rhewl (Clwyd) 50 SJ 1744
Rhiconich 110 NC 2552
Rhicullen 108 NH 6971
Rhifail 111 NC 7349
Rhigos 28 SN 9205
Rhilochan 108 NC 7407
Rhiwbryfdir 49 SH 6946
Rhiwderyn 28 ST 2587
Rhiwlas (Clwyd) 50 SJ 1931
Rhiwlas (Gwyn.) 48 SH 5765
Rhiwlas (Gwyn.) 49 SH 9237
Rhodes Minnis 15 TR 1542
Rhodesia 53 SK 5680
Rhodiad 24 SM 7627
Rhonehouse or Kelton Hill 69 NX 7459
Rhoose 28 ST 0666
Rhos (Dyfed) 26 SN 3835
Rhos (W Glam.) 25 SN 7303
Rhos-fawr 48 SH 3838
Rhos-on-Sea 49 SH 8480
Rhos-y-gwaliau 49 SH 9434
Rhos-y-llan 48 SH 2337
Rhoscolyn 48 SH 2675
Rhoscrowther 24 SM 9002
Rhosesmor 50 SJ 2168
Rhosgadfan 48 SH 5057
Rhosgoch (Gwyn.) 48 SH 4189
Rhoslan 48 SH 4841
Rhoslefain 38 SH 5705
Rhosllanerchrugog 50 SJ 2946
Rhosmeirch 48 SH 4677
Rhosneigr 48 SH 3172
Rhosnesni 50 SJ 3451
Rhossili 25 SS 4188
Rhosson 24 SM 7225
Rhostryfan 48 SH 4958
Rhostyllen 50 SJ 3148
Rhosybol 43 SH 4288
Rhu (Strath.) 90 NS 2783
Rhuallt 49 SJ 0774
Rhuddlan 49 SJ 0277
Rhulen 30 SO 1349
Rhunahaorine 81 NR 7048
Rhyd (Gwyn.) 48 SH 6341
Rhyd-Ddu 48 SH 5652
Rhyd-lydan 49 SH 8950
Rhyd-y-clafdy 48 SH 3235
Rhyd-y-meirch 29 SO 3107
Rhyd-yr-onnen 38 SH 6102
Rhydargaeau 25 SN 4326
Rhydcymerau 27 SN 5738
Rhydd 32 SO 8345
Rhydding 25 SS 7498
Rhydlewis 26 SN 3447
Rhydlios 48 SH 1830
Rhydowen 26 SN 4445
Rhydrosser 26 SN 5667
Rhydtalog 50 SJ 2354
Rhydycroesau 50 SJ 2330
Rhydyfelin (Dyfed) 26 SN 5979
Rhydyfro 25 SN 7105
Rhydymain 39 SH 7922
Rhydymwyn 50 SJ 2066
Rhyl 49 SJ 0181
Rhymney 28 SO 1107
Rhynd 92 NO 1520
Rhynie (Grampn.) 104 NJ 4927
Rhynie (Highld.) 108 NH 8578
Ribbesford 41 SO 7874
Ribbleton 57 SD 5630
Ribchester 58 SD 6435
Ribigill 111 NC 5854
Riby 61 TA 1807
Riccall 60 SE 6237
Riccarton (Strath.) 82 NS 4235
Richards Castle 40 SO 4969
Richmond 65 NZ 1701
Richmond upon Thames 21 TQ 1874
Rickarton 99 NO 8188
Rickinghall Inferior 37 TM 0475
Rickinghall Superior 37 TM 0475
Rickling 35 TL 4931
Rickmansworth 20 TQ 0594
Riddell 78 NT 5124
Riddlecombe 6 SS 6013
Riddlesden 59 SE 0742
Ridge (Dorset) 10 SY 9386
Ridge (Herts.) 21 TL 2100
Ridge (Wilts.) 10 ST 9531
Ridge Lane 43 SP 2994
Ridgehill (Avon) 17 ST 5362
Ridgemont 34 SP 9736
Ridgeway Cross 32 SO 7147
Ridgewell 36 TL 7340
Ridgewood 13 TQ 4719
Riding Mill 72 NZ 0161
Ridlington (Leic.) 44 SK 8402
Ridlington (Norf.) 47 TG 3430
Ridsdale 78 NY 9084
Rienachachait 110 NC 0530
Rievaulx 66 SE 5785
Rigg 70 NY 2966
Riggend 84 NS 7670
Righoul 103 NH 8851
Rigside 84 NS 8734
Rileyhill 42 SK 1115
Rilla Mill 4 SX 2973
Rillington 67 SE 8574
Rimington 58 SD 8045
Rimpton 9 ST 6021
Rimswell 61 TA 3128
Rinaston 24 SM 9825
Ring's End 45 TF 3902
Ringford 69 NX 6857
Ringland 47 TG 1313
Ringmer 13 TQ 4412
Ringmore 5 SX 6545
Ringorm 104 NJ 2644
Ringsfield 47 TM 4088
Ringsfield Corner 47 TM 4187
Ringshall (Bucks.) 34 SP 9814
Ringshall (Suff.) 37 TM 0452
Ringshall Stocks 37 TM 0551
Ringstead (Norf.) 46 TF 7040
Ringstead (Northants.) 44 SP 9875
Ringwood 10 SU 1405
Ringwould 15 TR 3648
Rinsey 2 SW 5927
Ripe 13 TQ 5010
Ripley (Derby.) 53 SK 3950
Ripley (Hants.) 10 SZ 1698
Ripley (N. Yorks.) 66 SE 2860
Ripley (Surrey) 20 TQ 0556
Riplingham 61 SE 9631
Ripon 66 SE 3171
Rippingale 45 TF 0927
Ripple (Here & W) 32 SO 8737
Ripple (Kent) 15 TR 3550
Ripponden 59 SE 0319

Risabus 249 Shabbington

Risabus 80 NR 3143
Risbury 31 SO 5455
Risby (Suff.) 36 TL 7966
Risca 28 ST 2391
Rise 61 TA 1541
Risegate 45 TF 2029
Riseley (Beds.) 35 TL 0463
Riseley (Berks.) 20 SU 7263
Rishangles 37 TM 1568
Rishton 58 SD 7229
Rishworth 59 SE 0317
Risley (Derby.) 53 SK 4635
Risplith 66 SE 2467
Rispond 110 NC 4565
Rivar 19 SU 3161
Rivenhall End 22 TL 8316
Riverhead 21 TQ 5156
Rivington 58 SD 6214
Roa Island 64 SD 2364
Roade 34 SP 7551
Roadmeetings 84 NS 8649
Roadside 112 ND 1560
Roadside of Kinneff 99 NO 8476
Roadwater 16 ST 0238
Roag 100 NG 2744
Roath 29 ST 1978
Roberton (Borders) 77 NT 4314
Roberton (Strath.) 76 NS 9428
Robertsbridge 14 TQ 7323
Roberttown 59 SE 1922
Robeston Cross 24 SM 8809
Robeston Wathen 24 SN 0815
Robin Hood's Bay 67 NZ 9505
Roborough 6 SS 5717
Roby 50 SJ 4291
Roby Mill 57 SD 5106
Rocester 52 SK 1039
Roch 24 SM 8821
Rochdale 58 SD 8913
Roche 3 SW 9860
Rochester (Kent) 14 TQ 7467
Rochester (Northum.) 78 NY 8397
Rochford (Essex) 22 TQ 8790
Rochford (Here & W) 41 SO 6268
Rock (Corn.) 3 SW 9475
Rock (Here & W) 41 SO 7371
Rock (Northum.) 79 NU 2020
Rock Ferry 50 SJ 3386
Rockbeare 8 SY 0195
Rockbourne 10 SU 1118
Rockcliffe (Cumbr.) 70 NY 3561
Rockcliffe (Dumf & G) 69 NX 8553
Rockfield (Gwent) 29 SO 4814
Rockfield (Highld.) 108 NH 9282
Rockhampton 29 ST 6593
Rockingham 44 SP 8691
Rockland All Saints 46 TL 9896
Rockland St. Mary 47 TG 3104
Rockland St. Peter 46 TL 9897
Rockley 18 SU 1571
Rockwell End 20 SU 7988
Rodbourne 18 ST 9383
Rodd 30 SO 3162
Roddam 79 NU 0220
Rodden 9 SY 6184
Rode 18 ST 8053
Rode Heath (Ches.) 51 SJ 8056
Rodeheath (Ches.) 51 SJ 8766
Rodel 113 NG 0483
Roden 41 SJ 5716
Rodhuish 16 ST 0139
Rodington 41 SJ 5814
Rodley 32 SO 7411
Rodmarton 18 ST 9397
Rodmell 13 TQ 4106
Rodmersham 14 TQ 9261
Rodney Stoke 17 ST 4849
Rodsley 53 SK 2040
Roecliffe 66 SE 3765
Roehampton 21 TQ 2373
Roewen 49 SH 7571
Roffey 12 TQ 1931
Rogart 108 NC 7303
Rogate 12 SU 8023
Rogerstone 28 ST 2688
Rogerton 84 NS 6256
Rogiet 29 ST 4587
Roker 72 NZ 4059
Rollesby 47 TG 4415
Rolleston (Leic.) 44 SK 7300
Rolleston (Notts.) 54 SK 7452
Rolleston (Staffs.) 42 SK 2327
Rolston 61 TA 2145
Rolvenden 14 TQ 8431
Rolvenden Layne 14 TQ 8530
Romaldkirk 72 NY 9921
Romanby 66 SE 3693
Romannobridge 85 NT 1547
Romansleigh 7 SS 7220
Romford 21 TQ 5188
Romiley 51 SJ 9390
Romsey 11 SU 3521
Romsley (Here & W) 41 SO 9679
Romsley (Salop) 41 SO 7883
Ronague 56 SC 2472
Rookhope 71 NY 9342
Rookley 11 SZ 5084
Rooks Bridge 17 ST 3752
Roos 61 TA 2830
Rootpark 84 NS 9554
Ropley 11 SU 6431
Ropley Dean 11 SU 6331
Ropsley 54 SK 9834
Rora 105 NK 0650
Rorrington 40 SJ 3000
Rose 2 SW 7754
Rose Ash 7 SS 7821
Roseacre 57 SD 4336
Rosebank 84 NS 8049
Rosebrough 87 NU 1326
Rosedale Abbey 66 SE 7296
Roseden 79 NU 0321
Rosehearty 105 NJ 9367
Rosehill 41 SJ 6630
Roseisle 104 NJ 1367
Rosemarket 24 SM 9508
Rosemarkie 103 NH 7357
Rosemary Lane 8 ST 1514
Rosemount (Strath.) 75 NS 3729
Rosemount (Tays.) 98 NO 2043
Rosewell 85 NT 2862
Roseworthy 2 SW 6139
Rosgill 63 NY 5316
Roshven 95 NM 7078
Roskhill 100 NG 2745
Rosley 70 NY 3245
Roslin 85 NT 2663
Rosliston 42 SK 2416
Rosneath 90 NS 2583
Ross (Dumf & G) 69 NX 6444
Ross (Northum.) 87 NU 1336
Ross (Tays.) 91 NN 7621
Ross-on-Wye 29 SO 6024
Rossett 50 SJ 3657
Rossington 60 SK 6298
Rosskeen 103 NH 6869
Roster 112 ND 2639
Rostherne 51 SJ 7483
Rosthwaite 62 NY 2514
Roston 52 SK 1241
Rosyth 85 NT 1183
Rothbury 79 NU 0601
Rotherby 43 SK 6716
Rotherfield 13 TQ 5529
Rotherfield Greys 20 SU 7282
Rotherfield Peppard 20 SU 7081
Rotherham 53 SK 4492
Rothersthorpe 34 SP 7156
Rotherwick 20 SU 7156
Rothes 104 NJ 2749
Rothesay 81 NS 0864
Rothiebrisbane 105 NJ 7437
Rothiemay 104 NJ 5447
Rothienorman 105 NJ 7235
Rothiesholm 113 HY 6123
Rothley 43 SK 5812
Rothmaise 105 NJ 6832
Rothwell (Lincs.) 61 TF 1599
Rothwell (Northants.) 44 SP 8181
Rothwell (W Yorks.) 59 SE 3428
Rotsea 67 TA 0651
Rottal 98 NO 3769
Rottingdean 13 TQ 3602
Rottington 62 NX 9613
Roud 11 SZ 5280
Rough Close 51 SJ 9239
Rougham 46 TF 8320
Rougham Green 36 TL 9061
Roughburn 96 NN 3781
Roughlee 58 SD 8440
Roughley 42 SP 1399
Roughsike 71 NY 5275
Roughton (Lincs.) 55 TF 2364
Roughton (Norf.) 47 TG 2136
Roughton (Salop) 41 SO 7594
Roundhay 59 SE 3235
Roundstreet Common 12 TQ 0528
Roundway 18 SU 0163
Rounton 66 NZ 4103
Rous Lench 32 SP 0153
Rousdon 8 SY 2990
Routenburn 82 NS 1961
Routh 61 TA 0842
Row (Corn.) 4 SX 0976
Row (Cumbr.) 63 SD 4589
Rowanburn 70 NY 4177
Rowde 18 ST 9762
Rowfoot 71 NY 6860
Rowhedge 23 TM 0221
Rowhook 12 TQ 1234
Rowington 42 SP 2069
Rowland 53 SK 2072
Rowland's Castle 12 SU 7310
Rowland's Gill 72 NZ 1658
Rowledge 12 SU 8243
Rowley (Humbs.) 61 SE 9732
Rowley (Salop) 40 SJ 3006
Rowley Regis 41 SO 9787
Rowlstone 29 SO 3727
Rowly 12 TQ 0441
Rowney Green 42 SP 0471
Rownhams 11 SU 3816
Rowsham 34 SP 8518
Rowsley 53 SK 2566
Rowston 54 TF 0856
Rowton (Ches.) 50 SJ 4464
Rowton (Salop) 41 SJ 6119
Roxburgh 86 NT 6930
Roxby (Humbs.) 60 SE 9217
Roxby (N Yorks.) 73 NZ 7616
Roxton 35 TL 1554
Roxwell 22 TL 6408
Roy Bridge 96 NN 2781
Royal Leamington Spa 43 SP 3166
Royal Tunbridge Wells 13 TQ 5839
Roydon (Essex) 35 TL 4009
Roydon (Norf.) 46 TF 7022
Roydon (Norf.) 37 TM 0980
Royston (Herts.) 35 TL 3541
Royston (S Yorks.) 59 SE 3611
Royton 58 SD 9207
Ruabon 50 SJ 3043
Ruaig 94 NM 0647
Ruan Lanihorne 3 SW 8942
Ruan Minor 2 SW 7115
Ruardean 29 SO 6117
Ruardean Woodside 29 SO 6216
Rubery 41 SO 9777
Ruckcroft 71 NY 5344
Ruckinge 15 TR 0233
Ruckland 55 TF 3378
Ruckley 40 SJ 5300
Ruddington 53 SK 5733
Rudge 18 ST 8252
Rudgeway 29 ST 6286
Rudgwick 12 TQ 0934
Rudhall 29 SO 6225
Rudry 28 ST 1986
Rudston 67 TA 0967
Rudyard 51 SJ 9557
Rufford 57 SD 4515
Rufforth 66 SE 5251
Rugby 43 SP 5075
Rugeley 42 SK 0418
Ruilick 102 NH 5046
Ruishton 8 ST 2624
Ruislip 20 TQ 0987
Rumbling Bridge 92 NT 0199
Rumburgh 47 TM 3581
Rumford 3 SW 8970
Rumney 28 ST 2179
Runcorn 50 SJ 5182
Runcton 12 SU 8802
Runcton Holme 46 TF 6109
Runfold 20 SU 8747
Runhall 47 TG 0507
Runham 47 TG 4610
Runnington 8 ST 1121
Runswick 73 NZ 8016
Runtaleave 98 NO 2867
Runwell 22 TQ 7494
Rush Green 21 TQ 5187
Rushall (Here & W) 31 SO 6434
Rushall (Norf.) 47 TM 1982
Rushall (W Mids.) 42 SK 0201
Rushall (Wilts.) 18 SU 1255
Rushbrooke 36 TL 8961
Rushbury 40 SO 5191
Rushden (Herts.) 35 TL 3031
Rushden (Northants.) 44 SP 9566
Rushford (Norf.) 46 TL 9281
Rushlake Green 13 TQ 6218
Rushmere 47 TM 4987
Rushmere St. Andrew 37 TM 2046
Rushmoor 12 SU 8740
Rushock 41 SO 8871
Rusholme 58 SJ 8494
Rushton (Ches.) 51 SJ 5863
Rushton (Northants) 44 SP 8483
Rushton (Salop) 41 SJ 6008
Rushton Spencer 51 SJ 9363
Rushwick 32 SO 8353
Rushyford 72 NZ 2828
Ruskie 90 NN 6200
Ruskington 54 TF 0850
Rusland 62 SD 3488
Rusper 13 TQ 2037
Ruspidge 29 SO 6512
Russell's Water 20 SU 7089
Rustington 12 TQ 0502
Ruston Parva 67 TA 0661
Ruswarp 67 NZ 8809
Rutherford 86 NT 6530
Rutherglen 84 NS 6161
Ruthernbridge 4 SX 0166
Ruthin 50 SJ 1257
Ruthrieston 99 NJ 9204
Ruthven (Grampn.) 104 NJ 5046
Ruthven (Tays.) 98 NO 2848
Ruthvoes 3 SW 9360
Ruthwell 70 NY 1067
Ruyton-XI-Towns 40 SJ 3922
Ryal 79 NZ 0174
Ryal Fold 58 SD 6621
Ryall (Dorset) 9 SY 4094
Ryarsh 14 TQ 6659
Rydal 62 NY 3606
Ryde 11 SZ 5992
Rye 14 TQ 9220
Rye Foreign 14 TQ 8822
Rye Harbour 15 TQ 9419
Ryhall 44 TF 0311
Ryhill 59 SE 3814
Ryhope 72 NZ 4152
Rylstone 65 SD 9758
Ryme Intrinseca 9 ST 5810
Ryther 60 SE 5539
Ryton (Glos.) 32 SO 7232
Ryton (N Yorks.) 67 SE 7975
Ryton (Salop) 41 SJ 7502
Ryton (Tyne and Wear) 72 NZ 1564
Ryton-on-Dunsmore 43 SP 3874

S

Sabden 58 SD 7737
Sacombe 35 TL 3419
Sacriston 72 NZ 2447
Sadberge 72 NZ 3416
Saddell 81 NR 7832
Saddington 43 SP 6591
Saddle Bow 46 TF 6015
Saffron Walden 35 TL 5438
Saham Hills 46 TF 9003
Saham Toney 46 TF 9002
Saighton 50 SJ 4462
Saint Hill (W. Susx.) 13 TQ 3835
Sainthury 32 SP 1139
Salcombe 5 SX 7338
Salcombe Regis 8 SY 1488
Salcott 23 TL 9413
Sale 51 SJ 7990
Sale Green 32 SO 9358
Saleby 55 TF 4578
Salehurst 14 TQ 7424
Salem (Dyfed) 25 SN 6226
Salem (Dyfed) 39 SN 6684
Salem (Gwyn.) 48 SH 5456
Salen (Highld.) 95 NM 6864
Salen (Island of Mull) 95 NM 5743
Salesbury 58 SD 6732
Salford (Beds.) 34 SP 9339
Salford (Gtr Mches.) 58 SJ 7796
Salford (Oxon.) 33 SP 2828
Salford Priors 32 SP 0751
Salfords 21 TQ 2846
Salhouse 47 TG 3114
Saline 92 NT 0292
Salisbury 10 SU 1429
Sall 47 TG 1024
Sallachy (Highld.) 101 NG 9130
Salmonby 55 TF 3273
Salmond's Muir 93 NO 5837
Salperton 32 SP 0720
Salph End 35 TL 0752
Salsburgh 84 NS 8262
Salt 41 SJ 9594
Saltash 4 SX 4258
Saltburn 103 NH 7269
Saltburn-by-the-Sea 73 NZ 6621
Saltby 44 SK 8426
Saltcoats 82 NS 2441
Saltdean 13 TQ 3802
Salter 64 SD 6063
Salterforth 58 SD 8845
Salterswall 51 SJ 6267
Saltfleet 55 TF 4593
Saltfleetby All Saints 55 TF 4590
Saltfleetby St. Clements 55 TF 4591
Saltfleetby St. Peter 55 TF 4389
Saltford 29 ST 6867
Salthouse 47 TG 0743
Saltmarshe 60 SE 7824
Saltness 113 ND 2790
Saltney 50 SJ 3864
Salton 66 SE 7180
Saltwick 79 NZ 1780
Saltwood 15 TR 1536
Salwarpe 32 SO 8762
Salwayash 9 SY 4596
Sambourne 32 SP 0561
Sambrook 41 SJ 7124
Samlesbury 57 SD 5829
Samlesbury Bottoms 58 SD 6229
Sampford Arundel 8 ST 1018
Sampford Brett 16 ST 0940
Sampford Courtnay 6 SS 6301
Sampford Peverell 8 ST 0214
Sampford Spiney 5 SX 5372
Samuelston 86 NT 4870
Sanaigmore 80 NR 2370
Sancreed 2 SW 4029
Sancton 60 SE 8939
Sand (Shetland Is.) 113 HU 3447
Sand Hutton (N Yorks.) 66 SE 6958
Sand Side 62 SD 2282
Sandbach 51 SJ 7560
Sandbank 82 NS 1580
Sandbanks 10 SZ 0487
Sandend 104 NJ 5566
Sanderstead 21 TQ 3461
Sandford (Avon) 17 ST 4159
Sandford (Cumbr.) 63 NY 7216
Sandford (Devon) 7 SS 8202
Sandford (Dorset) 10 SY 9289
Sandford (Strath.) 84 NS 7143
Sandford Orcas 9 ST 6220
Sandford St. Martin 33 SP 4226
Sandford-on-Thames 33 SP 5301
Sandfordhill 105 NK 1141
Sandgarth 113 HY 5215
Sandgate 15 TR 2035
Sandgreen 69 NX 5752
Sandhaven 105 NJ 9667
Sandhead 68 NX 0949
Sandhoe 72 NY 9766
Sandholme (Humbs.) 60 SE 8230
Sandholme (Lincs.) 55 TF 3337
Sandhurst (Berks.) 20 SU 8361
Sandhurst (Glos.) 32 SO 8223
Sandhurst (Kent) 14 TQ 8028
Sandhutton (N Yorks.) 66 SE 3881
Sandiacre 53 SK 4736
Sandilands 55 TF 5280
Sandiway 51 SJ 6070
Sandleheath 10 SU 1214
Sandleigh 33 SP 4501
Sandling 14 TQ 7558
Sandness 113 HU 1956
Sandon (Essex) 22 TL 7404
Sandon (Herts) 35 TL 3234
Sandon (Staffs.) 41 SJ 9429
Sandown 11 SZ 5984
Sandplace 4 SX 2457
Sandridge (Herts.) 35 TL 1710
Sandridge (Wilts.) 18 ST 9465
Sandringham 46 TF 6928
Sandsend 73 NZ 8512
Sandtoft 60 SE 7408
Sandvoe 113 HU 3692
Sandwich 15 TR 3358
Sandwick (Cumbr.) 62 NY 4219
Sandwick (Shetld) 113 HU 4323
Sandy 35 TL 1649
Sandy Lane (Wilts) 18 ST 9668
Sandycroft 50 SJ 3366
Sandygate 56 SC 3797
Sangobeg 110 NC 4266
Sanna 95 NM 4569
Sanquhar 76 NS 7809
Santon Bridge 62 NY 1001
Santon Downham 46 TL 8187
Sapcote 43 SP 4893
Sapey Common 32 SO 7064
Sapiston 36 TL 9175
Sapperton (Glos.) 32 SO 9403
Sapperton (Lincs.) 54 TF 0133
Saracen's Head 45 TF 3427
Sarclet 112 ND 3443
Sarisbury 11 SU 5008
Sarn (Mid Glam.) 28 SS 9083
Sarn (Powys) 40 SO 2090
Sarn Meyllteyrn 48 SH 2432
Sarn-bach 38 SH 3026
Sarnau (Dyfed) 25 SN 3151
Sarnau (Dyfed) 26 SN 3318
Sarnau (Gwyn.) 49 SH 9739
Sarnau (Powys) 40 SJ 2315
Sarnesfield 30 SO 3750
Saron (Dyfed) 26 SN 3738
Saron (Dyfed) 25 SN 6012
Sarratt 20 TQ 0499
Sarre 15 TR 2565
Sarsden 33 SP 2822
Satley 72 NZ 1143
Satterleigh 7 SS 6622
Satterthwaite 62 SD 3392
Sauchrie 75 NS 3014
Sauchen 105 NJ 7010
Saucher 92 NO 1933
Sauchieburn 99 NO 6669
Saughall 50 SJ 3669
Saughtree 78 NY 5696
Saul 32 SO 7409
Saundby 54 SK 7888
Saundersfoot 24 SN 1304
Saunderton 34 SP 7901
Saunton 6 SS 4537
Sausthorpe 55 TF 3869
Savalmore 108 NC 5908
Sawbridgeworth 35 TL 4814
Sawdon 67 SE 9485
Sawley (Lancs.) 58 SD 7746
Sawley (N Yorks.) 66 SE 2467
Sawston 35 TL 4849
Sawtry 45 TL 1683
Saxby (Leic.) 44 SK 8220
Saxby (Lincs.) 54 TF 0086
Saxby All Saints 61 SE 9816
Saxelbye 44 SK 7021
Saxilby 54 SK 8875
Saxlingham 46 TG 0239
Saxlingham Nethergate 37 TM 2397
Saxmundham 37 TM 3863
Saxon Street 36 TL 6859
Saxondale 53 SK 6839
Saxtead 37 TM 2665
Saxtead Green 37 TM 2564
Saxthorpe 46 TG 1130
Saxton 60 SE 4736
Sayers Common 13 TQ 2618
Scackleton 66 SE 6472
Scaftworth 53 SK 6691
Scagglethorpe 67 SE 8372
Scalasaig 88 NR 3894
Scalby (N. Yorks.) 67 TA 0090
Scaldwell 34 SP 7672
Scale Houses 71 NY 5845
Scaleby 71 NY 4563
Scalebyhill 70 NY 4363
Scales (Cumbr.) 64 SD 2772
Scalford 44 SK 7624
Scalloway 113 HU 4039
Scamblesby 55 TF 2778
Scampston 67 SE 8575
Scampton 54 SK 9479
Scar 113 HY 6745
Scarborough 67 TA 0388
Scarcliffe 53 SK 4968
Scarcroft 59 SE 3540
Scardroy 102 NH 2151
Scarfskerry 112 ND 2673
Scargill 72 NZ 0510
Scarinish 94 NM 0444
Scarisbrick 57 SD 3713
Scarning 46 TF 9512
Scarrington 54 SK 7341
Scarth Hill 57 SD 4206
Scartho 61 TA 2606
Scarwell 113 HY 2421
Scaur or Kippford 69 NX 8355
Scawby 61 SE 9605
Scawton 66 SE 5483
Scayne's Hill 13 TQ 3723
Scethrog 28 SO 1025
Scholes (W Yorks.) 59 SE 1507
Scholes (W Yorks.) 59 SE 3736
Sciberscross 108 NC 7810
Scleddau 24 SM 9434
Sco Ruston 47 TG 2821
Scole 37 TM 1579
Scolton 24 SM 9922
Sconser 100 NG 5232
Scopwick 54 TF 0658
Scorborough 61 TA 0145
Scorrier 2 SW 7244
Scorton (Lancs.) 57 SD 5048
Scorton (N Yorks.) 66 NZ 2400
Scotby 71 NY 4454
Scotforth 64 SD 4759
Scothern 54 TF 0377
Scotland Gate 79 NZ 2584
Scotlandwell 92 NO 1801
Scots' Gap 79 NZ 0486
Scotsburn 108 NH 7275
Scotscraig 93 NO 4428
Scotstown 95 NM 8263
Scotter 60 SE 8800
Scotterthorpe 60 SE 8701
Scotton (Lincs.) 60 SK 8899
Scotton (N Yorks.) 65 SE 1895
Scotton (N Yorks.) 66 SE 3259
Scottow 47 TG 2623
Scoughall 86 NT 6183
Scoulton 46 TF 9800
Scourie 110 NC 1544
Scousburgh 113 HU 3717
Scrabster 112 ND 0970
Scrainwood 79 NT 9909
Scrane End 55 TF 3841
Scraptoft 43 SK 6405
Scratby 47 TG 5115
Scrayingham 66 SE 7360
Scredington 55 TF 0940
Scremby 55 TF 4467
Scremerston 87 NU 0049
Screveton 54 SK 7343
Scriven 66 SE 3458
Scrooby 53 SK 6590
Scropton 52 SK 1930
Scrub Hill 55 TF 2355
Scruton 66 SE 2992
Sculthorpe 46 TF 8931
Scunthorpe 60 SE 8910
Sea Palling 47 TG 4327
Seaborough 9 ST 4205
Seacombe 50 SJ 3190
Seacroft (Lincs) 55 TF 5660
Seafield 85 NT 0066
Seaford 13 TV 4899
Seaforth 50 SJ 3297
Seagrave 43 SK 6117
Seaham 72 NZ 4149
Seahouses 87 NU 2132
Seal 21 TQ 5556
Sealand 50 SJ 3268
Seamer (N Yorks.) 73 NZ 4910
Seamer (N Yorks.) 67 TA 0183
Seamill 82 NS 2047
Searby 61 TA 0605
Seasalter 15 TR 0864
Seascale 62 NY 0301
Seathwaite (Cumbr.) 62 SD 2296
Seaton (Corn.) 4 SX 3054
Seaton (Cumbr.) 62 NY 0130
Seaton (Devon.) 8 SY 2490
Seaton (Durham) 72 NZ 4049
Seaton (Humbs.) 61 TA 1646
Seaton (Leic.) 44 SP 9098
Seaton (Northum.) 79 NZ 3276
Seaton Carew 73 NZ 5229
Seaton Delaval 79 NZ 3075
Seaton Ross 60 SE 7741
Seaton Sluice 79 NZ 3376
Seave Green 66 NZ 5600
Seavington St. Mary 9 ST 3914
Seavington St. Michael 9 ST 4015
Sebergham 70 NY 3541
Seckington 42 SK 2607
Sedbergh 63 SD 6592
Sedbusk 65 SD 8891
Sedgeberrow 32 SP 0238
Sedgebrook 54 SK 8537
Sedgefield 72 NZ 3528
Sedgeford 46 TF 7136
Sedgehill 10 ST 8627
Sedgley 41 SO 9193
Sedgwick 63 SD 5186
Sedlescombe 14 TQ 7818
Seend 18 ST 9460
Seend Cleeve 18 ST 9260
Seer Green 20 SU 9691
Seething 47 TM 3197
Sefton 57 SD 3500
Seghill 79 NZ 2874
Seighford 41 SJ 8725
Seisdon 41 SO 8394
Selattyn 50 SJ 2633
Selborne 12 SU 7433
Selby 60 SE 6132
Selham 12 SU 9320
Selkirk 77 NT 4728
Sellack 29 SO 5627
Sellindge 15 TR 0938
Selling 15 TR 0358
Sells Green 18 ST 9462
Selly Oak 42 SP 0482
Selmeston 13 TQ 5007
Selsden 21 TQ 3562
Selsey (W. Sussex) 12 SZ 8593
Selsfield Common 13 TQ 3434
Selston 53 SK 4553
Selworthy 16 SS 9146
Semer 36 TM 0046
Semington 18 ST 8960
Semley 10 ST 8926
Send 20 TQ 0155
Senghenydd 28 ST 1191
Sennen 2 SW 3525
Sennen Cove 2 SW 3425
Sennybridge 28 SN 9228
Sessay 66 SE 4575
Setchey 46 TF 6313
Setley 11 SU 3000
Setter 113 HU 4683
Settle 65 SD 8263
Settrington 67 SE 8370
Seven Kings 21 TQ 4586
Seven Sisters 28 SN 8108
Sevenhampton (Glos.) 32 SP 0321
Sevenhampton (Wilts.) 18 SU 2090
Sevenoaks 21 TQ 5355
Sevenoaks Weald 21 TQ 5351
Severn Beach 20 ST 5381
Severn Stoke 32 SO 8544
Sevington 15 TR 0340
Sewards End 36 TL 5738
Sewerby 67 TA 2068
Seworgan 2 SW 7030
Sewstern 44 SK 8821
Sezincote 33 SP 1731
Shabbington 34 SP 6606

Shackerstone 250 Spettisbury

Shackerstone 43 SK 3706
Shackleford 20 SU 9345
Shadforth 72 NZ 3441
Shadingfield 47 TM 4383
Shadoxhurst 15 TQ 9737
Shadwell 46 TL 9383
Shaftesbury 10 ST 8622
Shafton 59 SE 3810
Shalbourne 19 SU 3163
Shalcombe 11 SZ 3985
Shalden 20 SU 6941
Shaldon 8 SX 9272
Shalfleet 11 SZ 4189
Shalford (Essex) 22 TL 7229
Shalford (Surrey) 20 TQ 0047
Shalford Green 22 TL 7127
Shallowford 7 SS 7144
Shalstone 34 SP 6436
Shamley Green 12 TQ 0344
Shandon 90 NS 2586
Shangton 44 SP 7196
Shanklin 11 SZ 5881
Shap 63 NY 5615
Shapwick (Somer.) 17 ST 4137
Shardlow 53 SK 4330
Shareshill 41 SJ 9406
Sharlston 59 SE 3818
Sharnbrook 34 SP 9959
Sharnford 43 SP 4891
Sharoe Green 57 SD 5332
Sharow 66 SE 3271
Sharpenhoe 35 TL 0630
Sharperton 79 NT 9503
Sharpness 29 SO 6702
Sharpthorne 13 TQ 3732
Sharrington 47 TG 0337
Shatterford 41 SO 7980
Shaugh Prior 5 SX 5463
Shaughlaige-e-Caine 56 SC 3187
Shavington 51 SJ 6951
Shaw (Gtr Mches.) 58 SD 9308
Shaw (Wilts.) 18 ST 8865
Shaw Mills 66 SE 2562
Shawbost 109 NB 2646
Shawbury 40 SJ 5521
Shawell 43 SP 5480
Shawford 11 SU 4624
Shawforth 58 SD 8920
Shawhead 69 NX 8675
Shawwood 75 NS 5325
Shear Cross 18 ST 8642
Shearsby 43 SP 6291
Shebbear 6 SS 4309
Shebdon 41 SJ 7525
Shebster 112 ND 0164
Shedfield 11 SU 5512
Sheen 52 SK 1161
Sheepscombe 32 SO 8910
Sheepstor 5 SX 5567
Sheepwash 6 SS 4806
Sheepy Magna 43 SK 3201
Sheepy Parva 43 SK 3301
Sheering 22 TL 5013
Sheerness 23 TQ 9274
Sheet 12 SU 7524
Sheffield 53 SK 3587
Sheffield Bottom 19 SU 6469
Shefford 35 TL 1439
Sheigra 110 NC 1861
Sheinton 41 SJ 6104
Shelderton 40 SO 4077
Sheldon (Derby.) 52 SK 1768
Sheldon (Devon.) 8 ST 1208
Sheldon (W Mids.) 42 SP 1584
Sheldwich 15 TR 0156
Shelf 59 SE 1228
Shelfanger 47 TM 1083
Shelfield 42 SK 0302
Shelford (Notts.) 53 SK 6642
Shelley 59 SE 2011
Shellingford 19 SU 3193
Shellow Bowells 22 TL 6108
Shelsley Beauchamp 32 SO 7362
Shelsley Walsh 32 SO 7263
Shelton (Beds.) 34 TL 0368
Shelton (Norf.) 47 TM 2191
Shelton (Notts.) 54 SK 7844
Shelton Green 47 TM 2390
Shelve 40 SO 3399
Shelwick 31 SO 5243
Shenfield 22 TQ 6094
Shenington 33 SP 3642
Shenley 35 TL 1900
Shenley Brook End 34 SP 8335
Shenley Church End 34 SP 8336
Shenleybury 35 TL 1802
Shenmore 30 SO 3938
Shenstone (Here & W) 41 SO 8673
Shenstone (Staffs.) 42 SK 1004
Shenton 43 SK 3800
Shenval 104 NJ 2129
Shepherd's Green 20 SU 7183
Shepherdswell or Sibertswold 15 TR 2548
Shepley 59 SE 1909
Shepperdine 29 ST 6195
Shepperton 20 TQ 0867
Shepreth 35 TL 3947
Shepshed 43 SK 4719
Shepton Beauchamp 9 ST 4016
Shepton Mallet 17 ST 6143
Shepton Montague 17 ST 6731
Shepway 14 TQ 7753
Sheraton 73 NZ 4334
Sherborne (Dorset) 9 ST 6316
Sherborne (Glos.) 33 SP 1714
Sherborne St. John 19 SU 6155
Sherbourne 33 SP 2661
Sherburn (Durham) 72 NZ 3142
Sherburn (N Yorks.) 67 SE 9577
Sherburn in Elmet 60 SE 4933
Shere 20 TQ 0747
Shereford 46 TF 8829
Sherfield English 11 SU 2922
Sherfield on Loddon 19 SU 6757
Sherford 5 SX 7744
Sheriff Hutton 66 SE 6566
Sheriffhales 41 SJ 7512
Sheringham 47 TG 1543
Sherington 34 SP 8846
Shernborne 46 TF 7132
Sherrington 10 ST 9638
Sherston 18 ST 8585
Sherwood Green 6 SS 5520
Shettleston 84 NS 6464
Shevington 57 SD 5408
Shevington Moor 57 SD 5410
Sheviock 4 SX 3655
Shiel Bridge 101 NG 9318
Shieldaig 101 NG 8154
Shieldhill (Central) 84 NS 8976
Shielfoot 95 NM 6669
Shifnal 41 SJ 7507
Shilbottle 79 NU 1908
Shildon 72 NZ 2226
Shillingford (Devon.) 8 SS 9723
Shillingford (Oxon.) 19 SU 5992
Shillingford St. George 8 SX 9087
Shillingstone 10 ST 8211
Shillington 35 TL 1234
Shillmoor (Northum.) 78 NT 8807
Shilton (Oxon.) 33 SP 2608
Shilton (Warw.) 43 SP 4084
Shimpling (Norf.) 47 TM 1583
Shimpling (Suff.) 36 TL 8551
Shimpling Street 36 TL 8652
Shiney Row 72 NZ 3252
Shinfield 20 SU 7368
Shinness 111 NC 5314
Shipbourne 21 TQ 5952
Shipdham 46 TF 9607
Shipham 17 ST 4457
Shiphay 5 SX 8965
Shiplake 20 SU 7678
Shipley (Salop) 41 SO 8095
Shipley (W Susx.) 12 TQ 1422
Shipley (W Yorks.) 59 SE 1337
Shipmeadow 47 TM 3789
Shippon 19 SU 4898
Shipston on Stour 33 SP 2540
Shipton (Glos.) 32 SP 0318
Shipton (N Yorks) 66 SE 5558
Shipton (Salop) 40 SO 5591
Shipton Bellinger 18 SU 2345
Shipton Gorge 9 SY 4991
Shipton Green 12 SU 8000
Shipton Moyne 18 ST 8889
Shipton-on-Cherwell 33 SP 4716
Shipton-under-Wychwood 33 SP 2717
Shiptonthorpe 60 SE 8543
Shirburn 20 SU 6995
Shirdley Hill 57 SD 3612
Shire Oak 42 SK 0504
Shirebrook 53 SK 5267
Shirehampton 29 ST 5276
Shiremoor 79 NZ 3171
Shirenewton 29 ST 4793
Shirl Heath 30 SO 4359
Shirland 53 SK 3958
Shirley (Derby.) 53 SK 2141
Shirley (Hants.) 11 SU 4114
Shirley (W Mids.) 42 SP 1277
Shirrell Heath 11 SU 5714
Shirwell 6 SS 5937
Shiskine 74 NR 9129
Shobdon 30 SO 3961
Shobrooke 7 SS 8600
Shocklach 50 SJ 4348
Shoeburyness 23 TQ 9384
Sholden 15 TR 3552
Sholing 11 SU 4511
Shop (Corn.) 6 SS 2214
Shop (Corn.) 3 SW 8773
Shoreditch (Gtr. London) 21 TQ 3282
Shoreham 21 TQ 5261
Shoreham-by-Sea 13 TQ 2105
Shoresdean 87 NT 9546
Shoreswood 87 NT 9446
Shoretown 102 NH 6161
Shorncote 18 SU 0296
Shorne 14 TQ 6970
Short Heath (Leic.) 43 SK 3014
Short Heath (W Mids.) 42 SP 0992
Shortgate 13 TQ 4915
Shortlanesend 2 SW 8047
Shortlees 82 NS 4335
Shorwell 11 SZ 4582
Shoscombe 17 ST 7156
Shotesham 47 TM 2599
Shotgate 22 TQ 7692
Shotley Bridge 72 NZ 0752
Shotley Gate 37 TM 2433
Shotley Street 37 TM 2335
Shottenden 15 TR 0454
Shottermill 12 SU 8732
Shottery 32 SP 1854
Shotteswell 33 SP 4245
Shottisham 37 TM 3144
Shottle 53 SK 3149
Shotton (Clwyd) 50 SJ 3069
Shotton (Durham) 72 NZ 4139
Shotton (Northum.) 87 NT 8430
Shotton Colliery 72 NZ 3941
Shotts 84 NS 8760
Shotwick 50 SJ 3371
Shouldham 46 TF 6708
Shouldham Thorpe 46 TF 6607
Shoulton 32 SO 8058
Shrawley 32 SO 8064
Shrewley 42 SP 2167
Shrewsbury 40 SJ 4912
Shrewton 18 SU 0643
Shripney 12 SU 9302
Shrivenham 18 SU 2489
Shropham 46 TL 9893
Shroton or Iwerne Courtney 10 ST 8512
Shrub End 23 TL 9723
Shucknall 31 SO 5842
Shudy Camps 36 TL 6244
Shurdington 32 SO 9118
Shurlock Row 20 SU 8374
Shurrey 112 ND 0458
Shurton 16 ST 2044
Shustoke 42 SP 2290
Shut End 41 SO 9089
Shute (Devon) 8 SY 2597
Shutford 33 SP 3840
Shuthonger 32 SO 8935
Shutlanger 34 SP 7249
Shuttington 42 SK 2505
Shuttlewood 53 SK 4672
Sibbertoft 43 SP 6782
Sibdon Carwood 40 SO 4083
Sibertswold or Shepherdswell 15 TR 2548
Sibford Ferris 33 SP 3537
Sibford Gower 33 SP 3537
Sible Hedingham 36 TL 7734
Sibsey 55 TF 3551
Sibson (Cambs.) 45 TL 0997
Sibson (Leic.) 43 SK 3500
Sibthorpe 54 SK 7645
Sibton 37 TM 3669
Sicklesmere 36 TL 8760
Sicklinghall 59 SE 3548
Sidbury (Devon.) 8 SY 1491
Sidbury (Salop) 41 SO 6885
Sidcup 21 TQ 4672
Siddington (Ches.) 51 SJ 8470
Siddington (Glos.) 18 SU 0399
Sidestrand 47 TG 2539
Sidford 8 SY 1390
Sidlesham 12 SZ 8598
Sidley 14 TQ 7409
Sidmouth 8 SY 1287
Siefton 40 SO 4883
Sigford 5 SX 7773
Sigglesthorne 61 TA 1545
Silchester 19 SU 6462
Sileby 43 SK 6015
Silecroft 62 SD 1281
Silian 27 SN 5751
Silk Willoughby 54 TF 0542
Silkstone 59 SE 2905
Silloth 70 NY 1153
Sillyearn 104 NJ 5254
Silpho 67 SE 9692
Silsden 59 SE 0446
Silsoe 35 TL 0835
Silver End (Beds.) 35 TL 0942
Silver End (Essex) 22 TL 8019
Silverburn 85 NT 2060
Silverdale (Lancs.) 64 SD 4674
Silverdale (Staffs.) 51 SJ 8146
Silverford 105 NJ 7764
Silverley's Green 37 TM 2976
Silverstone 34 SP 6644
Silverton 8 SS 9502
Simonburn 78 NY 8773
Simonsbath 7 SS 7739
Simonstone (Lancs) 58 SD 7734
Simprim 87 NT 8545
Sinclairston 75 NS 4716
Sinderby 66 SE 3481
Sinderhope 71 NY 8452
Sindlesham 20 SU 7769
Singleton (Lancs.) 57 SD 3838
Singleton (W Susx) 12 SU 8713
Singlewell or Ifield (Kent) 22 TQ 6471
Sinnington 67 SE 7485
Sinton Green 32 SO 8160
Sipson 20 TQ 0877
Sirhowy 28 SO 1410
Sissinghurst 14 TQ 7937
Siston 29 ST 6875
Sithney 2 SW 6329
Sittenham 108 NH 6574
Sittingbourne 14 TQ 9163
Six Ashes 41 SO 6988
Six Mile Bottom 36 TL 5756
Sixhills 55 TF 1787
Sixpenny Handley 10 ST 9917
Sizewell 37 TM 4762
Skaill (Mainland) (Orkney) 113 HY 5806
Skaill (Westray) (Orkney) 113 HY 4552
Skares 75 NS 5217
Skateraw 86 NT 7375
Skeabost 100 NG 4148
Skeeby 65 NZ 1902
Skeffington 44 SK 7402
Skeffling 61 TA 3619
Skegby 53 SK 5060
Skegness 55 TF 5663
Skeldyke 55 TF 3337
Skellingthorpe 54 SK 9272
Skelmanthorpe 59 SE 2210
Skelmersdale 57 SD 4605
Skelmonae 105 NJ 8839
Skelmorlie 82 NS 1967
Skelmuir 105 NJ 9842
Skelpick 111 NC 7355
Skelton (Cleve.) 73 NZ 6518
Skelton (Cumbr.) 63 NY 4335
Skelton (N Yorks.) 65 NZ 0900
Skelton (N Yorks.) 66 SE 3568
Skelton (N Yorks.) 66 SE 5656
Skelwith Bridge 62 NY 3503
Skendleby 55 TF 4369
Skenfrith 29 SO 4520
Skerne 67 TA 0455
Skerray 111 NC 6563
Skerricha 110 NC 2351
Skewen 25 SS 7297
Skewsby 66 SE 6270
Skeyton 47 TG 2425
Skidbrooke 55 TF 4393
Skidby 61 TA 0133
Skigersta 109 NB 5461
Skilgate 16 SS 9827
Skillington 44 SK 8925
Skinburness 70 NY 1255
Skinidin 100 NG 2247
Skinningrove 73 NZ 7119
Skipness 81 NR 8957
Skipsea 67 TA 1655
Skipton 65 SD 9851
Skipton-on-Swale 66 SE 3679
Skipwith 60 SE 6538
Skirling 85 NT 0739
Skirmett 20 SU 7789
Skirpenbeck 67 SE 7457
Skirwith (Cumbr.) 63 NY 6132
Skirwith (N Yorks.) 64 SD 7073
Skirza 112 ND 3868
Skulamus 101 NG 6722
Skullomie 111 NC 6161
Skye of Curr 103 NH 9924
Slackhall 52 SK 0781
Slackhead 104 NJ 4063
Slacks of Cairnbanno 105 NJ 8546
Slad 32 SO 8707
Slade (Devon) 6 SS 5046
Slade Green 21 TQ 5276
Slaggyford 71 NY 6752
Slaidburn 65 SD 7152
Slaithwaite 59 SE 0714
Slaley 72 NY 9757
Slamannan 84 NS 8573
Slapton (Bucks.) 34 SP 9320
Slapton (Devon.) 5 SX 8244
Slapton (Northants.) 34 SP 6346
Slaugham 13 TQ 2528
Slawston 44 SP 7794
Sleaford (Hants.) 12 SU 8037
Sleaford (Lincs.) 54 TF 0645
Sleagill 63 NY 5919
Sleapford 41 SJ 6315
Sledge Green 32 SO 8134
Sledmere 67 SE 9364
Sleights 67 NZ 8607
Slickly 112 ND 2966
Sliddery 74 NR 9322
Sliemore 103 NJ 0320
Sligachan 100 NG 4829
Slimbridge 32 SO 7303
Slindon (Staffs.) 51 SJ 8232
Slindon (W Susx) 12 SU 9608
Slinfold 12 TQ 1131
Slingsby 66 SE 6974
Slioch (Grampn.) 104 NJ 5638
Slip End 35 TL 0818
Slipton 44 SP 9479
Slockavullin 89 NR 8297
Sloley 47 TG 2924
Sloothby 55 TF 4970
Slough 20 SU 9779
Slyne 64 SD 4765
Smailholm 86 NT 6436
Small Dole 13 TQ 2112
Small Hythe 14 TQ 8930
Smallbridge 58 SD 9114
Smallburgh 47 TG 3324
Smallburn (Grampn.) 105 NK 0141
Smallburn (Strath.) 76 NS 6827
Smalley 53 SK 4044
Smallfield 13 TQ 3243
Smallridge 8 ST 3001
Smarden 14 TQ 8842
Smeatharpe 8 ST 1910
Smeeth 15 TR 0739
Smeeton Westerby 43 SP 6792
Smerral 112 ND 1733
Smethwick 42 SP 0288
Smisby 43 SK 3419
Smithfield 71 NY 4465
Smithincott 8 ST 0611
Smithstown 109 NG 7879
Smithton 103 NH 7145
Snailbeach 40 SJ 3702
Snailwell 36 TL 6467
Snainton 67 SE 9182
Snaith 60 SE 6422
Snape (N Yorks.) 66 SE 2684
Snape (Suff.) 37 TM 3959
Snape Street 37 TM 3958
Snarestone 43 SK 3409
Snarford 54 TF 0482
Snargate 15 TQ 9928
Snave 15 TR 0130
Snead 40 SO 3191
Sneaton 67 NZ 8907
Sneaton Thorpe 67 NZ 9006
Snelland 54 TF 0780
Snelston 52 SK 1543
Snettisham 46 TF 6834
Snitter 79 NU 0203
Snitterby 54 SK 9894
Snitterfield 33 SP 2159
Snitton 40 SO 5575
Snodhill 30 SO 3140
Snodland 14 TQ 7061
Snowshill 32 SP 0933
Soberton 11 SU 6016
Soberton Heath 11 SU 6014
Soham 26 TL 5973
Soldon Cross 6 SS 3210
Soldridge 11 SU 6534
Sole Street 15 TR 0949
Solihull 42 SP 1479
Sollas 109 NF 8074
Sollers Dilwyn 30 SO 4255
Sollers Hope 31 SO 6033
Sollom 57 SD 4518
Solva 24 SM 8024
Somerby 44 SK 7710
Somercotes 53 SK 4253
Somerford Keynes 18 SU 0195
Somerley 12 SZ 8198
Somerleyton 47 TM 4897
Somersal Herbert 52 SK 1335
Somersby 55 TF 3472
Somersham (Cambs.) 45 TL 3677
Somersham (Suff.) 37 TM 0848
Somerton (Norf.) 47 TG 4719
Somerton (Oxon.) 33 SP 4928
Somerton (Somer.) 17 ST 4828
Sompting 12 TQ 1605
Sonning 20 SU 7575
Sonning Common 19 SU 7080
Sopley 10 SZ 1596
Sopworth 18 ST 8286
Sorbie 69 NX 4346
Sordale 112 ND 1462
Sorisdale 94 NM 2763
Sorn 75 NS 5526
Sornhill 82 NS 5134
Sortat 112 ND 2863
Sotby 55 TF 2078
Sots Hole 55 TF 1164
Sotterly 47 TM 4584
Soughton 50 SJ 2466
Soulbury 34 SP 8827
Soulby 63 NY 7410
Souldern 33 SP 5231
Souldrop 34 SP 9861
Soundwell 29 ST 6574
Sourhope 78 NT 8420
Sourton 5 SX 5390
Soutergate 62 SD 2281
South Acre 46 TF 8114
South Allington 5 SX 7938
South Alloa 91 NS 8791
South Ambersham 12 SU 9120
South Ballachulish 96 NN 0559
South Bank 73 NZ 5220
South Barrow 17 ST 6027
South Benfleet 22 TQ 7785
South Brent 5 SX 6960
South Burlingham 47 TG 3708
South Cadbury 17 ST 6325
South Cairn 68 NW 9768
South Carlton 54 SK 9476
South Cave 60 SE 9231
South Cerney 18 SU 0497
South Chard 8 ST 3205
South Charlton 79 NU 1620
South Cheriton 10 ST 6924
South Cliffe 60 SE 8736
South Clifton 54 SK 8270
South Cove 47 TM 5081
South Creake 46 TF 8536
South Croxton 43 SK 6810
South Dalton 67 SE 9645
South Darenth 21 TQ 5669
South Duffield 60 SE 6733
South Elkington 55 TF 2988
South Elmsall 60 SE 4711
South End (Berks.) 19 SU 5970
South End (Cumbr.) 64 SD 2063
South Fambridge 22 TQ 8694
South Fawley 19 SU 3980
South Ferriby 61 SE 9820
South Green (Essex) 22 TQ 6893
South Hanningfield 22 TQ 7497
South Harting 12 SU 7819
South Hayling 12 SZ 7299
South Heath 34 SP 9102
South Heighton 13 TQ 4503
South Hetton 72 NZ 3745
South Hiendley 59 SE 3812
South Hill 4 SX 3272
South Hole 6 SS 2219
South Holmwood 12 TQ 1745
South Hornchurch 21 TQ 5283
South Hylton 72 NZ 3556
South Kelsey 61 TF 0398
South Killingholme 61 TA 1416
South Kilvington 66 SE 4283
South Kilworth 43 SP 6082
South Kirkby 60 SE 4410
South Kirkton 105 NJ 7405
South Kyme 55 TF 1749
South Lancing 12 TQ 1804
South Leigh (Oxon.) 33 SP 3908
South Leverton 54 SK 7881
South Littleton 32 SP 0746
South Lopham 47 TM 0481
South Luffenham 44 SK 9402
South Malling 13 TQ 4211
South Marston 18 SU 1987
South Milford 60 SE 4931
South Milton 5 SX 7042
South Mimms 35 TL 2201
South Molton 7 SS 7125
South Moor 72 NZ 1952
South Moreton 19 SU 5688
South Mundham 8 SU 8800
South Muskham 54 SK 7957
South Newington 33 SP 4033
South Newton 10 SU 0834
South Normanton 53 SK 4456
South Norwood 21 TQ 3468
South Nutfield 21 TQ 3048
South Ockendon 21 TQ 5982
South Ormsby 55 TF 3675
South Otterington 66 SE 3787
South Oxhey 20 TQ 1193
South Perrott 9 ST 4706
South Petherton 9 ST 4316
South Petherwin 4 SX 3182
South Pickenham 46 TF 8504
South Pool 5 SX 7740
South Radworthy 7 SS 7432
South Raynham 46 TF 8723
South Reston 55 TF 4082
South Runcton 46 TF 6308
South Scarle 54 SK 8463
South Shields 72 NZ 3667
South Skirlaugh 61 TA 1439
South Somercotes 55 TF 4193
South Stainley 66 SE 3063
South Stoke (Avon) 18 ST 7461
South Stoke (Oxon.) 19 SU 6083
South Stoke (W Susx) 12 TQ 0210
South Street (E. Susx) 13 TQ 3918
South Tawton 5 SX 6594
South Thoresby 55 TF 4077
South Tidworth 18 SU 2347
South Town (Hants.) 11 SU 6536
South View 113 HU 3942
South Walsham 47 TG 3613
South Warnborough 20 SU 7247
South Weald 21 TQ 5793
South Weston 19 SU 7098
South Wheatley 4 SX 2492
South Widcombe 17 ST 5756
South Wigston 43 SP 5898
South Willingham 55 TF 1983
South Wingfield 53 SK 3755
South Witham 44 SK 9219
South Wonston 11 SU 4635
South Woodham Ferrers 22 TQ 8097
South Wootton 46 TF 6422
South Wraxall 18 ST 8364
South Zeal 5 SX 6593
South-haa 113 HU 3688
Southall 20 TQ 1280
Southam (Glos.) 32 SO 9725
Southam (Warw.) 33 SP 4161
Southampton 11 SU 4212
Southborough 13 TQ 5842
Southbourne (Dorset) 10 SZ 1491
Southbourne (W Susx) 12 SU 7705
Southbrecks 113 HY 3917
Southburgh 46 TG 0004
Southchurch 23 TQ 9186
Southcott (Devon) 6 SX 5495
Southease 13 TQ 4205
Southend (Strath.) 74 NR 6908
Southend-on-Sea 22 TQ 8885
Southerndown 28 SS 8874
Southerness 70 NX 9754
Southery 46 TL 6294
Southfleet 14 TQ 6171
Southgate (Gtr London) 21 TQ 3093
Southgate (Norf.) 46 TF 6833
Southgate (Norf.) 47 TG 1324
Southill 35 TL 1442
Southleigh (Devon) 8 SY 2093
Southminster 23 TQ 9699
Southoe 35 TL 1864
Southolt 37 TM 1968
Southorpe 45 TF 0803
Southowram 59 SE 1123
Southport 57 SD 3316
Southrepps 47 TG 2536
Southrey 55 TF 1366
Southrop 33 SP 1903
Southrope 19 SU 6744
Southsea 11 SZ 6498
Southwaite 71 NY 4445
Southwater 12 TQ 1526
Southway 17 ST 5142
Southwell (Dorset) 9 SY 6870
Southwell (Notts.) 53 SK 7053
Southwick (Hants.) 11 SU 6208
Southwick (Northants.) 44 TL 0192
Southwick (Tyne and Wear) 72 NZ 3758
Southwick (W Susx) 13 TQ 2405
Southwick (Wilts.) 18 ST 8354
Southwold 37 TM 5076
Southwood (Norf.) 47 TG 3905
Southwood (Somer.) 17 ST 5533
Soutra Mains 86 NT 4559
Sowerby (N Yorks.) 66 SE 4381
Sowerby (W Yorks.) 59 SE 0423
Sowerby Bridge 59 SE 0523
Sowerby Row 62 NY 3940
Sowton 8 SX 9792
Spa Common 47 TG 2930
Spacey Houses 36 SE 3151
Spalding 45 TF 2422
Spaldington 60 SE 7533
Spaldwick 45 TL 1272
Spalford 54 SK 8369
Sparham 47 TG 0619
Spark Bridge 62 SD 3084
Sparkford 17 ST 6026
Sparkwell 5 SX 5757
Sparrowpit 52 SK 0980
Sparsholt (Hants.) 11 SU 4331
Sparsholt (Oxon.) 19 SU 3487
Spaunton 66 SE 7289
Spaxton 16 ST 2236
Spean Bridge 96 NN 2281
Speen (Berks.) 19 SU 4568
Speen (Bucks.) 20 SU 8499
Speeton 67 TA 1574
Speke 50 SJ 4383
Speldhurst 13 TQ 5541
Spellbrook 35 TL 4817
Spelsbury 33 SP 3421
Spencers Wood 20 SU 7166
Spennithorne 65 SE 1489
Spennymoor 72 NZ 2533
Spetchley 32 SO 8953
Spettisbury 10 ST 9002

Spexhall 251 Stuartfield

Spexhall 37 TM 3780
Spey Bay 104 NJ 3866
Spilsby 55 TF 4066
Spindlestone 87 NU 1533
Spinningdale 108 NH 6789
Spirthill 18 ST 9975
Spital 112 ND 1654
Spithurst 13 TQ 4217
Spittal (Dyfed) 24 SM 9723
Spittal (Lothian) 86 NT 4677
Spittal (Northum.) 87 NU 0051
Spittal of Glenmuick 98 NO 3184
Spittal of Glenshee 98 NO 1070
Spittalfield 98 NO 1040
Spixworth 47 TG 2415
Spofforth 66 SE 3650
Spondon 53 SK 3935
Spooner Row 47 TM 0997
Sporle 46 TF 8411
Spott 86 NT 6775
Spratton 44 SP 7170
Spreakley 12 SU 8341
Spreyton 7 SX 6996
Spridlington 54 TF 0084
Springburn 81 NS 5968
Springfield (Fife.) 93 NO 3411
Springfield (Grampn.) 103 NJ 0559
Springfield (W Mids.) 42 SP 1082
Springholm 69 NX 8070
Springside 82 NS 3639
Springthorpe 54 SK 8789
Sproatley 61 TA 1934
Sproston Green 51 SJ 7367
Sprotbrough 60 SE 5302
Sproughton 37 TM 1244
Sprouston 86 NT 7375
Sprowston 47 TG 2412
Sproxton (Leic.) 44 SK 8524
Sproxton (N Yorks.) 66 SE 6181
Spurstow 51 SJ 5556
St. Abbs 87 NT 9167
St. Agnes (Corn.) 2 SW 7150
St. Albans 35 TL 1507
St. Allen 2 SW 8250
St. Andrews 93 NO 5016
St. Andrews Major 28 ST 1471
St. Ann's (Dumf & G) 77 NY 0793
St. Ann's Chapel 4 SX 4170
St. Anne's (Lancs.) 57 SD 3129
St. Anthony 2 SW 7725
St. Arvans 29 ST 5196
St. Asaph 49 SJ 0374
St. Athan 28 ST 0168
St. Austell 4 SX 0152
St. Bees 62 NX 9611
St. Blazey 4 SX 0654
St. Boswells 86 NT 5930
St. Breock 3 SW 9771
St. Breward 4 SX 0977
St. Briavels 29 SO 5504
St. Bride's Major 28 SS 8974
St. Brides 24 SM 8010
St. Brides Wentlooge 29 ST 2982
St. Brides-super-Ely 28 ST 1078
St. Budeaux 5 SX 4558
St. Clears 25 SN 2716
St. Cleer 4 SX 2468
St. Clement (Corn) 2 SW 8443
St. Clether 4 SX 2084
St. Colmac 81 NS 0467
St. Columb Major 3 SW 9163
St. Columb Minor 2 SW 8362
St. Columb Road 3 SW 9059
St. Combs 105 NK 0563
St. Cross South Elmham 47 TM 2984
St. Cyrus 99 NO 7464
St. Davids (Dyfed) 24 SM 7525
St. Davids (Tays.) 91 NN 9420
St. Day 2 SW 7242
St. Dennis 3 SW 9558
St. Dogmaels 26 SN 1646
St. Dogwells 24 SM 9728
St. Dominick 4 SX 3967
St. Donats 28 SS 9368
St. Edith's Marsh 18 ST 9764
St. Endellion 3 SW 9978
St. Enoder 3 SW 8956
St. Erme 2 SW 8449
St. Erth 2 SW 5435
St. Erth Praze 2 SW 5735
St. Ervan 3 SW 8870
St. Ewe 3 SW 9745
St. Fagans 28 ST 1177
St. Fergus 105 NK 0951
St. Fillans 91 NN 6942
St. Florence 24 SN 0801
St. Gennys 6 SX 1497
St. George (Clwyd) 49 SH 9775
St. Georges (S Glam.) 28 ST 0976
St. Germans 4 SX 3557
St. Giles in the Wood 6 SS 5318
St. Giles-on-the-Heath 4 SX 3677
St. Harmon 27 SN 9872
St. Helen Auckland 72 NZ 1826
St. Helena 47 TG 1816
St. Helens (I. of W.) 11 SZ 6288
St. Helens (Mers.) 50 SJ 5095
St. Hilary (Corn) 2 SW 5531
St. Hilary (S Glam.) 28 ST 0173
St. Illtyd 28 SO 2102
St. Ippollitts 35 TL 1927
St. Ishmaels 24 SM 8307
St. Issey 3 SW 9271
St. Ive (Corn.) 4 SX 3167
St. Ives (Cambs.) 45 TL 3171
St. Ives (Corn.) 2 SW 5140
St. Ives (Dorset) 10 SU 1203
St. James South Elmham 47 TM 3281
St. John (Corn.) 4 SX 4053
St. John's (I. of M.) 56 SC 2781
St. John's Chapel 63 NY 8837
St. John's Fen End 45 TF 5311
St. John's Highway 45 TF 5314
St. John's Town of Dalry 69 NX 6281
St. Johns (Here & W) 32 SO 8453
St. Jude's 56 SC 3996
St. Just (Corn.) 2 SW 8435
St. Just. (Corn.) 2 SW 3631
St. Katherines 105 NJ 7034
St. Keverne 2 SW 7821
St. Kew 4 SX 0276
St. Kew Highway 4 SX 0375
St. Keyne 4 SX 2460
St. Lawrence (Corn.) 4 SX 0466
St. Lawrence (Essex) 23 TL 9604
St. Lawrence (I. of W.) 11 SZ 5476
St. Lenords (Bucks.) 34 SP 9006
St. Leonards (Dorset) 10 SU 1002
St. Leonards (E Susx.) 14 TQ 8009
St. Levan 22 SW 3822
St. Lythans 28 ST 1073
St. Mabyn 4 SX 0373
St. Margaret South Elmham 47 TM 3183
St. Margarets 30 SO 3534
St. Margarets Hope (S Ronaldsay) 113 ND 4493
St. Margarets at Cliffe 15 TR 3644
St. Marks 56 SC 2976
St. Martin (Corn.) 4 SX 2555
St. Martin's Green 2 SW 7324
St. Martins (Salop) 50 SJ 3236
St. Martins (Tays.) 92 NO 1530
St. Mary Bourne 19 SU 4250
St. Mary Church 28 ST 0071
St. Mary Cray 21 TQ 4767
St. Mary Hill 28 SS 9678
St. Mary in the Marsh 15 TR 0628
St. Mary's (Orkney) 113 HY 4701
St. Mary's Bay 15 TR 0927
St. Mary's Hoo 22 TQ 8076
St. Marylebone 21 TQ 2881
St. Mawes 3 SW 8433
St. Mawgan 3 SW 8765
St. Mellion 4 SX 3865
St. Mellons 28 ST 2281
St. Merryn 3 SW 8874
St. Mewan 3 SW 9951
St. Michael Caerhays 3 SW 9642
St. Michael Penkevil 2 SW 8542
St. Michael South Elmham 47 TM 3483
St. Michaels (Here & W) 31 SO 5765
St. Michaels (Kent) 14 TQ 8835
St. Michaels on Wyre 57 SD 4640
St. Minver 3 SW 9677
St. Monans 93 NO 5201
St. Neot (Corn) 4 SX 1867
St. Neots (Cambs.) 35 TL 1860
St. Nicholas (Dyfed) 24 SM 9035
St. Nicholas (S Glam.) 28 ST 0874
St. Nicholas at Wade 15 TR 2666
St. Ninians 91 NS 7991
St. Osyth 23 TM 1215
St. Owens Cross 29 SO 5324
St. Paul's Walden 35 TL 1922
St. Pauls Cray 21 TQ 4768
St. Peter's 15 TR 3668
St. Petrox 24 SR 9797
St. Pinnock 4 SX 2063
St. Quivox 75 NS 3723
St. Stephen (Corn.) 3 SW 9453
St. Stephens (Corn.) 4 SX 3285
St. Stephens (Corn.) 4 SX 4158
St. Teath 4 SX 0680
St. Tudy 3 SX 0676
St. Vigeans 99 NO 6443
St. Wenn 3 SW 9664
St. Weonards 29 SO 4924
Stackhouse 65 SD 8165
Stacksteads 58 SD 8421
Staddiscombe 5 SX 5151
Staddlethorpe 60 SE 8428
Stadhampton 19 SU 6098
Staffield 71 NY 5442
Staffin 100 NG 4967
Stafford 41 SJ 9223
Stagsden 34 SP 9849
Stainburn (N. Yorks) 59 SE 2448
Stainby 44 SK 9022
Staincross 59 SE 3210
Staindrop 72 NZ 1220
Staines 20 TQ 0471
Stainfield (Lincs.) 45 TF 0724
Stainfield (Lincs.) 55 TF 1173
Stainforth (N Yorks.) 65 SD 8267
Stainforth (S Yorks.) 60 SE 6411
Staining 57 SD 3435
Stainland 59 SE 0719
Stainsacre 67 NZ 9108
Stainton (Cleve.) 73 NZ 4714
Stainton (Cumbr.) 63 NY 4827
Stainton (Cumbr.) 63 SD 5285
Stainton (Durham) 72 NZ 0718
Stainton (N Yorks.) 65 SE 1096
Stainton (S Yorks.) 53 SK 5593
Stainton by Langworth 54 TF 0577
Stainton le Vale 55 TF 1794
Stainton with Adgarley 64 SD 2472
Staintondale 67 SE 9898
Stair (Cumbr.) 62 NY 2321
Stair (Strath.) 75 NS 4323
Staithes 73 NZ 7818
Stake Pool 57 SD 4148
Stalbridge 9 ST 7317
Stalbridge Weston 9 ST 7216
Stalham 47 TG 3725
Stalham Green 47 TG 3824
Stalisfield Green 15 TQ 9652
Stalling Busk 65 SD 9185
Stallingborough 61 TA 2011
Stalmine 57 SD 3745
Stalybridge 58 SJ 9698
Stambourne 36 TL 7238
Stamford (Lincs) 44 TF 0207
Stamford Bridge (Humbs.) 66 SE 7155
Stamfordham 79 NZ 0772
Stanborough 35 TL 2210
Stanbridge (Beds.) 34 SP 9623
Stanbridge (Dorset) 10 SU 0003
Stand 84 NS 7668
Standburn 84 NS 9274
Standeford 41 SJ 9107
Standen 14 TQ 8540
Standford 12 SU 8134
Standish (Glos.) 57 SD 5609
Standlake 33 SP 3902
Standon (Hants.) 11 SU 4227
Standon (Herts.) 35 TL 3922
Standon (Staffs.) 51 SJ 8134
Stane 84 NS 8859
Stanfield 46 TF 9320
Stanford (Beds.) 35 TL 1641
Stanford (Kent) 15 TR 1238
Stanford Bishop 31 SO 6851
Stanford Bridge 32 SO 7165
Stanford Dingley 19 SU 5771
Stanford Rivers 22 TL 5301
Stanford in the Vale 19 SU 3493
Stanford le Hope 22 TQ 6882
Stanford on Avon 43 SP 5878
Stanford on Soar 43 SK 5422
Stanford on Teme 37 SO 7065
Stanghow 73 NZ 6715
Stanhoe 46 TF 8036
Stanhope 72 NY 9939
Stanhope 85 NT 1230
Stanion 44 SP 9187
Stanley (Derby.) 53 SK 4140
Stanley (Durham) 72 NZ 1953
Stanley (Staffs.) 51 SJ 9252
Stanley (Tays.) 92 NO 1033
Stanley (W Yorks.) 59 SE 3422
Stanmer 13 TQ 3309
Stanmore (Berks.) 19 SU 4778
Stanmore (Gtr London) 21 TQ 1692
Stannington (Northum.) 79 NZ 2179
Stannington (S Yorks.) 53 SK 2988
Stansbatch 30 SO 3461
Stansfield 36 TL 7852
Stanstead 36 TL 8449
Stanstead Abbots 35 TL 3811
Stansted 14 TQ 6062
Stansted Mountfitchet 22 TL 5124
Stanton (Glos.) 32 SP 0634
Stanton (Northum.) 79 NZ 1390
Stanton (Staffs.) 52 SK 1246
Stanton (Suff.) 36 TL 9673
Stanton Drew 17 ST 5963
Stanton Fitzwarren 18 SU 1790
Stanton Harcourt 33 SP 4105
Stanton Hill 53 SK 4860
Stanton Lacy 40 SO 4978
Stanton Long 41 SO 5690
Stanton Prior 17 ST 6762
Stanton St. Bernard 18 SU 0962
Stanton St. John 33 SP 5709
Stanton St. Quintin 18 ST 9079
Stanton Street 36 TL 9566
Stanton Wick 17 ST 6162
Stanton by Bridge 43 SK 3627
Stanton by Dale 53 SK 4637
Stanton in Peak 53 SK 2464
Stanton on the Wolds 53 SK 6330
Stanton under Bardon 43 SK 4010
Stanton upon Hine Heath 41 SJ 5624
Stanwardine in the Fields 40 SJ 4124
Stanway (Essex) 23 TL 9324
Stanway (Glos.) 32 SP 0532
Stanwell 20 TQ 0574
Stanwell Moor 20 TQ 0474
Stanwick 44 SP 9871
Stape 67 SE 7993
Stapehill 10 SU 0500
Stapeley 51 SJ 6749
Staple 15 TR 2756
Staple Cross (E. Susx.) 14 TQ 7822
Staple Fitzpaine 8 ST 2618
Staplefield 13 TQ 2728
Stapleford (Cambs.) 35 TL 4751
Stapleford (Herts.) 35 TL 3117
Stapleford (Leic.) 44 SK 8118
Stapleford (Lincs.) 54 SK 8757
Stapleford (Notts.) 53 SK 4837
Stapleford (Wilts.) 10 SU 0637
Stapleford Abbotts 21 TQ 5096
Stapleford Tawney 21 TQ 5098
Staplegrove 16 ST 2126
Staplehurst 14 TQ 7843
Staplers 11 SZ 5189
Stapleton (Avon) 17 ST 6175
Stapleton (Cumbr.) 71 NY 5071
Stapleton (Here & W) 30 SO 3265
Stapleton (Leic.) 43 SP 4398
Stapleton (N Yorks.) 72 NZ 2612
Stapleton (Salop) 40 SJ 4604
Stapleton (Somer.) 9 ST 4621
Stapley 8 ST 1813
Staploe 35 TL 1460
Star (Dyfed) 26 SN 2435
Star (Fife.) 93 NO 3103
Star (Somer.) 17 ST 4358
Starbotton 65 SD 9574
Starcross 8 SX 9781
Starston 47 TM 2384
Startforth 72 NZ 0416
Startley 18 ST 9482
Stathe 17 ST 3728
Stathern 54 SK 7731
Station Town 72 NZ 4036
Staughton Highway 35 TL 1364
Staunton (Glos.) 29 SO 5412
Staunton (Glos.) 32 SO 7929
Staunton on Arrow 30 SO 3660
Staunton on Wye 30 SO 3645
Staveley (Cumbr.) 62 SD 3786
Staveley (Cumbr.) 63 SD 4698
Staveley (Derby.) 53 SK 4374
Staveley (N Yorks.) 66 SE 3662
Staverton (Devon.) 5 SX 7964
Staverton (Glos.) 32 SO 9823
Staverton (Northants.) 33 SP 5461
Staverton (Wilts.) 17 ST 8560
Stawell 17 ST 3638
Staxigoe 112 ND 3852
Staxton 67 TA 0179
Staylittle 39 SN 8892
Staythorpe 54 SK 7554
Stean 65 SE 0873
Stearsby 66 SE 6171
Steart 17 ST 2745
Stebbing 22 TL 6624
Stedham 12 SU 8622
Steele Road 78 NY 5292
Steen's Bridge 31 SO 5457
Steep 12 SU 7525
Steeple (Dorset) 10 SY 9080
Steeple (Essex) 23 TL 9303
Steeple Ashton 18 ST 9056
Steeple Aston 33 SP 4725
Steeple Barton 33 SP 4424
Steeple Bumpstead 36 TL 6741
Steeple Claydon 34 SP 7027
Steeple Gidding 45 TL 1381
Steeple Langford 10 SU 0337
Steeple Morden 35 TL 2842
Steeton 59 SE 0344
Steinmanhill 105 NJ 7642
Stelling Minnis 15 TR 1446
Stenalees 4 SX 0157
Stenhousemuir 84 NS 8682
Stenness 113 HU 2176
Stenton 86 NT 6274
Steppingley 35 TL 0135
Stepps 84 NS 6668
Sternfield 37 TM 3861
Stert 18 SU 0259
Stetchworth 36 TL 6458
Stevenage 35 TL 2325
Stevenston 82 NS 2642
Steventon (Hants.) 19 SU 5547
Steventon (Oxon.) 19 SU 4691
Stevington 34 SP 9853
Stewartby 35 TL 0242
Stewarton (Strath.) 82 NS 4246
Stewton 55 TF 3687
Steyning 12 TQ 1711
Steynton 24 SM 9108
Stibb 6 SS 2210
Stibb Cross 6 SS 4314
Stibb Green 18 SU 2262
Stibbard 46 TF 9828
Stibbington 45 TL 0898
Stichill 86 NT 7138
Sticker 3 SW 9750
Stickford 55 TF 3560
Sticklepath (Devon) 5 SX 6394
Stickney 55 TF 3456
Stiffkey 46 TF 9743
Stifford's Bridge 32 SO 7348
Stillingarry 109 NF 7638
Stillingfleet 60 SE 5940
Stillington (Cleve.) 72 NZ 3723
Stillington (N Yorks.) 66 SE 5867
Stilton 45 TL 1689
Stinchcombe 29 ST 7298
Stinsford 9 SY 7191
Stirchley 41 SJ 6906
Stirling (Central) 91 NS 7993
Stisted 22 TL 8024
Stithians 2 SW 7336
Stivichall 43 SP 3376
Stixwould 55 TF 1765
Stoak 50 SJ 4273
Stobo 85 NT 1837
Stoborough 10 SY 9286
Stoborough Green 10 SY 9184
Stock (Essex) 22 TQ 6998
Stock Green 32 SO 9859
Stock Wood 32 SP 0058
Stockbridge (Hants.) 11 SU 3535
Stockbriggs 84 NS 7936
Stockbury 14 TQ 8461
Stockcross 19 SU 4368
Stockdalewath 70 NY 3845
Stockerston 44 SP 8397
Stocking Pelham 35 TL 4529
Stockingford 43 SP 3391
Stockland 8 ST 2404
Stockland Bristol 16 ST 2443
Stockleigh English 7 SS 8406
Stockleigh Pomeroy 7 SS 8703
Stockley 18 SU 0067
Stockport 51 SJ 8989
Stocksbridge 59 SK 2798
Stocksfield 72 NZ 0561
Stockton (Here & W) 30 SO 5161
Stockton (Norf.) 47 TM 3894
Stockton (Salop) 41 SO 7299
Stockton (Warw.) 33 SP 4363
Stockton (Wilts.) 10 ST 9738
Stockton Heath 51 SJ 6185
Stockton on Teme 41 SO 7167
Stockton on the Forest 66 SE 6556
Stockton-on-Tees 72 NZ 4419
Stockwith 54 SK 7994
Stodmarsh 15 TR 2160
Stody 41 TG 0535
Stoer 110 NC 0428
Stoford (Somer.) 9 ST 5613
Stoford (Wilts.) 10 SU 0835
Stogumber 16 ST 0937
Stogursey 16 ST 2042
Stoke (Devon.) 6 SS 2324
Stoke (Hants.) 19 SU 4051
Stoke (Hants.) 12 SU 7202
Stoke (Kent) 22 TQ 8275
Stoke Abbott 9 ST 4500
Stoke Albany 44 SP 8088
Stoke Ash 37 TM 1170
Stoke Bardolph 53 SK 6441
Stoke Bliss 31 SO 6562
Stoke Bruerne 34 SP 7450
Stoke Canon 8 SX 9397
Stoke Charity 11 SU 4839
Stoke Climsland 4 SX 3574
Stoke D'Abernon 20 TQ 1260
Stoke Doyle 44 TL 0286
Stoke Dry 44 SP 8597
Stoke Ferry 46 TF 7000
Stoke Fleming 5 SX 8648
Stoke Gabriel 5 SX 8457
Stoke Gifford 29 ST 6280
Stoke Golding 43 SP 3997
Stoke Goldington 34 SP 8348
Stoke Hammond 34 SP 8829
Stoke Holy Cross 47 TG 2301
Stoke Lacy 31 SO 6149
Stoke Lyne 33 SP 5628
Stoke Mandeville 34 SP 8310
Stoke Newington 21 TQ 3286
Stoke Orchard 32 SO 9128
Stoke Poges 20 SU 9884
Stoke Prior (Here & W) 30 SO 5256
Stoke Prior (Here & W) 41 SO 9467
Stoke Rivers 6 SS 6335
Stoke Rochford 44 SK 9127
Stoke Row 19 SU 6883
Stoke St. Gregory 17 ST 3426
Stoke St. Mary 8 ST 2622
Stoke St. Michael 17 ST 6646
Stoke St. Milborough 40 SO 5682
Stoke Talmage 19 SU 6799
Stoke Trister 17 ST 7328
Stoke by Clare 36 TL 7443
Stoke sub Hamdon 9 ST 4717
Stoke upon Tern 41 SJ 6327
Stoke-by-Nayland 36 TL 9836
Stoke-on-Trent 51 SJ 8745
Stokeford 10 SY 8787
Stokeham 54 SK 7876
Stokeinteignhead 8 SX 9170
Stokenchurch 20 SU 7596
Stokenham 5 SX 8042
Stokesay 40 SO 4381
Stokesby 47 TG 4310
Stokesley 66 NZ 5208
Stolford 16 ST 2245
Ston Easton 17 ST 6253
Stondon Massey 22 TL 5800
Stone (Bucks.) 34 SP 7812
Stone (Glos.) 29 ST 6895
Stone (Here & W) 41 SO 8675
Stone (Kent) 21 TQ 5774
Stone (Kent) 15 TQ 9427
Stone (Staffs.) 51 SJ 9034
Stone Allerton 17 ST 3950
Stone Cross 13 TQ 6104
Stone House (Cumbr.) 65 SD 7785
Stonebroom 53 SK 4159
Stonegate 13 TQ 6628
Stonegate Crofts 105 NK 0339
Stonegrave 66 SE 6577
Stonehaugh 78 NY 7976
Stonehaven 99 NO 8685
Stonehouse (Glos.) 32 SO 8005
Stonehouse (Northum.) 71 NY 6958
Stonehouse (Strath.) 76 NS 7546
Stoneleigh 43 SP 3272
Stonely 45 TL 1067
Stones Green 23 TM 1626
Stonesby 44 SK 8224
Stonesfield 33 SP 3917
Stoney Cross 11 SU 2511
Stoney Middleton 53 SK 2275
Stoney Stanton 43 SP 4894
Stoney Stratton 17 ST 6539
Stoney Stretton 40 SJ 3809
Stoneybridge 109 NF 7433
Stoneyburn 85 NS 9762
Stoneygate 43 SK 6102
Stoneyhills 23 TQ 9497
Stoneykirk 68 NX 0853
Stoneywood 105 NJ 8910
Stonham Aspal 37 TM 1359
Stonnall 42 SK 0603
Stonor 20 SU 7388
Stonton Wyville 44 SP 7395
Stony Stratford 34 SP 7840
Stoodleigh 8 SS 9218
Stopham 12 TQ 0219
Stopsley 35 TL 1023
Storeton 50 SJ 3084
Stornoway 109 NB 4333
Storridge 32 SO 7448
Storrington 12 TQ 0814
Storth 63 SD 4780
Stotfold 35 TL 2136
Stottesdon 41 SO 6782
Stoughton (Leic.) 43 SK 6402
Stoughton (Surrey) 20 SU 9851
Stoughton (W Susx) 12 SU 8011
Stoulton 32 SO 9049
Stour Provost 10 ST 7921
Stour Row 10 ST 8220
Stourbridge 41 SO 8984
Stourpaine 10 ST 8509
Stourport-on-Severn 41 SO 8171
Stourton (Here & W) 41 SO 8585
Stourton (Warw.) 33 SP 2936
Stourton (Wilts.) 17 ST 7733
Stourton Caundle 9 ST 7114
Stoven 47 TM 4481
Stow (Borders) 86 NT 4644
Stow (Lincs.) 54 SK 8781
Stow Bardolph 46 TF 6205
Stow Bedon 46 TL 9596
Stow Longa 45 TL 1171
Stow Maries 22 TQ 8399
Stow cum Quy 35 TL 5260
Stow-on-the-Wold 33 SP 1925
Stowbridge 46 TF 6007
Stowe (Salop) 40 SO 3173
Stowe (Staffs.) 42 SK 0027
Stowell 9 ST 6822
Stowford (Devon) 4 SX 4386
Stowlangtoft 36 TL 9568
Stowmarket 37 TM 0458
Stowting 15 TR 1241
Stowupland 37 TM 0659
Straad 81 NS 0462
Strachan 99 NO 6792
Strachur 89 NN 0901
Stradbroke 37 TM 2373
Stradishall 36 TL 7452
Stradsett 46 TF 6605
Stragglethorpe (Lincs.) 54 SK 9152
Straiton (Lothian) 85 NT 2766
Straiton (Strath.) 75 NS 3804
Straloch (Grampn.) 105 NJ 8621
Straloch (Tays.) 98 NO 0463
Stramshall 52 SK 0735
Stranraer 68 NX 0660
Strata Florida 27 SN 7465
Stratfield Mortimer 19 SU 6764
Stratfield Saye 19 SU 6961
Stratfield Turgis 19 SU 6959
Stratford St. Andrew 37 TM 3560
Stratford St. Mary 37 TM 0434
Stratford Tony 10 SU 0926
Stratford-upon-Avon 33 SP 2055
Strath 112 ND 2753
Strath Gairloch 106 NG 7977
Strathan (Highld.) 110 NC 0821
Strathaven 84 NS 7044
Strathblane (Central) 84 NS 5679
Strathcarron (Highld.) 101 NG 9442
Strathdon 104 NJ 3513
Strathkanaird (Highld.) 106 NC 1501
Strathkinness 93 NO 4516
Strathmiglo 92 NO 2109
Strathmore Lodge 113 ND 1048
Strathpeffer 102 NH 4858
Strathwhillan 81 NS 0235
Strathy 111 NC 8465
Strathyre 90 NN 5617
Stratton (Corn.) 6 SS 2306
Stratton (Dorset) 9 SY 6593
Stratton (Glos.) 32 SP 0103
Stratton Audley 34 SP 6026
Stratton St. Margaret 18 SU 1787
Stratton St. Michael 47 TM 2093
Stratton Strawless 47 TG 2220
Stratton-on-the-Fosse 17 ST 6550
Stravithie 93 NO 5311
Streat 13 TQ 3515
Streatham 21 TQ 2972
Streatley (Beds.) 35 TL 0728
Streatley (Berks.) 19 SU 5980
Street (Lancs.) 64 SD 5252
Street (Somer.) 17 ST 4836
Street End (W. Susx.) 12 SZ 8599
Streethay 42 SK 1410
Streetly 42 SP 0898
Strefford 40 SO 4485
Strensall 66 SE 6360
Strensham 32 SO 9040
Stretcholt 17 ST 2943
Strete 5 SX 8447
Stretford 51 SJ 7894
Stretford Court 30 SO 4455
Strethall 35 TL 4840
Stretham 45 TL 5174
Strettington 12 SU 8807
Stretton (Ches.) 50 SJ 4452
Stretton (Ches.) 51 SJ 6182
Stretton (Derby.) 53 SK 3961
Stretton (Leic.) 44 SK 9415
Stretton (Staffs.) 41 SJ 8811
Stretton (Staffs.) 42 SK 2526
Stretton Grandison 31 SO 6344
Stretton Heath 40 SJ 3610
Stretton Westwood 41 SO 5998
Stretton en le Field 43 SK 3012
Stretton on Fosse 33 SP 2238
Stretton under Fosse 43 SP 4581
Stretton-on-Dunsmore 43 SP 4072
Strichen 105 NJ 9455
Stringston 16 ST 1742
Strixton 34 SP 9061
Stroat 29 ST 5798
Stromeferry 101 NG 8634
Stromness (Orkney) 113 HY 2509
Stronachlachar 90 NN 4010
Strone (Highld.) 96 NN 1582
Strone (Strath.) 96 NS 1985
Stronenaba 96 NN 2084
Stronmilchan 89 NN 1528
Strontian 95 NM 8161
Strood 14 TQ 7369
Stroud (Glos.) 32 SO 8504
Stroud (Hants.) 12 SU 7223
Struan (Highld.) 100 NG 3438
Strubby 55 TF 4582
Strumpshaw 47 TG 3507
Strutherhill 84 NS 7650
Struy 102 NH 4039
Stuartfield 105 NJ 9745

Stubbington 252 Tilney St. Lawrence

Stubbington 11 SU 5503
Stubbins 58 SD 7918
Stubhampton 10 ST 9113
Stubton 54 SK 8748
Stuckton 10 SU 1613
Studham 34 TL 0215
Studland 10 SZ 0382
Studley (Oxen.) 34 SP 6012
Studley (Warw.) 32 SP 0763
Studley (Wilts.) 18 ST 9671
Studley Roger 66 SE 2970
Stump Cross 35 TL 5044
Stuntney 36 TL 5578
Sturbridge 51 SJ 8330
Sturmer 36 TL 6944
Sturminster Common 10 ST 7812
Sturminster Marshall 10 SY 9499
Sturminster Newton 10 ST 7813
Sturry 15 TR 1760
Sturton by Stow 54 SK 8980
Sturton le Steeple 54 SK 7884
Stuston 37 TM 1378
Stutton (N Yorks.) 60 SE 4741
Stutton (Suff.) 37 TM 1434
Stwekley 34 SP 8525
Styal 51 SJ 8383
Suckley 32 SO 7151
Sudborough 44 SP 9682
Sudbourne 37 TM 4153
Sudbrook (Gwent) 29 ST 5087
Sudbrooke 54 TF 0276
Sudbury (Derby.) 52 SK 1631
Sudbury (Suff.) 36 TL 8741
Suddie 103 NH 6654
Sudgrove 32 SO 9307
Suffield (Norf.) 47 TG 2332
Sugnall 41 SJ 7930
Sulby 56 SC 3994
Sulgrave 33 SP 5545
Sulham 19 SU 6474
Sulhamstead 19 SU 6368
Sullington 12 TQ 0913
Sullom 113 HU 3573
Sully 28 ST 1568
Summerbridge 65 SE 1962
Summercourt 3 SW 8856
Summerleaze 29 ST 4284
Summerseat 58 SD 7914
Summit 58 SD 9418
Sunadale 81 NR 8145
Sunbury 20 TQ 1069
Sunderland (Cumbr.) 62 NY 1735
Sunderland (Tyne and Wear) 72 NZ 3957
Sunderland Bridge 72 NZ 2637
Sundhope 77 NT 3324
Sundon Park 35 TL 0525
Sundridge 21 TQ 4854
Sunk Island 61 TA 2619
Sunningdale 20 SU 9567
Sunninghill 20 SU 9367
Sunningwell 33 SP 4900
Sunniside (Durham) 72 NZ 1438
Sunniside (Tyne and Wear) 72 NZ 2159
Sunny Bank 62 SD 2992
Sunnylaw 91 NS 7998
Sunnyside 13 TQ 3937
Surbiton 21 TQ 1867
Surfleet 45 TF 2528
Surfleet Seas End 45 TF 2628
Surlingham 47 TG 3106
Surrigarth 113 HY 4945
Sustead 47 TG 1837
Susworth 60 SE 8302
Sutcombe 6 SS 3411
Sutterton 55 TF 2835
Sutton (Beds.) 35 TL 2247
Sutton (Cambs.) 45 TL 4479
Sutton (Gtr London) 21 TQ 2463
Sutton (Kent) 15 TR 3349
Sutton (Norf.) 47 TG 3823
Sutton (Notts.) 53 SK 6784
Sutton (Notts.) 54 SK 7637
Sutton (Oxon.) 33 SP 4106
Sutton (Salop) 51 SJ 6631
Sutton (Salop) 40 SO 5082
Sutton (Salop) 41 SO 7286
Sutton (Staffs.) 41 SJ 7622
Sutton (Suff.) 37 TM 3046
Sutton (Surrey) 20 TQ 1046
Sutton (W Susx) 12 SU 9715
Sutton Bassett 44 SP 7790
Sutton Benger 18 ST 9478
Sutton Bonington 43 SK 5025
Sutton Bridge 45 TF 4821
Sutton Cheney 43 SK 4100
Sutton Coldfield 42 SP 1296
Sutton Courtenay 19 SU 5093
Sutton Crosses 45 TF 4321
Sutton Grange 66 SE 2874
Sutton Howgrave 66 SE 3179
Sutton Lane Ends 51 SJ 9270
Sutton Maddock 41 SJ 7201
Sutton Mallet 17 ST 3736
Sutton Mandeville 10 ST 9828
Sutton Montis 9 ST 6224
Sutton Scotney 11 SU 4539
Sutton St. Edmund 45 TF 3613
Sutton St. James 45 TF 3918
Sutton St. Nicholas 31 SO 5345
Sutton Valence 14 TQ 8148
Sutton Veny 18 ST 9041
Sutton Waldron 10 ST 8615
Sutton Weaver 50 SJ 5479
Sutton at Hone 21 TQ 5570
Sutton in Ashfield 53 SK 5058
Sutton on Sea 55 TF 5282
Sutton on Trent 54 SK 7965
Sutton on the Hill 53 SK 2333
Sutton upon Derwent 60 SE 7046
Sutton-in-Craven 59 SE 0044
Sutton-on-Hull 61 TA 1132
Sutton-on-the-Forest 66 SE 5864
Sutton-under-Brailes 33 SP 2937
Sutton-under-Whitestonecliffe 66 SE 4882
Swaby 55 TF 3877
Swadlincote 43 SK 3019
Swaffham 46 TF 8109
Swaffham Bulbeck 36 TL 5562
Swaffham Prior 36 TL 5764
Swafield 47 TG 2832
Swainby 66 NZ 4701
Swainsthorpe 47 TG 2101
Swainswick 29 ST 7568
Swalcliffe 33 SP 3738
Swalecliffe 15 TR 1367
Swallow 61 TA 1703
Swallowcliffe 10 ST 9626
Swallowfield 20 SU 7264
Swanage 10 SZ 0278
Swanbourne 34 SP 8027
Swanland 61 SE 9927
Swanley 21 TQ 5168
Swanmore 11 SU 5815
Swannington (Leic.) 43 SK 4116
Swannington (Norf.) 47 TG 1319
Swanscombe 21 TQ 6074
Swansea 25 SS 6593
Swanton Abbot 47 TG 2625
Swanton Morley 46 TG 0117
Swanton Novers 46 TG 0132
Swanwick (Derby.) 53 SK 4053
Swanwick (Hants.) 11 SU 5109
Swarby 54 TF 0440
Swardeston 47 TG 2002
Swarkestone 43 SK 3728
Swarland 79 NU 1601
Swarland Estate 79 NU 1603
Swaton 55 TF 1337
Swavesey 45 TL 3668
Sway 11 SZ 2798
Swayfield 44 SK 9822
Swaythling 11 SU 4315
Swefling 37 TM 3463
Swepstone 43 SK 3610
Swerford 33 SP 3731
Swettenham 51 SJ 8067
Swilland 37 TM 1853
Swillington 59 SE 3830
Swimbridge 6 SS 6230
Swinbrook 33 SP 2812
Swinderby 54 SK 8662
Swindon (Glos.) 32 SO 9325
Swindon (Staffs.) 41 SO 8690
Swindon (Wilts.) 18 SU 1484
Swine 61 TA 1335
Swinefleet 60 SE 7621
Swineshead (Beds.) 45 TL 0565
Swineshead Bridge 55 TF 2142
Swiney 112 ND 2335
Swinford (Leic.) 43 SP 5679
Swinford (Oxon.) 33 SP 4408
Swingfield Minnis 15 TR 2142
Swinhill 84 NS 7748
Swinhoe 87 NU 2028
Swinhope 55 TF 2196
Swinithwaite 65 SE 0489
Swinscoe 52 SK 1347
Swinstead 44 TF 0122
Swinton (Borders) 87 NT 8447
Swinton (Gtr Mches.) 58 SD 7701
Swinton (N Yorks.) 65 SE 2179
Swinton (N Yorks.) 67 SE 7573
Swinton (S Yorks.) 60 SK 4499
Swintonmill 87 NT 8145
Swithland 43 SK 5413
Swordale 102 NH 5765
Swordly 111 NC 7363
Sworton Heath 51 SJ 6884
Swyddffynnon 27 SN 6966
Swynnerton 51 SJ 8435
Swyre 9 SY 5288
Syde 32 SO 9411
Sydenham (Gtr London) 21 TQ 3571
Sydenham (Oxon.) 34 SP 7301
Sydenham Damerel 4 SX 4075
Syderstone 46 TF 8332
Sydling St. Nicholas 9 SY 6399
Sydmonton 19 SU 4857
Syerston 54 SK 7447
Syke 58 SD 8915
Sykehouse 60 SE 6216
Sylen 25 SN 5107
Symbister 113 HU 5362
Symington (Strath.) 82 NS 3831
Symington (Strath.) 85 NS 9935
Symonds Yat 29 SO 5516
Symondsbury 9 SY 4493
Synod Inn 26 SN 4054
Syre 111 NC 6843
Syreford 32 SP 0320
Syresham 34 SP 6241
Syston (Leic.) 43 SK 6211
Syston (Lincs.) 54 SK 9240
Sytchampton 32 SO 8466
Sywell 44 SP 8267

T

Tackley 33 SP 4720
Tacolneston 47 TM 1395
Tadcaster 60 SE 4843
Tadden 10 ST 9801
Taddington (Derby) 52 SK 1471
Taddington (Glos.) 32 SP 0831
Tadley 19 SU 6060
Tadlow 35 TL 2847
Tadmarton 33 SP 3937
Tadworth 21 TQ 2356
Tafarn-y-Gelyn 50 SJ 1861
Tafarnaubach 28 SO 1110
Taff's Well 28 ST 1283
Tafolwern 39 SH 8902
Tai'n-lon 48 SH 4450
Tai'r Bull 28 SN 9926
Tai-bach (Clwyd) 40 SJ 1528
Taibach (W Glam.) 28 SS 7789
Tain (Highld.) 112 ND 2266
Tain (Highld.) 108 NH 7782
Takeley 22 TL 5521
Tal-y-Bont (Gwyn.) 49 SH 7668
Tal-y-bont (Gwyn.) 38 SH 5921
Tal-y-cafn 49 SH 7971
Tal-y-llyn (Gwyn.) 39 SH 7109
Talachddu 27 SO 0733
Talacre 50 SJ 1284
Talaton 8 SY 0699
Talbenny 24 SM 8412
Talerddig 39 SH 9300
Talgarreg 26 SN 4251
Talgarth 30 SO 1534
Taliesin 39 SN 6591
Talisker 100 NG 3230
Talke 51 SJ 8253
Talkin 71 NY 5557
Talladale 106 NG 9270
Tallentire 62 NY 1035
Talley 27 SN 6332
Tallington 45 TF 0908
Talmine 111 NC 5862
Talog 25 SN 3325
Talsarn 26 SN 5456
Talsarnau 48 SH 6135
Talskiddy 3 SW 9165
Talwrn 48 SH 4876
Talybont (Dyfed) 39 SN 6589
Talybont-on-Usk 28 SO 1122
Talysarn 48 SH 4852
Talywern 39 SH 8200
Tamerton Foliot 5 SX 4761
Tamworth 42 SK 2004
Tan-y-fron 49 SH 9564
Tan-y-groes 26 SN 2849
Tandridge 21 TQ 3750
Tanfield 72 NZ 1855
Tangley 19 SU 3352
Tangmere 12 SU 9006
Tankersley 59 SK 3499
Tannach 112 ND 3247
Tannadice 99 NO 4758
Tannington 37 TM 2467
Tansley 53 SK 3259
Tansor 45 TL 0590
Tantobie 72 NZ 1754
Tanton 73 NZ 5210
Tanworth in Arden 42 SP 1170
Tanygrisiau 49 SH 6845
Taplow 20 SU 9182
Tarbert (Harris) 109 NB 1500
Tarbert (Jura) 88 NR 6082
Tarbert (Strath.) 81 NR 8668
Tarbet (Highld.) 110 NC 1648
Tarbet (Highld.) 95 NM 7992
Tarbet (Strath.) 90 NN 3104
Tarbock Green 50 SJ 4687
Tarbolton 75 NS 4327
Tarbrax 85 NT 0255
Tardebigge 41 SO 9969
Tarfside 99 NO 4979
Tarland 99 NJ 4804
Tarleton 57 SD 4420
Tarlscough 57 SD 4313
Tarlton 18 ST 9599
Tarnbrook 64 SD 5855
Tarporley 50 SJ 5562
Tarr 16 ST 1030
Tarrant Crawford 10 ST 9203
Tarrant Gunville 10 ST 9212
Tarrant Hinton 10 ST 9310
Tarrant Keynston 10 ST 9204
Tarrant Launceston 10 ST 9409
Tarrant Monkton 10 ST 9408
Tarrant Rawston 10 ST 9306
Tarrant Rushton 10 ST 9305
Tarring Neville 13 TQ 4404
Tarrington 31 SO 6140
Tarsappie 92 NO 1220
Tarskavaig 100 NG 5810
Tarves 105 NJ 8631
Tarvin 50 SJ 4867
Tasburgh 47 TM 2096
Tasley 41 SO 6994
Taston 33 SP 3521
Tatenhill 42 SK 2022
Tathwell 55 TF 3282
Tatsfield 21 TQ 4156
Tattenhall 50 SJ 4858
Tatterford 46 TF 8628
Tattersett 46 TF 8429
Tattershall 55 TF 2157
Tattershall Bridge 55 TF 1956
Tattershall Thorpe 55 TF 2159
Tattingstone 37 TM 1337
Taunton 8 ST 2324
Taverham 47 TG 1513
Tavernspite 24 SN 1812
Tavistock 5 SX 4774
Taw green 7 SX 6497
Tawstock 6 SS 5529
Taxal 52 SK 0079
Tayinloan 81 NR 6945
Taynton (Glos.) 32 SO 7221
Taynton (Oxon.) 33 SP 2313
Taynuilt 89 NN 0031
Tayport 93 NO 4528
Tayvallich 89 NR 7386
Tealby 55 TF 1590
Teangue 101 NG 6609
Tebay 63 NY 6104
Tebworth 34 SP 9926
Tedburn St. Mary 5 SX 8194
Teddington (Glos.) 32 SO 9632
Teddington (Gtr London) 21 TQ 1671
Tedstone Delamere 31 SO 6958
Tedstone Wafre 31 SO 6759
Teeton 43 SP 6970
Teffont Evias 10 ST 9831
Teffont Magna 10 ST 9832
Tegryn 26 SN 2233
Teigh 44 SK 8616
Teigngrace 5 SX 8474
Teignmouth 8 SX 9473
Telford 41 SJ 6909
Tellisford 18 ST 8055
Telscombe 13 TQ 4003
Templand 70 NY 0886
Temple (Corn.) 4 SX 1473
Temple (Lothian) 85 NT 3158
Temple (Strath.) 84 NS 5469
Temple Bar 26 SN 5354
Temple Cloud 17 ST 6157
Temple Ewell 15 TR 2844
Temple Grafton 32 SP 1254
Temple Guiting 32 SP 0928
Temple Hirst 60 SE 6025
Temple Normanton 53 SK 4167
Temple Sowerby 63 NY 6127
Templecombe 9 ST 7022
Templeton (Devon.) 7 SS 8813
Templeton (Dyfed) 24 SN 1111
Tempsford 35 TL 1653
Ten Mile Bank 46 TL 6097
Tenbury Wells 41 SO 5968
Tenby 24 SN 1300
Tendring 23 TM 1424
Tenterden 14 TQ 8833
Terling 22 TL 7715
Ternhill 51 SJ 6332
Terrington 66 SE 6670
Terrington St. Clement 45 TF 5520
Terrington St. John 45 TF 5416
Teston 14 TQ 7053
Testwood 11 SU 3514
Tetbury 18 ST 8993
Tetbury Upton 18 ST 8795
Tetchill 50 SJ 3832
Tetcott 6 SX 3396
Tetford 55 TF 3374
Tetney 61 TA 3101
Tetney Lock 61 TA 3402
Tetsworth 34 SP 6802
Teversal 53 SK 4861
Teversham 35 TL 4958
Teviothead 77 NT 4005
Tewin 35 TL 2714
Tewkesbury 32 SO 8933
Teynham 15 TQ 9663
Thakeham 12 TQ 1017
Thame 34 SP 7006
Thames Ditton 21 TQ 1567
Thames Haven 22 TQ 7581
Thamesmead 21 TQ 4779
Thaneston 99 NO 6375
Thanington 15 TR 1356
Thankerton 85 NS 9737
Tharston 47 TM 1894
Thatcham 19 SU 5167
Thatto Heath 50 SJ 5093
Thaxted 36 TL 6131
The City 20 SU 7896
Theakston 66 SE 3085
Thealby 60 SE 8917
Theale (Berks.) 19 SU 6371
Theale (Somer.) 17 ST 4646
Thearne 61 TA 0736
Theberton 37 TM 4365
Theddingworth 43 SP 6685
Theddlethorpe All Saints 55 TF 4688
Theddlethorpe St. Helen 55 TF 4788
Thelbridge Barton 7 SS 7812
Thelnetham 36 TM 0178
Thelwall 51 SJ 6587
Themelthorpe 47 TG 0524
Thenford 33 SP 5141
Therfield 35 TL 3337
Thetford 46 TL 8783
Theydon Bois 21 TQ 4598
Thickwood 18 ST 8272
Thimbleby (Linc.) 55 TF 2369
Thimbleby (N Yorks.) 66 SE 4495
Thirkleby 66 SE 4778
Thirlby 66 SE 4884
Thirlestane 86 NT 5647
Thirn 65 SE 2185
Thirsk 66 SE 4282
Thistleton (Leics.) 44 SK 9118
Thistley Green 36 TL 6776
Thixendale 67 SE 8461
Thockrington 78 NY 9579
Tholomas Drove 45 TF 4006
Tholthorpe 66 SE 4766
Thomas Chapel 24 SN 1008
Thomastown (Grampn.) 104 NJ 5737
Thompson 46 TL 9296
Thomshill 104 NJ 2157
Thong 14 TQ 6770
Thoralby 65 SE 0086
Thoresby 53 SK 6371
Thoresway 61 TF 1696
Thorganby (Lincs.) 61 TF 2097
Thorganby (N Yorks.) 60 SE 6841
Thorgill 66 SE 7096
Thorington 37 TM 4274
Thorington Street 36 TM 0135
Thorlby 65 SD 9652
Thorley 35 TL 4719
Thormanby 66 SE 4974
Thornaby-on-Tees 73 NZ 4518
Thornage 47 TG 0436
Thornborough (Bucks.) 34 SP 7433
Thornborough (N Yorks.) 66 SE 2979
Thornbury (Avon) 29 ST 6390
Thornbury (Devon.) 6 SS 4008
Thornbury (Here & W) 31 SO 6159
Thornby (Northants.) 43 SP 6675
Thorncliff 52 SK 0158
Thorncombe 8 ST 3703
Thorncombe Street 12 TQ 0042
Thorndon 37 TM 1469
Thorne 60 SE 6813
Thorne St. Margaret 8 ST 0920
Thorner 59 SE 3740
Thorney (Cambs.) 45 TF 2804
Thorney (Notts.) 54 SK 8572
Thorney Hill 11 SZ 2099
Thorney Island 12 SU 7503
Thornfalcon 8 ST 2723
Thornford 9 ST 6013
Thorngumbald 61 TA 2026
Thornham 46 TF 7343
Thornham Magna 37 TM 1071
Thornham Parva 37 TM 1072
Thornhaugh 45 TF 0600
Thornhill (Central) 91 NS 6699
Thornhill (Derby.) 52 SK 1983
Thornhill (Dumf & G) 16 NX 8795
Thornhill (Hants.) 11 SU 4612
Thornhill (Mid Glam.) 28 ST 1584
Thornhill (W Yorks.) 59 SE 2418
Thornicombe 10 ST 8703
Thornley (Durham) 72 NZ 1137
Thornley (Durham) 72 NZ 3639
Thornliebank 84 NS 5459
Thorns 36 TL 7455
Thornthwaite (Cumbr.) 62 NY 2225
Thornthwaite (N Yorks.) 65 SE 1858
Thornton (Bucks.) 34 SP 7535
Thornton (Fife.) 93 NT 2897
Thornton (Humbs.) 60 SE 7545
Thornton (Lancs.) 57 SD 3342
Thornton (Leic.) 43 SK 4607
Thornton (Lincs.) 55 TF 2467
Thornton (Mers.) 57 SD 3300
Thornton (Northum.) 87 NT 9547
Thornton (Tays.) 98 NO 3946
Thornton (W Yorks.) 59 SE 1032
Thornton Curtis 61 TA 0817
Thornton Dale 67 SE 8383
Thornton Hough 50 SJ 3080
Thornton Rust 65 SD 9788
Thornton Steward 65 SE 1787
Thornton Watlass 66 SE 2385
Thornton le Moor (Lincs.) 61 TF 0496
Thornton-in-Craven 58 SD 9048
Thornton-le-Beans 66 SE 3990
Thornton-le-Clay 66 SE 6875
Thornton-le-Moor (N Yorks.) 66 SE 3988
Thornton-le-Moors 50 SJ 4474
Thorntonhall 84 NS 5955
Thorntonloch 86 NT 7574
Thorntonpark 87 NT 9448
Thornwood Common 35 TL 4705
Thoroton 54 SK 7642
Thorp Arch 59 SE 4346
Thorpe (Derby.) 52 SK 1550
Thorpe (Humbs.) 61 SE 9946
Thorpe (Lincs.) 55 TF 4982
Thorpe (N Yorks.) 65 SE 0161
Thorpe (Norf) 47 TM 4398
Thorpe (Notts.) 54 SK 7649
Thorpe (Surrey) 20 TQ 0268
Thorpe Abbotts 37 TM 1979
Thorpe Acre 43 SK 5120
Thorpe Arnold 44 SK 7620
Thorpe Audlin 60 SE 4715
Thorpe Bassett 67 SE 8573
Thorpe Bay 23 TQ 9284
Thorpe Constantine 42 SK 2608
Thorpe End Garden Village 47 TG 2811
Thorpe Green (Suff.) 36 TL 9354
Thorpe Hesley 59 SK 3796
Thorpe Langton 44 SP 7492
Thorpe Larches 72 NZ 3862
Thorpe Malsor 44 SP 8379
Thorpe Mandeville 33 SP 5345
Thorpe Market 47 TG 2436
Thorpe Morieux 36 TL 9453
Thorpe Salvin 53 SK 5281
Thorpe Satchville 44 SK 7311
Thorpe St. Andrew 47 TG 2609
Thorpe St. Peter 55 TF 4861
Thorpe Thewless 72 NZ 4023
Thorpe Underwood (N. Yorks.) 66 SE 4659
Thorpe Waterville 44 TL 0281
Thorpe Willoughby 60 SE 5731
Thorpe by Water 44 SP 8996
Thorpe in Balne 60 SE 5910
Thorpe in the Fallows 54 SK 9180
Thorpe on the Hill 54 SK 9065
Thorpe-le-Soken 23 TM 1822
Thorpeness 37 TM 4759
Thorrington 23 TM 0920
Thorverton 8 SS 9202
Thrandeston 37 TM 1176
Thrapston 44 SP 9978
Threapwood 50 SJ 4345
Three Bridges 13 TQ 2837
Three Cocks 30 SO 1737
Three Crosses 25 SS 5794
Three Holes 45 TF 5000
Three Legged Cross (Dorset) 10 SU 0806
Three Mile Cross 20 SU 7168
Threekingham 54 TF 0836
Threlkeld 62 NY 3225
Threshfield 65 SD 9963
Thrigby 47 TG 4512
Thringarth 63 NY 9323
Thringstone 43 SK 4217
Thrintoft 66 SE 3293
Thriplow 35 TL 4446
Throcking 35 TL 3330
Throckley 72 NZ 1567
Throckmorton 32 SO 9749
Throop 10 SY 8292
Throphill 79 NZ 1385
Thropton 79 NU 0202
Throwleigh 5 SX 6690
Throwley 15 TQ 9955
Thrumpton 53 SK 5131
Thrumster 112 ND 3345
Thrunton 79 NU 0810
Thrupp (Glos.) 32 SO 8603
Thrupp (Oxon.) 33 SP 4715
Thrushelton 5 SX 4487
Thrushgill 64 SD 6462
Thrussington 43 SK 6416
Thruxton (Hants.) 19 SU 2845
Thruxton (Here & W) 30 SO 4334
Thrybergh 53 SK 4694
Thundersley 22 TQ 7788
Thurcaston 43 SK 5610
Thurcroft 53 SK 4988
Thurgarton (Norf.) 47 TG 1835
Thurgarton (Notts.) 53 SK 6949
Thurgoland 59 SE 2801
Thurlaston (Leic.) 43 SP 5099
Thurlaston (Warw.) 43 SP 4671
Thurlby (Lincs.) 54 SK 9061
Thurlby (Lincs.) 45 TF 1017
Thurleigh 35 TL 0558
Thurlestone 5 SX 6742
Thurlow 36 TL 6750
Thurloxton 17 ST 2730
Thurlstone 59 SE 2303
Thurlton 47 TM 4198
Thurmaston 43 SK 6109
Thurnby 43 SK 6404
Thurne 47 TG 4015
Thurnham (Kent) 14 TQ 8057
Thurnham (Lancs.) 64 SD 4554
Thurning (Norf.) 47 TG 0729
Thurning (Northants.) 45 TL 0883
Thurnscoe 60 SE 4605
Thursby 70 NY 3250
Thursford 46 TF 9833
Thursley 12 SU 9039
Thurso 12 ND 1168
Thurstaston 50 SJ 2483
Thurston 36 TL 9365
Thurstonfield 70 NY 3156
Thurstonland 59 SE 1610
Thurton 47 TG 3200
Thurvaston 53 SK 2437
Thuxton 47 TG 0307
Thwaite (N Yorks.) 65 SD 8998
Thwaite (Suff.) 37 TM 1168
Thwaite St. Mary 47 TM 3395
Thwing 67 TA 0570
Tibbermore 92 NO 0523
Tibberton (Glos.) 32 SO 7521
Tibberton (Here & W) 32 SO 9054
Tibberton (Salop) 41 SJ 6720
Tibbie Shiels Inn 77 NT 2320
Tibenham 47 TM 1389
Tibshelf 53 SK 4360
Tibthorpe 67 SE 9555
Ticehurst 13 TQ 6930
Tichborne 11 SU 5630
Tickencote 44 SK 9809
Tickenham 29 ST 4571
Tickhill 53 SK 5993
Ticklerton 40 SO 4890
Ticknall 43 SK 3524
Tickton 61 TA 0641
Tidcombe 19 SU 2858
Tiddington (Oxon.) 34 SP 6404
Tiddington (Warw.) 33 SP 2256
Tidebrook 13 TQ 6130
Tideford 4 SX 3459
Tidenham 29 ST 5596
Tideswell 52 SK 1575
Tidmarsh 19 SU 6374
Tidmington 33 SP 2538
Tidpit 10 SU 0718
Tiers Cross 24 SM 9010
Tiffield 34 SP 6951
Tifty 105 NJ 7740
Tigerton 99 NO 5364
Tigharry 109 NF 7171
Tighnabruaich 81 NR 9772
Tighnafiline 106 NG 8789
Tigley 5 SX 7560
Tilbrook 45 TL 0769
Tilbury 22 TQ 6376
Tile Cross 42 SP 1687
Tile Hill 43 SP 2777
Tilehurst 19 SU 6673
Tilford 12 SU 8743
Tillathrowie 104 NJ 4634
Tillicoultry 91 NS 9197
Tillingham 23 TL 9903
Tillington (Here & W) 30 SO 4645
Tillington (W Susx.) 12 SU 9621
Tillington Common 30 SO 4546
Tillyarblet 99 NO 5267
Tillycorthie 105 NJ 9123
Tillyfourie 104 NJ 6412
Tillygarmond 99 NO 6393
Tillygreig 105 NJ 8823.
Tilmanstone 15 TR 3051
Tilney All Saints 46 TF 5618
Tilney High End 46 TF 5617
Tilney St. Lawrence 46 TF 5414

Tilshead 253 Upton Lovell

Tilshead 18 SU 0347
Tilstock 50 SJ 5337
Tilston 50 SJ 4551
Tilstone Fearnall 51 SJ 5660
Tilsworth 34 SP 9724
Tilton on the Hill 44 SK 7405
Timberland 55 TF 1158
Timbersbrook 51 SJ 8962
Timberscombe 16 SS 9542
Timble 65 SE 1752
Timperley 51 SJ 7988
Timsbury (Avon) 17 ST 6658
Timsbury (Hants.) 11 SU 3424
Timworth Green 36 TL 8669
Tincleton 10 SY 7691
Tindale 71 NY 6159
Tingewick 34 SP 6533
Tingley 59 SE 2826
Tingrith 34 TL 0032
Tinhay 4 SX 4085
Tinshill 59 SE 2540
Tinsley 53 SK 3990
Tintagel 4 SX 0588
Tintern Parva 29 SO 5200
Tintern Parva 29 SO 5201
Tintinhull 9 ST 5019
Tintwistle 59 SK 0297
Tinwald 70 NY 0081
Tinwell 44 TF 0006
Tipperty 105 NJ 9627
Tipton 41 SO 9592
Tipton St. John 8 SY 0991
Tiptree 23 TL 8916
Tirabad 27 SN 8741
Tirley 32 SO 8328
Tirphil 28 SO 1303
Tirril 63 NY 5026
Tisbury 10 ST 9429
Tissington 52 SK 1752
Titchberry 6 SS 2427
Titchfield 11 SU 5305
Titchmarsh 44 TL 0279
Titchwell 46 TF 7543
Tithby 54 SK 6936
Titley 30 SO 3260
Titlington 79 NU 1015
Tittensor 51 SJ 8738
Tittleshall 46 TF 8920
Tiverton (Ches.) 50 SJ 5560
Tiverton (Devon.) 8 SS 9512
Tivetshall St. Margaret 47 TM 1787
Tivetshall St. Mary 47 TM 1686
Tixall 41 SJ 9722
Tixover 44 SK 9700
Toab 113 HU 3811
Tobermory 95 NM 5055
Toberonochy 89 NM 7408
Tocher 105 NJ 6932
Tockenham 18 SU 0379
Tockenham Wick 18 SU 0381
Tockholes 58 SD 6623
Tockington 29 ST 6186
Tockwith 66 SE 4652
Todber 10 ST 7920
Toddington (Beds.) 34 TL 0129
Toddington (Glos.) 32 SP 0432
Todenham 33 SP 2436
Todhills 70 NY 3663
Todmorden 58 SD 9324
Todwick 53 SK 4984
Toft (Cambs.) 35 TL 3655
Toft (Ches.) 51 SJ 7676
Toft (Lincs.) 45 TF 0617
Toft Monks 47 TM 4295
Toft next Newton 54 TF 0488
Toftrees 46 TF 8927
Tofts 112 ND 3768
Toftwood 46 TF 9811
Togston 79 NU 2401
Tokavaig 100 NG 6012
Tokers Green 20 SU 7077
Toll of Birness 105 NK 0034
Tolland 16 ST 1032
Tollard Royal 10 ST 9417
Toller Fratrum 9 SY 5797
Toller Porcorum 9 SY 5697
Tollerton (N Yorks.) 66 SE 5164
Tollerton (Notts.) 53 SK 6134
Tollesbury 23 TL 9510
Tolleshunt D'Arcy 23 TL 9312
Tolleshunt Major 23 TL 9011
Tolpuddle 10 SY 7994
Tolstachaolais 109 NB 1938
Tolworth 21 TQ 1965
Tomatin 103 NH 8028
Tombreck 103 NH 6934
Tomich (Highld.) 102 NH 5348
Tomich (Highld.) 108 NH 7071
Tomintoul (Grampn.) 104 NJ 1618
Tomintoul (Gramps.) 98 NO 1490
Tomnavoulin 104 NJ 2026
Ton 29 SO 3301
Tonbridge 14 TQ 5845
Tondu 28 SS 8984
Tong (Isle of Lewis) 109 NB 4436
Tong (Salop) 41 SJ 7907
Tonge 43 SK 4123
Tongham 20 SU 8848
Tongland 69 NX 6953
Tongue 111 NC 5957
Tongwynlais 28 ST 1581
Tonna 28 SS 7798
Tonwell 35 TL 3317
Tonypandy 28 SS 9992
Tonyrefail 28 ST 0188
Toot Baldon 33 SP 5600
Toot Hill (Essex) 22 TL 5102
Toot Hill (Hants.) 11 SU 3718
Topcliffe 66 SE 3976
Topcroft 47 TM 2693
Topcroft Street 47 TM 2692
Toppesfield 36 TL 7337
Toppings 58 SD 7213
Toprow 47 TM 1698
Topsham 8 SX 9788
Torbay 5 SX 8962
Torbeg 74 NR 8929
Torbryan 5 SX 8266
Torcastle 96 NN 1378
Torcross 5 SX 8242
Tore 107 NH 6052
Torksey 54 SK 8378
Torlundy 96 NN 1477
Tormarton 18 ST 7678
Tormitchell 75 NX 2394
Tormore 87 NR 8932
Tornagrain 108 NH 7649
Tornahaish 104 NJ 2908
Tornaveen 104 NJ 6106
Torness 102 NH 5727
Torpenhow 62 NY 2039
Torphichen 84 NS 9672
Torphins 99 NJ 6202
Torpoint 4 SX 4355
Torquay 8 SX 9164
Torquhan 86 NT 4447
Torran (Strath.) 89 NM 8704
Torrance 84 NS 6174
Torridon 101 NG 9055
Torrin 100 NG 5720
Torrisdale 111 NC 6761
Torrish 111 NC 9718
Torrisholme 64 SD 4464
Torroble 108 NC 5904
Torry (Grampn.) 104 NJ 4339
Torry (Grampn.) 105 NJ 9404
Torryburn 85 NT 0286
Torrylin 74 NR 9621
Torterston 105 NK 0747
Torthorwald 70 NY 0378
Tortington 12 TQ 0005
Tortworth 29 ST 6992
Torvaig 100 NG 4944
Torver 62 SD 2894
Torwood 84 NS 8484
Torworth 53 SK 6586
Toscaig 101 NG 7138
Toseland 35 TL 2362
Tosside 65 SD 7655
Tostock 36 TL 9563
Totaig 100 NG 2050
Tote 100 NG 4149
Totegan 111 NC 8268
Totland 11 SZ 3286
Totley 53 SK 3179
Totnes 5 SX 8060
Toton 53 SK 5034
Tottenham 21 TQ 3491
Tottenhill 46 TF 6310
Totteridge 21 TQ 2494
Totternhoe 34 SP 9921
Tottington 58 SD 7712
Totton 11 SU 3513
Tournaig 106 NG 8783
Toux (Grampn.) 104 NJ 5458
Toux (Grampn.) 105 NJ 9850
Tovil 14 TQ 7554
Tow Law 72 NZ 1139
Toward 82 NS 1368
Towcester 34 SP 6948
Towednack 2 SW 4838
Tower Hamlets 21 TQ 3582
Towersey 34 SP 7305
Towie 104 NJ 4412
Towiemore 104 NJ 3945
Town End (Cambs.) 45 TL 4195
Town End (Cumbr.) 63 SD 4483
Town Street 46 TL 7786
Town Yetholm 87 NT 8228
Townhead (Dumf & G) 69 NX 6946
Townhead of Greenlaw 69 NX 7465
Townhill 85 NT 1089
Townshend 2 SW 5932
Towthorpe 66 SE 6258
Towton 60 SE 4839
Towyn (Clwyd) 49 SH 9779
Toy's Hill 21 TQ 4751
Toynton All Saints 55 TF 3904
Toynton Fen Side 55 TF 3961
Toynton St. Peter 55 TF 4063
Trabboch 75 NS 4321
Traboe 2 SW 7421
Tradespark (Highld.) 103 NH 8656
Trafford Park 58 SJ 7996
Tranent 86 NT 4072
Trantlebeg 111 NC 9054
Trantlemore 111 NC 8853
Tranwell 79 NZ 1883
Trapp 25 SN 6519
Traprain 86 NT 5975
Traquair 85 NT 3334
Trawden 58 SD 9138
Trawsfynydd 49 SH 7035
Tre'r-ddol 39 SN 6592
Tre-groes 26 SN 4044
Trealaw 28 SS 9992
Treales 57 SD 4432
Trearddur Bay 48 SH 2478
Treaslane 100 NG 3953
Trebartha 4 SX 2677
Trebarwith 4 SX 0585
Trebetherick 3 SW 9377
Treborough 16 ST 0036
Trebudannon 3 SW 8961
Treburley 4 SX 3477
Trecastle 28 SN 8729
Trecwyn 24 SM 9632
Trecynon 28 SN 9903
Tredavoe 2 SW 4528
Treddiog 24 SM 8928
Tredegar 28 SO 1409
Tredington (Warw.) 33 SP 2543
Tredinnick (Corn.) 3 SW 9270
Tredomen 30 SO 1231
Tredunnock 29 ST 3795
Treen 2 SW 3923
Treeton 53 SK 4387
Trefdraeth 48 SH 4070
Trefecca 30 SO 1431
Trefeglwys 39 SN 9690
Trefenter 27 SN 6068
Treffgarne 24 SM 9523
Treffynnon 24 SM 8428
Trefil 28 SO 1212
Trefilan 26 SN 5457
Trefnannau 40 SJ 2015
Trefnant 49 SJ 0570
Trefonen 40 SJ 2526
Trefor 48 SH 3779
Trefriw 49 SH 7763
Tregadillett 4 SX 2983
Tregaian 48 SH 4579
Tregare 29 SO 4110
Tregaron 27 SN 6759
Tregarth 48 SH 6067
Tregeare 4 SX 2486
Tregeiriog 50 SJ 1733
Tregele 48 SH 3592
Tregidden 2 SW 7523
Treglemais 24 SM 8229
Tregole 6 SX 1998
Tregonetha 3 SW 9563
Tregony 3 SW 9244
Tregoyd 30 SO 1937
Tregurrian 2 SW 8465
Tregynon 39 SO 0998
Trehafod 28 ST 0491
Treharris 28 ST 1097
Treherbert (Mid Glam.) 28 SS 9398
Trelawnyd 49 SJ 0879
Trelech 26 SN 2830
Trelech a'r Betws 25 SN 3026
Treleddyd-fawr 24 SM 7528
Trelewis 28 ST 1197
Trelights 3 SW 9879
Trelill 4 SX 0477
Trelissick 2 SW 8339
Trelleck 29 SO 5005
Trelleck Grange 29 SO 4901
Trelogan 50 SJ 1180
Trelystan 40 SJ 2603
Tremadog 48 SH 5640
Tremail 4 SX 1686
Tremain 26 SN 2348
Tremaine 4 SX 2388
Tremar 4 SX 2568
Trematon 4 SX 3959
Tremeirchion 49 SJ 0773
Trenance 2 SW 8567
Trenarren 4 SX 0348
Trench 41 SJ 6913
Treneglos 4 SX 2088
Trenewan 4 SX 1753
Trent 9 ST 5918
Trentham 51 SJ 8640
Trentishoe 7 SS 6448
Treoes 28 SS 9478
Treorchy 28 SS 9596
Tresaith 26 SN 2751
Trescott 41 SO 8497
Trescowe 2 SW 5731
Tresham 18 ST 7991
Tresillian 3 SW 8646
Tresmeer 4 SX 2387
Tressait 97 NN 8160
Tresta (Fetlar) 113 HU 6190
Tresta (Shetld.) 113 HU 3650
Treswell 54 SK 7779
Trethurgy 4 SX 0355
Tretio 24 SM 7828
Tretire 29 SO 5124
Tretower 28 SO 1821
Treuddyn 50 SJ 2458
Trevalga 4 SX 0889
Trevanson 3 SW 9772
Trevarren 3 SW 9160
Trevarrick 3 SW 9843
Trevellas 2 SW 7452
Treverva 2 SW 7631
Trevethin 29 SO 2802
Trevigro 4 SX 3369
Trevine 24 SM 8432
Treviscoe 3 SW 9455
Trevone 3 SW 8975
Trevor 48 SH 3746
Trewarmett 4 SX 0686
Trewarthenick 3 SW 9044
Trewassa 4 SX 1486
Trewellard 2 SW 3733
Trewen 4 SX 2583
Trewidland 4 SX 2560
Trewint (Corn.) 6 SX 1897
Trewithian 3 SW 8737
Trewoon 3 SW 9952
Treyarnon 2 SW 8673
Treyford 12 SU 8218
Trickett's Cross 10 SU 0801
Trimdon 72 NZ 3634
Trimdon Colliery 72 NZ 3835
Trimdon Grange 72 NZ 3735
Trimingham 47 TG 2738
Trimley 37 TM 2736
Trimley Heath 37 TM 2737
Trimpley 41 SO 7978
Trimsaran 25 SN 4504
Trimstone 6 SS 5043
Trinant 28 SO 2000
Tring 34 SP 9211
Trinity (Tayside) 99 NO 6061
Trislaig 96 NN 0874
Trispen 2 SW 8450
Tritlington 79 NZ 2092
Trochrie 91 NN 9740
Troedyraur 26 SN 3245
Troedyrhiw 28 SO 0702
Trofarth 49 SH 8571
Troon (Corn.) 2 SW 6638
Troon (Strath.) 82 NS 3230
Troston 36 TL 8972
Trottiscliffe 14 TQ 6460
Trotton 12 SU 8322
Troutbeck 62 NY 4103
Troutbeck Bridge 62 NY 4000
Trow Green 29 SO 5706
Trowbridge 18 ST 8557
Trowle Common 18 ST 8358
Trows 86 NT 6932
Trowse Newton 47 TG 2406
Trudoxhill 18 ST 7443
Trull 8 ST 2122
Trumpan 100 NG 2261
Trumpet 31 SO 6539
Trumpington 35 TL 4455
Trunch 47 TG 2834
Truro 2 SW 8244
Trusham 5 SX 8582
Trusley 53 SK 2535
Trusthorpe 55 TF 5183
Trysull 41 SO 8494
Tubney 19 SU 4498
Tuckenhay 5 SX 8156
Tuddenham (Suff.) 36 TL 7371
Tuddenham (Suff.) 37 TM 1948
Tudeley 13 TQ 6245
Tudhoe 72 NZ 2635
Tudweiloig 48 SH 2336
Tuffley 32 SO 8315
Tugby 44 SK 7601
Tugford 40 SO 5587
Tullibody 91 NS 8595
Tullich (Highld.) 108 NH 8576
Tullich (Strath.) 89 NN 0815
Tullich Muir 108 NH 7373
Tulliemet 98 NN 9952
Tulloch (Grampn.) 99 NO 7671
Tullochgorm 89 NR 9695
Tulloes 99 NO 5145
Tullybannocher 91 NN 7521
Tullyfergus 98 NO 2149
Tullynessle 104 NJ 5519
Tumble 25 SN 5411
Tumby 55 TF 2359
Tumby Woodside 55 TF 2657
Tummel Bridge 97 NN 7659
Tunstall (Humbs.) 61 TA 3032
Tunstall (Kent) 14 TQ 8961
Tunstall (Lancs.) 64 SD 6073
Tunstall (N Yorks.) 65 SE 2195
Tunstall (Norf.) 47 TG 4107
Tunstall (Staffs.) 51 SJ 8551
Tunstall (Suff.) 37 TM 3655
Tunstead 47 TG 3022
Tunworth 19 SU 6748
Tupsley 31 SO 5340
Tur Langton 44 SP 7194
Turgis Green 19 SU 6959
Turin 99 NO 5352
Turkdean 32 SP 1017
Turnastone 30 SO 3536
Turnberry 75 NS 2005
Turnditch 53 SK 2946
Turner's Hill 13 TQ 3435
Turners Puddle 10 SY 8394
Turnworth 10 ST 8107
Turriff 105 NJ 7249
Turton Bottoms 58 SD 7315
Turvey 34 SP 9452
Turville 20 SU 7691
Turville Heath 20 SU 7391
Turweston 34 SP 6037
Tutbury 42 SK 2129
Tutnall 41 SO 9870
Tutshill 29 ST 5394
Tuttington 47 TG 2227
Tuxford 54 SK 7370
Twatt (Orkney) 113 HY 2624
Twechar 84 NS 6975
Tweedmouth 87 NT 9952
Tweedsmuir 77 NT 1024
Twelveheads 2 SW 7642
Twenty 45 TF 1520
Twerton 17 ST 7263
Twickenham 21 TQ 1473
Twigworth 32 SO 8421
Twineham 13 TQ 2519
Twinhoe 18 ST 7360
Twinstead 36 TL 8637
Twiss Green 58 SJ 6595
Twitchen (Devon.) 7 SS 7830
Twitchen (Salop) 40 SO 3679
Two Bridges 5 SX 6075
Two Dales 53 SK 2762
Two Gates 42 SK 2101
Twycross (Leic.) 43 SK 3305
Twyford (Berks.) 20 SU 7975
Twyford (Bucks.) 34 SP 6626
Twyford (Hants.) 11 SU 4724
Twyford (Leics.) 44 SK 7210
Twyford (Norf.) 46 TG 0124
Twyford Common 30 SO 5135
Twyn-y-Sheriff 29 SO 4005
Twynholm 69 NX 6654
Twyning 32 SO 8936
Twyning Green 32 SO 9037
Twynllanan 28 SN 7524
Twywell 44 SP 9578
Ty'n-y-groes 49 SH 7771
Ty-hen 48 SH 1731
Ty-nant (Clwyd) 49 SH 9944
Ty-nant (Gwyn.) 39 SH 9026
Ty-uchaf 39 SH 9922
Tyberton 30 SO 3739
Tyburn 42 SP 1490
Tycroes 25 SN 6010
Tycrwyn 40 SJ 1018
Tydd Gote 45 TF 4518
Tydd St. Giles 45 TF 4216
Tydd St. Mary 45 TF 4418
Tyldesley 58 SD 6902
Tyler Hill 15 TR 1460
Tylers Green (Bucks.) 20 SU 9094
Tylorstown 28 ST 0195
Tylwch 39 SN 9780
Tyn-y-ffridd 40 SJ 1230
Tyn-y-graig 27 SO 0149
Tyndrum 90 NN 3330
Tyneham 10 SY 8880
Tynehead 85 NT 3960
Tynemouth (Tyne and Wear) 72 NZ 3468
Tynewydd 28 SS 9399
Tyninghame 86 NT 6179
Tynribbie 95 NM 9446
Tynron 76 NX 8093
Tyringham 34 SP 8547
Tythegston 28 SS 8578
Tytherington (Avon) 29 ST 6788
Tytherington (Ches.) 51 SJ 9175
Tytherington (Somer.) 18 ST 7744
Tytherington (Wilts.) 18 ST 9140
Tytherleigh 8 ST 3203
Tywardreath 4 SX 0854
Tywyn (Gwyn) 38 SH 5800
Tywyn (Gwyn) 49 SH 7878

U

Ubbeston Green 37 TM 3271
Ubley 17 ST 5257
Uckerby 66 NZ 2402
Uckfield 13 TQ 4721
Uckington 32 SO 9224
Uddingston 84 NS 6960
Uddington 84 NS 8633
Udimore 14 TQ 8718
Udny Green 105 NJ 8726
Uffcott 18 SU 1277
Uffculme 8 ST 0612
Uffington (Lincs.) 45 TF 0608
Uffington (Oxon.) 19 SU 3089
Uffington (Salop) 40 SJ 5313
Ufford (Northants.) 45 TF 0904
Ufford (Suff.) 37 TM 2953
Ufton 33 SP 3762
Ufton Nervet 19 SU 6367
Ugadale 74 NR 7828
Ugborough 5 SX 6755
Uggeshall 37 TM 4580
Ugglebarnby 67 NZ 8707
Ugley 22 TL 5128
Ugley Green 22 TL 5227
Ugthorpe 73 NZ 7911
Uig (Isle of Lewis) 109 NB 0534
Uig (Isle of Skye) 100 NG 1952
Uig (Isle of Skye) 100 NG 3963
Ulbster 112 ND 3241
Ulceby (Humbs.) 61 TA 1014
Ulceby (Lincs.) 55 TF 4272
Ulcombe 14 TQ 8449
Uldale 62 NY 2536
Uley 18 ST 7898
Ulgham 79 NZ 2392
Ullapool 106 NH 1294
Ullenhall 42 SP 1267
Ullenwood 32 SO 9416
Ulleskelf 60 SE 5140
Ullesthorpe 43 SP 5087
Ulley 53 SK 4687
Ullingswick 31 SO 5950
Ullinish 100 NG 3237
Ullock 62 NY 0724
Ulpha 62 SD 1993
Ulrome 67 TA 1656
Ulsta 113 HU 4680
Ulverston 62 SD 2878
Umberleigh 6 SS 6023
Unapool 110 NC 2333
Under River 21 TQ 5552
Underbarrow 63 SD 4692
Underwood (Notts.) 53 SK 4750
Undy 29 ST 4386
Union Mills 56 SC 3578
Unstone 53 SK 3777
Up Cerne 9 ST 6502
Up Exe 8 SS 9302
Up Hatherley 32 SO 9120
Up Holland 57 SD 5105
Up Nately 20 SU 6951
Up Somborne 11 SU 3932
Up Sydling 9 ST 6201
Upavon 18 SU 1354
Upchurch 14 TQ 8467
Upcott (Here & W) 30 SO 3250
Upend 36 TL 7058
Uphall 85 NT 0571
Upham (Devon.) 7 SS 8808
Upham (Hants.) 11 SU 5320
Uphill (Avon) 17 ST 3158
Uplawmoor 82 NS 4355
Upleadon 32 SO 7527
Upleatham 73 NZ 6319
Uplees 15 TQ 9964
Uplowman 8 ST 0115
Uplyme 8 SY 3293
Upminster 21 TQ 5686
Upnor 14 TQ 7470
Upottery 8 ST 2007
Uppark 12 SU 7717
Upper Ardchronie 108 NH 6188
Upper Arley 41 SO 7680
Upper Astrop 33 SP 5137
Upper Basildon 19 SU 5976
Upper Beeding 12 TQ 1910
Upper Benefield 44 SP 9789
Upper Bentley 32 SO 9966
Upper Boddington 33 SP 4853
Upper Breakish 60 NG 6823
Upper Breinton 30 SO 4640
Upper Broughton 43 SK 6826
Upper Bucklebury 19 SU 5368
Upper Caldecote 35 TL 1645
Upper Chapel 27 SO 0040
Upper Chute 19 SU 2953
Upper Clatford 19 SU 3543
Upper Clynnog 48 SH 4746
Upper Cokeham 12 TQ 1605
Upper Cwmtwrch 28 SN 7611
Upper Dean 45 TL 0467
Upper Denby 59 SE 2207
Upper Derraid 103 NJ 0233
Upper Dicker 13 TQ 5510
Upper Elkstone 52 SK 0559
Upper End 52 SK 0876
Upper Ethie 103 NH 7663
Upper Farringdon 12 SU 7135
Upper Framilode 32 SO 7510
Upper Froyle 12 SU 7542
Upper Gravenhurst 35 TL 1136
Upper Green 19 SU 3663
Upper Hackney 53 SK 2961
Upper Hale 20 SU 8448
Upper Hambleton 44 SK 9007
Upper Hardres Court 15 TR 1550
Upper Hartfield 13 TQ 4634
Upper Heath 40 SO 5685
Upper Helmsley 66 SE 6956
Upper Heyford (Northants) 34 SP 6759
Upper Heyford (Oxon.) 33 SP 4926
Upper Hill 30 SO 4753
Upper Hopton 59 SE 1918
Upper Hulme 52 SK 0160
Upper Inglesham 18 SU 2096
Upper Killay 25 SS 5892
Upper Knockando 104 NJ 1843
Upper Lambourn 19 SU 3180
Upper Langwith 53 SK 5169
Upper Lochton 99 NO 6997
Upper Longdon 42 SK 0614
Upper Lydbrook 29 SO 6015
Upper Maes-coed 30 SO 3335
Upper Minety 18 SU 0091
Upper North Dean 20 SU 8598
Upper Poppleton 66 SE 5554
Upper Quinton 33 SP 1746
Upper Sapey 31 SO 6863
Upper Scoulag 82 NS 1059
Upper Seagry 18 ST 9580
Upper Shelton 34 SP 9943
Upper Sheringham 47 TG 1441
Upper Skelmorlie 82 NS 1968
Upper Slaughter 32 SP 1523
Upper Soudley 29 SO 6610
Upper Stondon 35 TL 1535
Upper Stowe 34 SP 6456
Upper Street (Hants.) 10 SU 1418
Upper Street (Norf.) 47 TG 3516
Upper Sundon 35 TL 0527
Upper Swell 32 SP 1726
Upper Tasburgh 47 TM 2095
Upper Tean 52 SK 0139
Upper Tillyrie 92 NO 1006
Upper Tooting 21 TQ 2772
Upper Town (Avon) 29 ST 5265
Upper Tysoe 33 SP 3343
Upper Upham 18 SU 2277
Upper Wardington 33 SP 4946
Upper Weald 34 SP 8037
Upper Weedon 34 SP 6258
Upper Wield 11 SU 6238
Upper Winchendon 34 SP 7414
Upper Woodford 10 SU 1237
Uppermill 59 SD 9906
Upperthong 59 SE 1208
Upperton 12 SU 9522
Uppertown (Stroma) 112 ND 3576
Uppingham 44 SP 8699
Uppington 41 SJ 5909
Upsall 66 SE 4587
Upshire 35 TL 4100
Upstreet 15 TR 2262
Upton (Berks.) 20 SU 9879
Upton (Bucks.) 34 SP 7711
Upton (Cambs.) 45 TL 1778
Upton (Ches.) 50 SJ 4069
Upton (Dorset) 10 SY 9893
Upton (Hants.) 19 SU 3555
Upton (Hants.) 11 SU 3716
Upton (Lincs.) 54 SK 8686
Upton (Mers.) 50 SJ 2687
Upton (Norf.) 47 TG 3912
Upton (Northants.) 34 SP 7160
Upton (Notts.) 54 SK 7354
Upton (Notts.) 54 SK 7476
Upton (Oxon.) 19 SU 5186
Upton (Somer.) 16 SS 9928
Upton (W Yorks.) 60 SE 4713
Upton Bishop 29 SO 6427
Upton Cheyney 29 ST 6969
Upton Cressett 41 SO 6592
Upton Cross 4 SX 2872
Upton Grey 19 SU 6948
Upton Hellions 7 SS 8303
Upton Lovell 18 ST 9440

Upton Magna 254 Westhead

Upton Magna 40 SJ 5512
Upton Noble 17 ST 7139
Upton Pyne 8 SX 9197
Upton Scudamore 18 ST 8647
Upton Snodsbury 32 SO 9454
Upton St. Leonards 32 SO 8615
Upton Warren 41 SO 9267
Upton upon Severn 32 SO 8540
Upwaltham 12 SU 9413
Upware 45 TL 5370
Upwell 45 TF 5002
Upwey 9 SY 6684
Upwood 45 TL 2582
Urchal 103 NH 7544
Urchany 103 NH 8849
Urchfont 18 SU 0356
Urdimarsh 31 SO 5249
Urmston 58 SJ 7695
Urquhart (Grampn.) 104 NJ 2863
Urra 66 NZ 5702
Urray 102 NH 5053
Urswick 64 SD 2674
Ushaw Moor 72 NZ 2342
Usk 29 SO 3701
Usselby 55 TF 0993
Utley 59 SE 0542
Uton 7 SX 8298
Utterby 55 TF 3093
Uttoxeter 52 SK 0933
Uwchmynydd (Gwyn.) 38 SH 1425
Uxbridge 20 TQ 0583
Uyeasound (Unst) 113 HP 5901
Uzmaston 24 SM 9714

V

Valley 48 SH 2979
Valleyfield 85 NT 0086
Valtos (Island of Skye) 100 NG 5163
Valtos (Isle of Lewis) 109 NB 0936
Vange 22 TQ 7287
Vardre 25 SN 6902
Varteg 28 SO 2506
Vatsetter 113 HU 5388
Vatten 100 NG 2843
Vauld, The 31 SO 5349
Vaynor 28 SO 0410
Velindre (Dyfed) 26 SN 1039
Velindre (Dyfed) 26 SN 3538
Velindre (Powys) 30 SO 1836
Vementry 113 HU 3159
Venn Ottery 8 SY 0791
Vennington 40 SJ 3309
Ventnor 11 SZ 5677
Vernham Dean 19 SU 3356
Vernham Street 19 SU 3457
Vernolds Common 40 SO 4780
Verwig 26 SN 1849
Verwood 10 SU 0908
Veryan 3 SW 9139
Vicarage 8 SY 2088
Vickerstown 64 SD 1868
Victoria 3 SW 9961
Vidlin 113 HU 4766
Viewpark 84 NS 7161
Villavin 6 SS 5816
Vine's Cross 13 TQ 5917
Vinehall Street 14 TQ 7520
Virginia Water 20 SU 9967
Virginstow 4 SX 3792
Vobster 17 ST 7048
Voe (Shetld.) 113 HU 4062
Vowchurch 30 SO 3636

W

Wackerfield 72 NZ 1522
Wacton 47 TM 1891
Wadborough 32 SO 8947
Waddesdon 34 SP 7416
Waddingham 61 SK 9896
Waddington (Lancs.) 58 SD 7243
Waddington (Lincs.) 54 SK 9764
Wadebridge 3 SW 9972
Wadeford 8 ST 3110
Wadenhoe 44 TL 0083
Wadesmill 35 TL 3517
Wadhurst 13 TQ 6431
Wadshelf 53 SK 3171
Wadworth 60 SK 5697
Waen Fach 40 SJ 2017
Wag 112 ND 0226
Wainfleet All Saints 55 TF 4959
Wainfleet Bank 55 TF 4759
Wainhouse Corner 6 SX 1895
Wainscott 22 TQ 7471
Wainstalls 59 SE 0428
Waitby 65 NY 7507
Wakefield 59 SE 3320
Wakerley 44 SP 9599
Wakes Colne 22 TL 8928
Walberswick 37 TM 4974
Walberton 12 SU 9705
Walcot (Lincs.) 54 TF 0535
Walcot (Lincs.) 55 TF 1256
Walcot (Salop) 41 SJ 5912
Walcot (Warw.) 32 SP 1258
Walcote 43 SP 5683
Walcott (Norf.) 47 TG 3632
Walden Head 65 SD 9880
Walden Stubbs 60 SE 5516
Walderslade 14 TQ 7563
Walderton 12 SU 7910
Walditch 9 SY 4892
Waldridge 72 NZ 2549
Waldringfield 37 TM 2744
Waldron 13 TQ 5419
Wales 53 SK 4782
Walesby (Lincs.) 55 TF 1392
Walesby (Notts.) 53 SK 6870
Walford (Here & W) 40 SO 3872
Walford (Here & W) 29 SO 5820
Walford (Salop) 40 SJ 4320
Walgherton 51 SJ 6948
Walgrave 44 SP 8071
Walk Mill 58 SD 8629
Walkden 58 SD 7303
Walker 72 NZ 2864
Walker Fold 58 SD 6742
Walker's Green 31 SO 5248
Walkerburn 85 NT 3637
Walkeringham 54 SK 7692
Walkerith 54 SK 7892
Walkern 35 TL 2926
Walkhampton 5 SX 5369
Walkington 61 SE 9936
Wall (Northum.) 71 NY 9168
Wall (Staffs.) 42 SK 0906
Wall Bank 40 SO 5092
Wallacetown (Strath.) 75 NS 3422
Wallasey 50 SJ 2992
Wallend 22 TQ 8775
Wallingford 19 SU 6089
Wallington (Gtr London) 21 TQ 2863
Wallington (Hants.) 11 SU 5806
Wallington (Herts.) 35 TL 2933
Wallis 24 SN 0125
Walliswood 12 TQ 1138
Walls 113 HU 2449
Wallsend 72 NZ 2766
Wallyford 85 NT 3671
Walmer 15 TR 3750
Walmer Bridge 57 SD 4724
Walmersley 58 SD 8013
Walmley 42 SP 1393
Walpole (Suff.) 37 TM 3674
Walpole Highway 45 TF 5113
Walpole St. Andrew 45 TF 5017
Walpole St. Peter 45 TF 5016
Walsall 42 SP 0198
Walsall Wood 42 SK 0403
Walsden 58 SD 9322
Walsgrave on Sowe 43 SP 3781
Walsham le Willows 36 TM 0071
Walsoken 45 TF 4710
Walston 85 NT 0545
Walterstone 29 SO 3425
Waltham (Humbs.) 61 TA 2503
Waltham (Kent) 15 TR 1148
Waltham Abbey 21 TL 3800
Waltham Chase 11 SU 5614
Waltham St. Lawrence 20 SU 8276
Waltham on the Wolds 44 SK 8025
Walthamstow 21 TQ 3788
Walton (Cumbr.) 71 NY 5264
Walton (Derby.) 53 SK 3569
Walton (Leic.) 43 SP 5987
Walton (Powys) 30 SO 2559
Walton (Salop) 41 SJ 5818
Walton (Somer.) 17 ST 4636
Walton (Suff.) 37 TM 2935
Walton (W Yorks.) 59 SE 3516
Walton (W Yorks.) 59 SE 4447
Walton (Warw.) 33 SP 2853
Walton Cardiff 32 SO 9032
Walton East 24 SN 0123
Walton Highway 44 TF 4912
Walton West 24 SM 8713
Walton on the Hill (Surrey) 21 TQ 2255
Walton on the Naze 23 TM 2521
Walton on the Wolds 43 SK 5919
Walton-in-Gordano 29 ST 4273
Walton-le-Dale 57 SD 5627
Walton-on-Thames 20 TQ 1066
Walton-on-Trent 42 SK 2118
Walton-on-the-Hill (Staffs.) 41 SJ 9520
Walworth 72 NZ 2218
Walwyn's Castle 24 SM 8711
Wambrook 8 ST 2907
Wanborough (Wilts) 18 SU 2082
Wandsworth 21 TQ 2673
Wangford 37 TM 4679
Wanlip 43 SK 5910
Wanlockhead 76 NS 8712
Wansford (Cambs.) 44 TL 0799
Wansford (Humbs.) 67 TA 0656
Wanstead 21 TQ 4087
Wanstrow 17 ST 7141
Wanswell 29 SO 6801
Wantage 19 SU 4087
Wapley 29 ST 7179
Wappenbury 43 SP 3769
Wappenham 34 SP 6245
Warbleton 13 TQ 6018
Warborough 19 SU 5993
Warboys 45 TL 3080
Warbstow 4 SX 2090
Warburton 51 SJ 7089
Warcop 63 NY 7415
Ward Green 37 TM 0564
Warden 15 TR 0271
Wardington 33 SP 4946
Wardle (Ches.) 51 SJ 6057
Wardle (Gtr Mches.) 58 SD 9116
Wardley 44 SK 8300
Wardlow 52 SK 1874
Wardy Hill 45 TL 4782
Ware 35 TL 3614
Wareham 10 SY 9287
Warehorne 15 TQ 9832
Waren Mill 87 NU 1534
Warenford 87 NU 1328
Warenton 87 NU 1030
Wareside 35 TL 3915
Waresley (Camb.) 35 TL 2454
Warfield 20 SU 8872
Wargrave 20 SU 7878
Warham All Saints 46 TF 9441
Warham St. Mary 46 TF 9441
Wark (Northum.) 87 NT 8238
Wark (Northum.) 78 NY 8576
Warkleigh 7 SS 6422
Warkton 44 SP 8980
Warkworth 79 NU 2406
Warlaby 66 SE 3591
Warland 58 SD 9419
Warleggan 4 SX 1569
Warley 42 SP 0086
Warlingham 21 TQ 3658
Warmfield 59 SE 3720
Warmingham 51 SJ 7161
Warmington (Northants.) 45 TL 0791
Warmington (Warw.) 33 SP 4147
Warminster 18 ST 8644
Warmsworth 60 SE 5400
Warmwell 9 SY 7585
Warndon 32 SO 8856
Warnford 11 SU 6223
Warnham 12 TQ 1633
Warninglid 13 TQ 2526
Warren (Ches.) 51 SJ 8870
Warren (Dyfed) 24 SR 9397
Warren Row 20 SU 8180
Warren Street 14 TQ 9253
Warrington (Bucks.) 34 SP 8954
Warrington (Ches.) 51 SJ 6088
Warsash 11 SU 4905
Warslow 52 SK 0858
Warsop 53 SK 5667
Warter 67 SE 8750
Warthill 66 SE 6755
Wartling 13 TQ 6509
Wartnaby 44 SK 7123
Warton (Lancs) 57 SD 4028
Warton (Lancs.) 64 SD 4972
Warton (Northum) 79 NU 0002
Warton (Warw) 42 SK 2803
Warwick (Cumbr.) 71 NY 4656
Warwick (Warw.) 33 SP 2865
Warwick Bridge 71 NY 4756
Washaway 4 SX 0369
Washbourne 5 SX 7954
Washfield 8 SS 9315
Washfold 65 NZ 0502
Washford 16 ST 0441
Washford Pyne 7 SS 8111
Washingborough 54 TF 0170
Washington (Tyne and Wear) 72 NZ 3356
Washington (W Susx) 12 TQ 1212
Wasing 19 SU 5764
Waskerley 72 NZ 0545
Wasperton 33 SP 2659
Wass 66 SE 5579
Watchet 16 ST 0743
Watchfield (Oxon.) 18 SU 2490
Watchfield (Somer.) 17 ST 3446
Watchgate 63 SD 5399
Water (Lancs.) 58 SD 8425
Water End (Herts.) 35 TL 0310
Water End (Herts.) 35 TL 2304
Water Meetings 76 NS 9513
Water Newton 45 TL 1097
Water Orton 42 SP 1791
Water Stratford 34 SP 6534
Water Yeat 62 SD 2889
Waterbeach 45 TL 4965
Waterbeck 70 NY 2477
Waterden 46 TF 8835
Waterfall 52 SK 0851
Waterfoot (Lancs.) 58 SD 8321
Waterfoot (Strath.) 84 NS 5654
Waterford 35 TL 3114
Waterheads 85 NT 2451
Waterhouses (Durham) 72 NZ 1841
Waterhouses (Staffs.) 52 SK 0850
Wateringbury 14 TQ 6853
Wateringhouse 113 ND 3090
Waterloo (Dorset) 10 SZ 0194
Waterloo (Mers.) 50 SJ 3297
Waterloo (Norf.) 47 TG 2219
Waterloo (Strath.) 84 NS 8153
Waterloo (Tays.) 92 NO 0636
Waterlooville 11 SU 6809
Waterperry 34 SP 6206
Waterrow 16 ST 0525
Waters Upton 41 SJ 6319
Watersfield 12 TQ 0115
Waterside (Strath.) 75 NS 4308
Waterside (Strath.) 82 NS 4843
Waterside (Strath.) 84 NS 5160
Waterside (Strath.) 84 NS 6773
Waterstock 34 SP 6305
Waterston 24 SM 9306
Watford (Herts.) 20 TQ 1196
Watford (Northants.) 43 SP 6069
Wath (N Yorks.) 66 SE 3277
Wath (N. Yorks.) 65 SE 1467
Wath Upon Dearne 59 SE 4300
Watlington (Norf.) 46 TF 6211
Watlington (Oxon.) 19 SU 6994
Watnall Chaworth 53 SK 5046
Watten 112 ND 2454
Wattisfield 36 TM 0174
Wattisham 36 TM 0151
Watton (Humbs.) 67 TA 0150
Watton (Norf.) 46 TF 9100
Watton-at-Stone 35 TL 3019
Wattston 84 NS 7770
Wattstown 28 ST 0194
Waunarlwydd 25 SS 6095
Waunfawr (Gwyn) 48 SH 5259
Wavendon 34 SP 9137
Waverton (Ches.) 50 SJ 4663
Waverton (Cumbr.) 70 NY 2247
Wawne 61 TA 0836
Waxham 47 TG 4326
Waxholme 61 TA 3229
Way Village 7 SS 8810
Wayford 9 ST 4006
Wealdstone 21 TQ 1689
Weare 17 ST 4152
Weare Giffard 6 SS 4721
Weasenham All Saints 46 TF 8421
Weasenham St. Peter 46 TF 8522
Weaverham 51 SJ 6173
Weaverthorpe 67 SE 9670
Webheath 42 SP 0266
Weddington 43 SP 3693
Wedhampton 18 SU 0557
Wedmore 17 ST 4347
Wednesbury 42 SP 0095
Wednesfield 41 SJ 9400
Weedon 34 SP 8118
Weedon Bec 34 SP 6259
Weedon Lois 33 SP 6047
Weeford 42 SK 1404
Week (Devon) 7 SS 7316
Week St. Mary 6 SX 2397
Weekley 44 SP 8880
Weeley 23 TM 1422
Weeley Heath 23 TM 1520
Weem 97 NN 8449
Weeping Cross 41 SJ 9421
Weeting 46 TL 7788
Weeton (Lancs.) 57 SD 3834
Weeton (W Yorks.) 59 SE 2846
Weir 58 SD 8724
Welbeck Colliery Village 53 SK 5869
Welborne 47 TG 0610
Welbourn 54 SK 9654
Welburn 66 SE 7168
Welbury 66 NZ 3902
Welby 54 SK 9738
Welches Dam 45 TL 4786
Welcombe 6 SS 2218
Weldon 44 SP 9289
Welford (Berks.) 19 SU 4073
Welford (Northants.) 43 SP 6480
Welford-on-Avon 32 SP 1552
Welham (Leic.) 44 SP 7692
Welham Green 35 TL 2305
Well (Hants.) 20 SU 7646
Well (Lincs.) 55 TF 4473
Well (N Yorks.) 66 SE 2682
Well Hill (Kent) 21 TQ 4963
Welland 32 SO 7940
Wellesbourne 33 SP 2755
Wellhill (Highld.) 108 NH 9962
Welling 21 TQ 4575
Wellingborough 44 SP 8968
Wellingham 46 TF 8722
Wellingore 54 SK 9856
Wellington (Here & W) 30 SO 4948
Wellington (Salop) 41 SJ 6411
Wellington (Somer.) 8 ST 1320
Wellington Heath 32 SO 7140
Wellow (Avon) 18 ST 7358
Wellow (I. of W.) 11 SZ 3887
Wellow (Notts.) 53 SK 6666
Wells 17 ST 5445
Wells of Ythan 104 NJ 6338
Wells-Next-The-Sea 46 TF 9143
Wellsborough 43 SK 3602
Wellwood 85 NT 0888
Welney 45 TL 5294
Welsh End 50 SJ 5035
Welsh Frankton 50 SJ 3633
Welsh Hook 24 SM 9327
Welsh Newton 29 SO 4918
Welsh St. Donats 28 ST 0276
Welshampton 50 SJ 4334
Welshpool (Trallwng) 40 SJ 2207
Welton (Cumbr.) 70 NY 3544
Welton (Humbs.) 61 SE 9527
Welton (Lincs.) 54 TF 0079
Welton (Northants.) 33 SP 5865
Welton le Marsh 55 TF 4768
Welton le Wold 55 TF 2787
Welwick 61 TA 3421
Welwyn 35 TL 2316
Welwyn Garden City 35 TL 2412
Wem 40 SJ 5129
Wembdon 17 ST 2837
Wembley 21 TQ 1985
Wembury 5 SX 5148
Wembworthy 7 SS 6609
Wemyss Bay 82 NS 1869
Wenallt 49 SH 9842
Wendens Ambo 35 TL 5036
Wendlebury 33 SP 5519
Wendling 46 TF 9213
Wendover 34 SP 8708
Wendron 2 SW 6731
Wendy 35 TL 3247
Wenhaston 37 TM 4275
Wennington (Cambs.) 45 TL 2379
Wennington (Essex) 21 TQ 5381
Wennington (Lancs.) 64 SD 6169
Wensley (Derby) 53 SK 2661
Wensley (N Yorks) 65 SE 0989
Wentbridge 60 SE 4817
Wentnor 40 SO 3892
Wentworth (Cambs.) 45 TL 4878
Wentworth (S Yorks.) 59 SK 3898
Wenvoe 28 ST 1272
Weobley 30 SO 4051
Weobley Marsh 30 SO 4151
Wereham 46 TF 6801
Wergs 41 SJ 8601
Wernffrwd 25 SS 5193
Wernheolydd 29 SO 3913
Werrington (Devon.) 4 SX 3287
Werrington (Staffs.) 51 SJ 9647
Wervin 50 SJ 4171
Wesham 57 SD 4132
Wessington 53 SK 3757
West Acre 46 TF 7715
West Allerdean 87 NT 9646
West Alvington 5 SX 7243
West Anstey 7 SS 8527
West Ashby 55 TF 2672
West Ashling 12 SU 8007
West Ashton 18 ST 8755
West Auckland 72 NZ 1826
West Bagborough 16 ST 1633
West Barkwith 55 TF 1580
West Barns 86 NT 6578
West Barsham 46 TF 9033
West Bay 9 SY 4690
West Beckham 47 TG 1339
West Bergholt 23 TL 9527
West Bexington 9 SY 5386
West Bilney 46 TF 7115
West Blatchington 13 TQ 2706
West Bradenham 46 TF 9208
West Bradford 58 SD 7444
West Bradley 17 ST 5536
West Bretton 59 SE 2813
West Bridgford 53 SK 5837
West Bromwich 42 SP 0091
West Buckland (Devon) 7 SS 6531
West Buckland (Somer.) 8 ST 1720
West Burton (N Yorks) 65 SE 0186
West Burton (W Susx) 12 TQ 0014
West Caister 47 TG 5011
West Calder 85 NT 0163
West Camel 9 ST 5724
West Challow 19 SU 3688
West Charleton 5 SX 7542
West Chelborough 9 ST 5405
West Chevington 79 NZ 2297
West Chiltington 12 TQ 0918
West Chinnock 9 ST 4613
West Clandon 20 TQ 0452
West Cliffe 15 TR 3445
West Clyne 108 NC 8906
West Clyth 112 ND 2736
West Coker 9 ST 5113
West Compton (Dorset) 9 SY 5694
West Compton (Somer.) 17 ST 5942
West Cross 25 SS 6189
West Curry 4 SX 2893
West Curthwaite 70 NY 3248
West Dean (W Susx) 12 SU 8512
West Dean (Wilts.) 11 SU 2526
West Deeping 45 TF 1009
West Derby 50 SJ 3993
West Dereham 46 TF 6500
West Ditchburn 79 NU 1320
West Down (Devon) 6 SS 5142
West Drayton (Gtr London) 20 TQ 0679
West Drayton (Notts.) 54 SK 7074
West Dunnet 112 ND 2273
West End (Avon) 29 ST 4469
West End (Beds.) 34 SP 9853
West End (Hants) 11 SU 4614
West End (Herts.) 35 TL 3306
West End (Norf.) 47 TG 4911
West End (Oxon.) 33 SP 4204
West End (Surrey) 20 SU 9461
West End Green 19 SU 6661
West Farleigh 14 TQ 7152
West Felton 40 SJ 3425
West Firle 13 TQ 4707
West Geirnish 109 NF 7741
West Ginge 19 SU 4386
West Grafton 18 SU 2460
West Green 20 SU 7456
West Grimstead 11 SU 2026
West Grinstead 12 TQ 1721
West Haddlesey 60 SE 5526
West Haddon 43 SP 6371
West Hagbourne 19 SU 5187
West Hallam 53 SK 4341
West Halton 60 SE 9020
West Ham (Gtr London) 21 TQ 4083
West Handley 53 SK 3977
West Hanney 19 SU 4092
West Hanningfield 22 TQ 7399
West Harnham 10 SU 1229
West Harptree 17 ST 5556
West Hatch 8 ST 2820
West Helmsdale 112 ND 0114
West Hendred 19 SU 4488
West Heslerton 67 SE 9175
West Hill 8 SY 0694
West Hoathly 13 TQ 3632
West Holme 10 SY 8885
West Horndon 22 TQ 6288
West Horrington 17 ST 5747
West Horsley 20 TQ 0753
West Hougham 15 TR 2640
West Humble 21 TQ 1652
West Hyde 20 TQ 0391
West Ilsley 19 SU 4682
West Itchenor 12 SU 7900
West Kennet 18 SU 1167
West Kilbride 82 NS 2048
West Kingsdown 21 TQ 5762
West Kington 18 ST 8077
West Kirby 50 SJ 2186
West Knighton 9 SY 7387
West Knoyle 10 ST 8532
West Langdon 15 TR 3247
West Langwell 108 NC 6909
West Lavington (W Susx.) 12 SU 8920
West Lavington (Wilts.) 18 SU 0052
West Layton 72 NZ 1409
West Leake 43 SK 5226
West Lexham 46 TF 8417
West Lilling 66 SE 6465
West Linton (Borders) 85 NT 1551
West Littleton 29 ST 7575
West Looe 4 SX 2553
West Lulworth 10 SY 8280
West Lutton 67 SE 9269
West Lynn 46 TF 6120
West Mains (Strath.) 84 NS 9550
West Malling 14 TQ 6857
West Malvern 32 SO 7646
West Marden 12 SU 7613
West Markham 54 SK 7272
West Marton 65 SD 8850
West Meon 11 SU 6424
West Mersea 23 TM 0112
West Milton 9 SY 5096
West Monkton 16 ST 2528
West Moors 10 SU 0802
West Muir (Tays.) 99 NO 5661
West Newton (Humbs.) 61 TA 2038
West Newton (Norf.) 46 TF 6927
West Norwood 21 TQ 3171
West Ogwell 5 SX 8170
West Overton 18 SU 1367
West Parley 10 SZ 0997
West Peckham 14 TQ 6452
West Pennard 17 ST 5438
West Pentire 2 SW 7760
West Perry 25 TL 1466
West Putford 6 SS 3515
West Quantoxhead 16 ST 1141
West Rainton 72 NZ 3246
West Rasen 54 TF 0589
West Raynham 46 TF 8725
West Row 36 TL 6775
West Rudham 46 TF 8127
West Runton 47 TG 1842
West Saltoun 86 NT 4667
West Sandwick 113 HU 4488
West Scrafton 65 SE 0783
West Stafford 9 SY 7289
West Stoke 12 SU 8208
West Stonesdale 65 NY 8802
West Stoughton 17 ST 4149
West Stour 10 ST 7822
West Stourmouth 15 TR 2562
West Stow 36 TL 8170
West Stowell 18 SU 1362
West Street 14 TQ 9054
West Tanfield 66 SE 2778
West Tarbert 81 NR 8467
West Thorney 12 SU 7602
West Thurrock 21 TQ 5877
West Tilbury 22 TQ 6677
West Tisted 11 SU 6429
West Tofts 92 NO 1134
West Torrington 55 TF 1381
West Town (Avon) 29 ST 4767
West Tytherley 11 SU 2730
West Tytherton 18 ST 9474
West Walton 45 TF 4713
West Wellow 11 SU 2818
West Wemyss 93 NT 3294
West Wick (Avon) 17 ST 3661
West Wickham (Cambs.) 36 TL 6149
West Wickham (Gtr. London) 21 TQ 3866
West Winch 46 TF 6316
West Winterslow 11 SU 2232
West Wittering 12 SZ 7898
West Witton 65 SE 0688
West Woodburn 78 NY 8986
West Woodhay 19 SU 3962
West Worldham 12 SU 7436
West Wratting 36 TL 6052
West Wycombe 20 SU 8394
Westbere 15 TR 1961
Westbourne (Dorset) 10 SZ 0690
Westbourne (W Susx.) 12 SU 7507
Westbury (Salop) 50 SJ 3509
Westbury (Wilts.) 18 ST 8751
Westbury Leigh 18 ST 8649
Westbury-on-Severn 32 SO 7114
Westbury-sub-Mendip 17 ST 5049
Westby 57 SD 3731
Westcliff-on-Sea 22 TQ 8685
Westcombe 17 ST 6739
Westcote 33 SP 2120
Westcott (Bucks.) 34 SP 7117
Westcott (Devon) 8 ST 0104
Westcott (Surrey) 20 TQ 1348
Westcott Barton 33 SP 4224
Westdean (E Susx) 13 TV 5299
Wester Culbeuchly Crofts 104 NJ 6562
Wester Denoon 98 NO 3543
Wester Fintray 105 NJ 8116
Wester Gruinards 108 NH 5292
Wester Lonvine 108 NH 7172
Westerdale (Highld.) 112 ND 1251
Westerdale (N Yorks.) 66 NZ 6605
Westerfield (Suff.) 37 TM 1747
Westergate 12 SU 9305
Westerham 14 TQ 4454
Westerleigh 29 ST 6979
Westerloch 112 ND 3358
Westerton 99 NO 6654
Westfield (Caithness) 112 ND 0564
Westfield (E Susx.) 14 TQ 8115
Westfield (Lothian) 84 NS 9372
Westfield (Norf.) 46 TF 9909
Westgate (Durham) 63 NY 9038
Westgate (Humbs.) 60 SE 7707
Westgate (Norf.) 46 TF 9740
Westgate on Sea 15 TR 3270
Westhall (Cumbr.) 71 NY 5667
Westhall (Suff.) 47 TM 4280
Westham (E Susx.) 13 TQ 6404
Westham (Somer.) 17 ST 4046
Westhampnett 12 SU 8706
Westhay 17 ST 4342
Westhead 57 SD 4407